Advanced Database Systems

The Morgan Kaufmann Series in Data Management Systems
Series Editor, Jim Gray

Advanced Database Systems

Carlo Zaniolo

Stefano Ceri

Christos Faloutsos

Richard T. Snodgrass

V. S. Subrahmanian

Roberto Zicari

Yun chi

Morgan Kaufmann Publishers, Inc.
San Francisco, California

Sponsoring Editor Diane D. Cerra
Production Manager Yonie Overton
Production Editor Julie Pabst
Editorial Assistant Antonia Richmond
Cover Design Ross Carron Design
Copyeditor Ken DellaPenta
Proofreaders Judith Abrahms, Jennifer McClain, and Gary Morris
Indexer Ty Koontz
Printer Courier Corporation

This book was typeset by the authors, using LaTeX 2_ε.

Figure Credits: Figure 7.1 was adapted from Elmasri and Navathe, *Fundamentals of Database Systems*, p. 31. Figures 18.4, 18.5, 18.7, and 18.8 are reprinted with permission from the VLDB Endowment.

Morgan Kaufmann Publishers, Inc.
Editorial and Sales Office
340 Pine Street, Sixth Floor
San Francisco, CA 94104-3205
USA
Telephone 415/392-2665
Facsimile 415/982-2665
WWW http://www.mkp.com
Email mkp@mkp.com
Order toll free 800/745-7323

Library of Congress Cataloging-in-Publication Data is available for this book.
ISBN 1-55860-443-X

Contents

Preface

In the last 20 years, the database field has experienced rapid growth and seen major advances in applications, technology, and research. This volume provides an integrated introduction to many such advances, and it is designed as a textbook for a graduate course on databases.

The book is intended for computer science students and professionals who have already acquired a basic background on databases (e.g., by taking an introductory database course). The book introduces a reader to the most advanced concepts and research issues in several areas of database technology, including the following: active database systems and rule design, temporal databases and query languages, complex queries and nonmonotonic reasoning, indexing and content-based retrieval for multimedia databases, uncertainty in databases and knowledge bases, and object-oriented databases and the management of changes in schemas and data.

The book was jointly written by leading specialists in such areas; the authors contributed to the development of the enabling technology for those areas, wrote several papers and monographs on the topics covered in the book, and accumulated much experience in teaching these subjects in graduate database courses. Building on such experience, we have organized the presentation of each advanced topic in a gradual and didactic progression, with numerous examples, references, and a list of exercises and projects for class assignment. A rich set of supporting materials, including problem solutions, information about systems, prototypes, and useful resources, and a complete set of lecture slides, has also been prepared for instructors.

The genesis of this volume can be traced back to the sun-drenched island of Lipari, in the Mediterranean. Lipari is the inspiration for the cover of this volume. On this island in July 1995, an International School for Computer Science Researchers was held on "Databases and Knowledge Bases." The school was jointly taught by us, the six authors of this book, and organized as a graduate course, including homework assignments, projects, and final exams. The success of that course, where classroom discussion and students' projects often combined topics from different specialties, served as a proof-of-concept of the desirability of this course and its supporting textbook. In the two years that followed this motivating experience, we improved, integrated, and completed our initial set of notes into a comprehensive textbook where advanced and specialty topics are combined in a volume designed for classroom teaching.

Each author was responsible for a different specialty area. In particular, Stefano Ceri covered Active Databases (Part I), Richard Snodgrass covered Temporal Databases (Part II), and Carlo Zaniolo covered Complex Queries and Reasoning (Part III). Part IV (Spatial, Text, and Multimedia Databases) was covered by Christos Faloutsos, Part V (Uncertainty in Database and Knowledge Bases) was covered by V. S. Subrahmanian, and Part VI (Schema and Database Evolution in Object Database Systems) was covered by Roberto Zicari and Fabrizio Ferrandina.

How to Use this Book

Since each part of this volume is self-contained and organized in a didactic fashion, the book lends itself to multiple uses. Professionals and researchers interested in learning about a new area will benefit from the gradual progression of chapters in each part and from the extensive list of references included for further readings. The instructor, who wants to focus on one or few topics, can use each part of the book as a core introduction to a topic before tackling research papers and monographs. The most natural use of the book, however, could be for a course offering a broad introduction to several areas of database research. In this case, the instructor might only use a subset of the chapters in each part and then expand on the many opportunities for comparisons and synergism among the topics covered in the book.

Errors

We would appreciate hearing about any errors that you find in the book, as well as receiving any other constructive suggestions you may have. Suggestions for additional problems would be especially welcome. Please send errors or suggestions to us at zaniolo@mkp.com.

Acknowledgments

We would like to express our appreciation to the many colleagues and friends who contributed to this volume.

Elena Baralis, Piero Fraternali, Rainer Manthey, Stefano Paraboschi, Letizia Tanca, Jennifer Widom, and the IDEA Team at the Politecnico di Milano have offered many contributions and comments to Part I of this book.

The TSQL2 language presented in Part II was designed by a committee consisting of Ilsoo Ahn, Gad Ariav, Don Batory, James Clifford, Curtis E. Dyreson, Ramez Elmasri, Fabio Grandi, Christian S. Jensen, Wolfgang Käfer, Nick Kline, Krishna Kulkarni, Ting Y. Cliff Leung, Nikos Lorentzos, John F. Roddick, Arie Segev, R. T. Snodgrass (chair), Michael D. Soo, and Surynarayana M. Sripada.

This committee should also be credited with various refinements to the example in Chapter 6, while Ilsoo Ahn, Curtis E. Dyreson, Christian S. Jensen, Nick Kline, Edwin L. McKenzie, and Michael D. Soo made several other contributions to understanding of temporal databases presented in Part II.

Jan Chomicki, Sergio Greco, Daniel Jameson, Nanni Mirko, Domenico Saccà, and several students have contributed to Part III by suggesting many corrections and improvements.

We thank Alex Dekhtyar and Maria-Luisa Sapino for carefully reading Part V of the book and providing detailed feedback. We also thank Howard Blair, Melvin Fitting, Michael Kifer, Laks Lakshmanan, Nicola Leone, Raymond Ng, and Robert Ross for many years of discussions on uncertainty in databases, which have played a significant role in shaping this part of the book.

Thomas Golob and Markus Michalek should be acknowledged for their help in producing the artwork for Part VI.

We thank Panos Chrysanthis, Kia Makki, Sharad Mehrotra, Daniel Miranker, Patrick O'Neil, M. Tamer Özsu, Niki Pissinou, Dimitrios Plexousakis, Rahul Simha, and C. Thomas Wu for their reviews and comments on the book.

Finally, we want to express our deep gratitude to Alfredo Ferro, who laid the seeds of this volume by organizing and hosting the event that brought us together in Lipari during the first two weeks of July 1995.

CZ, SC, CF, RTS, VSS, RZ

Chapter 1

Introduction

The area of database systems has experienced sustained vigorous growth during the last three decades because of the strong pull of commercial applications and the incessant push of technology and research advances. Databases have also gained much recognition as a field for computer science research and university teaching. Introductory database courses are now a part of most undergraduate computer science curricula, and many graduate courses are now being offered in the database area.

However, the transition from undergraduate to graduate teaching of database topics poses unusual didactic challenges, which can be partially ascribed to the past research visibility and current commercial dominance of relational databases. Therefore, most introductory database courses focus on relational databases—and so do the many excellent textbooks written for such courses. But databases have experienced a major research growth since the mid-1970s, when the relational technology was developed, and these developments have been pushing the field toward specialized subareas, such as active, temporal, and object-oriented databases. This fracturing of the field into specialties makes it harder to produce balanced and comprehensive database courses beyond the introductory undergraduate level.

This volume addresses this problem by providing a graduate textbook of broad coverage tailored for classroom teaching. Through a gradual progression of chapters, supported by examples and exercises, the book introduces students to the research issues at the forefront of database technology. The book is written by a team of six authors who are leading specialists in the areas covered by the book and who have accumulated extensive experience in teaching graduate courses in those areas.

This book assumes a college-level knowledge of databases and SQL and seeks the following objectives:

- to provide an introduction to several fields of current research in database systems and intelligent information systems, so as to prepare students for research work and more advanced graduate courses

- to provide both researchers and practitioners with a better understanding of technological advances that are expected to reshape commercial database systems in the coming years

Motivated by the second objective, the authors have often used SQL as a beacon of reference throughout the book, where topics range from active database rules, which are now viewed as an integral part of relational databases, to object-oriented systems, which can either be viewed as a replacement for relational technology or as blueprints for its future evolution.

The first area covered in the volume is active databases, which support active rules and triggers to enable the database system to respond to new events in an intelligent and timely fashion. The actions taken include logging of important events, warnings sent to other systems or supervisors, and corrective actions to enforce the integrity and security of the information stored in the database. Active rules and triggers are already a part of the relational systems supplied by many commercial vendors, and they are viewed as a key feature of SQL3. Many difficult research problems, however, remain unsolved for active databases, hindering the deployment of this powerful technology. The existence of several activation semantics for rules represents one problem. Another is the difficulty of controlling and predicting the behavior of large sets of rules, leading to unexpected behaviors such as nontermination. Chapters 2 and 3 of this book provide a thorough introduction to active database rules and their problems. Then, in Chapter 4, a methodology is presented for the analysis and design of active rules for reliable applications.

Time is a very pervasive aspect of reality, and the inclusion of temporal support in the next generation of database systems is dictated by a growing number of application areas requiring the management of time-varying information. Chapter 5 of this book illustrates the difficulties that a developer encounters when implementing in SQL an information system that provides the temporal support required by many application areas—including accounting, banking, inventory control, econometrics, law, medical records, airline reservations, and geographic information systems. Chapter 6 surveys approaches proposed in the past to support temporal and historical queries, and then elucidates TSQL2, which represents the leading temporal extension proposed for SQL. Chapter 7 discusses implementation strategies for temporal database management systems.

The third part of this volume is concerned with the problem of extending relational query languages to support more complex queries and reasoning. This is achieved by extending the logic of relational query languages to express deductive rules and recursion (Chapter 8). The following chapter discusses implementation techniques for these language extensions, and shows that they are applicable to deductive databases and SQL systems alike. Finally, in Chapter 10, this approach is combined with nonmonotonic reasoning techniques from AI, temporal reasoning, and active rules to provide a powerful framework for the analysis and design of future database and knowledge base systems.

The demand for multimedia information systems has experienced an explosive growth in the last decade, and so has the interest in multimedia database systems. Multimedia databases face the problems of storing and searching large volumes of very diverse information. In fact, multimedia information includes, among other things, digitized 2-D and 3-D images, time series, large collections of sensor data from scientific measurements, audio and video, unstructured text, and DNA sequences. Chapter 11 of this volume provides an introduction to these assorted multimedia database problems. Then, the following chapter provides a unifying solution to the indexing and searching problems of multimedia databases.

Most of current database systems are only capable of answering queries under the assumption that the database is complete and completely accurate. Unfortunately, as the size and the scope of databases grow to include larger and larger domains, and as the information is frequently gathered from more and more heterogeneous data sources, the assumption of completeness and accuracy becomes unrealistic. Part V of this volume deals with these problems and the different techniques used to solve them. In particular, the book discusses fuzzy extensions and probabilistic extensions to the relational model and proposes extensions to SQL to express them. The final chapter of this part (Chapter 15) is devoted to the study of extensions of knowledge bases to deal with fuzzy sets and probabilistic models.

No course in advanced databases could be complete without a discussion of the object-oriented approach. Since an object-oriented database provides for complete integration with a powerful object-oriented programming language, the designer of an advanced information system is given a unsurpassed degree of control and flexibility. In addition to the control made available through the programming language, object-oriented databases deal

effectively with software evolution and schema changes. Following an introduction to object-oriented databases, the last part of this book presents an
in-depth discussion of the topic of schema evolution.

In introducing these areas of database research, we have built on our
extensive experience in teaching these advanced topics in regular courses.
The various parts are structured in a didactic progression that offers the
flexibility of stopping at a level selected by the course instructor; moreover, each chapter is endowed with an extensive bibliography and a rich set
of exercises. Many exercises combine problems from different parts of the
book, thus reinforcing the many technical threads that connect the various
topics of the book and bringing different areas of database research a step
closer together.

Part I

Active Databases

The first part of this book consists of Chapters 2, 3, and 4, which are dedicated to active databases. Active databases provide a facility, tightly integrated with the database system software, for creating and executing production rules. These rules follow the so-called *Event-Condition-Action* paradigm; they autonomously react to events occurring on the data, by evaluating a data-dependent condition, and by executing a reaction whenever the condition evaluation yields a truth value. The processing of rules is performed by an *active rule engine*, which monitors events caused by database transactions and schedules rules according to given policies; the resulting processing guarantees a *reactive database behavior*, which contrasts with the passive behavior of conventional database systems.

When a database exhibits a reactive behavior, a large fraction of the semantics that is normally encoded within applications can be expressed by means of active rules, giving to database applications a new independence dimension, called *knowledge independence*: applications are freed from the need of expressing the knowledge about reactive processing, which is instead coded in the form of active rules. Consequently, knowledge is encoded once and for all in the schema and is automatically shared by all users; knowledge modification is managed by changing the content of rules and not by changing applications. Clearly, knowledge independence introduces a new style in database programming; for this reason, active rule design becomes a relevant part of database design. This explains why in the final chapter of this part (Chapter 4) we concentrate on design methods for active rules.

This part of the book is organized as follows. Chapter 2 provides an introduction to the alternative semantics and basic features of active rules and discusses current trends toward commercial consolidation and standardization of these features. The chapter is organized bottom up; first, four active rule systems are presented in turn, and next their common features are abstracted and generalized, introducing as well some features not present in any of these four systems. Our bottom-up approach is motivated by the lack of a universal model for active databases, in spite of the existence of many research prototypes and commercial products. Indeed, the search for higher conceptual models and for a unifying theory is one of the factors that make active databases an interesting open field for research.

Chapter 3 is dedicated to the applications of active rules and introduces the classical uses of active rules for modeling integrity maintenance, data derivation, data replication, workflow management, and business rules. A large example shows the use of active rules for energy management.

Chapter 4, the final chapter of this part, is dedicated to active rule design methods and concentrates on rule analysis, modularization, and prototyping. With this shift of the discussion, we describe general concepts and problems, such as modularization and termination, that apply to all the different active database systems. At the end of the chapter, we sketch the features of the IDEA Methodology for active rule design, prototyping, and implementation, and the tools that can be used for supporting the methodology.

Chapter 2

Syntax and Semantics
of Active Databases

The first chapter of this part is dedicated to the understanding of the syntax and semantics of active rules. This topic is developed by examples, through the careful analysis of four representative active database systems. We start with the Starburst active rule system and conclude with Chimera. These are research prototypes for relational and object-oriented databases, respectively, that emphasize advanced semantic features, such as set-oriented database processing, sophisticated event composition and management, and the ability to access transition values representing past states. In between these research prototypes, we present Oracle and DB2, two of the most popular relational products. The emphasis on relational products is justified by the fact that all relational products support *triggers*. By this term they denote active rules; therefore we will use the terms "trigger" and "active rule" as synonyms. We will conclude this chapter with a comparative review of the various features of active rules and triggers that were progressively introduced.

It is interesting to position the two relational systems relative to the evolution of the SQL3 standard. An effort for defining a standard for SQL triggers has been ongoing since the late 1980s; however, triggers missed the publication deadline for SQL-92, probably because of the inadequacy of the standard document, which was very intricate, especially in a section listing measures for avoiding mutual triggering. Given the importance of standard compliance, all vendors have tried to produce systems as close as possible to the preliminary standard document by disregarding some of its most exotic features, but the document left a number of open issues, resolved by vendors in different ways. Oracle is a typical example of a system that was carefully developed along the guidelines of the SQL3 standard document dominating between 1990 and 1995.

More recently, in the summer of 1996, the designers of DB2 presented a change proposal for the SQL3 standard that introduces a novel semantics of triggering, in particular with respect to integrity checking. This proposal, which adapts well to the features of most relational products, was recently evaluated and accepted by the SQL3 standard body. Thus, the definition of triggers for DB2 gives us the most recent snapshot on the current SQL3 proposal for triggers, both syntactically and semantically; we cannot easily predict now when and how such a standard proposal will become definitive and be published.

2.1   Starburst

Starburst is the name of a project developed at the IBM Almaden Research Center; an active database extension developed in this framework, called the Starburst Active Rule System, has gained popularity mainly because of its simple syntax and semantics, which adopts the classical set-oriented syntax and semantics of relational databases.

The Active Rule System component extends the data definition language (DDL) of Starburst by enabling the creation and deletion of active rules. Active rules are based on the Event-Condition-Action (ECA) paradigm:

- Events are SQL data manipulation primitives (**INSERT, DELETE, UPDATE**).

- The condition is a boolean predicate on the database state, expressed in SQL.

- Actions may perform arbitrary SQL queries (including **SELECT, INSERT, DELETE, UPDATE**); in addition, actions may include rule manipulation statements and the transactional instruction **ROLLBACK WORK**.

The ECA paradigm has a simple, intuitive semantics: *when* the event occurs, *if* the condition is satisfied, *then* perform the action. This basic semantics is followed by most active rule systems; we say that a rule is *triggered* when its relevant event occurs, is *considered* when its condition is evaluated, and is *executed* when its action is performed. However, as it will become clear, there are subtle differences in the way in which different systems define the semantics of triggering, consideration, and execution of active rules.

Active rules are added to the schema and shared by all applications; however, each transaction can dynamically activate and deactivate existing rules. In Starburst, rules can be grouped, and a user can selectively activate and deactivate the rules of a group.

As an initial example, consider the following SalaryControl rule, which monitors the hiring, firing, and change of salary of employees. The rule is defined by a conservative manager who keeps the salary of his employees under control by imposing a salary reduction whenever the average salary goes beyond a given threshold.

Example 2.1   Salary control rule

> **CREATE RULE** SalaryControl **ON** Emp
> **WHEN INSERTED, DELETED, UPDATED** (Sal)
> **IF**   (**SELECT AVG** (Sal) **FROM** Emp) > 100
> **THEN   UPDATE** Emp
>   **SET** Sal = .9 * Sal

We now proceed with a systematic description of the syntax and semantics of active rules in Starburst.

2.1.1   Syntax of the Starburst **CREATE RULE** Statement

The main DDL extension for active rules enables the creation of active rules. Its syntax is defined in the following:[1]

> <Starburst-rule> ::=**CREATE RULE** <rule-name> **ON** <table-name>
>   **WHEN** <triggering-operations>
>   [**IF** <SQL-predicate>]
>   **THEN** <SQL-statements>
>   [**PRECEDES** <rule-names>]
>   [**FOLLOWS** <rule-names>]

---

[1]Throughout this part of the book we adopt a simple BNF notation where optionality is denoted by square brackets and alternatives by curly brackets; pluralized grammar production names (such as <rule-names>) indicate one or more repetitions of that grammatic construct, separated by commas.

<triggering-operation> ::= **INSERTED** | **DELETED** |

UPDATED [(<column-names>)]

Each active rule in Starburst has a unique name and is associated to a specific table, called the rule's *target*. Each rule monitors multiple events, specified as the rule's triggering operations; the same SQL statement can be monitored by multiple rules. The ordering of rules is regulated by means of a *partial order* between rules; at rule creation time, it is possible to specify that a given rule precedes given rules and follows given rules. The precedence relationships must be acyclic.

2.1.2   Semantics of Active Rules in Starburst

Rules in Starburst are processed in the context of a given transaction; rule processing is implicitly initiated when the transaction issues a **COMMIT WORK** command, thus yielding to a *deferred* execution; in addition, rule processing can be initiated with an explicit **PROCESS RULES** command.

A rule is either *triggered* or *untriggered*; it is untriggered at the transaction's start, and it becomes triggered because of the occurrence of its triggering events (we will define triggering more precisely later). The triggered rules at a given time form the *conflict set*. Starburst's rule processing algorithm consists of the iteration of the following steps:

Algorithm 2.1 *Starburst's rule processing algorithm*

While the conflict set is not empty

1. *Select one rule R from the conflict set among those rules at highest priority; R's state becomes untriggered.*

2. *Evaluate the condition of R.*

3. *If the condition of R is true, then execute the action of R.*

Rule selection at step 1 of the above algorithm produces one of the rules at highest priority (i.e., those rules in the conflict set that are not preceded by any other rule in the set); given that rules are partially ordered by their rule creation statements, there may be many rules that satisfy the above condition. In order to guarantee repeatability of execution (i.e., the same system's behavior on the same database state and input transaction), the system maintains a total order of rules, consistent with the user-specified partial order; rules at the same user-specified priority level are further ordered by the system on the basis of their creation time.

Action execution may cause the triggering of rules, including the re-triggering of the rule being executed. Thus, the above algorithm could lead to an infinite execution, caused by rules that cyclicly trigger each other; in this case, we say that the rule execution is *nonterminating*. As we will see, ensuring termination is one of the main problems of active rule design. When instead rule execution terminates with an empty conflict set, we denote the corresponding database state as a *quiescent state*.

The precise notion of rule triggering requires the definition of *state transitions*; these are transformations from a given state S_1 of the database to another state S_2 because of the execution of SQL statements by transactions. State transitions are defined by means of the sets *inserted, deleted,* or *updated*; these sets include the tuples that are, respectively, inserted, deleted, or updated by the SQL data manipulation operations that transform S_1 into S_2. From the set *updated* we can extract subsets containing tuples affected by updates on specific attributes, for example, *updated*(Sal).

Rules consider the *net effect* of operations between two well-defined database states; the net effect is obtained by composing multiple operations occurring on the same tuple. Because of the net effect, each tuple affected by a database operation appears at most in one of the above *inserted, deleted,* and *updated* sets. For instance, the net effect of the insertion of a tuple t followed by its deletion is null, while the insertion of a tuple t_1 followed by the update of t_1 into t_2 appears as the insertion of the tuple t_2.

We are now in the position of specifying whether a given rule is triggered. Intuitively, a rule R is triggered if any of the sets corresponding to its triggering operations is not empty, relative to a given state transition. At the first consideration of a rule we consider the transition from the initial state S_0 of the transaction to the state S_1 that exists when R is selected by the rule processing algorithm; this is called the *initial transition* for R. After consideration, R is detriggered (regardless of whether the rule is executed or not). In order to determine whether R is triggered in a later state S_2, we consider the transition from S_1 to S_2, and so on, until rule processing terminates on a quiescent state S_f, in which rule R, as well as all other rules, is not triggered.

The use of net effects and the notion of transitions as defined above has the consequence that each rule processes each database change to individual tuples exactly once.

In the condition or action parts of the rule, it is possible to make references to temporary relations storing the instances of the tuples that characterize state transitions. More precisely, four transition tables are defined, respectively called **INSERTED**, **DELETED**, **OLD-UPDATED**, and **NEW-**

UPDATED. The **INSERTED** and **DELETED** transition tables store the tuples belonging to the sets of *inserted* and *deleted* tuples as defined above; **OLD-UPDATED** stores the content of these tuples *before* the update, while **NEW-UPDATED** stores the content of updated tuples *after* the update. Referring to transition tables within SQL statements of active rules may be more efficient than referring to the current content of regular tables because transition tables are usually small and are resident in main memory. Transition tables are not defined outside of the scope of active rules.

2.1.3   Other Active Rule Commands

The DDL extensions provided by the Active Rule Language of Starburst also include commands for dropping, altering, activating, and deactivating rules:

<deactivate-rule> ::= **DEACTIVATE RULE** <rule-name> **ON** <table>

<activate-rule> ::= **ACTIVATE RULE** <rule-name> **ON** <table>

<drop-rule> ::= **DROP RULE** <rule-name> **ON** <table>

Rules in Starburst can be organized within a *ruleset*. Rulesets are created and manipulated by DDL instructions:

<create-ruleset> ::= **CREATE RULESET** <ruleset-name>

<alter-ruleset> ::= **ALTER RULESET** <ruleset-name>

[**ADDRULES** <rule-names>]

[**DELRULES** <rule-names>]

<drop-ruleset> ::= **DROP RULESET** <ruleset-name>

Rule processing can be invoked within a transaction on a specific ruleset, or even on a specific rule, by means of commands:

<rule-processing-commands> ::= **PROCESS RULES**

| **PROCESS RULESET** <ruleset-name>

| **PROCESS RULE** <rule-name>

2.1.4   Examples of Active Rule Executions

Let us consider an active rule system with only one rule, the SalaryControl rule presented before and repeated here for convenience:

CREATE RULE SalaryControl **ON** Emp
WHEN INSERTED, **DELETED**, **UPDATED** (Sal)
IF   (**SELECT AVG** (Sal) **FROM** Emp) > 100
THEN UPDATE Emp
         SET Sal = .9 * Sal

Consider the following initial database state:

Employee	Sal
Stefano	90
Patrick	90
Michael	110

Consider a transaction that performs the inserts of tuples (Rick,150) and (John,120). The insertion triggers the rule, which is selected at step 1 of the rule processing algorithm. The condition holds (the average is now 112), and the action is executed; the new database state is shown below:

Employee	Sal
Stefano	81
Patrick	81
Michael	99
Rick	135
John	108

The action again triggers the rule, this time because of an **UPDATE** operation to the Sal attribute; the rule is again considered, the condition holds again (the average is now 101, which is still too high), and the action is again executed, yielding the database state below:

Employee	Sal
Stefano	73
Patrick	73
Michael	89
Rick	121
John	97

At this point, the action again triggers the rule, the rule is again considered, but the condition evaluation yields **FALSE** (the average is 91); thus, rule processing terminates on a quiescent state. Note that termination occurs because the rule's action decreases the average salary and the rule's condition checks that the average salary is below a given threshold; thus, rule processing *converges* to a quiescent state where the rule's condition is met. If, instead, the multiplicative factor were equal to or greater than 1 in the action, then the execution would have been infinite. Generally, it is the responsibility of the rule designer to ensure that all executions terminate.

Let us consider now the effect of adding to the active database the rule HighPaid, which inserts within a view the tuples of those newly inserted employees whose salary exceeds 100.

Example 2.2   High paid rule

    CREATE RULE HighPaid **ON** Emp
    WHEN INSERTED
    IF   EXISTS (SELECT * FROM INSERTED
                WHERE Sal > 100)
    THEN INSERT INTO HighPaidEmp
                (SELECT * FROM INSERTED
                WHERE Sal > 100)
    FOLLOWS AvgSal

Consider again the transaction adding tuples for Rick and John to a database storing tuples for Stefano, Patrick, and Michael as illustrated above. Both rules SalaryControl and HighPaid are triggered by the insert, but the latter follows the former in rule ordering. Thus, rule SalaryControl is considered twice by the rule processing algorithm, yielding to the same final state relative to the Emp table. At this point, rule SalaryControl is not triggered, while rule HighPaid is still triggered because of the initial **INSERT** operations. Thus, the rule is considered, and its condition is satisfied. Because of net effects, the rule considers as **INSERTED** the following temporary table:

Employee	Sal
Rick	122
John	97

Note that this table is quite different from the value of the tuples that were actually inserted, as it reflects the application of two updates to each of the inserted tuples. The rule's action is executed next, causing the tuple (Rick,122) to be inserted into the view HighPaid. The tuple (John,97) is not inserted, although John was originally inserted by the transaction with a salary that was higher than 100, because this salary was rectified by the execution of the SalaryControl rule. Rule prioritization, in this case, serves the purpose of enabling the consideration of rule HighPaid only after the (recursive) consideration and execution of rule SalaryControl.

2.2   Oracle

Oracle supports general-purpose triggers, developed according to preliminary documents on the SQL3 standard for triggers. Triggers in Oracle may execute actions that contain arbitrary PL/SQL code; this feature makes triggers in Oracle particularly powerful and expressive. Triggers in Oracle respond to data manipulation operations (insert, delete, update) on a given target table. They support two distinct granularities, *row-level* and *statement-level*. With row-level triggers, triggering occurs for each row that is affected by the operation; thus, row-level triggers have an *instance-oriented semantics*, different from the one supported by Starburst. On the other hand, statement-level triggers have a set-oriented semantics, as in Starburst.

Another distinguishing feature of triggers in Oracle is that they are *immediate*: trigger consideration is tightly coupled with the execution of the triggering SQL statement. Recall that, in contrast, Starburst has a *deferred* execution mode, where triggers are executed either because of an explicit transactional statement or at commit time. In particular, triggers in Oracle can be considered and executed either *before* or *after* the triggering operation. Thus, by combining two granularities and two raising times, we get four possible combinations:

1. row-level before-triggers
2. statement-level before-triggers
3. row-level after-triggers
4. statement-level after-triggers

2.2.1   Syntax of the Oracle **CREATE TRIGGER** Statement

The syntax for creating triggers in Oracle is

<Oracle-trigger> ::= **CREATE TRIGGER** <trigger-name>
                     { **BEFORE** | **AFTER** } <trigger-events>
                     ON <table-name>
                     [[**REFERENCING** <references>]
                     FOR EACH ROW
                     [**WHEN** (<condition>)]] <PL/SQL block>

<trigger event> ::= **INSERT** | **DELETE** | **UPDATE**
                    [**OF** <column-names>]

<reference> ::=   **OLD AS** <old-value-tuple-name> |

                       NEW AS <new-value-tuple-name>

Let us discuss each syntactic feature in detail. Each trigger may monitor any combination of the three data manipulation operations (insert / delete / update) on the target table; when the trigger's reaction to events being monitored depends on the event and the trigger is row-level, special predicates **INSERTING**, **DELETING**, and **UPDATING** may be used in the action to detect which of the triggering events has occurred.

The granularity of the trigger is dictated by the clause **FOR EACH ROW**, which needs to be included for tuple-level triggers; when this clause is omitted, the granularity is statement-level. A condition is optionally supported only when the trigger is row-level, and consists of a simple row-level predicate that has to be true in order for the action to be executed on the specific row. For statement-level triggers, the condition part is not present; a condition can nonetheless be expressed within the action as a **WHERE** clause of an SQL statement, but in this case its failure does not prevent the action from being taken, which may result in the endless activation of the trigger.

For both row- and statement-level triggers, the action is an arbitrary block written in PL/SQL, with the limitation that the block should not include DDL or transactional commands.

References to past states are possible only when the trigger is row-based, and they are restricted to the specific tuple being changed; it can be referenced by means of correlation variables introduced by the **REFERENCING** clause, or implicitly by built-in variables called **OLD** and **NEW**.

2.2.2   Semantics of Oracle Triggers

Oracle versions prior to 7.1 impose a severe limitation, namely, that each operation can be monitored by at most one trigger per mode; thus, each operation has at most four associated triggers, corresponding to the options defined above. The limitation on the number of triggers is dropped in Oracle 7.2 and subsequent versions, however without providing an explicit mechanism for prioritizing the triggers that respond to the same event and mode, whose order is system-controlled and cannot be influenced by the database administrator.

The execution of a specific SQL statement is interleaved with the execution of triggers according to the following approach:

Algorithm 2.2 *Oracle's rule processing algorithm*

1. *Execute the statement-level before-triggers.*

2. *For each row in the target table:*

   a. *Execute the row-level before-triggers.*

   b. *Perform the modification of the row and row-level referential integrity and assertion checking.*

   c. *Execute the row-level after-triggers.*

3. *Perform statement-level referential integrity and assertion checking.*

4. *Execute the statement-level after-triggers.*

Each database manipulation performed from within the action part may cause the activation of other triggers; in this case, the execution of the current trigger is suspended and the other triggers are considered by applying to them the execution algorithm illustrated above. The maximum number of *cascading* (i.e., activated) triggers is 32; when the system reaches this threshold, which indicates the possibility of nontermination, execution is suspended and a specific exception is raised. If an exception is raised or an error occurs during trigger execution, then all database changes performed as a result of the original SQL operation and all the subsequent triggered actions are rolled back. Thus, Oracle supports partial (per statement) rollbacks instead of transactional rollbacks.

2.2.3 Example of Trigger Executions

The following trigger Reorder is used to automatically generate a new order (by inserting a tuple into the table PendingOrders) whenever the available quantity (PartOnHand) for a given part in the Inventory table goes below a given threshold (ReorderPoint). The attribute Part is the key of both tables Inventory and PendingOrders.

Example 2.3   Reorder rule

```
CREATE TRIGGER Reorder
AFTER UPDATE OF PartOnHand ON Inventory
WHEN (New.PartOnHand < New.ReorderPoint)
FOR EACH ROW
    DECLARE NUMBER X
    BEGIN
        SELECT COUNT(*) INTO X
```

```
          FROM PendingOrders
          WHERE Part = New.Part;
      IF X=0
      THEN
          INSERT INTO PendingOrders
          VALUES (New.Part, New.OrderQuantity, SYSDATE)
      END IF;
  END;
```

The above trigger has a row-level granularity and is considered immediately after each update to the PartOnHand attribute. The condition is checked for each row by taking into account the values that are produced by the update, denoted by means of the New correlation variable. The action contains code in PL/SQL, which however is straightforward; a variable X is declared and then used to store the number of pending orders for the particular part. If that number is equal to zero (i.e., if there are no pending orders for that part), then a new order is issued by inserting into PendingOrders a tuple with the name of the part, the (fixed) part's reorder quantity, and the current date. It is assumed that tuples in the PendingOrders table are deleted by a suitable application when parts are received at the inventory. Note that values of the row that is associated to the trigger's execution can be accessed in the action part of the trigger by means of the New correlation variable.

Consider the following initial state for the Inventory table; assume that PendingOrders is initially empty:

Part	PartOnHand	ReorderPoint	ReorderQuantity
1	200	150	100
2	780	500	200
3	450	400	120

Consider the following transaction (executed on October 10, 1996):

T_1: **UPDATE** Inventory
    SET PartOnHand = PartOnHand - 70
    WHERE Part = 1

This transaction causes the trigger Reorder to be executed, resulting in the insertion into PendingOrders of the tuple (1,100,1996-10-10). Next, assume that the following transaction is executed on the same day:

T_2: **UPDATE** Inventory
    SET PartOnHand = PartOnHand - 60
    WHERE Part >= 1

At this point, the trigger is executed upon all the tuples, and the condition holds for parts 1 and 3. However, no new order is issued for part 1 (because of the order pending to this part), while a new order is issued for part 3, resulting in the new tuple (3,120,1996-10-10), which is also inserted into the table PendingOrders. Note that, although T_1 and T_2 are separately committed, the effects of T_1 are seen by T_2, since the two transactions share the tables of the database, and active rules run within the scope of their triggering transactions.

2.3 DB2

Triggers for DB2 Common Servers were recently defined at the IBM Almaden Research Center; efforts were focused on giving to triggers a precise, unambiguous semantics, especially with respect to integrity constraint maintenance, by taking into account the experience gained in the earlier development of the Starburst system.

2.3.1 Syntax of the DB2 **CREATE TRIGGER** Statement

Every trigger in DB2 monitors a single event, which can be any SQL data manipulation statement; updates can be optionally qualified by a list of column names. As in Oracle, triggers are activated either **BEFORE** or **AFTER** their event, and have either a row- or a statement-level granularity. The syntax of triggers in DB2 is shown below:

    <DB2-trigger> ::= **CREATE TRIGGER** <trigger-name>
                          { **BEFORE** | **AFTER** } <trigger-event>
                          ON <table-name>
                          [**REFERENCING** <references>]
                          FOR EACH { **ROW** | **STATEMENT** }
                          WHEN (<SQL-condition>)
                          <SQL-procedure-statements>

<trigger-event> ::= **INSERT** | **DELETE** | **UPDATE**
[**OF** <column-names>]

<reference> ::=   **OLD AS** <old-value-tuple-name> |
NEW AS <new-value-tuple-name> |
OLD_TABLE AS <old-value-table-name> |
NEW_TABLE AS <new-value-table-name>

We notice the presence of transition values both at row- and statement-level granularities. **OLD** and **NEW** introduce correlation variables describing tuple values, as in Oracle, while **OLD_TABLE** and **NEW_TABLE** describe the tuples before and after a set-oriented update statement. An insert statement is described only by the **NEW_TABLE**, and a delete statement is described only by the **OLD_TABLE**. The content of these tables is similar to the content of Starburst's **INSERTED**, **DELETED**, **OLD_UPDATED**, and **NEW_UPDATED** tables, but these three tables can all be present within a Starburst trigger, which can monitor multiple events, while a DB2 trigger is relative to only one event. Triggers cannot perform data definition or transactional commands; however, they can raise errors, which in turn can cause statement-level rollbacks.

2.3.2   Semantics of DB2 Triggers

Before-triggers are typically used to detect error conditions and to condition input values; an assignment statement allows the body of these triggers to set the values of **NEW** transition variables. Before-triggers appear to execute entirely before the event that they monitor; thus, their conditions and actions must read the database state prior to any modification made by the event. They cannot modify the database by using **UPDATE**, **DELETE**, and **INSERT** statements, so that they do not recursively activate other triggers.

After-triggers embed part of the application logic in the database; their condition is evaluated and their action is possibly executed after the event's modification. The state of the database prior to the event can be reconstructed from transition values; for instance, for a given target table T, the before state is (T **MINUS NEW_TABLE**) **UNION OLD_TABLE**.

Several triggers (with either row- or statement-level granularity) can monitor the same event. They are considered according to a system-determined total order, which takes into account the triggers' definition time.

Row- and statement-level triggers are intertwined in the total order.[2] Row-level triggers are considered and possibly executed once for each tuple, while statement-level triggers are considered and possibly executed once per statement. If the action of a row-level trigger has multiple statements, all statements are executed for one row before considering the next row.

When triggers activate each other, if a modification statement S in the action A of a trigger causes an event E, then the following procedure takes place

Procedure 2.3 *DB2's statement processing procedure*

1. *Suspend the execution of A, and save its working storage on a stack.*

2. *Compute transition values (**OLD** and **NEW**) relative to event E.*

3. *Consider and execute all before-triggers relative to event E, possibly changing the **NEW** transition values.*

4. *Apply **NEW** transition values to the database, thus making the state change associated to event E effective.*

5. *Consider and execute all after-triggers relative to event E. If any of them contains an action A_i that activates other triggers, then invoke this processing procedure recursively for A_i.*

6. *Pop from the stack the working storage for A and continue its evaluation.*

Steps 1 and 6 of the above procedure are not required when the statement S is part of a user's transaction; if any error occurs during the chain of processing caused by S, then processing of S returns an error condition and the database state prior to the execution of S is restored.

This execution procedure is modified when the statement S, applied at step 4, violates constraints defined in the SQL-92 standard, such as referential constraints, check constraints, and views with check option. Thus, after step 4 in the above procedure, the *compensating actions* invoked by these constraints are performed until a fixpoint is reached where all integrity constraints are satisfied. The computation of these actions, however, may activate both before- and after-triggers; thus, the following processing takes place:

---

[2]Recall that in Oracle, instead, the interleaving of row- and statement-level triggers is fixed, defined by the rule processing algorithm.

Procedure 2.4 *Revised step 4 of DB2's statement processing*

4. *Apply the* **NEW** *transition values to the database, thus making the state change associated to event E effective. For each integrity constraint IC violated by the current state, consider the action A_j that compensates the integrity constraint IC.*

   a. *Compute the transition values (***OLD*** and* ***NEW***) relative to A_j.*

   b. *Execute the before-triggers relative to A_j, possibly changing the* ***NEW*** *transition values.*

   c. *Apply* ***NEW*** *transition values to the database, thus making the state change associated to A_j effective.*

   d. *Push all after-triggers relative to action A_j into a queue of suspended triggers.*

At this point, several after-triggers may be pending, due not only to the original statement S, but also to compensating actions A_j; they are processed according to their priority until a quiescent point is reached where all the integrity constraints violated in the course of the computation are compensated.

This integration of trigger management and integrity checking was recently submitted to the SQL3 standard body and accepted for incorporation into the SQL3 standard.

2.3.3   Examples of Trigger Executions

Consider a database schema including tables Part, Distributor, and Audit. The Part table includes PartNum as primary key, and the attributes Supplier and Cost; assume that HDD is the default supplier. Integrity contraints include a referential integrity constraint from Part to Distributor, with the following clause included into Part's schema:

FOREIGN KEY (Supplier)
REFERENCES Distributor
ON DELETE SET DEFAULT

Consider the following initial state for the Part and Distributor tables; assume that Audit is initially empty:

PartNum	Supplier	Cost
1	Jones	150
2	Taylor	500
3	HDD	400
4	Jones	800

Distributor	City	State
Jones	Palo Alto	California
Taylor	Minneapolis	Minnesota
HDD	Atlanta	Georgia

Next, consider two triggers. The before-trigger OneSupplier avoids a change of the Supplier value to **NULL** by raising an exception that forces a statement-level rollback; note that this trigger does not prevent the insertion of tuples with a null value for Supplier.

Example 2.4   Supplier rule

> **CREATE TRIGGER** OneSupplier
> **BEFORE UPDATE OF** Supplier **ON** Part
> **REFERENCING NEW AS** N
> **FOR EACH ROW**
> **WHEN** (N.Supplier **IS NULL**)
>   **SIGNAL SQLSTATE** '70005' ('Cannot change supplier to NULL')

The after-trigger AuditSupplier enters into the Audit table, for each update to Supplier, the user's name, current date, and total number of updated tuples.

Example 2.5   Audit rule

> **CREATE TRIGGER** AuditSupplier
> **AFTER UPDATE ON** Part
> **REFERENCING OLD_TABLE AS** OT
> **FOR EACH STATEMENT**
>   **INSERT INTO** Audit
>   **VALUES(USER, CURRENT_DATE,**
>   (**SELECT COUNT(*) FROM** OT))

Consider the following transaction (executed by user Bill on October 10, 1996):

T_1: **DELETE FROM** Distributor
     WHERE State = 'California'

This transaction causes the deletion of supplier Jones, which violates referential integrity; because of the foreign key specification, the Supplier of rows with PartNum 1 and 4 is set to the default value HDD; this compensating action triggers both OneSupplier and AuditSupplier. The former, a before-trigger, is executed twice, for each row of the updated parts; since the value of column Supplier in table Part is set to HDD, for each row the trigger's condition is invalid, and consequently the action is not performed. Next, the statement-level after-trigger is executed once, causing the entering in the **Audit** table of one tuple, as shown below:

User	CurrentDate	UpdatedTuples
Bill	1996-10-10	2

2.4 Chimera

Unlike the other three languages, which are all extensions of the relational query language SQL, Chimera is an object-oriented database language, integrating an object-oriented data model, a declarative query language, and an active rule language. Active rules in Chimera, called *triggers*, are set-oriented; they have several new features compared to active rules of Starburst and triggers of Oracle and DB2:

- They take advantage of object identifiers for describing the objects that are affected by events; object identifiers provide a *binding passing mechanism* for linking events to conditions and conditions to actions.

- They support different modes for processing events, called *event consumption modes*.

- They support both immediate and deferred trigger execution.

- They support mechanisms for accessing *intermediate database states*.

- They may optionally support the net effect of event computation; net effect computation is invoked by means of special predicates.

2.4.1 Summary of Chimera

Chimera is an expressive object-oriented language. In the following, we give a short summary of the essential notions that are required in order to be able to write simple schemas, triggers, and transactions in Chimera. Although this summary is fully self-contained, some of the notions introduced in this section (such as type constructors and classes) will be defined more extensively in Part VI, dedicated to object-oriented databases; declarative expressions supported by Chimera are inspired by deductive databases, which are the subject of Part III.

Schemas in Chimera include the definition of several *object classes*. An object class has a state consisting of attributes of arbitrary type, built through type constructors **record**, **set**, and **list**; atomic types include the classical types of programming languages and the names of classes in the schema. For instance:

define object class Employee
attributes Name: **string**,
          Salary: **integer**
end;

define object class Department
attributes Name: **string**,
          Employees: **set-of**(Employee)
end;

Classes are organized within generalization hierarchies, and class definitions include, in addition to the state, the definition of operations, constraints, and triggers that are *targeted* to the class; these features are not further discussed since they are not essential for this chapter.

Declarative expressions in Chimera are composed of two main syntactic categories: terms and formulas. *Terms* are atomic or complex. Atomic terms include constants and variables; complex terms include functional terms built from constructors (set, list, record) or evaluable terms built by means of functions available in Chimera (attributes, selectors, predefined operators). In particular, *attribute terms* extract specific attribute values for given object identifiers (for example, X.name).

Atomic formulas are composed of a predicate symbol and a list of parameter terms; they include type, class, comparison, and membership formulas:

- *Type formulas* introduce variables ranging over types; for example, integer(X).

- *Class formulas* introduce variables ranging over classes. For example, Employee(X) indicates that variable X ranges over the object identifiers of the class Employee. All variables in declarative expressions are defined by either type or class formulas.

- *Comparison formulas* are built between two scalar terms by means of classical comparison operators; for example, X.Name = 'John'.

- *Membership formulas* are built between two terms such that the first one is a scalar and the second one is a set or list; for example, Y **in** X.Departments.

Complex formulas are constructed from atomic formulas by means of connectives expressing conjunction and negation; negation is only applicable to atomic formulas. For instance:

Employee(X), Department(Y), Y.Name= 'Toys', **not** (X **in** Y.Employees)

Formulas are evaluated over a database state by matching variables to the values that are stored in the database; after evaluation, variables become bound to values that satisfy the formula. The meaning of declarative expressions of the Chimera language does not depend on the order of evaluation of component formulas and of their terms, with the exception of a few terms that are evaluable only when some of their arguments are bound.

Procedural expressions are composed of primitive database statements (i.e., of updates, queries, and operation calls):

- *Select primitives* produce bindings upon variables, defined in the *target list* of the select and such that a selection formula holds; the target list and selection formula are separated by the **where** keyword. For example:
  select(X **where** Employee(X), X.Name='John')

- *Create primitives* have three arguments: the class name, the state of the object being created, and an output variable that is bound to the object identifier of the newly created object after the execution of the create statement. For example:
  create(Employee, ['John',45000], X)

- *Delete primitives* have two arguments: the class name and the name of the variable that is bound, by a select primitive, to the object identifiers of objects that should be deleted. For example:
  delete(Employee, X)

- *Modify primitives* have three arguments: the name of the attribute being modified, a variable bound to the identifiers of objects to be modified, and the term indicating the value that is taken by the attribute after the update. For example:
  modify(Employee.Salary, X, X.Salary * 1.01)

Procedural expressions are organized into *transaction lines*, which are chains of primitive statements syntactically separated by commas and concluded by a semicolon; a transaction line is the smallest state transition that can be observed by triggers. The scope of variables is defined within a transaction line, and variable bindings obtained by means of **select** or **create** primitives are passed from one statement in the chain to the next.

2.4.2   Syntax of the Chimera **Define Trigger** Statement

Triggers are defined in DDL by means of the following statement:

<define-trigger> ::= **define** <option> **trigger** <trigger-name>
       [**for** <class-name>]
       events <triggering-events>
       condition <formula>
       actions <procedural-expression>
       [{ **before** | **after** } <trigger-names>]
       end

<triggering-event> ::= **create** | **delete** | **modify** [(<attr-name>)]

<option> ::=   [<consumption-opt>] [<execution-opt>]

<consumption-opt> ::= **event-consuming** | **event-preserving**

<execution-opt> ::= **deferred** | **immediate**

Events in Chimera include, in addition to the **create**, **delete**, and **modify** primitives, also the **display**, **generalize**, and **specialize** primitives and operation calls, but these are not further discussed. Triggers in Chimera can be either *targeted* or *untargeted*; in the former case, the name of the target class is indicated in the **for class** clause, and events are restricted to primitives applicable to that class, for example, **create**. In the latter case, instead, events in the condition part of a trigger can refer to different classes; in this case, triggering events must include the class name in addition to the primitive name, for example, **create**(Employee).

The condition is an arbitrary formula; the action is an arbitrary procedural expression. When a trigger is targeted, a variable named Self can be used, which implicitly ranges over the target class. Variables introduced in the condition can be used in the action, carrying along from the condition to the action the bindings induced by the computation of the condition. The **before** and **after** clauses introduce, as in Starburst, a partial order between triggers, which is useful during rule processing when multiple triggers are in the triggered state. As in Starburst, the precedence relationship induced by the **before** and **after** clauses must be acyclic. Special binary predicates **occurred** and **holds** can be used within the conditions of triggers. These predicates have two arguments: a list of events relative to a class, and a variable, called the *event variable*, which ranges over the identifiers of the object instances affected by these events:

<event-formula> ::= { **occurred** | **holds** }
(<event-names> , <variable-name>)

2.4.3   Semantics of Chimera Triggers

Triggers in Chimera are processed in the context of a given transaction; processing of immediate triggers is implicitly initiated at the end of each transaction line, while processing of deferred triggers is initiated when the transaction issues a **commit** or **savepoint** command. During the execution of deferred triggers, the immediate triggers that are triggered by a trigger's actions are considered together with deferred triggers.

A trigger is untriggered at the transaction's start, and it becomes triggered by the occurrence of any one of its triggering events. As in Starburst, the set of triggers that are triggered at a given time form the *conflict set*; this may be limited to immediate triggers or include both immediate and deferred triggers. Differently from Starburst, triggers are never detriggered because of net effect computation; thus, once a trigger is in the triggered state, it will be eventually considered by trigger processing.

Trigger processing consists, as in Starburst, of the iteration of the following steps:

> **Algorithm 2.5** *Chimera's trigger processing algorithm*
>
> *While the conflict set is not empty do:*
>
> *1. Select one trigger T from the conflict set among those rules at highest priority; T's state becomes untriggered.*
>
> *2. Evaluate the condition of T.*
>
> *3. If the condition of T is true, then execute the action of T.*

Trigger selection at step 1 of the above algorithm produces one of the triggers at highest priority from all the triggers that are considered by the trigger processing algorithm; **before** and **after** clauses introduce a partial order between both immediate and deferred triggers. As in Starburst, when two triggers are not totally ordered, the system uses an internal ordering, which cannot be influenced by the user, so that two executions of the same transaction on the same database state with the same set of triggers are repeated identically.

The *execution mode* of triggers is either immediate or deferred. Immediate triggers are considered after the completion of each transaction line; deferred triggers are considered only after the issuing of the **commit** primitive or after an explicit **savepoint** primitive.

Predicates **occurred** and **holds** are used to inspect the events that have occurred during a transaction. The predicate **occurred** binds the event variable to the OIDs of all objects affected by the specified events. The predicate **holds** binds the event variable to the OIDs of a subset of the objects affected by the specified events, based on the evaluation of net effect, where

- a sequence of **create** and **delete** primitives on the same object, possibly with an arbitrary number of intermediate **modify** primitives on that object, has a null net effect

- a sequence of **create** and several **modify** primitives on the same object has the net effect of a single create operation

- a sequence of several **modify** and a **delete** primitives on the same object has the net effect of a single delete operation on that object

Two distinct *event consumption modes* are possible for each trigger:

- When events are *consumed*, each instance of an event (e.g., the update to a specific object) is considered by a trigger only at its first consideration after the event, and then disregarded.

- When events are *preserved*, all instances of the event since the transaction start are considered at each consideration of the trigger.

This feature is only relevant when a given trigger is considered multiple times in the context of the same transaction, as it influences the computation of predicates **occurred** and **holds**:

- In the event-preserving case, the variable in the last argument of predicates **occurred** and **holds** becomes bound to all the object identifiers of objects affected by events since the transaction's start.

- In the event-consuming case, that variable becomes bound only to the object identifiers of objects affected by events that occurred since the last consideration.

Defaults for execution and consumption modes are set to *deferred* and *consuming*; alternative modes must be specified explicitly.

References to past database states are supported by the special function **old** applied to simple terms, applicable in the condition part of triggers. If the trigger is event-consuming, then the old state is the state of the last consideration of the trigger. For the first consideration of a trigger, the old state refers to the state at transaction start. If the trigger is event-preserving, then the old state always refers to the state at transaction start.

2.4.4   Examples of Trigger Executions

All examples refer to the following database schema and initial state:

define object class Employee
attributes Name: **string**,
            Salary: **integer**,
            Mgr: Employee
end;

define object class SpecialEmp
attributes Name: **string**
end;

define object class Department
attributes Name: **string**,
            Employees: **set-of**(Employee)
end;

Class Employee: { (o1,'john',3500,o2) ,
                (o2,'tom',4500,null) ,
                (o3,'bob',4300,o2) }
Class SpecialEmp: { }
Class Department: { (o4,'toys',{o1,o2,o3}) }

Let us consider first a trigger targeted on the Employee class, which monitors creation and salary modification. If the employee's salary exceeds the salary of the manager, then the salary is reduced to make it identical to the manager's salary.

Example 2.6   Adjust salary rule

> **define trigger** AdjustSalary **for** Employee
>   **events**   **create**, **modify**(Salary)
>   **condition**   Self.Salary > Self.Mgr.Salary
>   **actions**   **modify**(Employee.Salary,Self,Self.Mgr.Salary)
> **end**;

Consider the following transaction T_1, consisting of two transaction lines, each introducing the modification to the salary of an employee:

> T_1: **begin transaction**;
>   **select**(X **where** employee(X), X.name='tom'),
>   **modify**(Employee.Salary,X,5000);
>   **select**(X **where** employee(X), X.name='john'),
>   **modify**(Employee.Salary,X,5300);
>   **commit**;

The trigger AdjustSalary is triggered by the first **modify** primitive but, being deferred, is considered only at commit. Recall that the manager of John and Bob is Tom. At commit time, which occurs after the execution of the second transaction line, variable Self in the condition ranges over the object identifiers of class Employee (i.e., on o1, o2, and o3); the condition evaluation binds Self to o1 (John), and the salary of the corresponding object is modified and set to 5000, the current salary of o1's manager (Tom).

We next consider the variant ImmAdjSalary, where the execution mode is set to immediate and the predicate **occurred** is used to identify object instances that are affected by the event.

Example 2.7   Immediate adjust salary rule

> **define immediate trigger** ImmAdjustSalary **for** Employee
>   **events**   **create**, **modify**(Salary)
>   **condition**   **occurred**(**create**, **modify**(Salary),Self)
>   Self.Salary > Self.Mgr.Salary
>   **actions**   **modify**(Employee.Salary,Self,Self.Mgr.Salary)
> **end**;

We consider again transaction T_1. In this case, ImmAdjSalary is triggered immediately after the first modification, and the variable Self in the trigger's condition is bound to o2, but then the condition produces no binding and so the action is not executed. ImmAdjSalary becomes triggered again after the second modification, and this time the variable Self is bound to o1; then the condition is satisfied, and the action yields to the same final database state as in the previous example of execution.

Both the previous examples are event-consuming; we turn now to an event-preserving trigger, which monitors change of salaries and inserts employees whose salary has a rise of 5000 into a class SpecialEmp.

Example 2.8   Special employee rule

> **define immediate event-preserving trigger** SpecialEmp **for** Employee
> **events**   **modify**(Salary)
> **condition**   **occurred**(**modify**(Salary),Self)
>   Self.Salary - **old**(Self.Salary) > 5000
> **actions**   **create**(specialEmp, [Self.name], Z)
> **before**   AdjustSalary
> **end**;

Consider an active database consisting of triggers AdjustSalary and SpecialEmp and the following transaction:

T_2: **begin transaction**;
    select(X **where** Employee(X), X.Name='john'),
       modify(Employee.Salary,X,X.Salary+3000);
    select(X **where** Employee(X), X.Name='john'),
       modify(Employee.Salary,X,X.Salary+4500);
    commit;

Trigger SpecialEmp becomes triggered after the first modification and is immediately considered, but its condition is false. Next, SpecialEmp is reconsidered after the second modification, which affects the same object o1. This time, the condition is true, since **old** refers to the initial database state, and o1's salary has increased by more than 5000 since the transaction's start. Thus, the object <o5, john> is created in the class SpecialEmp. Finally, on commit, o1's salary is found to be greater than the salary of o1's manager, and thus trigger AdjustSalary sets o1's salary back to 5000.

Consider now what happens if SpecialEmp is turned into an event-consuming trigger. In this case, each event is independently monitored, and thus even at the second consideration the condition of the trigger is false; thus, no object is inserted into the SpecialEmp class. However, if SpecialEmp is turned into an event-consuming, deferred trigger, then it is triggered only once by the transaction, on commit; **old** refers this time to the initial state, and thus the condition is again true.

Consider next the case when both AdjustSalary and SpecialEmp are deferred and assume now that there is no partial order between them; then, the outcome of the transaction depends on the internal ordering between the two triggers, which is defined by the system. Although the old salary does not change, the current salary is different depending on whether AdjustSalary is considered before or after SpecialEmp, and this changes the truth value of the comparison predicate in the condition of the trigger SpecialEmp. Thus, we cannot determine a priori whether the class SpecialEmp will contain one object or instead be empty. We say that their execution is not *confluent*; confluence will be discussed in Chapter 4. This example shows that imposing a partial order between triggers is essential to control their behavior in case of conflict.

Finally, we show an untargeted trigger monitoring events on more than one class. The trigger forces a rollback if the sum of salaries of employees of the "toys" department exceeds 500,000.

Example 2.9   Excessive salary rule

> **define trigger** ExcessiveSalary
> **events**   **create**(Employee), **modify**(Employee.Salary),
>   **modify**(Department.Employees)
> **condition**   Department(Y), Y.Name='toys', Employee(X),
>   X **in** Y.Employees, **sum**(X.Salary) > 500000
> **action**   **rollback**
> **end**;

2.5   Taxonomy of Active Database Concepts

We summarize the main features of active databases that were progressively introduced in the preceding sections.

We start with the fundamental features of active databases: events, conditions, and actions:

- The typical *events* considered by active rules are primitives for database state changes; several systems can also monitor retrievals, some systems monitor time-related events (e.g., at 5 p.m., every Friday), and some systems monitor application-defined, external events explicitly raised by applications.

- The *condition* is either a database predicate or a query. A condition returns a truth value: a query is interpreted as TRUE if it contains some tuples and as FALSE if it is empty.

- The *action* is an arbitrary data manipulation program; it may include transactional commands (such as **ROLLBACK WORK**) or rule manipulation commands (such as the activation or deactivation of active rules or of groups of active rules), and sometimes may activate externally defined procedures.

Some rules are limited to monitoring a single event. However, in most cases, rules monitor a collection of events, with an implicit disjunctive semantics: they become triggered if any one of the monitored events occurs. In some systems, it is possible from within the condition to test on the specific event occurrence that has caused the triggering of the rule. Some systems support rich *event languages*, in which complex events are built from simple events by means of an event calculus supporting conjunction, disjunction, negation, or precedence between events. With complex events, the rule processing system must include a sophisticated mechanism in order to check whether a given rule is triggered at a given point of the transaction's execution.

Consideration of active rules relative to the event being monitored can be immediate, deferred, or detached:

- *Immediate consideration* can occur **BEFORE** the event being monitored, **AFTER** the event, or **INSTEAD OF** the event; in this last option, the event primitive is not executed, and the rule's action is executed instead.

- *Deferred consideration* can occur at the end of a transaction (started by the **COMMIT WORK** transactional command), after user-defined commands, or following a user-defined command starting rule processing (e.g., the **PROCESS RULES** command).

- *Detached consideration* occurs in the context of a separate transaction that is spawned from the initial transaction after the event occurrence. There can be *causal dependencies* between the initial transaction and the detached transaction, for instance, postponing the commit of the detached transaction until after the commit of the initial transaction, or forcing the detached transaction to roll back if the initial transaction rolls back.

Execution of the action relative to the condition's consideration can be immediate, deferred, or detached as well:

- *Immediate execution*, where the action's execution immediately follows the condition's consideration, is used in almost all cases.

- *Deferred execution* postpones the action's execution until the end of the transaction or a user-defined command starting rule processing.

- *Detached execution* occurs in the context of a separate transaction that is spawned from the initial transaction after the rule consideration. In this case, there can be causal dependencies as well between the initial transaction and the detached transaction.

In most cases, events being monitored are changes of the database state; active rules may monitor state changes at different *levels of granularity*:

- State changes can be monitored at the *instance level* (i.e., changes affecting individual rows within tables or individual objects within classes).

- Alternatively, state changes can be monitored at the *statement level*, considering data manipulation statements as events.

Transition values are temporary data describing the state changes performed by a transaction, whose content is affected by the rule's level of granularity:

- When changes are monitored at the instance level, transition values are changes affecting a single tuple or object, typically accessed by means of the **OLD** and **NEW** correlation variables.

- When changes are monitored at the statement level, transition values are collective changes, collected into temporary structures such as the tables **INSERTED** and **DELETED**. Updates can be treated explicitly (e.g., by means of two tables **OLD-UPDATED** and **NEW-UPDATED**) or implicitly (e.g., by adding their before state to the **DELETED** table and their after state to the **INSERTED** table).

In many systems, multiple rules can be triggered at the same time; we say that these rules form a *conflict set*, and the rule processing algorithm must have a given policy for selecting rules out of the conflict set. In active databases, the selection of the next rule to be processed typically occurs after each rule consideration and possible execution. In this way, the next rule to be processed at a generic step of the processing could be triggered by the action of the last rule that was executed. Alternatively, rule selection can be done at given points of the rule processing algorithm, thus building a list of triggered rules that are next considered one after the other, until the list is emptied. This selection alternative is typically used by expert systems in the context of applications of artificial intelligence.

The selection of rules from the conflict set is influenced by *priorities*. The following alternatives are offered:

- Rules can be specified together with a numeric priority that defines their *total ordering*.

- Rules can be specified together with numeric or relative priorities that define a *partial ordering*. In this case, either the system keeps a system-defined total order that is consistent with the user-defined partial order, or else it selects top-level priority rules nondeterministically.

- Finally, rules could have no explicit prioritization mechanism. In this case also, either the system keeps a system-defined total order, or else it selects all rules nondeterministically.

Normally, systems have a system-defined prioritization. In such cases, executions are *repeatable*: two executions of the same transaction on the same database state with the same set of triggers yield the same execution sequence (and the same quiescent state, if it exists). However, some systems indicate their ordering criterion explicitly (i.e., based on rule creation time), while other systems do not indicate their ordering criterion.

In some systems, rules can be dynamically *deactivated* and then *activated*. Rule deactivation, however, is extremely dangerous, since one of the typical applications of active rules is integrity maintenance; in this case, rules preserving database integrity should not be arbitrarily deactivated by any database user. For this reason, active rules (as well as all database objects) are subject to the authorization mechanisms of the database; in particular, privileges of rule creation, altering, deletion, activation, and deactivation can be given only to database administrators, or else can be delegated to other users (e.g., through explicit **GRANT PRIVILEGE** commands).

Rules can be clustered into *groups*. Once a group is formed, it can be separately processed, activated, and deactivated; groups are also useful devices for assigning creation or execution privileges to users in a systematic way.

2.6   Bibliographic Notes

Reference [455] provides a complete and up-to-date treatment of active rules; the book includes chapters dedicated to the systems Postgres, Ariel, Starburst, A-RDL, Chimera, Hipac, and Ode, and then chapters on the description of general active rule features (including their implementation), on commercial systems, and on applications.

The four systems selected in this chapter for illustrating the syntax and semantics of active rules are described in the following research papers and manuals:

- The Starburst language is described in [457]. The implementation techniques used in the Starburst prototype are described in [456]. Priority management is discussed in [5].

- Oracle is defined in the manuals [320] and [319], while the problem of mutating tables is described in [327].

- Triggers for DB2 are illustrated in [114] and in the manual [220].

- Chimera is described in [94] and [95].

Among other relational systems supporting active rules, we mention Informix [222], Sybase [426], and Illustra [221]; among object-oriented research prototypes, we mention Reach [72], Ode [185], and NAOS [119].

Overviews of the various features of active databases, with a description of the concepts and terminology, are given in [332] (where various dimensions are given for an understanding of active behavior) and in [131] (where active database features are classified as either essential or optional, and an applicative classification of active database systems is proposed).

2.7 Exercises

2.1. Given the relational database schema

Employee(<u>Name</u>, Salary, Department)
Department(<u>Dept-No</u>, Manager)

define the following active rules in Starburst, Oracle, and DB2:

    a. A rule that, whenever a department is deleted from the database, sets to null the value of the Department attribute for those tuples in relation Employee having the number of the deleted department.

    b. A rule that, whenever a department is deleted from the database, deletes all employees in the deleted department.

    c. A rule that, whenever the salary of an employee exceeds the salary of its manager, sets the salary of the employee to the salary of the manager.

d. A rule that, whenever salaries are updated, if the total of the updated salaries exceeds their total before the updates, then gives all the employees of the 'Research' department a 5% salary cut.

Complete this exercise by writing the same triggers in Chimera on the following object-oriented schema (which is equivalent to the previous relational schema):

create object class Employee
attributes Name: **string**,
           Salary: **integer**,
           Department: Dept
end;

create object class Dept
attributes Manager: Employee
end;

2.2. Referring to the relational schema above, define in Starburst or Chimera a deferred trigger R_1 that, whenever an employee who is a manager is deleted, also deletes all employees in the department managed by the deleted employee, along with the department itself.

Then define another deferred trigger R_2 that, whenever salaries are updated, checks the average of the updated salaries; if it exceeds 50,000, then it deletes all employees whose salary was updated and now exceeds 80,000.

Consider next a database state containing six employees: Jane, Mary, Bill, Jim, Sam, and Sue, with the following management structure:

- Jane manages Mary and Jim.
- Mary manages Bill.
- Jim manages Sam and Sue.

Now suppose that a user transaction deletes employee Jane and updates salaries in a way such that the average updated salary exceeds 50,000 and Mary's updated salary exceeds 80,000. Describe the trigger processing started at the end of this transaction.

2.3. Given the Chimera class Employee, with an attribute Salary and a class RichEmployee with the same schema, define in Chimera a set of triggers ensuring that in any database state the set of instances of the class

RichEmployee coincides with the set of instances of the class Employee whose value for attribute Salary is greater than 50,000.

Chapter 3

Applications of Active Databases

Active rules satisfy different application needs. Broadly speaking, we distinguish between internal and external applications of active rules:

- The applications of active rules to support classical database management features, such as integrity maintenance, derived data maintenance, and replication management, are denoted as *internal*; these rules are often system-generated and hidden to the user, and the generation process is fully automatic. In many cases, internal rules can be *declaratively specified* (e.g., in the format of integrity constraints, data derivation rules, or requirements on replicated copies). Although not yet widespread, several other internal applications of active rules can be envisioned, including version maintenance, security administration, demand logging, and event tracking. The class of internal applications can be extended to incorporate rules that, although not relevant to database management, can be built from abstract specifications, such as rules for workflow management.

- Other rules embed applicative knowledge, and are classified as *external*; these are often called *business rules*, as they perform a part of the business computation that normally would be contained in the application code. Examples of business rules are trading rules following bond fluctuations, inventory management rules following stock variations, and energy management rules to respond to changes in power distribution requirements. A significant class of business rules is *alerters*; actions of these rules consist of simply giving a warning or displaying a message, without changing the database content. Business rules are most advantageous when they support policies that are shared by all applications, so that these policies are centralized once and for all. *Knowledge independence* is the extraction of knowledge from applications and the encoding of it in rules; it will be further discussed in Section 4.4.

The examples in this chapter are written either in Starburst or in Chimera and use set-oriented triggers.

3.1 Integrity Management

Integrity maintenance is the most significant internal application. Constraints are expressed declaratively through predicates, also called *integrity rules*, that give a specification of the conditions that must hold on the database. In particular, constraints may be classified as static or dynamic:

- *Static constraints* are predicates evaluated on database states.

- *Dynamic constraints* are predicates on state transitions, which compare two subsequent database states produced by a transaction.

Integrity constraints are further classified as built-in or generic:

- *Built-in constraints* are fixed; they are specified by special language constructs of the data definition language. In relational databases, these include keys, unique attributes, notnull attributes, and referential integrity, all of which are allowed, for example, in SQL-92.

- *Generic constraints* are arbitrary, specified by generic predicates or queries. Examples are the check clauses and the assertions supported by the SQL-92 standard.

Integrity is enforced by the system, either during transaction execution (immediate constraints) or at the commit time of the transaction (deferred constraints). Many systems, however, check the constraints with internally generated triggers. For instance, Oracle uses this means to check referential integrity constraints. Moreover, many systems support only limited forms of generic constraints, as they do not support assertions and provide only check clauses whose scope is limited to a single row. In this case, the only possibility for specifying generic integrity constraints consists in encoding them by means of active rules.

3.1.1 Rule Generation

Rules for integrity constraints can be generated in a semiautomatic manner. The designer is initially concerned with the understanding of the declarative formula of the constraint, which corresponds to the *condition* part of the rule. Next, he must concentrate on the causes that may violate the constraint; these contribute to the *event* part of the rule and can be syntactically determined by analyzing the condition. Finally, he is concerned about the actions that ensure the constraint is no longer violated, which contribute to the *action* part of the rule. This last step normally requires a good understanding of the application, since repair actions encompass a critical part of the application's semantics; however, a standard repair action can be automatically generated that consists of forcing a transactional or statement-level rollback.

Integrity constraints can be managed by active rules with two different approaches:

- At the simplest level, constraints can be encoded as simple triggers, called *abort rules*. They are activated by any event that can violate the constraint. Their precondition tests for the actual occurrence of violations; if a violation is detected, then the rule issues a rollback command. Thus, abort rules can be syntactically generated from declarative constraints and faithfully implement the behavior of declarative constraints. The disadvantage of this approach is that it causes frequent transactional or statement-level rollbacks.

- At the most sophisticated level, constraints are specified together with a maintenance policy that indicates an action to be performed on the database state when the constraint is violated, so that database integrity is restored. Typical examples are the referential integrity constraints of SQL-92, which are specified together with a repair action. In this case, constraints can be encoded as *repair rules*; these have the same precondition and triggering events as abort rules, but their action contains database manipulations for repairing constraint violations. For instance, repair actions for referential integrity reflect the semantics of the SQL-92 clauses **CASCADE**, **RESTRICT**, **SET NULL**, or **SET DEFAULT**, which represent four policies for correcting violations to referential integrity.

3.1.2   Example

Let us consider a simple referential integrity constraint expressed in Starburst. Consider the "classical" tables Emp (employee) and Dept (department) with an attribute DeptNo of Emp, which expresses a reference to the attribute Dno of Dept; the referential integrity constraint states that all employees must be assigned to a department. The operations that can violate the constraint are

1. insertions into Emp
2. deletions from Dept
3. updates to Emp.DeptNo
4. updates to Dept.Dno

The condition is expressed as a predicate on tuples of the Emp table, stating that each tuple must be associated with a department:

Emp: **EXISTS** (**SELECT** * **FROM** Dept **WHERE** Dno = Emp.DeptNo)

Note that this predicate indicates a property that must be **TRUE** for all legal employees; however, in an active rule we are interested in determining those employees who violate the constraint; for them, the predicate must be **FALSE**. Thus, we really consider the following condition, obtained by negating the previous formula:

Emp: **NOT EXISTS** (**SELECT** * **FROM** Dept **WHERE** Dno = Emp.DeptNo)

The above formula is called the *denial form* of the integrity constraint.

In order to be compliant with the Starburst syntax, where all rules need to be targeted to one specific table, we need to introduce two rules, one for Emp and one for Dept; each rule monitors the events relevant to its target table. Thus, we can automatically produce the following abort rules:

Example 3.1   Abort rules

```
CREATE RULE DeptEmp1 ON Emp
WHEN INSERTED, UPDATED(DeptNo)
IF      EXISTS (SELECT * FROM Emp WHERE NOT EXISTS
            (SELECT * FROM Dept
            WHERE Dno = Emp.DeptNo))
```

```
CREATE RULE DeptEmp2 ON Dept
WHEN DELETED, UPDATED(Dno)
IF      EXISTS (SELECT * FROM Emp
WHERE NOT EXISTS
              (SELECT * FROM Dept
               WHERE Dno = Emp.DeptNo))
THEN  ROLLBACK
```

Note that these rules are not efficient. Whenever an event occurs that could violate the constraint, they compute the condition relative to the entire database, without taking into account transition values. Instead, rules could be coded by assuming that the constraint holds on the initial state; in that case, it is sufficient to compute the condition relative to transition values.

Next we write four optimized maintenance rules for the same example, which use transition values for achieving efficiency in the computation. Events and conditions do not change, but the action is generated according to the referential integrity policy. Note that, in order to implement these policies, each of the events producing a violation is associated with a different active rule.

We start with the two rules targeted on Emp; we choose to set the department number of new employees to **NULL**, and to set the department number of employees who violate the constraint because of a change of department number to a default value of 99. Note that strict referential integrity as in SQL-92 forces the partial rollback of these operations, but the trigger designer can override this policy.

Example 3.2 Repair rules on table Emp

```
CREATE RULE DeptEmp1 ON Emp
WHEN INSERTED
IF      EXISTS ( SELECT * FROM INSERTED
                WHERE NOT EXISTS
                      (SELECT * FROM Dept
                       WHERE Dno = Emp.DeptNo))
THEN  UPDATE Emp
      SET DeptNo = NULL
      WHERE EmpNo IN
            (SELECT EmpNo FROM INSERTED)
      AND NOT EXISTS
            (SELECT * FROM Dept
             WHERE Dno = Emp.DeptNo))
```

CREATE RULE DeptEmp2 **ON** Emp
WHEN UPDATED(DeptNo)
IF　　**EXISTS (SELECT * FROM NEW-UPDATED**
　　　　　　　　WHERE NOT EXISTS
　　　　　　　　(SELECT * FROM Dept
　　　　　　　　　　　　WHERE Dno = Emp.DeptNo))
THEN　UPDATE Emp
　　　　SET DeptNo = 99
　　　　WHERE EmpNo **IN**
　　　　　　　(SELECT EmpNo **FROM NEW-UPDATED)**
　　　　AND NOT EXISTS
　　　　　　　(SELECT * FROM Dept
　　　　　　　WHERE Dno = Emp.DeptNo))

For the rules targeted on the Dept table, we opt for a *cascade delete* policy, which consists in deleting the employees who remain "orphans" after a deletion of their department. The condition is optimized by introducing a test on the existence of deleted or updated departments, under the assumption that attribute DeptNo is a key of table Dept; thus, if a given department number is deleted or updated, employees with that department number certainly remain orphans, and therefore they must be deleted as well.

Example 3.3　Repair rules on table Dept

CREATE RULE DeptEmp3 **ON** Dept
WHEN DELETED
IF　　**EXISTS (SELECT * FROM** Emp **WHERE EXISTS**
　　　　　　　(SELECT * FROM DELETED
　　　　　WHERE Dno = Emp.DeptNo))
THEN　DELETE FROM Emp
　　　　WHERE EXISTS
　　　　　　　(SELECT * FROM DELETED
　　　　　　　WHERE Dno = Emp.DeptNo)

CREATE RULE DeptEmp4 **ON** Dept
WHEN UPDATED(Dno)
IF　　**EXISTS (SELECT * FROM** Emp **WHERE EXISTS**
　　　　　　　(SELECT * FROM OLD-UPDATED
　　　　　WHERE Dno = Emp.DeptNo))
THEN　DELETE FROM Emp
　　　　WHERE EXISTS

(SELECT * FROM OLD-UPDATED
WHERE Dno = Emp.DeptNo)

3.2 Derived Data Maintenance

Another important internal application of rules is view and derived data maintenance. A *view* is a query on the database; the query returns a table (in the relational model) or class (in the object-oriented model) whose content is derived from the content of the database; views, however, can be transparently used by applications as any other relation or class of the database. Similarly, a *derived attribute* is an attribute of a relation or class whose content can be derived by means of a derivation formula, which can be transparently used by applications as any other attribute of the database. Data derivations for views or derived attributes can be expressed by declarative query languages such as SQL; alternatively, they can be expressed by *deductive rules* (i.e., declarative rules expressing how derived data should be deduced from source data). Deductive rules enhance the power of SQL by adding various features, the most important of which is *recursion*, extensively described in Part III.

In order to support views and derived data, a database management system can use two strategies:

- Derived data can be *virtually supported*; in this case, their content is computed on demand, whenever the application issues a query that uses either a view or a derived attribute.

- Alternatively, derived data can be *materialized*; their content is persistently stored in the database. Materialized data can be accessed as any other data, but their content must be recomputed whenever the source data from which they are derived is changed.

3.2.1 Rule Generation

Active rules can be used both for data derivation and for data materialization; virtual data derivation by active rules is, however, currently supported only for views in the Illustra database system. Illustra supports two features that are very useful for this purpose: the ability of rules to be triggered by **SELECT** queries, and the clause **INSTEAD OF** for indicating that the action should be executed instead of the triggering event. Thus, whenever an application queries a view, a rule is triggered on the **SELECT** and provides, instead of access to the view, access to the underlying source tables.

In general, however, active rules are most used for the materialization of derived data. Data materialization is either through refresh or through incremental maintenance.

- The *refresh* approach consists in recomputing from scratch derived data from the source tables after each update of the source data.
- The *incremental* approach consists in computing the change to the view from the change to the source table. This approach requires computing the positive and negative *deltas*, consisting of the tuples that should be, respectively, inserted into or deleted from the view.

Rule generation for the materialization of derived data can be fully automatic: once the derivation rule is specified and the causes that make the rule invalid are syntactically determined, actions that make the view up-to-date can also be generated automatically. Refresh rules are very simple, while incremental rules are more complex and must be generated specifically for given structures of derivation rules; difficulties arise mainly from recursion and from the existence of duplicates and/or of multiple derivations for the same tuple of a view. A theory of incremental rules for derived data maintenance is outside the scope of this book.

These techniques give us devices for transforming deductive rules expressing data derivations into active rules; such transformation is particularly useful when deductive rules are not directly supported by a target database system.

3.2.2   Example

Let us consider the relational view selecting those departments that have at least one "rich" employee (who earns more than 50,000):

DEFINE VIEW HighPaidDept **AS**
     (**SELECT DISTINCT** Dept.Name
    FROM Dept, Emp
    WHERE Dept.Dno = Emp.DeptNo
    AND Emp.Sal > 50K)

The events that may cause the recomputation of the view are

1. insertions into Emp
2. insertions into Dept
3. deletions from Emp
4. deletions from Dept
5. updates to Emp.DeptNo

6. updates to Emp.Sal
7. updates to Dept.Dno

The refresh rules for this view, written in Starburst, are the following:

Example 3.4 Refresh rules

    CREATE RULE RefreshHighPaidDept1 **ON** Dept
    WHEN INSERTED, **DELETED**,
        UPDATED(DeptNo), **UPDATED**(Sal)
    THEN DELETE * **FROM** HighPaidDept;
        INSERT INTO HighPaidDept:
          (**SELECT DISTINCT** Dept.Name
          FROM Dept, Emp
          WHERE Dept.Dno = Emp.DeptNo
          AND Emp.Sal > 50K)

    CREATE RULE RefreshHighPaidDept2 **ON** Emp
    WHEN INSERTED, **DELETED**, **UPDATED**(Dno)
    THEN DELETE * **FROM** HighPaidDept;
        INSERT INTO HighPaidDept:
          (**SELECT DISTINCT** Dept.Name
          FROM Dept, Emp
          WHERE Dept.Dno = Emp.DeptNo
          AND Emp.Sal > 50K)

An incremental rule is easily written for the **INSERT** event on Dept, shown below, but it is more complex for other events.

Example 3.5 Incremental refresh rule

    CREATE RULE IncrRefreshHighPaidDept1 **ON** Dept
    WHEN INSERTED
    THEN INSERT INTO HighPaidDept:
        (**SELECT DISTINCT** Dept.Name
        FROM INSERTED, Emp
        WHERE INSERTED.Dno = Emp.DeptNo
        AND Emp.Sal > 50K)

3.3 Replication

Replication is a particular form of data derivation between several copies of the same information, which must be kept aligned. In general, replication is used in distributed systems: two or more copies of the same information are kept on different database servers. In a distributed system, keeping copies synchronized at all times is too expensive, and typically not required from an applicative viewpoint, since copies do not need to be identical at all times. Therefore, asynchronous techniques are used for propagating changes from one copy to another, rather than synchronizing them in the context of distributed transactions. Two replication schemes are used:

- The most widely used approach to replication distinguishes between a *primary copy* and one or more *secondary copies*. All changes are performed on the primary copy, while the secondary copy is asynchronously updated by the replication manager and is read-only for all applications. Changes to the primary copy are first monitored by a *capture module* installed at the primary copy site and then propagated to the copy by an *apply module* installed on the sites storing the secondary copies. Typically, the change capture occurs in the context of applications that modify the primary copies, while the change application is performed asynchronously.

- A more recent approach is *symmetric replication*, in which two copies can asynchronously accept changes. Thus, each of them in turn plays the role of both primary and secondary copy, and each has both a capture and an apply module. Concurrent updates can be performed on the copies without requiring their synchronization; obviously, this can cause losses of consistency between the copies, which must be recognized and reported to applications.

Active rules provide an efficient mechanism for implementing the capture module; they run in the context of transactions that perform the changes to source data, and construct the positive and negative deltas (i.e., the tuples that should be added to or dropped from the secondary copy in order to make it consistent with the primary). Deltas are next applied to secondary copies. The following active rules, written in Starburst, perform the capture function:

Example 3.6   Capture rules

```
CREATE RULE Capture1 ON Primary
WHEN INSERTED
THEN  INSERT INTO PosDelta
        (SELECT * FROM INSERTED)
```

```
CREATE RULE Capture2 ON Primary
WHEN DELETED
THEN  INSERT INTO NegDelta
      (SELECT * FROM DELETED)


CREATE RULE Capture3 ON Primary
WHEN UPDATED
THEN INSERT INTO PosDelta
      (SELECT * FROM NEW-UPDATED);
      INSERT INTO NegDelta
      (SELECT * FROM OLD-UPDATED)
```

3.4 Workflow Management

Workflow managers are emerging software systems for organizing the working activities within enterprises. They support a description of the process, and they help its execution and management by monitoring the assignment of tasks to users and by assisting their coordination through document and message exchange.

The workflow management paradigm is a reactive one: workflow managers monitor the events that occur in the system and then perform the required event management activities. Events can be *internal* (i.e., generated from within the workflow manager while workflows are progressing) or *external* (i.e., representing the interaction of the workflow manager with the external world). In particular, events may represent exceptions to the normal execution of workflows. For the features described above, workflow management is a very promising field of application for active databases.

An example of an internal event representing an exceptional situation is the sudden unavailability of an agent who is performing an urgent task; in such a case, the task is assigned to the agent's substitute, provided that he is in turn available. With suitable Chimera classes describing agents and tasks, the following trigger performs the required exception management:

```
define trigger WF1 for Agent
    events      modify(Agent.Availability)
    condition   Agent(A), occurred(modify(Agent.Availability),A),
                A.Availability=FALSE, task(T), T.Responsible=A,
                T.Type='Urgent', Agent(B), A.Substitute=B,
                B.Availability=TRUE
```

```
    actions      modify(Task.Responsible, T, B)
end;
```

An exceptional situation in a car rental workflow occurs when one of the company's cars is damaged in an accident and that car is booked for a car rental. In such a case, the workflow system creates a warning message that includes the booking number and responsible agent; based on that message, the agent will find a substitute for the car or inform the client. The following trigger performs the required exception management:

```
define trigger WF2 for Accident
    events       create(Accident)
    condition    Accident(A), occurred(create, A),
                 Booking(B), B.Car=A.DamagedCar,
    actions      create(Warning,[B.Number,B.Agent],X)
end;
```

3.5 Business Rules

Business rules model the reaction to events that occur in the real world, with tangible side effects on the database content, so as to encapsulate the application's reactive behavior to such events. Their organization and content are not regular and cannot be anticipated or declaratively specified. Representative examples of business rules, from real-life applications, include rules for stock and bond trading in financial applications, for airway assignment to flights in air traffic control systems, for order management in inventory control systems, and so on. The common feature of these rules is to respond to external events by pursuing certain objectives: profit maximization, flight safety, optimal warehouse logistics, and so on.

Generation of business rules is a critical process; the designer should be concerned with the portion of application-specific reactive processing, modeled by active rules rather than supported by the applications. We will come back to the design of business rules in the next chapter; in particular, Section 4.4 presents a methodology for the generation of business rules.

3.5.1 A Case Study: Energy Management System (EMS)

We conclude this chapter with an example of an application that is modeled with active rules covering the business process. We will look at a fragment of the Energy Management System (EMS), a system managing the Italian electrical power distribution network. The EMS network is composed of *sites* and *branches* connecting site pairs. Sites can be power stations, where power is generated; intermediate nodes, used for power distribution throughout the network; or final users, which make use of electrical power. The operating conditions of the network are monitored daily, with frequent reconfigurations; the topology is modified only once per month. An "operational network" has a radial topology (a forest of trees connecting power stations to users), although many other branches exist that can be dynamically added to or dropped from the network. The purpose of the network is to transfer the exact power from distributors to users through nodes and (directed) branches connecting node pairs. To this purpose, several wires are placed along the branches; wires are of given types, and each type carries a maximum power. Active rules are used to respond to input transactions asking for reconfigurations due to new users, or to changes in their required power, or to changes in the assignments of wires and tubes; note that in this example the same rules serve several different input transactions.

3.5.2 Database Schema for the EMS Case Study

We give a flat representation of the schema, without using generalization hierarchies. Nodes of the network are described by the classes Distributor, User, and Node. The class Distributor describes electrical power generators that provide power to the network, while the class User describes consumers of the network power. The class Node describes intermediate sites, where power is transferred in order to be distributed.

```
create object class IntNode
attributes NodeId: Site,
           BranchIn: Branch,
           Power: real
end;

create object class User
attributes UserId: Site,
           BranchIn: Branch,
           Power: real
end;

create object class Distributor
attributes NodeId: Site,
           Power: real,
           MaxPower: real
end;
```

The topology of the network is described in the class Branch, which contains all the connections between site pairs. The connections are described in the class Wire and can have a type described in the class WireType.

create object class Branch
attributes From: Site,
                 To: Site,
                 Power: **real**
end;

create object class Wire
attributes From: Site,
                 To: Site,
                 Type: WireType,
                 Power: **real**
end;

Create object type WireType
attributes MaxPower: **real**
end;

3.5.3 Business Rules for the EMS Case Study

The application gathers several users' requests and then applies all of them within a transaction; business rules propagate changes in the users' requirements up in the trees connecting users to distributors. The transaction fails if the maximum power of some distributors is exceeded because this situation forces the network's redesign, which is done manually. Otherwise, rules adapt the network to the new needs. In order to avoid an early propagation of increased requests that may lead to unnecessary rollbacks, rules propagate the reductions of power first and the increases of power next. If the requested power on wires exceeds the maximum power that can be carried by them, then rules automatically change or add wires in the relevant branches. These specifications yield to the following 11 rules, described first in natural language (for ease of understanding) and next in Chimera. Priorities require that rules R_2, R_3, and R_4 precede rules R_5, R_6, and R_7.

R_1: *If a new user node requires power, connect it to the closest node.*
R_2: *If a user or a node requires less power, change the power of the user or node and propagate the change to its input branch.*

R_3: *If a branch requires less power, change the power of the branch and propagate the change to its input node.*

R_4: *If the power required from a distributor is decreased, change its output power accordingly.*

R_5: *If a user or node requires more power, change the power of the user or node and propagate the change to its input branch.*

R_6: *If a branch requires more power, change the power of the branch and propagate the change to its input node.*

R_7: *If the power required from a distributor is increased, change its output power accordingly.*

R_8: *If a distributor's power exceeds its maximum, rollback the entire transaction.*

R_9: *If a branch's power is changed, change the power of some of its wires accordingly.*

R_{10}: *If a wire's power is above its threshold, change wire type.*

R_{11}: *If there's no suitable wire type, add another wire to the branch.*

We next show these rules written in Chimera. This is a nontrivial rule set that serves the purpose of showing a complex application of active rules; it can be skipped by the uninterested reader. Several user-defined functions and procedures are not further defined: function closest(U,N) finds the node N closest to a given user U; function one(set) returns an element randomly selected among the set of elements passed as arguments. Rules R_2 and R_5 have two versions, each targeted on a different class.

Example 3.7   Business rules for the EMS case study

```
define trigger R1 for User
    events      create
    condition   User(U), occurred(create,U),
                Node(N), closest(U,N),
    actions     create(Branch,[U.UserId,N.NodeId,U.Power],X),
                create(Wire,[U.UserId,N.UserId,'default',U.Power],Y)
    end;
```

Trigger R1 reacts to the creation of a new user; it determines the node N in the network that is closest to the new user and connects the new user to N with a branch and a wire.

define trigger R2.1 **for** User
    events   **modify**(Power)
    condition   User(U), **occurred**(**modify**(Power),U),
               real(R), R=**old**(U.Power)-U.Power, R > 0,
               Branch(B), U.BranchIn=B
    actions   **modify**(Branch.Power,B,B.Power-R)
before R5.1,R5.2,R6,R7
end;

Trigger R2.1 reacts to a decrease in the power requested by a user; it selects the branch incoming to the user and propagates the power decrease to the branch.

define trigger R2.2 **for** IntNode
    events   **modify**(Power)
    condition   IntNode(N), **occurred**(**modify**(Power),N),
               real(R), R=**old**(N.Power)-N.Power, R > 0,
               Branch(B), N.BranchIn=B
    actions   **modify**(Branch.Power,B,B.Power-R)
before R5.1,R5.2,R6,R7
end;

Trigger R2.2 reacts to a decrease in power requested by a node; it selects the branch incoming to the node and propagates the power decrease to the branch.

define trigger R3 **for** Branch
    events   **modify**(Power)
    condition   Branch(B), **occurred**(**modify**(Power),B),
               real(R), R=**old**(B.Power)-B.Power, R > 0,
               IntNode(N), N.From=B
    actions   **modify**(IntNode.Power,N,N.Power-R)
before R5.1,R5.2,R6,R7
end;

Trigger R3 reacts to a decrease in power transmitted along a branch; it selects the source node of the branch and propagates the power decrease to the node.

define trigger R4 **for** Branch
    events   **modify**(Power)
    condition   Branch(B), **occurred**(**modify**(Power),B),
                  real(R), R=**old**(B.Power)-B.Power, R > 0,
                  Distributor(D), D.From=B
    actions   **modify**(Distributor.Power,D,D.Power-R)
before R5.1,R5.2,R6,R7
end;

Trigger R4 reacts to a decrease in power transmitted along a branch directly connected to a distributor; it selects the distributor and propagates the power decrease to it.

define trigger R5.1 **for** User
    events   **create**, **modify**(Power)
    condition   User(U), **occurred**(**modify**(Power),U),
                  real(R), R=**old**(U.Power)-U.Power, R < 0,
                  Branch(B), U.BranchIn=B
    actions   **modify**(Branch.Power,B,B.Power-R)
before R5.1,R5.2,R6,R7
end;

Trigger R5.1 reacts to the creation of a new user or to the increase in power requested by a user; it behaves like trigger R2.1.

define trigger R5.2 **for** IntNode
    events   **modify**(Power)
    condition   IntNode(N), **occurred**(**modify**(Power),N),
                  real(R), R=**old**(N.Power)-N.Power, R < 0,
                  Branch(B), N.BranchIn=B
    actions   **modify**(Branch.Power,B,B.Power-R)
end;

Trigger R5.2 reacts to a decrease in power requested at a node; it behaves like trigger R2.2.

define trigger R6 **for** Branch
    events   **modify**(Power)
    condition   Branch(B), **occurred**(**modify**(Power),B),
                  real(R), R=**old**(B.Power)-B.Power, R < 0,
                  IntNode(N), N.From=B

   actions   **modify**(IntNode.Power,N,N.Power-R)
end;

Trigger R6 reacts to an increase in power transmitted along a branch; it
behaves like trigger R3.

define trigger R9 **for** Branch

define trigger R7 **for** Branch
   events   **modify**(Power)
   condition   Branch(B), **occurred**(**modify**(Power),B),
                 real(R), R=**old**(B.Power)-B.Power, R < 0,
                 Distributor(D), D.From=B
   actions   **modify**(Distributor.Power,D,D.Power-R)
end;

Trigger R7 reacts to a decrease in power transmitted along a branch directly
connected to a distributor; it behaves like trigger R4.

define trigger R8 **for** Distributor
   events   **modify**(Power)
   condition   Distributor(D), **occurred**(**modify**(Power),D),
                 D.Power > D.MaxPower
   actions   **rollback**
end;

Trigger R8 reacts to a request for an increase in power at a distributor that
exceeds the distributor's maximum power; it rolls the transaction back.

define trigger R9 **for** Branch
   events   **modify**(Power)
   condition   Branch(B), **occurred**(**modify**(Power),B),
                 real(R), R=**old**(B.Power)-B.Power,
                 Wire(W), W.From=B.From, W.To=B.To,
                 integer(C), C=count(W)
   actions   **modify**(Wire.Power,W,W.Power-(R/C))
end;

Trigger R9 reacts to the change in power transferred along a given branch
by propagating the change to the wires placed along the branch; the change
is equally distributed to all the wires of the branch.

define trigger R10 **for** Wire
   events   **create**, **modify**(Power), **modify**(Type)

condition	Wire(W), **occurred**(**create**, **modify**(Power),
	modify(Type), W),
	W.Power > W.Type.MaxPower, WireType(WT1),
	WT1.MaxPower = **min**(R **where** real(R), WireType(WT2),
	R = WT2.MaxPower, R > W.Power),
actions	**modify**(Wire.Type,W,one(WT1))

end;

Trigger R10 reacts to the creation of wires or to the change in power carried by a wire when the power exceeds the maximum for its wire type and a wire type exists that can support the new power request. In that case, one suitable wire type is selected, and then the wire type of the selected wire is modified.

define trigger R11 **for** Wire
events	**create**, **modify**(Power), **modify**(Type)
condition	Wire(W), **occurred**(**create**, **modify**(Power),
	modify(Type), W),
	W.Power > **max**(R **where** real(R), WireType(WT),
	R=WT.MaxPower)
actions	**modify**(Wire.Power,W,0.8×W.Type.MaxPower),
	create(Wire,[W.From, W.To, W.Type,
	(W.Power-0.8×W.Type.MaxPower)],X)

end;

Trigger R11 reacts to the change in power carried by a given wire when the power exceeds the maximum for its wire type and no wire type exists that can support the new power request. In that case, that wire is assigned to 80 percent of its maximum power, and the remaining power is carried by another wire that is created and placed on the given branch. This change triggers R10, which checks that the power carried by the newly introduced wire does not exceed its maximum power.

3.6 Bibliographic Notes

The "declarative approach" to active rule generation, which consists in giving a declarative specification of active rules and then automatically or semi-automatically generating them by appropriate translation, is described in [96] (relative to integrity constraint management) and [97] (relative to view maintenance). Incremental view maintenance is discussed in [201] and [98]; problems due to the existence of duplicates in views are focused on in [200] and [195]. A technique for the automatic generation of repair actions for integrity constraints, which takes into account the user's informal indications on the semantics of desired repair rules, is discussed in [93].

The use of active rules for workflow enactment is suggested in [125] and carefully specified in [86]; this paper is developed in the context of the WIDE Esprit project, whose aim is to use active rules and enhanced transactions in support of workflow management systems. The use of active rules for implementing active agents is discussed in [188], which uses workflow management as an example of application of the active agent paradigm.

The EMS application, summarized in this chapter, is further described in [292] and [36]. A significant application of active rules to building design is presented in [421]; the peculiarity of that approach is that rulesets can be dynamically activated and deactivated in order to adapt to the progression of the design.

3.7   Exercises

3.1. Given the relational database schema

> Ph.D. Student(<u>Email</u>, Name, Area, Supervisor)
> Prof(<u>Email</u>, Name, Area)
> Course(<u>Title</u>, Prof)
> CoursesTaken(<u>PhDSt</u>, <u>Course</u>)

derive the triggers for maintaining the following integrity constraints:

   a. Each Ph.D. student must work in the same area as their supervisor.

   b. Each Ph.D. student must take at least one course.

   c. Each Ph.D. student must take the courses taught by their supervisor.

3.2. Given the relational database schema

> Employee(<u>Name</u>, DeptCode)
> Department(<u>DeptCode</u>, DeptName, City, Budget)

and the view MilanEmp, defined as

SELECT Name
FROM Employee, Department

WHERE Employee.DeptCode = Department.DeptCode
    AND Department.City = 'Milano'

    a. define the triggers for incrementally maintaining the view

    b. define the triggers for handling updates (insertions and deletions) through the view

3.3. Consider the set of rules specified in Section 3.5.3. Draw a simple energy management network consisting of a few nodes and connections, then populate the corresponding classes in Chimera. Think of simple update operations and generate the corresponding execution trace, listing triggers that are subsequently considered and executed; show the final quiescent state obtained at the end of rule processing. Think of one update operation that causes the execution of the abort trigger R8.

Chapter 4

Design Principles
for Active Rules

The previous chapters have shown that the technology and availability of active databases—both research prototypes and commercial products—have grown tremendously and that active rules offer a wide range of applications; however, the impact of this technology has been marginal so far, certainly below its potential. For the vendors of relational products, trigger systems are an essential part of their software, requested by the market and available on all products; however, database administrators and application developers still make little use of the triggers. Their general fear is that, once significant portions of the application's semantics are modeled as active rules, then the application itself is less performing and less "under control."

Researchers and professionals have reached a consensus that design methods and tools are the key for warranting a larger exposure of technology to the end users—a large community of experts in database design and programming. The above considerations motivate the focus of this chapter on design methods for active rules. Throughout this chapter, we deliberately use examples described in the various active database languages presented in Chapter 2, thus showing that design principles do not specifically address the syntax or semantics of one system, but rather they constitute a theory applicable to any active rule system.

4.1 Properties of Active Rule Execution

Designing individual active rules is not too difficult, once it is well understood that the rule reacts to a given event, tests a given condition, and performs a given action. However, understanding the collective behavior of active rules is much more difficult than just observing them individually because rule interactions are often subtle and unexpected. Thus, the main problem in the design of an active rule set regards their collective behavior. Termination, confluence, and observable determinism are the most relevant properties for understanding the collective behavior of a set of active rules:

- A rule set guarantees *termination* when, for any user-defined transaction triggering the processing of rules, the processing eventually terminates, producing a final state.

- A rule set guarantees *confluence* when, for any user-defined transaction triggering the processing of rules, the processing eventually terminates, producing a unique final state that does not depend on the order of execution of the rules.

- A rule set guarantees *observable determinism* when, in addition to confluence, for any user-defined transaction, all visible actions performed by rules (including alerting by means of messages or output production) are the same.

These abstract properties are not equally important or desirable; in the following, we consider each of them separately. The process of checking, at rule design time, that the above properties hold is termed *rule analysis*. Rule analysis is performed through both formal, automatic techniques and informal reasoning.

4.1.1   Termination

Termination is the key design principle for active rules. In many cases, the first set of rules delivered by designers is subject to endless loop behaviors, even after a careful design, because of unexpected interactions between rules; reasoning about termination forces the designer to reason about rule interactions and indirectly results in a better understanding of rules.

A *triggering graph* is an effective representation of rules for reasoning about termination. Nodes of this graph are rules themselves; an edge connects two rules R_1 and R_2 whenever the execution of R_1 may cause the triggering of R_2. This property can be observed syntactically in any of the four active database systems presented in the previous chapter. For instance, in the following example we consider two rules T1 and T2 written in Starburst; an edge of the triggering graph is established between T1 and T2 because the action of T1 causes the triggering of T2.

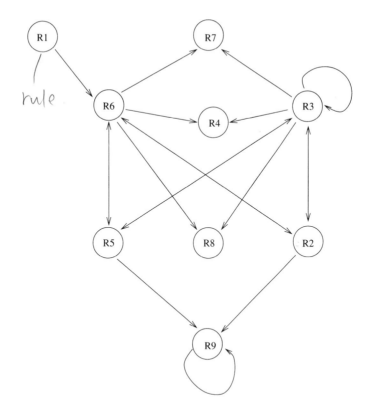

Figure 4.1: Example of a triggering graph

CREATE RULE T1 **FOR** Table1
WHEN ...
IF ...
THEN UPDATE Table1.Attr1 ...

CREATE RULE T2 **FOR** Table1
WHEN UPDATED(Attr1)
IF ...
THEN ...

Formally, given an arbitrary active rule set, the triggering graph is a directed graph $\{N, E\}$, where each node $n_i \in N$ corresponds to a rule $r_i \in R$. A directed arc $\langle r_j, r_k \rangle \in E$ means that the action of rule r_j generates events that trigger rule r_k. An example of a triggering graph is provided in Figure 4.1.

If the triggering graph is acyclic, then the number of rules that can be transitively triggered by a transaction is bound by some upper limit. However, it is not true that all executions of rules associated with a cyclic triggering graph will last forever. There are many cases of cyclic triggering graphs that correspond to a terminating behavior because at rule execution time the rules do not actually trigger each other.

Let us consider again the rule SalaryControl that was introduced in Section 2.1, repeated here for convenience.

CREATE RULE SalaryControl **ON** Emp
WHEN INSERTED, DELETED, UPDATED (Sal)
IF   (**SELECT AVG** (Sal) **FROM** Emp) > 100
THEN UPDATE Emp
          SET Sal = .9 * Sal

The triggering graph associated with this singleton rule set has only one node and one edge, but it is cyclic; thus, from the triggering graph we cannot determine whether the rule set guarantees termination. In Section 2.4 we argued that termination is guaranteed because the rule's action decreases the average salary and the rule's condition checks that the average salary is below a given threshold; thus, rule processing converges to a quiescent state. However, the rule SalaryControl2, described below, which is associated with the same triggering graph, has a quite different behavior.

Example 4.1   Revised salary control rule

　　CREATE RULE SalaryControl2 **ON** Emp
　　WHEN INSERTED, DELETED, UPDATED (Sal)
　　IF   (**SELECT AVG** (Sal) **FROM** Emp) > 100
　　THEN UPDATE Emp
　　 SET Sal = 1.1 * Sal

In the above rule, if the condition is TRUE for whatever reason, then the action causes the retriggering of the rule and, at the same time, changes the value of the attribute Sal but does not change the truth value of the condition, thus yielding an infinite loop; termination is clearly not guaranteed, although some transactions could still safely terminate.

In general, the analysis of triggering graphs is very conservative; many cycles of the triggering graph do not correspond to endless executions. Thus, cycles in triggering graphs give hints on possible causes of nontermination; then the designer can focus on a restricted number of "dangerous" cases, and either realize that rule processing terminates because of the actual semantics of the rules, or change the rule design.

Several techniques exist for improving rule analysis through "semantic reasoning," as illustrated by the previous example. Such semantic reasonings, based on rule semantics, improve a purely syntactic analysis and allow us to conclude at rule compilation time that termination occurs even with cyclic triggering graphs. Unfortunately, the problem is undecidable in general, since it includes as a required step the proof of implication between the predicates of first-order logic. The semantic techniques defined in the literature follow a finite number of approaches, yet they cover a relevant subset of all possible cases.

The first possible improvement consists in testing, for each arc $< r_i, r_j >$ in the triggering graph, whether we can conclude that the condition of r_j is guaranteed to be false after the execution of r_i, even if r_j is triggered by r_i's action; in this case, the arc can be removed from the graph.

Consider the following DB2 triggers, which maintain the consistency between several Grades, supposed of numeric type and stored within the Exam table, and the AvgGrade value in the student's general record.

Example 4.2   Grade consistency rules

```
CREATE TRIGGER AlignAvgGrade
AFTER UPDATE OF Grade ON Exam
REFERENCING NEW AS N
FOR EACH ROW
    UPDATE Student
    SET AvgGrade = SELECT AVG(Grade)
                   FROM Exam
                   WHERE StudentNumber = N.StudentNumber


CREATE TRIGGER CheckGrade
AFTER UPDATE OF AvgGrade ON Student
REFERENCING NEW AS N
FOR EACH ROW
WHEN (AvgGrade <> SELECT AVG(Grade)
                  FROM EXAM
                  WHERE StudentNumber = N.StudentNumber)
    UPDATE Student
    SET AvgGrade = SELECT AVG(Grade)
        FROM Exam
        WHERE StudentNumber = N.StudentNumber
```

We first discuss termination, then make some comments about the applicative adequacy of these triggers. The triggering graph of the above rule set includes two nodes (for rules AlignAvgGrade and CheckGrade) and two edges (from the former rule to the latter, and a ring on the latter). However, both edges can be removed after semantic analysis, because the actions of both rules make the condition of CheckGrade certainly false.

From an application-oriented viewpoint, the above rules seem to be in excess: if we could safely assume, possibly by suitable authorization commands, that the values of attribute AvgGrade are changed only as the effect of the rule AlignAvgGrade, then we could safely remove the rule CheckGrade, whose only purpose is to react to other sources of change of the attribute AvgGrade (for instance, an explicit update by a malicious student). Indeed, CheckGrade is always triggered by AlignAvgGrade, but this produces no effect other than the unnecessary processing of the query in CheckGrade's condition. However, CheckGrade is probably automatically generated as the effect of compiling a **CHECK** statement in SQL, which specifies declaratively a constraint on the AvgGrade field of the Student table. This example shows that active rules interact in subtle ways with integrity maintenance, but also that active rules can be very effective in restoring integrity, as noted in the previous chapter.

The above analysis can be further improved by considering that we do not really need to guarantee, for a given edge $< r_i, r_j >$, that the condition of r_j is always false; it is sufficient to guarantee that the new data produced by r_i do not satisfy the condition of r_j. In this way, r_j executes only because of the data that are resident in the database or generated by the triggering transaction or by other rules, but r_i does not contribute to repeated executions of r_j; for termination analysis, the edge $< r_i, r_j >$ can be removed.

For example, consider the following two DB2 triggers, which are used to set all out-of-scale values of attribute Grade in the Exam table to **NULL**. Assume that grades range, as in Italy, between 18 and 30.

Example 4.3   Grade range rules

```
CREATE TRIGGER CheckGradeDomain1
AFTER UPDATE OF Grade ON Exam
REFERENCING NEW AS N
FOR EACH ROW
WHEN (N.Grade > 30)
     UPDATE Exam
     SET Grade = NULL
     WHERE ExamNumber = N.ExamNumber
```

```
CREATE TRIGGER CheckGradeDomain2
AFTER UPDATE OF Grade ON Exam
REFERENCING NEW AS N
FOR EACH ROW
WHEN (N.Grade < 18)
THEN UPDATE Exam
    SET Grade = NULL
    WHERE ExamNumber = N.ExamNumber
```

Although the action of each of the two triggers CheckGradeDomain does not make the condition of the other one false, it does not add tuples that could satisfy the condition of the other one; both triggers could execute once and then be retriggered once, but both triggers at the second retriggering would have a false condition, thereby guaranteeing termination. Thus, the two edges between the two rules can be removed from the triggering graph for termination analysis.

4.1.2 Confluence

Confluence of set-oriented rules follows immediately from their termination if the rules are totally ordered; in this case, whenever multiple rules are triggered, one of them is deterministically selected for consideration and/or execution. Most set-oriented rules supported by database systems are deterministically scheduled by the system (although sometimes the rule sequence is not easily controlled by the user), and therefore set-oriented rule execution is normally confluent. This is the case with Chimera and Starburst and also with the set-oriented triggers of Oracle and DB2.

However, confluence is much harder to ensure in the presence of row-level granularity rules (or the object-oriented rules of some object-oriented research prototypes). In this case, confluence requires that each rule produce a final state regardless of the order in which tuples are accessed, which is typically determined by the database system. Ensuring this property is very hard, especially when rules trigger each other: a tuple change may trigger a rule that performs another tuple change and thus activates another rule, and so on; in such a context, at a given point of rule processing, there may be tuples that have been the source of complex rule chains, and other tuples of the same relation that are still waiting to be processed. Some relational products raise an exception, called a *mutating table exception*, when a table that is currently being updated also needs to be changed by a rule; this, however, imposes severe limitations on the possible computations that may

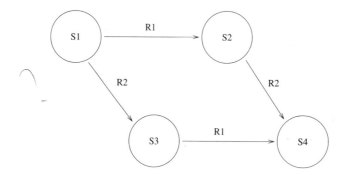

Figure 4.2: Commutative rules

be performed by the active rule system, and so should be considered as an overly restrictive requirement for providing confluence.

From an applicative point of view, confluence is not necessarily desirable: there are many applications where any one of the final states produced by a terminating rule set is equally acceptable. As an example, in a workflow application where each task must be assigned to some employee, it may be acceptable to assign tasks to employees and aim only at equalizing their global load, without really worrying about which employee is assigned to which task. In this case, confluence to an identical final solution is inessential. Thus, the use of tuple-oriented rules is best associated with applications that admit nondeterminism and abandon confluence.

With tuple-oriented rules or partially ordered set-oriented rules, non-determinism can occur. Under these assumptions, sufficient conditions for confluence can be defined. The basic notion is to determine whether two rules can commute; we say that two rules r_i and r_j are *commutative* within a given rule set R if, given any database state, considering rule r_i and then rule r_j produces the same database as considering rule r_j and then rule r_i (see Figure 4.2). Given any rule set for which termination is guaranteed, a sufficient condition for confluence requires that all rules commute. Such a condition is too restrictive, as it is sufficient to impose commutativity to a smaller set of rules, whose identification, however, is rather complex and will not be discussed here. An example of commutative rules in Chimera is the following:

Example 4.4   Commutative rules

```
create trigger T1 for C1
    events      modify(A1)
    condition   C1(X), X.A1=7
```

```
    actions        modify(C1.A2,X,A2+1)
  end;
```

```
  create trigger T2 for C1
     events        modify(A1)
     condition     C1(X), X.A1=7
     actions        modify(C1.A2,X,A2+2)
  end;
```

The above rules are both triggered on changes to attribute A1 of class C1, and both perform a change to attribute A2 of the same class; given that increments and decrements are commutative, they may execute in any order, and still the final value of A2 for all affected objects will not change. Thus, if we had a rule system consisting of rules T1 and T2 only, we could conclude that it is confluent.

4.1.3   Observable Determinism

Observable determinism is a stronger condition than confluence, as it prescribes that, for any input application, rule processing execution terminates in the same final state with the same output sequence; examples of outputs include messages produced by rules or display activities, such as reports. Observable determinism is easily achieved with set-oriented rules by imposing a total ordering on them. Most applications do not require observable determinism, since the order in which outputs are produced is irrelevant as long as the same outputs are produced for the same transaction.

For instance, the following two rules are confluent but do not satisfy the requirements of observable determinism because the display actions reveal the contents of the intermediate states reached after the execution of either one of the rules, and the intermediate states are different.

Example 4.5   Commutative rules with display action

```
  create trigger T1 for C1
     events        modify(A1)
     condition     C1(X), X.A1=7
     actions        modify(C1.A2,X,A2+1),
                    display(I where integer(I), I=X.A2)
  end;
```

```
  create trigger T2 for C1
     events        modify(A1)
```

condition   C1(X), X.A1=7
actions   **modify**(C1.A2,X,A2+2),
                 display(I **where** integer(I), I=X.A2)
end;

4.2   Rule Modularization

Modularization is a key design principle in software design. It enables the designer to focus on subsets of the original problem, thus partitioning a large design space; in software engineering, modularization enables the separation of programming "in the small" from programming "in the large." With active rules, modules (or *groups*) typically consist of subsets of the entire active rule set, which are put together due to shared properties (e.g., all rules dealing with a given applicative problem, or defined by a given user, or relative to a given target). In this section, we discuss modularization relative to termination, which is the main design problem of active rules.

The modularization approaches of active rules for providing termination are called *stratifications*. The term "stratification" was introduced in deductive databases to denote the partitioning of deductive rules into components, so that the ordering of components indicates a precedence in the evaluation of rules; when rules are not stratified, their semantics relevant to negation or aggregates gives rise to a number of problems, discussed in Part III. Stratification in active databases induces a partitioning of active rules into components, so that termination can be determined by reasoning only within components; the designer can abstract rule behavior by reasoning locally on each individual stratum separately, and then reasoning globally on the behavior across strata. The ordering of components in the stratification of active rules yields a "preferred order" for their evaluation. Three approaches to stratification are possible:

- *Behavioral stratification* associates each stratum to a particular applicative task; each stratum is responsible for performing the task. Global termination requires that interleaved executions of rules from different strata be under control, so that the task being pursued by one stratum is not compromised by rules from other strata.

- *Assertional stratification* associates each rule to an assertion, called the stratum's *postcondition*. Global termination requires that interleaved executions of rules from different strata do not compromise the postconditions that were already established.

- *Event-based stratification* defines a stratum in terms of the input/
  output relationship between its triggering events and its actions. Global
  termination requires that input/output events of all strata have some
  global acyclicity property.

Behavioral stratification is a more general principle, which subsumes both
assertional and event-based stratifications, as it is possible to automatically
derive a behavioral stratification for any given assertional or event-based
stratification. However, assertional and event-based stratifications may be
easier criteria to use in specific applications and/or contexts.

Different stratification methods can be hierarchically applied. For instance, a large set of active rules could be behaviorally stratified, and then
each stratum could be further stratified according to an arbitrary stratification technique.

Stratification is a particularly powerful abstraction when rules are modified. Indeed, adding a rule to, or dropping a rule from, an existing rule
set is very difficult, since understanding the side effects of changes is hard,
even when changes are small and apparently under control. The designer
should try to introduce the change within one stratum, by checking that the
stratum still locally converges after the change, and that the change does
not alter the relationships already established with any higher-order strata.
This methodology enables a controlled evolution of the knowledge expressed
by means of active rules. Unfortunately, in some cases, it is not possible to
operate within a stratum; however, even in these cases, stratification techniques may have a positive influence on rule maintenance.

4.2.1 Behavioral Stratification

Behavioral stratification aims at mapping groups of rules to applicative tasks,
so that the actions performed by rules in each stratum cooperate in their
execution. Convergence is described by a metric m_S, a finite function that
is computed on an arbitrary database state and returns a natural number.
The metric is defined on each stratum as if the rules of the stratum were the
only rules in the system.

Within this smaller rule set, we require that the metric be *strictly decreasing* whenever any rule of the stratum executes and produces a change of
database state; more precisely, it is required that when any rule of the stratum executes, eventually a database state is reached whose metric is strictly
less than the initial value. With such a property, we say that the stratum
is *locally converging*. Given that the metric is a natural number and cannot
become negative, after a finite number of executions, the metric evaluation

returns a minimum (possibly zero) and cannot further improve; we could regard this situation as the stratum's *fixpoint*. This property ensures that, whenever the rules of the stratum are in charge of execution, some progress toward the achievement of the task is performed.

Intuitively, the metric measures the distance from the current database state to the stratum's fixpoint. Determining the metric requires a good degree of understanding and intuition; the designer must be able to put the content of the database in relationship with the activity performed by the rules. Pragmatically, most metrics count given objects or tuples in the database, so that this number is indeed positive and at most becomes zero, when the convergence is achieved.

In order to guarantee that strata are somehow separated from each other, we further require that strata be ordered by the designer, and then rules be assigned priorities so that if the stratum S_1 has higher priority than the stratum S_2, then all the rules of stratum S_1 have higher priority than all the rules of stratum S_2. Once strata are ordered, the final condition for achieving a behavioral stratification requires that strata mutually *conserve the metric*. This requirement imposes that a rule running in one stratum does not decrease the metrics of strata with higher priority.

We now show an example of behavioral stratification, based on the following example application: A company receives and then processes client orders; order processing transforms pending orders into accepted orders when certain conditions on the client's credit and trustworthiness are met. Order processing is automatically performed by active rules: orders are accepted if they are within the allocated credit of clients, or if a client is trusted. We assume the following object-oriented schema:

Example 4.6   Order processing database

define object class Order
attributes OrderNumber: **integer**,
        Issuer: Client,
        Amount: **integer**,
        Status: (accepted, pending, rejected)
end;

define object class Client
attributes Name: **string**,
        Credit: **integer**,
        Trusted: **boolean**
end;

Triggers are encoded in Chimera. T1 monitors the creation of orders from trusted clients, which are immediately accepted regardless of the client's status; T2 monitors changes to orders of trusted clients, which are accepted as well. T3 monitors the creation of orders from all other clients, which are accepted only if the client has a positive credit; finally, T4 monitors the changes to orders of these clients, which again are accepted only if the credit is positive.

Example 4.7   Order processing triggers

```
create trigger T1 for Order
    events      create
    condition   Order(O), Client(C), holds(create, O),
                O.Status=pending, O.Issuer=C, C.Trusted=true
    actions     modify(Order.Status, O, accepted),
                modify(Client.Credit, C, C.Credit - O.Amount)
end;


create trigger T2 for Order
    events      modify(Amount), modify(Status)
    condition   Order(O), Client(C), holds(modify,O),
                integer(I), I=O.Amount-old(O.Amount),
                C.Trusted=true
    actions     modify(Order.Status, O, accepted),
                modify(Client.Credit, C, C.Credit - I)
end;


create trigger T3 for Order
    events      create
    condition   Order(O), Client(C), holds(create,O),
                C.Credit > A.Amount
    actions     modify(Order.Status, O, accepted),
                modify(Client.Credit, C, C.Credit - O.Amount)
end;


create trigger T4 for Order
    events      modify(Amount), modify(Status)
    condition   Order(O), Client(C), C=O.Issuer, holds(modify,O),
                integer(I), I=O.Amount-old(O.Amount), C.Credit > I
    actions     modify(Order.Status, O, accepted),
                modify(Client.Credit, C, C.Credit - I)
end;
```

These triggers have an applicative objective, namely, to accept as many orders as possible. Thus, they are all inserted within a single stratum, whose metric measures the maximized count of accepted orders; to ensure that the metric is a positive integer decreasing to a minimum value, we compute it as the difference between the count of all orders and the count of accepted orders:

Metric: count(Orders) - count(AcceptedOrders)

Assume now a change in the company's policy, due to recession. The new policy states: When the client's credit falls below 50K, then their orders are suspended, regardless of the client's trust. The trigger expressing this new policy is the following:

Example 4.8   Trigger for the new policy

> **create trigger** T5 **for** Client
>   **events**   **modify**(Credit)
>   **condition**   Client(C), **holds**(**modify**(Client.Credit),C),
>   C.Credit $<$ -50K, Order(O), O.Issuer$=$C
>   **actions**   **modify**(Order.Status, O, pending)
>   **before** T1, T2, T3, T4
> **end**;

We notice that T5 violates the metric of the stratum, because it reduces the number of accepted orders; this is a symptom of possible nonterminating behaviors. And indeed, when a trusted client falls below the 50K credit threshold, rules T2 and T5 loop indefinitely, with the corresponding orders being accepted by T2 and suspended by T5. An obvious correction is to delete the fact that a client is trusted as part of the rule's action; this correction is expressed by the following rule:

Example 4.9   Corrected trigger

> **create trigger** T5 **for** Client
>   **events**   **modify**(Credit)
>   **condition**   Client(C), **holds**(**modify**(Client.Credit),C),
>   C.Credit $<$ -50K, Order(O), O.Issuer$=$C
>   **actions**   **modify**(Order.Status, O, pending),
>   **modify**(Client.Trusted, C, false)
>   **before** T1, T2, T3, T4
> **end**;

Next, we give these rules a modularization, by placing T5 on the higher priority stratum and the remaining rules in the lower priority stratum. We keep for the lower priority module the metric defined above, while we give to the higher priority stratum the metric of minimizing the number of trusted clients. Thus, the modularization is defined by

Stratum S_1 T5
Metric m_1: count(TrustedClients)

Stratum S_2: T1 through T4
Metric m_2: count(Orders) - count(AcceptedOrders)

The stratification is correct, since the two strata locally converge and the rules of stratum S_2 do not change the metric of stratum S_1 (they do not change the status of clients).

The business rules presented in Section 3.5.3 for the Energy Management System can be stratified according to their behavior. The first rule is used to propagate requests from new users, and as such it constitutes a distinct stratum. Next, rules R_2 through R_7 propagate changes along the power distribution network, and rule R_8 may force the rollback; these rules belong to a second stratum. Finally, rules R_9 through R_{11} manage the wires within branches, once branches have an assigned power; these rules thus constitute stratum S_3. For the prioritization, S_1 precedes S_2, and S_2 precedes S_3; this order in rule processing is the most efficient because each rule does not run unnecessarily (i.e., on an ill-defined problem).

We can show that the above stratification is behavioral; strata accomplish the following tasks (stated informally):

S_1: *Connects new users to the power distribution network.*
S_2: *Propagates power requests along the distribution network.*
S_3: *Matches requests of power distribution along branches with suitable wires.*

The metrics of the three strata are the following:

S_1: count(disconnected new users)
S_2: count(nodes with unbalanced power distribution)
S_3: count(wires that cannot carry the required power)

Rules of strata S_2 and S_3 preserve the metric of stratum S_1 (since they do not deal with disconnected users); rules of stratum S_3 preserve the metric of stratum S_2 (since they don't change the power of nodes and branches).

4.2.2   Assertional Stratification

With assertional stratification, rules belonging to one stratum establish the truth of a given predicate, called the stratum's postcondition p_S; if p_S becomes **TRUE** as the result of rule execution, we say that the stratum *locally converges*, and at that point no rule of the stratum should execute its action. This condition is trivially satisfied when p_S implies that the conditions of the rules in the stratum are false, thus inhibiting their execution.

In order to guarantee that strata are somehow separated from each other, we further require that strata be ordered by the designer, and then rules be assigned priorities so that if the stratum S1 has higher priority than the stratum S2 and rules of stratum S2 execute, then the truth value of p_{S1} does not change from **TRUE** to **FALSE**. If this property holds, we say that the lower priority stratum *preserves the postcondition* of the high priority stratum.

The behavioral stratification of the EMS business rules, presented in the previous subsection, is also assertional, since the three strata S_1, S_2, and S_3 establish the following postconditions (stated informally):

S_1: *All users are connected to the power distribution network.*
S_2: *Power distribution at all branches and sites is balanced.*
S_3: *All wires are appropriate to carry the required power.*

It is easy to verify that, if the stratum's postcondition is true, then no rule of the stratum can execute any action (as the stratum's postcondition implies that each rule's condition is false). Further, S_2 conserves the postcondition of S_1 (while the opposite is not true, since S_1 may generate a user with unmatched power, thus violating the postcondition of S_2), and S_3 conserves the postconditions of S_1 and S_2 (while the opposite is not true, since S_2 may cause the change of wire types, thus violating the postcondition of S_3).

4.2.3   Event-Based Stratification

Event-based stratification associates events to strata rather than rules, and then considers the acyclicity of a triggering graph having strata as nodes. We denote as *input events* of a stratum the set of all events triggering any rule in the statum, and as *output events* the set of all operations that are performed within the action of any rule in the stratum. Therefore, each stratum establishes an input/output relationship between sets of events; event-based stratification requires the input/output relationship to be acyclic.

In addition, as usual, we require that each stratum locally converges (i.e., that its rules, considered separately from all other rules, terminate on any input transaction); local convergence can be established with any method, for example, by validating the cycles of the triggering graph inside each stratum to ensure that rule execution within a stratum is finite.

We can show that the stratification of the EMS business rules is also event-based, since the three strata S_1, S_2, and S_3 are characterized by the following input/output events:

Stratum S_1: *IN* **create**(user)
 OUT **create**(branch), **create**(wire)

Stratum S_2: *IN* **create**(user), **modify**(user.power), **modify**(intNode.power), **modify**(branch.power), **modify**(distributor.power)
 OUT **modify**(branch.power), **modify**(intNode.power), **modify**(distributor.power)

Stratum S_3: *IN* **modify**(branch.power), **create**(wire), **modify**(wire.power), **modify**(wire.wireType)
 OUT **modify**(wire.power), **create**(wire)

We notice that stratum S_1 must precede stratum S_3 because of the event **create**(Wire), which is included in the input events of S_3 and in the output events of S_1. We also notice that stratum S_2 must precede stratum S_3 because of the event **modify**(Branch.Power), which is included in the input events of S_3 and in the output events of S_2. These partial ordering relationships are consistent with the total ordering $S_1 < S_2 < S_3$, yielding an event-based stratification.

4.3 Rule Debugging and Monitoring

Although rule analysis and modularization, performed at compile time, should drive active rule design, the run-time debugging and monitoring of active rules is sometimes required in order to tune their behavior. Commercial systems, however, are rather inadequate for this purpose. Often, they do not even offer a trace facility for knowing which active rules have been running, so the only monitoring that can be performed is by looking at the rules' actions, which, in turn, become known only through the inspection of the database. In contrast, several research prototypes are focused on rule debugging; in particular, we present the features of the debugger of Chimera.

The debugger can be invoked by a user by issuing a special command, or it can be started during rule processing when given rules are being considered or executed. In order to do so, it is possible to set *spy points* in the rules. When the debugger is called into action, the execution of the current rule is completed (if rules are being processed), after which execution proceeds interactively; execution of rules is available at two levels of granularity:

- At the *rule step* level: After each rule execution, rule processing is halted and the situation is presented to the user. At this level there is no possibility of interrupting the run-time system during the computation of triggered rules and the evaluation of rules' conditions.

- At the *intra-rule step* level: Rule processing is halted at each of the three fundamental moments of rule execution (triggering, condition evaluation, and action execution). The user can obtain information on the state of rule processing and influence (in a limited way) the behavior of the rule executor.

The following functionalities are available in both modes:

- *Information on rules*: The system displays all available information about rules, including their source code, triggering time, and event consumption mode.

- *Commands for rule activation and deactivation*: Rules can be explicitly deactivated during debugging, so that they are disregarded during subsequent rule processing. A deactivated rule can be reactivated at any time.

- *Inspection of the conflict set*: The system displays all rules that are currently triggered in order of priority.

- *Inspection of the deferred conflict set*: The system displays those triggered rules whose execution is deferred.

- *Inspection of the trace*: The system displays all rules that were considered or executed since the last quiescent point.

- *Information on occurred events*: The system lists all events since the beginning of the transaction. Each event is described by its event type, the list of the OIDs of the objects affected by the event, and the indication of the database state in which the event has occurred. For identifying the various states of the database, all intermediate states since the beginning of the transaction are numbered progressively. Events are listed in order of occurrence.

When the debugging mode is intra-rule step, the following additional options are available:

- *Display of the processing status*: A graphical icon is used to show the current point of execution, either the computation of triggered rules, the evaluation of a rule's condition, or the execution of a rule's action.

- *Detection of the next executable rule*: Finds the rule with highest priority, among those that have not been considered yet, whose condition is satisfied in the current database state.

- *Modification of dynamic priorities*: Alters the chosen priority of triggered rules with equal static priority. In this way, it is possible to force the selection of a different rule from the one that would be chosen using the built-in conflict resolution strategy.

- *Information on bindings produced by the condition's consideration*: Enables the inspection of the objects that are bound by the evaluation of the rule's condition.

Debugging techniques are, as usual, dedicated to determining whether a given active rule set is terminating. To this purpose, a user should try all different types of transactions with all different types of input parameters— quite a difficult verification task. For a given rule processing execution, a situation of nontermination is suggested when a given rule sequence is repeated; this situation is easily recognized by inspecting the trace. At that point, a further suggestion of nontermination may come from the inspection of event instances and of the database state—which normally, in a looping situation, have a "periodic" behavior.

Consider rules that are totally ordered and have the property of not generating new terms. When a situation occurs where the database state and conflict set are identical at different stages of rule processing, then the system is certainly in an infinite loop. This theoretical result has inspired a technique, called a *cycle monitor*, where a particular cycle can be monitored by inspecting just one of its rules; it is sufficient to find the same database state and conflict set twice in order to conclude that the rules are in an endless loop. This test can be made very efficient by comparing only state changes, by means of transition values.

4.4 IDEA Methodology

The use of objects and rules in modern database systems is the main focus of the IDEA Esprit Project. In particular, it inspired the IDEA Methodology, a comprehensive and systematic approach to the design of database applications that use both deductive and active rules. The IDEA Methodology

reconciles deductive and active rules by assigning them the role of expressing knowledge about the application domain, either with a purely declarative
style or with a more procedural style.

The IDEA Methodology extends recently published object-oriented software engineering methodologies, targeted toward arbitrary software systems
and typically leading to implementations supported by an object-oriented
programming language, such as C++ or SmallTalk. Conversely, the IDEA
Methodology focuses on information systems (e.g., software systems managing large amounts of structured data).

Objects, deductive rules, and active rules are the three ingredients of
the IDEA Methodology; each of them is fundamental for a precise conceptual description of an information system. Objects provide encapsulation
as a form of abstraction that enables the designer to structure its applications. Deductive and active rules can be used to establish and enforce data
management policies, as they can provide a large amount of the semantics that normally needs to be coded with application programs; this trend
in designing database applications, called *knowledge independence*, brings
the nice consequence that data management policies can effectively evolve
just by modifying rules instead of application programs. Even if objects
and rules are not yet fully supported by products, nevertheless their combined use at the conceptual level generates a better understanding of the
overall application.

Like most object-oriented methodologies, the IDEA Methodology includes the three classical phases of analysis, design, and implementation.
In addition, it includes prototyping as an intermediate phase, placed between design and implementation, and dedicated to verification and critical
assessment of the conceptual schemas.

1. *Analysis* is devoted to the collection and specification of requirements
   at the conceptual level. This phase is focused on modeling reality
   with semiformal, expressive representation devices, aiming at a natural
   and easy-to-understand representation of the "universe of discourse."
   Therefore, this phase uses conceptual models with an associated graphical representation that are well established in software engineering
   practice, such as the Entity-Relationship model and Statecharts.

2. *Design* is the process of translating requirements into design documents
   that provide a precise, unambiguous specification of the application.
   Design is conducted by mapping from semiformal specifications into
   fully formal, computer-processable specifications. The process is divided into schema design (concerned mostly with types, classes, re-

lationships, and operations) and rule design (further subdivided into deductive rule design and active rule design).

3. *Rapid prototyping* is the process of testing, at a conceptual level, the adequacy of design results with respect to the actual user needs. A variety of formal transformation methods can be applied to improve the quality of the design, to verify its formal properties, or to transform design specifications into equivalent specifications that exhibit different features. Tools, which are available on the Internet, assist the automatic generation and analysis of active rules, and enable the prototyping of applications written in Chimera.

4. *Implementation* is the process of mapping conceptual specifications into schemas, objects, and rules of existing database platforms; the process is influenced by the features of the specific target environments that were selected. These include Oracle, Illustra, and DB2, three classic relational products supporting triggers; ODE, an object-oriented database available on the Internet to universities and research institutes; and Validity, the first deductive and object-oriented database system that will be soon be brought to the market.

4.4.1 Active Rule Design

Active rule design in the IDEA Methodology considers two different approaches for internal and external rules.

The design of external rules follows a declarative approach, consisting of giving a declarative specification of active rules and then semiautomatically generating them with generation algorithms (supported by suitable rule generation tools). The rationale of this approach is that a generation algorithm is able to generate rules that satisfy given quality criteria, in particular guaranteeing termination and/or confluence.

Integrity constraints constitute a natural application of this approach. A constraint on a database can be represented as a condition that must always be false. From a declarative specification of constraints, a user can easily generate a set of active rules capable of guaranteeing the consistency of the database; it is sufficient to write an abort rule as defined in Section 3.1. This simple solution to the problem does not use all the power of active rules because the reaction consists simply in discarding all the work done by the transaction; thus, a tool developed for assisting the IDEA Methodology is able to automatically generate repair rules, as defined in Section 3.1, implementing repairing policies that heuristically try to maximize the user's satisfaction, expressed informally.

Maintenance of materialized views is another classical application of rule generators; several approaches have been developed for the incremental maintenance of materialized views, as defined in Section 3.2. In the IDEA Methodology we classify rules into classes and then generate active rules to maintain views according to the mapping technique that applies to each class.

The design of business rules requires understanding the business process, and in particular the applicative goal that is pursued by the rules. In order to understand this goal, it is convenient to associate rules with a metric that measures the progress in achieving the task's objective. This goal-directed design of active rules is useful both for designing individual rules and for understanding their interaction and modularization. The following overall design strategy is suggested:

1. Identify applicative tasks for active rules. Associate each task to the condition under which the task should be executed. Give a simple description of the task in the form: "if condition, then action."

2. For each task, detect the events that cause the task to be executed; for each task, identify a metric that indicates the "progress" toward the solution of the task.

3. Generate active rules responding to the events that are associated with the task. The designer should constantly check that rules, if running, improve the metric and thus "progress" toward the task's solution.

The above strategy is extended to take into account modularization, as discussed in the previous section, when rules pursue multiple applicative tasks. Step 3 of the above procedure is refined into the following:

3.1 Define the "natural order" of tasks as a total order such that, if all tasks must be performed in the context of the application, then the tasks that do not need contributions from other tasks are first in the order.

3.2 Generate active rules responding to the events that are associated with the task. Constantly check that the following two conditions are satisfied:

3.2.1 Rules, if running, eventually improve the metric and thus "progress" toward the task's solution.

3.2.2 Rules, if running, do not decrease the metric of any task preceding the current task in the natural order defined at step 3.

Step 3.2.2 may cause the refinement of the natural task order tentatively defined at step 3.1; at all times, new tasks may be identified, or previously identified tasks may be refined.

4.4.2 Active Rule Prototyping

Prototyping denotes a methodological phase in which design results are tested; to this purpose, design results are implemented on a small scale, typically with rapid prototyping software, and their adequacy and conformity to requirements are evaluated by designers and by users. During prototyping we look at rule collections, regardless of the techniques that are required in order to collect them; thus, we consider a new aspect of knowledge design, called *knowledge design in the large*; in contrast, the design techniques for individual active and deductive rules can be regarded as *knowledge design in the small*.

Active rule prototyping in the IDEA Methodology has two facets: *compile-time rule analysis*, which can be used in order to prove properties of active rules, and *run-time testing*, which can be used to experiment with rules in order to assess and fine-tune their behavior. Both analysis and testing are assisted by rapid prototyping environments made available by the IDEA Project.

4.4.3 Active Rule Implementation

During the final implementation phase, the conceptual specifications are mapped into schemas, objects, and rules of five existing database platforms. Although all the selected database platforms implement some form of active rules, the mapping of active rules is difficult and problematic because of the intrinsically operational nature of active rule semantics, which is quite different in the five proposed systems, and also because of the heavy limitations that each product is introducing with respect to active rules supported in the conceptual model. In the end, two specific mapping techniques have emerged, used primarily for the mapping to relational products.

- *Meta-triggering* uses the native active rule engine in order to detect events, but then requires a second active engine in order to render the semantics of conceptual rules; in practice, the second active engine is capable of executing the Chimera rule processing algorithm on each of the selected target systems. In this way, meta-triggering preserves all features of conceptual active rules. Typically, the second active engine is programmed by using stored procedures and imperative language attachments; it is application-independent and therefore can be reused for developing arbitrary applications.

- *Macro-triggering* uses instead just the native active rule engine available on each target system; conceptual triggers are aggregated to constitute macro-triggers, defined on each target system. Macro-triggers normally do not have the same semantics as the conceptual active rules, but differences are well identified.

4.4.4   Design Tools Supporting the IDEA Methodology

A complete tool environment for assisting the design of active rules applications was developed at Politecnico di Milano in the context of the IDEA Project, for supporting the IDEA Methodology. The architecture of the tools provided in the IDEA design environment is represented in Figure 4.3.

Iade is used during analysis in order to collect the schema specifications by means of the Object Model (an extended entity-relationship model). These specifications are semiautomatically mapped into schema declarations in Chimera and into constraints and triggers useful to preserve schema integrity.

Argonaut supports the generation of active rules from the declarative specification of integrity constraints and views. In the former case, active rules correct integrity violations; in the latter case, they incrementally maintain materialized views corresponding to both nonrecursive and recursive deductive rules.

Arachne supports the compile-time termination analysis of a set of Chimera active rules. The tool determines the potential causes of infinite executions originating from the mutual interaction of active rules. Two different types of analysis are performed: a syntactic analysis that compares the events produced by rule actions with the events triggering the rules, and a more complex analysis that also considers rule conditions in order to detect irrelevant interactions in advance.

The Algres Testbed is an execution environment that permits the rapid prototyping of the design specifications. It provides functionalities for browsing schemas and rules and for monitoring the execution of transactions and active rules. The run-time debugger includes several features for temporarily changing the parameters of active rules (their coupling mode, priority, and event consumption mode). If any active rule is modified during the testing

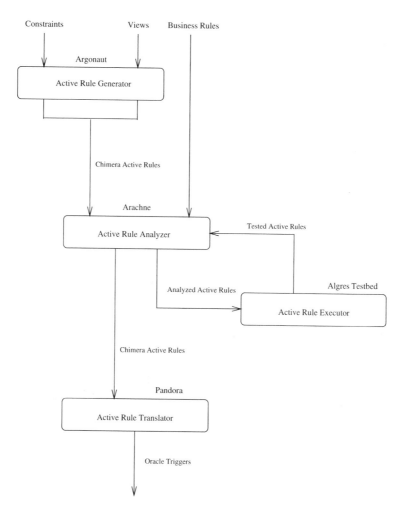

Figure 4.3: Tools architecture

session, the Arachne rule analyzer can be interactively called to analyze the new rule set, thus verifying the correctness of the performed modifications.

Pandora translates Chimera applications into Oracle, one of the target systems of the IDEA Methodology. Pandora requires user interaction for some optimization decisions, since the translation to Oracle presents several options and sometimes requires ad hoc redesign in order to fulfill the requirements of the target system.

In the remainder of this chapter, we focus on Arachne (Active Rules Analyzer for Chimera). Arachne accepts as input a set of active rules and detects rules that may exhibit a nonterminating behavior, using several analysis

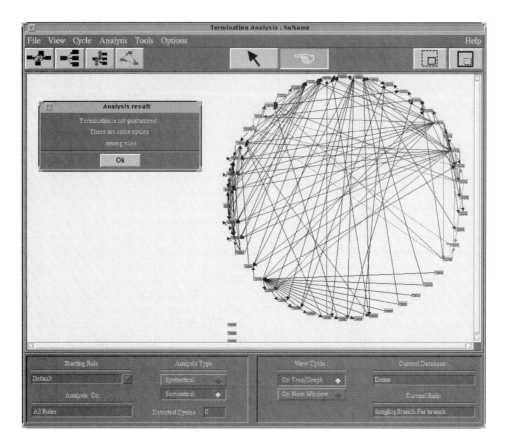

Figure 4.4: Description of an active rule set with Arachne

techniques. Arachne supports *event-based analysis*, which performs a simple, syntax-based analysis of the triggering graph, and *condition-based analysis*, which refines the analysis performed by event-based analysis by discarding superfluous arcs from the triggering graph after more sophisticated testing, as we have discussed in Section 4.1.1.

The tool proposes a graphical representation of active rules and highlights all cycles in the triggering graph as candidate sources of nontermination. It is the responsibility of the designer either to modify the active rule set, or to notify the system that a particular set of rules produces a terminating behavior.

Figure 4.4 shows Arachne applied to a large case study, consisting of over 50 triggers; such a large number of triggers and of interactions may appear too intricate, but indeed Arachne is very effective in highlighting the critical

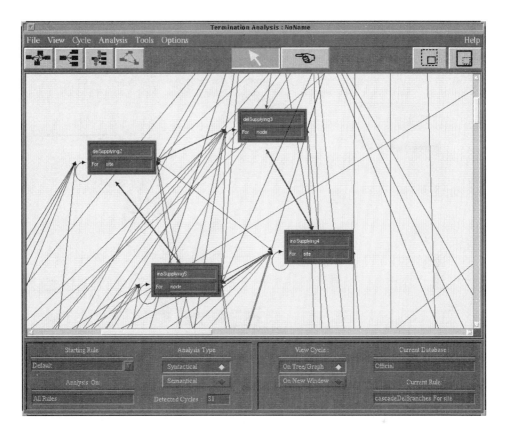

Figure 4.5: Cycle analysis with Arachne

parts of the triggering graph. Cycle analysis in this case reveals 24 cycles that are all caused by four rules, shown in Figure 4.5.

Once a cycle is detected by the tool, it is the user's responsibility to check for termination; however, Arachne is very effective in isolating this cluster of rules from the other 50 or so triggers and enables the designer to focus on the relevant issues, discarding all the noise induced by the other 50 triggers. The analysis of a cycle can be performed quite effectively: the cycle itself is graphically represented by Arachne as a chain of event/action pairs, as illustrated in Figure 4.6.

4.5 Summary and Open Problems

Active databases pose a number of theoretic and pragmatic problems and challenges to database researchers.

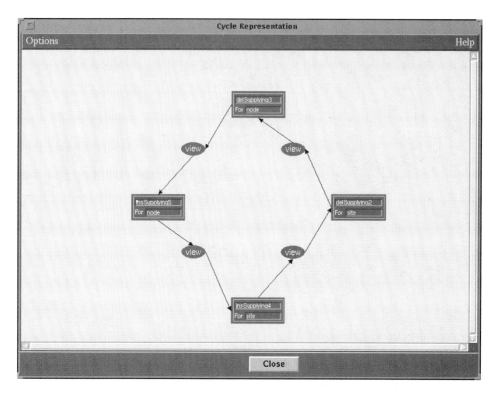

Figure 4.6: Zoom on a cycle in the triggering graph

The large number of options that characterize the semantics of active rules and their triggering call for a unifying theory, currently being attempted by several researchers. A promising approach consists in defining precisely the semantics of a "core active rule system," and then defining several semantic options, as supported by the various active rule systems and prototypes, by translating them into the few features supported by the core system; this approach guarantees comparability among the various alternative behaviors of active databases. Important efforts are also being made for bridging deductive to active rules at a more fundamental level, by defining suitable extensions of logic programming that support database updates and capture the same expressive power as active rules. As a consequence, active rule systems are guaranteed a clear (although operational) semantics and can be formally analyzed (e.g., for termination).

The concept of detached rules needs to be more fully understood and deepened, and in particular its transactional implications in light of the current evolution of transaction-based systems. Rules triggered by time or external events typically occur in a transactional space that is different from the one causing the triggering. Some commercial systems (including Oracle) are evolving in the direction of supporting time-related transaction scheduling as a new component, separate from their trigger system; however, the combination of active rules and time-based transactional services will give the same computational power as detached rules.

Another open research issue is the modeling of complex triggering events. The approach currently used by commercial systems (and presented in Chapter 2 of this book) consists in managing simple events—which capture all changes—and then supporting arbitrarily complex conditions. An alternative approach, recently proposed by researchers and currently adopted only in a few research prototypes, consists instead of supporting a sophisticated event calculus. In order for this second solution to become successful, two prerequisites are needed: the event language must be consolidated, and the event monitoring techniques must be made solid and efficient. Attempts are also being made for supporting the incremental evaluation of conditions through auxiliary data structures derived from discrimination networks in artificial intelligence (the Rete and TREAT algorithms); however, their successful application to generalized database systems is quite questionable.

Although triggers are already present in relational products and are being used in many applications, two factors are expected to influence their evolution and consolidation:

- The publishing of the SQL3 standard and the subsequent adaptation of existing products will remove the current diffidence toward the various incarnations of triggers supported in the various products. We expect that adaptation will occur and will be relatively fast because there are no fundamental reasons that motivate the differences among relational products—which were produced almost by accident in the absence of a solid standardization proposal.

- In addition, the development of tools for the designing and debugging of trigger-based applications (e.g., simplified versions of the IDEA tools illustrated in Section 4.4.4) will be fundamental in making the design, testing, and use of triggers by real applications easier and more widespread.

4.6 Bibliographic Notes

The definitions of termination, confluence, and observable determinism are given in [14]. This paper has also introduced termination analysis, based on the simple detection of cycles in the triggering graph, and confluence analysis, based on the definition of commutative rules. This event-based technique is implemented in Arachne. More sophisticated rule analysis techniques, constituting the theoretical foundation of condition-based analysis supported by Arachne, are described in [41].

Among other approaches to rule analysis, we mention [239], reducing active rules to term-rewriting systems. Condition-action rules (i.e., with events defined implicitly) are considered in [433]; the analysis is based on the construction of an activation graph that represents the mutual interaction among rules, built considering the semantics of the conditions and actions. A similar approach is extended to ECA rules in [38], which presents the most accurate approach to termination analysis. Also [439] proposes analysis techniques for rules with implicit events in an object-oriented context.

Modularization of active rules is defined in [40], and run-time monitoring of active rules is discussed in [39].

Some tools have been implemented to support the construction of applications based on active rules. DEAR [130] is an active rule debugger developed in the context of the active DBMS Exact; it provides a graphical representation of rule interaction during execution. VITAL [51] is a tool for active rule analysis and debugging; the analysis is based on the construction of the triggering graph, while debugging operates by simulating the execution of rules. VITAL also offers a graphical representation of the evolution of the database content. The active DBMS Sentinel includes a visualization and explanation tool [99], which supports a posteriori analysis of rule execution; the tool is being extended to become a rule debugger for the run-time analysis of rules.

The IDEA Methodology extends the new-generation object-oriented software design methodologies, such as OMT [369], Fusion [118], Syntropy [121], and the Booch method [69]. It is the main outcome of the Esprit Project IDEA, funded by the European Community, with the participation of three research partners and five industrial partners from five European countries. The IDEA Methodology is presented in the forthcoming book [92]; a short description is presented in [91]. The tools assisting the IDEA Methodology are available on the Internet, at the site http://www.elet.polimi.it/idea. The organization of the tool environment is described in [35]; Arachne is described in [37].

The use of a core model for explaining active database behaviors is presented in [174]. Studies for relating deductive and active rules are presented in [466, 468]. Proposals for the use of complex event calculus are given in

[72, 185, 297]. A description of the Rete and TREAT approaches and their comparison is given in [453].

4.7 Exercises

4.1. Show the triggering graph of the following set of rules:

- r_1:
    - — event: $U(B)$
    - — condition: $B = 1$
    - — action: $A = 0, B = 1$
- r_2:
    - — event: $U(C)$
    - — condition: $B = 1$
    - — action: $A = 1, B = O$
- r_3:
    - — event: $U(A)$
    - — condition: $A = 1$
    - — action: $A = 0, B = 1, C = 1$

4.2. Discuss the termination of the EMS rules described in Section 3.5.3. Describe the triggering graph associated with the rules, and analyze its cycles; show that, although the graph is cyclic, the rule set is actually terminating.

4.3. Given the relational database schema

Acct(<u>Num</u>, Name, Bal, Rate)
LowAcct(<u>Num</u>, Date)

define the following active rules in Starburst:

a. Define a rule BadAccount, stating that if an account has a balance less than 500 and an interest rate greater than 0%, then the account interest rate is set to 0%.

b. Define a rule RaiseRate, stating that if an account has an interest rate greater than 1% but less than 2%, then the interest rate is raised to 2%.

c. Define a rule AddBad, stating that if an account has a balance less than 500 and it is not yet recorded in the LowAcct relation, then the information on that account is inserted into the LowAcct relation, timestamped with the current date.

d. Define a rule DelBad, stating that if an account in the LowAcct relation has a balance of at least 500 in the Acct relation, then the account is deleted from the LowAcct relation.

e. Discuss the behavior of the set of triggers with respect to termination.

4.4. Consider a repair and maintenance system, in which a fault is characterized by the part that has failed and by the time required by a maintenance team to replace it. When a fault is generated, if there is a spare part in stock, then the maintenance team is urgently called to perform the replacement; otherwise an order is issued to buy the part.

The parts may also be replaced as part of preventive maintenance. Two dates are associated with each renewable part: a date on which the part should be replaced, and a date on which a part reaches the end of its service life and must be urgently replaced.

When a replacement becomes urgent, if the spare is available, then a maintenance team is urgently called. If a part should be replaced and it is not available in stock, then an order is issued. When a part is delivered, then the stock is updated.

Repairs are scheduled when a maintenance team is available; urgent calls have higher priority than preventive maintenance. When repairs are terminated, maintenance teams become available again.

Consider the following relational database schema for the repair and maintenance system. Relation Fault contains failed parts; Stock describes the stock of spare parts; Order and Deliver contain parts that are ordered and delivered. Relation ProgrammedReplacement contains the schedule of replacements for a part. Two dates are provided: at the first date a replacement can be executed, and at the second date the replacement becomes urgent. Relation UrgentCall contains the urgent repairs needed; Available lists the maintenance teams that are available. Finally, TimeRequired indicates the time required for each part's replacement; ScheduledRepair lists the assignments of teams to maintenance tasks.

Fault(<u>Part</u>)
Stock(<u>Part</u>,SerialNo)
Order(<u>OrderCode</u>,Part)
Deliver(<u>OrderCode</u>,Part,SerialNo)
ProgrammedReplacement(<u>Part</u>,Date,DateUrg)
UrgentCall(<u>Part</u>,SerialNo)
Available(<u>Team</u>)
TimeRequired(<u>Part</u>,Time)
ScheduledRepair(<u>Part</u>,SerialNo,Team,DayIn,DayOut)

Consider a set of business rules that perform the above process, with rules organized within four strata:

- *Stratum S_1*

  R_{11} If a part is delivered, insert it into the stock and delete the corresponding order.

- *Stratum S_2*

  R_{21} If a part fails and a spare is not available in the stock, issue an order.

  R_{22} If a part fails and a spare is available in the stock, issue an urgent call.

- *Stratum S_3*

  R_{31} If a part has terminated its service life and a spare is not available in the stock, issue an order.

  R_{32} If a part has terminated its service life and a spare is available in the stock, issue an urgent call.

  R_{33} If a part can be preventively replaced and a spare is not available in the stock, issue an order.

- *Stratum S_4* (with priorities $R_{41} < R_{42}$)

  R_{41} If a maintenance team becomes available and there is an unserviced urgent call, assign the maintenance team to the call.

  R_{42} If a maintenance team becomes available, a part can be preventively replaced, and a spare part is available in the stock, assign the maintenance team to the preventive maintenance.

a. Define the active rules specified above.

b. Discuss their modularization and termination.

Part II

Temporal Databases

Time is a pervasive aspect of reality. Events occur at specific points in time; objects and the relationships among objects exist over time. The ability to model this temporal dimension of the real world is essential to many computer applications, such as accounting, banking, inventory control, econometrics, law, medical records, land and geographical information systems, and airline reservations.

A *temporal database* is one that supports some aspect of time. This part summarizes the major concepts, approaches, and implementation strategies underlying temporal databases.

This part commences with a case study that illustrates the difficulties a developer encounters when implementing via SQL an application that manages time-varying information. We then consider time itself, in particular how it is modeled. The design space of temporal data models is surveyed. Chapter 5 ends by listing the many temporal query languages that have been defined.

In Chapter 6, we focus on one language, TSQL2, in detail. Then Chapter 7 considers implementation strategies for a temporal database management system.

Chapter 5

Overview of Temporal Databases

Time is an important aspect of all real-world phenomena. Database applications must capture the time-varying nature of the phenomena they model.

As one example, every university maintains a temporal database recording the courses taken by each student and the grades that student received. This information certainly varies over time: courses are taken during a particular semester, and indeed a course may be taken several times by a student. While the registrar may be most interested in the current semester—what students are signed up for what classes—graduating students are probably more interested in getting printouts of their entire transcript. And department heads often look at enrollment statistics over time to better plan future staffing.

As another example, advertising agencies plan very carefully when advertisements will run. Television advertisements are especially expensive (an advertisement during the Super Bowl costs about $2 million a minute; advertising during a prime-time show can cost $100,000 to $600,000 a minute); print media are also costly. Agencies store media plans in databases, recording which advertisements are to appear when, the costs involved, and an estimate of the number of people, in various categories, that will see each advertisement. Analyses are run against this information, such as determining the advertising budget over time (is it relatively flat, or are there peaks and valleys?), estimating the total number of people in each category that will be exposed to the product, and evaluating the integration with print advertisements (do television advertisements run prior to, during, or after the appearance of print advertisements?). Both the underlying information and the queries over this information are inherently temporal.

Conventional (nontemporal) databases represent the state of an enterprise at a single moment in time. Although the contents of the database continue to change as new information is added, these changes are viewed as modifications to the state, with the old, out-of-date data being deleted from the database. The current content of the database may be viewed as a snapshot of the enterprise. As we will see shortly in a case study, when a conventional database is used, the attributes involving time are manipulated solely by the application programs, with little help from the database management system (DBMS).

From the academic database example, the current state contains information about the semester in progress. Queries and updates concern this semester. Information on previous semesters can be stored by associating a column identifying the relevant semester. However, in a nontemporal DBMS, this column must be explicitly manipulated by the user. Obtaining enrollment statistics over time requires complex application code.

A *temporal database* is one that supports some aspect of time. We will shortly encounter more specific characterizations that concern the kind(s) of time supported. Queries over previous states are easy to specify. Also, modifications to previous states (if an error is detected, or if more information becomes available) and to future states (for planning purposes) are also easier to express using a temporal DBMS.

A temporal DBMS allows sophisticated queries over time to be stated. As an example, using the media planning database, we may want to determine the well-established shows, to potentially use for our advertising. More specifically, we request all shows broadcast by NBC that ran continuously for at least two years, as well as the day that they began that run. A more sophisticated query would be to calculate the advertising budget for each month for the major television networks (ABC, CBS, NBC, Fox). Such queries using a temporal query language are but a few lines long.

Almost all database applications concern time-varying information. In fact, it is difficult to identify applications that do not involve the management of time-varying data. The advantages provided by built-in temporal support include higher-fidelity data modeling, more efficient application development, and a potential increase in performance.

5.1 A Case Study

We first demonstrate the need for temporal databases with a case study that illustrates the pitfalls of using a conventional DBMS to underlie a time-varying application.

The University of Arizona's Office of Appointed Personnel (OAP) has information concerning university employees in a database; this information includes the employee's name, their current salary, and their current title. In the relational model, this can be represented by a simple, three-column relation:

Employee(Name, Salary, Title)

Each tuple (row) of this relation provides information on one employee; different tuples are associated with distinct employees.

Given this relation, finding the employee's salary is easy when a relational query language such as SQL is used:

Example 5.1   What is Bob's salary?

> **SELECT** Salary
> **FROM** Employee
> **WHERE** Name = 'Bob'

Now the OAP wishes to record the date of birth. To do so, a column is added to the relation, yielding the following schema:

Employee(Name, Salary, Title, DateofBirth **DATE**)

Finding the employee's date of birth is analogous to determining the salary:

Example 5.2   What is Bob's date of birth?

> **SELECT** DateofBirth
> **FROM** Employee
> **WHERE** Name = 'Bob'

This illustrates the (limited) temporal support available in SQL (more precisely, in the SQL-92 standard, as well as in all major commercial DBMSs), that of the column type **DATE**. As we will see later, other temporal types are available, but they are not sufficient for ease in querying time-varying data. Rather, a temporal query language is required.

The OAP wishes to record the employment history. To do so, they append two columns, one indicating when the information in the tuple became valid, the other indicating when the information was no longer valid.

Employee (Name, Salary, Title, DateofBirth, Start **DATE**, Stop **DATE**)

To the data model, these new columns are identical to DateofBirth. However, their presence has far-ranging consequences.

5.1.1   Temporal Projection

To find the employee's current salary, things are more difficult:

Example 5.3   What is Bob's current salary?

> **SELECT** Salary
> **FROM** Employee
> **WHERE** Name = 'Bob' **AND** Start <= **CURRENT_DATE**
>   **AND CURRENT_DATE** <= Stop

This query is more complicated than the previous one. The culprit is obviously the two new columns.

The OAP wants to distribute to each employee their salary history. Specifically, for each person, the maximal periods of time for each salary needs to be determined. Unfortunately, this is very difficult in SQL. An employee could have arbitrarily many title changes between salary changes, as shown below:

Name	Salary	Title	DateofBirth	Start	Stop
Bob	60000	Assistant Provost	1945-04-09	1995-01-01	1995-06-01
Bob	70000	Assistant Provost	1945-04-09	1995-06-01	1995-10-01
Bob	70000	Provost	1945-04-09	1995-10-01	1996-02-01
Bob	70000	Professor	1945-04-09	1996-02-01	1997-01-01

Note that there are three tuples in which Bob's salary remained constant at $70,000. Hence, the result should be two tuples for Bob:

Name	Salary	Start	Stop
Bob	60000	1995-01-01	1995-06-01
Bob	70000	1996-06-01	1997-01-01

Here is one possible solution. The intuition is that we find those time periods with the same salary value that overlap or are adjacent, and merge those periods by extending the earlier period. This process is repeated until maximal periods are constructed. At that point, the nonmaximal periods are removed. This process is termed *coalescing*.

Example 5.4   What is Bob's salary history (first attempt)?

    CREATE TABLE Temp(Salary, Start, Stop)
    AS   SELECT Salary, Start, Stop
        FROM Employee
        WHERE Name = 'Bob';

repeat
    UPDATE Temp T1
    SET (T1.Stop) = (**SELECT MAX**(T2.Stop)
        FROM Temp **AS** T2
        WHERE T1.Salary = T2.Salary **AND** T1.Start < T2.Start
            AND T1.Stop >= T2.Start **AND** T1.Stop < T2.Stop)
    WHERE EXISTS (**SELECT** *
        FROM Temp **AS** T2
        WHERE T1.Salary = T2.Salary **AND** T1.Start < T2.Start
            AND T1.Stop >= T2.Start **AND** T1.Stop < T2.Stop)
until *no tuples updated*;

    DELETE FROM Temp T1
    WHERE EXISTS (**SELECT** *
        FROM Temp **AS** T2
        WHERE T1.Salary = T2.Salary
          AND ((T1.Start > T2.Start **AND** T1.Stop <= T2.Stop)
          OR (T1.Start >= T2.Start **AND** T1.Stop < T2.Stop))

Assume that Bob had many tuples with the same salary, but with different titles. The Temp relation would initially contain nonoverlapping time periods:

After the first iteration of the repeat-until loop, the Temp relation would contain

Note how the Stop time is extended when a *value-equivalent* tuple (one with identical values for the nontimestamp attributes, in this case the Salary attribute) meets or overlaps it.

After the second iteration, some periods are further extended:

The next iteration does not change any stop time, and so the repeat-until loop is terminated. The **DELETE** statement removes the nonmaximal value-equivalent periods, retaining only the last one shown above.

One problem with this approach is that it uses a non-SQL statement, the repeat-until loop. For a time, it was thought impossible to express this query completely in SQL. A solution was discovered just a few years ago, involving complex, multiply nested **NOT EXISTS** subclauses:

Example 5.5   What is Bob's salary history (entirely in SQL)?

```
CREATE TABLE Temp(Salary, Start, Stop)
AS   SELECT Salary, Start, Stop
     FROM Employee
     WHERE Name = 'Bob';

SELECT DISTINCT F.Salary, F.Start, L.Stop
FROM Temp AS F, Temp AS L
WHERE F.Start < L.Stop
    AND F.Salary = L.Salary
    AND NOT EXISTS (SELECT *
      FROM Temp AS M
      WHERE M.Salary = F.Salary
         AND F.Start < M.Start AND M.Start < L.Stop
         AND NOT EXISTS (SELECT *
           FROM Temp AS T1
           WHERE T1.Salary = F.Salary
              AND T1.Start < M.Start AND M.Start <= T1.Stop))
    AND NOT EXISTS (SELECT *
      FROM Temp AS T2
      WHERE T2.Salary = F.Salary
         AND ((T2.Start < F.Start AND F.Start <= T2.Stop) OR
              (T2.Start < L.Stop AND L.Stop < T2.Stop)))
```

In this query, we search for two (possibly the same) value-equivalent tuples (represented by the correlation names F, for *first*, and L, for *last*) defining start point F.Start and end point L.Stop of a coalesced tuple. The first **NOT EXISTS** ensures that there are no holes between F.Start and L.Stop (i.e., no time points where the respective fact does not hold). This guarantees that all start points M.Start between F.Start and L.Stop of value-equivalent tuples are extended (toward F.Start) by another value-equivalent tuple. This is illustrated below:

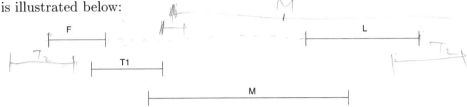

In this subclause, T1 may in fact be F. It may also be the case that F itself overlaps L, in which case the **NOT EXISTS** is certainly true.

The second **NOT EXISTS** ensures that only maximal periods result (i.e., F and L cannot be part of a larger value-equivalent tuple T2).

A third alternative is to use SQL only to open a cursor on the relation. A linked list of periods is maintained, each with a salary. This linked list should be initialized to empty.

Example 5.6 What is Bob's salary history (using a cursor)?

```
DECLARE emp_cursor CURSOR FOR
    SELECT Salary, Title, Start, Stop
    FROM Employee
    WHERE Name = 'Bob';


OPEN emp_cursor;


loop:
    FETCH emp_cursor INTO :salary, :start: stop;
    if no data returned then goto finished;
    find position in linked list to insert this information;
    goto loop;


finished:
CLOSE emp_cursor;
iterate through linked list, printing out dates and salaries
```

The linked list is unnecessary if the cursor is **ORDER BY** Start.

In all cases, the query is quite complex for such a simple English equivalent. The reason is that SQL is a nontemporal query language. The language has no facilities for timestamped tuples.

The query is trivial in TSQL2, a temporal query language that will be discussed in depth later:

Example 5.7 What is Bob's salary history (in TSQL2)?

> **SELECT** Salary
> **FROM** Employee
> **WHERE** Name = 'Bob'

5.1.2 Temporal Join

A more drastic approach avoids the problem in SQL of extracting the salary history by reorganizing the schema to separate salary, title, and date of birth information.

Employee1 (Name, Salary, Start **DATE**, Stop **DATE**)
Employee2 (Name, Title, Start **DATE**, Stop **DATE**)

With this change, getting the salary information is now easy.

Example 5.8 What is Bob's salary history (using Employee1)?

> **SELECT** Salary, Start, Stop
> **FROM** Employee1
> **WHERE** Name = 'Bob'

But what if the OAP wants a relation of salary/title periods? Using SQL, the query must do a case analysis of how each tuple of Employee1 overlaps each tuple of Employee2; there are four possible cases.

Example 5.9 Provide the salary and department history for all employees

> **SELECT** Employee1.Name, Salary, Dept, Employee1.Start, Employee1.Stop
> **FROM** Employee1, Employee2
> **WHERE** Employee1.Name = Employee2.Name
>   **AND** Employee2.Start <= Employee1.Start
>   **AND** Employee1.Stop <= Employee2.Stop
> **UNION**
> **SELECT** Employee1.Name, Salary, Dept, Employee1.Start, Employee2.Stop
> **FROM** Employee1, Employee2
> **WHERE** Employee1.Name = Employee2.Name
>   **AND** Employee1.Start > Employee2.Start
>   **AND** Employee2.Stop < Employee1.Stop
>   **AND** Employee1.Start < Employee2.Stop

```
UNION
SELECT Employee1.Name, Salary, Dept, Employee2.Start, Employee1.Stop
FROM Employee1, Employee2
WHERE Employee1.Name = Employee2.Name
    AND Employee2.Start > Employee1.Start
    AND Employee1.Stop < Employee2.Stop
    AND Employee2.Start < Employee1.Stop
UNION
SELECT Employee1.Name, Salary, Dept, Employee2.Start, Employee2.Stop
FROM Employee1, Employee2
WHERE Employee1.Name = Employee2.Name
    AND Employee2.Start >= Employee1.Start
    AND Employee2.Stop <= Employee1.Stop
```

In the first case, the period associated with the **Employee2** tuple entirely contains the period associated with the **Employee1** tuple. Since we are interested in those times when both the salary and the department are valid, the intersection of the two periods is the contained period, that is, the period from Employee1.Start to Employee1.Stop:

In the second case, neither period contains the other:

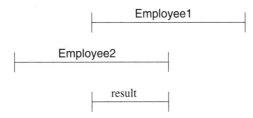

The other cases similarly identify the overlap of the two periods.

While this query is not as complex as those given before, it still requires care to get the eleven inequalities and the four select lists correct.

In a temporal query language such as TSQL2, performing a temporal join is just what one would expect:

Example 5.10   Provide the salary and department history for all employees (in TSQL2)

> **SELECT** Employee1.Name, Salary, Dept
> **FROM** Employee1, Employee2
> **WHERE** Employee1.Name = Employee2.Name

5.1.3   Summary

Time-varying data is common, and applications that manage such data abound. However, nontemporal DBMSs and their query languages provide inadequate support for such applications. If a temporal DBMS is used, the data model more accurately reflects reality, SQL queries are much simpler, and significantly less application code is required. This enables developers to more easily write, debug, and maintain applications.

In the remainder of this part of the book, we will discuss the foundations of temporal databases, survey the many temporal data models that have been developed, delve into the TSQL2 temporal query language, and discuss implementation strategies for temporal DBMSs.

5.2   The Time Domain

Here we focus on time itself: how it is modeled and how it is represented. Section 5.4 will then combine time with facts, to model time-varying information.

Models of time in a temporal logic represent time as an arbitrary set of instants with an imposed partial order. Additional axioms introduce other, more refined models of time. For example, *linear* time can be specified by adding an axiom imposing a total order on this set. In the linear model, time advances from the past to the future in a step-by-step fashion. In the *branching* model, also termed the *possible futures* or *hypothetical* model, time is linear from the past to now, where it then divides into several time lines, each representing a potential sequence of events. Along any future path, additional branches may exist. The structure of branching time is a tree rooted at now. Generalizations allow branches in the past, or allow branches to join. Recurrent processes may be associated with a *cyclic* model of time. An example is a week, in which each day recurs every seven days.

Axioms may also be added to temporal logics to characterize the *density* of the time line. Combined with the linear model, *discrete* models of time are isomorphic to the natural numbers, implying that each point in time has a single successor. *Dense* models of time are isomorphic to either the rationals or the reals: between any two moments of time another moment exists. *Continuous* models of time are isomorphic to the reals, that is, they are both dense and, unlike the rationals, contain no "gaps."

In the continuous model, each real number corresponds to a "point" in time; in the discrete model, each natural number corresponds to a nondecomposable unit of time with an arbitrary duration. Such a nondecomposable unit of time is referred to as a *chronon*. A chronon is the smallest duration of time that can be represented in this model. It is not a point, but a line segment on the time line.

Although time itself is perceived by most to be continuous, the discrete time model is generally used. Several practical arguments justify this choice. First, measures of time are inherently imprecise. Clocking instruments invariably report the occurrence of events in terms of chronons, not time "points." Hence, events, even so-called instantaneous events, can at best be measured as having occurred during a chronon. Second, most natural language references to time are compatible with the discrete time model. For example, when we say that an event occurred at 4:30 PM, we usually don't mean that the event occurred at the "point" in time associated with 4:30 PM, but at some time in the chronon (perhaps minute) associated with 4:30 PM. Third, the concepts of chronon and period allow us to naturally model events that are not instantaneous but have duration. Finally, any implementation of a data model with a temporal dimension will of necessity have to have some discrete encoding for time.

Axioms can also be placed on the *boundedness* of time. Time can be bounded orthogonally in the past and in the future. A finite encoding implies bounds from the left (i.e., the existence of a time origin) and from the right. Models of time may include the concept of *distance*, though most temporal logics do not do so.

Finally, one can differentiate *relative* time from *absolute* time (more precise terms are *unanchored* and *anchored*). For example, "9 AM, January 1, 1996" is an absolute time, and "9 hours" is a relative time. This distinction, though, is not as crisp as we would hope, because absolute time is with respect to another time (in this example, midnight, January 1, AD 1), termed an *anchor*. Relative time can be distinguished from distance in that the former has a direction. For example, you could envision a relative time of −9 hours, but distance is unsigned.

5.3   Time Data Types

Several temporal data types have proven useful. The most basic is a time *instant*, which is a particular chronon on the time line. An *event* is an instantaneous fact, that is, something occurring at an instant. The *event occurrence time* of an event is the instant at which the event occurs in the real world.

SQL-92 provides three instant data types: **DATE** (a particular day, with a year in the range AD 1–9999), **TIME** (a particular second within a range of 24 hours), and **TIMESTAMP** (a particular fraction of a second, defaulting to microsecond, of a particular day).

A *time period* is the time between two instants. In some of the literature, this notion is called a *time interval*, but this usage conflicts with the SQL-92 data type **INTERVAL**, which is a different concept altogether. SQL-92 does not include periods, but periods are now part of the evolving SQL3 specification.

A *time interval* is a directed duration of time, that is, an amount of time with a known length, but not specific starting or ending instants. A positive interval denotes forward motion of time, toward the future. SQL-92 supports two kinds of intervals, month-year and second-day intervals.

Two final temporal data types are *instant sets*, which are (logically!) sets of instants, and *temporal elements*, which are finite unions of periods.

Temporal types must be representable. A bounded discrete representation, as an integer count of the instants since the origin, is the simplest option. A bounded dense representation is also not difficult to manage, as all rationals may be expressed as the ratio between two integers. A floating point representation may also be employed. A continuous representation is the most difficult to implement.

5.4   Associating Facts with Time

The previous sections discussed the time domain itself. We now turn to associating time with facts.

5.4.1   Dimensionality

In the context of databases, two time dimensions are of general interest: the valid time dimension and the transaction time dimension.

Valid time concerns the time a fact was true in reality. The valid time of an event is the time at which the event occurred in the real world, indepen-

Figure 5.1: Structure of a snapshot relation

dent of the recording of that event in some database. Valid times can also be in the future, if it is expected that some fact will be true at a specified time after now.

Transaction time concerns the time the fact was present in the database as stored data. The transaction time (a period) of a fact identifies the transaction that inserted the fact into the database and the transaction that removed this fact from the database.

These two dimensions are orthogonal. A data model supporting neither is termed *snapshot*, as it captures only a single snapshot in time of both the database and the enterprise that the database models. A data model supporting only valid time is termed *valid-time*, one that supports only transaction time is termed *transaction-time*, and one that supports both valid and transaction time is termed *bitemporal*. *Temporal* is a generic term implying some kind of time support.

Figure 5.1 illustrates the structure of a (three-column) conventional relation. A relation consists of a number of tuples (rows), each having the same number of attribute values (columns). Each tuple captures a fact that is currently thought to be true in the modeled reality. As reality changes, the relation changes, with tuples added, removed, or modified.

Figure 5.2 illustrates the structure of a transaction-time relation, which is a sequence of snapshot states, indexed over transaction time. The relation started out as an empty relation. A transaction inserted three tuples, resulting in the first state being appended to the sequence, with an associated transaction time of the commit time of that transaction. A later transaction inserted one tuple, resulting in the second state being appended. A subsequent transaction then deleted the first tuple and inserted yet another tuple, resulting in the third state.

This figure emphasizes the semantics of transaction time. Unlike snapshot relations, transactions do not alter existing data in transaction-time relations. Rather, the change is made to the current snapshot state, resulting in a new snapshot state that is appended to the relation. In this sense, transaction-time relations are append-only, and thus amenable to be-

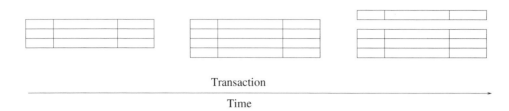

Transaction

Time

Figure 5.2: Structure of a transaction-time relation

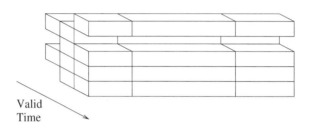

Valid
Time

Figure 5.3: Structure of a valid-time relation

ing implemented on write-once media such as optical disks. This kind of
relation supports transaction-time queries that extract information from the
state of the relation at some point in the past. While we'll consider only
linear transaction time, an alternative, branching transaction time, provides
a useful model for versioning in computer-aided design tasks.

Figure 5.3 also depicts a three-dimensional structure, although here time
does not proceed horizontally, but rather perpendicularly, out of the page.
The valid time of a tuple is the time in reality when the fact represented by
the tuple was valid. Any portion can be corrected, as new knowledge about
reality becomes available. This kind of relation supports valid-time queries,
which concern facts that were true in the past or will be true in the future.
Note that it is not possible to determine what the state of the database was
at a previous time, as that information is not retained.

Figure 5.4 illustrates the structure of a single bitemporal relation composed of a sequence of valid-time states indexed by transaction time. It is,
in fact, a four-dimensional structure: tuples, attribute values, valid time,
and transaction time. This particular relation is the result of four transactions starting from an empty relation: (1) three tuples were added, (2) one
tuple was added, (3) one tuple was added and an existing one terminated
(logically deleted), and (4) the starting time of a previous tuple, the middle

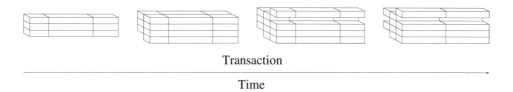

Transaction

Time

Figure 5.4: The structure of a bitemporal relation

one added in the first transaction, was changed to a somewhat later time (presumably the original starting time was incorrect) and a tuple (the top one) was inserted. Each update operation involves copying the valid-time state, then applying the update to the newly created state. Of course, less redundant representations than the one shown are possible.

As with transaction-time relations, bitemporal relations are append-only and support transaction-time queries. As with valid-time relations, bitemporal relations support valid-time queries and permit facts to be true in the past and in the future.

While valid time may extend into the future, transaction time is defined only until now. Specifically, transaction time starts when the database is created (before which time, nothing was stored) and doesn't extend past now (no facts are known to have been stored in the future). Changes to the database state are required to be stamped with the current transaction time. As the database state evolves, transaction times grow monotonically. In contrast, successive transactions may mention widely varying valid times. For instance, the fourth transaction in Figure 5.4 added information to the database that was transaction timestamped with time 4, while changing a valid time of one of the tuples to 2.

The two time dimensions are not homogeneous; transaction time has a different semantics than valid time. Valid and transaction time are orthogonal, though there are generally some application-dependent correlations between the two times. As a simple example, consider the situation where a fact is recorded as soon as it becomes valid in reality. In such a *specialized* bitemporal database, termed *degenerate*, the valid and transaction times of a fact are identical. As another example, if a cloud cover measurement is recorded at most 2 days after it was valid in reality, and if it takes at least 6 hours from the measurement time to record the measurement, then such a relation is characterized as "delayed strongly retroactively bounded with bounds 6 hours and 2 days."

Data model name	Temporal dimension(s)	Identifier
Accounting Data Model	Both	ADM
—	Both	Ahn
Temporally Oriented Data Model	Both	Ariav
—	Valid	Bassinouni
—	Both	Bhargava
Bitemporal Conceptual Data Model	Both	BCDM
Time Relational Model	Both	Ben-Zvi
DATA	Transaction	DATA
DM/T	Transaction	DM/T
Extensional Data Model	Both	EDM
Homogeneous Relational Model	Valid	Gadia-1
Heterogeneous Relational Model	Valid	Gadia-2
Historical Data Model	Valid	HDM
Historical Relational Data Model	Valid	HRDM
—	Valid	Jones
—	Transaction	Lomet
Temporal Relational Model	Valid	Lorentzos
—	Valid	Lum
—	Both	McKenzie
Temporal Relational Model	Valid	Navathe
—	Valid	Sadeghi
—	Valid	Sarda
Temporal Data Model	Valid	Segev
—	Both	Snodgrass
—	Valid	Tansel
Time Oriented Databank Model	Valid	Wiederhold
—	Both	Yau

Table 5.1: Temporal relational data models

5.4.2   Underlying Data Model

Time has been added to many data models: the entity-relationship model, semantic data models, knowledge-based data models, and deductive data models. However, by far the majority of work in temporal databases is based on the relational and object-oriented models. For this reason, we focus on these two data models in our subsequent discussion.

Table 5.1 lists most of the temporal relational data models that have appeared in the literature. Some models are defined only over valid time or transaction time; others are defined over both. The last column indicates a short identifier that denotes the model; the table is ordered on this column.[1]

---

[1]If the model has not been given a name, we use the name of the first designer of the model as an identifier; this is also done for models with identical acronyms. Citations of

Data model name	Temporal dimension(s)	Identifier	Transaction timestamp representation
—	Both	Caruso	Chronon
IRIS	Transaction	IRIS	Chronon, identifier
—	Transaction	Kim	Version hierarchy
MATISSE	Transaction	MATISSE	Chronon, identifier
OODAPLEX	Arbitrary	OODAPLEX	Arbitrary
OSAM*/T	Valid	OSAM*/T	N/A
OVM	Transaction	OVM	Identifier
Postgres	Transaction	Postgres	Period
—	Arbitrary	Sciore-1	Arbitrary
—	Both	Sciore-2	Chronon
TEDM	Valid	TEDM	N/A
TIGUKAT	Both	TIGUKAT	Identifier
TMAD	Valid	TMAD	N/A
Temporal Object-Oriented Data Model	Both	TOODM	Temporal element

Table 5.2: Temporal object-oriented data models

We classify the extant object-oriented temporal data models in Table 5.2. The last column will be discussed shortly. Those with "arbitrary" indicated in the temporal dimensions and transaction timestamp representation columns support time with user- or system-provided classes; hence, anything is possible. N/A denotes "not applicable."

Valid Time

These models may be compared along the valid-time dimension by asking two basic questions: how is valid time represented and how are facts associated with valid time. Table 5.3 categorizes most of the data models along these two aspects. We do not include the OODAPLEX, Sciore-1, and TIGUKAT data models, as these two aspects are arbitrarily specifiable in these models.

Valid times can be represented with single chronon identifiers (i.e., instant timestamps), with periods (i.e., as period timestamps), or as *valid-time elements*, which are finite sets of periods. Valid time can be associated with

---

papers describing these models may be found in the bibliographic notes at the end of this chapter.

	Single chronon	Period (pair of chronons)	Valid-time element (set of periods)
Timestamped attribute values	ADM Caruso Lorentzos	Bassiouni Gadia-2 McKenzie Tansel	Bhargava Gadia-1 HRDM TOODM
Timestamped groups of attributes	Sciore-2		
Timestamped tuples	Ariav EDM HDM Lum Sadeghi Segev Wiederhold	Ahn Ben-Zvi Jones Navathe Sarda Snodgrass Yau	BCDM
Timestamped objects	TEDM	OSAM*/T TMAD	

Table 5.3: Valid time in temporal data models

individual attribute values, with groups of attributes, or with an entire tuple or object. Finally, constraints over the integers (or reals) may be used to express the times at which a tuple is valid. The solutions of the constraints are time points. The relational algebra can then be extended by manipulating these constraints. Other alternatives, such as associating valid time with sets of tuples (i.e., relations) or with object graphs (i.e., a set of objects, with an attribute of one object referencing another object in the set, forming a connected graph), have not been incorporated into any of the proposed data models, primarily because they introduce considerable data redundancy.

Transaction Time

The same general issues are involved in transaction time, but there are about three times as many alternatives. The choices made in the various data models are characterized in Table 5.4. OODAPLEX is not included, as it can support virtually any of these options (while that is also possible in TIGUKAT, specific support for versioning has been added to the data model and language). Transaction time may be represented with the following alternatives:

- The transaction timestamp may be a single chronon, which implies

	Single chronon	Period	Three chronons	Transaction-time element (set of periods)	Other
Timestamped attribute values	Caruso			Bhargava TOODM	Sciore-1
Timestamped groups of attributes	Sciore-2				OVM
Timestamped tuples	Ariav DATA DM/T EDM Lomet	Postgres Snodgrass Yau	Ben-Zvi	BCDM	
Timestamped objects	IRIS TIGUKAT				IRIS Kim
Timestamped sets of tuples	ADM Ahn	McKenzie			
Object graph	MATISSE TIGUKAT				MATISSE
Timestamped schema	MATISSE TIGUKAT	McKenzie Postgres		BCDM	MATISSE

Table 5.4: Transaction time in temporal data models

that tuples inserted on each transaction signify the termination (logical deletion) of previously current tuples with identical keys, with the timestamps of these previously recorded tuples not requiring change.

- The timestamp may be a period. A newly inserted tuple would be associated with the period starting at now and ending at the special value *U.C.* (*until changed*).

- The timestamp may consist of three chronons. Ben-Zvi's model records (1) the transaction time when the valid start time was recorded, (2) the transaction time when the valid stop time was recorded, and (3) the transaction time when the tuple was logically deleted.

- The timestamp may be a transaction-time element, which is a set of periods.

More detail on the representation of "Other" may be found in the last column of Table 5.2. Specifically, those data models supporting versions often allow arbitrary user-supplied identifiers to be associated with versions. One model even allows an entire version hierarchy to be associated with a version.

5.4.3   Representative Data Models

To ground this discussion, let's examine five representative models. One of the simplest is Segev's valid-time data model, in which tuples are time-stamped with the instant that the tuple became valid. This allows the history of the attribute values of a key to be succinctly captured. In the following relation instance, we see that Eric started working in the shoe department on June 1 (in these examples, we omit the month and year from the timestamp). He moved to the book department on June 6, and returned to the shoe department on June 11. He resigned on June 13; this requires a separate tuple, with null values for all the nonkey attributes.

Name	Dept	Time
Eric	Shoe	1
Eric	Book	6
Eric	Shoe	11
Eric	Null	13

This data model can use such a simple timestamp because it does not permit multiple values at any point in time. By using period timestamps, as for example in Sarda's data model, multiple values can be accommodated. The following shows the same information as above, in a period-timestamped model.

Name	Dept	Time
Eric	Shoe	[1–5]
Eric	Book	[6–10]
Eric	Shoe	[11–13]

Note that null values are not required in Sarda's model when an employee resigns.

Several of the models timestamp attribute values instead of tuples. This allows more history to be captured in a single tuple. In the HRDM, attribute values are functions from time to a value domain:

Name	Dept	Valid Time	Transaction Time
Eric	Shoe	1	1
Eric	Shoe	2	1
...	...	...	...
Eric	Shoe	1	2
Eric	Shoe	2	2
...	...	...	...
Eric	Shoe	1	8
...	...	...	...
Eric	Shoe	5	8
Eric	Book	6	8
Eric	Book	7	8
...	...	...	...
Eric	Shoe	1	9
...	...	...	...
Eric	Shoe	5	9
Eric	Book	6	9
Eric	Book	7	9
...	...	...	...

Figure 5.5: The extensional data model

Name	Dept
1 → Eric	1 → Shoe
...	...
12 → Eric	5 → Shoe
	6 → Book
	...
	10 → Book
	11 → Shoe
	12 → Shoe

Eric's entire employment history is captured in a single tuple. Another advantage of attribute value timestamping is that attributes that vary independently, termed *asynchronous attributes*, do not require an additional tuple when an attribute value changes.

The above data models are all valid-time models. As a simple example of a bitemporal data model, the extensional data model timestamps each tuple with a single valid-time chronon and a single transaction-time chronon.

Name	Dept
$[1,11] \times [1,\infty]$ Eric	$[1,7] \times [1,\infty]$ Shoe
$[12,\nearrow] \times [1,12]$ Eric	
	$[8,9] \times [1,\infty]$ Shoe
	$[8,9] \times [6,\infty]$ Book
	$[10,10] \times [1,5]$ Shoe
	$[10,10] \times [6,10]$ Book
	$[11,12] \times [1,5]$ Shoe
	$[11,12] \times [6,10]$ Book
	$[11,12] \times [11,\infty]$ Shoe
	$[12,\nearrow] \times [1,5]$ Shoe
	$[11,\nearrow] \times [6,10]$ Book
	$[11,\nearrow] \times [11,\infty]$ Shoe

Figure 5.6: Bhargava's data model

In the example shown in Figure 5.5, Eric was hired in the shoe department on June 1. At that time, we didn't know what would happen in the future, so the valid time is assumed to be from June 1 to the maximum time. On June 2, nothing had changed, and so those same valid times are repeated. On June 8, we find out that Eric had been working in the book department since June 6.

This data model captures all the information about what was true and when it was known, but does so in a very space-inefficient manner. However, this data model is also extremely simple, and so is useful when describing the semantics of query languages.

Bhargava's model (see Figure 5.6) is also a bitemporal data model, yet uses attribute value timestamping. The same information present above in many, many tuples in the extensional data model can be represented in a single, complex tuple in Bhargava's model.

In Bhargava's model, the value of an attribute is a set of values from the value domain, each associated with a rectangle in bitemporal space. Each rectangle is shown here as a period in transaction time × a period in valid time. The value Eric is timestamped with two rectangles. The first is from June 1 to June 11 in transaction time and from June 1 to forever (represented as "∞") in valid time. This means that the information about Eric was stored in the database on June 1 and was assumed to be true in reality from June 1 to forever. June 11 was the last day that was known to be true. The second rectangle is associated with a transaction time from June 12 to forever (represented as "↗") and with a valid time from June 1 to June 12. While this representation stores the same information as the relation instance in the extensional data model, by employing rectangles and attribute value timestamping, a much more compact representation is achieved.

5.5 Temporal Query Languages

A data model consists of a set of objects with a specified structure, a set of constraints on those objects, and a set of operations on those objects. In the two previous sections we have investigated in detail the structure of, and constraints on, the objects of temporal databases. Here, we complete the picture by discussing the operations, specifically temporal query languages.

Many temporal query languages have been proposed. In fact, it seems that each researcher feels it necessary to define a new data model and query language.

Table 5.5 lists the major temporal query language proposals to date. The underlying data model is a reference to Table 5.1. The next column lists the conventional query language the temporal proposal is based on. Most of the query languages have a formal definition.

Table 5.6 lists the object-oriented query languages that support time. Note that many "nested" relational query languages and data models, such as HQuel, HRDM, HTQuel, TempSQL, and TBE, have features that might be considered to be object-oriented.

The data model and conventional query language on which the temporal query language is based are identified in the second and third columns. The fourth column indicates whether the language has been implemented. It is rare for an object-oriented query language to have a formal semantics. Also in contrast to temporal relational query languages, most object-oriented query languages have been implemented.

5.6 Summary

A temporal data model attempts to simultaneously satisfy many goals. It should capture the semantics of the application to be modeled in a clear and concise fashion. It should be a consistent, minimal extension of an existing data model, such as the relational model. It is best if the tempo-

Name	Underlying data model	Based on	Formal semantics
HQL	Sadeghi	DEAL	✓
HQuel	Tansel	Quel	✓
HSQL	Sarda	SQL	
HTQuel	Gadia-1	Quel	✓
IXSQL	Lorentzos	SQL-92	✓
Legol 2.0	Jones	Relational Algebra	
TDM	Segev	SQL	✓
Temporal Relational Algebra	Lorentzos	Relational Algebra	✓
TempSQL	Yau	SQL	✓
Time-By-Example	Tansel	QBE	✓
TOSQL	Ariav	SQL	
TQuel	Snodgrass	Quel	✓
TSQL	Navathe	SQL	
TSQL2	BCDM	SQL-92	
—	ADM	Relational Algebra	✓
—	Bassiouni	Quel	✓
—	Ben-Zvi	SQL	✓
—	DM/T	Relational Algebra	✓
—	Gadia-2	Quel	
—	HDM	IL_s	✓
—	HRDM	Relational Algebra	✓
—	McKenzie	Relational Algebra	✓

Table 5.5: Temporal relational query languages

Name	Underlying data model	Based on	Implemented
MATISSE	MATISSE	SQL	✓
OODAPLEX	OODAPLEX	DAPLEX	
OSQL	IRIS	SQL	✓
OQL	OVM	SQL	✓
OQL/T	OSAM*/T	OSAM*/OQL	
Orion	Kim	SQL	✓
PICQUERY+	TEDM	PICQUERY	✓
Postquel	Postgres	Quel	✓
TMQL	TMAD	SQL	
TQL	TIGUKAT	SQL	✓
TOOSQL	TOODM	SQL	✓
TOSQL	TOODM	SQL	
VISION	Caruso	Metafunctions	✓
—	Sciore-1	Annotations	
—	Sciore-2	EXTRA/EXCESS	

Table 5.6: Temporal object-oriented query languages

ral data model presents all the time-varying behavior of a fact or object coherently. The data model should be easy to implement, while attaining high performance.

The experience of the last 15 years and some 40 data models appearing in the literature argues that designing a temporal data model with all of these characteristics is elusive at best, and probably not possible. The objectives appear to be contradictory.

Simultaneously focusing on data presentation (how temporal data is displayed to the user), on data storage (with its requisite demands of regular structure), and on efficient query evaluation has complicated the central task of capturing the time-varying semantics of data. The result has been, as we have seen, a plethora of incompatible data models, with many query languages, and a corresponding surfeit of database design and implementation strategies that may be employed across these models.

In the next chapter, we will see a different approach that exploits the advantages of each model.

5.7 Bibliographic Notes

A series of six bibliographies concerning temporal databases [67, 280, 415, 410, 248, 435] references some 1,100 papers through January 1996. A bibliography on space and time in databases [15] lists 144 spatio-temporal database papers. An annotated bibliography on schema evolution [362] includes eight temporal database papers.

The book edited by Tansel et al. provides a snapshot of temporal database research as of 1993 [427]. Chapters of that book provide excellent surveys on temporal reasoning [291] and on temporal deductive databases [46]. The glossary that was initially prepared for that book has since been considerably expanded; the most recent version appeared in *SIGMOD Record* [230].

Other extant surveys include those on temporal data models [233, 406], temporal query languages [107, 281, 407], and temporal access methods [383]. A recent survey covers both temporal and real-time databases [328]; that survey contains references to all the data models discussed here (in Tables 5.1, 5.2, 5.5, and 5.6). The solution in Example 5.5 was discovered independently by Böhlen [64] and by Rozenshtein, Abramovich, and Birger [90, 368]. The relative performance of many algorithms for coalescing has been compared [66].

Van Benthem's book is an excellent introduction to temporal logic [438], as is an earlier one by Rescher [357]. An extensive literature has since developed.

While previous authors had mentioned various kinds of time, Snodgrass and Ahn showed that there were two principal types, valid time and transaction time [408]. The concepts of temporal specialization and generalization, which characterize correlations between the valid and transaction times of a fact, were introduced by Jensen and Snodgrass [231]. Later they summarized the general topic of the semantics of time-varying data, including logical and physical design [232].

Time has been added to many data models, in addition to the relational and object-oriented data models discussed in the chapter. The entity-relationship model, semantic data models, knowledge-based data models, and deductive database models have been extended. References to these data models may be found in the survey [328]. More information on the five models discussed in Section 5.4.3 is available: Segev [395], Sarda [385], HRDM [110], EDM [111], and Bhargava [56]. There are also several data models involving constraints [235, 255, 256]. The relational algebra may be extended to manipulate these constraints.

SQL-92 is described in Melton and Simon's book [285]. References to the query languages mentioned in this chapter may be found in the survey [328].

We did not consider the related topic of *temporal reasoning* (also termed *inferencing* or *rule-based search*) [236, 263, 291, 414], which uses artificial intelligence techniques to perform more sophisticated analyses of temporal relationships, generally with much lower query processing efficiency. Also not included are knowledge representation languages, such as Telos [300] or TSOS [43], which, while supporting either valid or transaction time, or both, are not strictly query languages.

Oversimplifying, the history of temporal databases can be seen as comprising four overlapping phases. The first, from 1956 to 1985, focused on concept development, considering the multiple kinds of time and conceptual modeling. The second, from 1978 to 1994, contained two subphases: 1978 to 1990 saw the design of many relational temporal query languages, while 1990 to 1994 experienced the introduction of object-oriented temporal query languages. The third phase, from 1988 to the present, considered implementation aspects, in particular storage structures, operator algorithms, and temporal indexes. The final phase is one of consolidation, starting with the infrastructure workshop in 1993 and continuing to the present. In this phase a consensus glossary, query language test suite, and TSQL2 emerged. The number of temporal database papers continues to increase at a superlinear rate, as it has for the past two decades.

5.8 Exercises

5.1. In Example 5.4, the repeat-until loop updates the Stop time.

    a. Revise the **UPDATE** statement to update the Start time instead. Argue the correctness of your solution.

    b. Combine the approaches to simultaneously update both the Start and Stop times.

5.2. Five ways were presented to perform coalescing: (1) updating the Stop time (Example 5.4), (2) **SELECT DISTINCT** (Example 5.5), (3) using a cursor (Example 5.6), (4) updating the Start time (Exercise 5.1a), and (5) updating both the Start and Stop times (Exercise 5.1b). What is the worst-case complexity of each of these five approaches, for n value-equivalent tuples? To determine their relative average-case efficiency, run each on a conventional DBMS.

5.3. The UA Office of Appointed Personnel is asked, "What is the maximum salary?"

    a. Give this query in SQL on a snapshot database, storing only the current information.

    b. Now that the salary history is stored, we'd like a history of the maximum salary over time. The problem, of course, is that SQL does not provide temporal aggregates. One way to do this is indirectly, by converting the snapshot aggregate query into a nonaggregate query, then converting that into a temporal query. The nonaggregate query finds those salaries for which a greater salary does not exist. Write this query in SQL, again, on a snapshot database.

    c. Now convert this latter query into a temporal query. This is quite challenging.

    d. How do you think this query could be expressed in TSQL2?

    e. Why doesn't the trick in (c) work when asked to compute the average salary over time?

5.4. Show how, by using derived tables, i.e., **FROM (SELECT ...) AS** F, Example 5.5 can be expressed in a *single* SQL statement. Why doesn't this transformation work for Example 5.4?

5.5. Remove the linked list from the code in Example 5.6, using **ORDER BY** Start. Run both versions on a conventional DBMS to determine their relative efficiency.

5.6. Pick your favorite application. Be creative.

   a. What aspects of this application require storing historical or future information?

   b. Specify an SQL schema for several historical relations, using columns of type **DATE** or **TIMESTAMP**.

   c. Populate these relations with sample data.

   d. Provide some interesting English prose queries, along with the results that should be returned when evaluated on the same data.

   e. Express your queries in SQL. Evaluate the difficulty of using SQL for your application.

   f. Discuss how valid and transaction time relate to your application. Which relations should support valid time, which should support transaction time, and which should support both?

   g. Extend your sample data to include both valid and transaction time.

Chapter 6

TSQL2

The Temporal Structured Query Language, or TSQL2, was designed by a committee of 18 researchers who had individually designed many of the languages listed in the previous chapter. The goal of TSQL2 was to consolidate approaches to temporal data models and calculus-based query languages, to achieve a consensus extension to SQL-92 and an associated data model upon which future research could be based. Additionally, TSQL2 is being incorporated into the evolving SQL3 standard.

6.1 Time Ontology

TSQL2 uses a linear time structure, bounded on both ends. The origin is 18 billion years ago, when the Big Bang is thought to have occurred; the time line extends 18 billion years into the future.

The TSQL2 time line is a discrete representation of the real time line, which can be considered to be discrete, dense, or continuous. The TSQL2 time line consists of atomic (nondecomposable) chronons. Consecutive chronons may be grouped together into *granules*, with different groupings yielding distinct granularities. TSQL2 allows a value of a temporal data type to be converted from one granularity to another.

TSQL2 is carefully designed not to require choosing among the discrete, dense, and continuous time ontologies. Rather, TSQL2 permits no question to be asked that would differentiate among these three ontologies. For example, it is not possible to ask if an instant a precedes an instant b. It is only possible to ask that question in terms of a specified granularity, such as seconds, days, or years. Different granularities could yield different answers to this question. Similarly, distance is in terms of a specified granularity, and is represented as an integral number of granules.

TSQL2 inherits the temporal types in SQL-92, **DATE**, **TIME**, **TIME-STAMP**, and **INTERVAL**, and adds the **PERIOD** data type.

6.2   Data Model

TSQL2 employs a very simple underlying data model. This data model retains the simplicity and generality of the relational model. It has no illusions of being suitable for presentation, storage, or query evaluation. Instead, separate, representational data models, of equivalent expressive power, are employed for implementation and for ensuring high performance. Other presentational data models may be used to render time-varying behavior to the user or application. A coordinated suite of data models can achieve in concert goals that no single data model could attain.

This conceptual model, termed the *Bitemporal Conceptual Data Model* (*BCDM*), timestamps tuples with bitemporal elements, which are sets of bitemporal chronons. Each bitemporal chronon represents a tiny rectangle in valid-time/transaction-time space. Because no value-equivalent tuples are allowed in a bitemporal relation instance, the full time history of a fact is contained in a single tuple. Equivalently, we say that the BCDM is a coalesced data model. In Table 5.3, the conceptual temporal data model occupies the entry corresponding to timestamping tuples with valid-time elements, and it occupies the entry in Table 5.4 corresponding to timestamping tuples with transaction-time elements.

Example 6.1   A bitemporal relation

Consider an Employee relation recording information such as "Jake works for the shipping department." We assume that the granularity of chronons is 1 day for both valid time and transaction time, and the period of interest is some given month in a given year (e.g., the integer 15 in a timestamp represents the date June 15, 1996).

Figure 6.1 shows how the bitemporal element in an employee's department tuple changes. In graphical representations of bitemporal space, we choose the x-axis as the transaction-time dimension, and the y-axis as the valid-time dimension. Hence, the ordered pair (t, v) represents the bitemporal chronon with transaction time t and valid time v.

Employee Jake was hired by the company as temporary help in the shipping department for the period from time 10 to time 15, and this fact became current in the database at time 5. This is shown in Figure 6.1(a). The arrows pointing to the right signify that the tuple has not been logically deleted; it continues through to the transaction time *until changed* (*U.C.*).

Figure 6.1(b) shows a correction. The personnel department discovers that Jake had really been hired from time 5 to time 20, and the database is corrected beginning at time 10. Later, the personnel department is informed that the correction was itself incorrect; Jake really was hired for the original time period, time 10 to time 15, and the correction took effect in the database at time 15. This is shown in Figure 6.1(c). Lastly, Figure 6.1(d) shows the result of three updates to the relation, all of which become current starting at time 20. (The same transaction could have caused all three of these updates.) While the period of validity was correct, it was discovered that Jake was not in the shipping department, but in the loading department. Consequently, the fact (Jake,Ship) is removed from the current state and the fact (Jake,Load) is inserted. A new employee, Kate, is hired for the shipping department for the period from time 25 to time 30.

We note that the number of bitemporal chronons in a given bitemporal element is the area enclosed by the bitemporal element. The bitemporal element for (Jake,Ship) contains 140 bitemporal chronons.

The actual bitemporal relation corresponding to the graphical representation in Figure 6.1(d) is shown in Figure 6.2. This relation contains three facts. The timestamp attribute T shows each transaction-time chronon associated with each valid-time chronon as a set of ordered pairs.

It is possible to demonstrate equivalence mappings between the conceptual model and several representational models. Mappings have been demonstrated for five bitemporal data models: BenZvi (five timestamps per tuple), Bhargava (attribute timestamping, illustrated in the previous chapter), Jensen (tuple timestamping with a single transaction chronon), McKenzie (transaction timestamping of states, valid timestamping of attributes), and Snodgrass (tuple timestamping, with period valid and transaction times). This equivalence is based on *snapshot equivalence*, which says

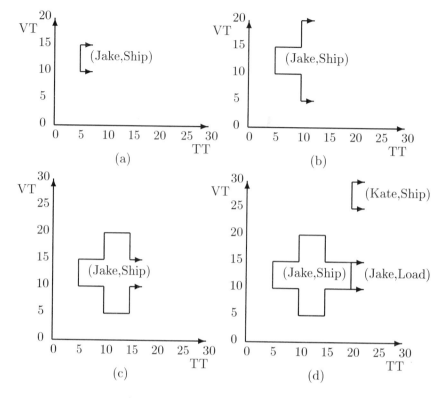

Figure 6.1: Bitemporal elements

Emp	Dept	T
Jake	Ship	$\{(5,10),\ldots,(5,15),\ldots,(9,10),\ldots,(9,15),$ $(10,5),\ldots,(10,20),\ldots,(14,5),\ldots,(14,20),$ $(15,10),\ldots,(15,15)\ldots,(19,10),\ldots,(19,15)\}$
Jake	Load	$\{(U.C.,10),\ldots,(U.C.,15)\}$
Kate	Ship	$\{(U.C.,25),\ldots,(U.C.,30)\}$

Figure 6.2: A bitemporal relation instance

that two relation instances are equivalent if their snapshots, taken at all times (valid and transaction), are identical. Snapshot equivalence provides a natural means of comparing rather disparate representations.

In essence, this model moves the distinction among the various existing temporal data models from a semantic basis to a physical, performance-relevant basis, utilizing the proposed conceptual data model to capture the time-varying semantics. Data presentation, storage representation, and time-varying semantics can be considered in isolation, utilizing different data models. Semantics, specifically as determined by logical database design, is expressed in the conceptual model. Multiple presentation formats are available, as different applications require different ways of viewing the data. The storage and processing of bitemporal relations are performed in a data model that emphasizes efficiency, as discussed in the next chapter.

6.3 Language Constructs

We now turn to the statements available in TSQL2.

6.3.1 Schema Definition

This language is a strict superset of SQL-92, and so it supports conventional relations in all their grandeur. To explore the temporal features of TSQL2, we'll need a temporal relation. Envision a patient database at a doctor's office. Included in this database is information on the drugs prescribed to each patient.

Example 6.2 Define the Prescription **relation**

> **CREATE TABLE** Prescription (Name **CHAR**(30),
>   Physician **CHAR**(30), Drug **CHAR**(30), Dosage **CHAR**(30),
>   Frequency **INTERVAL MINUTE**)
> **AS VALID STATE DAY AND TRANSACTION**

The Name column specifies the patient's name. The Frequency is the number of minutes between drug administrations.

The **AS** clause is new in TSQL2. The valid time specifies the period(s) during which the drug was prescribed. The transaction time specifies when this information was recorded as current in the database. Tuples that have not been updated or deleted will have a transaction time that includes now.

The valid time has a granularity of 1 day. The granularity of the transaction time is system-dependent, but most likely will be no coarser than a millisecond, to differentiate consecutive transactions.

The Prescription relation is a bitemporal state relation, as it includes both kinds of time. There are six kinds of relations:

- snapshot relations, which have no temporal support

- valid-time state relations, specified with **AS VALID STATE** (**STATE** is optional)

- valid-time event relations, specified with **AS VALID EVENT**

- transaction-time relations, specified with **AS TRANSACTION**

- bitemporal state relations, specified with **AS VALID STATE AND TRANSACTION**

- bitemporal event relations, specified with **AS VALID EVENT AND TRANSACTION**

The type of a relation can be changed at any time, using the **ALTER TABLE** statement.

6.3.2   The **SELECT** Statement

To obtain a snapshot result from a temporal relation, specify the new reserved word **SNAPSHOT**.

Example 6.3   Who has been prescribed drugs?

> **SELECT SNAPSHOT** Name
> **FROM** Prescription

This will return the names of all patients who have been prescribed drugs, now or in the past.

Example 6.4   Who is or was taking the drug Proventil?

> **SELECT SNAPSHOT** Name
> **FROM** Prescription
> **WHERE** Drug = 'Proventil'

Again, a simple list of names results.
   The history can also be requested:

Example 6.5   Who has been prescribed drugs, and when?

> **SELECT** Name
> **FROM** Prescription

The default is to return the history, so omitting **SNAPSHOT** does the trick. TSQL2 performs automatic coalescing, so the result is a set of tuples, each associated with one or more maximal periods, during which time the patient was prescribed at least one drug.

When more than one correlation name is mentioned, the default is to identify those moments when all of the underlying tuples are valid. We are interested in the interactions of Proventil with other drugs.

Example 6.6 **What drugs have been prescribed with Proventil?**

    SELECT P1.Name, P2.Drug
    FROM Prescription **AS** P1, Prescription **AS** P2
    WHERE P1.Drug = 'Proventil' **AND** P2.Drug <> 'Proventil'
        AND P1.Name = P2.Name

The result is a set of tuples, each specifying a patient and a drug, along with the maximal period(s) during which both that drug and Proventil were prescribed to that patient.

6.3.3 Restructuring

One of the most powerful constructs of TSQL2 is *restructuring*. Whereas TSQL2 automatically performs coalescing on the result of a query, restructuring in the **FROM** clause allows coalescing to be performed on the underlying tuples.

Example 6.7 **Who has been on a drug for more than a total of six months?**

    SELECT Name, Drug
    FROM Prescription(Name, Drug) **AS** P
    WHERE CAST(**VALID**(P) **AS INTERVAL MONTH**)
        > **INTERVAL** '6' **MONTH**

[handwritten margin notes:]
— because we need Valid(P)
so we have to restruct P
for this P, Valid (P) is
not period, but time-element

Notice that the **FROM** clause mentions in parentheses several of the attributes of the Prescription relation. This clause projects out the Name and Drug attributes, then coalesces the result, which is then manipulated in the remainder of the query. By restructuring on Name and Drug, the timestamp associated with each name-drug pair indicates the maximal period(s) when that patient was prescribed that drug, independent of the prescribing physician, the dosage, or the frequency. Hence, a single pair may be computed from many pairs of the underlying Prescription relation. The other attributes are not available via P.

    The new **VALID**(P) construct returns the valid-time element (set of maximal periods) associated with P. Then, the **CAST** operator converts it to the type **INTERVAL MONTH** by summing the durations (in months) of each of the maximal periods. This computes the total number of months that patient has been prescribed that drug, ignoring gaps when the drug was not prescribed. This total is compared with the interval constant 6 months.

    The result is a relation with two columns, the patient's name and the drug, along with a timestamp specifying when that drug was prescribed.

However, only drugs that have been prescribed for at least a total of 6 months will appear in the result.

Correlation names can be *coupled* (one correlation name is defined in terms of another correlation name) with further restructuring.

Example 6.8   Who has been on Proventil throughout their drug regime?

> **SELECT SNAPSHOT** P1.Name
> **FROM** Prescription(Name) **AS** P1, P1(Drug) **AS** P2
> **WHERE** P2.Drug = 'Proventil' **AND VALID**(P2) = **VALID**(P1)

The first portion of the **FROM** clause projects out just the Name and coalesces, with the resulting timestamp indicating when that patient was prescribed any drug, by any physician, at any frequency and dosage. The correlation name P2 is defined in terms of P1. P2 adds the Drug attribute, and hence is similar to the P correlation name defined in the previous query, as it is restructured on both Name (from P1) and Drug. Also, since P2 was defined in terms of P1, TSQL2 ensures that the common attributes—in this case, Name—have the same value for both. So P1 captures when the patient was prescribed any drug, and P2 captures when that patient was prescribed the drug Proventil. The **WHERE** clause stipulates that the valid times (both of which are sets of maximal periods) must be the same, meaning that whenever the patient was prescribed any drug, she was prescribed Proventil.

It is always the case that **VALID**(P1) CONTAINS **VALID**(P2), by virtue of P2 being a further restructuring of P1, but only for some patients will the two temporal elements be equal.

Finally, note that **SNAPSHOT** is specified, so the result is simply a set of patient names.

Interestingly, both restructuring and coupled correlation names are syntactic sugar. The above query can be rephrased without using either construct.

Example 6.9   The same query as Example 6.8, but without using restructuring or coupled correlation names

> **SELECT SNAPSHOT** P1.Name
> **FROM (SELECT** Name **FROM** Prescription) **AS** P1,
>   **(SELECT** Name, Drug **FROM** Prescription) **AS** P2
> **WHERE** P1.Name = P2.Name **AND** P2.Drug = 'Proventil'
>   **AND VALID**(P2) = **VALID**(P1)

Hence, restructuring is effectively a nested **SELECT** clause, to perform the projection and coalescing. Coupling correlation names implies equality of their shared attributes.

Intuitively, P1 ranges over Name and is timestamped with a temporal element indicating when the value of the Name attribute remained constant. P2 ranges over different values of Drug, with the timestamp of P2 being a subset (proper or otherwise) of the timestamp of P1.

6.3.4 Partitioning

Regardless of whether the correlation name has been restructured, the timestamp is still a temporal element. Often we wish to examine the constituent maximal periods of the timestamp. This can be accomplished by *partitioning*, which is denoted with (**PERIOD**).

Example 6.10 Who has been on the same drug for more than 6 consecutive months?

> **SELECT SNAPSHOT** Name, Drug, **VALID**(P)
> **FROM** Prescription(Name, Drug)(**PERIOD**) **AS** P
> **WHERE CAST**(**VALID**(P) **AS INTERVAL MONTH**)
> > **INTERVAL** '6' **MONTH**

It is useful to compare the English and TSQL2 versions of this query with those of the previous query. We first restructure on Name and Drug, computing a temporal element for each name-drug pair. Then each maximal period is extracted, so that P contains potentially many tuples with identical name-drug values, but timestamped with different maximal periods. **VALID**(P) is then of type period, rather than a temporal element. The **WHERE** clause considers the duration of an individual period, rather than the total of all periods, thus capturing the notion of 6 consecutive months.

The result is a snapshot relation, with a **PERIOD** value in the last attribute. This result may contain several tuples with the same Name and Drug values, but with different values for the third attribute.

Alternatively, we could have requested a valid-time relation:

Example 6.11 Who has been on the same drug for more than 6 consecutive months?

> **SELECT** Name, Drug
> **FROM** Prescription(Name, Drug)(**PERIOD**) **AS** P
> **WHERE CAST**(**VALID**(P) **AS INTERVAL MONTH**)
> > **INTERVAL** '6' **MONTH**

In this case, only one tuple for each name-drug pair would be returned, with an associated temporal element timestamp, containing only those maximal periods of duration greater than 6 months.

Partitioning, however, is not syntactic sugar. The intermediate relation (the result of the **FROM** clause) violates the data model, since it produces value-equivalent tuples. Note that the underlying and resulting relations are always coalesced, so this violation is isolated to the query evaluation.

To summarize, **VALID**(P) evaluates to the timestamp associated with the correlation name P. For state relations associated with unpartitioned correlation names (whether or not restructured), this evaluates to a temporal element. For state relations partitioned by (**PERIOD**), this evaluates to a single period.

In the above example, **VALID**(P) was used in the **SELECT** list. This is permitted because P was partitioned. An attribute cannot be of type temporal element, and so this usage would not have been correct if P was not partitioned.

6.3.5   The **VALID** Clause

To this point, the timestamp of the resulting tuples has defaulted to the intersection of the timestamps of the underlying tuples associated with the correlation name(s). This default can be overridden via a **VALID** clause.

Example 6.12   What drugs was Melanie prescribed during 1996?

```
SELECT Drug
VALID INTERSECT(VALID(Prescription), PERIOD '[1996]' DAY)
FROM Prescription
WHERE Name = 'Melanie'
```

The result is a list of drugs, each associated with a set of the periods during 1996 during which the drug was prescribed to Melanie. Those drugs that were prescribed only before or after 1996 will not be included, because the intersection will result in an empty temporal element, which is disallowed as a timestamp. This intersection is between a temporal element and a specified period. It is possible that multiple periods of the temporal element will intersect the year 1996, with the result containing multiple periods.

6.3.6   The Modification Statements

The SQL modification statements, **INSERT**, **DELETE**, and **UPDATE**, apply to temporal relations.

Example 6.13   Insert a prescription today

> **INSERT INTO** Prescription
> **VALUES** ('Melanie', 'Dr. Beren', 'Proventil', '100mg',
>   **INTERVAL** '8:00' **MINUTE**)

In this example, we didn't specify a timestamp, so the timestamp defaults to

VALID PERIOD(CURRENT_TIMESTAMP,
    NOBIND(CURRENT_TIMESTAMP))

Assume that the clock on the wall says that it is currently July 9, 1996, at 1:30 PM. The prescription starts on **DATE** '1996-07-09' (it is a date because that is the valid-time granularity of the Prescription relation). It is valid until **NOBIND(CURRENT_TIMESTAMP)**, which is the way in TSQL2 that you specify storing the variable now. This value is bound whenever it is retrieved from the database. So if we evaluated the following query,

SELECT *
FROM Prescription

we would see that that prescription went from July 9 to July 9. If we executed the same query 3 days from now (i.e., on July 12), we would see that the prescription went from July 9 to July 12. This is because we don't know what will happen in the future, so the default is to indicate that the tuple was valid until now.

Of course, most prescriptions are not open-ended, and so a terminating date is generally known.

Example 6.14   Insert a prescription with a known period of validity

> **INSERT INTO** Prescription
> **VALUES** ('Melanie', 'Dr. Beren', 'Proventil', '100mg',
>   **INTERVAL** '8:00' **MINUTE**)
> **VALID PERIOD** '[1996-01-01 - 1996-06-30]'

We use the **VALID** clause, introduced earlier for the **SELECT** statement.

Since TSQL2 automatically coalesces, if there was a value-equivalent tuple already in the relation, its temporal element timestamp would be coalesced with the inserted period. Only if a value-equivalent tuple was not already present would this **INSERT** statement result in a new tuple being added to the relation.

In both cases, the transaction time of the new tuple has a value identical to the valid-time default. That is, the tuple was inserted at **CURRENT_TIMESTAMP** and is in the database through *U.C.*; we have no way of knowing whether it will still be in the database tomorrow. It is not possible to specify a transaction time, as that semantics of transaction time must be ensured by the DBMS.

The **VALID** clause can also be used in the **DELETE** and **UPDATE** statements:

Example 6.15   Melanie wasn't prescribed anything for June 1996

>   **DELETE FROM** Prescription
>   **WHERE** Name = 'Melanie'
>   **VALID PERIOD** '[1996-06-01 - 1996-06-30]'

The month of June 1996 is removed from the timestamp of each tuple for the patient named Melanie. Some tuples might not be affected at all (if they do not overlap June 1996), some might be removed entirely (if they were valid only for June 1996, or a part thereof), and some might have a portion of their timestamp removed (if a portion of the timestamp overlapped June 1996). TSQL2 takes care of the details in these three cases.

The semantics of the **UPDATE** statement is quite similar, but the mechanics are more involved:

Example 6.16   Change the Proventil dosage to 50 mg

>   **UPDATE** Prescription
>   **SET** Dosage **TO** '50 mg'
>   **WHERE** Name = 'Melanie' **AND** Drug = 'Proventil'

This changes all current and future Proventil prescriptions to a dosage of 50 milligrams. Prescriptions valid in the past are unaffected. If there were no tuples currently existing with such a dosage, this might actually cause a tuple to be inserted into the relation.

Example 6.17   Change the dosage for March through May

>   **UPDATE** Prescription
>   **SET** Dosage **TO** '50 mg'
>   **VALID PERIOD** '[1996-03-01 - 1996-05-30]'
>   **WHERE** Name = 'Melanie' **AND** Drug = 'Proventil'

Here the dosages before March 1996 and after May 1996 are unaffected.

6.3.7   Event Relations

To this point, we have considered only the Prescription relation, which is a bitemporal state relation, recording facts that are true over time. *Event relations* record instantaneous events. Event relations are timestamped with *instant sets*, which are simply sets of instants. Each tuple identifies a particular kind of event, and the timestamp of that tuple specifies the instant(s) when that event occurred.

Example 6.18 **Define the LabTest event relation**

> **CREATE TABLE** LabTest (Name **CHAR**(30), Physician **CHAR**(30),
> TestID **INTEGER**)
> **AS VALID EVENT HOUR AND TRANSACTION**

A lab test occurs at a particular hour (we are not interested in a finer granularity) and is ordered by a physician for a patient. TestID identifies a particular kind of test (e.g., blood test), which might possibly be administered several times to a particular patient.

Event relations can also be restructured and partitioned.

Example 6.19 **Were any patients the sole receivers of tests ordered by a physician?**

> **SELECT** L1.Name, L2.Physician
> **FROM** LabTest(Name) **AS** L1, L1(Physician) **AS** L2,
> LabTest(Physician) **AS** L3
> **WHERE VALID**(L1) = **VALID**(L2) **AND** L2.Physician = L3.Physician
> **AND VALID**(L1) = **VALID**(L3)

VALID(L1) is an event set containing all tests done on a particular patient, because of the restructuring on Name. Thus, the event sets of all tuples with the same Name are coalesced into a single event set. **VALID**(L2) is an event set containing all tests done on the same patient as in L1, but ordered by a particular physician. In both cases, the TestID is ignored. Because of the semantics of coupled correlation names, it must be the case that **VALID**(L1) CONTAINS **VALID**(L2). Finally, **VALID**(L3) is an event set containing all tests ordered by a particular physician, ignoring the patient.

The predicate **VALID**(L1) = **VALID**(L2) requires that all tests administered to the patient be ordered by L2.Physician. The predicate **VALID**(L1) = **VALID**(L3) requires that all those tests be ordered by L3.Physician.

6.3.8 Transaction-Time Support

To this point, we haven't discussed the implications of the Prescription relation supporting transaction time. In particular, all the queries have implicitly applied to the current state of the relation, ignoring older, corrected tuples.

Example 6.20   **What is Melanie's prescription history?**

> **SELECT** Drug
> **FROM** Prescription
> **WHERE** Name = 'Melanie'

This returns the prescription history as best known, taking into account all corrections that have been entered.

We can roll back the database to its contents stored at a previous point in time.

Example 6.21   **What did the physician believe on June 1, 1996, was Melanie's prescription history?**

> **SELECT** Drug
> **FROM** Prescription **AS** P
> **WHERE** Name = 'Melanie'
>   **AND TRANSACTION**(P) **OVERLAPS DATE** '1996-06-01'

TRANSACTION(P) is allowed only on transaction-time and bitemporal relations, and returns the maximal period in transaction time when the values of the attributes and the valid time associated with the tuple (if present) remained constant.

The default predicate is

TRANSACTION(P) **OVERLAPS CURRENT_TIMESTAMP**

In the above example, we specified a different transaction time. Note that the result could contain drugs that we determined later had not in fact been prescribed to Melanie.

Auditing can be done on previously corrected data.

Example 6.22   **When was Melanie's data, valid on June 1, 1996, last corrected?**

> **SELECT SNAPSHOT BEGIN(TRANSACTION**(P2))
> **FROM** Prescription **AS** P P2
> **WHERE** P1.Name = 'Melanie' **AND** p2.Name = 'Melanie'
>   **AND VALID**(P1) **OVERLAPS DATE** '1996-06-01'
>   **AND VALID**(P2) **OVERLAPS DATE** '1996-06-01'
>   **AND TRANSACTION**(P1) **MEETS TRANSACTION**(P2)

We are interested in data concerning the state of the modeled reality for Melanie on June 1, 1996, and so both P1 and P2 are required to be valid on that date, with a Name of Melanie. The predicate **TRANSACTION**(P1) **MEETS TRANSACTION**(P2) says that the tuple associated with P1 was corrected, with the new value of one of the other attributes recorded in the tuple associated with P2. The actual transaction performing the update of this tuple has a transaction time of **BEGIN(TRANSACTION**(P2)). Note that the tuple associated with P2 may also be incorrect, in which case there will be yet another tuple whose transaction time period meets that of P2.

Note that the transaction time of tuples is supplied by the system. Hence, there is no transaction clause that mirrors the valid clause discussed above for **SELECT** and modification statements.

6.3.9 Aggregates

SQL-92 supports the aggregates **MIN**, **MAX**, **COUNT**, **SUM**, and **AVG**. These aggregates return time-varying results when applied to temporal relations.

Example 6.23   How many drugs has Melanie been taking?

> **SELECT COUNT**(*)
> **FROM** Prescription
> **WHERE** Name = 'Melanie'

This is a conventional SQL-92 query applied to a bitemporal state relation. The current valid-time state is queried; tuples whose transaction time does not overlap now are ignored. A valid-time state relation will be returned, providing a time-varying count of the number of prescriptions valid at any point in time.

Aggregates may also have a **GROUP BY** clause:

Example 6.24   How many people were taking each drug?

> **SELECT** Drug, **COUNT**(*)
> **FROM** Prescription
> **GROUP BY** Drug

Again, the result is a valid-time state relation, showing the history of the count for each drug.

TSQL2 adds one aggregate, **RISING**, which evaluates to the longest period during which the specified attribute was monotonically rising.

Example 6.25   When was Melanie's Proventil dosage rising the longest?

> **SELECT SNAPSHOT RISING**(Dosage)
> **FROM** Prescription
> **WHERE** Name = 'Melanie' **AND** Drug = 'Proventil'

This query returns a set of periods, indicating those stretches of time when the dosage was rising. If the dosage rose (or stayed level), then fell, then rose, the result would consist of two periods.

6.3.10 Schema Evolution and Versioning

SQL permits the schema to be changed by using the **ALTER** statement, termed *schema evolution*. Only one schema is in effect at any time; a schema change causes the previous schema to be lost. In TSQL2, if the relation has transaction-time support (i.e., if it is a transaction-time or bitemporal relation), then the schema is *versioned* for that relation. Effectively, the schema itself becomes a set of transaction-time relations.

The Prescription relation now has five attributes. A sixth attribute is later added:

Example 6.26   Add a column to the Prescription relation on August 20, 1996

> **ALTER TABLE** Prescription **ADD COLUMN** Identifier **INTEGER**

Both the previous schema, with five attributes, and the new schema, with six attributes, are retained. Since data in a relation that supports transaction time cannot be modified after it is stored (since such relations are append-only), a schema change can affect only data written by the transaction effecting the schema change, or by future transactions.

Legacy applications written before August 20 may want to use the old schema in force when the application was developed. They can do so by specifying **SET SCHEMA DATE** '1996-08-19'. This allows data written after (or before) that date to be viewed as of the schema in effect on that date. TSQL2 transforms data of different schemas into the schema associated with the query. In the case of the one attribute being added, using the old schema simply means that that attribute is unavailable to the query. Some schema changes cannot be accommodated; an example is a change that splits one relation into two. In such situations, the query's schema must match the data's schema.

6.4   Other Constructs

We end with a brief discussion of some additional features of TSQL2.

A *surrogate* is a unique value that can be compared for equality but is otherwise not visible to users. Surrogates are useful for identifying objects when the primary key of the object is time-varying. TSQL2 adds a new column type, **SURROGATE**, as well as a unary function, **NEW**, that supplies a surrogate value that has never been used before.

A *temporal granularity* is a partitioning of the time line into *granules*; examples include seconds, hours, academic semesters, and fiscal quarters. An instant is represented by an integral number of granules from an identified granularity anchor, which is a fixed point on the time line. Granularities are provided by *calendars*, which also supply mappings between granularities. The granularities together form a lattice, which ensures that it is possible to convert a temporal value in any granularity into any other granularity.

Calendars are gathered into *calendric systems*, which can be then selected by the user. The default is the provided SQL-92 calendric system, which defines the granularities already present in SQL-92: **SECOND**, **MINUTE**, **HOUR**, **DAY**, **MONTH**, and **YEAR**.

Operands of predicates (e.g., **PRECEDES**) must be *comparable*, that is, must have the same granularity. The predicate is performed at this implicit granularity. The user can change the granularity of the operands, and thus of the operation.

Temporal indeterminacy is "don't know when" information. Examples include "between 2 PM and 4 PM" and "around the middle of August." Note that in both cases the event is known to have happened; it is not certain when, or more precisely, exactly when, the event occurred. Temporal indeterminacy interacts closely with granularity. "Some time during the first week in January 1996" is indeterminate at a granularity of days, but it is determinate at the granularity of weeks. Section 14.3 discusses temporal indeterminacy in the general context of uncertainty in databases.

There are two conversion functions available: **CAST** and **SCALE**. **CAST** always results in a determinate value; **SCALE** preserves as much information as possible, which may require indeterminacy. Scaling an instant to a coarser granularity may cause an indeterminate instant to become determinate; scaling to a finer granularity always introduces indeterminacy. As an example, **CAST**(**TIMESTAMP** '04-19-1996 15:24:00' **AS DAY**) results in '04-19-1996'; the same value results if **SCALE** is used. However, **CAST**(**DAY** '04-19-1996' **AS SECOND**) results in the first second of that day; **SCALE** will result in an indeterminate instant occurring during an unspecified second of the 86,400 seconds of that day.

SQL-92 includes the nullary functions **CURRENT_DATE**, **CURRENT_-TIME**, and **CURRENT_TIMESTAMP**, but doesn't allow these variables to be stored in relations. As discussed above, TSQL2 does allow these values to be stored, via **NOBIND**. In addition, TSQL2 supports more general versions of these now variables—specifically, now-relative values such as 'now - 3' days as well as indeterminate versions.

Relations supporting transaction time are append-only, growing monotonically. This behavior can cause problems. The most obvious ramification is that data could outgrow the available storage media. Even if the data fits, more data means slower querying and update. Finally, many countries have strict laws that necessitate the physical deletion of old data, to prevent particular data from being retained longer than a specified time interval. Hence, there is the need to remove data that is no longer useful from the database.

Vacuuming is the process of removing obsolete data. Note that data with a transaction end time of *now* can easily be removed by simply using the **DELETE** statement. If the relation has transaction-time support, however, this data will be retained, with a transaction end time of the transaction in which the delete occurred. A separate vacuuming statement is available in TSQL2 to eliminate data with a transaction end time before a specified date.

6.5   Summary

Here are the major concepts underlying TSQL2:

- *State relations* are timestamped with temporal elements, which are sets of periods.

- Conventional (non-time-varying) relations can be derived from time-varying relations by specifying **SNAPSHOT** in the **SELECT** clause. Conventional relations can participate along with time-varying relations in a query or modification statement.

- *Periods* are anchored durations of time. This is a new data type, augmenting SQL's datetimes and intervals.

- *Restructuring* merges the timestamps of value-equivalent tuples, and is specified by listing column names in the **FROM** clause.

- *Coupled correlation names* permit a further restructuring on additional columns, while ensuring that the tuples associated with the two correlation names agree on the values of the original coalescing columns.

- *Partitioning* extracts maximal period(s) from a valid-time element timestamp for a tuple, and is specified by (**PERIOD**) in the **FROM** clause.

- *Valid-time selection* enables tuples to be selected by predicates on their timestamps, within the **WHERE** clause.

- *Valid-time projection* specifies the period of validity of a derived relation, via the **VALID** clause.

- *Event relations* are timestamped with sets of instants.

- *Bitemporal relations* are timestamped with both valid time and transaction time.

- *Transaction-time selection* permits specification of previous versions.

- *Time-varying aggregates* can be computed. *Grouping* can be over columns or over tuple timestamps.

- *Schema versioning* allows relations timestamped with transaction time to be accessed and modified through previous schemas, thereby supporting legacy applications.

- *Surrogates* identify objects when the primary key is time-varying.

- A *granularity* is a partitioning of the time line.

- *Calendars* provide a collection of granularities and conversions between those granularities.

- *Temporal indeterminacy* allows "don't know precisely when" information to be recorded and queried.

- *Now-relative* times are bound during query evaluation.

- Relations timestamped with transaction time may be *vacuumed* to remove old versions.

6.6 Bibliographic Notes

TSQL2 is described thoroughly in a book devoted to the language [409]. The TSQL2 data model is further elaborated in [234]. Constructs in the language are being incorporated into a new part of SQL3 called SQL/Temporal [284]. As of January 1997, SQL/Temporal includes the **PERIOD** data type.

6.7 Exercises

6.1. This exercise concerns the personnel database introduced in Chapter 5 (see Exercise 5.3).

  a. Define the Employee relation as a bitemporal table using TSQL2's **CREATE TABLE** statement.

  b. Express the following in TSQL2 on this relation:

     i. What is the history of the maximum salary?

     ii. What is the history of the average salary?

6.2. Show, with a concrete example relation, how a **DELETE** statement with a specified valid time can

  a. not affect some tuples at all

  b. remove some tuples entirely

  c. remove a portion of some tuples

Show this relation before and after the update (see Example 6.15).

6.3. Show how the **UPDATE** statement in Example 6.17, executed on September 15, 1996, affects the following Prescription relation:

Name	Drug	Valid Time	Transaction Time
Melanie	Proventil	[1996-01-01 - 1996-08-31]	[1996-06-01 - until changed]

6.4. Provide an example where

CAST(VALID(A) AS ?) PRECEDES CAST(VALID(B) AS ?)

could yield different results for different granularities replacing the "?".

6.5. From the Employee relation shown in Figure 6.2, give the following queries in TSQL2 and provide the resulting relations:

  a. As known on June 7, in which department and for what time was Jake working?

  b. As known on June 12, . . .

  c. As known on June 17, . . .

  d. As best known, . . .

    e. Which departments did we think, as of various times in the past, that Jake worked in?

6.6. This exercise concerns the personnel database introduced in Chapter 5 (see Exercise 5.6).

    a. Translate your relational schema to TSQL2.

    b. Express your original queries in TSQL2. Evaluate the use of TSQL2 for your application.

    c. Show how restructuring, partitioning, and aggregation could be used in your application.

    d. Add sample data and queries, expressed in English and in TSQL2, with results shown, for the following aspects:

        i. temporal indeterminacy

        ii. temporal granularity

        iii. event relations

6.7. Section 5.1 illustrated how a temporal query language can greatly simplify temporal queries. However, when a relation is **ALTER**ed to be a temporal table, the existing application breaks: queries that before returned a snapshot relation of the current state now return a time-varying valid-time relation. An alternative to using **ALTER** is to retain the original Employee relation, recoding the current situation, and create a new table, EmployeeHistory, which stores the historical information.

    a. Create this new table using TSQL2.

    b. We wish to avoid changing the original personnel application to maintain this new table. Define rules, using Starburst, Oracle, DB2, or Chimera syntax, that can automatically maintain the EmployeeHistory relation in the presence of modifications to the snapshot Employee relation.

6.8. TSQL2, being an extension of SQL-92, did not consider triggers. Revisit the description of DB2 triggers in Section 2.3, and for each element of the syntax and the semantics, discuss what changes are necessary, if any, when the underlying table is a temporal table. Consider valid-time and transaction-time support separately.

Chapter 7

Implementation

Chapter 5 sketched the boundaries of a temporal data model by examining the temporal domain and how facts may be associated with time. Chapter 6 considered how temporal information may be stored and queried. In this chapter, we now turn to the implementation of a temporal DBMS.

7.1 System Architecture

Adding temporal support to a DBMS impacts virtually all of its components. Figure 7.1 provides a simplified architecture for a conventional DBMS. The *database administrator (DBA)* and her staff design the database, producing a physical schema specified in a *data definition language (DDL)*, which is processed by the *DDL compiler* and stored, generally as system relations, in the *data dictionary*. Users prepare queries, either ad hoc or embedded in procedural code, which are submitted to the *query compiler*. The query is first lexically and syntactically analyzed, using information from the system catalog, then optimized for efficient execution. A query evaluation plan is sent to the *run-time evaluator*. For ad hoc queries, this occurs immediately after processing; for embedded queries, this occurs when the cursor associated with a particular query is opened. The run-time evaluator is usually an interpreter for a form of the relational algebra annotated with access methods and operator strategies. While evaluating the query, this component accesses the database via a *transaction and data manager*, which implements concurrency control, transaction management, recovery, buffering, and the available data access methods.

7.2   Adding Temporal Support

In the following, we visit each of these components in turn, reviewing what changes need to be made to add temporal support.

7.2.1   DDL Compiler

The changes to support time involve adding temporal domains, such as periods, and adding constructs to specify support for transaction and valid time in the definition of relations. A more substantial change is the data dictionary, which must now consist of transaction-time relations. Schema versioning concerns only the recording of the data, and hence does not involve valid time. The attributes and their domains, the indexes, and even the names of the relations vary over transaction time.

7.2.2   Query Compiler

Optimization of temporal queries is more involved than that of conventional queries, for several reasons. First, optimization of temporal queries is more critical, and thus easier to justify expending effort on, than conventional optimization. The relations that temporal queries are defined over are larger, and are growing monotonically, with the result that unoptimized queries take longer and longer to execute. This justifies trying harder to optimize the queries, and spending more execution time to perform the optimization.

Second, the predicates used in temporal queries are harder to optimize. In traditional database applications, predicates are usually equality predicates (hence the prevalence of equijoins and natural joins); if a less-than join is involved, it is rarely in combination with other less-than predicates. On the other hand, in temporal queries, less-than joins appear more frequently, as a conjunction of several inequality predicates. As an example, the TSQL2 **OVERLAPS** operator is translated into two "$\leq$" predicates on the underlying timestamps (see Example 5.3). Optimization techniques in conventional databases focus on equality predicates, and often implement inequality joins as Cartesian products, with their associated inefficiency.

However, there is greater opportunity for query optimization when time is present. Time advances in one direction; the time domain is continuously expanding, and the most recent time point is the largest value in the domain. This implies that a natural clustering or sort order will manifest itself, which can be exploited during query optimization and evaluation. The integrity constraint **BEGIN**(p) **PRECEDES END**(p) holds for every period p. Also, for many relations, the periods associated with a key are contiguous in time,

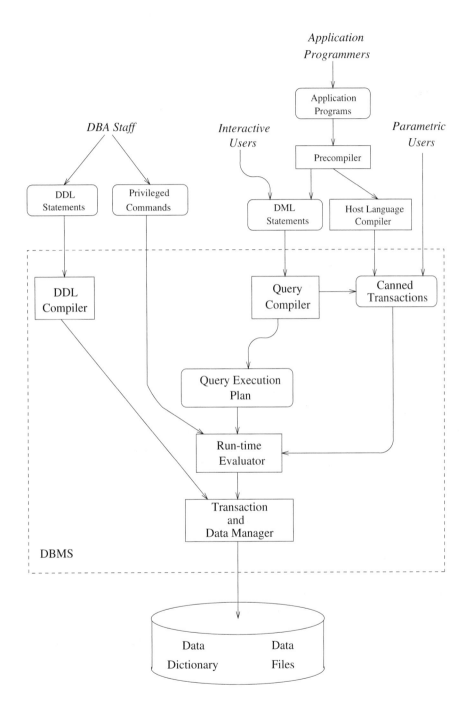

Figure 7.1: Components of a database management system

with one period starting exactly when the previous period ended. An example is salary data, where the periods associated with the salaries for each employee are contiguous. Semantic query optimization can exploit these integrity constraints, as well as additional ones that can be inferred.

The importance of efficient query optimization and evaluation for temporal databases was underscored by an initial study that analyzed the performance of a brute-force approach to adding time support to a conventional DBMS. In this study, the university Ingres DBMS was extended in a minimal fashion to support TQuel. The results were discouraging. Sequential scans, as well as access methods such as hashing and ISAM, suffered from rapid performance degradation due to ever-growing overflow chains. Because adding time creates multiple tuple versions with the same key, reorganization did not help to shorten overflow chains. The objective of work in temporal query evaluation, then, is to avoid looking at all of the data, because the alternative implies that queries will continue to slow down as the database accumulates facts. We emphasize that these results do not imply that a time-varying database implemented on a conventional DBMS will be much less efficient than that database implemented on a brute-force temporal DBMS. In fact, simulating a time-varying database on a conventional DBMS, which is currently the only alternative available to application programmers, will encounter all of the problems listed above.

A single query can be optimized by replacing the algebraic expression with an equivalent one that is more efficient, by changing an access method associated with a particular operator, or by adopting a particular implementation of an operator. The first alternative requires a definition of equivalence in the form of a set of tautologies. Tautologies have been identified for many of the algebras listed in Table 5.5. Some of these temporal algebras support the tautologies defined in the standard relational algebra, enabling existing query optimizers to be used.

To determine which access method is best for each algebraic operator, *metadata*, that is, statistics on the stored temporal data, and *cost models*, that is, predictors of the execution cost for each operator implementation/access method combination, are needed. Temporal data requires additional metadata, such as the time period over which the relation is defined (termed the *lifespan*), the lifespans of the tuples, the surrogate and tuple arrival distributions, the distributions of the time-varying attributes, regularity and granularity of temporal data, and the frequency of the null values that are sometimes introduced when attributes within a tuple aren't synchronized. Such statistical data may be updated by random sampling or by a scan through the entire relation. In particular, selectivity estimates on the size of the results of various temporal joins have been derived.

7.2.3 Run-Time Evaluator

A wide variety of binary joins have been considered, including *time-join* and *time-equijoin* (TE-join), *event-join* and *TE-outerjoin, contain-join, contain-semijoin* and *intersect-join,* and *temporal natural join.* The various algorithms proposed for these joins have generally been extensions to nested loop or merge joins that exploit sort orders or local workspace, as well as hash joins.

Several approaches have been proposed for implementing temporal joins. Some of these exploit ordering of the input tables to achieve higher efficiency. If the underlying tables are ordered, coalescing can be handled in a manner similar to that for projection.

Coalescing is an important operation, since value-equivalent tuples may be present in the representation. Also, the semantics of some queries demand that the input relations be coalesced prior to evaluation. If prior coalescing is required, this is most easily accomplished if the input relation is sorted on the explicit attribute values. The temporal element associated with the conceptual tuple is easily reconstructed during a scan of the relation. If indexes or precomputed results are available, then it may be possible to avoid the relation scan.

We note that for many predicates prior coalescing is not required. For example, if a predicate references only the explicit attributes of a relation, then the coalescing operation can be eliminated.

Conventional indexes have long been used to reduce the need to scan an entire relation to access a subset of its tuples. Indexes are even more important in temporal relations that grow monotonically in size. Many temporal indexing strategies are available. Most of the indexes are based on B^+-trees, which index on values of a single key; the remainder are based on R-trees, which index on ranges (periods) of multiple keys. The worst-case performance for most proposals has been evaluated in terms of total space required, update per change, and several important queries.

7.3 Minimal Support Needed for TSQL2

The preceding discussed in general terms how a conventional DBMS could be extended to provide temporal support. In the remainder of this chapter, we describe the minimal changes needed by each component of the architecture to support a specific temporal query language: TSQL2.

Note that the precompiler and host language compiler are largely independent of the database query language—they require only small changes to support temporal literal/timestamp conversion. For each of the remaining components, the data dictionary and data files, as well as those within the DBMS proper, we describe the minimal modifications needed by these components to support TSQL2 queries.

7.3.1   Data Dictionary and Data Files

The data dictionary and data files contain the database, the actual data managed by the DBMS. The data dictionary records schema information such as file structure and format, the number and types of attributes in a table, integrity constraints, and associated indexes. The data files contain the physical tables and access paths of the database.

For a minimal extension, the data files require no revision. We can store tuple-timestamped temporal tables in conventional tables, where the timestamp attributes are stored as explicit atomic attributes. However, the data dictionary must be extended in a number of ways to support TSQL2. The most significant extensions involve schema versioning, multiple granularities, and vacuuming.

For schema versioning, the data dictionary must record, for each table, all of its schemas and when they were current. The data files associated with a schema must also be preserved. This is easily accomplished by making a transaction-time table recording the schemas for a single table. The transaction time associated with a tuple in this table indicates the time when the schema was current.

Multiple granularities are associated in a lattice structure specified at system generation time. A simple option is to store the lattice as a data structure in the data dictionary. Alternatively, if the lattice is fixed (i.e., new granularities will not be added after the DBMS is generated), then the lattice can exist as a separate data structure outside of the data dictionary.

Vacuuming specifies what information should be physically deleted from the database. Minimally, this requires a timestamp, the cutoff time, to be stored for each transaction-time or bitemporal table cataloged by the data dictionary. The cutoff time indicates that all data current in the table before the value of the timestamp has been physically deleted from the table.

7.3.2 DDL Compiler

The DDL compiler translates TSQL2 **CREATE** and **ALTER** statements into executable transactions. Each of these statements affects both the data dictionary and the data files. The **CREATE** statement adds new definitions, of either tables or indexes, to the data dictionary and creates the data files containing the new table or index. The **ALTER** variants change an existing schema by updating the data dictionary, and possibly updating the data file containing the table.

Numerous changes are needed by the DDL compiler, but each is straightforward and extends existing functionality in small ways. First, the syntactic analyzer must be extended to accommodate the extended TSQL2 syntax for each of the **CREATE** and **ALTER** statements. The semantic analyzer must be extended in a similar manner, for example, to ensure that an existing table being transformed into a valid-time state table with the **ADD VALID STATE** command is not already a valid-time table.

7.3.3 Query Compiler

The query compiler translates TSQL2 data manipulation language (DML) statements into an executable, and semantically equivalent, internal form called the *query execution plan*. As with the DDL compiler, each phase of the query compiler—syntactic analysis, semantic analysis, and query plan generation—must be extended to accommodate TSQL2 queries.

We use the model that the initial phase of the compilation, syntactic analysis, creates a tree-structured query representation, which is then referenced and augmented by subsequent phases. Abstractly, the query compiler performs the following steps:

1. Parse the TSQL2 query. The syntactic analyzer, extended to parse the TSQL2 constructs, produces an internal representation of the query, the parse tree.

2. Semantically analyze the constructed parse tree. The parse tree produced by the syntactic analyzer is checked for types and other semantic constraints, and simultaneously augmented with semantic information.

3. Lastly, a query execution plan, essentially an algebraic expression that is semantically equivalent to the original query, is produced from the augmented parse tree by the query plan generator.

The minimal changes required by the query compiler are summarized as follows:

- The syntactic and semantic analyzers must be extended to support TSQL2.

- The query execution plan generator must be extended to support the extended TSQL2 algebra, including the new coalescing, join, and slicing operations. In a minimally extended system, it may be acceptable to use existing algebraic equivalences for optimization, even with the extended operator set. Such an approach preserves the performance of conventional snapshot queries. Later inclusion of optimization rules for the new operators would be beneficial to the performance of temporal queries.

- Support for vacuuming must be included in the compiler. Query modification, which normally occurs after semantic analysis and prior to query optimization, must be extended to include vacuuming support.

The need to extend the syntactic and semantic analyzers is self-evident and straightforward. Extending the query plan generator to use the extended algebra is also straightforward, assuming that temporal aspects of the query are not considered during query optimization. In the worst case, the same performance would be encountered when executing a temporal query on a purely snapshot database. Lastly, in order to support vacuuming, the query compiler, within its semantic analysis phase, must support automated query modification based on vacuuming cutoff times stored in the data dictionary.

7.3.4 Run-Time Evaluator

The run-time evaluator interprets a query plan produced by the query compiler. The run-time evaluator calls the transaction and data manager to retrieve data from the data dictionary and data files.

We assume that the run-time evaluator makes no changes to the query plan as received from the query compiler; that is, the query plan, as generated by the query compiler, is optimized and represents the best possible evaluation plan for the query. As such, the changes required for the run-time evaluator are small. In particular, since evaluation plans for any new operators have already been selected by the query compiler, the run-time evaluator must merely invoke these operations in the same manner as non-temporal operations. Additionally, evaluation algorithms for new temporal operators (e.g., coalescing) are similar to well-known algorithms for snapshot operators. For example, coalescing can be implemented with slightly modified duplicate elimination algorithms, which have been studied thoroughly.

7.3.5 Transaction and Data Manager

The transaction and data manager performs two basic tasks: it manages the transfer of information to and from disk and main memory, and it ensures the consistency of the database in light of concurrent access and transaction failure.

Again, at a minimum, little needs to be modified. We assume that the conventional buffer management techniques are employed. Supporting transaction time requires the following small extension to the concurrency control mechanism.

For correctness, transaction times are assigned at commit time. To avoid having to reread modified tuples, the executing transaction can instead write tuples without filling in the transaction timestamp of the tuples. When the transaction later commits, the transaction times of affected tuples are then updated. This is accomplished by maintaining a (reconstructible) table of tuple-ids written by the transaction. This table is read by an asynchronous background process that performs the physical update of the tuples' transaction timestamp. Correctness only requires that the transaction times for all written tuples be filled in before they are read by a subsequent transaction. While this simple extension suffices, more complex and efficient methods have been proposed. Notice also that this algorithm does not affect the recovery mechanism used by the DBMS, assuming that the transaction time of a committed transaction is logged along with the necessary undo/redo information.

We anticipate that the performance of the minimally extended architecture will rival the performance of conventional systems. Snapshot queries on the current database state may suffer a slight performance penalty because of the additional temporal support. However, since we are able to use existing optimization techniques, evaluation algorithms, and storage structures, we expect snapshot queries on the temporal DBMS to approach the performance of identical queries on a conventional DBMS.

7.4 Summary and Open Problems

The first section considered the changes necessitated by adding temporal support to the DDL compiler, the query compiler, and the run-time evaluator. We then described how a canonical DBMS architecture can be extended to support TSQL2. The changes described are minimal; they represent the smallest necessary extensions to support the functionality of TSQL2. Because the extensions are small, we believe that, as a first step, TSQL2 can be supported for a relatively low development cost. While there are many opportunities for improvement, we believe that temporal queries on the minimally extended architecture will show reasonable performance. In particular, the architecture can employ new evaluation and optimization techniques for temporal queries. With the addition of temporally optimized storage structures, we expect further performance improvements.

We conclude this part with a list of accomplishments and a list of disappointments, which can also serve as pointers to future work.

There have been many significant accomplishments over the past 15 years of temporal database research:

- The semantics of the time domain, including its structure, dimensionality, and indeterminacy, is well understood.

- A great amount of research has been expended on temporal data models, addressing this extraordinarily complex and subtle design problem.

- The semantics of temporal relational schemas and their logical design are well understood. The Bitemporal Conceptual Data Model is gaining acceptance as the appropriate model in which to consider data semantics.

- Many temporal query languages have been proposed. The numerous types of temporal queries are fairly well understood. Half of the proposed temporal query languages have a strong formal basis.

- The TSQL2 query language has achieved acceptance. Constructs from that language are being incorporated into a new part of SQL3, called SQL/Temporal.

- Representational issues of timestamps have recently been resolved. Operations on timestamps are now well understood, and efficient implementations exist.

- Temporal joins, aggregates, and coalescing are well understood, and efficient implementations exist.

- More than a dozen temporal index structures have been proposed, supporting valid time, transaction time, or both.

- A handful of prototype temporal DBMS implementations have been developed.

- Several commercial object-oriented DBMSs now on the market include some temporal support.

There have also been some disappointments:

- The user-defined time support in the SQL2 standard is poorly designed. The representation specified in that standard suffers from inadequate range, excessive space requirements, and inefficient operations.

- In contrast to temporal relational query languages, the specification of temporal object-oriented query languages is quite informal. No temporal object-oriented data model or query language has a formal semantics.

- There is no consensus temporal object-oriented query language, in contrast to TSQL2.

- More empirical studies are needed to compare join algorithms, and to possibly suggest even more efficient variants. More work is also required on temporal difference, which has attracted little attention to date.

- While preliminary performance studies have been carried out for each of the proposed temporal indexes in isolation, there has been little effort to empirically compare them.

- While there are a host of individual approaches to isolated portions of a DBMS, no coherent architecture has arisen. While the analysis given in this chapter may be viewed as a starting point, much more work is needed to integrate these approaches into a cohesive structure.

- Conceptual and physical database design of temporal schemas are still in their infancy. In the past, such investigation has been hindered by the plethora of temporal data models.

- Little has been done in integrating spatial, temporal, and active data models, query languages, and implementation techniques.

- There is as yet no prominent commercial temporal relational DBMS, despite the obvious need in the marketplace.

- There has been little work on adding time to so-called fourth-generation languages that are revolutionizing user interfaces for commercially available DBMSs.

- To date, most research has assumed that applications will be designed using a new temporal data model, implemented using novel temporal query languages, and run on as yet nonexistent temporal DBMSs. In the short to medium term, this is an unrealistic assumption. Approaches for transitioning legacy applications will become increasingly sought after as temporal technology moves from research to practice.

7.5   Bibliographic Notes

The performance of the TQuel [405] implementation was evaluated in [11]. Selectivity estimates have been investigated by Gunadhi and Segev [196, 394]. Temporal joins have been extensively studied [110, 197, 265, 411]. Efficient evaluation of coalescing has been recently considered [66]. The processing of temporal aggregates has also been studied [249]. B^+-trees were first described by Comer [120], and R-trees by Guttman [202]. Worst-case performance of many temporal indexes is summarized by Salzberg and Tsotras [383]. Nine temporal DBMS prototypes are summarized by Böhlen [65].

7.6   Exercises

7.1. Compare and contrast the following two ways to implement a temporal DBMS;

    a. During DDL and query processing, map schema specifications, queries, and modification statements to equivalent ones in standard SQL.

    b. Augment the DBMS internally to support time by extending the catalog, query optimization strategies, and storage structures and indexes.

7.2. Why must transaction times be commit times? Why can't the transaction start time be used as the transaction time? What are the performance implications of this?

7.3. Consider the design of temporal triggers in Exercise 6.8. What further extensions to those discussed in Section 7.3 are needed to minimally support temporal triggers?

Part III

Complex Queries
and Reasoning

The importance of complex queries in advanced database systems cannot be overstated. At the introduction of the relational model, powerful logic-based queries were primarily motivated by their importance for end users. Subsequently, a long experience with SQL and large-scale commercial applications has shown that powerful query languages are essential in modern databases that use distributed environments, parallel machines, and client/server architectures.

Since support for complex queries means support for complex reasoning on large databases, this line of database work is also tackling problems previously addressed in research domains, such as knowledge representation, nonmonotonic reasoning, and expert systems. The next three chapters provide a unified introduction to the complex field of database and knowledge-based systems. In Chapter 8, we revisit relational query languages and extend them with more powerful constructs such as recursion, complex objects, and flexible set aggregates. In Chapter 9, we discuss the implementation of these extended queries in deductive databases and SQL systems. Finally, in Chapter 10, we explore recent advances in nonmonotonic reasoning that provide a unified model for temporal reasoning, active databases, and nondeterministic queries.

Chapter 8

The Logic of Query Languages

First-order logic provides a conceptual foundation for relational query languages. This foundation was established from the very first introduction of the relational data model by E. F. Codd, who introduced the parallel notions of relational calculus and relational algebra. Relational calculus provides a logic-based model for declarative query languages; relational algebra provides its operational equivalent: safe queries in predicate calculus can be transformed into equivalent relational expressions, and vice versa. The transformation of a calculus expression into an equivalent relational algebra expression represents the first step in efficient query implementation and optimization.

However, relational calculus has limited expressive power and cannot express many important queries, such as transitive closures and generalized aggregates. This situation has led to the design of more powerful logic-based languages that subsume relational calculus. First among these is the rule-based language Datalog, which is the focus of a large body of research and also of this chapter.

8.1   Datalog

In a Datalog representation, the database is viewed as a set of facts, one fact for each tuple in the corresponding table of the relational database, where the name of the relation becomes the predicate name of the fact. For instance, the facts in Example 8.2 correspond to the relational database of Example 8.1.

Example 8.1   **A relational database about students and the courses they took**

student		
Name	*Major*	*Year*
Joe Doe	cs	senior
Jim Jones	cs	junior
Jim Black	ee	junior

took		
Name	*Course*	*Grade*
Joe Doe	cs123	2.7
Jim Jones	cs101	3.0
Jim Jones	cs143	3.3
Jim Black	cs143	3.3
Jim Black	cs101	2.7

Example 8.2   **The Datalog equivalent of Example 8.1**

```
student('Joe Doe', cs, senior).
student('Jim Jones', cs, junior).
student('Jim Black', ee, junior).
took('Joe Doe', cs123, 2.7).
took('Jim Jones', cs101, 3.0).
took('Jim Jones', cs143, 3.3).
took('Jim Black', cs143, 3.3).
took('Jim Black', cs101, 2.7).
```

facts

Predicate name of facts

→ tenary predicates

A *fact* is a logical predicate having only constants (i.e., no variables) as its arguments. We will use the accepted convention of denoting constants by tokens that begin with lowercase characters or numbers, while denoting variables by tokens that begin with uppercase. Thus, in a predicate such as

```
took(Name, cs143, Grade)
```

Name and Grade denote variables, while cs143 denotes a constant. However, tokens in quotes, such as 'Jim Black', denote constants. Also, Name, cs143, and Grade are, respectively, the first, second, and third argument of the ternary predicate took. Both student and took are three-argument predicates, or equivalently, ternary predicates, or predicates with arity 3.

Rules constitute the main construct of Datalog programs. For instance, Example 8.3 defines all students at the junior level who have taken cs101 and cs143. Thus, firstreq(Name) is the head; student(Name, Major, junior), took(Name, cs101, Grade1), and took(Name, cs143, Grade2) are, respectively, the first, second, and third goal of the rule. Together, these three goals form the body of the rule.

Example 8.3   Find the name of junior-level students who have taken both cs101 and cs143

```
firstreq(Name) ←  student(Name,Major,junior),
                  took(Name,cs101,Grade1),
                  took(Name,cs143,Grade2).
```

The commas separating the goals stand for logical conjuncts. Therefore, the order in which the goals appear in the rule is immaterial. Since the commas separating the goals stand for logical AND, the symbols "∧" and "&" are often used in their place. Another common notational variation is the use of the symbol ":-" instead of the arrow to separate the head from the body of the rule.

A logical disjunct is represented via multiple rules with the same head predicate (i.e., sharing the same predicate name and arity). Thus, to find those juniors who took either course cs131 or course cs151, with grade better than 3.0, we would write the following:

Example 8.4   Junior-level students who took course cs131 or course cs151 with grade better than 3.0

```
scndreq(Name) ←  took(Name,cs131,Grade),Grade > 3.0,
                 student(Name,Major,junior).
scndreq(Name) ←  took(Name,cs151,Grade),Grade > 3.0,
                 student(Name,_,junior).
```

Observe that in the first rule of Example 8.4, the variable Major occurs only once; therefore, it can be replaced with the symbol "_", which is called an *anonymous* variable, and stands for a uniquely named variable that does not appear anywhere else in the rule (see the second rule of Example 8.4). The set of rules having as their heads a predicate with the same name p is called the definition of p. Thus, the definition of a derived predicate is similar to the definition of a virtual view in relational databases. The meaning of such a definition is independent of the order in which these rules are listed, and independent of the order in which the goals appear in the rules. Table 8.1 displays the corresponding nomenclatures of Datalog and the relational model. Therefore, *base predicates* correspond to database relations and are defined by the database schema, while *derived predicates* are defined by rules. It is also common to use the terms *extensional database* and *intensional database* to refer to base predicates and derived predicates, respectively. In deductive databases, the assumption normally made is that these two form disjoint sets: that is, base predicates never appear in the heads of rules.

Datalog	Relational Model
Base predicate	Table or relation
Derived predicate	View
Fact	Row or tuple
Argument	Column or attribute

Table 8.1: The terminology of Datalog versus the relational model

Since rules are merely definitional devices, concrete Datalog programs also contain one or more query goals to specify which of the derived relations must actually be computed. Query goals can have different forms. A query that contains no variables is called a *boolean query* or a *closed query*; the answer to such a query is either yes or no. For instance,

$$?firstreq('Jim Black')$$

is a closed query with answer yes or no depending on whether 'Jim Black' has satisfied the first requirement. On the other hand, consider the goal

$$?firstreq(X)$$

Since X is a variable, the answer to this query is a (possibly empty) set of facts for the students who satisfy the first requirement, as follows:

$$firstreq('Jim Jones')$$
$$firstreq('Jim Black')$$

In general, query goals will mix variables and constants in their arguments.

Rules represent a powerful formalism from both theoretical and practical viewpoints. Their practical appeal follows from the ability to view goals in rules as search patterns. For instance, in the second rule of Example 8.4, we are searching for **took** tuples with **cs151** as their second argument, and a grade greater than 3.0. Also, we are looking for the pattern **junior** in the third column of **student**, where the first attribute in this tuple is identical to the first value in the tuple of **took**, since all occurrences of the same variable in a rule must be assigned the same value. The scope of variables, however, is local to rules, and identically named variables in different rules are considered independent.

The second important benefit of the Datalog formalism is its ability to break up the problem into smaller subproblems, each expressed by simple rules. Thus, complex patterns of computation and logical decisions can be achieved through rather simple Datalog rules that are stacked one upon another in a rich semantic structure.

For instance, say that in order to take the individual-study course cs298, a junior must have satisfied both requirements. Then we can simply write the following:

Example 8.5   Both requirements must be satisfied to enroll in cs298

```
req_cs298(Name) ← firstreq(Name), scndreq(Name).
```

Therefore, derived relations can be used as goals in rules in the same fashion as database relations.

Datalog rules discussed so far are nonrecursive rules without negation. Additional expressive power can be achieved by allowing recursion and negation in Datalog. We will next discuss negation; we discuss recursion later in this chapter.

Negation in Datalog rules can only be applied to the goals of the rule. Negation can never be used in the heads of rules. For instance, in Example 8.6, the second goal of the second rule is negated. This rule is meant to compute junior students who did not take course cs143.

Example 8.6   Junior-level students who did not take course cs143

```
hastaken(Name, Course) ←   took(Name, Course, Grade).
lacks_cs143(Name) ←        student(Name, _, junior),
                           ¬hastaken(Name, cs143).
```

Thus, `hastaken` defines the courses completed by a student, independent of the final grade. Then, the second rule selects those students for whom the pattern `cs143` does not appear in the second column.

A frequent use of negation is in conjunction with universally quantified queries that are often expressed by words such as "each" and "every." For instance, say we would like to express the following query: "find the senior students who completed all requirements for a cs major."

The universally quantified condition "all requirements must be satisfied" can only be expressed in Datalog by transforming it into an equivalent condition where universal quantification is replaced by existential quantification and negation. This transformation normally requires two steps.

The first step is that of formulating the complementary query. For the example at hand, this could be "find students who did not take some of the courses required for a cs major." This can be expressed using the first rule in Example 8.7. Having derived those senior students who are missing some required courses, as the second step, we can now reexpress the original query as "find the senior students who are NOT missing any requirement for a cs major." This corresponds to the second rule in Example 8.7.

Example 8.7 **Find the senior students who completed all the requirements for the cs major: ?all_req_sat(X)**

$$\text{req\_missing}(\text{Name}) \leftarrow \text{student}(\text{Name}, \_, \text{senior}),$$
$$\text{req}(\text{cs}, \text{Course}),$$
$$\neg\text{hastaken}(\text{Name}, \text{Course}).$$
$$\text{all\_req\_sat}(\text{Name}) \leftarrow \text{student}(\text{Name}, \_, \text{senior}),$$
$$\neg\text{req\_missing}(\text{Name}).$$

Turning a universally quantified query into a doubly negated existential query is never without difficulty, but this is a skill that can be mastered with some practice. Indeed, such a transformation is common in natural languages, particularly in euphemistic nuances. For instance, our last sentence, " ... is never without difficulty," was obtained by rephrasing the original sentence " ... is always difficult."

8.2   Relational Calculi

Relational calculus comes in two main flavors: the domain relational calculus (DRC) and the tuple relational calculus (TRC). The main difference between the two is that in DRC variables denote values of single attributes, while in TRC variables denote whole tuples.

For instance, the DRC expression for a query ?firstreq(N) is

$$\{(N) \mid \exists G_1(took(N, cs101, G_1)) \wedge \exists G_2(took(N, cs143, G_2)) \wedge$$
$$\exists M(student(N, M, junior)) \quad\quad \}$$

The query ?scndreq(N) can be expressed as follows:

$$\{(N) \mid \exists G, \exists M(took(N, cs131, G) \wedge G > 3.0 \wedge student(N, M, junior)) \vee$$
$$\exists G, \exists M(took(N, cs151, G) \wedge G > 3.0 \wedge student(N, M, junior))\}$$

There are obvious syntactic differences that distinguish DRC from Datalog, including the use of set definition by abstraction instead of rules.

Furthermore, DRC formulas contain many additional constructs such as explicit quantifiers, nesting of parentheses, and the mixing of conjunctions and disjunctions in the same formula.

Negation and universal quantification are both allowed in DRC. Therefore, the query ?all_req_sat(N) can be expressed either using double negation, or directly using the universal quantifier as shown in Example 8.8. This formula also features the implication sign $\rightarrow$, where $p \rightarrow q$ is just a shorthand for $\neg p \vee q$.

Example 8.8 **Using a universal quantifier to find the seniors who completed all cs requirements**

$$\{(N)| \quad \exists M(student(N, M, senior)) \wedge$$
$$\forall C(req(cs, C) \rightarrow \exists G(took(N, C, G)))\} \tag{8.1}$$

↳ universal quantifier makes it possible, not "→"

The additional syntactic complexity of DRC does not produce a more powerful language. In fact, for each domain predicate calculus expression there is an equivalent, nonrecursive Datalog program. The converse is also true, since a nonrecursive Datalog program can be mapped into an equivalent DRC query.

Relational calculus languages are important because they provide a link to commercial database languages. For instance, Query-By-Example (QBE) is a visual query language based on DRC. However, languages such as QUEL and SQL are instead based on TRC.

In TRC, variables range over the tuples of a relation. For instance, the TRC expression for a query ?firstreq(N) is the following:

Example 8.9 **The TRC equivalent of the query ?firstreq(N) in Example 8.3**

course

$$\{(t[1])| \quad \exists u \exists s(took(t) \wedge took(u) \wedge student(s) \wedge t[2] = cs101 \wedge$$
$$u[2] = cs143 \wedge t[1] = u[1] \wedge s[3] = junior \wedge s[1] = t[1])\}$$

Name

In Example 8.9, t and s are variables denoting, respectively, tuples in took and student. Thus, $t[1]$ denotes the first component in t (i.e., that corresponding to attribute Name); $t[2]$ denotes the Course value of this tuple. In general, if $j_1, \ldots, j_n$ denote columns of a relation R, and $t \in R$, then we will use the notation $t[j_1, \ldots, j_n]$ to denote the n-tuple $(t[j_1], \ldots, t[j_n])$.

The main difference between DRC and TRC is that TRC requires an explicit statement of equality, while in DRC equality is denoted implicitly by the presence of the same variable in different places. For instance, in

Example 8.9, the explicit conditions $t[1] = u[1]$ and $s[1] = t[1]$ are needed to express equality joins. Once again, however, these differences do not change the power of the language: TRC and DRC are equivalent, and there are mappings that transform a formula in one language into an equivalent one in the other.

8.3   Relational Algebra

Datalog rules and DRC or TRC formulas are declarative logic-based languages, but relational algebra (RA) is an operator-based language. However, formulas in logical languages can be implemented by transforming them into equivalent RA expressions.

The main operators of relational algebra can be summarized as follows:

1. *Union.* The union of relations R and S, denoted $R \cup S$, is the set of tuples that are in R, or in S, or in both. Thus, it can be defined using TRC as follows:

$$R \cup S = \{t | t \in R \vee t \in S\}$$

   This operation is defined only if R and S have the same number of columns.

2. *Set difference.* The difference of relations R and S, denoted $R - S$, is the set of tuples that belong to R but not to S. Thus, it can be defined as follows: ($t = r$ denotes that both t and r have n components and $t[1] = r[1] \wedge \ldots \wedge t[n] = r[n]$):

$$R - S = \{t | t \in R \wedge \neg \exists r (r \in S \wedge t = r)\}$$

   This operation is defined only if R and S have the same number of columns (arity).

3. *Cartesian product.* The Cartesian product of R and S is denoted $R \times S$.

$$R \times S = \{t | (\exists r \in R)(\exists s \in S)(t[1, \ldots, n] = r \wedge t[n+1, \ldots, n+m] = s)\}$$

   If R has n columns and S has m columns, then $R \times S$ contains all the possible $m + n$ tuples whose first m components form a tuple in R and the last n components form a tuple in S. Thus, $R \times S$ has $m + n$ columns and $|R| \times |S|$ tuples, where $|R|$ and $|S|$ denote the respective cardinalities of the two relations.

4. *Projection.* Let R be a relation with n columns, and $L = \$1, \ldots, \$n$ be a list of the columns of R. Let L' be a sublist of L obtained by (1) eliminating some of the elements, and (2) reordering the remaining ones in an arbitrary order. Then, the projection of R on columns L', denoted $\pi_{L'}$, is defined as follows:

$$\pi_{L'} R = \{r[L'] \mid r \in R\}$$

5. *Selection.* $\sigma_F R$ denotes the selection on R according to the selection formula F, where F obeys one of the following patterns:

   (i) $\$i\theta C$, where i is a column of R, θ is an arithmetic comparison operator, and C is a constant, or

   (ii) $\$i\theta\$j$, where $\$i$ and $\$j$ are columns of R, and θ is an arithmetic comparison operator, or

   (iii) an expression built from terms such as those described in (i) and (ii), above, and the logical connectives $\vee$, $\wedge$, and $\neg$.

Then,
$$\sigma_F R = \{t \mid t \in R \wedge F'\}$$

where F' denotes the formula obtained from F by replacing $\$i$ and $\$j$ with $t[i]$ and $t[j]$.

For example, if F is "$\$2 = \$3 \wedge \$1 = bob$", then F' is "$t[2] = t[3] \wedge t[1] = bob$". Thus $\sigma_{\$2=\$3 \wedge \$1=bob} R = \{t \mid t \in R \wedge t[2] = t[3] \wedge t[1] = bob\}$.

Additional operators of frequent use that can be derived from these are discussed next.

The *join operator* can be constructed using Cartesian product and selection. In general, a join has the following form: $R \bowtie_F S$, where $F = \$i_1\theta_1\$j_1 \wedge \ldots \wedge i_k\theta_k\$j_k$; $i_1, \ldots, i_k$ are columns of R; $j_1, \ldots, i_k$ are columns of S; and $\theta_1, \ldots, \theta_k$ are comparison operators. Then, if R has arity m, we define $F' = \$i_1\theta_1\$(m + j_1) \wedge \ldots \wedge \$i_k\theta_k\$(m + j_k)$. Therefore,

$$R \bowtie_F S = \sigma_{F'}(R \times S)$$

The *intersection* of two relations can be constructed either by taking the equijoin of the two relations in every column (and then projecting out duplicate columns) or by using the following property: $R \cap S = R - (R - S) = S - (S - R)$.

The *generalized projection* of a relation R is denoted $\pi_L(R)$, where L is a list of column numbers and constants. Unlike ordinary projection, components might appear more than once, and constants as components of the list L are permitted (e.g., $\pi_{\$1,c,\$1}$ is a valid generalized projection). Generalized projection can be derived from the other operators (see Exercise 8.6).

8.4   From Safe Datalog to Relational Algebra

Relational algebra provides a very attractive operational target language onto which the logic-based queries can be mapped. However, only *safe* Datalog programs can be mapped into equivalent relational algebra expressions. From a practical viewpoint, this is hardly a limitation, since enforcing the safety requirement on programs enables the compiler-time detection of rules and queries that are inadequately specified.

For instance, to find grades better than the grade Joe Doe got in cs143, a user might write the following rule:

$$\texttt{bettergrade(G1)} \leftarrow \texttt{took('Joe Doe', cs143, G), G1 > G.}$$

This rule presents the following peculiar traits:

1. *Infinite answers.* Assuming that, say, Joe Doe got the grade of 3.3 (i.e., B+) in course cs143 then there are infinitely many numbers that satisfy the condition of being greater than 3.3.

2. *Lack of domain independence.* A query formula is said to be *domain independent* when its answer only depends on the database and the constants in the query, and not on the domain of interpretation. Clearly, the set of values for G1 satisfying the rule above depends on what domain we assume for numbers (e.g., integer, rational, or real). Thus, there is no domain independence.

3. *No relational algebra equivalent.* Only database relations are allowed as operands of relational algebra expressions. These relations are finite, and so is the result of every RA expression over these relations. Therefore, there cannot be any RA expression over the database relations that is equivalent to the rule above.

In practical languages, it is desirable to allow only safe formulas, which avoid the problems of infinite answers and loss of domain independence. Unfortunately, the problems of domain independence and finiteness of answers

(handwritten: → non recursive queries / could be not safe)

are undecidable even for nonrecursive queries. Therefore, necessary and sufficient syntactic conditions that characterize safe formulas cannot be given in general. In practice, therefore, we must use sufficient conditions (i.e., conditions that once satisfied ensure domain independence and finiteness of the answers), although such properties might also be satisfied by formulas that do not obey those conditions. A set of simple sufficient conditions for the safety of Datalog programs is presented next.

Definition 8.1 *Safe Datalog. The following is an inductive definition of safety for a program* P*:*

1. *Safe predicates: A predicate q of P is safe if*

    (i) q is a database predicate, or

    (ii) every rule defining q is safe.

2. *Safe variables: A variable X in rule r is safe if*

    (i) X is contained in some *positive goal* $q(t_1, \ldots, t_n)$, where the predicate $q(A_1, \ldots, A_n)$ is safe, or

    (ii) r contains some equality goal $X = Y$, where Y is safe.

3. *Safe rules: A rule r is safe if all its variables are safe.*

4. *The goal* $?q(t_1, \ldots, t_n)$ *is safe when the predicate* $q(A_1, \ldots, A_n)$ *is safe.*

For every safe Datalog program, there is an equivalent relational algebra expression, generated using the following algorithm:

Algorithm 8.2 *Mapping a safe, nonrecursive Datalog program P into RA*

step 1. P is transformed into an equivalent program P' that does not contain any equality goal by replacing equals with equals and removing the equality goals. For example,

$$r : \mathsf{s}(Z, b, W) \leftarrow \mathsf{q}(X, X, Y), \mathsf{p}(Y, Z, a), W = Z, W > 24.3 .$$

is translated into

$$r : \mathsf{s}(Z, b, Z) \leftarrow \mathsf{q}(X, X, Y), \mathsf{p}(Y, Z, a), Z > 24.3 .$$

step 2. The body of a rule r is translated into the RA expression $Body_r$. $Body_r$ consists of the Cartesian product of all the base or derived relations in the body, followed by a selection σ_F, where F is the conjunction of the following conditions: (i) inequality conditions for each such goal (e.g., $Z > 24.3$), (ii) equality conditions between columns containing the same variable, and (iii) equality conditions between a column and the constant occurring in such a column.

For the example at hand, (i) the condition $Z > 24.3$ translates into the selection condition $\$5 > 24.3$, while (ii) the equality between the two occurrences of X translates into $\$1 = \$2$, while the equality between the two Ys maps into $\$3 = \$4$, and (iii) the constant in the last column of p maps into $\$6 = a$. Thus we obtain:

$$Body_r = \sigma_{\$1=\$2,\$3=\$4,\$6=a,\$5>24.3}(Q \times P)$$

step 3. Each rule r is translated into a generalized projection on $Body_r$, according to the patterns in the head of r. For the rule at hand, we obtain:

$$S = \pi_{\$5,b,\$5}Body_r$$

step 4. Multiple rules with the same head are translated into the union of their equivalent expressions.

The mapping just described can be generalized to translate rules with negated goals, as described next. Say that the body of some rule contains a negated goal, such as the following body:

$$r : \ldots \leftarrow \quad \mathsf{b1(a, Y), b2(Y), \neg b3(Y)}.$$

Then we consider a *positive body*, that is, one constructed by dropping the negated goal,

$$rp : \ldots \leftarrow \quad \mathsf{b1(a, Y), b2(Y)}.$$

and a *negative* body, that is, one obtained by removing the negation sign from the negated goal,

$$rn : \ldots \leftarrow \quad \mathsf{b1(a, Y), b2(Y), b3(Y)}.$$

The two bodies so generated are safe and contain no negation, so we can transform them into equivalent relational algebra expressions as per step 2 of Algorithm 8.2; let $Body_{rp}$ and $Body_{rn}$ be the RA expressions so obtained.

Then the body expression to be used in step 3 of said algorithm is simply $Body_r = Body_{rp} - Body_{rn}$.

Finally, observe that by repeating this mapping for each negated goal in the rule we can translate rules with several negated goals. Therefore, we can state the following:

Theorem 8.3 *Let P be a safe Datalog program without recursion or function symbols. Then, for each predicate in P, there exists an equivalent relational algebra expression.*

Safety conditions similar to those described for Datalog can also be generated for DRC and TRC formulas. Thus, safe formulas in each language can be translated into RA, and vice versa (see Exercise 8.9).

The safety conditions used here can be relaxed in several ways to improve the flexibility and ease-of-use of the language. One such extension, discussed in the next chapter, achieves safety by using bindings that are passed in a top-down fashion. Another important extension is to allow the negated goals in a rule to contain existential variables, that is, variables that do not appear anywhere else in the rule. For instance, to express the query "find all senior students that did not take cs143," we might write the first rule in the following example:

Example 8.10   Two equivalent uses of negation

$$\text{student}(\text{Nme}, \text{Yr}) \leftarrow \text{student}(\text{Nme}, \text{cs}, \text{Yr}), \neg\text{took}(\text{Nme}, \text{cs143}, \text{G}).$$

$$\text{project\_took}(\text{Nme}, \text{cs143}) \leftarrow \text{took}(\text{Nme}, \text{cs143}, \text{G}).$$
$$\text{student}(\text{Nme}, \text{Yr}) \leftarrow \qquad \text{student}(\text{Nme}, \text{cs}, \text{Yr}),$$
$$\neg\text{project\_took}(\text{Nme}, \text{cs143}).$$

The first rule in Example 8.10, where G does not appear in any positive goal, will be viewed as a convenient shorthand for the other two rules in the same example, which are safe by our previous definition. These last two rules, therefore, define the meaning and the RA equivalent of the first rule.

8.4.1   Commercial Query Languages

Relational query languages represent the results of protracted efforts to simplify the DRC and TRC and make them more user-friendly. For instance, QBE is generally regarded as a very attractive rendering of DRC. Instead, languages such as QUEL and SQL are derived from TRC via simple syntactic modifications. The main modification consists of ensuring that every tuple variable is *range quantified*; that is, it is explicitly associated with a relation over which it ranges, thus ensuring the safety of the resulting TRC expressions. For instance, the query of Example 8.9 can be rearranged as follows:

Example 8.11 **A range-quantified version of Example 8.9**

$$\{(t[1])| \tag{8.2}$$
$$t \in took \ \exists u \in took \ \exists s \in student \tag{8.3}$$
$$(t[2]=cs101 \wedge u[2]=cs143 \wedge t[1]=u[1] \wedge$$
$$s[3] = junior \wedge s[1] = t[1])\} \tag{8.4}$$

Thus, t and u range over took, while s ranges over student. Then our TRC query consists of three parts: (1) a target-list (8.2), (2) tuple range declaration (8.3), and (3) the conditions (8.4). These are, respectively, mapped into the three basic parts of the SQL query: (1) the **SELECT** part, (2) the **FROM** part, and (3) the **WHERE** part. Also, if $t \in R$, and Name is the name of the jth column of R, then the notation t.Name denotes $t[j]$. Therefore, from Example 8.11, we obtain the SQL query of Example 8.12:

Example 8.12   The SQL translation of Example 8.11

    SELECT t.Name
    FROM took t, took u, student s
    WHERE t.Course= 'cs101' **AND**
            u.Course= 'cs143' **AND**
            t.Name = u.Name **AND**
            s.Year = 'junior' **AND**
            s.Name = t.Name

While the need for explicit quantifiers was eliminated in SQL through the use of the **FROM** clause, **EXISTS** and **ALL** are allowed in nested SQL queries. However, the query from Example 8.7 ("find the seniors who satisfied all requirements for a cs degree") cannot be expressed using **ALL**, but must instead be expressed using double negation and existential quantifiers as shown in Example 8.13.

Indeed, while SQL supports the construct **ALL**, various syntactic restrictions limit its applicability to the point that it cannot be used to express universal quantification in many queries, including the current one. In fact, with the exception of set aggregates, the many additional constructs cluttering SQL do not extend the expressive power of the language beyond that of relational algebra or nonrecursive Datalog rules. Therefore, the current

Example 8.13 **Find senior students where there is no required cs course our senior has not taken**

SELECT Name
FROM student
WHERE Year = 'senior' **AND** Name **NOT IN**
    (**SELECT** s.Name
    FROM student s, req r
    WHERE r.Major = 'cs' **AND** s.Year = 'senior' **AND**
      NOT EXISTS
        (**SELECT** t.*
      FROM took t
      WHERE t.Course=r.Course **AND**
      t.Name = s.Name
)
)

practice in developing database applications is to rely on procedural languages, with embedded SQL subqueries. The interface between the procedural language and SQL must overcome an impedance mismatch, that is, a mismatch between their respective data types and computational paradigms. More powerful query languages are expected to ameliorate these problems because they allow a larger portion of the application to be developed in the database query language. Better data independence and distributed processing are also expected as a result.

In the sections that follow, we will investigate the design of more powerful database query languages, building on Datalog, which, in terms of syntax and semantics, provides a better formal vehicle for such study than SQL and other languages presented so far. This effort will lead to (1) the design of logic-based rule languages similar to Datalog, which have been proven effective in the development of advanced data-intensive applications, and (2) the design of SQL extensions that significantly enhance its power as a relational query language.

8.5 Recursive Rules

Bill of materials (BoM) problems are related to assemblies containing super-parts composed of subparts that are eventually composed of basic parts. Consider Example 8.14. The base predicate `assembly(Part, Subpart, Qty)` in the parts database contains parts, their immediate subparts, and the quantity of subparts needed to assemble the part. The base predicate `part_cost(BasicPart, Supplier, Cost, Time)` describes the basic parts,

Example 8.14   Relational tables for a BoM application

part_cost			
BASIC_PART	*SUPPLIER*	*COST*	*TIME*
top_tube	cinelli	20.00	14
top_tube	columbus	15.00	6
down_tube	columbus	10.00	6
head_tube	cinelli	20.00	14
head_tube	columbus	15.00	6
seat_mast	cinelli	20.00	6
seat_mast	cinelli	15.00	14
seat_stay	cinelli	15.00	14
seat_stay	columbus	10.00	6
chain_stay	columbus	10.00	6
fork	cinelli	40.00	14
fork	columbus	30.00	6
spoke	campagnolo	0.60	15
nipple	mavic	0.10	3
hub	campagnolo	31.00	5
hub	suntour	18.00	14
rim	mavic	50.00	3
rim	araya	70.00	1

assembly		
PART	*SUBPART*	*QTY*
bike	frame	1
bike	wheel	2
frame	top_tube	1
frame	down_tube	1
frame	head_tube	1
frame	seat_mast	1
frame	seat_stay	2
frame	chain_stay	2
frame	fork	1
wheel	spoke	36
wheel	nipple	36
wheel	rim	1
wheel	hub	1
wheel	tire	1

that is, parts bought from external suppliers rather than assembled internally. This relation describes the suppliers of each part, and for each supplier the price charged for it and time needed to deliver it.

Assume now that we want to find all the subparts of a given part—not just immediate subparts. Then recursive rules, such as those in Example 8.15, are needed to express this transitive closure query. The second rule in Example 8.15 inductively defines the transitive closure of all subparts; this rule is recursive since the head predicate also appears in the body of the rule.

A nonrecursive rule defining a recursive predicate, such as the first rule in Example 8.15, is called an *exit rule*. Thus, an exit rule provides the base case in the inductive definition of a recursive predicate.

Example 8.15   All subparts: a transitive closure query

$$\text{all\_subparts(Part, Sub)} \leftarrow \quad \text{assembly(Part, Sub, \_).}$$
$$\text{all\_subparts(Part, Sub2)} \leftarrow \quad \text{all\_subparts(Part, Sub1),}$$
$$\text{assembly(Sub1, Sub2, \_).}$$

Once we view `assembly(Sub1, Sub2, _)` as defining an arc from Sub1 to Sub2, we see that we are basically computing the transitive closure of a graph. Transitive closure computations and its variations are very common in actual applications. Queries involving aggregates are common in BoM applications. For instance, say that a user needs to compute how long it takes to obtain all the basic subparts of an assembly part. (Assuming that the actual assembly time is negligible, this will allow us to estimate how soon an order can be filled.) Then, we can begin with rules that define basic subparts as follows:

Example 8.16 **For each part, basic or otherwise, find its basic subparts (a basic part is a subpart of itself)**

$$basic\_subparts(BasicP, BasicP) \leftarrow part\_cost(BasicP, \_, \_, \_).$$

$$basic\_subparts(Prt, BasicP) \leftarrow assembly(Prt, SubP, \_),$$
$$basic\_subparts(SubP, BasicP).$$

Now, we want to find the absolutely shortest time in which we can obtain a basic part, given that the time for delivery might be a function of supplier or even the price charged (fast deliveries might command a premium price). The least-time condition can be expressed using negation, by requiring that there is no faster time for this part.

Example 8.17 **For each basic part, find the least time needed for delivery**

$$fastest(Part, Time) \leftarrow part\_cost(Part, Sup, Cost, Time),$$
$$\neg faster(Part, Time).$$
$$faster(Part, Time) \leftarrow part\_cost(Part, Sup, Cost, Time),$$
$$part\_cost(Part, Sup1, Cost1, Time1),$$
$$Time1 < Time.$$

Then, by combining the last two examples, we can build for each part the list of its basic components, with each component listed with the least time required to get that component.

Example 8.18 **Times required for basic subparts of the given assembly**

$$timeForbasic(AssPart, BasicSub, Time) \leftarrow$$
$$basic\_subparts(AssPart, BasicSub),$$
$$fastest(BasicSub, Time).$$

Thus, the time required to have all the basic parts of a given part is just the longest time required for any such part.

Example 8.19   The maximum time required for basic subparts of the given assembly

$$
\begin{aligned}
\mathtt{howsoon(AssPart, Time)} \leftarrow\ & \mathtt{timeForbasic(AssPart, \_, Time)}, \\
& \mathtt{\neg larger(AssPart, Time)}. \\
\mathtt{larger(Part, Time)} \leftarrow\ & \mathtt{timeForbasic(Part, \_, Time)}, \\
& \mathtt{timeForbasic(Part, \_, Time1)}, \\
& \mathtt{Time1 > Time}.
\end{aligned}
$$

Another family of queries of interest are set aggregates. As seen in Examples 8.17 and 8.19, nonrecursive Datalog with negation can express `min` and `max`. Other aggregates, such as `count` or `sum`, require stratified Datalog with arithmetic. However, counting the elements in a set modulo an integer does not require arithmetic. The program in Example 8.20 determines whether a given base relation `br(X)` contains an even number of elements (i.e., counts the cardinality of this relation *mod* 2). The `next` predicate in the example sorts the elements of `br` into an ascending chain, where the first link of the chain connects the distinguished node `nil` to the least element in `br` (third rule in the example).

Example 8.20   The parity query

$$
\begin{aligned}
\mathtt{between(X, Z)} \leftarrow\ & \mathtt{br(X), br(Y), br(Z), X < Y, Y < Z}. \\
\mathtt{next(X, Y)} \leftarrow\ & \mathtt{br(X), br(Y), X < Y, \neg between(X, Y)}. \\
\mathtt{next(nil, X)} \leftarrow\ & \mathtt{br(X), \neg smaller(X)}. \\
\mathtt{smaller(X)} \leftarrow\ & \mathtt{br(X), br(Y), Y < X}. \\
\mathtt{even(nil)}. & \\
\mathtt{even(Y)} \leftarrow\ & \mathtt{odd(X), next(X, Y)}. \\
\mathtt{odd(Y)} \leftarrow\ & \mathtt{even(X), next(X, Y)}. \\
\mathtt{br\_is\_even} \leftarrow\ & \mathtt{even(X), \neg next(X, Y)}.
\end{aligned}
$$

Observe that Example 8.20 relies on the assumption that the elements of `br` are totally ordered by $>$, and can therefore be visited one at a time using this order.

8.6   Stratification

The predicate dependency graph for a program P is denoted $pdg(P)$ and is defined as follows:

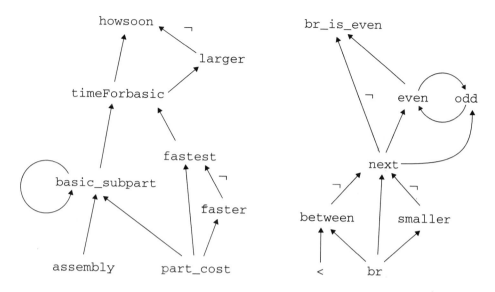

Figure 8.1: Predicate dependency graphs for the BoM query and the parity query

Definition 8.4 *The* predicate dependency graph *for a program P is a graph having as nodes the names of the predicates in P. The graph contains an arc $g \rightarrow b$ if there exists a rule r where g is the name of some goal of r and h is the name of the head of r. If the goal is negated, then the arc is marked as a negative arc.*

The nodes and arcs of the strong components of $pdg(P)$, respectively, identify the recursive predicates and recursive rules of P. Let r be a rule defining a recursive predicate p. The number of goals in r that are mutually recursive with p will be called the *rank* of r.

If $rank(r) = 0$, then r is an exit rule; otherwise, it is a recursive rule. A recursive rule r is called *linear* when $rank(r) = 1$; it is called *nonlinear* when $rank(r) > 1$. Rules with rank 2 and 3 are also called quadratic rules and cubic rules, respectively.

For the BoM program defined by Examples 8.16–8.19, the only recursive predicate is **basic_subparts** and is identified by a loop in the left graph of Figure 8.1. The predicate dependency graph for the parity query program, also shown in Figure 8.1, has a strong component having as nodes the mutually recursive predicates **even** and **odd**.

Observe that in Figure 8.1 no arc marked with negation belongs to a strong component of the graph (a directed cycle). Under this situation the program is said to be *stratifiable*. As discussed in later chapters, programs that are stratifiable have a clear meaning, but programs that are not stratifiable are often ill defined from a semantic viewpoint. In fact, when an arc in a strong component of $pdg(P)$ is marked with negation, then P contains a rule where a predicate p is defined in terms of a goal $\neg p$, or of a goal $\neg q$, where q is mutually recursive with p. Because of the nonmonotonic nature of negation, this might cause contradictions and other semantic problems that will be discussed in more detail later.

Given a stratifiable program P, by applying a topological sorting on $pdg(P)$, the nodes of P can be partitioned into a finite set of n strata $1, \ldots, n$, such that, for each rule $r \in P$, the predicate name of the head of r belongs to a stratum that

(i) is $\geq$ to each stratum containing some positive goal of r, and also

(ii) is strictly $>$ than each stratum containing some negated goal of r.

The strata of P are used to structure the computation so that the predicates of stratum j are used only after every predicate at the lower stratum has been computed. Violations of this rule can produce meaningless results. For our BoM example, for instance, a stratification is shown in Figure 8.1. Observe, for example, that in order to compute `howsoon`, we need to have completed the computation of `larger`, which, in turn, requires the computation of `timeForbasic` and `basic_subpart`. This is a recursive predicate, and many iterations might be needed before its computation is completed. The computation of `howsoon` must wait until such completion; indeed, it is not possible to compute the maximum time required by `basic_subpart` before all basic subparts are known.

A stratification of a program will be called *strict* if every stratum contains either a single predicate or a set of predicates that are mutually recursive.

total order?

8.7   Expressive Power and Data Complexity

The *expressive power of a language* L is the set of functions that can be written (programmed) in L. Determining the expressive power of a language and its constructs is fundamental in understanding the limitations of the language and the computational complexity of queries written in such a language.

For instance, transitive closure queries can be expressed using recursive Datalog rules. Moreover, recursive rules are also indispensable for the task, insofar as transitive closures cannot be computed in Datalog or SQL without recursion. Characterizing the expressive power of a query language is often difficult because proving the impossibility of expressing certain classes of queries frequently represents an open research challenge, and much current work is devoted to this topic. This section provides a very short overview of the most basic results on this subject.

A basic requirement for query languages is that they should be able to express all queries expressed by relational algebra. Languages having this property are said to be *relationally complete*. All languages discussed so far meet this requirement, since safe DRC and TRC have the same expressive power as relational algebra, and nonrecursive Datalog with negation is also equivalent to these. The term *first-order* (FO) *languages* is often used to denote the class of these equivalent languages.

At the introduction of the relational model, relational completeness for query languages was viewed as a difficult objective to meet, insofar as many of the early query languages were not relationally complete. Nowadays, commercial languages, such as SQL, are relationally complete, and they also support set aggregate constructs that cannot be expressed by relational algebra but are frequently needed in queries. Thus, the objective of today's advanced database systems is to go well beyond relational completeness. In particular, it is desirable that query languages express every query that can be computed in a polynomial number of steps in the size of the database. These are called *DB-PTIME queries*, and are discussed next.

The notion of *data complexity* is defined by viewing query programs as mappings from the database (the input) to the answer (the output). Thus, complexity measures, such as the big O, are evaluated in terms of the size of the database, which is always finite.[1]

Therefore, a Turing machine is used as the general model of computation, and a database of size n is encoded as a tape of size $O(n)$. Then, all computable functions on the database can be implemented as Turing machines. Some of these machines halt (complete their computation) in a polynomial

---

[1]Concretely, we might want to measure the database size by the number of characters in the database, or the number of elements in relation columns, or the number of tuples in relations. Assuming that there is a finite number of relations, each with a finite number of columns, and an upper bound to the length of the items in the columns, then these three measures only differ by multiplicative constants of no consequence in normal complexity measures.

number of steps, that is, at most in $O(n^k)$ steps, with k a positive integer; other machines halt in an exponential number of steps; others never halt.

The set of machines that halt in a number of steps that is polynomial in n defines the class of DB-PTIME functions. A language L is said to be in DB-PTIME if every function it computes is polynomial in n. L is said to be *DB-PTIME complete* if L is in DB-PTIME and L can express all DB-PTIME computable functions.

It is easy to prove that FO languages are in DB-PTIME. Actually, sophisticated query optimization strategies and storage structures are used by commercial DBMSs to keep the exponents and coefficients of the polynomials low. But FO languages are not DB-PTIME complete. For instance, they cannot express transitive closures.

As we will show later, recursive Datalog with stratified negation is in DB-PTIME. However, there are still some polynomial queries, such as the parity query, that this language cannot express. The parity query determines whether a set contains an even number of elements. To perform this computation, you need the ability to process the elements in a relation one at a time. Unfortunately, RA operates in the set-at-a-time mode, and Datalog does, too, since its rules can be translated into RA. One way to overcome this limitation is to assume that the elements in the set belong to a totally ordered domain, (i.e., for every two distinct elements, x and y, in the domain, either $x \leq y$ or $y \leq x$). Then the elements of any set can be visited one at a time with the technique illustrated by the parity query (Example 8.20).

In fact, if constants in the database belong to a totally ordered domain, then stratified Datalog can express all polynomial functions, that is, it is DB-PTIME complete.

While assuming that the universe is totally ordered (e.g., in some lexicographical way) is, in itself, not an unreasonable assumption, it leads to a violation of the principle of genericity of queries, which causes the loss of data independence. Therefore, a preferable solution, discussed in later chapters, is that of introducing nondeterministic constructs in Datalog. Nondeterminism can also be used to express more complex queries, including exponential-time queries in Datalog.

Finally, to achieve Turing completeness, and have a language that can express every possible query, an infinite computation domain must be used. In Datalog this can be achieved by using functors.

8.7.1 Functors and Complex Terms

In base relations, functors can be used to store complex terms and variable-length subrecords in tuples. For instance, consider the database of flat assembly parts in Example 8.21. Each planar part is described by its geometric shape and its weight. Different geometric shapes require a different number of parameters. Also actualkg is the actual weight of the part, but unitkg is the specific weight, from which the actual weight can be derived by multiplying it by the area of the part. For simplicity, we will assume that all parts described are flat in shape and can therefore be described by their planar geometry.

Example 8.21   **Flat parts, their number, shape, and weight, following the schema: part(Part#, Shape, Weight)**

> part(202, circle(11), actualkg(0.034)).
> part(121, rectangle(10, 20), unitkg(2.1)).
> part_weight(No, Kilos) ← part(No, _, actualkg(Kilos)).
> part_weight(No, Kilos) ← part(No, Shape, unitkg(K)),
>   area(Shape, Area), Kilos = K * Area.
>
> area(circle(Dmtr), A) ←   A = Dmtr * Dmtr * 3.14/4.
> area(rectangle(Base, Height), A) ← A = Base * Height.

The complex terms circle(11), actualkg(0.034), rectangle(10, 20), and unitkg(2.1) are in logical parlance called *functions* because of their syntactic appearance, consisting of a function name (called the *functor*) followed by a list of arguments in parentheses. In actual applications, these complex terms are not used to represent evaluable functions; rather, they are used as variable-length subrecords. Thus, circle(11) and rectangle(10, 20), respectively, denote that the shape of our first part is a circle with diameter 11 cm, while the shape of the second part is a rectangle with base 10 cm and height 20 cm. Any number of subarguments is allowed in such complex terms, and these subarguments can, in turn, be complex terms. Thus, objects of arbitrary complexity, including solid objects, can be nested and represented in this fashion.

As illustrated by the first two rules in Example 8.21, functors can also be used as case discriminants to prescribe different computations. The weight of a part is computed in two different ways, depending on whether the third argument of part contains the functor actualkg or unitkg. In the first case, the weight of the part is the actual argument of the functor (e.g., 0.034 for part 202). In the latter case, the argument gives the specific weight per cm^2, and its actual weight is computed by multiplying the specific weight by the `Area` of the part. Now, `Area` is derived from `Shape`, according to the computation prescribed by the last two rules, which have been written assuming a top-down passing of parameters from the goal `area(Shape, Area)` to the heads of the rules (the top-down passing of parameters will be further discussed in later sections). Thus, if `Shape` is instantiated to `circle(11)` by the execution of the first goal in the second rule, then the first `area` rule is executed; but if `Shape` = `rectangle(10, 20)`, then the second rule is executed. This example also illustrates the ability to mix computation with retrieval in a seamless fashion.

The full power of functors comes to life when they are used to generate recursive objects such as lists. Lists can be represented as complex terms having the following form: `list(nil)` (the empty list), and `list(Head, Tail)` for nonempty lists. Given the importance of lists, most logic programming languages provide a special notation for these. Thus, [ ] stands for the empty list, while [Head|Tail] represents a nonempty list. Then, the notation [mary, mike, seattle] is used as a shorthand for [mary, [mike, [seattle, [ ]]]].

Lists or complex terms are powerful constructs and can be used to write very sophisticated applications; however, they are also needed in basic database applications, such as constructing nested relations from normalized ones. This problem is solved in the following examples:

Example 8.22   A list-based representation for suppliers of `top_tube`

part_sup_list(top_tube, [cinelli, columbus, mavic]).

Transforming a nested-relation representation into a normalized relation, such as the `ps` relation in Example 8.23, is quite simple.

Example 8.23   Normalizing a nested relation into a flat relation

flatten(P, S, L) ←   part_sup_list(P, [S|L]).
flatten(P, S, L) ←   flatten(P, _, [S|L]).
ps(Part, Sup) ←   flatten(Part, Sup, _).

The application of these rules to the facts of Example 8.22 yields

ps(top_tube, cinelli)
ps(top_tube, columbus)
ps(top_tube, mavic)

However, the inverse transformation (i.e., constructing a nested relation from a normalized relation such as ps above) is not so simple. It requires an approach similar to that used in Example 8.20:

Example 8.24 From a flat relation to a nested one

$$\begin{aligned}
&\texttt{between(P, X, Z)} \leftarrow &&\texttt{ps(P, X), ps(P, Y), ps(P, Z), X < Y, Y < Z.} \\
&\texttt{smaller(P, X)} \leftarrow &&\texttt{ps(P, X), ps(P, Y), Y < X.} \\
&\texttt{nested(P, [X])} \leftarrow &&\texttt{ps(P, X), ¬smaller(P, X).} \\
&\texttt{nested(P, [Y|[X|W]])} \leftarrow &&\texttt{nested(P, [X|W]), ps(P, Y), X < Y,} \\
& &&\texttt{¬between(P, X, Y).} \\
&\texttt{ps\_nested(P, W)} \leftarrow &&\texttt{nested(P, W), ¬nested(P, [X|W]).}
\end{aligned}$$

Simple extensions of RA are needed to support Datalog with arithmetic and function symbols (see Exercise 8.11).

8.8 Syntax and Semantics of Datalog Languages

Following the general introduction to logic-based query languages in the previous sections, we can now present a more formal definition for such languages. Thus, we relate the syntax and semantics of query languages to those of first-order logic. Then, we introduce the model-theoretic semantics of Datalog programs and present a fixpoint theorem that provides the formal link to the bottom-up implementation of such programs.

8.8.1 Syntax of First-Order Logic and Datalog

First-order logic follows the syntax of context-free languages. Its alphabet consists of the following:

1. *Constants.*
2. *Variables*: In addition to identifiers beginning with uppercase, x, y, and z also represent variables in this section.
3. *Functions*, such as $f(t_1, \ldots, t_n)$, where f is an n-ary functor and $t_1, \ldots, t_n$ are the arguments.
4. *Predicates.*
5. *Connectives*: These include basic logical connectives $\lor$, $\land$, $\lnot$, and the implication symbols $\leftarrow$, $\rightarrow$, and $\leftrightarrow$.
6. *Quantifiers*: $\exists$ denotes the existential quantifier and $\forall$ denotes the universal quantifier.
7. Parentheses and punctuation symbols, used liberally as needed to avoid ambiguities.

A *term* is defined inductively as follows:

- A variable is a term.
- A constant is a term.
- If f is an n-ary functor and $t_1, \ldots, t_n$ are terms, then $f(t_1, \ldots, t_n)$ is a term.

Well-formed formulas (WFFs) are defined inductively as follows:

1. If p is an n-ary predicate and $t_1, \ldots, t_n$ are terms, then $p(t_1, \ldots, t_n)$ is a formula (called an *atomic formula* or, more simply, an *atom*).

2. If F and G are formulas, then so are $\neg F$, $F \vee G$, $F \wedge G$, $F \leftarrow G$, $F \rightarrow G$, and $F \leftrightarrow G$.

3. If F is a formula and x is a variable, then $\forall x \ (F)$ and $\exists x \ (F)$ are formulas. When so, x is said to be *quantified* in F.

Terms, atoms, and formulas that contain no variables are called *ground*.

Example 8.25   Well-formed formulas in first-order logic

$$\exists G_1(took(N, cs101, G_1)) \wedge \ \exists G_2(took(N, cs143, G_2)) \wedge$$
$$\exists M(student(N, M, junior)) \qquad (8.5)$$

$$\exists N, \exists M(student(N, M, senior) \wedge \forall C(req(cs, C) \rightarrow \exists G(took(N, C, G))))$$

$$\forall x \forall y \forall z \ (p(x, z) \vee \neg q(x, y) \vee \neg r(y, z)) \qquad (8.6)$$

$$\forall x \forall y \ (\neg p(x, y) \vee q(f(x, y), a)) \qquad (8.7)$$

A WFF F is said to be a *closed formula* if every variable occurrence in F is quantified. If F contains some variable x that is not quantified, then x is said to be a (quantification-) free variable in F, and F is not a closed formula. The variable N is not quantified in the first formula in Example 8.25 (8.5), so this formula is not closed. The remaining three WFFs in Example 8.25 are closed.

A *clause* is a closed WFF of the form

$$\forall x_1, \ldots, \forall x_s \ (A_1 \vee \ \ldots \ \vee A_k \vee \neg B_1 \vee \ \ldots \ \vee \neg B_n)$$

where $A_1, \ldots, A_k, B_1, \ldots, B_n$ are atoms and $x_1, \ldots, x_s$ are all the variables occurring in these atoms. Thus, a clause is the disjunction of positive and negated atoms, whose every variable is universally quantified. A clause is called a *definite clause* if it contains exactly one positive atom and zero or more negated atoms. Thus a definite clause has the form

$$\forall x_1, \ldots, \forall x_s \, (A \; \vee \neg B_1 \vee \; \ldots \; \vee \neg B_n)$$

Since $F \leftarrow G \equiv F \vee \neg G$, the previous clause can be rewritten in the standard rule notation:

$$A \leftarrow B_1, \; \ldots, \; B_n.$$

A is called the *head*, and $B_1, \; \ldots, \; B_n$ is called the *body* of the rule.

In Example 8.25, only the WFFs 8.6 and 8.7 are clauses and are written as follows:

Example 8.26 **The rule-based representation of clauses 8.6 and 8.7**

$$p(x, z) \leftarrow q(x, y), r(y, z).$$

$$q(f(x, y), a) \leftarrow p(x, y).$$

A definite clause with an empty body is called a *unit clause*. It is customary to use the notation "A." instead of the more precise notation "$A \leftarrow .$" for such clauses. A *fact* is a unit clause without variables (see Example 8.27).

Example 8.27 **A unit clause (everybody loves himself) and three facts**

$$\text{loves}(X, X).$$
$$\text{loves}(\text{marc}, \text{mary}).$$
$$\text{loves}(\text{mary}, \text{tom}).$$
$$\text{hates}(\text{marc}, \text{tom}).$$

Definition 8.5 *A positive logic program is a set of definite clauses.*

We will use the terms *definite clause program* and *positive program* as synonyms.

8.8.2 Semantics

Positive logic programs have a very well defined formal semantics since alternative plausible semantics proposed for these programs have been shown to be equivalent. More general programs (e.g., those containing negation) are less well behaved and more complex in this respect and will be discussed in later chapters. For the rest of this chapter, the word "program" simply means a positive logic program (i.e., a set of definite clauses).

We will discuss the model-theoretic and fixpoint-based semantics of programs. The former provides a purely declarative meaning to a program, while the latter provides the formal link to the bottom-up implementation of deductive databases. The proof-theoretic approach, which leads to SLD-resolution and top-down execution, will be covered in the next chapter.

8.8.3   Interpretations

The notion of an interpretation for a program P is defined with respect to the constant symbols, function symbols, and predicate symbols that are contained in P. In a slightly more general context, we also define interpretations for any first-order language L, given its set of constant symbols, function symbols, and predicate symbols.

Then the first step for assigning an interpretation to L (and every program written in L) is to select a nonempty set of elements U, called the *universe* (or *domain*) of interpretation. Then, an *interpretation* of L consists of the following:

1. For each constant in L, an assignment of an element in U

2. For each n-ary function in L, the assignment of a mapping from U^n to U

3. For each n-ary predicate q in L, the assignment of a mapping from U^n into true, false (or, equivalently, a relation on U^n)

For definite clause languages and programs, however, it is sufficient to consider Herbrand interpretations, where constants and functions represent themselves. Under Herbrand interpretations, functors are viewed as variable-length subrecords, rather than evaluable functions. Therefore, `rectangle(10, 20)` denotes the actual rectangle rather than a two-place function that computes on its arguments 10 and 20.

Then, the *Herbrand universe* for L, denoted U_L, is defined as the set of all terms that can be recursively constructed by letting the arguments of the functions be constants in L or elements in U_L. (In the case that L has no constants, we add some constant, say, a, to form ground terms.)

Then the *Herbrand base* of L is defined as the set of atoms that can be built by assigning the elements of U_L to the arguments of the predicates.

Therefore, given that the assignment of constants and function symbols is fixed, a (*Herbrand interpretation*) is defined by assigning to each n-ary predicate q, a relation Q of arity n, where $q(a_1, \ldots, a_n)$ is true iff $(a_1, \ldots, a_n) \in Q$, $a_1, \ldots, a_n$ denoting elements in U_L. Alternatively, a Herbrand interpretation of L is a subset of the Herbrand base of L.

For a program P, the Herbrand universe, U_P, and the Herbrand base, B_P, are, respectively, defined as U_L and B_L of the language L that has as constants, functions, and predicates those appearing in P.

Example 8.28   **Let P be the following program:**

$$
\begin{aligned}
\text{anc}(X, Y) &\leftarrow & \text{parent}(X, Y). \\
\text{anc}(X, Z) &\leftarrow & \text{anc}(X, Y), \text{parent}(Y, Z). \\
\text{parent}(X, Y) &\leftarrow & \text{father}(X, Y). \\
\text{parent}(X, Y) &\leftarrow & \text{mother}(X, Y). \\
\text{mother}&(\text{anne}, \text{silvia}). \\
\text{mother}&(\text{anne}, \text{marc}).
\end{aligned}
$$

In this example, $U_P = \{anne, silvia, marc\}$, and

$$
\begin{aligned}
B_P = \ & \{parent(x, y) | x, y \in U_P\} \cup \{father(x, y) | x, y \in U_P\} \cup \\
& \{mother(x, y) | x, y \in U_P\} \cup \{anc(x, y) | x, y \in U_P\}
\end{aligned}
$$

Since in Example 8.28 there are four binary predicates, and three possible assignments for the first arguments and three for their second arguments, then $|B_P| = 4 \times 3 \times 3 = 36$. Since there are $2^{|B_P|}$ subsets of B_P, there are 2^{36} Herbrand interpretations for the program in Example 8.28.

Example 8.29   **A program P with an infinite B_P and an infinite number of interpretations**

$$
\begin{aligned}
\text{p}(\text{f}(x)) &\leftarrow & \text{q}(x). \\
\text{q}(\text{a}) &\leftarrow & \text{p}(x).
\end{aligned}
$$

Then,

$$
U_P = \{a, f(a), \ldots, f^n(a), \ldots\}
$$

where $f^0(a), f^1(a)$, and $f^2(a), \ldots$, stand for $a, f(a)$, and $f((a))$, and so on. Moreover,

$$
B_P = \{p(f^n(a)) \,|n \geq 0\} \cup \{q(f^m(a)) \mid m \geq 0\}.
$$

8.9   The Models of a Program

Let r be a rule in a program P. Then $ground(r)$ denotes the set of ground instances of r (i.e., all the rules obtained by assigning values from the Herbrand universe U_P to the variables in r).

Example 8.30   Let r be the fourth rule in the Example 8.28

Since there are two variables in said r and $|U_P| = 3$, then $ground(r)$ consists of 3×3 rules:

$$\texttt{parent(anne, anne)} \leftarrow \qquad \texttt{mother(anne, anne)}.$$
$$\texttt{parent(anne, marc)} \leftarrow \qquad \texttt{mother(anne, marc)}.$$
$$\cdots$$
$$\texttt{parent(silvia, silvia)} \leftarrow \texttt{mother(silvia, silvia)}.$$

The ground version of a program P, denoted $ground(P)$, is the set of the ground instances of its rules:

$$ground(P) = \{ground(r) \mid r \in P\}$$

For the program P of Example 8.28, $ground(P)$ contains 9 instantiations of the first rule (since it has two variables and $|U_P| = 3$), 27 instantiations of the second rule, 9 instantiations of the third rule, and 9 of the fourth one, plus the two original facts.

Let I be an interpretation for a program P. Then, every ground atom $a \in I$ is said to be true (or satisfied); if $a \notin I$, then a is said to be false (or not satisfied). Then a formula consisting of ground atoms and logical connectives is defined as true or false (satisfied or not satisfied) according to the rules of propositional logic. Therefore,

Definition 8.6 (*Satisfaction*) *A rule $r \in P$ is said to hold true in interpretation I, or to be satisfied in I, if every instance of r is satisfied in I.*

Definition 8.7 (*Model.*) *An interpretation I that makes true all rules P is called a* model *for P.*

Observe that I is a model for P iff it satisfies all the rules in $ground(P)$.

Example 8.31   Interpretations and models for Example 8.28

- If $I_1 = \emptyset$, then every instance of the first and second rules in the example are satisfied since the bodies are always false. I_1, however, is not a model since the third and fourth rules in the example (i.e., the facts) are not satisfied. Thus every interpretation aspiring to be a model must contain every fact in the program.

- Consider now $I_2 = \{mother(anne, silvia), mother(anne, marc)\}$. The first rule is satisfied since the body is always false. However, consider the following instance of the second rule: `parent(anne,silvia)` ← `mother(anne,silvia)`. Here every goal in the body is satisfied, but the head is not. Thus, I_2 is not a model.

- Now consider $I_3 = \{mother(anne, silvia), \; mother(anne, marc), \; parent(anne, silvia), \qquad parent(anne, marc), \qquad anc(anne, silvia), \; anc(anne, marc)\}$. This is a model.

- $I_4 = I_3 \cup \{anc(silvia, marc)\}$ is also a model, but it is not a minimal one since it contains a redundant atom.

Lemma 8.8 *Model intersection property. Let P be a positive program, and M_1 and M_2 be two models for P. Then, $M_1 \cap M_2$ is also a model for P.*

Definition 8.9 *Minimal model and least model. A model M for a program P is said to be a* minimal model *for P if there exists no other model M' of P where $M' \subset M$. A model M for a program P is said to be its* least model *if $M' \supseteq M$ for every model M' of P.*

Then, as a result of the last lemma we have the following:

Theorem 8.10 *Every positive program has a least model.*

Proof.   Since B_P is a model, P has models, and therefore minimal models. Thus, either P has several minimal models, or it has a unique minimal model, the least model of P. By contradiction, say that M_1 and M_2 are two distinct minimal models, then $M_1 \cap M_2 \subset M_1$ is also a model. This contradicts the assumption that M_1 is a minimal model. Therefore, there cannot be two distinct minimal models for P. □

Definition 8.11 *Let P be a positive program. The least model of P, denoted M_P, defines the meaning of P.*

8.10   Fixpoint-Based Semantics

The least-model semantics provides a logic-based declarative definition of the meaning of a program. We need now to consider constructive semantics and effective means to realize the minimal model semantics. A constructive semantics follows from viewing rules as constructive derivation patterns, whereby, from the tuples that satisfy the patterns specified by the goals in a rule, we construct the corresponding head atoms. As previously discussed, relational algebra can be used to perform such a mapping from the body relations to the head relations. For instance, in Example 8.28, `parent` can be derived through a union operator. Then `grandparent` can be derived from these. However, the recursive predicate `anc` is both the argument and the result of the relational algebra expression. Therefore, we have a *fixpoint equation*, that is, an equation of the form $x = T(x)$, where T is a mapping $U \to U$. A value of x that satisfies this equation is called a *fixpoint* for T; for an arbitrary T, there might be zero or more fixpoints.

For a positive program P, it is customary to consider the mapping T_P, called the *Immediate consequence operator*, for P, defined as follows:

$$T_P(I) = \{A \in B_P \mid \exists r : A \leftarrow A_1, \ldots, A_n \in ground(P), \{A_1, \ldots, A_n\} \subseteq I\}$$

Thus, T_P is a mapping from Herbrand interpretations of P to Herbrand interpretations of P.

Example 8.32   Let P be the program of Example 8.28

For $I = \{anc(anne, marc), parent(marc, silvia)\}$, we have

$$T_P(I) = \{anc(marc, silvia), anc(anne, silvia),$$
$$mother(anne, silvia), mother(anne, marc)\}$$

Thus, in addition to the atoms derived from the applicable rules, T_P always returns the database facts and the ground instances of all unit clauses.

Example 8.33   Let P be the program of Example 8.29

Then, $U_P = \{a, f(a), \ldots, f^n(a), \ldots\}$

If $I = \{p(a) \}$, then $T_P(I) = \{q(a)\}$.
If $I_1 = \{p(x)|x \in U_P\} \cup \{q(y)|y \in U_P \}$,
   then $T_P(I_1) = \{q(a)\} \cup \{p(f^n(a)) \mid n \geq 1\}$.
If $I_2 = \emptyset$, then $T_P(I_2) = \emptyset$.
If $I_3 = T_P(I_1)$, then $T_P(I_3) = \{q(a)\} \cup \{p(f(a))\}$.

Under the fixpoint semantics, we view a program P as defining the following *fixpoint equation* over Herbrand interpretations:

$$I = T_P(I)$$

In general, a fixpoint equation might have no solution, one solution, or several solutions. However, our fixpoint equation is over Herbrand interpretations, which are subsets of B_P, and thus partially ordered by the set inclusion relationship $\subseteq$. In fact, $(2^{|B_P|}, \subseteq)$ is a partial order (transitive, reflexive, and antisymmetric) and a lattice, where intersection $I_1 \cap I_2$, and union $I_1 \cup I_2$, respectively, define the *lub* and *glb* of the lattice. Furthermore, given a set of elements in 2^{B_P}, there exists the union and intersection of such a set, even if it contains infinitely many elements. Thus, we have a *complete* lattice. Therefore, we only need to observe that T_P for definite clause programs is monotonic (i.e., if $N \leq M$, then $T_P(N) \leq T_P(M)$) to conclude that Knaster/Tarski's theorem applies, yielding the following result:

Theorem 8.12 *Let P be a definite clause program. There always exists a least fixpoint for T_P, denoted $lfp(T_P)$.*

The least-model semantics and the least-fixpoint semantics for positive programs coincide:

Theorem 8.13 *Let P be a definite clause program. Then $M_P = lfp(T_P)$.*

Proof. Let I be a fixpoint for T_P. If I is not a model, then there exists a rule $r \in ground(P)$, where the body of r is satisfied by I but the head $h(r)$ is not in I. Then I cannot be a fixpoint. Thus, every fixpoint is also a model. Vice versa, let M_P be the least model for P. Observe that if $a \in M_P$ and $a \notin T_P(M_P)$, then there is no rule in $ground(P)$ with head a and body satisfied by M_P. Thus, $M_P - \{a\}$ would also be a model—a contradiction. Thus, $T_P(M_P) \supseteq M_P$; but if $T_P(M_P) \supset M_P$, then M_P cannot be a model. Thus, $T_P(M_P) = M_P$. Therefore, M_P is a fixpoint; now, we need to prove that it is the least fixpoint. In fact, $M_P \supset lfp(T_P)$ yields a contradiction, since every fixpoint is a model, and $lfp(T_P)$ would be a smaller model than M_P. Thus, $M_P = lfp(T_P)$. □

In conclusion, the least-fixpoint approach and the least-model approach assign the same meaning to a positive program P: $lfp(T_P) = M_P$.

8.10.1 Operational Semantics: Powers of T_P

For positive programs, $lfp(T_P)$ can simply be computed by repeated applications of T_P. The result of n applications of T_P is called the nth power of T_P, denoted $T_P^{\uparrow n}$, defined as follows:

$$T_P^{\uparrow 0}(I) \;=\; I$$

$$\cdots$$

$$T_P^{\uparrow n+1}(I) \;=\; T_P(T_P^{\uparrow n}(I))$$

Moreover, with ω denoting the first limit ordinal, we define

$$T_P^{\uparrow \omega}(I) \;=\; \bigcup \{T^{\uparrow n}(I) \mid n \geq 0\}$$

Of particular interest are the powers of T_P starting from the empty set (i.e., for $I = \emptyset$).

Theorem 8.14 *Let P be a definite clause program. Then $lfp(T_P) = T_P^{\uparrow \omega}(\emptyset)$.*

Proof.   To show that $T_P^{\uparrow \omega}(\emptyset) \subseteq T_P(T_P^{\uparrow \omega}(\emptyset))$, let $a \in T_P^{\uparrow \omega}(\emptyset)$. Then, for some integer $k > 0$, $a \in T_P^{\uparrow k}(\emptyset)$. But $T_P^{\uparrow k}(\emptyset) = T_P(T_P^{\uparrow k-1}(\emptyset)) \subseteq T_P(T_P^{\uparrow \omega}(\emptyset))$, since T_P is monotonic and $T_P^{\uparrow k-1}(\emptyset) \subseteq T_P^{\uparrow \omega}(\emptyset)$. Thus, $a \in T_P(T_P^{\uparrow \omega}(\emptyset))$.

Now, to show that $T_P^{\uparrow \omega}(\emptyset) \supseteq T_P(T_P^{\uparrow \omega}(\emptyset))$, observe that every atom in the latter set must be the head of some rule $r \in ground(P)$ whose goals are in $T_P^{\uparrow \omega}(\emptyset)$. Now, observe that $a \in T_P^{\uparrow \omega}(\emptyset)$ iff $a \in T_P^{\uparrow k}(\emptyset)$ for some integer k. Therefore, since r has a finite number of goals, there is an integer k for which all the goals of r are in $T_P^{\uparrow k}(\emptyset)$. Then, for the head of r we have $h(r) \in T_P^{\uparrow k+1}(\emptyset) \subseteq T_P^{\uparrow \omega}(\emptyset)$.

Therefore, we have proven that $T_P^{\uparrow \omega}(\emptyset)$ is a fixpoint for T_P. To prove that it is the least fixpoint, let us show that if $N = T_P(N)$, then $N \supseteq T_P^{\uparrow \omega}(\emptyset)$. Indeed, if $N = T_P(N)$, then $N = T_P^{\uparrow \omega}(N)$. But, since $T_P^{\uparrow \omega}$ is monotonic, $T_P^{\uparrow \omega}(N) \supseteq T_P^{\uparrow \omega}(\emptyset)$.   □

The equality $M_P = lfp(T_P) = T_P^{\uparrow \omega}(\emptyset)$ outlines a simple algorithm for computing the least model of a definite clause program. In fact, given that T_P is monotonic, and that $T_P^{\uparrow 0}(\emptyset) \subseteq T_P^{\uparrow 1}(\emptyset)$, by induction it follows that $T_P^{\uparrow n}(\emptyset) \subseteq T_P^{\uparrow n+1}(\emptyset)$. Thus, the successive powers of T_P form an ascending chain. Moreover,

$$T_P^{\uparrow k} (\emptyset) \;=\; \bigcup_{n \leq k} T_P^{\uparrow n} (\emptyset)$$

Observe that if $T_P^{\uparrow n+1}(\emptyset) = T_P^{\uparrow n}(\emptyset)$, then $T_P^{\uparrow n}(\emptyset) = T_P^{\uparrow \omega}(\emptyset)$. Thus, the least fixpoint and least model can be computed by starting from the bottom and iterating the application of T ad infinitum—or until no new atoms are obtained and the $(n+1)^{th}$ power is identical to the nth power.

Since $T_P^{\uparrow k}$ is also monotonic, for all integers k and for $k = \omega$, we have the following:

Lemma 8.15 *Let P be a definite clause program, with least model M_P. Then, $T_P^{\uparrow \omega}(M) = M_P$ for every $M \subseteq M_P$.*

Proof. Since $\emptyset \subseteq M \subseteq M_P$, then $T_P^{\uparrow \omega}(\emptyset) \subseteq T_P^{\uparrow \omega}(M) \subseteq T_P^{\uparrow \omega}(M_P)$, where $T_P^{\uparrow \omega}(\emptyset) = T_P^{\uparrow \omega}(M_P)$. □

8.11 Bibliographic Notes

The logic-based foundations for the relational data model and query languages were established by E. F. Codd, who introduced the relational calculus and relational algebra and proved their equivalence [115, 116, 117]. Several textbooks, including [437, 2], provide an extensive coverage of these topics.

The topic of logic and databases has been the area of much research work; an incomplete list of published works that explore this area include [182, 183, 308, 355]. A recent survey of the topic can be found in [289]. An interest in logic-based languages for databases was renewed in the 1980s, in part as a result of the emergence of the Prolog language [309, 112, 418]. The design approaches followed by these languages and their supporting deductive database systems are discussed and contrasted with those of Prolog in [296, 465, 302].

The topic of expressive power and computational complexity of query languages is extensively covered in [2]; proofs that transitive closures cannot be expressed in FO languages are presented in [13, 100].

The equivalence of least-fixpoint and least-model semantics for logic programs was proven in [441]; the least-fixpoint theorem for monotonic functions in a lattice is primarily credited to Tarski [428]. Lattices are treated in [60] and in Part V of this volume.

8.12   Exercises

8.1. Using the part_cost relation of Example 8.14, write safe Datalog rules to find those suppliers who supply all basic parts.

8.2. Write a Datalog query to find students who have taken at least two classes, and got the highest grade (possibly with others) in every class they took.

8.3. Express the previous query in SQL using the **EXISTS** construct.

8.4. Universally quantified queries can also be expressed in SQL using the set aggregate **COUNT**. Reformulate the last query and that of Example 8.13 in SQL, using the **COUNT** aggregate.

8.5. A relationally complete relational algebra (RA) contains set union, set difference, set intersection, Cartesian product, selection, and projection.

    a. Show that the expressive power of RA does not change if we drop set intersection.

    b. List the monotonic operators of RA.

    c. Show that there is a loss in expressive power if we drop set difference from the RA described above.

8.6. Define generalized projection using the other RA operators.

8.7. Which of the following rules and predicates are safe if b1 and b2 are database predicates?

$$r_1 : p(X, X) \leftarrow \quad b2(Y, Y, a), b1(X), X > Y.$$
$$r_2 : q(X, Y) \leftarrow \quad p(X, Z), p(Z, Y).$$
$$r_3 : s(X) \leftarrow \quad b2(Y, Y, a), X > Y, \neg b1(X).$$

Translate the safe Datalog rules and predicates in this program into equivalent relational algebra expressions.

8.8. Improve the translation proposed for negated rule goals into RA by minimizing the number of columns in the relations involved in the set difference. Translate the following rule:

$$r_4 : n(X, X) \leftarrow \quad b2(X, Y, \_), \neg b2(X, a, \_).$$

8.9. Prove the converse of Theorem 8.3: that is, show that for every RA expression, there exists an equivalent Datalog program, which is safe and nonrecursive.

8.10. Express in Datalog the division operation $R(A, B) \div S(B)$. By translating the rules so obtained into RA, express relation division in terms of the other RA operators.

8.11. Generalize the safety conditions for Datalog to include function symbols. Then extend the RA with the following two operators: the *extended projection*, which extracts the subarguments of a complex term, and the *combine* operator (denoted by γ), which builds complex terms from simple tokens. For instance, if a relation R only contains the tuple ('Jones', degree_year(ba, 1996)), then $S = \pi_{\$1,\$1.0,\$1.1} R$ contains the tuple ('Jones', degree_year, ba). Then $\gamma_{\mathsf{degree}(\$3)} S$ returns the tuple ('Jones', degree(ba)). Prove that every safe nonrecursive Datalog program can be mapped into extended RA algebra expressions.

8.12. The following employee relation, emp(Eno, Ename, MgNo), specifies the name and manager number of each employee in the company. The management structure in this company is a strict hierarchy. Write transitive closure rules to construct emp_all_mgrs(Eno, AllMangrs), where AllMangrs is a list containing the employee numbers for all managers of Eno in the management chain.

8.13. Write a Datalog program to compute how many courses required for a cs degree each senior cs student is missing.

8.14. Prove the model intersection property.

8.15. Show that for each positive program P,

$$T_p^{\uparrow n+1}(\emptyset) \supseteq T_p^{\uparrow n}(\emptyset)$$

8.16. Let P be a positive Datalog program. Show that $T_P^{\uparrow \omega}$ can be computed in time that is polynomial in the size of P's Herbrand base.

Chapter 9

Implementation of Rules and Recursion

9.1 Operational Semantics: Bottom-Up Execution

In the last chapter, we saw that the least model for a program P can be computed as $T_P^{\uparrow k}(\emptyset)$, where k is the lowest integer for which $T_P^{\uparrow k}(\emptyset) = T_P^{\uparrow k+1}(\emptyset)$, if such an integer exists, or the first ordinal ω otherwise. The need to compute to the first ordinal can only occur in the presence of an infinite Herbrand universe (e.g., when there are function symbols). For basic Datalog, without function symbols or arithmetic, the universe is finite, and the computation of the least model of a program ends after a finite number of steps k.

This property forms the basis for the bottom-up computation methods used by deductive databases. Several improvements and tuning for special cases are needed, however, to make this computation efficient. This chapter describes these improved bottom-up execution techniques and other execution techniques that are akin to top-down execution strategies used in Prolog.

9.2 Stratified Programs and Iterated Fixpoint

In most systems, $T_P^{\uparrow \omega}(\emptyset)$ is computed by strata. Unless otherwise specified, we will use strict stratifications in the discussion that follows.

The stratified computation is *inflationary*, in the sense that the results of the previous iterations on T_P are kept and augmented with the results of the new iteration step. This yields the concept of the inflationary immediate consequence operator.

Definition 9.1 *Let P be program. The* inflationary immediate consequence operator *for P, denoted Υ_P, is a mapping on subsets of B_P defined as follows:*

$$\Upsilon_P(I) = T_P(I) \cup I$$

It is easy to prove by induction that $\Upsilon_P^{\uparrow n}(\emptyset) = T_P^{\uparrow n}(\emptyset)$. (The computation $T_P^{\uparrow \omega}(\emptyset)$ is frequently called *inflationary fixpoint* computation.) Thus, we have the following properties:

$$M_P = lfp(T_P) = T_P^{\uparrow \omega}(\emptyset) = lfp(\Upsilon_P) = \Upsilon_P^{\uparrow \omega}(\emptyset)$$

Algorithm 9.2 *Iterated fixpoint for program P stratified in n strata. Let P_j, $1 \leq j \leq n$, denote the rules with their head in the jth stratum. Then, M_j is inductively constructed as follows:*

1. $M_0 = \emptyset$ *and*

2. $M_j = \Upsilon_{P_j}^{\uparrow \omega}(M_{j-1})$.

Theorem 9.3 *Let P be a positive program stratified in n strata, and let M_n be the result produced by the iterated fixpoint computation. Then, $M_P = M_n$, where M_P is the least model of P.*

Proof.   We want to prove that, for all $1 \leq j \leq n$, $M_j = \Upsilon_{\leq j}^{\uparrow \omega}(M_{j-1})$, where $\Upsilon_{\leq j}$ denotes the inflationary immediate consequence operator for the rules up to the jth stratum. The property is trivial for $j = 1$. Now assume that it holds for every M_i, where $0 \leq i \leq j - 1$. Now, the equality $\Upsilon_{P_j}^{\uparrow k}(M_{j-1}) = \Upsilon_{\leq j}^{\uparrow k}(M_{j-1})$ holds for $k = 0$, and we will next prove that if it holds for k, then it also holds for $k+1$. Indeed, then $\Upsilon_{\leq j}^{\uparrow k+1}(M_{j-1}) = \Upsilon_{\leq j}(\Upsilon_{\leq j}^{\uparrow k}(M_{j-1})) = \Upsilon_{\leq j}(\Upsilon_{P_j}^{\uparrow k}(M_{j-1}))$. But every rule with its head in a stratum $< j$ produces atoms that are already in M_{j-1}. Thus, $\Upsilon_{\leq j}(\Upsilon_{P_j}^{\uparrow k}(M_{j-1})) = \Upsilon_{P_j}(\Upsilon_{P_j}^{\uparrow k}(M_{j-1}))$, and $M_j = \Upsilon_{\leq j}^{\uparrow \omega}(M_{j-1})$.

Therefore, by using double induction over the n strata, we conclude that $M_n = \Upsilon_{\leq n}^{\uparrow \omega}(M_{n-1})$. But $M_n = \Upsilon_{\leq n}^{\uparrow \omega}(M_{n-1}) = \Upsilon_P^{\uparrow \omega}(M_{n-1})$. But since $\emptyset \subseteq M_{n-1} \subseteq M_P$, then $\Upsilon_P^{\uparrow \omega}(M_{n-1}) = M_P$, by Lemma 8.15. $\square$

The iterated fixpoint computation defined by Algorithm 9.2 terminates whenever the original fixpoint computation terminates. However, when this requires an infinite number of steps, then the iterated fixpoint will not go past the first stratum, requiring infinitely many iterations. In this case, we have a transfinite computation that is more accurately described by the term "procedure," than by "algorithm."

9.3 Differential Fixpoint Computation

The algorithm for computing $\Upsilon_{P_j}^{\uparrow \omega}(M_j)$ for stratum j of the iterated fixpoint computation is given by Algorithm 9.4, where for notational expediency, we let Υ stand for Υ_{P_j} and M stand for M_{j-1}.

Algorithm 9.4 *The inflationary fixpoint computation for each stratum*

$$S := M;$$
$$S' := \Upsilon(M)$$
$$\textbf{while } (S \subset S')$$
$$\{$$
$$\qquad S := S';$$
$$\qquad S' := \Upsilon(S)$$
$$\}$$

This computation can be improved by observing that $T(M) = T_E(M)$ and $\Upsilon(M) = \Upsilon_E(M)$, where T_E denotes the immediate consequence operator for the exit rules and Υ_E denotes its inflationary version. Conversely, let T_R denote the immediate consequence operator for the recursive rules and let Υ_R be its inflationary version. Then, $\Upsilon(S)$ in the **while** loop can be replaced by $\Upsilon_R(S)$, while $\Upsilon(M)$ outside the loop can be replaced by $\Upsilon_E(M)$. For instance, for the linear ancestor rules of Example 9.1, Υ_E and Υ_R are defined by rules r_1 and r_2, respectively.

Example 9.1 Left-linear ancestor rules

$$r_1 : \mathtt{anc(X,Y)} \leftarrow \mathtt{parent(X,Y)}.$$
$$r_2 : \mathtt{anc(X,Z)} \leftarrow \mathtt{anc(X,Y), parent(Y,Z)}.$$

Even after this first improvement, there is still significant redundancy in the computation. In fact, before entering the loop, the set S contains the pairs parent/person. After the first iteration, this contains the pairs grandparent/person, along with the old pairs parent/person. Thus, at the second iteration, the recursive rule produces the pairs great-grandparent/person, but also produces the old pairs great-grandparent/person from previous iterations. In general, the jth iteration step also recomputes all atoms obtained *and therefore all $j-2^{th}$ step ......, i.e., all previous results*

in the $j-1^{th}$ step. This redundancy can be eliminated by using finite differences techniques, which trace the derivations over two steps. Let us use the following notation:

1. S is a relation containing the atoms obtained up to step $j-1$.

2. $S' = \Upsilon_R(S)$ is a relation containing the atoms produced up to step j.

3. $\delta S = \Upsilon_R(S) - S = T_R(S) - S$ denotes the atoms newly obtained at step j (i.e., the atoms that were not in S at step $j-1$). *at the begining of step j (at the end of step $j-1$)*

4. $\delta'S = \Upsilon_R(S') - S' = T_R(S') - S'$ are the atoms obtained at step j. *at the end of step j*

We can now rewrite Algorithm 9.4 as follows:

Algorithm 9.5 *Differential fixpoint*

> $S := M;$ *or $T_E(M)$*
> $\delta S := \Upsilon_E(M) - M;$
> $S' := \delta S \cup S;$
> **while** $(\delta S \neq \emptyset)$
> {
> $\delta'S := T_R(S') - S';$ *$\delta'S$*
> $S := S';$
> $\delta S := \delta'S;$
> $S' := S \cup \delta S$
> }

For Example 9.1, let anc, δanc, and anc′, respectively, denote ancestor atoms that are in S, δS, and $S' = S \cup \delta S$. Then, when computing $\delta S' := T_R(S') - S'$ in Algorithm 9.5, we can use a T_R defined by the following rule:

$$\delta'\text{anc}(X, Z) \leftarrow \text{anc}'(X, Y), \text{parent}(Y, Z).$$

Now, we can split anc′ into anc and δanc, and rewrite the last rule into the following pairs:

$$\delta'\text{anc}(X, Z) \leftarrow \delta\text{anc}(X, Y), \text{parent}(Y, Z).$$
$$\delta'\text{anc}(X, Z) \leftarrow \text{anc}(X, Y), \text{parent}(Y, Z).$$

The second rule can now be eliminated, since it produces only atoms that were already contained in anc′ (i.e., in the S' computed in the previous iteration). Thus, in Algorithm 9.5, rather than using $\delta'S := T_R(S') - S'$, we can write $\delta'S := T_R(\delta S) - S'$ to express the fact that the argument of T_R is the set of delta tuples from the previous step, rather the set of all tuples obtained so far. This transformation holds for all linear recursive rules.

Consider now a quadratic rule (i.e., one where the recursive predicate appears twice in the body). Say, for instance, that we have the following:

Example 9.2   Quadratic ancestor rules

$$\text{ancs}(X, Y) \leftarrow \text{parent}(X, Y).$$
$$\text{ancs}(X, Z) \leftarrow \text{ancs}(X, Y), \text{ancs}(Y, Z).$$

The recursive rule can be transformed for Algorithm 9.5 as follows:

$$r : \delta'\text{ancs}(X, Z) \leftarrow \text{ancs}'(X, Y), \text{ancs}'(Y, Z).$$

By partitioning the relation corresponding to the first goal into an ancs part and a δancs part, we obtain:

$$r_1 : \delta'\text{ancs}(X, Z) \leftarrow \delta\text{ancs}(X, Y), \text{ancs}'(Y, Z).$$
$$r_2 : \delta'\text{ancs}(X, Z) \leftarrow \text{ancs}(X, Y), \text{ancs}'(Y, Z).$$

Now, by the same operation on the second goal, we can rewrite the second rule just obtained into

$$r_{2,1} : \delta'\text{ancs}(X, Z) \leftarrow \text{ancs}(X, Y), \delta\text{ancs}(Y, Z).$$
$$r_{2,2} : \delta'\text{ancs}(X, Z) \leftarrow \text{ancs}(X, Y), \text{ancs}(Y, Z).$$

Rule $r_{2,2}$ produces only "old" values, and can thus be eliminated; we are then left with rules r_1 and $r_{2,1}$, below:

$$\delta'\text{ancs}(X, Z) \leftarrow \delta\text{ancs}(X, Y), \text{ancs}'(Y, Z).$$
$$\delta'\text{ancs}(X, Z) \leftarrow \text{ancs}(X, Y), \delta\text{ancs}(Y, Z).$$

Thus, for nonlinear rules, the immediate consequence operator used in Algorithm 9.5 has the more general form $\delta'S := T_R(\delta S, S, S') - S'$, where $\delta S = S' - S$.

Observe that even if S and S' are not totally eliminated, the resulting computation is usually much more efficient, since it is typically the case that $n = |\delta S| \ll N = |S| \approx |S'|$. The original ancs rule, for instance, requires the equijoin of two relations of size N; after the differentiation we need to compute two equijoins, each joining a relation of size n with one of size N.

Observe also that there is a simple analogy between the symbolic differentiation of these rules and the chain rule used to differentiate expressions in calculus. For instance, the body of the left-linear anc rule of Example 9.1

consists of the conjunction of a recursive predicate anc (a variable predicate) followed by a constant predicate. Thus, we have a pattern $x \cdot c$, where x stands for a variable and c for a constant. Therefore, $\delta(x \cdot c) = (\delta x) \cdot c$. For the quadratic rule defining ancs in Example 9.2, we have instead the pattern $\delta(x \cdot y) = \delta x \cdot y + \delta y \cdot x$, where the symbol '+' should be interpreted as set union.

The general expression of $T_R(\delta S, S, S')$ for a recursive rule of rank k is as follows. Let

$$r : Q_0 \leftarrow c_0, Q_1, c_1, Q_2, \ldots, Q_k, c_k$$

be a recursive rule, where $Q_1, \ldots, Q_k$ stand for occurrences of predicates that are mutually recursive with Q_0, and $c_1, \ldots, c_k$ stand for the remaining goals. Then, r is symbolically differentiated into k rules as follows:

$$
\begin{aligned}
&r_1 : \delta'Q_0 \leftarrow c_0, \; \delta Q_1, \; c_1, \; Q_2', & \ldots & \quad Q_k', \; c_k \\
&r_2 : \delta'Q_0 \leftarrow c_0, \; Q_1, \; c_1, \; \delta Q_2, & \ldots & \quad Q_k', \; c_k \\
& & \ldots & \\
&r_j : \delta'Q_0 \leftarrow \qquad \ldots & \delta Q_j & \quad Q_k', \; c_k \\
& & \ldots & \\
&r_k : \delta'Q_0 \leftarrow c_0, \; Q_1, \; c_1, \; Q_2, & \ldots & \quad \delta Q_k, \; c_k
\end{aligned}
$$

Observe the pattern of delta predicates on the main diagonal, unprimed predicates to the left of the diagonal, and primed predicates to its right. This result was obtained by expanding each goal Q_j' into δQ_j and Q_j for ascending js. If we perform the expansion by descending js, the deltas become aligned along the other diagonal.

In terms of implementation, the differential fixpoint is therefore best realized by rewriting the original rules. Alternatively you can first transform the original rules into relational algebra expressions and apply symbolic differentiation to those.

9.4   Top-Down Execution

In the top-down procedural semantics of logic programs, each goal in a rule body is viewed as a call to a procedure defined by other rules in the same stratum or in lower strata. Consider, for instance, the rules from Example 9.3. The goal area(Shape, Area) in rule r_2 can be viewed as a call to the procedure area defined by rules r_3 and r_4. At the time when the procedure is called, Shape is instantiated to values such as circle(11) or

Example 9.3 The rules of Example 8.21

$r_1 : \texttt{part\_weight}(\texttt{No}, \texttt{Kilos}) \leftarrow \texttt{part}(\texttt{No}, \_, \texttt{actualkg}(\texttt{Kilos})).$
$r_2 : \texttt{part\_weight}(\texttt{No}, \texttt{Kilos}) \leftarrow \texttt{part}(\texttt{No}, \texttt{Shape}, \texttt{unitkg}(\texttt{K})),$
$\qquad\qquad\qquad\qquad\qquad\qquad \texttt{area}(\texttt{Shape}, \texttt{Area}),$
$\qquad\qquad\qquad\qquad\qquad\qquad \texttt{Kilos} = \texttt{K} * \texttt{Area}.$

$r_3 : \texttt{area}(\texttt{circle}(\texttt{Dmtr}), \texttt{A}) \leftarrow \qquad \texttt{A} = \texttt{Dmtr} * \texttt{Dmtr} * 3.14/4.$
$r_4 : \texttt{area}(\texttt{rectangle}(\texttt{Base}, \texttt{Height}), \texttt{A}) \leftarrow \texttt{A} = \texttt{Base} * \texttt{Height}.$

$\texttt{rectangle}(10, 20)$ by the execution of r_3 and r_4 goals. The argument $\texttt{Area}$ is instead assigned a value by the execution of the two called $\texttt{area}$ rules. Thus, $\texttt{A}$ and $\texttt{Area}$ can be viewed as what in procedural languages are respectively called formal parameters and actual parameters. Unlike procedural languages, however, the arguments here can be complex, and the passing of parameters is performed through a process known as *unification*. For instance, if $\texttt{Shape} = \texttt{rectangle}(10, 20)$, this will be made equal to (unified to) the first argument of the second $\texttt{area}$ rule, $\texttt{rectangle}(\texttt{Base, Height})$, by setting $\texttt{Base} = 10$ and $\texttt{Height} = 20$.

9.4.1 Unification

Definition 9.6 *A substitution θ is a finite set of the form $\{v_1/t_1, \ldots, v_n/t_n\}$, where each v_i is a distinct variable, and each t_i is a term distinct from v_i. Each t_i is called a* binding *for v_i. The substitution θ is called a* ground *substitution if every t_i is a ground term.*

Let E be a term [atom?] and θ a substitution for the variables of E. Then, $E\theta$ denotes the result of applying the substitution θ to E (i.e., of replacing each variable with its respective binding). For instance, if $E = p(x, y, f(a))$ and $\theta = \{x/b, y/x\}$, then $E\theta = p(b, x, f(a))$. If $\gamma = \{x/c\}$, then $E\gamma = p(c, y, f(a))$. Thus, variables that are not part of the substitution are left unchanged.

Definition 9.7 *Let $\theta = \{u_1/s_1, \ldots, u_m/s_m\}$ and $\delta = \{v_1/t_1, \ldots, v_n/t_n\}$ be substitutions. Then the composition $\theta\delta$ of θ and δ is the substitution obtained from the set*

$$\{u_1/s_1\delta, \ldots, u_m/s_m\delta, v_1/t_1, \ldots, v_n/t_n\}$$

by deleting any binding $u_i/s_i\delta$ for which $u_i = s_i\delta$ and deleting any binding v_j/t_j for which $v_j \in \{u_1, \ldots, u_m\}$.

i.e., v_j/t_j extends $\{u_1, \cdots, u_m\}$, not redefine $\{u_1, \cdots u_m\}$ for $v_j \notin \{u_1, \cdots u_m\}$, net result is just v_j/t_j for input v_j.

→ then given z, $(z\theta)\delta = z\,\delta = b$ $z(\theta\delta) = b$!

208   9. *IMPLEMENTATION OF RULES AND RECURSION*

how about $\theta = \{x/z\},\ \delta = \{z/b,\ b/c\} \Rightarrow \theta\delta = \{x/b, z/b, b/c\}$

For example, let $\theta = \{(x/f(y), y/z)\}$ and $\delta = \{x/a, y/b, z/y\}$. Then $\theta\delta = \{x/f(b), z/y\}$.

Definition 9.8 *A substitution θ is called a* unifier *for two terms A and B if $A\theta = B\theta$.*

Definition 9.9 *A unifier θ for these two terms is called a* most general unifier *(mgu), if for each other unifier γ, there exists a substitution δ such that $\gamma = \theta\delta$.*

For example, the two terms $p(f(x), a)$ and $p(y, f(w))$ are not unifiable because the second arguments cannot be unified.

The two terms $p(f(x), z)$ and $p(y, a)$ are unifiable, since $\delta = \{y/f(a), x/a, z/a)\}$ is a unifier. A most general unifier is $\theta = \{y/f(x), z/a\}$. Note that $\delta = \theta\{x/a\}$.

There exist efficient algorithms to perform unification; such algorithms either return a most general unifier or report that none exists.

9.4.2   SLD-Resolution

Consider a rule $r : A \leftarrow B_1, \ldots, B_n$, and a query goal $\leftarrow g$, where r and g have no variables in common (we can rename the variables of r to new distinct names to satisfy this requirement). If there exists an mgu δ that unifies A and g, then the *resolvent* of r and g is the goal list:

$$\leftarrow B_1\delta, \ldots, B_n\delta.$$

The following abstract algorithm describes the top-down proof process for a given program P and a goal list **G**.

Algorithm 9.10 *SLD-resolution*

    Input: *A first-order program P and a goal list* **G**.
    Output: *Either an instance* **G**δ *that was proved from P, or* failure.
begin *Set* Res $=$ **G**;
      While Res *is not empty, repeat the following:*
          Choose a goal g from Res;
          Choose a rule $A \leftarrow B_1, \ldots, B_n(n \geq 0)$ from P
               such that A and g unify under the mgu δ,
               (renaming the variables in the rule as needed);

> If no such rule exists, then
>   output failure and exit;
> else Delete g from Res;
> Add $B_1, \ldots, B_n$ to Res; ← *for ground rule, this "add" will*
> Apply δ to Res and **G**; *produce no more new goals*
> If Res is empty, then output $\mathbf{G}\delta$

end

Example 9.4 SLD-resolution on a program with unit clauses

$$s(X, Y) \leftarrow p(X, Y), q(Y).$$
$$p(X, 3).$$
$$q(3).$$
$$q(4).$$

Let us consider the top-down evaluation of the goal $?s(5, X)$ as applied to this program:

1. The initial goal list is

$$\leftarrow s(5, W)$$

2. We choose $s(5, W)$ as our goal and find that it unifies with the first rule under the substitution $\{X/5, Y/W\}$. The new goal list is

$$\leftarrow p(5, W), q(W)$$

3. This time, say that we choose $q(W)$ as a goal and find that it unifies with the fact $q(3)$, under the substitution $\{W/3\}$. (This goal also unifies with $q(4)$, under the substitution $\{W/4\}$, but say that we choose the first substitution). Then, the new goal list is

$$\leftarrow p(5, 3)$$

which unifies with the fact $p(X, 3)$ under the substitution $\{X/5\}$. At this point, the goal list becomes empty and we report success. Thus, a top-down evaluation returns the answer $\{W/3\}$ for the query $\leftarrow s(5, W)$ from the example program.

However, if in the last step above, we choose instead the fact $q(4)$, then under substitution $\{W/4\}$, we obtain the following goal list:

$$\leftarrow p(5, 4)$$

This new goal cannot unify with the head of any rule; thus SLD-resolution returns failure.

Therefore, at each step, SLD-resolution chooses nondeterministically

- a next goal from the goal list, and
- a next rule from those whose head unifies with the goal just selected.

Therefore, a single instance of an SLD-resolution can return either success or failure, depending on the choices made. However, say q is a predicate without bound arguments. Then we can consider all possible choices and collect the results returned by successful instances of SLD-resolution starting from the goal $\leftarrow q$. This is known as the *success set* for q; the union of the success sets for all the predicates in program P is equal to the least model of P. This ensures the theoretical equivalence of top-down semantics and bottom-up semantics.

The generation of the success set for a given predicate is possible (e.g., using breadth-first search); however, this is considered too inefficient for most practical applications. Thus, systems such as Prolog use depth-first exploration of alternatives, whereby goals are always chosen in a left-to-right order and the heads of the rules are also considered in the order they appear in the program. Then, the programmer is given responsibility for ordering the rules and their goals in such a fashion as to guide Prolog into successful and efficient searches. The programmer must also make sure that the procedure never falls into an infinite loop. For instance, say that our previous ancestor example is written as follows:

$$\mathrm{anc}(X, Z) \leftarrow \; \mathrm{anc}(X, Y), \mathrm{parent}(Y, Z).$$
$$\mathrm{anc}(X, Z) \leftarrow \; \mathrm{parent}(X, Y).$$

and that our goal is $?\mathrm{anc}(\mathrm{marc}, \mathrm{mary})$. By computing the resolvent of this goal with the head of the first rule, we obtain

$$?\mathrm{anc}(\mathrm{marc}, Y_1), \mathrm{parent}(Y_1, \mathrm{mary}).$$

By replacing the first goal with its resolvent with the head of the first rule, we obtain the following goals:

$$?\mathrm{anc}(\mathrm{marc}, Y_2), \mathrm{parent}(Y_2, Y_1), \mathrm{parent}(Y_1, \mathrm{mary}).$$

An additional resolution of the first goal with the first rule yields

$$?\mathrm{anc}(\mathrm{marc}, Y_3), \mathrm{anc}(Y_3, Y_2), \mathrm{parent}(Y_2, Y_1), \mathrm{parent}(Y_1, \mathrm{mary}).$$

Thus at each step we construct a longer and longer list, without ever returning a single result. When working with Prolog, however, the programmer is aware of the fact that the goals are visited from left to right, and the rule heads are searched in the same order as they are written. Thus, the programmer will list the rules and order the goals in the rules so as to avoid infinite loops. In our case, this means the exit rule is placed before the recursive one and the parent goal is placed before the recursive anc goal, yielding the following:

Example 9.5 Computing ancestors using Prolog

$$\text{anc}(X, Z) \leftarrow \text{parent}(X, Y).$$
$$\text{anc}(X, Z) \leftarrow \text{parent}(Y, Z), \text{anc}(X, Y).$$

In many cases, however, rule reordering does not ensure safety from infinite loops. Take, for instance, the nonlinear version of ancestor:

$$\text{anc}(X, Z) \leftarrow \text{parent}(X, Y).$$
$$\text{anc}(X, Z) \leftarrow \text{anc}(Y, Z), \text{anc}(X, Y).$$

This will first produce all the ancestors pairs; then it will enter a perpetual loop. (This is best seen by assuming that there is no parent fact. Then, the recurring failure of the first rule forces the second rule to call itself in an infinite loop.)

Even when the rules are properly written, as in Example 9.5, directed cycles in the underlying parent relation will cause infinite loops. In the particular case of our parent relation, cycles are not expected, although they might result from homonyms and corrupted data. But the same rules could also be used to compute the transitive closures of arbitrary graphs, which normally contain cycles.

Therefore, the bottom-up computation works in various situations where the top-down approach flounders in infinite loops. Indeed, the bottom-up operational semantics is normally more robust than the top-down semantics. However, the top-down approach is superior in certain respects—particularly with its ability to take advantage of constants and constraints that are part of the query goals to reduce the search space. This can be illustrated by the following example:

Example 9.6 Blood relations

$$\text{anc}(\text{Old}, \text{Young}) \leftarrow \text{parent}(\text{Old}, \text{Young}).$$
$$\text{anc}(\text{Old}, \text{Young}) \leftarrow \text{anc}(\text{Old}, \text{Mid}), \text{parent}(\text{Mid}, \text{Young}).$$
$$\text{grandma}(\text{Old}, \text{Young}) \leftarrow \text{parent}(\text{Mid}, \text{Young}), \text{mother}(\text{Old}, \text{Mid}).$$
$$\text{parent}(F, Cf) \leftarrow \text{father}(F, Cf).$$
$$\text{parent}(M, Cm) \leftarrow \text{mother}(M, Cm).$$

[Handwritten margin notes:]

left linear, so if ask anc(marc, Who), then can replace all rules with Old/marc: base case gets marc's children, recursive case gets marc's descendent step by step.

t! if ask anc(Who marc), we couldn't do that; we replace the 2nd argument of anc with marc; base case gives us marc's parent,

recursive rule goal #2 gives Mid = marc's parent, then ask for anc(Old, Mid), but it is not in anc database yet, so stuck, which is wrong.

In a query such as ?grandma(GM, marc), marc unifies with Young, which in turn unifies first with Cf and then with Cm. This results in the father relation being searched for tuples where the second component is marc—an efficient search if an index is available on this second column. If this search yields, say, tom, then this value is also passed to Mid, which is instantiated to tom. Thus, the goal mother(Old, tom) is now solved, and if, say, ann is the mother of tom, then the value GM = ann is returned. For the sake of discussion, say that several names are found when searching for the father of marc; then each of these names is passed to the goal mother, and new answers are generated for each new name (assuming that Prolog is in an all-answers mode). When no more such names are found, then the substitution M = marc is attempted, and the second parent rule is processed in similar fashion.

The passing of constants from the calling goals to the defining rules can also be used in the execution of some recursive predicates. For instance, say that in Example 9.6, we have a query ?anc(milton, SV). Then, milton must unify with the first argument in anc, through zero or more levels of recursive calls, until, via the exit rule, it is passed to the first argument of parent, and from there to the base relations.

Advanced deductive database systems mix the basic bottom-up and top-down techniques to combine their strengths. Some systems adopt Prolog's SLD-resolution extended with memorization to overcome various problems, such as those created by cycles in the database. Many systems keep the bottom-up, fixpoint-based computation, but then use special methods to achieve a top-down propagation of query constants similar to that described in this section. The next sections describe these methods, beginning with techniques used for nonrecursive predicates, and proceeding to those used for recursive predicates of increasing complexity.

9.5   Rule-Rewriting Methods

The grandma predicate can be computed using the following relational algebra expression:

$$GRANDMA = \pi_{\$3,\$2}((FATHER \cup MOTHER) \bowtie_{\$1=\$2} MOTHER)$$

which is the result of replacing selections on Cartesian products with equivalent joins in the RA expression produced by Algorithm 8.2. Then the answer to the query goal ?grandma(marc, GM) is $\sigma_{\$2=marc} GRANDMA$. But this approach is inefficient since it generates all pairs grandma/grand-child, even if most of them are later discarded by the selection $\sigma_{\$2=marc}$. A better approach is to transform the original RA expression by pushing selection into the expression as is currently done by query optimizers in relational databases. Then we obtain the equivalent expression:

$$\pi_{\$3,\$2}((\sigma_{\$2=marc}FATHER \cup \sigma_{\$2=marc}MOTHER) \bowtie_{\$1=\$2} MOTHER)$$

In the RA expression so obtained, only the parents of marc are selected from the base relations mother and father and processed through the rest of the expression. Moreover, since this selection produces a binary relation where all the entries in the second column are equal to marc, the projection $\pi_{\$1}$ could also be pushed into the expression along with selection.

The optimization performed here on relational algebra can be performed directly by specializing the original rules via an SLD-like pushing of the query constants downward (i.e., into the rules defining the goal predicate); this produces the following program, where we use the notation X/a to denote that X has been instantiated to a:

Example 9.7   Find the grandma of marc

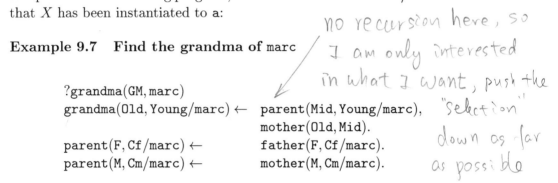

no recursion here, so I am only interested in what I want, push the "selection" down as far as possible

```
?grandma(GM, marc)
grandma(Old, Young/marc) ←    parent(Mid, Young/marc),
                              mother(Old, Mid).
parent(F, Cf/marc) ←          father(F, Cf/marc).
parent(M, Cm/marc) ←          mother(M, Cm/marc).
```

Thus, the second argument in the predicate parent is set equal to the constant marc.

9.5.1   Left-Linear and Right-Linear Recursion

If, in Example 9.6, we need to compute all the anc pairs, then a bottom-up approach provides a very effective computation for this recursive predicate. However, consider the situation where the goal contains some constant; for example, say that we have the query ?anc(tom, Desc). As in the case of nonrecursive rules, we want to avoid the wasteful approach of generating all the possible ancestor/person pairs, later to discard all those whose first component is not tom. For the recursive anc rule of Example 9.6, we can observe that the value of Old in the head is identical to that in the body; thus we can specialize our recursive predicate to anc(tom, _) throughout the fixpoint computation. Therefore, the anc rules can be specialized into those of Example 9.8, where constant tom has been pushed into the recursive predicate.[1]

Example 9.8   The descendants of tom

can be removed

```
?anc(tom, Desc).
anc(Old/tom, Young) ←  parent(Old/tom, Young).
anc(Old/tom, Young) ←  anc(Old/tom, Mid), parent(Mid, Young).
```

As previously discussed, Prolog performs this operation during execution. Most deductive databases prefer a compilation-oriented approach where the program is compiled for a *query form*, such as anc($Name, X). The dollar sign before Name denotes that this is a deferred constant, i.e., a parameter whose value will be given at execution time. Therefore, deferred constants are treated as a constant by the compiler, and the program of Example 9.8 is rewritten using $Name as the first argument of anc.

Transitive-closure-like computations can be expressed in several equivalent formulations; the simplest of these use recursive rules that are either left-linear or right-linear. The left-linear version of anc is that of Example 9.6. Consider now the right-linear formulation of ancestor:

Example 9.9   Right-linear rules for the descendants of tom

```
anc(Old, Young) ←  parent(Old, Young).
anc(Old, Young) ←  parent(Old, Mid), anc(Mid, Young).
```

With the right-linear rules of Example 9.9, the query ?anc($Name, X) can no longer be implemented by specializing the rules. (To prove that, say that we replace Old with the constant $Name = tom; then, the transitive closure cannot be computed using parent(tom, Mid), which only yields children of tom, while the grandchildren of tom and their children are also needed.)

While it is not possible to specialize the program of Example 9.9 for a query ?anc($Name, X), it is possible to transform it into an equivalent program for which such a specialization will work. Take, for instance, the right-linear program of Example 9.9; this can be transformed into the equivalent left-linear program of Example 9.6, on which the specialization approach can then be applied successfully. While recognizing the equivalence of programs is generally undecidable, many simple left-linear rules can be detected and

---

[1]As a further improvement, the constant first argument might also be dropped from the recursive predicate.

transformed into their equivalent right-linear counterparts. Symmetric conclusions follow for the left-linear program of Example 9.6, which, for a query such as ?anc(Y, $D), is transformed into its right-linear equivalent of Example 9.9. Techniques for perfoming such transformations will be discussed in Section 9.6.

After specialization, left-linear and right-linear rules can be be supported efficiently using a single fixpoint computation. However, more complex recursive rules require more sophisticated methods to exploit bindings in query goals. As we shall see in the next section, these methods generate a pair of fixpoint computations.

9.5.2 Magic Sets Method

To illustrate the basic idea behind magic sets, let us first consider the following example, consisting of two nonrecursive rules that return the names and addresses of senior students:

Example 9.10 **Find the graduating seniors and the addresses of their parents**

$$\text{snr\_par\_add(SN, PN, Paddr)} \leftarrow \text{senior(SN), parent(PN, SN),}$$
$$\text{address(PN, Paddr).}$$
$$\text{senior(SN)} \leftarrow \text{student(SN, \_, senior), graduating(SN).}$$

A bottom-up computation on the rules of Example 9.10 determines graduating seniors, their parents, and the parents' addresses in an efficient manner. But, say that we need to find the address of a particular parent, for example, the address of Mr. Joe Doe, who has just called complaining that he did not get his invitation to his daughter's graduation. Then, we might have the following query: ?snr_par_add (SN, 'Joe Doe', Addr). For this query, the first rule in Example 9.10 can be specialized by letting PN = 'Joe Doe'. Yet, using a strict bottom-up execution, the second rule still generates all names of graduating seniors and passes them up to the senior(SN) of the first rule. An optimization technique to overcome this problem uses an auxiliary "magic" relation computed as follows:

Example 9.11 **Find the children of Joe Doe, provided that they are graduating seniors**

$$\text{snr\_par\_add\_q('Joe Doe').}$$
$$\text{m.senior(SN)} \leftarrow \text{snr\_par\_add\_q(PN), parent(PN, SN).}$$

The fact snr_par_add_q('Joe Doe') stores the bound argument of the original query goal. This bound argument is used to compute a value of SN that is then passed to m.senior(SN) by the bottom-up rule in Example 9.11, emulating what the first rule in Example 9.10 would do in a top-down computation. We can now improve the second rule of Example 9.10 as follows:

Example 9.12   Restricting search via magic sets

$$senior(SN) \leftarrow m.senior(SN),$$
$$student(SN, \_, senior), graduating(SN).$$

Therefore, the bottom-up rules of Example 9.12 are designed to emulate the top-down computation where the binding is passed from SN in the head to the first goal of parent. This results in the instantiation of SN, which is then passed to the argument of senior.

The "magic sets" notion is very important for those recursive predicates that are not amenable to the specialization treatment used for left-linear and right-linear rules. For instance, the recursive rule in Example 9.13 is a linear rule that is neither left-linear nor right-linear.

Example 9.13   People are of the same generation if their parents are of the same generation

```
?sg(marc, Who).
sg(X, Y) ← parent(XP, X), sg(XP, YP), parent(YP, Y).
sg(A, A).
```

The recursive rule here states that X and Y are of the same generation if their respective parents XP and YP also are of the same generation. The exit rule sg(X, X) states that every element of the universe is of the same generation as itself. Obviously this rule is unsafe, and we cannot start a bottom-up computation from it. However, consider a top-down computation on these rules, assuming for simplicity that the fact parent(tom, marc) is in the database. Then, the resolvent of the query goal with the first rule is ← parent(XP, marc), sg(XP, YP), parent(YP, Y). Then, by unifying the first goal in this list with the fact parent(tom, marc), the new goal list becomes ← sg(tom, YP), parent(YP, Y). Thus, the binding was passed from the first argument in the head to the first argument of the recursive predicate in the body. Now, the recursive call unfolds as in the previous case, yielding the parents of tom, who are the grandparents of marc. In summary, the top-down computation generates all the ancestors of marc using the recursive rule. This computation causes the instantiation of variables X and XP, while Y and YP remain unbound. The basic idea of magic sets is to emulate this top-down binding passing using rules to be executed in a bottom-up fashion. Therefore, we can begin by restricting our attention to the bound arguments and use the following rule: $sg(X) \leftarrow parent(XP, X), sg(XP)$. Then, we observe that the top-down process where bindings are passed from X to XP through parent can be emulated by the bottom-up execution of the magic rule $m.sg(XP) \leftarrow m.sg(X), parent(XP, X)$; the rule is constructed from the last one by exchanging the head with the recursive goal (and adding the prefix "m."). Finally, as the exit rule for the magic predicate, we add the fact $m.sg(marc)$, where marc is the query constant.

In summary, the magic predicate m.sg is computed as shown by the first two rules in Example 9.14. Example 9.14 also shows how the original rules are rewritten with the addition of the magic goal m.sg to restrict the bottom-up computation.

Example 9.14   The magic sets method applied to Example 9.13

$$m.sg(marc).$$
$$m.sg(XP) \leftarrow \quad m.sg(X), parent(XP, X).$$
$$sg'(X, X) \leftarrow \quad m.sg(X).$$
$$sg'(X, Y) \leftarrow \quad parent(XP, X), sg'(XP, YP), parent(YP, Y), m.sg(X).$$
$$?sg'(marc, Z).$$

Observe that, in Example 9.14, the exit rule has become safe as a result of the magic sets rewriting, since only people who are ancestors of marc are considered by the transformed rules. Moreover, the magic goal in the recursive rule is useful in narrowing the search because it eliminates people who are not ancestors of marc.

Following our strict stratification approach, the fixpoint for the magic predicates will be computed before that of the modified rules. Thus, the magic sets method can be viewed as an emulation of the top-down computation through a cascade of two fixpoints, where each fixpoint is then computed efficiently using the differential fixpoint computation.

The fixpoint computation works well even when the graph representing parent is a directed acyclic graph (DAG) or contains directed cycles. In the case of a DAG, the same node and its successors are visited several times using SLD-resolution. This duplication is avoided by the fixpoint computation, since every new result is compared against those previously memorized. In the presence of directed cycles, SLD-resolution flounders in an infinite loop, while the magic sets method still works.

An additional virtue for the magic sets method is its robustness, since the method works well in the presence of multiple recursive rules and even nonlinear rules (provided that the binding passing property discussed in Section 9.6 holds).

One problem with the magic sets method is that the computation performed during the first fixpoint might be repeated during the second fixpoint. For the example at hand, for instance, the ancestors of marc are computed during the computation of ms.sg and revisited again as descendants of those ancestors in the computation of sg'. The counting method and the supplementary magic sets technique discussed next address this problem.

9.5.3   The Counting Method

The task of finding people who are of the same generation as marc can be reexpressed as that of finding the ancestors of marc and their levels, where marc is a zero-level ancestor of himself, his parents are first-generation (i.e., first-level) ancestors, his grandparents are second-generation ancestors, and so on. This computation is performed by the predicate sg_up in Example 9.15:

Example 9.15   Find ancestors of marc, and then their descendants

$$
\begin{aligned}
&\texttt{sg\_up}(0, \texttt{marc}).\\
&\texttt{sg\_up}(J+1, XP) \leftarrow \texttt{parent}(XP, X), \texttt{sg\_up}(J, X).\\
&\texttt{sg\_dwn}(J, X) \leftarrow \texttt{sg\_up}(J, X).\\
&\texttt{sg\_dwn}(J-1, Y) \leftarrow \texttt{sg\_dwn}(J, YP), \texttt{parent}(YP, Y).\\
&\texttt{sg\_dwn}(0, Z).
\end{aligned}
$$

Here, we have used sg_up to replace the top-down computation in the original example; thus, sg_up computes the ancestors of marc while increasing the level of ancestors. Then, the original exit rule (every person is of the same generation as himself) was used to switch to the computation of descendants. This computation is performed by sg_dwn, which also decreases the level counter at each application of the recursive rule. Once we return to level zero, we have a person who is of the same generation as marc, as per the modified query goal in Example 9.15. Here we have two fixpoint computations, where the second fixpoint does not duplicate the first computation, except for reversing the original counting of levels. It should be understood that, while the meaning of our same-generation example helps us to recognize the equivalence between the original program and the rewritten program, this equivalence nevertheless holds for all programs that obey the same patterns of bound arguments. As discussed in later sections, an analysis of patterns of bound arguments that occur during a top-down computation is performed by the compiler to decide the applicability of methods such as magic sets or counting, and to implement these methods by rewriting the original rules into modified rules that yield the same query results.

The counting method mimics the original top-down SLD-resolution to such an extent that it also shares some of its limitations. In particular, cycles in the database will throw the rewritten rules into a perpetual loop; in fact, if sg_up(J, XP) is true and XP is a node in the loop, then sg_up(J + K, XP), with K the length of the cycle, holds as well.

Another problem with counting is its limited robustness, since for more complex programs, the technique becomes inapplicable or requires several modifications. For instance, let us revise Example 9.13 by adding the goal XP ≠ YP to the recursive rule, to avoid the repeated derivation of people who are of the same generation as themselves. Then, the rules defining sg_up must be modified to memorize the values of XP, since these are needed in the second fixpoint. By contrast, the supplementary magic technique discussed next disregards the level information and instead relies on the systematic memorization of results from the first fixpoint, to avoid repeating the same computation during the second fixpoint.

9.5.4 Supplementary Magic Sets

In addition to the magic predicates, supplementary predicates are used to store the pairs bound-arguments-in-head/bound-arguments-in-recursive-goal produced during the first fixpoint. For instance, in Example 9.16, we compute spm.sg, which is then used during the second fixpoint computation, since the join of spm.sg with sg' in the recursive rule returns the memorized value of X for each new XP.

Example 9.16 **The supplementary magic method applied to Example 9.13**

```
m.sg(marc).
m.sg(XP) ←        m.sg(X), parent(XP, X).
spm.sg(X, XP) ←   parent(XP, X), m.sg(X).
sg'(X, X) ←       m.sg(X).
sg'(X, Y) ←       sg'(XP, YP), spm.sg(X, XP), parent(YP, Y).
?sg'(marc, Z).
```

The supplementary magic rules used in Example 9.16 are in a form that illustrates that this is a refinement of the basic magic sets method previously described, and in fact the two terms are often used as synonyms. Frequently, the magic predicate and the supplementary magic predicate are written in a mutually recursive form. Thus, for Example 9.16, we have the following rules:

Example 9.17   The magic and supplementary magic rules for 9.13

$$m.sg(marc).$$
$$spm.sg(X, XP) \leftarrow \quad m.sg(X), parent(XP, X)$$
$$m.sg(XP) \leftarrow \qquad spm.sg(X, XP).$$

To better understand how the method works, let us revise the previous example. Say that we only want to search up to k^{th} generations where the parents and their children lived in the same state. Then, we obtain the following program:

Example 9.18   People who are of the same generation through common ancestors who are less than 12 levels remote and always lived in the same state

$$?stsg(marc, 12, Z).$$
$$stsg(X, K, Y) \leftarrow \qquad parent(XP, X), K > 0, KP = K - 1,$$
$$born(X, St), born(XP, St),$$
$$stsg(XP, KP, YP),$$
$$parent(YP, Y).$$
$$stsg(X, K, X).$$

Given that the first two arguments of stsg are bound, the supplementary magic method yields:

Example 9.19   The supplementary magic method for Example 9.18

$$m.stsg(marc, 12).$$
$$spm.stsg(X, K, XP, KP) \leftarrow \quad m.stsg(X, K),$$
$$parent(XP, X), K > 0, KP = K - 1,$$
$$born(X, St), born(XP, St).$$
$$m.stsg(X, K) \leftarrow \qquad spm.stsg(X, K, XP, KP).$$

$$stsg(X, K, X) \qquad\qquad m.stsg(X, K).$$
$$stsg(X, K, Y) \leftarrow \qquad stsg(XP, KP, YP), spm.stsg(X, K, XP, KP),$$
$$parent(YP, Y).$$

As illustrated by this example, not all the bound arguments are memorized. Only those that are needed for the second fixpoint are stored in the supplementary magic relations. In our case, for instance, St is not included.

Because of its generality and robustness, the supplementary magic technique is often the method of choice in deductive databases. In fact, the method works well even when there are cycles in the underlying database. Moreover, the method entails more flexibility with arithmetic predicates. For instance, the expression KP = K − 1 is evaluated during the first fixpoint, where K is given and the pair (K, KP) is then memorized in the supplementary relations for use in the second fixpoint. However, with the basic magic sets method from the second fixpoint, K can only be computed from the values of KP taken from δstsg(XP, KP, YP), provided that the equation KP = K − 1 is first solved for K. Since this is a simple equation, solving it is a simple task for a compiler; however, solving more general equations might either be very difficult or impossible. An alternative approach consists in using the arithmetic equality as is, by taking each value of K from the magic set and computing K − 1. However, this computation would then be repeated with no change at each step of the second fixpoint computation. The use of supplementary magic predicates solves this problem in a uniform and general way since the pairs K, KP are stored during the first fixpoint and then used during the second fixpoint.

The supplementary magic method can be further generalized to deal with nonlinear rules, including nonlinear rules as discussed in the next section (see also Exercise 9.7).

9.6 Compilation and Optimization

Most deductive database systems combine bottom-up techniques with top-down execution. Take for instance the flat parts program shown in Example 9.3, and say that we want to print a list of part numbers followed by their weights using the following query: ?part_weight(Part, Weight). An execution plan for this query is displayed by the *rule-goal graph* of Figure 9.1.

The graph depicts a top-down, left-to-right execution, where all the possible unifications with rule heads are explored for each goal. The graph shows the names of the predicates with their bound/free *adornments* positioned as superscripts. Adornments are vectors of f or b characters. Thus, a kth character in the vector being equal to b or f denotes that the kth argument in the predicate is respectively bound or free. An argument in a predicate is said to be *bound* when all its variables are instantiated; otherwise the argument is said to be *free*, and denoted by f.

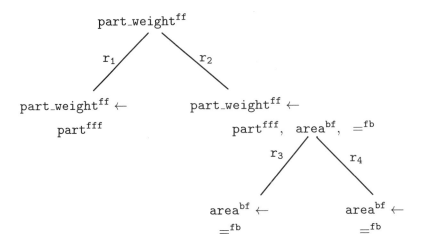

Figure 9.1: The rule-goal graph for Example 9.3

9.6.1   Nonrecursive Programs

The rule-goal graph for a program P is denoted $rgg(P)$. The rule-goal graph for a nonrecursive program is constructed as follows:

Algorithm 9.11 *Construction of the rule-goal graph $rgg(P)$ for a nonrecursive program P.*

1. *Initial step:* The query goal is adorned according to the constants and deferred constants (i.e., the variables preceded by \$), and becomes the root of $rgg(P)$.

2. *Bindings passing from goals to rule heads:* If the calling goal g unifies with the head of the rule r, with mgu γ, then we draw an edge (labeled with the name of the rule, i.e., r) from the adorned calling goal to the adorned head, where the adornments for $h(r)$ are computed as follows: (i) all arguments bound in g are marked bound in $h(r)\gamma$; (ii) all variables in such arguments are also marked bound; and (iii) the arguments in $h(r)\gamma$ that contain only constants or variables marked bound in (ii) are adorned b, while the others are adorned f.

   For instance, say that our goal is $g = p(f(X_1), Y_1, Z_1, a)$, and the head of r is $h(r) = p(X_2, g(X_2, Y_2), Y_2, W_2)$. (If g and $h(r)$ had variables in common, then a renaming step would be required here.) A most general unifier exists for the two: $\gamma = \{X_2/f(X_1), Y_1/g(f(X_1), Y_2), Z_1/Y_2, W_2/a\}$; thus, bindings might be passed from this goal to this

head in a top-down execution, and the resulting adornments of the
head must be computed.

The unified head is $h(r)\gamma = p(f(X_1), g(f(X_1), Y_2), Y_2, a)$. For instance,
say that the goal was adorned p^{bffb}; then variables in the first argument
of the head (i.e., X_1) are bound. The resulting adorned head is p^{bffb},
and there is an edge from p^{bffb} to $p^{bffb} \leftarrow$. But if the adorned goal is
p^{fbfb}, then all the variables in the second argument of the head (i.e.,
X_1, Y_2) are bound. Then the remaining arguments of the head are
bound as well. In this case, there is an edge from the adorned goal
p^{fbfb} to the adorned head $p^{bbbb} \leftarrow$.

3. *Left-to-right passing of bindings to goals:* A variable X is bound after
   the nth goal in a rule, if X is among the bound head variables (as for
   the last step), or if X appears in one of the goals of the rule preceding
   the nth goal.

   The $(n + 1)^{th}$ goal of the rule is adorned on the basis of the variables
   that are bound after the nth goal.

For simplicity of discussion, we assume that the rule-goal graph for a
nonrecursive program is a tree, such as that of Figure 9.1. Therefore, rather
than drawing multiple edges from different goals to the same adorned rule
head, we will duplicate the rule head to ensure that a tree is produced, rather
than a DAG.

The rule-goal graph determines the safety of the execution in a top-down
mode and yields an overall execution plan, under the simplifying assumption
that the execution of a goal binds all the variables in the goal. The safety
of the given program (including the bound query goal) follows from the fact
that certain adorned predicates are known to be safe a priori.

For instance, base predicates are safe for every adornment. Thus, `part`^{fff}
is safe. Equality and comparison predicates are treated as binary predicates.
The pattern θ^{bb} is safe for θ denoting any comparison operator, such as $\leq$ or
$>$. Moreover, there is the special case of $=^{bf}$ or $=^{fb}$ where the free argument
consists of only one variable; in either case the arithmetic expression in the
bound argument can be computed and the resulting value can be assigned
to the free variable.[2]

Then, we have the following definition of safety for a program whose
rule-goal graph is a tree:

---

[2]These represent basic cases that can be treated by any compiler. As previously indicated, a sophisticated compiler could treat an expression, such as $2 * X + 7 = 35$, as safe, if rewriting it as $X = (35 - 7)/2$ is within the capabilities of the compiler.

Definition 9.12 *Let P be a program with rule-goal graph $rgg(P)$, where $rgg(P)$ is a tree. Then P is safe if the following two conditions hold:*
  (i) Every leaf node of $rgg(P)$ is safe a priori, and
  (ii) every variable in every rule in $rgg(P)$ is bound after the last goal.

Given a safe $rgg(P)$, there is a simple execution plan to compute rules and predicates in the program. Basically, every goal with bound adornments generates two computation phases. In the first phase, the bound values of a goal's arguments are passed to its defining rules (its children in the rule-goal graph). In the second phase, the goal receives the values of the f-adorned arguments from its children. Only the second computation takes place for goals without bound arguments. Observe that the computation of the heads of the rules follows the computation of all the goals in the body. Thus, we have a strict stratification where predicates are computed according to the postorder traversal of the rule-goal graph.

Both phases of the computation can be performed by a relational algebra expression. For instance, the set of all instances of the bound arguments can be collected in a relation and passed down to base relations, possibly using the magic sets technique—resulting in the computation of semijoins against the base relations. In many implementations, however, each instance of bound arguments is passed down, one at a time, to the children, and then the computed values for the free arguments are streamed back to the goal.

9.6.2   Recursive Predicates

The treatment of recursive predicates is somewhat more complex because a choice of recursive methods must be performed along with the binding passing analysis.

The simplest case occurs when the goal calling a recursive predicate has no bound argument. In this case, the recursive predicate, say p, and all the predicates that are mutually recursive with it, will be computed in a single differential fixpoint. Then, we fall back into the treatment of rules for the nonrecursive case, where

1. step 3 of Algorithm 9.11 is performed assuming that rule heads have no bound argument

2. safety analysis is performed by treating the recursive goals (i.e., p and predicates mutually recursive with it) as safe a priori—in fact, they are bound to the values computed in the previous step.

When the calling goal has some bound arguments, then, a *binding passing analysis* is performed to decide which method should be used for the case at

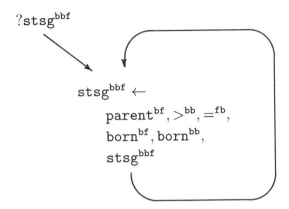

Figure 9.2: Binding passing analysis for the program of Example 9.19

hand. After this analysis, the program is rewritten according to the method selected.

Figure 9.2 illustrates how the binding passing analysis is performed on recursive rules. The binding passing from a goal to the recursive rule heads remains the same as that used for the nonrecursive case (step 2 in Algorithm 9.11). There are, however, (two) important differences. The first is that we allow cycles in the graph, to close the loop from a calling recursive goal to a matching adorned head already in the graph. The second difference is that the left-to-right binding passing analysis for recursive rules is more restrictive than that used at step 3 of Algorithm 9.11; only particular goals (called chain goals) can be used.

An adorned goal q^γ in a recursive rule r is called a *chain goal* when it satisfies the following conditions:

1. *SIP independence of recursive goals:* q is not a recursive goal (i.e., not the same predicate as that in the head of r, nor a predicate mutually recursive with q; however, recursive predicates of lower strata can be used as chain goals).

2. *Selectivity:* q^γ has some argument bound (according to the bound variables in the head of r and the chain goals to the left of q^γ).

3. *Safety:* q^γ is a safe goal.[3]

---

[3]If q is not a recursive predicate, then safety is defined above. If q is a recursive goal, then it belongs to a lower stratum; therefore, safety can be determined independently of the safety of q.

The basic idea behind the notion of chain goals is that the binding in the head will have to reduce the search space. Any goal that is called with all its adornment free will not be beneficial in that respect. Also, there is no sideway information passing (SIP) between two recursive goals; bindings come only from the head through nonrecursive goals.

The algorithm for adorning the recursive predicates and rules constructs a set of adorned goals $\mathbf{A}$ starting from the initial query goal (or a calling goal) q that has adornment γ, where γ contains some bound argument.

Algorithm 9.13 *Binding passing analysis for recursive predicates*

1. *Initially $\mathbf{A} = \{q^\gamma\}$, with q^γ the initial goal, where q is a recursive predicate and γ is not a totally free adornment.*

2. *For each $h \in \mathbf{A}$, pass the binding to the heads of rules defining q.*

3. *For each recursive rule, determine the adornments of its recursive goals (i.e., of q or predicates mutually recursive with q).*

4. *If the last step generated adornments not currently in $\mathbf{A}$, add them to $\mathbf{A}$ and resume from step 2. Otherwise halt.*

The calling goal g is said to have the *binding passing property* when $\mathbf{A}$ does not contain any recursive predicate with totally free adornment. In this case, we say that g has the *unique* binding passing property when $\mathbf{A}$ contains only one adornment for each recursive predicate.

When the binding passing property does not hold, then a totally free adornment occurs, and mutually recursive predicates must be computed as if the calling goal had no bound arguments. Otherwise, the methods described in the previous sections are applicable, and the recursive program is rewritten according to the method selected.

9.6.3 Selecting a Method for Recursion

For simplicity of discussion, we assume that the unique binding passing property holds and concentrate on the rewriting for the magic sets method, which can then be used as the basis for other methods.

Let $q^\gamma \in \mathbf{A}$, and r be a recursive rule defining q. Then, if the recursive rank of r is k, then there are k magic rules corresponding to r: one for each recursive goal in r. If p is one of these goals, then the head of the magic rule is named $m.p$, and has as arguments the arguments of p bound according to q^γ. The body of the magic rule consists of the following goals: the recursive goal $m.q$ with the bound arguments in q^γ, and the chain goals of r.

The (one and only) exit rule for all the magic predicates is actually the fact $m.g'$, where g' is obtained from the calling goal by eliminating its free arguments.

Finally, each original rule r is augmented with the addition of a magic goal as follows. Say that q is the head of r, $q^\gamma \in \mathbf{A}$, and q' is obtained from $h(r)$ by eliminating all the arguments that are free (i.e., denoted by an f in γ); then, $m.q'$ is the magic goal added to r.

The rewriting methods for supplementary magic predicates, and for the counting method, can be derived as simple modifications of the templates for magic sets. While the counting method is limited to the situation where we have only one recursive rule and this rule is linear, the other two methods are applicable whenever the binding passing property holds (see Exercise 9.7).

The magic sets method can also be used as the basis for detecting and handling the special cases of left-linear and right-linear rules. For instance, if we write the magic rules for Example 9.8, we obtain:

$$m.anc(tom).$$
$$m.anc(Old) \leftarrow m.anc(Old).$$

Obviously the recursive magic rule above is trivial and can be eliminated. Since the magic relation anc now contains only the value tom, rather than appending the magic predicate goal to the original rules, we can substitute this value directly into the rules. It is simple for a compiler to recognize the situation where the body and the head of the rule are identical, and then to eliminate the magic rule and perform the substitution.

Consider now the application of the magic sets method to Example 9.8. We obtain

$$m.anc(tom).$$
$$m.anc(Mid) \leftarrow parent(Old, Mid), m.anc(Old).$$
$$anc'(Old, Young) \leftarrow m.anc(Old), parent(Old, Young).$$
$$anc'(Old, Young) \leftarrow parent(Old, Mid), anc'(Mid, Young),$$
$$m.anc'(Old).$$
$$?anc'(tom, Young).$$

Observe that the recursive rule defining anc' here plays no useful role. In fact, the second argument of anc' (i.e., Young) is simply copied from the goal to the head of the recursive rule. Moreover, once this second argument is dropped, then this rule simply revisits the magic set computation leading back to tom. Thus, every value of Young produced by the exit rule satisfies the query. Once the redundant recursive rule is eliminated, we obtain the following program:

m.anc(tom).
m.anc(Mid) ←   m.anc(Old), parent(Old, Mid).
anc'(Old, Young) ←   m.anc(Old), parent(Old, Young).
?anc'(tom, Young).

In general, for the recursive rule to be dropped, the following two conditions must hold: (1) all the recursive goals in the recursive rule have been used as chain goals (during the binding passing analysis), and (2) the free arguments in the recursive goal are identical to those of the head. These are simple syntactic tests for a compiler to perform. Therefore, the transformation between right-linear recursion and left-linear recursion can be compiled as a special subcase of the magic sets method.

9.6.4   Optimization Strategies and Execution Plan

Several variations are possible in the overall compilation and optimization strategy described in the previous sections. For instance, the requirement of having the unique binding passing property can be relaxed easily (see Exercise 9.9). The supplementary magic method can also be generalized to allow the passing of bindings between recursive goals in the same rule; however, the transformed programs so produced can be complex and inefficient to execute.

A topic that requires further research is query optimization. Most relational databases follow the approach of estimating the query cost under all possible join orders and then selecting the plan with the least-cost estimate. This approach is not commonly used in deductive database prototypes because of its prohibitive cost for large programs and the difficulty of obtaining reliable estimates for recursive predicates. Therefore, many systems use instead simple heuristics to select an order of execution for the goals. For instance, to select the next goal, precedence is given to goals that have more bound arguments and fewer unbound arguments than the other goals.

In other systems, the order of goal execution is that in which they appear in the rule (i.e., the Prolog convention also followed in the rule-goal graph of Figure 9.1). This approach leaves the control of execution in the hands of the programmer, with all the advantages and disadvantages that follow. A promising middle ground consists of using the optimization techniques of relational systems for simple rules and queries on base predicates, while letting the programmer control the execution of more complex programs, or predicates more remote from the base predicates.

Although different systems often use a different mix of recursive methods, they normally follow the same general approach to method selection. Basically, the different techniques, each with its specific applicability preconditions, are ranked in order of desirability; the first applicable method in the list is then selected. Therefore, the binding passing property is tested first, and if this is satisfied, methods such as those for left-linear and right-linear recursion are tried first; then if these fail, methods such as magic sets and supplementary magic are tried next. Several other techniques have been proposed for recursion, and novel approaches and refinements are being proposed frequently—although it is often difficult to evaluate the comparative effectiveness of the different techniques.

An additional generalization that should be mentioned allows some arguments of a goal to remain uninstantiated after its execution. In this approach, variables not bound by the execution of the goal will need to be bound by later goals, or will be returned to the head of the rule, and then to the calling goal, as unbound variables.

In addition to the global techniques discussed above, various optimizations of a local and specialized nature can be performed on Datalog-like languages. One such technique consists in avoiding the generation of multiple bindings for existential variables, such as variables that occur only once in a rule. Techniques for performing intelligent backtracking have also been used; these can, for example, simulate multiway joins in a tuple-at-a-time execution model. Therefore, many of the local optimization techniques used are specific to the low-level execution model adopted by the system; this, in turn, depends on many factors, including whether the system is primarily designed for data residing on secondary storage or data already loaded in main memory. These alternatives have produced the assortment of techniques and design choices explored by current deductive database prototypes.

9.7 Recursive Queries in SQL

The new SQL3 standards include support for recursive queries. For instance, the BoM program of Example 8.15 is expressible in SQL3, using the view construct as follows:

Example 9.20 **Recursive views in SQL3**

```
CREATE RECURSIVE view all_subparts(Major, Minor) AS
    SELECT PART SUBPART
    FROM assembly
UNION
```

SELECT all.Major assb.SUBPART
FROM all_subparts all, assembly assb
WHERE all.Minor= assb.PART

The **SELECT** statement before **UNION** is obviously equivalent to the exit rule in Example 8.15, while the **SELECT** statement after **UNION** corresponds to the recursive rule. Therefore we will refer to them as *exit select* and *recursive select*, respectively.

Since all_subparts is a virtual view, an actual query on this view is needed to materialize the recursive relation or portions thereof. For instance, the query of Example 9.21 requests the materialization of the whole relation.

Example 9.21   Materialization of the view of Example 9.20

SELECT *
FROM all_subparts

The **WITH** construct provides another way, and a more direct one, to express recursion in SQL3. For instance, a query to find all the superparts using 'top_tube' can be expressed as follows:

Example 9.22   Find the parts using 'top_tube'

WITH RECURSIVE all_super(Major, Minor) **AS**
       (**SELECT** PART, SUBPART
       FROM assembly
       UNION
       SELECT assb.PART, all.Minor
       FROM assembly assb, all_super all
       WHERE assb.SUBPART = all.Major
)
SELECT *
WHERE Minor = 'top_tube'

9.7.1   Implementation of Recursive SQL Queries

The compilation techniques developed for Datalog apply directly to recursive SQL queries. For instance, the query of Example 9.21 on the view defined in Example 9.20 requires the materialization of the whole transitive closure, and can thus be implemented efficiently using the differential fixpoint Algorithm 9.5. Then, $T_E(S')$ and $T_R(S')$ are, respectively, computed from the exit select and the recursive select in Example 9.20. Here too, the computation of $T_R(S') - S'$ will be improved using the differential fixpoint technique. In fact, this step is simple to perform since there is only one recursive relation in the **FROM** clause of Example 9.20; therefore, this is a case of linear recursion. Thus, the recursive relation all_subparts in the **FROM** clause is replaced with δall_subparts, which contains new tuples generated in the previous iteration of Algorithm 9.5.

Consider now Example 9.22. This requires the passing of the condition Minor= 'top_tube' into the recursive SQL query defined using **WITH**. Now, the recursive select in Example 9.22 uses right-linear recursion, whereby the second argument of the recursive relation is copied unchanged by T_R. Thus, the condition Minor = 'top_tube' can simply be attached unchanged to the **WHERE** clause of the exit select and the recursive select, yielding the following equivalent SQL program:

Example 9.23   Specialization of the query of Example 9.22

    WITH RECURSIVE all_super(Major, Minor) **AS**
        (**SELECT** PART, SUBPART
            FROM assembly
            WHERE SUBPART = 'top_tube'
            UNION
            SELECT assb.PART, all.Minor
            FROM assembly assb, all_super all
            WHERE assb.SUBPART = all.Major
            AND all.Minor = 'top_tube'
)
    **SELECT *

However, say that the same query is expressed against the virtual view of Example 9.20, as follows:

    **SELECT *
    FROM all_subparts
    WHERE Minor = 'top_tube'

Since all_subparts is defined in Example 9.20 using left-linear recursion, the addition of the condition Minor = 'top_tube' to the recursive select would not produce an equivalent query. Instead, the SQL compiler must transform the original recursive select into its right-linear equivalent before the condition Minor = 'top_tube' can be attached to the **WHERE** clause. The compilation techniques usable for such transformations are basically those previously described for Datalog.

9.8   Bibliographic Notes

The notion of differential fixpoint based on the "derivatives" of set-valued operations was proposed in different contexts by [172, 330]. The use of the technique for improving naive fixpoint computation was studied by Bayer [47] and by Bancilhon, who coined the name "semi-naive" [28]. The idea of direct differentiation on the rules was introduced by Balbin [24], and the rewriting presented in this chapter is due to Saccà and Zaniolo [373].

The best-known algorithm for unification is due to Martelli and Montanari [277].

The magic sets technique was introduced by Bancilhon, Maier, Sagiv, and Ullman [29]; supplementary predicates were introduced by Saccà and Zaniolo [373]. The generalized magic sets method is credited to Beeri and Ramakrishnan [49]. The counting algorithm was proposed in [29] and generalized in [374]. Approaches to ensure that the counting method can deal with cycles are presented in [372, 203, 16, 194]. An evaluation of the counting method and other techniques is presented in [275].

Techniques for efficient support of recursion with a combination of top-down, bottom-up, and memoing have been the focus of a large body of research. Here we only mention the work by Henschen and Naqvi [212], the query-subquery approach by Vielle [449], and the approach based on the parsing technique called "Early Deduction" by Pereira and Warren [336]. A survey of early techniques was presented in [30].

The notion of "separable" recursion introduced by Naughton [303] includes left-linear rules, right-linear rules, and mixed left- and right-linear rules, which can be implemented by a single fixpoint. Similar recursive rules are also treated by Han [207], using the notion of chain queries. The simplified compilation presented here for left-linear and right-linear rules are based on the techniques presented in [194].

The NAIL! project introduced the use of rule-goal graph for compilation and the use of capture rules for optimization [296, 295]. Various optimization techniques for Datalog were also explored in [104, 348]. Techniques for safety analysis of bottom-up and top-down queries are discussed in [464, 347]. A more general notion of safety is discussed in [445].

Among the more influential prototypes of deductive databases, we can mention NAIL!/Glue [296, 338], LDL/LDL++ [105, 469], and CORAL [349, 350]. A more extensive overview of different systems can be found in [351].

Many novel applications of deductive databases have been discussed in the literature. An early overview was presented by Tsur [436], and a more recent book on the subject is [346].

The recursive extensions of SQL3, discussed here, are based on the proposal by Finkelstein, Mattos, Mumick, and Pirahesh [168].

9.9 Exercises

9.1. Use the `emp_all_mgrs(Eno, AllManagers)` relation of Exercise 8.12 to construct a combined list of managers for employees 'Joe Doe' and 'Tom Jones'. First write the rules to perform a bottom-up list append of the manager list for the first employee with that of second employee. Then refine this program to ensure that no duplicate manager is inserted in the list.

9.2. A better-known list append is the top-down one used in Prolog. Write (top-down) recursive rules to compute $app(L1, L2, L3)$, which appends two lists L1 and L2, giving L3.

9.3. Write Prolog and Datalog rules to generate all positive integers up to a given integer K—in ascending and descending order.

9.4. Write nonlinear Prolog rules to compute the first K Fibonacci numbers in a bottom-up fashion.

9.5. Write linear rules to compute efficiently the first K Fibonacci numbers in Prolog. Solve the same problem for Datalog.

9.6. Describe how the binding passing analysis will be performed on Exercise 9.2, and which compilation methods can be used. Transform the original programs according to compilation methods selected.

9.7. An arithmetic expression such as $y \times y + c$ might be parsed and represented internally as a complex term such as

$$plus(times(var(y), var(y)), cost(c)).$$

Write rules to perform a symbolic differentiation of such expressions. Thus our original query goal might be `?derivation($Expr, Derivt)`. If the previous expression is given as the first argument, the second argument returned should be

$$plus(plus(times(cost(1), var(y)), times(var(y), cost(1))), cost(0)).$$

Just give the basic top-down rules for addition and multiplication. The most direct formulation requires nonlinear rules that cannot be supported in Prolog; explain why.

9.8. Perform the binding analysis for Exercise 9.7, and show how this leads to the application of the magic sets method or supplementary magic technique. Rewrite the original programs according to both methods.

9.9. Explain how the magic sets and related methods are also applicable to programs that have the binding passing property, but not the unique binding passing property. Apply the magic sets method to the following example:

$$?\,\mathtt{sg(marc, Who)}.$$
$$\mathtt{sg(X, Y)} \leftarrow \qquad \mathtt{parent(XP, X), sg(YP, XP), parent(YP, Y)}.$$
$$\mathtt{sg(A, A)}.$$

Chapter 10

Database Updates and Nonmonotonic Reasoning

Two important problems have been left open in previous chapters. One is how to relax the restriction that negation and other nonmonotonic constructs can only appear in stratified programs, which represents a serious limitation in many practical applications. The other problem is that, so far, we have neglected the dynamic aspects of database systems, such as database updates and active database rules. In this chapter, we fill these lacunas and develop a unified approach to reasoning with nonmonotonic knowledge, nondeterministic constructs, database updates, active rules, and database histories.

10.1 Nonmonotonic Reasoning

The issue of nonmonotonic reasoning is a difficult problem that databases share with several other areas, including artificial intelligence, knowledge representation, and logic programming. Much previous research has focused on the problems of correct semantics and logical consistency. To address the efficiency and scalability requirements of databases, we will also stress issues such as computational complexity, expressive power, amenability to efficient implementation, and usability.

Negation represents the quintessential nonmonotonic construct; as we shall see later, issues regarding other nonmonotonic constructs, such as set aggregates or updates, can be reduced to issues regarding negation.

Most of the technical challenges posed by negation follow from the fact that information systems normally do not store negative information explicitly. Rather, they normally store only positive information, and negative information is derived implicitly via some form of default, such as the closed-world assumption. For instance, in our university database of Example 8.1, we see that only courses actually taken by students are stored. Thus, if for a certain student there is no "cs123" entry in the database, then the conclusion follows that the student has not taken the course.

Two different views of the world are possible.

- *Open world:* What is not part of the database or the program is assumed to be unknown.

- *Closed world:* What is not part of the database or the program is assumed to be false.

Databases and other information systems adopt the closed-world assumption (CWA). Thus, if p is a base predicate with n arguments, then the CWA prescribes that $\neg p(a_1, \ldots, a_n)$ holds iff $p(a_1, \ldots, a_n)$ is not true, that is, is not in the database. This assumption is natural and consistent, provided that a *unique name axiom* is also satisfied. The unique name assumption specifies that two constants in the database cannot stand for the same semantic object. According to the unique name assumption, for instance, the absence of coolguy('Clark Kent') from the database implies ¬coolguy('Clark Kent'), even though the database contains a fact coolguy('Superman'). This negative conclusion does not follow in a system that does not adopt the unique name assumption, and, for instance, treats 'Superman' and 'Clark Kent' as different references to the same underlying entity.[1]

As we shall see next, the extension of the CWA to programs where rules contain negation might lead to inconsistencies. The CWA for a positive program P is as follows:

Definition 10.1 *Let P be a positive program; then for each atom $a \in B_P$,*
  (i) a is true iff $a \in T_P^{\uparrow\omega}(\emptyset)$, and
  (ii) $\neg a$ is true iff $a \notin T_P^{\uparrow\omega}(\emptyset)$.

Definition 10.1 basically states that every conclusion derivable from the given program is true, and everything else is false. This definition is consistent when P is a positive program. However, contradictions may arise when P is a general program where rules are allowed to contain negated goals.

---

[1] Lois Lane's unique name assumption has provided the theme and romantic plot for many Superman movies. Also Herbrand interpretations follow this approach by letting constants represent themselves.

Consider for instance the classical paradox of the village where the barber shaves everyone who does not shave himself:

grou nd_m (P)

Example 10.1   Every villager who does not shave himself is shaved by the barber

shaves (miller, miller),
villager (miller),
villager (Smith),

```
                    shaves(barber,X) ←         villager(X),¬shaves(X,X).
shaves(barber, smith)  shaves(miller,miller).
shaves(miller,miller),  villager(miller).
villager(miller),      villager(smith).
villager(smith),?      villager(barber).
villager(smith).?
```

Model
shaves (barber, Smith),
shaves (miller, miller),
villager (miller),
villager (smith).?

shaves (b, b) ← villager (b), ¬shaves(b, b).
shaves (b, S) ← villager(S), ¬shave (S,S).
shaves (b, m) ← villager(m), ¬shave (m,m)

if not exist

There is no problem with villager(miller), who shaves himself, and therefore does not satisfy the body of the first rule. For villager(smith), given that shaves(smith, smith) is not in our program, we can assume that ¬shaves(smith, smith). Then, the body of the rule is satisfied, and the conclusion shaves(barber, smith) is reached. There is no problem with this conclusion, since it is consistent with all the negative assumptions previously made.

However, consider villager(barber). If we make the assumption that ¬shaves(barber, barber), the rule yields shaves(barber, barber), which directly contradicts the initial assumption. However, if we do not assume ¬shaves(barber, barber), then we cannot derive shaves(barber, barber) using this program. Therefore, by the CWA policy we must conclude that ¬shaves(barber, barber), which is again a contradiction. There is no way out of this paradox, and thus, there is no reasonable semantics for self-contradictory programs, such as that of Example 10.1, under the CWA. The *stable model semantics* discussed next characterizes programs that are free of such contradictions.

i.e., we have
to draw
conclusion
that
¬shave (b, b)

→ depends on interperation, or model in definition 10.3

Definition 10.2 (*Stability transformation*) *Let P be a program and $I \subseteq B_P$ be an interpretation of P. Then ground$_I$(P) denotes the program obtained from ground(P) by the following transformation, called the* stability transformation:

→ why ground

  1. *Remove every rule having as a goal some literal ¬q with $q \in I$.*
  2. *Remove all negated goals from the remaining rules.*

Example 10.2   A program $P = ground(P)$

→ Since there is no variable in P, P = ground (P)

i.e., ¬8, 9∈I, is false
¬9, 8∉I, is true.

$$p \leftarrow \neg q$$
$$q \leftarrow \neg p$$

For the program in Example 10.2, the stability transformation yields the following:

For $I = \emptyset$, $ground_I(P)$ is $p.$ $q.$

For $I = \{p\}$, $ground_I(P)$ is $p.$

For $I = \{p, q\}$, $ground_I(P)$ is the empty program.

given M, $\Rightarrow$ $ground_M(P)$, if still M $\Rightarrow$ stable Model

Definition 10.3 (*Stable models.*) *Let P be a program with model M. M is said to be a stable model for P when M is the least model of $ground_M(P)$.*

Observe that $ground_M(P)$ is a positive program, by construction. So, it has a least model that is equal to $T^{\uparrow \omega}(\emptyset)$, where T here denotes the immediate consequence operator of $ground_M(P)$.

Every stable model for P is a minimal model for P and a minimal fixpoint for T_P; however, minimal models or minimal fixpoints need not be stable models, as in the example that follows:

Example 10.3 $M = \{a\}$ **is the only model and fixpoint for this program**

$$r_1 : a \leftarrow \neg a.$$
$$r_2 : a \leftarrow a.$$

M is the only model and fixpoint for the program in Example 10.3. But $ground_M(P)$ contains only rule r_2; thus, its least model is the empty set, and M is not a stable model. *empty is not stable model either, empty is not model at all.*

A given program can have no stable model, a unique stable model, or multiple stable models. For instance, the program in Example 10.1 has no stable model, but it has a unique stable model after we eliminate the fact `villager(barber)`. The program of Example 10.3 has no stable model. The program of Example 10.2 has two stable models: $M_1 = \{p\}$ and $M_2 = \{q\}$. Thus there are two symmetric ways to give a logical meaning to this program: one where p is true and q is false, and the other where p is false and q is true. Since either solution can be accepted as the meaning of the program, we see that stable model semantics also brings the notion of nondeterminism to logic-based languages. This topic will be revisited in later sections.

The notion of stable models can be defined directly using a modified version of the immediate consequence operator (ICO) as follows: With r being a rule of P, let $h(r)$ denote the head of r, $gp(r)$ denote the set of positive goals of r, and $gn(r)$ denote the set of negated goals of r without their negation sign. For instance, if $r : a \leftarrow b, \neg c, \neg d.$, then $h(r) = a$, $gp(r) = \{b\}$, and $gn(r) = \{c, d\}$.

Definition 10.4 *Let P be a program and $I \subseteq B_P$. Then the explicit nega-tion ICO for P under a set of negative assumptions $N \subseteq B_P$ is defined as follows:*

$$\Gamma_{P(N)}(I) = \{h(r) \mid r \in ground(P), \ gp(r) \subseteq I, \ gn(r) \subseteq N\}$$

We will keep the notation T_P to denote the *implicit negation ICO* of P, defined as follows:

$$T_P(I) = \Gamma_{P(\bar{I})}(I), \ \text{where } \bar{I} = B_P - I$$

While Γ can also be viewed as a two-place function (on I and N), in the following theorem we view it as a function of I only, since N is kept constant (the proof of the theorem follows directly from the definitions):

Theorem 10.5 *Let P be a logic program with Herbrand base B_P and $\overline{M} = B_P - M$. Then, M is a stable model for P iff*

$$\Gamma_{P(\overline{M})}^{\uparrow\omega}(\emptyset) = M$$

Thus, Theorem 10.5 states that M is a stable model if it can be obtained as the ω-power of the explicit negation ICO, where the set of false atoms is kept constant and equal to the set of atoms not in M. This theorem can be used to check whether an interpretation I is a stable model without having first to construct $ground_P(I)$. Furthermore, the computation of the ω-power of the positive consequence operator has polynomial data complexity (see Exercise 10.1); thus, checking whether a given model is stable can be done in polynomial time. However, deciding whether a given program has a stable model is, in general, $\mathcal{NP}$-complete; thus, finding any such model is $\mathcal{NP}$-hard.

Therefore, much research work has been devoted to the issue of finding polynomial-time algorithms that compute stable models for classes of pro-grams of practical interest. The challenges posed by this problem can be appreciated by observing how techniques, such as SLD-resolution, that work well for positive programs run into difficulties when faced with programs with negation.

Prolog and other top-down systems use SLD-resolution with negation by failure (SLD-NF) for negative programs. In a nutshell, SLD-NF operates as follows: When presented with a goal $\neg g$, SLD-NF tries instead to prove g. Then, if g evaluates to true, $\neg g$ evaluates to false; however, if g evaluates to false, $\neg g$ evaluates to true. The answers returned by the SLD-resolution are correct in both these cases, but there is also the case where SLD-resolution flounders in an infinite loop, and then no answer is returned. Unfortunately, this case is common when the Herbrand universe is infinite and can also occur when the universe is finite. For instance, if the program consists of only one rule $p \leftarrow p$, then the query $?\neg p$ flounders in an infinite loop and SLD-NF never returns any answer. Since the least model of the program $p \leftarrow p$ is the empty set, $?\neg p$ should evaluate to true under the CWA. Therefore, this example illustrates how SLD-NF does not provide a complete implementation of the CWA even for simple positive programs. A similar problem occurs when a goal like $\neg$anc(marc, mary) is expressed against the program of Example 9.5. SLD-NF flounders if marc and mary are nodes in a directed cycle of a graph corresponding to the parent relation. Both these two queries, where SLD-NF fails, can be supported by the iterated fixpoint used in the bottom-up computation of stratified programs.

10.2   Stratification and Well-Founded Models

Stable model semantics is very powerful, and various nonmonotonic knowledge representation formalisms such as prioritized circumscription, default theory, and autoepistemic logic can be reduced to it.

But given the exponential complexity of computing a stable model, current research is seeking more restrictive classes of programs capable of expressing the intended applications while having stable models computable in polynomial time. In this chapter, we consider stratified and locally stratified programs, and the notion of well-founded models.

A stratified program has a stable model that can be computed using the iterated fixpoint computation (Algorithm 9.2). Furthermore, we will prove later that such a model is unique.

Theorem 10.6 *Let P be a stratified program. Then P has a stable model that is equal to the result of the iterated fixpoint procedure.*

Proof.   Let Σ be a stratification for P, and let M be the result of the iterated fixpoint on P according to Σ. Since the iterated fixpoint on $ground(P)$ according to Σ also yields M, let $r \in ground(P)$ be a rule used in the latter computation, where $h(r)$ belongs to a stratum i. If $\neg g$ is a goal of r, then the predicate name of g belongs to a stratum lower than i, and thus g cannot be generated by the iterated fixpoint computation of strata $\geq i$. Therefore, for each rule r used in the iterated fixpoint computation of $ground(P)$, $r' \in ground_M(P)$, where r' is the rule obtained from r by removing its negated goals. Therefore, the iterated fixpoint computation on the iterated fixpoint on $ground_M(P)$ according to Σ also yields M. Therefore, M is a stable model. $\square$

Since the class of stratified programs is too restrictive in many applications, we now turn to the problem of going beyond stratification and allowing the usage of negated goals that are mutually recursive with the head predicates.

10.2.1 Locally Stratified Programs

The notion of local stratification provides a generalization where atoms are stratified on the basis of their argument values, in addition to the names of their predicates.

Definition 10.7 *Local stratification. A program P is locally stratifiable iff B_P can be partitioned into a (possibly infinite) set of strata $S_0, S_1, \ldots,$ such that the following property holds: For each rule r in $ground(P)$ and each atom g in the body of r, if $h(r)$ and g are, respectively, in strata S_i and S_j, then*

(i) $i \geq j$ if $g \in pg(r)$, and

(ii) $i > j$ if $g \in ng(r)$.

Example 10.4   A locally stratified program defining integers

$$\text{even}(0).$$
$$\text{even}(\text{s}(J)) \leftarrow \neg\text{even}(J).$$

The program in Example 10.4 has an obvious local stratification, obtained by assigning $\text{even}(0)$ to S_0, $\text{even}(\text{s}(0))$ to S_1, and so on.

The program in Example 10.5 attempts an alternative definition of integers; this program is not locally stratified (see Exercise 10.6).

Example 10.5   A program that is not locally stratified

$$\text{even}(0).$$
$$\text{even}(J) \leftarrow \neg\text{even}(\text{s}(J)).$$

Theorem 10.8 *Every locally stratified program has a stable model that is equal to the result of the iterated fixpoint computation.*

The proof of this last theorem is the same as the proof of Theorem 10.6. This underscores the conceptual affinity existing between stratified programs and locally stratified programs. The two classes of programs, however, behave very differently when it comes to actual implementation. Indeed, a program P normally contains a relatively small number of predicate names. Thus, the verification that there is no strong component with negated arcs in $pdg(P)$ and the determination of the strata needed for the iterated fixpoint computation are easy to perform at compile-time. However, the question of whether a given program can be locally stratified is undecidable when the Herbrand base of the program is infinite. Even when the universe is finite, the existence of a stable model cannot be checked at compile-time, since it often depends on the database content. For instance, in Example 10.1, the existence of a stable model depends on whether villager(barber) is in the database.

predicate dependency graph

Much research work has been devoted to finding general approaches for the efficient computation of nonstratified programs. The concept of well-founded models represents a milestone in this effort.

10.2.2   Well-Founded Models

The basic equality $lfp(T_P) = T_P^{\uparrow\omega}$, which was the linchpin of the bottom-up computation, no longer holds in the presence of negation. One possible solution to this dilemma is to derive from T_P a new operator that is monotonic. This leads to the notion of alternating fixpoint and well-founded models, discussed next.

The operator $\Gamma_{P(N)}^{\uparrow\omega}(\emptyset)$ is monotonic in N. Thus

$$S_P(N) = B_P - \Gamma_{P(N)}^{\uparrow\omega}(\emptyset)$$

is antimonotonic in N (i.e., $S_P(N') \subseteq S_P(N)$ for $N' \supseteq N$). Therefore, the composition of an even number of applications of S_P yields a monotonic mapping, while the composition of an odd number of applications yields an antimonotonic mapping. In particular,

$$A_P(N) = S_P(S_P(N))$$

is monotonic in N. Thus, by Knaster-Tarski's theorem, A_P has a least fixpoint $lfp(A_P)$. Actually, A_P might have several fixpoints:

Lemma 10.9 *Let $(M, \overline{M})$ be a dichotomy of B_P. Then, M is a stable model for P iff $\overline{M}$ is a fixpoint for S_P. Also, every stable model for P is a fixpoint of A_P.*

Proof. By Theorem 10.5, M is a stable model for P iff $\Gamma_{P(\overline{M})}^{\uparrow\omega}(\emptyset) = M$. This equality holds iff $B_P - \Gamma_{P(\overline{M})}^{\uparrow\omega}(\emptyset) = B_P - M = \overline{M}$, i.e., iff $S_P(\overline{M}) = \overline{M}$. Finally, every fixpoint for S_P is also a fixpoint for A_P. $\qquad\square$

The least fixpoint $lfp(A_P)$ can be computed by (possibly transfinite) applications of A_P. Furthermore, every application of A_P in fact consists of two applications of S_P. Now, since $A_P^{\uparrow n-1}(\emptyset) \subseteq A_P^{\uparrow n}(\emptyset)$, the even powers of S_P

$$A_P^{\uparrow n}(\emptyset) = S_P^{\uparrow 2 \times n}(\emptyset)$$

define an ascending chain. The odd powers of S_P

$$S_P(A_P^{\uparrow n}(\emptyset)) = S_P^{\uparrow 2 \times n+1}(\emptyset)$$

define a descending chain. Furthermore, it is easy to show that every element of the descending chain is $\supseteq$ than every element of the ascending chain. Thus we have an increasing chain of underestimates dominated by a decreasing chain of overestimates. If the two chains ever meet,[2] they define the (total) well-founded model[3] for P.

Definition 10.10 *Well-founded model. Let P be a program and W be the least fixpoint for A_P. If $S_P(W) = W$, then $B_P - W$ is called the* well-founded *model for P.*

$B_P - S_P(\overline{M}) = B_P - \overline{M} = M$. But $B_P - S_P(\overline{M}) = \Gamma_{P(\overline{M})}^{\uparrow\omega}(\emptyset)$.

Theorem 10.11 *Let P be a program with well-founded model M. Then M is a stable model for P, and P has no other stable model.*

Proof. The fact that M is a stable model was proven in Lemma 10.9. Now, by the same lemma, if N is another stable model, then $\overline{N}$ is also a fixpoint for A_P; in fact, $\overline{N} \supseteq \overline{M}$, since $\overline{M}$ is the least fixpoint of A_P. Thus, $N \subseteq M$; but, $N \subset M$ cannot hold, since M is a stable model, and every stable model is a minimal model. Thus $N = M$. $\qquad\square$

The computation of $A_P^{\uparrow\omega}(\emptyset)$ is called the *alternating fixpoint computation*. The alternating fixpoint computation for the program of Example 10.2 is shown in Example 10.6.

---

[2]Including the situation where they meet beyond the first infinite ordinal.

[3]The term *well-founded model* is often used to denote the *partial well-founded model*, defined as having as negated atoms $M^- = lfp(A_P)$ and positive atoms $M^+ = B_P - S_P(M^-)$; thus, the atoms in $B_P - (M^+ \cup M^-)$ are undefined in the partial well-founded model, while this set is empty in the total well-founded model.

Example 10.6   **The alternating fixpoint computation for Example 10.2**

$$S_P(\emptyset) = \{p, q\}$$

$$A_P(\emptyset) = S_P(S_P(\emptyset)) = S_P(\{p, q\}) = \emptyset$$

Then, the situation repeats itself, yielding

$$A_P^{\uparrow k}(\emptyset) = A_P(\emptyset) \subset S_P(A_P^{\uparrow k}(\emptyset))$$

Since the overestimate and underestimate never converge, this program does not have a (total) well-founded model.

Indeed, Example 10.2 has two stable models; thus, by Theorem 10.11, it cannot have a well-founded model.

Stratified and locally stratified programs always have a well-founded model (and therefore a unique stable model) that can be computed using the alternating fixpoint procedure:

Theorem 10.12 *Let P be a program that is stratified or locally stratified. Then P has a well-founded model.*

Proof (Sketch). If P is a program that is stratified or locally stratified, then the alternating fixpoint procedure emulates the stratified fixpoint procedure.

□

While the notion of a well-founded model is significant from a conceptual viewpoint, it does not provide a simple syntactic criterion that the programmer can follow (and the compiler can exploit) when using negation in recursive rules, so as to ensure that the final program has a clear semantics. The objective of achieving local stratification through the syntactic structure of the rules can be obtained using Datalog$_{1S}$.

10.3   Datalog$_{1S}$ and Temporal Reasoning

In Datalog$_{1S}$, predicates have a distinguished argument, called the *temporal argument*, where values are assumed to be taken from a discrete temporal domain. The discrete temporal domain consists of terms built using the constant 0 and the unary function symbol +1 (written in postfix notation). For the sake of simplicity, we will write n for

$$(\ldots((0 \overbrace{+1) + 1)\ldots + 1}^{n \ times})$$

Also, if T is a variable in the temporal domain, then T, $T+1$, and $T+n$ are valid temporal terms, where $T+n$ is again a shorthand for

$$\overbrace{(\dots((T+1)+1)\dots+1)}^{n\ times}$$

The following Datalog program models the succession of seasons:

Example 10.7   The endless succession of seasons

```
quarter(0, winter).
quarter(T + 1, spring) ←   quarter(T, winter).
quarter(T + 1, summer) ←   quarter(T, spring).
quarter(T + 1, fall) ←     quarter(T, summer).
quarter(T + 1, winter) ←   quarter(T, fall).
```

Therefore, Datalog₁S provides a natural formalism for modeling events and history that occur in a discrete time domain (i.e., a domain isomorphic to integers). The granularity of time used, however, depends on the application. In the previous example, the basic time granule was a season. In the next example, which lists the daily schedule of trains to Newcastle, time granules are hours.

Trains for Newcastle leave every two hours, starting at 8:00 AM and ending at 10:00 PM (last train of the day). Here we use midnight as our initial time, and use hours as our time granules. Then we have the following daily schedule:

Example 10.8   Trains for Newcastle leave daily at 800 hours and then every two hours until 2200 hours (military time)

```
before22(22).
before22(H) ←     before22(H + 1).
leaves(8, newcastle).
leaves(T + 2, newcastle) ←   leaves(T, newcastle),
                             before22(T).
```

Thus the query ?leaves(When, newcastle) will generate the daily departure schedule for Newcastle.

This example also illustrates how Datalog₁S models the notion of before 10 PM (2200 hours in military time), and after 8 AM.

So Datalog1S program could be not Stratifiable.

Datalog$_{1S}$ is standard Datalog, to which a particular temporal interpretation is attached. In fact, we have already encountered Datalog$_{1S}$ programs. For instance, the programs in Examples 10.4 and 10.5 are Datalog$_{1S}$ programs where $s(J)$ is used instead of $J+1$ to model the notion of successor (actually the name Datalog$_{1S}$ originated from this alternate notation). Also the programs in Example 9.15 are Datalog$_{1S}$, since the pairs $J-1$ and J in the counting rules can be replaced by I and $I+1$ without changing their meaning.

Remarkably, Datalog$_{1S}$ represents as powerful a language for temporal reasoning as special-purpose temporal languages with modal operators. Take for instance Propositional Linear Temporal Logic (PLTL).

PLTL is based on the notion that there is a succession of states $H = (S_0, S_1, \ldots)$, called a *history*. Then, modal operators are used to define in which states a predicate p holds true.

For instance, the previous example of trains to Newcastle can be modeled by a predicate *newcstl* that holds true in the following states: $S_8, S_{10},$ $S_{12}, S_{14}, S_{16}, S_{18}, S_{20}, S_{22}$, and it is false everywhere else.

Then temporal predicates that hold in H are defined as follows:

1. *Atoms:* Let p be an atomic propositional predicate. Then p is said to hold in history H when p holds in H's initial state S_0.

In addition to the usual propositional operators $\vee, \wedge,$ and $\neg$, PLTL offers the following operators:

2. *Next:* Next p, denoted $\bigcirc p$, is true in history H, when p holds in history $H_1 = (S_1, S_2, \ldots)$.

   Therefore, $\bigcirc^n p$, $n \geq 0$, denotes that p is true in history $(S_n, S_{n+1}, \ldots)$.

3. *Eventually:* Eventually q, denoted $\mathcal{F}q$, holds when, for some n, $\bigcirc^n q$.

4. *Until:* p until q, denoted $p \, \mathcal{U} \, q$, holds if, for some n, $\bigcirc^n q$, and for every state $k < n$, $\bigcirc^k p$.

Other important operators can be derived from these. For instance, the fact that q will never be true can simply be defined as $\neg \mathcal{F}q$; the fact that q is always true is simply described as $\neg \mathcal{F}(\neg q))$; the notation $\mathcal{G}q$ is often used to denote that q is always true.

The operator p before q, denoted $p\mathcal{B}q$ can be defined as $\neg((\neg p) \, \mathcal{U} \, q)$— that is, it is not true that p is false until q.

PLTL finds many applications, including temporal queries and proving properties of dynamic systems. For instance, the question "Is there a train to Newcastle that is followed by another one hour later?" can be expressed by the following query:

$$?\mathcal{F}(newcstl \wedge \bigcirc newcstl)$$

Every query expressed in PLTL can also be expressed in propositional Datalog$_{1S}$ (i.e., Datalog with only the temporal argument). For instance, the previous query can be turned into the query ?`pair_to_newcstl` where

$$\texttt{pair\_to\_newcstl} \leftarrow \texttt{newcstl}(J) \wedge \texttt{newcstl}(J+1).$$

Therefore, the interpretation "for some J" assigned to the temporal argument J of a Datalog$_{1S}$ predicate is sufficient to model the operator $\mathcal{F}$ of PLTL, while $\bigcirc$ is now emulated by $+1$.

The translation of the other operators, however, is more complex. Say, for instance, that we want to model $p \, \mathcal{U} \, q$. By the definition, p must be true at each instant in history, until the first state in which q is true.

Example 10.9 $p \, \mathcal{U} \, q$ **in Datalog$_{1S}$**

$$
\begin{aligned}
\texttt{post\_q}(J+1) &\leftarrow & \texttt{q}(J). \\
\texttt{post\_q}(J+1) &\leftarrow & \texttt{post\_q}(J). \\
\texttt{first\_q}(J) &\leftarrow & \texttt{q}(J), \neg\texttt{post\_q}(J). \\[4pt]
\texttt{pre\_first\_q}(J) &\leftarrow & \texttt{first\_q}(J+1). \\
\texttt{pre\_first\_q}(J) &\leftarrow & \texttt{pre\_first\_q}(J+1). \\[4pt]
\texttt{fail\_p\_Until\_q} &\leftarrow & \texttt{pre\_first\_q}(J), \neg\texttt{p}(J). \\
\texttt{p\_Until\_q} &\leftarrow & \texttt{pre\_q}(0), \neg\texttt{fail\_p\_Until\_q}.
\end{aligned}
$$

Therefore, we used recursion to reason back in time and identify all states in history that precede the first occurrence of q. Then, $p \, \mathcal{U} \, q$ was defined using double negation, yielding a program with stratified negation (although this is not necessary; see Exercise 10.8). A similar approach can be used to express other operators of temporal logic. For instance, $p \, \mathcal{B} \, q$ can be defined using the predicates in Example 10.9 and the rule

$$\texttt{p\_Before\_q} \leftarrow \texttt{p}(J), \texttt{pre\_first\_q}(J).$$

10.4 XY-Stratification

The main practical limitation of semantics based on concepts such as well-founded models is that there is no simple way to decide whether a program obeys such a semantics, short of executing the program. This is in sharp contrast with the concept of stratified negation, where a predicate dependency graph free of cycles provides a simple criterion for the programmer to follow in writing the program, and for the compiler to check and use in validating and optimizing the execution of the program. We will next discuss a particular mixture of Datalog$_{1S}$ and stratification that has great expressive power but preserves much of the simplicity of stratified programs.

For instance, the ancestors of marc, and the number of generations that separates them from marc, can be computed using the following program, which also includes the differential fixpoint improvement:

Example 10.10   Ancestors of marc and the generation gap including the differential fixpoint improvement

$$r_1 : \text{delta\_anc}(0, \text{marc}).$$
$$r_2 : \text{delta\_anc}(J + 1, Y) \leftarrow \text{delta\_anc}(J, X), \text{parent}(Y, X),$$
$$\neg \text{all\_anc}(J, Y).$$
$$r_3 : \text{all\_anc}(J + 1, X) \leftarrow \text{all\_anc}(J, X).$$
$$r_4 : \text{all\_anc}(J, X) \leftarrow \text{delta\_anc}(J, X).$$

This program is locally stratified by the first argument in anc that serves as temporal argument. The zeroth stratum consists of atoms of nonrecursive predicates such as parent and of atoms that unify with all_anc(0, X) or delta_anc(0, X), where X can be any constant in the universe. The kth stratum consists of atoms of the form all_anc(k, X), delta_anc(k, X). Thus, this program is locally stratified, since the heads of recursive rules belong to strata that are one above those of their goals. Also observe that the program of Example 10.4 has this property, while the program of Example 10.5 does not.

So far, we have studied the case where all recursive atoms with the same temporal argument belong to the same stratum. This structure can be generalized by partitioning atoms with the same temporal argument into multiple substrata. For instance, in Example 10.10, a strict stratification would place delta_anc(k, X) in a stratum lower than all_anc(k, X). In fact, if the goal ¬delta_anc(J + 1, X) is added to the third rule (this will not change the meaning of the program), having the former atoms in a lower stratum becomes necessary to preserve local stratification.

From these examples, therefore, we can now describe the syntactic structure of our programs as follows:

Definition 10.13 *XY-programs. Let P be a set of rules defining mutually recursive predicates. Then we say that P is an XY-program if it satisfies the following conditions:*

1. *Every recursive predicate of P has a distinguished temporal argument.*

2. *Every recursive rule r is either an X-rule or a Y-rule, where*

   - *r is an X-rule when the temporal argument in every recursive predicate in r is the same variable (e.g., J),*
   - *r is a Y-rule when (i) the head of r has as temporal argument J + 1, where J denotes any variable, (ii) some goal of r has as temporal argument J, and (iii) the remaining recursive goals have either J or J + 1 as their temporal arguments.*

For instance, the program in Example 10.10 is an XY-program where r_4 is an X-rule while r_2 and r_3 are Y-rules.

Therefore, exit rules establish initial values for the temporal argument; then the X-rules are used for reasoning within the same state (i.e., the same value of temporal argument) while the Y-rules are used for reasoning from one state to the successor state.

There is a simple test to decide whether an XY-program P is locally stratified. The test begins by labeling the recursive predicates in P to yield the *bi-state program* P_{bis}, computed as follows: For each $r \in P$,

1. Rename all the recursive predicates in **r** that have the same temporal argument as the head of r with the distinguished prefix new_ .

2. Rename all other occurrences of recursive predicates in **r** with the distinguished prefix old_.

3. Drop the temporal arguments from the recursive predicates.

For instance, the bi-state version for the program in Example 10.10 is as follows:

Example 10.11   The bi-state version of the program in Example 10.10

```
new_delta_anc(marc).
new_delta_anc(Y) ←    old_delta_anc(X), parent(Y, X),
                      ¬old_all_anc(Y).
new_all_anc(X) ←      new_delta_anc(X).
new_all_anc(X) ←      old_all_anc(X).
```

Definition 10.14 *Let P be an XY-program. P is said to be XY-stratified when P_{bis} is a stratified program.*

The program of Example 10.11 is stratified with the following strata: $S_0 = \{\texttt{parent}, \texttt{old\_all\_anc}, \texttt{old\_delta\_anc}\}$, $S_1 = \{\texttt{new\_delta\_anc}\}$, and $S_2 = \{\texttt{new\_all\_anc}\}$. Thus, the program in Example 10.10 is locally stratified.

Theorem 10.15 *Let P be an XY-stratified program. Then P is locally stratified.*

Proof.   Let Σ be a stratification of P_{bis} in $n + 1$ strata numbered from 0 to n, where we can assume, without loss of generality, that if p is a recursive predicate, then old_p along with every nonrecursive predicate belongs to stratum 0. Then, a local stratification for P can be constructed by assigning every recursive atom with predicate name, say, q, to the stratum $j \times n + k$, where k is the stratum of Σ to which new_q belongs and j is the temporal argument in q. Nonrecursive predicates are assigned to stratum 0. Then, by construction, the head of every rule $r \in ground(P)$ belongs to a stratum that is higher than the strata containing positive goals of r and strictly higher than the strata containing negated goals of r.   □

Thus, the program of Example 10.10 is locally stratified with strata

$$
\begin{aligned}
S_0 &= \{\texttt{parent}\} \\
S_1 &= \{\texttt{delta\_anc}(0, \ldots)\} \\
S_2 &= \{\texttt{all\_anc}(0, \ldots)\} \\
S_3 &= \{\texttt{delta\_anc}(1, \ldots)\} \\
S_4 &= \{\texttt{all\_anc}(1, \ldots)\}
\end{aligned}
$$

$$\cdots$$

$$
\begin{aligned}
S_{j \times 2 + 1} &= \{\texttt{delta\_anc}(\texttt{j}, \ldots)\} \\
S_{j \times 2 + 2} &= \{\texttt{all\_anc}(\texttt{j}, \ldots)\}
\end{aligned}
$$

For an XY-stratified program P, the iterated fixpoint of Algorithm 9.2 becomes quite simple; basically it reduces to a repeated computation over the stratified program P_{bis}. However, since the temporal arguments have been removed from this program, we need to (1) store the temporal argument as an external fact $\texttt{counter}(\texttt{T})$, and (2) add a new goal $\texttt{counter}(\texttt{I}_r)$ to each exit rule r in P_{bis}, where $\texttt{I}_r$ is the temporal argument in the original rule r. The program so constructed will be called the *synchronized* version of P_{bis}.

For instance, to obtain the synchronized version of the program in Example 10.11, we need to change the first rule to

$$\texttt{new\_delta\_anc(marc)} \leftarrow \texttt{counter(0)}.$$

since the temporal argument in the original exit rule was the constant 0.

Then, the iterated fixpoint computation for an XY-stratified program can be implemented by the following procedure:

Procedure 10.16 *Computing the well-founded model of an XY-stratified program P*

> **Inititialize***: Set $T = 0$ and insert the fact* `counter(T)`.

> **Forever repeat the following two steps:**

> > 1. *Apply the iterated fixpoint computation to the synchronized program P_{bis}, and for each recursive predicate* q, *compute* new_q. *Return the* new_q *atoms so computed, after adding a temporal argument* T *to these atoms; the value of* T *is taken from* `counter(T)`.

> > 2. *For each recursive predicate* q, *replace* old_q *with* new_q, *computed in the previous step. Then, replace* `counter(T)` *with* `counter(T + 1)`.

Thus, for Example 10.10, the goal `counter(0)` ensures that the exit rule only fires once immediately after the initialization step. However, we might have exit rules where the temporal argument is a constant greater than zero, or even is not a constant, and then the exit rules might produce results at later steps, too.

For the program in Example 10.4, Procedure 10.16 cannot terminate since it must compute all integers. However, for practical applications we need to have simple sufficient conditions that allow us to stop the computation. An effective condition can be formulated as follows: For each rule, there is at least one positive goal that cannot be satisfied for any value of its variables. Then, the following two conditions need to be checked: (i) the exit rules cannot produce any new values for values of T greater than the current one, and (ii) for each recursive rule, there is a positive goal, say, q, for which no new_q atoms were obtained at the last step. For Example 10.10, condition (i) is satisfied since the temporal argument is a constant; however, the third rule forever fails condition (ii), causing an infinite computation. Thus, the programmer should add the goal delta_anc(J, _) to this rule. Once no new arcs are found, then because of the negated goal in the second rule, there is no new_delta_anc(J, _) atom and the computation stops.

The computation of Procedure 10.16 can be made very efficient by some simple improvements. The first improvement consists in observing that the replacement of old_q with new_q described in the last step of the procedure can become a zero-cost operation if properly implemented (e.g., by switching the reference pointers to the two relations). A second improvement concerns copy rules such as the last rule in Example 10.10. Observe that the body and the head of this rule are identical, except for the prefixes new or old, in its bi-state version (Example 10.11). Thus, in order to compute new_all_anc, we first execute the copy rule by simply setting the pointer to new_all_anc to point to old_all_anc—a zero-cost operation. The third rule is executed after that, since it can add tuples to new_all_anc.

In the next example, we use XY-stratified programs to compute temporal projections. Say, for instance, that we have a temporal relation as follows: emp_dep_sal (Eno, Dept, Sal, From, To). Now, say that

$$emp\_dep\_sal(1001, shoe, 35000, 19920101, 19940101).$$
$$emp\_dep\_sal(1001, shoe, 36500, 19940101, 19960101).$$

represent two tuples from this relation. The first fact denotes that employee with Eno = 1001 has kept the same salary ($35,000) and department (shoe) from 1992/01/01 (year/month/day) till 1994/01/01.[4] According to the second fact, this employee, still in the shoe department, then received a salary of $36,500 from 1994/01/01 till 1996/01/01. If we now project out the salary and department information, these two intervals must be merged together. In this example, we have intervals overlapping over their endpoints. In more general situations, where a temporal projection eliminates some key attributes, we might have intervals overlapping each other over several time granules.

Thus, we use the program of Example 10.12, which iterates over two basic computation steps. The first step is defined by the overlap rule. This determines pairs of distinct overlapping intervals, where the first interval precedes (i.e., contains the start) of the second interval. The second step consists of deriving a new interval that begins at the start of the first interval, and ends at the later of the two endpoints. Finally, there is a copy rule that copies those intervals that do not overlap other intervals.

---

[4] In a Datalog system that supports the temporal data types discussed in Part II, those should be used instead of this crude representation.

This example uses the auxiliary predicates `distinct` and `select_larger`. The first verifies that two intervals are not the same interval. The second selects the larger of a pair of values. The program P of Example 10.12 is XY-stratified since the nodes of P_{bis} can be sorted into the following strata $\sigma_0 = \{\text{distinct}, \text{select\_larger}, \text{old\_overlap}, \text{old\_e\_hist}\}$, $\sigma_1 = \{\text{new\_overlap}\}$, $\sigma_2 = \{\text{new\_e\_hist}\}$.

Example 10.12 **Merging overlapping periods into maximal periods after a temporal projection**

$$\text{e\_hist}(0, \text{Eno}, \text{Frm}, \text{To}) \leftarrow \quad \text{emp\_dep\_sal}(\emptyset, \text{Eno}, \text{D}, \text{S}, \text{Frm}, \text{To}).$$

$$\text{overlap}(\text{J} + 1, \text{Eno}, \text{Frm1}, \text{To1}, \text{Frm2}, \text{To2}) \leftarrow$$
$$\text{e\_hist}(\text{J}, \text{Eno}, \text{Frm1}, \text{To1}),$$
$$\text{e\_hist}(\text{J}, \text{Eno}, \text{Frm2}, \text{To2}),$$
$$\text{Frm1} \leq \text{Frm2}, \text{Frm2} \leq \text{To1},$$
$$\text{distinct}(\text{Frm1}, \text{To1}, \text{Frm2}, \text{To2}).$$

$$\text{e\_hist}(\text{J}, \text{Eno}, \text{Frm1}, \text{To}) \leftarrow \quad \text{overlap}(\text{J}, \text{Eno}, \text{Frm1}, \text{To1}, \text{Frm2}, \text{To2}),$$
$$\text{select\_larger}(\text{To1}, \text{To2}, \text{To}).$$
$$\text{e\_hist}(\text{J} + 1, \text{Eno}, \text{Frm}, \text{To}) \leftarrow \quad \text{e\_hist}(\text{J}, \text{Eno}, \text{Frm}, \text{To}),$$
$$\text{overlap}(\text{J} + 1, \_, \_, \_, \_, \_),$$
$$\neg \text{overlap}(\text{J} + 1, \text{Eno}, \text{Frm}, \text{To}, \_, \_),$$
$$\neg \text{overlap}(\text{J} + 1, \text{Eno}, \_, \_, \text{Frm}, \text{To}).$$

$$\text{final\_e\_hist}(\text{Eno}, \text{Frm}, \text{To}) \leftarrow \quad \text{e\_hist}(\text{J}, \text{Eno}, \text{Frm}, \text{To}),$$
$$\neg \text{e\_hist}(\text{J} + 1, \_, \_, \_).$$

$$\text{distinct}(\text{Frm1}, \text{To1}, \text{Frm2}, \text{To2}) \leftarrow \quad \text{To1} \neq \text{To2}.$$
$$\text{distinct}(\text{Frm1}, \text{To1}, \text{Frm2}, \text{To2}) \leftarrow \quad \text{Frm1} \neq \text{Frm2}.$$

$$\text{select\_larger}(\text{X}, \text{Y}, \text{X}) \leftarrow \quad \text{X} \geq \text{Y}.$$
$$\text{select\_larger}(\text{X}, \text{Y}, \text{Y}) \leftarrow \quad \text{Y} > \text{X}.$$

Thus, in the corresponding local stratification, the atoms `distinct` and the atoms `select_larger` go to the bottom stratum S_0. Then the atoms in σ_1 are in strata $S_{j \times 2 + 1}$, while those in σ_2 are now in strata $S_{j \times 2 + 2}$ (j denotes the temporal argument of these atoms).

The second `e_hist` rule in Example 10.12 is a qualified copy rule; that is, the head is copied from the body provided that certain conditions are satisfied. This can be implemented by letting `new_e_hist` and `old_e_hist` share the same table, and use deletion-in-place for those tuples that do not satisfy the two negated goals. The goal `overlap(J, _, _, _, _)` ensures that the computation stops as soon as no more overlapping intervals are found.

As demonstrated by these examples, XY-stratified programs allow an efficient logic-based expression of procedural algorithms.

10.5 Updates and Active Rules

In general, logic-based systems have not dealt well with database updates. For instance, Prolog resorts to its operational semantics to give meaning to `assert` and `retract` operations. Similar problems are faced by deductive database systems, which, however, concentrate on changes in the base relations, rather than facts and rules as in Prolog. Active database rules contain updates in both their bodies and their heads. Much current research work pursues the objective of providing a unified treatment for active rules, dealing with updates, and deductive rules, dealing with queries. The two are now viewed as separate areas of database technology, although they often use similar techniques and concepts (see, for instance, the uses of stratification in Section 4.2). This section outlines a simple solution to these problems using Datalog$_{1S}$ and XY-stratification.

The approach here proposed is driven by the threefold requirement of (1) providing a logical model for updates, (2) supporting the same queries that current deductive databases do, and (3) supporting the same rules that active databases currently do.

The first requirement can be satisfied by using history relations as extensional data. Thus, for each base relation R in the schema, there is a *history relation*, which keeps the history of all changes (updates) on R. For our university database, instead of having a `student` relation with facts of the following form:

```
student('Jim Black', cs, junior).
```

we have a `student_hist` relation containing the history of changes undergone by `Jim Black`'s record. Example 10.13 shows a possible history.

Example 10.13 The history of changes for `Jim Black`

```
student_hist(2301,+, 'Jim Black', ee, freshman).

student_hist(4007,-, 'Jim Black', ee, freshman).
student_hist(4007,+, 'Jim Black', ee, sophomore).
```

```
student_hist(4805,-, 'Jim Black', ee, sophomore).
student_hist(4805,+, 'Jim Black', cs, sophomore).

student_hist(6300,-, 'Jim Black', cs, sophomore).
student_hist(6300,+, 'Jim Black', cs, junior).
```

Thus, 'Jim Black' joined as a freshman in ee. The first column, 2301, is a change counter that is global for the system—that is, it is incremented for each change request. In fact, several changes can be made in the same SQL update statement: for instance, it might be that all the ee freshmen have been updated to sophomore in the same request. Thus, one year later, as Jim moves from freshman to sophomore, the change counter has been set to 4007. Therefore, there has been a total of $4,007 - 2,301$ database changes during the course of that year. Thus, we represent here deletions by the "$-$" sign in the second column and inserts by the "$+$" sign in the same column. An update is thus represented by a delete/insert pair having the same value in the temporal argument. Different representations for updates and other database events (e.g., representing the update directly, and timestamping the tuples) could also be handled in this modeling approach.

The remaining history of Jim Black's records states that he became a sophomore, and then he changed his major from ee to cs. Finally Jim became a junior—and that represents the current situation.

For a history database to be correct, it must satisfy a *continuity axiom*, which basically states that there is no jump in the change counters. This can be expressed through a predicate that registers when there is some change in some database relation. For instance, say that our university database, in addition to the tables

$$\text{student}(\text{Name}, \text{Major}, \text{Year}); \text{took}(\text{Name}, \text{Course}, \text{Grade})$$

discussed in Chapter 8, also contains the relation

$$\text{alumni}(\text{Name}, \text{Sex}, \text{Degree}, \text{ClassOf})$$

which obviously records the alumni who graduated from college in the previous years. Then we will need three rules to keep track of all changes:

$$\begin{aligned}
\text{change}(\text{J}) &\leftarrow \text{student\_hist}(\text{J}, \_, \_, \_, \_). \\
\text{change}(\text{J}) &\leftarrow \text{took\_hist}(\text{J}, \_, \_, \_, \_). \\
\text{change}(\text{J}) &\leftarrow \text{alumni\_hist}(\text{J}, \_, \_, \_, \_, \_).
\end{aligned}$$

Thus, there is a rule for each history relation. A violation to the continuity axiom can be expressed as follows:

$$\texttt{bad\_history} \leftarrow \ \texttt{change}(J+1), \neg\texttt{change}(J).$$

Let us turn now to the second requirement: the support of deductive queries against the current database. This is achieved through snapshot predicates, derived from the history relations using frame axioms.

For the student relation, for instance, we have the following rules:

Example 10.14   Snapshot predicates for student via frame axioms

$$
\begin{aligned}
&\texttt{student\_snap}(J+1, \texttt{Name}, \texttt{Major}, \texttt{Level}) \leftarrow \\
&\qquad\qquad \texttt{student\_snap}(J, \texttt{Name}, \texttt{Major}, \texttt{Level}), \\
&\qquad\qquad \neg\texttt{student\_hist}(J+1, -, \texttt{Name}, \texttt{Major}, \texttt{Level}). \\
&\texttt{student\_snap}(J, \texttt{Name}, \texttt{Major}, \texttt{Level}) \leftarrow \\
&\qquad\qquad \texttt{student\_hist}(J, +, \texttt{Name}, \texttt{Major}, \texttt{Level}).
\end{aligned}
$$

These rules express what are commonly known as *frame axioms*. Basically, the content of a database relation after some change is the same as that in the previous state, minus the deleted tuples, and plus the inserted tuples. Observe that the recursive student_snap rules so obtained are XY-stratified. Furthermore, observe the first rule in Example 10.14, which computes the effects of deletions. This is a copy rule and, therefore, it will be implemented by removing the tuples satisfying the negated goal (i.e., the deleted tuples) and leaving the rest of the relation unchanged. Similar frame axiom rules will be defined for each relation in the schema.

Deductive queries are then answered against the current content of the database (i.e., the final value of the change counter).

Example 10.15   The current content of the relation student

$$
\begin{aligned}
\texttt{current\_state}(J) \leftarrow \ & \texttt{change}(J), \neg\texttt{change}(J+1). \\
\texttt{student}(\texttt{Name}, \texttt{Major}, \texttt{Year}) \leftarrow \ & \texttt{student\_snap}(J, \texttt{Name}, \texttt{Major}, \texttt{Year}), \\
& \texttt{current\_state}(J).
\end{aligned}
$$

Because of the continuity axiom, $\texttt{change}(J), \neg\texttt{change}(J+1)$ defines the current state J. Similar rules will be written for the remaining relations in the database. The predicates so derived are then used in deductive rules described in the previous chapters.

We can now turn to the problem of modeling active rules. Here we limit our discussion to *Event-Condition-Action* rules, under the immediate-after activation semantics, that were discussed in Chapter 2. These can be modeled naturally in this framework, since conditions can be expressed against the snapshot relations, while events and actions can be expressed against history relations. For instance, say that we have the following active rules:

A_1 : *If a student is added to the alumni relation, then delete his name from the student relation, provided that this is a senior-level student.*

A_2 : *If a person takes a course, and the name of this person is not in the student relation, then add that name to the student relation, using the (null) value* tba *for Major and Level.*

Under the "immediately after" activation semantics, discussed in Section 2.2, these rules can be modeled as follows:

Example 10.16   Active rules on histories and snapshots

A_1 : student_hist$(\mathtt{J} + 1, -, \mathtt{Name}, \mathtt{Major}, \mathtt{senior}) \leftarrow$
$\qquad\qquad$ alumni_hist$(\mathtt{J}, +, \mathtt{Name}, \_, \_, \_)$,
$\qquad\qquad$ student_snap$(\mathtt{J}, \mathtt{Name}, \mathtt{Major}, \mathtt{senior})$.

A_2 : student_hist$(\mathtt{J} + 1, +, \mathtt{Name}, \mathtt{tba}, \mathtt{tba}) \leftarrow$
$\qquad\qquad\qquad$ took_hist$(\mathtt{J}, +, \mathtt{Name}, \_, \_)$,
$\qquad\qquad\qquad \neg$student_snap$(\mathtt{J}, \mathtt{Name}, \_, \_)$.

Let $\mathcal{A}$ be an active program, that is, the logic program consisting of (1) the history relations, (2) the change predicates, (3) the snapshot predicates, and (4) the active rules. Because of its XY-stratified structure, this program has a unique stable model M, which defines the meaning of the program.

Now assume that a new tuple is added to the history relation. Active rules might trigger changes and then tuples are added to the history relations until no more rules can fire. However, only the external changes requested by a user, and those triggered by active rules, can be in the history relations. Therefore, an active database $\mathcal{A}$ must satisfy the following two axioms:

1. *Completeness Axiom.* The history relations in $\mathcal{A}$ must be identical to the history relations in the stable model of $\mathcal{A}$.

2. *External Causation Axiom.* Let $\mathcal{A}_{ext}$ be the logic program obtained from $\mathcal{A}$ by eliminating from the history relations all changes but the external changes requested by users. Then, the stable model of $\mathcal{A}_{ext}$ and the stable model of the original $\mathcal{A}$ must be identical.

Thus, while predicates defined by deductive rules behave as virtual views, the history relations behave as concrete views. Whenever a new change is requested by users, all changes implied by the active rules are also added to the history relations. The complete set of new entries added to the history relations define the response of the system to the changes requested by the user.

10.6   Nondeterministic Reasoning

Say that, with relation student(Name, Major, Year), our university database contains the relation professor(Name, Major). In fact, say that our toy database contains only the following facts:

> student('Jim Black', ee, senior).   professor(ohm, ee).
>
>   professor(bell, ee).

Now, the rule is that the major of a student must match his/her advisor's major area of specialization. Then eligible advisors can be computed as follows:

> elig_adv(S, P) ← student(S, Major, Year), professor(P, Major).

This yields

> elig_adv('Jim Black', ohm).
> elig_adv('Jim Black', bell).

But, since a student can only have one advisor, the goal choice((S), (P)) must be added to force the selection of a unique advisor, out of the eligible advisors, for a student.

Example 10.17   Computation of unique advisors by choice rules

> actual_adv(S, P) ← student(S, Major, Levl), professor(P, Major),
>   choice((S), (P)).

student 1 — professor
student 2
fcn dep . m to 1

The goal $\texttt{choice}((\texttt{S}),(\texttt{P}))$ can also be viewed as enforcing a functional dependency (FD) $\texttt{S} \to \texttt{P}$; thus, in $\texttt{actual\_adv}$, the second column (professor name) is functionally dependent on the first one (student name).

The result of executing this rule is *nondeterministic*. It can either give a singleton relation containing the tuple $(\texttt{'JimBlack'}, \texttt{ohm})$ or that containing the tuple $(\texttt{'JimBlack'}, \texttt{bell})$.

A program where the rules contain choice goals is called a *choice program*. The semantics of a choice program P can be defined by transforming P into a program with negation, $SV(P)$, called the *stable version* of a choice program P. $SV(P)$ exhibits a multiplicity of stable models, each obeying the FDs defined by the choice goals. Each stable model for $SV(P)$ corresponds to an alternative set of answers for P and is called a *choice model* for P. $SV(P)$ is defined as follows:

Definition 10.17 *The stable version $SV(P)$ of a choice program P is obtained by the following transformation. Consider a choice rule r in P:*

$$r : A \leftarrow B(Z), \ choice((X_1),(Y_1)), \ \ldots, \ choice((X_k),(Y_k)).$$

where,

(i) $B(Z)$ denotes the conjunction of all the choice goals of r that are not choice goals, and

(ii) X_i, Y_i, Z, $1 \leq i \leq k$, denote vectors of variables occurring in the body of r such that $X_i \cap Y_i = \emptyset$ and $X_i, Y_i \subseteq Z$.

Then the original program P is transformed as follows:

1. *Replace r with a rule r' obtained by substituting the choice goals with the atom $chosen_r(W)$:*

$$r' : A \leftarrow B(Z), \ chosen_r(W).$$

where $W \subseteq Z$ is the list of all variables appearing in choice goals, i.e., $W = \bigcup_{1 \leq j \leq k} X_j \cup Y_j$.

2. *Add the new rule*

$$chosen_r(W) \leftarrow B(Z), \ \neg diffChoice_r(W).$$

3. *For each choice atom $choice((X_i),(Y_i))$ $(1 \leq i \leq k)$, add the new rule*

$$diffChoice_r(W) \leftarrow chosen_r(W'), \ Y_i \neq Y_i'.$$

where (i) the list of variables W' is derived from W by replacing each $A \in Y_i$ with a new variable $A' \in Y_i'$ (i.e., by priming those variables), and (ii) $Y_i \neq Y_i'$ is true if $A \neq A'$, for some variable $A \in Y_i$ and its primed counterpart $A' \in Y_i'$.

The stable version of Example 10.17 is given in Example 10.18, which can be read as a statement that a professor will be assigned to each student if a different professor has not been assigned to the same student.

Example 10.18   The stable version of the rule in Example 10.17

$$\begin{aligned}
\texttt{actual\_adv(S,P)} &\leftarrow \texttt{student(S,Majr,Yr), professor(P,Majr),} \\
&\quad \texttt{chosen(S,P).} \\
\texttt{chosen(S,P)} &\leftarrow \texttt{student(S,Majr,Yr), professor(P,Majr),} \\
&\quad \neg\texttt{diffChoice(S,P).} \\
\texttt{diffChoice(S,P)} &\leftarrow \texttt{chosen(S,P'), P} \neq \texttt{P'.}
\end{aligned}$$

In general, the program $SV(P)$ generated by the transformation discussed above has the following properties:

- $SV(P)$ has one or more total stable models.

- The chosen atoms in each stable model of $SV(P)$ obey the FDs defined by the choice goals.

The stable models of $SV(P)$ are called *choice models* for P.

Stratified Datalog programs with choice are in DB-PTIME: actually they can be implemented efficiently by producing chosen atoms one at a time and memorizing them in a table. The diffchoice atoms need not be computed and stored; rather, the goal ¬diffchoice can simply be checked dynamically against the table chosen.

The use of choice is critical in many applications. For instance, the following nonrecursive rules can be used to determine whether there are more boys than girls in a database containing the unary relations boy and girl:

Example 10.19   Are there more boys than girls in our database?

$$\begin{aligned}
\texttt{match(Bname,Gname)} &\leftarrow \texttt{boy(Bname), girl(Gname).} \\
&\quad \texttt{choice((Bname),(Gname)),} \\
&\quad \texttt{choice((Gname),(Bname)).} \\
\texttt{matched\_boy(Bname)} &\leftarrow \texttt{match(Bname,Gname).} \\
\texttt{moreboys} &\leftarrow \texttt{boy(Bname), } \neg\texttt{matched\_boy(Bname).}
\end{aligned}$$

The most significant applications of choice involve the use of choice in recursive predicates. For instance, the following program computes the spanning tree, starting from the source node a, for a graph where an arc from node b to d is represented by the database fact g(b, d).

Example 10.20   Computing a spanning tree

```
st(root, a).
st(X, Y) ←   st(_, X), g(X, Y), Y ≠ a, choice((Y), (X)).
```

In this example, the goal Y ≠ a ensures that, in st, the end-node for the arc produced by the exit rule has an in-degree of one; likewise, the goal choice((Y), (X)) ensures that the end-nodes for the arcs generated by the recursive rule have an in-degree of one.

Stratified Datalog programs with choice are also DB-PTIME complete, without having to assume that the universe is totally ordered. Indeed, the following program defines a total order for the elements of a set d(X) by constructing an immediate-successor relation for its elements (root is a distinguished new symbol):

Example 10.21   Ordering a domain

```
ordered_d(root, root).
ordered_d(X, Y) ←   ordered_d(_, X), d(Y),
                    choice((X), (Y)), choice((Y), (X)).
```

The choice goals in Example 10.21 ensure that once an arc (X, Y) is generated, this is the only arc leaving the source node X and the only arc entering the sink node Y.

Set aggregates on the elements of the set d(X), including the parity query, are easily computed using the relation ordered_d. Alternatively, these aggregates can be computed directly using a program similar to that of Example 10.21. For instance, the sum of all elements in d(X) can be computed as follows:

Example 10.22   The sum of the elements in d(X)

```
sum_d(root, root, 0) ←   d(_).
sum_d(X, Y, SY) ←   sum_d(_, X, SX), d(Y),
                    choice((X), (Y)), choice((Y), (X)), SY = SX + Y.
total_d(Sum) ←   sum_d(_, X, Sum), ¬sum_d(X, _, _).
```

If we eliminate the choice goal from the program P of Example 10.22, we obtain a program P' that is stratified with respect to negation. Therefore, the original P is called a *stratified choice program*. Stratified choice programs always have stable models. Moreover, these stable models can be computed by an iterated fixpoint computation that computes choice models for strata where rules have choice goals. For instance, in Example 10.22, the choice model of the sum_d stratum is computed first, and the next stratum containing total_d is computed after that. Likewise, choice goals can be added to XY-stratified programs, yielding programs that have multiple stable models. These models can be computed by Procedure 10.16, which is now iterating over stratified choice programs.

The choice construct is significant for both nondeterministic and deterministic queries. A nondeterministic query is one where any answer out of a set is acceptable. This is, for instance, the case of Example 10.17, where an advisor has to be assigned to a student. Example 10.22 illustrates the use of choice to compute a deterministic query; in fact, the sum of the elements of the set is independent from the order in which these are visited.

Since stratified Datalog on an ordered domain is DB-PTIME complete, Example 10.21 ensures that stratified choice programs are also DB-PTIME complete for deterministic queries. Furthermore, the use of choice, unlike the assumption of an underlying ordered domain, also ensures the *genericity* of queries. Basically, a query is said to be generic if it is independent of permutations of the order of constants in the database.

When choice is used in the computation of stratified or XY-stratified programs, no previously made choice needs to be repudiated later, since the iterated fixpoint always generates a stable model. This produces "don't care" nondeterminism, generating polynomial-time computations.

In the more general case, however, finding a stable model for a program requires the use of intelligent (oracle-type) nondeterminism; in practice, this can only be realized by an exponential search. For instance, the following program determines if there exists a Hamiltonian path in a graph. A graph has a Hamiltonian path iff there is a simple path that visits all nodes exactly once.

Example 10.23   Hamiltonian path in a directed graph g(X, Y)

```
simplepath(root, root).
simplepath(X, Y) ←  simple_path(_, X), g(X, Y),
                    choice((X), (Y)), choice((Y), (X)).
nonhppath ←   n(X), ¬ simplepath(_, X).
q ←    ¬q, nonhppath.
```

Let M be a model for this program. If `nonhppath` is true in M, then rule q $\leftarrow$ $\neg$q must also be satisfied by M. Thus, M cannot be a stable model. Thus, this program has a stable model iff there exists a Hamiltonian path. Thus, searching for a stable model of this program might require all alternative choices to be explored for each possible node (e.g., using backtracking). This generates an exponential computation. In fact, since the Hamiltonian path problem is known to be $\mathcal{NP}$-complete, the stable version of Example 10.23 provides a simple proof that deciding whether a stable model exists for a program is $\mathcal{NP}$-hard.

10.7 Research Directions

The main focus of current research is breaking through the many barriers that have limited the application of logic-oriented databases in various domains. Developing a logic-based theory of database changes and events and supporting the integration of active and deductive databases represent two important objectives in this effort. In contrast with the simple approach described in this chapter, many of the approaches proposed in the past have been very sophisticated and complex. A major line of AI research uses situation calculus, where function symbols are used to represent changes and histories. In addition to modeling database updates, this approach has been used for integrity constraints, AI planning, reasoning with hypothetical updates, and other difficult problems. A logic-based framework for modeling changes and frame axioms in situation calculus can follow an open-world approach with explicit-negation, or take the implicit-negation approach, often in conjunction with stable model semantics. The transaction logic approach developed by Bonner and Kifer recasts some of this power and complexity into a path-based formalism (Datalog$_{1S}$ is state-oriented) attuned to database transactions.

Support for temporal and spatial reasoning in databases represents a promising area of current research, and so is the topic of reasoning with uncertainty, discussed in Part V. These lines of research often tackle issues of partial order, since nonmonotonic programs written to reason with time or uncertainty, for example, can become monotonic once the appropriate lattice-based representation is found. A closely related research line investigates the problem of monotonic aggregation in databases.

In the previous chapter we discussed some of the technical challenges facing the design of deductive database systems and of recursive extensions for SQL3. It is reasonable to expect that the next generation of system prototypes will resolve those problems and move toward the integration of the active, deductive, and temporal capabilities previously outlined. Furthermore, object-oriented features will be included in these systems. The integration of deductive and object-oriented databases has been a topic of active research and will remain so for the near future.

In the end, future developments in the field will be driven more by applications than by technological advances. In particular, the uses of deductive systems to realize distributed mediators and to perform knowledge discovery from databases are emerging as very promising application domains for the technology.

10.8   Bibliographic Notes

The CWA was proposed by Reiter [354] and was later generalized by Minker [288]. The notion of stratification has seen several independent discoveries, including those by Chandra and Harel [101], Apt, Blair and Walker [20], Naqvi [301], Van Gelder [442], and Przymusinski [341], who is also credited with the notion of locally stratified programs. The undecidability of this class of program was proven in [61]. A study of SLD-NF and its limitations can be found in [109] and [269]. Well-founded models (partial and total) were introduced by Van Gelder, Ross, and Schlipf, using the notion of unfounded sets [444]; the alternating fixpoint is due to Van Gelder [443]. The notion of modular stratification is a significant step toward practical realizations of well-founded semantics [364]. Implementations of this semantics in the top-down framework were also studied in [103].

The notion of stable models is due to Gelfond and Lifschitz [186]. This concept distills in a simple definition many AI ideas following McCarthy's notion of circumscription [279]. The definition of stable models can also be generalized to partial models, which exist for every program but contain undefined atoms. Three-valued logic provides a convenient tool to define partial stable models [342], although two-valued logic is quite up to the task [376]. An in-depth treatment of nonmonotonic formalisms, including defaults, can be found in [276].

A survey of query languages based on temporal logic can be found in [107]. Different kinds of temporal logic, including PLTL, are surveyed in [357] and [142]. Temporal applications of Datalog$_{1S}$ and its underlying theory were elucidated by Chomicki [106, 46].

The notion of XY-stratification is due to Zaniolo, Arni, and Ong [469]. The related concept of explicitly locally stratified programs was investigated in [241]. The use of XY-stratified programs to model updates and active rules was explored in [466, 467]. Brogi, Subrahmanian, and Zaniolo extended XY-stratification with the choice construct to model various planning problems [80]. The logic of actions has been the focus of a large body of research; the use of situation calculus and classical logic was explored by Reiter [339, 354]. Among the many approaches using implicit negation, we will only mention [33, 187, 34].

Transaction logic is described in [68]. F-logic represents a leading proposal in the area of deductive and object-oriented databases [243]. An introduction to the problem of monotonic aggregation can be found in [365].

The concept of choice, first proposed by Krishnamurthy and Naqvi [257], was then revised by Saccà and Zaniolo [375] using the stable-model semantics; the concept of dynamic choice was introduced by Giannotti, Pedreschi, Saccá and Zaniolo in [189], and its expressive power was studied in [123]. Other nondeterministic extensions to Datalog languages were investigated by Abiteboul and Vianu [4].

10.9 Exercises

10.1. Let P be a Datalog program. Show that $\Gamma_P^{\uparrow \omega}$ can be computed in time that is polynomial in the size of P's Herbrand base.

10.2. Use Example 10.23 and the results from Exercise 10.1 to show that deciding whether stable models exist for a given program is $\mathcal{NP}$-complete.

10.3. Consider the program

$$
\begin{aligned}
c &\leftarrow a, \neg c.\\
a &\leftarrow \neg b.\\
b &\leftarrow a, \neg c.
\end{aligned}
$$

For this program, write all models, minimal models, fixpoints, minimal fixpoints, and stable models, if any. Also give $T_P^{\uparrow \omega}$.

10.4. Prove that every stable model is a minimal model.

10.5. Prove that every stable model for P is a minimal fixpoint for T_P.

10.6. Prove that the program in Example 10.5 is not locally stratified.

10.7. Explain how the alternating fixpoint computes the stable model for a stratified program. Perform the computation on Example 8.7.

10.8. The until ($\mathcal{U}$) operator of PLTL is monotonic; give a positive program that expresses this operator.

10.9. Write an XY-stratified program for the BoM Example 8.19, where the computation of longest time required for all subparts of a given part is performed in the recursive rules. What are the local strata for the resulting program?

10.10. Given a directed graph $g(a, b, d)$, where a and b are nodes, and d is their distance, determine

   a. the least distances of a given node to all other nodes of the graph, and

   b. the distances between all node pairs.

   Express various algorithms for computing such distances by XY-stratified programs.

10.11. For the active program $\mathcal{A}$ described in Section 10.5, derive A_{bis} and its synchronized version. Explain why the program is XY-stratified and how the actual computation will take place.

10.12. Given the relation club_member(Name, Sex), write a nonrecursive Datalog program to determine whether there is exactly the same number of males and females in the club. Use choice but not function symbols.

10.13. Use choice to write a recursive program that takes a set of database predicates $b(X)$ and produces a relation $sb(X, I)$, with I a unique sequence number attached to each X.

10.14. Express the parity query using choice (do not assume a total order of the universe).

10.15. Write a program with choice and stratified negation that performs the depth-first traversal of a directed graph.

Part IV

Spatial, Text, and Multimedia Databases

The problem we focus on in this part is the design of fast searching methods that will search a database of spatial, text, or multimedia objects to locate those that match a query object, exactly or approximately. Objects can be 2-dimensional color images, gray-scale medical images in 2-D or 3-D (e.g., MRI brain scans), 1-dimensional time series, digitized voice or music, video clips, and so on. A typical query by content would be "in a collection of color photographs, find ones with the same color distribution as a sunset photograph."

Specific applications include the following:

- Image databases, where we would like to support queries on color, shape, and texture.

- Financial, marketing and production time series, such as stock prices, sales numbers, and so on. In such databases, typical queries would be "find companies whose stock prices move similarly," or "find other companies that have sales patterns similar to our company," or "find cases in the past that resemble last month's sales pattern of our product."

- Scientific databases, with collections of sensor data. In this case, the objects are time series, or, more generally, *vector fields*, that is, tuples of the form, for example, $< x, y, z, t, pressure, temperature, \ldots >$. For example, in weather, geological, environmental, astrophysics databases, and so on, we want to ask queries like "find past days in which the solar magnetic wind showed patterns similar to today's pattern" to help in predictions of the earth's magnetic field.

- Multimedia databases, with audio (voice, music), video, and so on. Users might want to retrieve similar music scores or video clips.

- Medical databases, where 1-D objects (e.g., ECGs), 2-D images (e.g., X rays), and 3-D images (e.g., MRI brain scans) are stored. The ability to retrieve quickly past cases with similar symptoms would be valuable for diagnosis, as well as for medical teaching and research purposes.

- Text and photograph archives. Digital libraries with ASCII text, bitmaps, and gray-scale and color images.

- DNA databases, where there is a large collection of long strings (hundreds or thousands of characters long) from a four-letter alphabet (A,G,C,T); a new string has to be matched against the old strings to find the best candidates. The distance function is the editing distance (smallest number of insertions, deletions, and substitutions that are needed to transform the first string to the second).

This part is organized as follows: Chapter 11 describes traditional access methods, for secondary keys, spatial data, and text. Chapter 12 describes the GEMINI method for indexing multimedia data types and its applications to time sequences and images.

Chapter 11

Traditional Indexing Methods

In this chapter, we examine older database access methods. Specifically, Section 11.1 describes secondary key access methods, Section 11.2 lists spatial access methods, and Section 11.3 surveys text retrieval methods.

11.1 Secondary Keys

Access methods for secondary key retrieval have attracted much interest. The problem is stated as follows: Given a file, say, EMPLOYEE(name, salary, age), organize the appropriate indices so that we can answer efficiently queries on any and all of the available attributes. Rivest [359] classified the possible queries into the following classes, in increasing order of complexity:

- *Exact match* query, when the query specifies all the attribute values of the desired record. For example,

$$\text{name} = \text{'Smith' and salary} = 40{,}000 \text{ and age} = 45$$

- *Partial match* query, when only some of the attribute values are specified. For example,

$$\text{salary} = 40{,}000 \text{ and age} = 45$$

- *Range queries*, when ranges for some or all of the attributes are specified. For example,

$$35{,}000 \leq \text{salary} \leq 45{,}000 \text{ and age} = 45$$

- *Boolean queries*:

$$((\text{not name} = \text{'Smith'}) \text{ and salary} \geq 40{,}000) \text{ or age} \geq 50$$

In the above classification, each class is a special case of the next class. A class of queries outside the above hierarchy is the *nearest neighbor*, or *best match*, query. For example,

$$\text{salary} \approx 45{,}000 \text{ and age} \approx 55$$

where the user specifies some of the attribute values and asks for the best match(es), according to some prespecified distance/dissimilarity function.

   In this chapter, first we mention inverted files, which are the industry workhorse. Then we describe some methods that treat records as points in k-D space (where k is the number of attributes); these methods are known as *point access methods* (PAMs) [393] and are closely related to the upcoming *spatial access methods* (SAMs). Specifically, we present grid files and k-D trees.

11.1.1 Inverted Files

This is the most popular approach in database systems. An inverted file on a given attribute (say, salary) is built as follows: For each distinct attribute value, we store

1. a list of pointers to records that have this attribute value *(postings list)*

2. optionally, the length of this list

The set of distinct attribute values is typically organized as a B-tree or as a hash table. The postings lists may be stored at the leaves, or in a separate area on the disk. Figure 11.1 shows an index on the salary of an EMPLOYEE table. A list of unique salary values is maintained, along with the postings lists.

   Given indices on the query attributes, complex Boolean queries can be resolved by manipulating the lists of record pointers before accessing the actual records. Notice that indices can be created automatically by a relational DBMS, with the SQL command **CREATE INDEX**.

11.1.2 Grid File

A fruitful point of view is to envision a record with k attributes as a point in k-dimensional space. Then, there are several methods that can handle

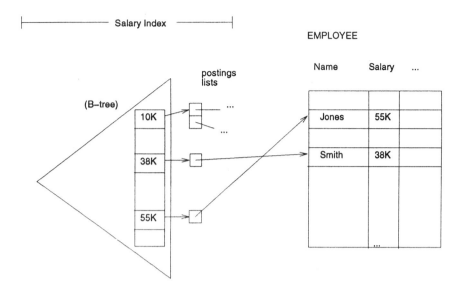

Figure 11.1: Illustration of inversion: a B-tree index on salary

points, the so-called *point access methods* (PAMs) [393]. Since most of them can also handle spatial objects (rectangles, polygons, etc.) in addition to points, we postpone their description for the next chapter. Next we briefly describe two of the PAMs, the grid files and the k-D trees. They both are mainly designed for points, and they have suggested important ideas that several SAMs have subsequently used.

The grid file [310] can be envisioned as the generalization of extendible hashing [145] in multiple dimensions. The idea is that it imposes a grid on the address space; the grid adapts to the data density by introducing more divisions on areas of high data density. Each grid cell corresponds to one disk page, although two or more cells may share a page. To simplify the record keeping, the cuts are allowed only on predefined points ($\frac{1}{2}$, $\frac{1}{4}$, $\frac{3}{4}$, etc., of each axis), and they cut all the way through, to form a grid. Thus, the grid file needs only a list of cut points for every axis, as well as a directory. The directory has one entry for every grid cell, containing a pointer to the disk page that contains the elements of the grid cell. Figure 11.2 illustrates a grid file on two attributes.

The grid file has the following desirable properties:

- It guarantees two disk accesses for exact match queries.

- It is symmetric with respect to the attributes.

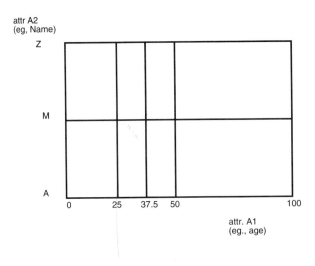

Figure 11.2: Illustration of a grid file with two attributes

- It adapts to nonuniform distributions.

However, it suffers from two disadvantages:

- It does not work well if the attribute values are correlated (e.g., age and salary might be linearly correlated in an EMPLOYEE file).

- It might need a large directory if the dimensionality of the address space is high ("dimensionality curse").

However, for a database with low-dimensionality points and uncorrelated attributes, the grid file is a solution to consider.

11.1.3   *k*-D Trees

This is the only main-memory access method that we shall describe in this book. We make this exception because *k*-D trees suggest elegant ideas that have been used subsequently in several access methods for disk-based data. Moreover, extensions of the original *k*-D tree method have been proposed [53] to group and store *k*-D tree nodes on disk pages, at least for static data.

The *k*-D tree [52] divides the address space in disjoint regions, through "cuts" on alternating dimensions/attributes. Structurally, it is a binary tree, with every node containing a data record, a left pointer and a right pointer. At every level of the tree, a different attribute is used as the discriminator, typically in a round-robin fashion.

Let n be a node, r be the record in this node, and A be the discriminator for this node. Then, the left subtree of the node n will contain records with smaller A values, while the right subtree will contain records with greater or equal A values. Figure 11.3(a) illustrates the partitioning of the address space by a k-D tree: the file has two attributes (e.g., age and salary), and it contains the following records (in insertion order): (40,50), (20,30), (10,10). Figure 11.3(b) shows the equivalent k-D tree as a binary tree.

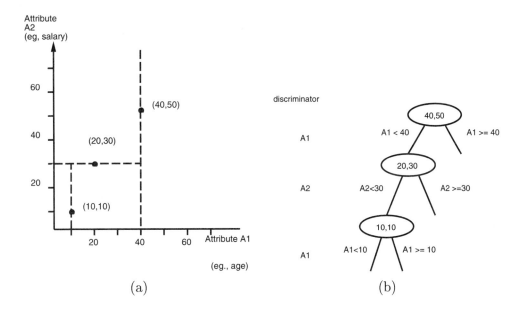

Figure 11.3: Illustration of a k-D tree: (a) the divisions in the address space and (b) the tree itself

The k-D tree can easily handle exact-match queries, range queries, and nearest-neighbor queries [52]. The algorithms are elegant and intuitive, and they typically achieve good response times, thanks to the efficient pruning of the search space that the k-D tree leads to.

Several disk-based PAMs have been inspired by or used k-D trees. The k-D B-trees [360] divide the address space in m regions for every node (as opposed to just two that the k-D tree does), where m is the fanout of the tree. The hB-tree [271] divides the address space in regions that may have "holes"; moreover, the contents of every node/disk page are organized into a k-D tree.

11.1.4   Conclusions

With respect to secondary-key methods, inversion with a B-tree (or hashed) index is automatically provided by commercial DBMSs with the create index SQL command. The rest of the point access methods are typically used in stand-alone systems. Their extensions, the spatial access methods, are examined next.

11.2   Spatial Access Methods (SAMs)

In the previous section, we examined the secondary-key access methods, which handle queries on keys that may have duplicates (e.g., salary, or age, in an EMPLOYEE file). As mentioned, records with k numerical attributes can be envisioned as k-dimensional points. Here we examine *spatial access methods*, which are designed to handle multidimensional points, lines, rectangles, and other geometric bodies.

There are numerous applications that require efficient retrieval of spatial objects:

- Traditional relational databases, where, as we mentioned, records with k-attributes become points in k-D spaces.

- Geographic information systems (GISs), which contain, for example, point data, such as cities on a 2-dimensional map.

- Medical image databases with, for example, 3-dimensional MRI brain scans, which require the storage and retrieval of point sets, such as digitized surfaces of brain structures [21].

- Multimedia databases, where multidimensional objects can be represented as points in feature space [227, 157]. For example, 2-D color images correspond to points in (R,G,B) space (where R, G, and B are the average amount of red, green, and blue [152]).

- Time-sequence analysis and forecasting [452, 87], where k successive values are treated as a point in k-D space; correlations and regularities in this k-D space help in characterizing the dynamical process that generates the time series.

- Temporal databases (see Part II), where events correspond to time intervals [252] or even to 2-D rectangles, if we consider transaction time and valid time [258]. See [383] for a survey and recent developments.

- Rule indexing in expert database systems [420] where rules can be represented as ranges in address space (e.g., "all the employees with salary in the range 10K–20K and age in the range 30–50 are entitled to specific health benefits").

In a collection of spatial objects, there are additional query types that are of interest. The following query types seem to be the most frequent:

1. *Range* queries, a slight generalization of the range queries we saw in secondary key retrieval. For example, "find all cities within 10 miles of Washington DC," or "find all rivers in Canada." Thus, the user specifies a region (a circle around Washington, or the region covered by Canada) and asks for all the objects that intersect this region. The *point query* is a special case of the range query, when the query region collapses to a point. Typically, the range query requests all the spatial objects that intersect a region; similarly, it could request the spatial objects that are completely contained, or that completely contain the query region. We mainly focus on the "intersection" variation; the remaining two can usually be easily answered by slightly modifying the algorithm for the "intersection" version.

2. *Nearest neighbor* queries, again a slight generalization of the nearest neighbor queries for secondary keys. For example, "find the five closest post offices to our office building." The user specifies a point or a region, and the system has to return the k closest objects. The distance is typically the Euclidean distance (L_2 norm), or some other distance function (e.g., city-block distance L_1, or the L_∞ norm).

3. *Spatial joins*, or *overlays*. For example, in a CAD design, "find the pairs of elements that are closer than ϵ" (and thus create electromagnetic interference to each other). Or, given a collection of lakes and a collection of cities, "find all the cities that are within 10km of a lake."

The proposed methods in the literature form the following classes (for a recent, extensive survey, see [180]):

- Methods that use space-filling curves (also known as *z-ordering* or *linear quadtrees*)

- Methods that use treelike structures: R-trees and its variants

The next two subsections are dedicated to each of the above classes. For each class, we discuss the main idea and its most successful variations, and sketch the algorithms to handle the above query types. In the third subsection we present the idea of transforming spatial objects into higher-dimensionality points. In the last subsection we give the conclusions for this section.

11.2.1   Space-Filling Curves

This method has attracted a lot of interest, under the names of N-trees [454], linear quadtrees [184], z-ordering [321, 324, 322, 323], and so on. The fundamental assumption is that there is a finite precision in the representation of each coordinate, say, K bits. The terminology is easiest described in 2-D address space; the generalizations to n dimensions should be obvious. Following the quadtree literature, the address space is a square, called an *image*, and it is represented as a $2^K \times 2^K$ array of 1×1 squares. Each such square is called a *pixel*.

Figure 11.4 gives an example for $n = 2$ dimensional address space, with $K = 2$ bits of precision. Next, we describe how the method handles points and regions.

Handling Points

The space-filling curve tries to impose a linear ordering on the resulting pixels of the address space, so as to translate the problem into a primary-key access problem.

One such obvious mapping is to visit the pixels in a row-wise order. A better idea is to use bit interleaving [325]. Then, the *z-value* of a pixel is the value of the resulting bit string, considered as a binary number. For example, consider the pixel labeled A in Figure 11.4, with coordinates $x_A = 00$ and $y_A = 11$. Suppose that we decide to shuffle the bits, starting from the x-coordinate first, that is, the order with which we pick bits from the coordinates is "1,2,1,2" ("1" corresponds to the x-coordinate and "2" to the y-coordinate). Then, the z-value z_A of pixel A is computed as follows:

$$z_A = \text{Shuffle } (\text{``1,2,1,2''}, x_A, y_A) =$$

that is,

$$z_A = \text{Shuffle } (\text{``1,2,1,2''}, 00, 11) = 0101 = (5)_{10}$$

Visiting the pixels in ascending z-value order creates a self-similar trail, as depicted in Figure 11.4 with a dashed line; the trail consists of "N" shapes,

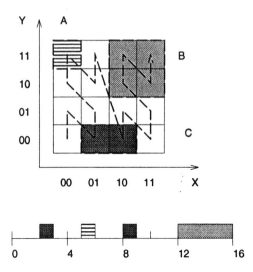

Figure 11.4: Illustration of z-ordering

organized to form larger "N" shapes recursively. Rotating the trail by 90 degrees gives "z" shapes, which is probably the reason that the method was named *z-ordering*. Figure 11.5 shows the trails of the z-ordering for a 2 × 2, a 4 × 4, and an 8 × 8 grid. Notice that each larger grid contains four miniature replicas of the smaller grids, joined in an "N" shape.

Figure 11.5: Z-order curves for 2 x 2, 4 x 4, and 8 x 8 grids

We have just described one method to compute the z-value of a point in 2-D address space. The extension to n-D address spaces is obvious: we just shuffle the bits from each of the n dimensions, visiting the dimensions in a round-robin fashion. The inverse is also obvious: given a z-value, we translate it to a binary number and unshuffle its bits to derive the n coordinate values.

Handling Regions

A region typically breaks into one or more pieces (blocks), each of which can be described by a z-value. A *block* is a square region that is the result of one or more quadtree subdivisions of the original image. Pixels are clearly 1×1 blocks. For example, the region labeled C in Figure 11.4 breaks into two pixels, C_1 and C_2, with z-values

$$z_{C_1} = 0010 = (2)_{10}$$
$$z_{C_2} = 1000 = (8)_{10}$$

The region labeled B consists of four pixels, which have the common prefix 11 in their z-values; in this case, the z-value of B is exactly this common prefix,

$$z_B = \; 11$$

or, using "*" as the "don't care" character,

$$z_B = 11**$$

A large region may be decomposed in many such pieces; for efficiency reasons (e.g., see [322, 323]), we typically approximate such a region with a coarser-resolution region.

In conclusion, each object (and range query) can be uniquely represented by the z-values of its blocks. Each such z-value can be treated as a primary key of a record of the form (z-value, object-id, other attributes ...), and it can be inserted in a primary-key file structure, such as a B^+-tree. Additional objects in the same address space can be handled in the same way; their z-values will be inserted into the same B^+-tree.

Algorithms

The z-ordering method can handle all the queries that we have listed earlier:

- *Range queries:* The query shape is translated into a set of z-values as if it were a data region. Typically, we opt for an approximate representation of it, trying to balance the number of z-values and the amount of extra area in the approximation [323]. Then, we search the B^+-tree with the z-values of the data regions for matching z-values. The matching is done efficiently, because of the following observation: Let z_1 and z_2 be two z-values, and let z_1 be the shortest one, without loss of generality; then, for the corresponding regions (i.e., blocks) r_1 and r_2, there are only two possibilities: (1) either r_1 completely contains r_2, if z_1 is the prefix of z_2, or (2) the two regions are disjoint. See Orenstein and Manola [324] for the detailed algorithm for matching.

- *Nearest neighbor queries:* The sketch of the basic algorithm is as follows: Given a query point P, we compute its z-value and search the B^+-tree for the closest z-value; then, we compute the actual distance r, and issue a range query centered at P with radius r.

- *Spatial joins:* The algorithm for spatial joins is a generalization of the algorithm for the range query. Let S be a set of spatial objects (e.g., lakes) and R be another set (e.g., railways line segments). The spatial join "find all the railways that cross lakes" is handled as follows: the elements of set S are translated into z-values, sorted; the elements of set R are also translated into a sorted list of z-values; the two lists of z-values are merged. The "don't care" character "*" has to be treated carefully; see [321, 324] for the details.

Variations and Improvements

We have seen that if we traverse the pixels in ascending z-value order, we obtain a trail as shown in Figure 11.4. This trail imposes a mapping from n-D space onto a 1-D space; ideally, we would like a mapping with distance-preserving properties; that is, pixels that are near in address space should have nearby z-values. The reason is that good clustering will make sure that "similar" pixels will end up in the same or nearby leaf pages of the B^+-tree, thus greatly accelerating the retrieval on range queries.

The z-ordering indeed imposes a good such mapping: It does not leave a quadrant unless it has visited all its pixels. However, it has some long, diagonal jumps, which maybe could be avoided. This observation prompted the search for better space-filling curves. Alternatives included a curve using Gray codes [148]; the best performing one is the Hilbert curve [159], which has been shown to achieve better clustering than the z-ordering and the Gray codes curve. It is the only one that we shall describe.

Figure 11.6 shows the Hilbert curves of order 1, 2, and 3: The order k curve is derived from the original order 1 curve by substituting each of its four points with an order $k - 1$ curve, appropriately rotated or reflected. In the limit, the resulting curve has fractal dimension = 2 [274], which intuitively means that it is so intertwined and dense that it behaves like a 2-D object. Notice also that the trail of a Hilbert curve does not have any abrupt jumps, like the z-ordering does. Thus, intuitively it is expected to have better distance-preserving properties than the z-ordering. Experiments have shown that the claim holds for the reported settings [159].

Algorithms to compute the Hilbert value of an n-D pixel have been published [57, 83]; source code in the C programming language is available for

$n = 2$ dimensions [226]. The complexity of all these algorithms, as well as their inverses, is $O(b)$ where b is the total number of bits of the z/Hilbert value. The proportionality constant is small (a few operations per bit for the z-value, a few more for the Hilbert value). For both curves, the time to compute a z/Hilbert value is negligible compared to the disk access time.

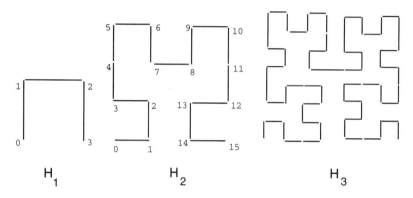

Figure 11.6: Hilbert curves of order 1, 2, and 3

There are several analytical and simulation studies of space-filling curves: Faloutsos and Roseman [159] used exhaustive enumeration to study the clustering properties of several curves, showing that the Hilbert curve is best; Jagadish [226] provides analysis for partial match and 2×2 range queries; Rong and Faloutsos [363] derive closed formulas for the z-ordering; Moon et al. [294] derive closed formulas for range queries on the Hilbert curve.

Also related is the analytical study for quadtrees, trying to determine the number of quadtree blocks that a spatial object will be decomposed into [218, 137, 398, 150, 155, 179, 154]. The common observation is that the number of quadtree blocks and the number of z/Hilbert values that a spatial object requires is proportional to the measure of its boundary (e.g., perimeter for 2-D objects, surface area for 3-D, etc.). As intuitively expected, the constant of proportionality is smaller for the Hilbert curve compared to the z-ordering.

11.2.2   R-Trees

The R-tree was proposed by Guttman [202]. It can be thought of as an extension of the B-tree for multidimensional objects. A spatial object is represented by its minimum bounding rectangle (MBR). Nonleaf nodes contain entries of the form (ptr, R), where ptr is a pointer to a child node in the R-tree; R is the MBR that covers all rectangles in the child node. Leaf nodes

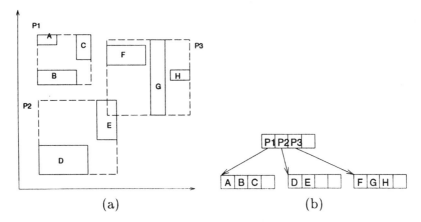

Figure 11.7: (a) Data (solid-line rectangles) organized in an R-tree with fanout = 4; (b) the resulting R-tree on disk

contain entries of the form $(obj - id, R)$ where $obj - id$ is a pointer to the object description, and R is the MBR of the object. The main innovation in the R-tree is that parent nodes are allowed to overlap. This way, the R-tree can guarantee good space utilization and remain balanced. Figure 11.7(a) illustrates data rectangles (solid boundaries), organized in an R-tree with fanout 3, while Figure 11.7(b) shows the file structure for the same R-tree, where nodes correspond to disk pages.

The R-tree inspired much subsequent work, whose main focus was to improve the search time. A packing technique is proposed in [367] to minimize the overlap between different nodes in the R-tree for static data. The idea was to order the data in, say, ascending x-low value, and scan the list, filling each leaf node to capacity. An improved packing technique based on the Hilbert curve is proposed in [237]: the idea is to sort the data rectangles on the Hilbert value of their centers.

A class of variations consider more general minimum bounding shapes, trying to minimize the dead space that an MBR may cover. Günther proposed the cell trees [198], which introduce diagonal cuts in arbitrary orientation. Jagadish proposed the polygon trees (P-trees) [225], where the minimum bounding shapes are polygons with slopes of sides 0, 45, 90, and 135 degrees. Minimum bounding shapes that are concave or even have holes have been suggested (e.g., in the hB-tree [271]).

One of the most successful ideas in R-tree research is the idea of deferred splitting: Beckmann et al. proposed the R^*-tree [48], which was reported to outperform Guttman's R-trees by $\approx 30\%$. The main idea is the concept of *forced reinsert*, which tries to defer the splits to achieve better utilization: When a node overflows, some of its children are carefully chosen, and they are deleted and reinserted, usually resulting in a better-structured R-tree. The idea of deferred splitting was also exploited in the Hilbert R-tree [238]; there, the Hilbert curve is used to impose a linear ordering on rectangles, thus defining who the sibling of a given rectangle is, and subsequently applying the 2-to-3 (or s-to-$(s + 1)$) splitting policy of the B^*-trees. Both methods achieve higher space utilization than Guttman's R-trees, as well as better response time (since the tree is shorter and more compact).

Finally, analysis of the R-tree performance has attracted a lot of interest: Faloutsos et al. [160] provide formulas, assuming that the spatial objects are uniformly distributed in the address space. Faloutsos and Kamel relaxed the uniformity assumption in [156]; there it was shown that the fractal dimension is an excellent measure of the nonuniformity, and that it leads to accurate formulas to estimate the average number of disk accesses of the resulting R-tree. The fractal dimension also helps estimate the selectivity of spatial joins [50]. When the sizes of the MBRs of the R-tree are known, formulas for the expected number of disk access are given in [329] and [237].

Algorithms

Since the R-tree is one of the most successful spatial access methods, we describe the related algorithms in some more detail:

- *Insertion:* When a new rectangle is inserted, we traverse the tree to find the most suitable leaf node; we extend its MBR if necessary, and store the new rectangle there. If the leaf node overflows, we split it, as discussed next.

- *Split:* This is one of the most crucial operations for the performance of the R-tree. Guttman suggested several heuristics to divide the contents of an overflowing node into two sets and store each set in a different node. Deferred splitting, as mentioned in the R^*-tree and in the Hilbert R-tree, will improve performance. Of course, as in B-trees, a split may propagate upwards.

- *Range queries:* The tree is traversed, comparing the query MBR with the MBRs in the current node; thus, nonpromising (and potentially large) branches of the tree can be pruned early.

- *Nearest Neighbors:* The algorithm follows a "branch and bound" technique similar to [178] for nearest-neighbor searching in clustered files.

The algorithm works roughly as follows: given the query point Q, we examine the MBRs of the highest-level parents; we proceed in the most promising parent, estimating the best-case and worst-case distance from its contents, and using these estimates to prune out non-promising branches of the tree. Roussopoulos et al. [366] give the detailed algorithm for R-trees.

- *Spatial Joins:* Given two R-trees, the obvious algorithm builds a list of pairs of MBRs that intersect; then, it examines each pair in more detail, until we reach the leaf level. Significantly faster methods than the above straightforward method have been suggested [79, 78]. Lo and Ravishankar [270] proposed an efficient method to perform a spatial join when only one of the two spatial data sets has an R-tree index on it.

Conclusions

R-trees are one of the most promising SAMs. Among its variations, the R^*-trees and the Hilbert R-trees seem to achieve the best response time and space utilization, in exchange for more elaborate splitting algorithms.

11.2.3   Transformation to Higher-D Points

The idea is to transform 2-D rectangles into 4-D points [213], by using the low and high values for each axis; then, any point access method (PAM) can be used. In general, an n-dimensional rectangle will become a $2n$-dimensional point. The original and final space are called *native* and *parameter* space, respectively [323]. A range query in native space can also be translated to a range query in parameter space [213, 151].

The strong point of this idea is that we can turn any PAM into an SAM with very little effort. This approach has been used or suggested in several settings, for example, with grid files [213], B-trees [158], and hB-trees [271] as the underlying PAM.

The weak points are the following: First, the parameter space has high dimensionality, inviting "dimensionality curse" problems earlier on (see the discussion in Section 11.2.4). Second, except for range queries, there are no published algorithms for nearest-neighbor and spatial join queries. Nevertheless, it is a clever idea, which can be valuable for a stand-alone, special-purpose system, operating on a low-dimensionality address space. Such an application could be, for example, a temporal database system [435] where the spatial objects are 1-dimensional time segments [258].

11.2.4   Conclusions

From a practical point of view, the most promising methods seem to be the following:

- Z-ordering: Z-ordering and, equivalently, linear quadtrees have been very popular for 2-dimensional spaces. One of the major applications is in geographic information systems: linear quadtrees have been used both in production systems, like the TIGER system at the U.S. Bureau of Census [454], which stores the map and statistical data of the United States, as well as research prototypes such as QUILT [399], PROBE [324], and GODOT [181]. For higher dimensions, oct-trees have been used in 3-D graphics and robotics [27], and in databases of 3-D medical images [22]. Z-ordering performs very well for a low dimensionality and for points. It is particularly attractive because it can be implemented on top of a B-tree with relatively little effort. However, for objects with nonzero area (= hypervolume), the practitioner should be aware of the fact that each such object may require a large number of z-values for its exact representation; the recommended approach is to approximate each object with a small number of z-values [322, 323].

- R-trees and variants: They operate on the native space (requiring no transforms to high-dimensionality spaces), and they can handle rectangles and other shapes without the need to divide them into pieces. Cutting data into pieces results in an artificially increased database size (linear on the number of pieces); moreover, it requires a duplicate-elimination step because a query may retrieve the same object-id several times (once for each piece of the qualifying object). R-trees have been tried successfully for 20- to 30-dimensional address spaces [152, 337]. Thanks to the properties mentioned above, R-trees have been incorporated in academic as well as commercial systems, like POSTGRES and Illustra/Informix.

Before we close this section, we should mention the "dimensionality curse." Unfortunately, all the SAMs will suffer for high dimensionalities n: For the z-ordering, the range queries of radius r will require effort proportional to the hypersurface of the query region $O(r^{(n-1)})$. Similarly, for the R-trees, as the dimensionality n grows, each MBR will require more space; thus, the fanout of each R-tree page will decrease. This will make the R-tree taller and slower. However, as mentioned, R-trees have been successfully used for 20–30 dimensions [152, 337]. In the published literature, performance results for the z-ordering method are available for low dimensionalities only (typically, $n = 2$). A comparison of R-trees versus z-ordering for high dimensionalities is an interesting research question.

11.3 Text Retrieval

Here we present the main ideas for text retrieval methods. See Section 11.5 for citations to recent surveys. Access methods for text are interesting for three reasons:

1. Multimedia objects often have captions in free text; exploiting these captions may help retrieve some additional relevant objects [317].

2. Research in text retrieval has led to some extremely useful ideas, like the relevance feedback and the vector space model that we discuss next.

3. Text retrieval has several applications in itself, including library automation [381], searching on the World-Wide Web and the Internet (veronica [316], lycos, etc.), automated law and patent offices [214, 210], electronic encyclopedias [143] and dictionaries [192], and information filtering [126, 171]).

In text retrieval, the queries can be classified as follows [147]:

- Boolean queries: For example, "(data or information) and retrieval and (not text)." Here, the user specifies terms, connected with Boolean operators. Some additional operators are also supported, like adjacent, or within *n* words or within sentence, with the obvious meanings. For example, the query "data within sentence retrieval" will retrieve documents that contain a sentence with both the words "data" and "retrieval."

- Keyword search: Here, the user specifies a set of keywords, e.g., "data, retrieval, information"; the retrieval system should return the documents that contain as many of the above keywords as possible. This interface offers less control to the user, but it is more user-friendly because it does not require familiarity with Boolean logic.

Several systems typically allow for prefix matches; for example, "organ*" will match all the words that start with "organ," like "organs," "organization," "organism," and so on. We shall use the asterisk "*" as the variable-length "don't care" character.

The rest of this section is organized as follows: In the next three subsections we discuss the main three methods for text retrieval, namely, full text scanning, inversion, and signature files. In the last section we discuss the clustering approach.

11.3.1   Full Text Scanning

According to this method, no preprocessing of the document collection is required. When a query arrives, the whole collection is inspected until the matching documents are found.

When the user specifies a pattern that is a regular expression, the textbook approach is to use a finite state automaton (FSA) [215, pp. 29–35]. If the search pattern is a single string with no "don't care" characters, faster methods exist, like the Knuth, Morris, and Pratt algorithm [251], and the fastest of all, the Boyer and Moore algorithm [71] and its recent variations [425, 217].

For multiple query strings, the algorithm by Aho and Corasick [12] builds a finite state automaton in time linear on the total length of the strings, and reports all the matches in a single pass over the document collection.

Searching algorithms that can tolerate typing errors have been developed by Wu and Manber [460] and Baeza-Yates and Gonnet [23]. The idea is to scan the database one character at a time, keeping track of the currently matched characters. The algorithm can retrieve all the strings within a desired *editing distance* from the query string. The editing distance of two strings is the minimum number of insertions, deletions, and substitutions that are needed to transform the first string into the second [205, 272, 384]. The method is flexible and fast, requiring a few seconds for a few megabytes of text on a SUN-class workstation. Moreover, its source code is available through anonymous ftp from the University of Arizona (ftp://cs.arizona.edu/agrep).

In general, the advantage of every full text scanning method is that it requires no space overhead and minimal effort on insertions and updates, since no indices have to be changed. The price is that the response time is slow for large databases. Therefore, full text scanning is typically used for small databases (a few megabytes in size), or in conjunction with another access method (e.g., inversion) that would restrict the scope of searching.

11.3.2 Inversion

In inversion, each document can be represented by a list of keywords, which describe the contents of the document for retrieval purposes. Fast retrieval can be achieved if we invert on those keywords: The keywords are stored (e.g., alphabetically) in the index file; for each keyword, we maintain a list of pointers to the qualifying documents in the postings file. Figure 11.8 illustrates the file structure, which is very similar to the inverted index for secondary keys (see Figure 11.1).

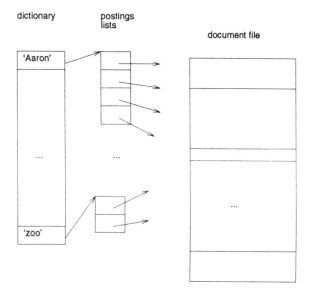

Figure 11.8: Illustration of inversion

Typically, the index file is organized using sophisticated primary-key access methods, such as B-trees, hashing, TRIEs [175], or variations and combinations of these (e.g., see [250, pp. 471–542]).

The advantages are that inversion is relatively easy to implement, it is fast, and it supports synonyms easily (e.g., the synonyms can be organized as a threaded list within the dictionary). For the above reasons, the inversion method has been adopted in most of the commercial systems such as DIALOG, BRS, MEDLARS, ORBIT, and STAIRS [381, Chapter 2].

The disadvantages of this method are the storage overhead and the cost of updating and reorganizing the index if the environment is dynamic. Techniques to achieve fast insertions incrementally include the work by Tomasic et al. [430], Cutting and Pedersen [124], and Brown et al. [81]. Typically, these methods try to exploit the skewness of the distribution of the postings list, treating the few long lists differently than the many short ones. Compression methods have also been suggested to minimize the size of the indices: Zobel et al. [474] use Elias's [140] compression scheme for postings lists, reporting small space overheads for the index. Finally, the glimpse package [273] uses a coarse index plus the agrep package [460] for approximate matching. Like the agrep package, glimpse is also available from the University of Arizona.

11.3.3   Signature Files

The idea behind signature files is to create a "quick and dirty" filter, which will be able to quickly eliminate most of the nonqualifying documents. As we shall see next and in Section 12.1, this idea has been used several times in very different contexts, often with excellent results. A recent survey on signature files is in [149].

The method works as illustrated in Figure 11.9: For every document, a short, typically hash-coded version of it is created (its *document signature*); document signatures are typically stored sequentially and are searched upon a query. The signature test returns all the qualifying documents, plus (hopefully, few) false matches, or *false alarms* or *false drops*. The documents whose signatures qualify are further examined, to eliminate the false drops.

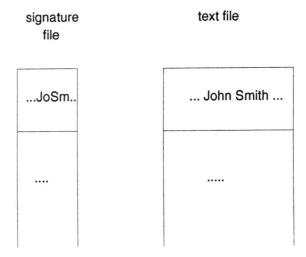

Figure 11.9: Example of signature files. For illustration, the signature of a word is decided to be its first two letters.

Figure 11.9 shows a naive (and not recommended) method of creating signatures, namely, by keeping the first two letters of every word in the document. One of the best methods to create signatures is *superimposed coding* [293]. Following the notation in [108], each word yields a bit pattern (*word signature*) of size F, with m bits set to one and the rest left as zero. These bit patterns are OR-ed to form the document signature. Figure 11.10 gives an example for a toy document with two words: "data" and "base."

Word	Signature
data	001 000 110 010
base	000 010 101 001
document signature	001 010 111 011

Figure 11.10: Illustration of superimposed coding: $F = 12$ bits for a signature, with $m = 4$ bits per word set to one

On searching for a word, say "data," we create its word signature and exclude all the document signatures that do not have a one at the corresponding bit positions. The choice of the signature length F depends on the desirable false-drop rate; the m parameter is chosen such that, on the average, half of the bits should be one in a document signature [419].

The method has been studied and used extensively in text retrieval: on bibliographic entries [167], for fast substring matching [208, 240], and in office automation and message filing [434, 153]. It has been used in academic [378, 377] as well as commercial systems [416, 247].

The advantages of the signature file approach are the simplicity of its implementation and the efficiency in handling insertions. In addition, the method is trivially parallelizable [416]. The disadvantage is that it may be slow for large databases, unless the sequential scanning of the signature file is somehow accelerated [378, 262, 470].

11.3.4 Vector Space Model and Clustering

The vector space model is very popular in information retrieval [380, 381, 446], and it is well suited for keyword queries. The motivation behind the approach is the *cluster hypothesis*: closely associated documents tend to be relevant to the same requests. Grouping similar documents accelerates the searching.

An important contribution of the vector space model is to envision each document as a V-dimensional vector, where V is the number of terms in the document collection. The procedure of mapping a document into a vector is called *indexing* (overloading the word!); indexing can be done either manually (by trained experts) or automatically, using a stop list of common

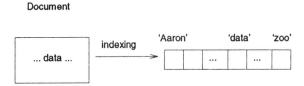

Figure 11.11: Illustration of the indexing process in information retrieval

words, some stemming algorithm, and possibly a thesaurus of terms. The final result of the indexing process is that each document is represented by a V-dimensional vector, where V is the number of permissible index terms (see Figure 11.11). Absence of a term is indicated by a 0 (or by minus 1 [122]); presence of a term is indicated by a 1 (for binary document vectors) or by a positive number (term weight), which reflects the importance of the term for the document.

The next step in the vector space model is to decide how to group similar vectors together (cluster generation); the last step is to decide how to search a cluster hierarchy for a given query (cluster search). For both the above problems, we have to decide on a document-to-document similarity function and on a document-to-cluster similarity function. For the document-to-document similarity function, several choices are available, with very similar performance (see [381, pp. 202–203] and [446, p. 38]). Thus, we present only the *cosine similarity function* [380], which seems to be the most popular:

$$\cos(\vec{x}, \vec{y}) = \vec{x} \circ \vec{y} / (\| \, \vec{x} \, \| \quad \| \, \vec{y} \, \|) \tag{11.1}$$

where $\vec{x}$ and $\vec{y}$ are two V-dimensional document vectors, $\circ$ stands for the inner product of two vectors and $\| \, . \, \|$ for the Euclidean norm of its argument. There are also several choices for the document-to-cluster distance/similarity function. The most popular seems to be the method that treats the centroid of the cluster as a single document, and then applies the document-to-document similarity/distance function. Other choices include the *single link method*, which estimates the minimum distance (= dissimilarity) of the document from all the members of the cluster, and the *all link method*, which computes the maximum of the above distances.

An interesting and effective recent development is *latent semantic indexing* (LSI), which applies the singular value decomposition (SVD) on the document-term matrix and automatically groups co-occurring terms. These groups can be used as a thesaurus, to expand future queries. Experiments showed up to 30% improvement over the traditional vector model [171].

More details on the method are in [151], along with the description of the SVD.

In the next subsections, we briefly describe the main ideas behind the cluster generation algorithms, the cluster search algorithms, and the evaluation methods of the clustering schemes.

Cluster Generation

Several cluster generation methods have been proposed; recent surveys can be found in [353, 299, 446]. Following Van Rijsbergen [446], we distinguish two classes: sound methods, which are based on the document-to-document similarity matrix, and iterative methods, which are more efficient and proceed directly from the document vectors, but are sensitive to the insertion order:

- *Sound methods*: If N is the number of documents, these methods usually require $O(N^2)$ time (or more) and apply graph theoretic techniques. A simplified version of such a clustering method would work as follows [135, p. 238]: An appropriate threshold is chosen, and two documents with a similarity measure that exceeds the threshold are assumed to be connected with an edge. The connected components (or the maximal cliques) of the resulting graph are the proposed clusters.

- *Iterative methods*: This class consists of methods that are faster: on the average $O(N \log N)$ or $O(N^2/\log N)$. They are based directly on the object (document) descriptions and they do not require the similarity matrix to be computed in advance. The typical iterative method works as follows:

  1. Choose some seeds (e.g., from sound clustering on a sample).

  2. Assign each vector to the closest seed (possibly adjusting the cluster centroid).

  3. Possibly, reassign some vectors, to improve clusters.

Several iterative methods have been proposed along these lines. The simplest and fastest one seems to be the *single pass method* [382]: Each document is processed once and is either assigned to one (or more, if overlap is allowed) of the existing clusters, or it creates a new cluster.

Cluster Searching

Searching in a clustered file is much simpler than cluster generation (see Figure 11.12). The input query is represented as a V-dimensional vector, and it is compared with the cluster centroids. The searching proceeds in the most similar clusters (i.e., those whose similarity with the query vector exceeds a threshold). As mentioned, a typical cluster-to-query similarity function is the cosine function (see Equation 11.1).

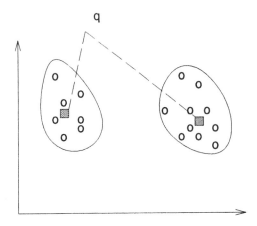

Figure 11.12: Searching in clustered files (for the query vector q, searching continues in the closest cluster at the left)

The vector representation of queries and documents has led to two important ideas: ranked output and relevance feedback. The first idea, ranked output, comes naturally because we can always compute the distance/similarity of the retrieved documents to the query, and we can sort them (most similar first) and present only the first screenful to the user.

The second idea, relevance feedback, is even more important because it can easily increase the effectiveness of the search [361]: The user pinpoints the relevant documents among the retrieved ones, and the system reformulates the query vector and starts searching from the beginning. To carry out the query reformulation, we operate on the query vector and add (vector addition) the vectors of the relevant documents and subtract the vectors of the nonrelevant ones. Experiments indicate that the above method gives excellent results after only two or three iterations [379].

11.3.5 Conclusions

We have discussed several methods for text searching and information retrieval. Among them, the conclusions for a practitioner are as follows:

- Full text scanning is suitable for small databases (up to a few megabytes); agrep is a recent, excellent freeware search package. Its scaled-up version, glimpse, allows fast searching for up to a few gigabytes of size.

- Inversion is the industry workhorse for larger databases.

- Signatures can provide a quick-and-dirty test when false alarms are tolerable or when they can be quickly discarded.

- The major ideas from the vector space model are two: relevance feedback and the ability to provide ranked output (i.e., documents sorted on relevance order).

11.4 Summary and Future Research

In this chapter, we have surveyed methods for secondary-key retrieval, for spatial data, for text objects.

For secondary-key access methods, inversion is the industry workhorse. For spatial access methods, z-ordering and R-trees have started making their way into commercial database systems. Between the two, R-trees have been tried for higher dimensionalities, while z-ordering has typically been used for 2-D and 3-D spaces. For text access methods, inversion is typically the method of choice for commercial systems; the most successful of them also incorporate the ideas of relevance feedback and ranked output, which the vector space model had long ago suggested.

For future research, spatial access methods would benefit from studies on the dimensionality curse, that is, access methods for high dimensionalities. In addition, the use of fractals for the analysis of spatial access methods seems like a promising direction.

For text, the technology for keyword matching in a centralized database is mature, with several commercial products. Some very interesting problems include how to find duplicates or near duplicates; how to handle the resulting huge indices, possibly through parallelism; how to handle queries and documents on multiple languages; and whether natural language processing (NLP) methods will help improve the precision and recall.

11.5   Bibliographic Notes

Surveys and descriptions for secondary-key retrieval methods appear in text-books for data structures and databases; for example, see Knuth [250]; and Korth and Silberschatz [253]. For a recent, very thorough survey of spatial access methods, see Gaede and Günther [180]. For text retrieval, see the survey in [147], the book by Frakes and Baeza-Yates [173], as well as the older books by Salton and McGill [381] and by Van Rijsbergen [446].

11.6   Exercises

11.1. Implement a k-D tree package, with insertion and range search routines. Again, let the number of dimensions n be defined on run-time by the user. (See [52] for more details on k-D trees.)

11.2. What is the z-value of the pixel (11, 00) in Figure 11.4? What is its Hilbert value?

11.3. Design an algorithm for the spatial join in R-trees.

11.4. Implement the code for the Hilbert curve for 2 dimensions.

11.5. Implement the code for the Hilbert curve for n dimensions.

11.6. Implement the straightforward method for full text scanning. That is, implement the function int find(char *s, char *p), which should scan the string s, locate the first occurrence of the pattern p, and return the matching position, or -1 if p is not a substring of s.

11.7. Implement the function int editDist (char *s, char *t), which will compute the editing distance of the two strings s and t. The editing distance is defined as the minimum number of insertions, deletions, or substitutions that are needed to transform one string to the other. (Hint: Use recursion; see the discussion by Hall and Dowling [205].)

Chapter 12

Multimedia Indexing

This chapter examines methods for searching multimedia data types by content. Section 12.1 describes the main idea behind GEMINI, a generic approach to indexing multimedia objects. Section 12.2 gives more details on GEMINI for whole-match queries. Section 12.3 illustrates the application of GEMINI for 1-D time series indexing. Section 12.4 focuses on indexing color images. Section 12.5 examines subpattern matching.

12.1 Basic Idea

For the rest of this part, we focus on multimedia objects, namely, time sequences and images. In this chapter we illustrate GEMINI, a generic approach to achieve fast searching in multimedia databases.

As mentioned in the introduction of this part, searching in multimedia databases is essential because it helps in predictions, computer-aided medical diagnosis and teaching, hypothesis testing, and, in general, in "data mining" [7, 8, 9] and rule discovery.

Of course, the distance of two objects has to be quantified. We rely on a domain expert to supply such a distance function $\mathcal{D}()$:

Definition 12.1 *Given two objects, O_A and O_B, the distance (= dissimilarity) of the two objects is denoted by*

$$\mathcal{D}(O_A, O_B) \tag{12.1}$$

For example, if the objects are two (equal-length) time series, the distance $\mathcal{D}()$ could be their Euclidean distance (sum of squared differences). Similarity queries can be classified into two categories:

- *Whole match:* Given a collection of N objects $O_A, O_B, \ldots, O_N$ and a query object Q, we want to find those data objects that are within distance ϵ from Q. Notice that the query and the objects are of the same type: for example, if the objects are 512×512 gray-scale images, so is the query.

- *Subpattern match:* Here the query is allowed to specify only part of the object. Specifically, given N data objects (e.g., images) $O_A, O_B, \ldots, O_N$, a query (sub-)object Q and a tolerance ϵ, we want to identify the parts of the data objects that match the query. If the objects are, for example, 512×512 gray-scale images (like medical X rays), in this case the query could be a 16×16 subpattern (e.g., a typical X ray of a tumor).

Additional types of queries include the nearest-neighbor queries (e.g., "find the five most similar stocks to IBM's stock") and the "all pairs" queries or spatial joins (e.g., " report all the pairs of stocks that are within distance ϵ from each other"). Both the above types of queries can be supported by our approach: As we shall see, we reduce the problem into searching for multidimensional points, which will be organized in R-trees; in this case, nearest-neighbor search can be handled with a branch-and-bound algorithm (e.g., [178], [52]), and the spatial join query can be handled with recent, highly fine-tuned algorithms [78]. Thus, we do not put much emphasis on nearest-neighbor and "all pairs" queries.

For both whole match and subpattern match, the ideal method should fulfill the following requirements:

- It should be fast. Sequential scanning and distance calculation with each and every object will be too slow for large databases.

- It should be "correct." In other words, it should return all the qualifying objects, without missing any (i.e., no false dismissals). Notice that false alarms are acceptable, since they can be discarded easily through a postprocessing step.

- The ideal method should require a small space overhead.

- The method should be dynamic. It should be easy to insert, delete, and update objects.

12.2   GEMINI for Whole Match Queries

To illustrate the basic idea, we shall focus on whole match queries. There, the problem is defined as follows:

- We have a collection of N objects: O_A, O_B, ..., O_N.

- The distance/dissimilarity between two objects (O_i, O_j) is given by the function $\mathcal{D}(O_i, O_j)$, which can be implemented as a (possibly slow) program.

- The user specifies a query object Q and a tolerance ϵ.

Our goal is to find the objects in the collection that are within distance ϵ from the query object. An obvious solution is to apply sequential scanning: For each and every object O_i $(1 \leq i \leq N)$, we can compute its distance from Q and report the objects with distance $\mathcal{D}(Q, O_i) \leq \epsilon$.

However, sequential scanning may be slow, for two reasons:

1. The distance computation might be expensive. For example, the editing distance in DNA strings requires a dynamic programming algorithm, which grows like the product of the string lengths (typically, in the hundreds or thousands for DNA databases).

2. The database size N might be huge.

Thus, we are looking for a faster alternative. The approach is based on two ideas, each of which tries to avoid each of the two disadvantages of sequential scanning:

- A quick-and-dirty test, to discard quickly the vast majority of non-qualifying objects (possibly allowing some false alarms)

- The use of spatial access methods, to achieve faster-than-sequential searching, as suggested by Jagadish [227]

The case is best illustrated with an example. Consider a database of time series, such as yearly stock price movements, with one price per day. Assume that the distance function between two such series S and Q is the Euclidean distance:

$$\mathcal{D}(S, Q) \equiv \left(\sum_{i=1}^{l} (S[i] - Q[i])^2 \right)^{1/2} \tag{12.2}$$

where $S[i]$ stands for the value of stock S on the ith day. Clearly, computing the distance of two stocks will take 365 subtractions and 365 squarings in our example.

The idea behind the quick-and-dirty test is to characterize a sequence with a single number, which will help us discard many nonqualifying sequences. Such a number could be, for example, the average stock price over the year; clearly, if two stocks differ in their averages by a large margin, it is impossible that they will be similar. The converse is not true, which is exactly the reason we may have false alarms. Numbers that contain some information about a sequence (or a multimedia object, in general) will be referred to as "features" for the rest of this chapter. Using a good feature (like the average, in the stock prices example), we can have a quick test that will discard many stocks with a single numerical comparison for each sequence (a big gain over the 365 subtractions and squarings that the original distance function requires).

If using one feature is good, using two or more features might be even better, because they may reduce the number of false alarms (at the cost of making the quick-and-dirty test a bit more elaborate and expensive). In our stock prices example, additional features might be the standard deviation, or, even better, some of the discrete Fourier transform (DFT) coefficients, as we shall see in Section 12.3.

The end result of using k features for each of our objects is that we can map each object into a point in k-dimensional space. We shall refer to this mapping as $F()$:

Definition 12.2 *Let $F()$ be the mapping of objects to k-D points; that is, $F(O)$ will be the k-D point that corresponds to object O.*

This mapping provides the key to improve on the second drawback of sequential scanning: by organizing these k-D points into a spatial access method, we can cluster them in a hierarchical structure, like the R-trees. Upon a query, we can exploit the R^*-tree to prune out large portions of the database that are not promising. Such a structure will be referred to by "F-index" (for "Feature index"). Thus, we do not even have to do the quick-and-dirty test on all of the k-D points!

Figure 12.1 illustrates the basic idea: Objects (e.g., time series that are 365-points long) are mapped into 2-D points (e.g., using the average and standard deviation as features). Consider the whole match query that requires all the objects that are similar to S_n within tolerance ϵ: this query becomes a k-D sphere in feature space, centered on the image $F(S_n)$ of S_n. Such queries on multidimensional points are exactly what R-trees and other SAMs are designed to answer efficiently. More specifically, the search algorithm for a whole match query is as follows:

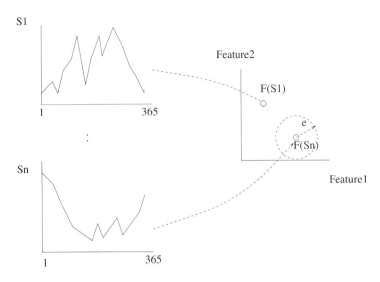

Figure 12.1: Illustration of basic idea: a database of sequences S_1, ..., S_n; each sequence is mapped to a point in feature space; a query with tolerance ϵ becomes a sphere of radius ϵ

Search an F-index

1. Map the query object Q into a point $F(Q)$ in feature space.

2. Using the SAM, retrieve all points within the desired tolerance ϵ from $F(Q)$.

3. Retrieve the corresponding objects, compute their actual distance from Q, and discard the false alarms.

Intuitively, an F-index has the potential to relieve both problems of the sequential scan, presumably resulting in much faster searches. The only step that we have to be careful with is that the mapping $F()$ from objects to k-D points does not distort the distances. Let $\mathcal{D}()$ be the distance function of two objects, and $\mathcal{D}_{feature}()$ be the (say, Euclidean) distance of the corresponding feature vectors. Ideally, the mapping should preserve the distances exactly, in which case the SAM will have neither false alarms nor false dismissals. However, requiring perfect distance preservation might be troublesome or very difficult; for example, it is not obvious which features we have to use to match the editing distance between two DNA strings. Even if the features are obvious, there might be practical problems. For example, in the stock price example, we could treat every sequence as a 365-dimensional vector; although in theory an SAM can support an arbitrary number of dimensions, in practice they all suffer from the dimensionality curse, as discussed earlier.

The crucial observation is that we can guarantee that the F-index method will not result in any false dismissals, if the distance in feature space matches or underestimates the distance between two objects. Intuitively, this means that our mapping $F()$ from objects to points should make things look closer.

Mathematically, let O_A and O_B be two objects (e.g., same-length sequences) with distance function $\mathcal{D}()$ (e.g., the Euclidean distance), and let $F(O_1)$ and $F(O_2)$ be their feature vectors (e.g., their first few Fourier coefficients), with distance function $\mathcal{D}_{feature}()$ (e.g., the Euclidean distance, again). Then we have the following:

Lemma 12.3 *To guarantee no false dismissals for whole match queries, the feature extraction function $F()$ should satisfy the following formula:*

$$\mathcal{D}_{feature}(F(O_1), F(O_2)) \leq \mathcal{D}(O_1, O_2) \tag{12.3}$$

Proof.   See [157].   □

In conclusion, the approach to indexing multimedia objects for fast similarity searching is as follows (named GEMINI, for "GEneric Multimedia object INdexIng"):

GEMINI

1. Determine the distance function $\mathcal{D}()$ between two objects.

2. Find one or more numerical feature extraction functions to provide a quick-and-dirty test.

3. Prove that the distance in feature space lower-bounds the actual distance $\mathcal{D}()$, to guarantee correctness.

4. Choose a SAM, and use it to manage the k-D feature vectors.

In the next sections, we show how the GEMINI approach was applied to 1-D time series and to 2-D color images. We shall see that the philosophy of the quick-and-dirty filter, in conjunction with the lower-bounding lemma, can lead to solutions to two problems:

- the dimensionality curse (time series)

- the "cross talk" of features (color images)

For each case, we describe the objects and the distance function, show how to apply the lower-bounding lemma, and mention related experimental results.

12.3   1-D Time Series

Here the goal is to search a collection of (equal-length) time series, to find the ones that are similar to a desirable series. For example, in a collection of yearly stock price movements, we want to find the ones that are similar to IBM. For the rest of the section, we shall use the following notational conventions: If S and Q are two sequences, then

- $Len(S)$ denotes the length of S

- $S[i : j]$ denotes the subsequence that includes entries in positions i through j

- $S[i]$ denotes the ith entry of sequence S

- $\mathcal{D}(S, Q)$ denotes the distance of the two (equal-length) sequences S and Q

12.3.1   Distance Function

According to the GEMINI algorithm, given at the end of Section 12.2, the first step is to determine the distance measure between two time series. This is clearly application-dependent. Several measures have been proposed for 1-D and 2-D signals. In a recent survey for images (2-D signals), Brown [82, p. 367, Section 4.2] mentions that one of the typical similarity measures is the cross-correlation (which reduces to the Euclidean distance, plus some additive and multiplicative constants).

As in [6], we chose the Euclidean distance because (1) it is useful in many cases, as is, and (2) it is often the case that other similarity measures can be expressed as the Euclidean distance between feature vectors after some appropriate transformation (e.g., see [229]).

Formally, for two sequences S and Q of the same length l, we define their distance $\mathcal{D}(S, Q)$ as their Euclidean distance (see Equation 12.2).

Additional, more elaborate distance functions (including time-warping [384], etc.) are the topic of future research. However, even for these distance functions, our method will work if we manage to lower-bound them with some Euclidean distance function.

12.3.2   Feature Extraction and Lower-Bounding

Having decided on the Euclidean distance as the dissimilarity measure, the next step is to find some features that can lower-bound it. We would like a set

of features that (1) preserve/lower-bound the distance and (2) carry much
information about the corresponding time series (so that the false alarms
are few). The second requirement suggests that we use "good" features
that have much discriminatory power. In the stock price example, a "bad"
feature would be, for example, the first day's value because two stocks might
have similar first-day values, yet they may differ significantly from then on.
Conversely, two otherwise similar sequences may agree everywhere, except
for the first day's values.

Clearly, we need some better features. A natural feature to use is the
average. By the same token, additional features could be the average of the
first half, of the second half, of the first quarter, and so on. These features
resemble the first coefficients of the Hadamard transform [135]. In signal
processing, the most well-known transform is the Fourier transform, and,
for our case, the discrete Fourier transform (DFT). Before we describe the
desirable features of the DFT, we proceed with its definition and some of its
properties:

12.3.3   Introduction to DFT

The n-point discrete Fourier transform [206, 318] of a signal $\vec{x} = [x_i]$, $i = 0, \ldots, n - 1$ is defined to be a sequence $\vec{X}$ of n complex numbers X_f, $f = 0, \ldots, n - 1$, given by

$$X_f = 1/\sqrt{n} \sum_{i=0}^{n-1} x_i \exp\left(-j 2\pi f i/n\right) \quad f = 0, 1, \ldots, n - 1 \qquad (12.4)$$

where j is the imaginary unit $j = \sqrt{-1}$. The signal $\vec{x}$ can be recovered by
the inverse transform:

$$x_i = 1/\sqrt{n} \sum_{f=0}^{n-1} X_f \exp\left(j 2\pi f i/n\right) \quad i = 0, 1, \ldots, n - 1 \qquad (12.5)$$

X_f is a complex number (with the exception of X_0, which is real if the signal
$\vec{x}$ is real). The energy $E(\vec{x})$ of a sequence $\vec{x}$ is defined as the sum of energies
(squares of the amplitude $|x_i|$) at every point of the sequence:

$$E(\vec{x}) \equiv \parallel \vec{x} \parallel^2 \equiv \sum_{i=0}^{n-1} |x_i|^2 \qquad (12.6)$$

A fundamental theorem for the correctness of our method is Parseval's
theorem [318], which states that the DFT preserves the energy of a signal:

Theorem 12.4 (Parseval's theorem) *Let $\vec{X}$ be the discrete Fourier transform of the sequence $\vec{x}$. Then*

$$\sum_{i=0}^{n-1} |x_i|^2 = \sum_{f=0}^{n-1} |X_f|^2 \tag{12.7}$$

Since the DFT is a linear transformation [318], Parseval's theorem implies that the DFT also preserves the Euclidean distance between two signals $\vec{x}$ and $\vec{y}$:

$$\mathcal{D}(\vec{x}, \vec{y}) = \mathcal{D}(\vec{X}, \vec{Y}) \tag{12.8}$$

where $\vec{X}$ and $\vec{Y}$ are Fourier transforms of $\vec{x}$ and $\vec{y}$, respectively.

Thus, if we keep the first k coefficients of the DFT as the features, we have

$$
\begin{aligned}
\mathcal{D}_{feature}(F(\vec{x}), F(\vec{y})) &= \sum_{f=0}^{k-1} |X_f - Y_f|^2 \\
&\leq \sum_{f=0}^{n-1} |X_f - Y_f|^2 = \\
&= \sum_{i=0}^{n-1} |x_i - y_i|^2 \equiv \mathcal{D}(\vec{x}, \vec{y})
\end{aligned} \tag{12.9}
$$

that is, the resulting distance in the k-D feature space will clearly underestimate the distance of two sequences. Thus, there will be no false dismissals, according to Lemma 12.3.

Note that we can use *any* orthonormal transform, such as the discrete cosine transform (DCT) [450], the wavelet transform [371] and so on, because they all preserve the distance between the original and the transformed space. In fact, the response time will improve with the ability of the transform to concentrate the energy: the fewer the coefficients that contain most of the energy, the fewer the false alarms, and the faster our response time.

We have chosen the DFT because it is the most well known, its code is readily available (e.g., in the *Mathematica* package [459] or in C [340]), and it does a good job of concentrating the energy in the first few coefficients, as we shall see next. In addition, the DFT has the attractive property that the amplitude of the Fourier coefficients is invariant under time shifts. Thus, using the DFT for feature extraction has the potential that our technique can be extended to finding similar sequences ignoring shifts.

12.3.4   Energy-Concentrating Properties of DFT

Thus far, we have proved that keeping the first few DFT coefficients will lower-bound the actual distance. The topic we address next is how good DFT is, that is, whether it allows few false alarms. To achieve that, we have to argue that the first few DFT coefficients will usually contain much information about the signal.

The worst-case signal for our method is white noise, where each value x_i is completely independent of its neighbors x_{i-1}, x_{i+1}. The energy spectrum of white noise follows $O(f^0)$ [392]; that is, it has the same energy in every frequency. This is bad for the F-index because it implies that all the frequencies are equally important. However, we have strong reasons to believe that real signals have a skewed energy spectrum. For example, random walks (also known as *brown noise* or *brownian walks*) exhibit an energy spectrum of $O(f^{-2})$ [392], and therefore an amplitude spectrum of $O(f^{-1})$. Random walks follow the formula

$$x_i = x_{i-1} + z_i \qquad\qquad (12.10)$$

where z_i is noise, that is, a random variable. Stock movements and exchange rates have been successfully modeled as random walks (e.g., [102, 274]).

In addition to stock price movements, other real signals have also a skewed amplitude spectrum. Birkhoff's theory [392] claims that "interesting" signals, such as musical scores and other works of art, consist of *pink noise*, whose energy spectrum follows $O(f^{-1})$. In addition to the above, there is another group of signals, called *black noise* [392]. Their energy spectrum follows $O(f^{-b})$, $b2$, which is even more skewed than the spectrum of brown noise. Such signals model successfully, for example, the water level of rivers as they vary over time [274].

12.3.5   Experiments

Experiments have shown that the response time has a (rather flat) minimum when we retain $k = 2$ or 3 features, and that the resulting method is faster than sequential scanning [6]. The major conclusions from the application of the GEMINI approach on time series are the following:

1. The approach can be successfully applied to time series, and specifically to the ones that behave like "colored noises" (stock price movements, currency exchange rates, water level in rivers, etc.).

2. For signals with skewed spectrum like the above ones, the minimum in the response time is achieved for a small number of Fourier coefficients

($k = 1$ to 3). Moreover, the minimum is rather flat, which implies that a suboptimal choice for k will give search time that is close to the minimum.

12.4 2-D Color Images

The goal is to study ways to query large on-line image databases using the images' content as the basis of the queries. Examples of the content we use include color, texture, shape, position, and dominant edges of image items and regions. Potential applications include medical ("give me other images that contain a tumor with a texture like this one"), photojournalism ("give me images that have blue at the top and red at the bottom"), and many others in art, fashion, cataloging, retailing, and industry.

Querying image databases by their image content is an active area of research. In terms of features to use, it benefits from the large body of work in machine vision on feature extraction and similarity measures (see, e.g., [27, 135]). Recently, several papers (such as [228, 307]) comment on the need for increased communication between the machine vision and the database communities for such problems. This is exactly one of the goals of this chapter.

Next we describe how to accelerate the search on color images. We focus on whole match queries, where the user specifies a whole image (either by sketching it, or by choosing it from a collection after browsing) and asks for similar images. More specifically, we examine queries on color. Details for queries on shape and texture can be found in [152, 170].

12.4.1 Image Features and Distance Functions

We describe the feature sets we use to characterize images, and the associated distance functions that try to capture the similarity that a human perceives. The features are computed once during the feature computation step (at insertion time), and the matching functions are applied using those features at query time. We mainly focus on the color features because color presents an interesting problem (namely, the "cross talk" of features), which can be resolved using the GEMINI approach (see Section 12.2).

One of the methods we used is to compute an h-element color histogram for each item and scene. Conceptually, h can be as high as 16×10^6 colors, with each color being denoted by a point in a 3-dimensional color space. In practice, we cluster similar colors together using an agglomerative clustering technique [135], and choose one representative color for each bucket (= "color bin"). In our experiments, we concentrated on using $h = 256$ and $h = 64$ color clusters. Each component in the color histogram is the percentage of pixels that are most similar to that color. Figure 12.2 gives an example of such a histogram of a fictitious photograph of a sunset; there are many red, pink, orange, and purple pixels, but only a few white and green ones. Once these histograms are computed, one method to measure the distance between two histograms ($h \times 1$ vectors) $\vec{x}$ and $\vec{y}$ is given by

$$d_{hist}^2(\vec{x}, \vec{y}) = (\vec{x} - \vec{y})^t \mathbf{A}(\vec{x} - \vec{y}) = \sum_i^h \sum_j^h a_{ij}(x_i - y_i)(x_j - y_j) \qquad (12.11)$$

where the superscript t indicates matrix transposition, and the color-to-color similarity matrix $\mathbf{A}$ has entries a_{ij}, which describe the similarity between color i and color j.

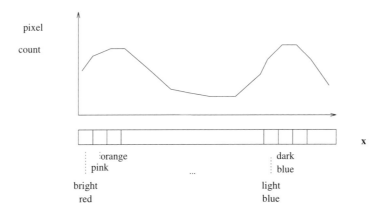

Figure 12.2: An example of a color histogram of a fictitious sunset photograph: many red, pink, orange, purple, and bluish pixels; few yellow, white, and greenish ones

12.4.2   Lower-Bounding

As mentioned before, we focus on indexing on the color; the texture creates no indexing problems, while the shapes present only the dimensionality curse ($k \approx 20$ features), which can be resolved with an energy-concentrating transformation. We have used the Karhunen-Loeve (K-L) transform [135]; our experiments on a collection of 1,000 and 10,000 shapes showed that an R^*-tree with the first $k = 2$ K-L coefficients gives the best overall response time [152].

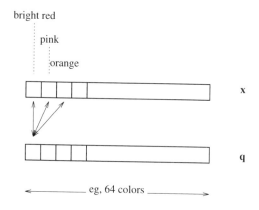

Figure 12.3: Illustration of the cross talk between two color histograms

In applying the F-index method for color indexing, there are two ob-
stacles: the dimensionality curse (k may be large, e.g., 64 or 256 for color
features) and, most importantly, the quadratic nature of the distance function. The distance function in the feature space involves cross talk among
the features (see Equation 12.11), and it is thus a full quadratic form involving all cross terms. Not only is such a function much more expensive to
compute than a Euclidean (or any L_p) distance, but it also precludes efficient
implementation of commonly used multikey indexing methods (SAMs). Figure 12.3 illustrates the situation: to compute the distance between the two
color histograms **x** and **q**, the bright-red component of **x** has to be compared
not only to the bright-red component of **q**, but also to the pink, orange, and
so on, components of **q**.

To resolve the cross-talk problem, we try to apply the GEMINI algorithm.
As we shall see, the algorithm solves both the dimensionality curse as well
as the cross-talk problems simultaneously. The first step of the algorithm
has been done: the distance function between two color images is given by
Equation 12.11: $\mathcal{D}() = d_{hist}()$. The next step is to find one or more numerical
features whose Euclidean distance would lower-bound $d_{hist}()$. Intuitively,
the question is again: If we are allowed to use only one numerical feature to
describe each color image, what should this feature be?

A natural choice is to consider some average value, or the first few
2-D DFT coefficients. Since we have three color components, (e.g., red,
green, and blue), we could consider the average amount of red, green, and
blue in a given color image. The average color of an image or item $\bar{x} =$

$(R_{avg}, G_{avg}, B_{avg})^t$ is defined in the obvious way, with

$$R_{avg} = (1/N) \sum_{p=1}^{N} R(p), \ G_{avg} = (1/N) \sum_{p=1}^{N} G(p), \ B_{avg} = (1/N) \sum_{p=1}^{N} B(p)$$

where there are N pixels in the item, and $R(p)$, $G(p)$, and $B(p)$ are the red, green, and blue components (intensities typically in the range 0–255), respectively, of the pth pixel. Given the average colors $\bar{x}$ and $\bar{y}$ of two items, we define $d_{avg}()$ as the simple Euclidean distance between the 3-dimensional average color vectors:

$$d_{avg}^2(\bar{x}, \bar{y}) = (\bar{x} - \bar{y})^t (\bar{x} - \bar{y}) \tag{12.12}$$

The next step of the GEMINI algorithm is to prove that our simplified distance $d_{avg}()$ lower-bounds the actual distance $d_{hist}()$. Indeed, this is true, as an application of the quadratic distance bounding theorem; see [152] for the details.

The result is that, given a color query, our retrieval proceeds by first filtering the set of images based on their average (R, G, B) color, then doing a final, more accurate matching using their full k-element histogram.

12.4.3   Experiments and Conclusions

Experiments on color retrieval on a collection of approximately 1,000 images are reported in [152]. Using a filter based on the RGB, the resulting method required at most 4 seconds, while sequential scanning took $\approx$ 10 seconds. Thus, the conclusions are the following:

- The idea to extract some features for a quick-and-dirty test motivated a fast method, using the average RGB distance; it also motivated a strong theorem [152], which guarantees the correctness in our case.

- Resolving the cross-talk problem has several benefits:

  — It allows indexing with SAMs.

  — It solves the dimensionality curse problem, as well.

  — It saves CPU time, since $d_{hist}()$ is quadratic on the number of colors ($O(h^2)$).

12.5 Subpattern Matching

Up to now, we have examined the whole match case. The question is, Could we extend the philosophy of the quick-and-dirty test, so that we can handle subpattern matching queries?

Let's focus on 1-D time series to illustrate the problem and the solution more clearly. Then, the problem is defined as follows:

- We are given a collection of N sequences of real numbers S_1, S_2, ..., S_N, each one of potentially different length.

- The user specifies query subsequence Q of length $Len(Q)$ (which may vary) and the tolerance ϵ, that is, the maximum acceptable dissimilarity (= distance).

- We want to find quickly all the sequences S_i $(1 \leq i \leq N)$, along with the correct offsets k, such that the subsequence $S_i[k : k + Len(Q) - 1]$ matches the query sequence: $\mathcal{D}(Q, S_i[k : k + Len(Q) - 1]) \leq \epsilon$.

As in Section 12.3, we use the Euclidean distance as the dissimilarity measure. The brute-force solution is to examine sequentially every possible subsequence of the data sequences for a match. We shall refer to this method as the "sequential scan method." Next, we describe a method that uses a small space overhead to achieve order of magnitudes savings over the sequential scan method.

12.5.1 Sketch of the Approach—ST-Index

Without loss of generality, we assume that the minimum query length is w, where w (≥ 1) depends on the application. For example, in stock price databases, analysts are interested in weekly or monthly patterns because shorter patterns are susceptible to noise [139]. Notice that we never lose the ability to answer shorter than w queries because we can always resort to sequential scanning.

Generalizing the reasoning of the method for whole matching, we use a sliding window of size w and place it at every possible position (offset), on every data sequence. For each such placement of the window, we extract the features of the subsequence inside the window. Thus, a data sequence of length $Len(S)$ is mapped to a trail in feature space, consisting of $Len(S) - w + 1$ points: one point for each possible offset of the sliding window. Figure 12.4 gives an example of a trail: Consider the sequence S_1, and assume that we keep the first $k = 2$ features (e.g., the amplitude of the

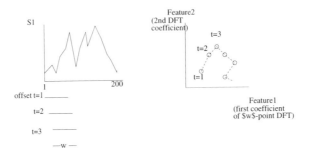

Figure 12.4: Illustration of the way that trails are created in feature space

first and second coefficient of the w-point DFT). When the window of length w is placed at offset $= 0$ on S_1, we obtain the first point of the trail; as the window slides over S_1, we obtain the rest of the points of the trail.

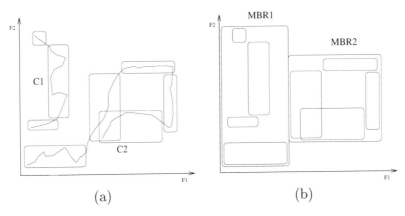

Figure 12.5: Example of (a) dividing trails into subtrails and MBRs, and (b) grouping of MBRs into larger ones

The straightforward way to index these trails would be to keep track of the individual points of each trail, storing them in a spatial access method. We call this method the "I-naive method," where "I" stands for "Index" (as opposed to sequential scanning). However, storing the individual points of the trail in an R^*-tree is inefficient, both in terms of space as well as search speed. The reason is that almost every point in a data sequence will correspond to a point in the f-dimensional feature space, leading to an index with a 1:k increase in storage requirements. Moreover, the search performance will also suffer because the R^*-tree will become tall and slow. As shown in [157], the I-naive method ended up being almost twice as slow as the sequential scan method. Thus, we want to improve the I-naive method by making the representation of the trails more compact.

Here is where the idea of a quick-and-dirty test leads to a solution. Instead of laboriously keeping track of each and every point of a trail in feature space, we propose to exploit the fact that successive points of the trail will probably be similar because the contents of the sliding window in nearby offsets will be similar. We propose to divide the trail of a given data sequence into subtrails and represent each of them with its minimum bounding (hyper-)rectangle (MBR). Thus, instead of storing thousands of points of a given trail, we shall store only a few MBRs. More importantly, at the same time we still guarantee no false dismissals. When a query arrives, we shall retrieve all the MBRs that intersect the query region; thus, we shall retrieve all the qualifying subtrails, plus some false alarms (subtrails that do not intersect the query region, while their MBR does).

Figure 12.5(a) gives an illustration of the proposed approach. Two trails are drawn: the first curve, labeled *C1* (on the northwest side), has been divided into three subtrails (and MBRs); the second one, labeled *C2* (in the southeast side), has been divided into five subtrails. Notice that it is possible that MBRs belonging to the same trail may overlap, as C2 illustrates.

Thus, we propose to map a data sequence into a set of rectangles in feature space. This yields significant improvements with respect to space, as well as with respect to response time, as shown in [157]. Each MBR corresponds to a whole subtrail, that is, points in feature space that correspond to successive positionings of the sliding window on the data sequences.

These MBRs can be subsequently stored in a spatial access method. We have used R^*-trees [48], in which case these MBRs are recursively grouped into parent MBRs, grandparent MBRs, and so on. Figure 12.5(b) shows how the eight leaf-level MBRs of Figure 12.5(a) will be grouped to form two MBRs at the next higher level, assuming a fanout of 4 (i.e., at most four items per nonleaf node). Note that the higher-level MBRs may contain leaf-level MBRs from different data sequences. For example, in Figure 12.5(b) we remark how the left-side MBR1 contains a part of the southeast curve C2.

This completes the sketch of the proposed index structure. We shall refer to it as "ST-index," for subtrail index. There are two questions that we have to answer to complete the description of our method:

- Insertions: When a new data sequence is inserted, what is a good way to divide its trail in feature space into subtrails? The idea [157] is to use an adaptive, heuristic algorithm, which will break the trail into subtrails, so that the resulting MBRs of the subtrails have small volume (and, therefore, result in few disk accesses on search).

- Queries: How to handle queries, and especially the ones that are longer than w? Figure 12.6 shows how to handle queries of length w. The query subsequence is translated into a point Q in feature space; all the MBRs that are within radius ϵ from Q are retrieved. Searching for longer queries is handled by the following algorithm:

  — Break the query subsequence into p disjoint pieces of length w each (ignoring the last piece if it is shorter than w).
  — Search for each piece, with tolerance $\epsilon/\sqrt{p}$.
  — OR the results and discard false alarms.

  Figure 12.7 illustrates the algorithm: the query sequence is broken into $p = 2$ pieces, each of length w; each piece gives rise to a range query in feature space.

Justifications and correctness proofs for the above algorithms are omitted for brevity (see [157]).

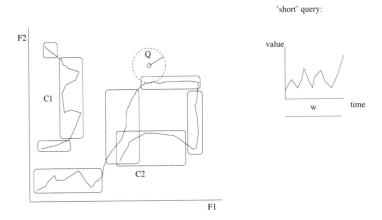

Figure 12.6: Illustration of the search algorithm for minimum-length queries: the query becomes a sphere of radius ϵ in feature space

12.5.2   Experiments

Experiments on real data (stock prices) are reported in [157]. The ST-index method outperforms sequential scanning by 3 to 100 times.

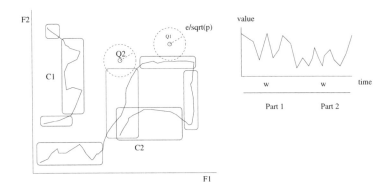

Figure 12.7: Illustration of the search algorithm for a longer query: the query is divided in $p = 2$ pieces of length w each, giving rise to p range queries in feature space

Using a quick-and-dirty filter pays off again. Every sequence is represented coarsely by a set of MBRs in feature space; despite the loss of information, these MBRs provide the basis for quick filtering, which eventually achieves large savings over the sequential scanning.

12.6 Summary and Future Research

In this chapter, we have considered the problem of fast searching in multimedia data types. We have focused on the GEMINI approach, to accelerate queries by content on multimedia databases. Target queries are, for example, "find images with a color distribution of a sunset photograph," or "find companies whose stock price moves similarly to a given company's stock."

The GEMINI approach combines two ideas:

- The first is to devise a quick-and-dirty test, which will eliminate several nonqualifying objects. To achieve that, we should extract k numerical features from each object, which should somehow describe the object (for example, the first few DFT coefficients for a time sequence, or for a gray-scale image).

- The second idea is to further accelerate the search by organizing these k-dimensional points using state-of-the-art spatial access methods (SAMs), like the R^*-trees. These methods typically group neighboring points together, thus managing to discard large unpromising portions of the address space early.

The above two ideas achieve fast searching, and, if the lower-bounding lemma is observed, GEMINI is not only fast, but also "correct," in the sense that it will not miss any qualifying object (false alarms are acceptable because they can be discarded, with the obvious way).

Finally, we mentioned case studies, where the GEMINI approach was applied to time sequences and color images.

There are several open problems for future research: How to handle distance functions other than the Euclidean (such as the string-editing distance, or distances involving time-warping [384]); data mining on signals to detect correlations; medical applications; and similarity searching for audio/music, as well as video signals.

12.7   Bibliographic Notes

For signal processing, see the textbooks by Oppenheim [318] and Hamming [206]. For textbooks on machine vision and pattern classification, see Duda and Hart [135], Ballard and Brown [27], and Fukunaga [177].

Multimedia indexing has only recently started to attract interest. The most accessible citation is probably the special issue of *IEEE Computer* dedicated to image databases; Flickner et al. [170] describe the QBIC system of IBM, which is operational and available on the Web. In the same issue, Ogle and Stonebraker [317] describe the extension of a relational database system, so that it can retrieve images by content as well as by caption. The monograph by Faloutsos [151] provides an extensive treatment of the topics in this part of the book.

12.8   Exercises

12.1. Implement a package to compute the DFT of a time sequence (an $O(N^2)$ algorithm is acceptable).

12.2. Use the above package to compute the 32-point DFT of a sinusoidal function $f(i) = 5\sin(2\pi 4i/32)$, $i = 0, \ldots, 31$. List your observations.

12.3. Use the above package to compute the DFT of a stock price sequence. Compare the amplitude spectrum with the $1/f$ line.

12.4. Extend the definition of the DFT to 2 dimensions; implement a package to do the 2-D DFT transform, and apply it on a gray-scale image. (Hint: see [318] or [340].)

Part V

Uncertainty in Databases and Knowledge Bases

Most research into the development of databases has assumed, by and large, that the database is "complete" and "perfect" in the sense that no data items are missing and that all the data contained in the database is perfectly accurate. However, real-world information is rarely complete, and its accuracy is very difficult to guarantee. This is particularly true in today's age, where data is often gathered from multiple, heterogeneous data sources, some of which are more reliable than others.

Part V of this book presents techniques by which databases may be extended to handle uncertain data. Chapter 13 introduces different models of uncertainty studied in the literature. Rather than cover the hundreds of uncertainty models proposed by researchers, it instead focuses on a few of the best-known paradigms. Chapter 14 then shows how the relational model of data may be extended to handle these models of uncertainty. Finally, Chapter 15 specifies how the deductive database paradigm may be extended to handle uncertain data.

also, more accurate infor may be more expensive

Chapter 13

Models of Uncertainty

13.1 Introduction

A database is a representation of data collected from one or more sources, by one or more individuals, over a potentially extensive period of time. To date, most treatments of databases have assumed that databases are "complete" in the sense that there are no missing pieces of information. Furthermore, they assume that the data present in the database is "perfect" in the sense that it is error-free. While these two assumptions are certainly reasonable as a starting point for the management of data, there are a variety of applications where we must account for the fact that data may be missing and/or erroneous.

Uncertain information may arise in databases in a wide variety of ways. Below, we present three different scenarios by which uncertainty may arise in databases, and later use the first of the three as a running example throughout the rest of Part V of this book.

13.1.1 Uncertainty in DBs: An Image Database Example

For example, consider the problem of representing image content (see Part IV) in a relational database. Consider a very simple relation called `face` that specifies which persons' faces are contained in which image files. Such a relation may have the schema

$$(\texttt{File}, \texttt{Person}, \texttt{LLx}, \texttt{LLy}, \texttt{URx}, \texttt{URy})$$

and a simple instance of the `face` relation is shown below:

File	Person	LLx	LLy	URx	URy
im1.gif	John Smith	10	10	20	20
im1.gif	Mark Bloom	10	10	20	20
im1.gif	Mark Bloom	30	10	40	20
im1.gif	Ted Lewis	30	10	40	20
im2.gif	Mark Bloom	50	10	60	20
im2.gif	Ted Lewis	10	10	20	20
im3.gif	Lynn Bloom	10	10	20	20
im3.gif	Elsa Bloom	10	10	20	20

The attribute names may be interpreted as follows:

- `File` is the name of an image file (e.g., `im1.gif`).

- `(LLx,LLy)` and `(URx,URy)` specify the lower-left corner and the upper-right corner of a rectangle (with sides parallel to the x- and y-axes) that bounds a particular person's face. Thus, in the above example, the first tuple indicates that there is a face (in `im1.gif`) in the rectangular region whose lower-left corner is at (10,10) and whose upper-right corner is at (20,20). Thus, the `(LLx,LLy)` and `(URx,URy)` components of any tuple uniquely capture a rectangle within the specified image.

- `Person` specifies the name of the person whose face occurs in the rectangle specified by a tuple in this relation. Thus, for instance, the first tuple in the `face` relation states that the person in the rectangular region whose lower-left corner is at (10,10) and whose upper-right corner is at (20,20) is John Smith.

In general, as stated in Part IV of this book, the identification of image subpatterns in a complex image is usually performed by an automatic image processing program. It is well known that such programs are only partially accurate—in particular, they can rarely make perfectly accurate identifications of the patterns involved. Consequently, if we are to consider an image processing program that processes a set of image files and stores the results in a table such as the relation `face` presented above, we must take into account the fact that these programs may be highly inaccurate. Furthermore, you may have already observed that the `face` relation is making a strange claim—after all, if we assume that each rectangle captures only one person's face, then tuples 1 and 2 of the `face` relation say that the person in the rectangular region whose lower-left corner is at (10,10) and whose upper-right corner is at (20,20) is simultaneously both John Smith and Mark Bloom, which is an apparent inconsistency. However, an image processing program may very well identify the person in this rectangle to be John Smith (with a certain confidence level) and Mark Bloom (with a possibly different confidence level). Consequently, both the tuples in the relation above are feasible, but each is "correct" only up to a certain confidence level.

13.1.2 Uncertainty in DBs: A Temporal Database Example

Part II of this book dealt extensively with temporal databases and introduced the concept of valid time. Often, a tuple in a relational database is timestamped with an interval of time. This often denotes the fact that the tuple was true at some time instant in that interval. For example, we may have a temporal relation called `shipping` that is maintained by a factory. This relation may have the schema

$$(\texttt{Item}, \texttt{Destination}).$$

When extended to handle temporal information, we may have a new additional attribute called `ShipDate` that denotes the date on which the item was shipped. The expanded `shipping` relation may contain the following tuples:

Item	Destination	When
widget-1	Boston	Jan. 1 ~ Jan. 7, 1996
widget-1	Chicago	Jan. 2, 1996
widget-2	Omaha	Feb. 1 ~ Feb. 7, 1996
widget-2	Miami	Feb. 18 ~ Feb. 21, 1996

The first tuple above says that the factory shipped an order of widget-1 to Boston sometime between January 1 and January 7 (inclusive). However, the precise date is unknown. Consider now the query "find all places to which widget-1 was shipped on or before January 5, 1996." As we will see below, some different answers are possible:

1. If we were to assume that the probability of being shipped on any given day is equally likely, then there is a $\frac{5}{7}$ probability that the Boston shipment was on or before January 5. Thus, we should return the answer

Destination	Prob
Boston	$\frac{5}{7}$
Chicago	1

2. On the other hand, if we know that nothing is shipped from the factory over the weekend, then we know, since January 1, 1996, was a Monday, that the probability of the shipment going out between January 1 and January 5 is 1, and we should return the answer

Destination	Prob
Boston	1
Chicago	1

In both cases, however, we needed to use probabilistic reasoning to determine what the answer should be. Furthermore, we assumed that there was a probability distribution over the values that could occur in a particular slot in the shipping relation.

13.1.3   Uncertainty in DBs: A Null-Value Example

As you are probably aware, it is not always possible to associate a value with each and every column of each and every tuple in a given relation. For example, because of some unforeseen conditions (e.g., a coffee spill), the destination of a particular shipment may not be deducible from a given shipping invoice. However, the name of the intended recipient may be visible, leading the database administrator to conclude that the shipment was intended for one of the two factories of that company, located in New York and Denver. The database administrator, after speaking to the shipping department, may conclude that most likely the shipment was intended for Denver (with 90% certainty). In this case, the following data may be entered into the database.

Item	Destination	When	Prob
widget-3	Denver	Jan. 25, 1996	0.9
widget-3	New York	Jan. 25, 1996	0.1

Any algorithm that now accesses this table will need to take into account the uncertainty inherent in this data when performing computations in response to user queries.

In the rest of this chapter, we will attempt to lay out formal definitions of some of the informal terms we have used above. In particular, the expression "confidence level" could be interpreted in terms of fuzzy set theory, members of some lattice of truth values, or probability theory. Each of these paradigms has some advantages and some disadvantages. Each of them leads to different extensions of the relational algebra and the relational calculus.

This chapter will introduce these different models of uncertainty and show how relational databases and deductive databases may be extended to handle these concepts.

The rest of this chapter is organized as follows. First, we introduce the three basic models of uncertainty. Subsequently, we show how relational databases may be extended to handle each of these uncertainty models. We then show how the concept of deductive databases, introduced in Chapter 3, may be extended to incorporate these different styles of uncertainty as well.

13.2 Models of Uncertainty

In this section, we introduce three models of uncertainty. The first of these is called fuzzy sets. The second, which is based on a concept called lattices, generalizes fuzzy sets. The third is based on probabilities.

13.2.1 Fuzzy Sets

We are all familiar with standard set theory (usually called *naive* set theory). Given a set S, we may associate with S a *characteristic function* χ_S, defined as

$$\chi_S(x) = \begin{cases} 1 & \text{if } x \in S \\ 0 & \text{otherwise} \end{cases}$$

Thus, all elements x are either in the set S or not.

In contrast to the above behavior, in fuzzy sets, the function χ_S may assign any real number in the unit interval $[0, 1]$ to element x. Thus, a fuzzy set S has an associated characteristic function, χ_S, that assigns *grades* or *levels* of membership to elements x. Intuitively, if $\chi_S(x) = 0$, then this means that x is definitely not in set S; if $\chi_S(x) = 1$, then this means that x is definitely in set S and if $\chi_S(x_1) = 0.3$ while $\chi_S(x_2) = 0.4$, then the degree of membership of x_1 in S is somewhat less than the degree of membership of x_2 in S.

In standard set theory, the concepts of union, intersection, and difference are defined in the standard ways:

$$S_1 \cup S_2 = \{x \mid x \in S_1 \text{ or } x \in S_2\}$$
$$S_1 \cap S_2 = \{x \mid x \in S_1 \text{ and } x \in S_2\}$$
$$\overline{S} = \{x \mid x \notin S\}$$

In contrast, we define union, intersection, and difference of fuzzy sets by specifying their associated characteristic functions, $\chi_{S_1 \cup S_2}$, $\chi_{S_1 \cap S_2}$, and $\chi_{\overline{S}}$. Fuzzy set theory does this in the following way:

$$\chi_{S_1 \cup S_2}(x) = \max(\chi_{S_1}(x), \chi_{S_2}(x))$$
$$\chi_{S_1 \cap S_2}(x) = \min(\chi_{S_1}(x), \chi_{S_2}(x))$$
$$\chi_{\overline{S}} = 1 - \chi_S(x)$$

Though we wish to pass no judgement on the epistemic basis underlying fuzzy set theory, we would like to make a couple of observations:

- First of all, in fuzzy sets, it is entirely possible that $\chi_{S \cap \overline{S}}(x)$ could be greater than zero. For instance, suppose S is a fuzzy set such that

$$\chi_S(a) = 0.5$$

  Then it is easy to see that $\chi_{\overline{S}} = 0.5$, which means that according to the above definition of fuzzy intersection,

$$\chi_{S \cap \overline{S}}(a) = \min(0.5, 0.5) = 0.5$$

  However, this seems to say that a enjoys a 50% membership grade in both S and its complement, which seems counterintuitive to many.

- Second, it is entirely possible that $\chi_{S \cup \overline{S}}(x)$ could be less than 1. Using the same example as above,

$$\chi_{S \cup \overline{S}}(a) = \max(0.5, 0.5) = 0.5$$

  This derived quantity seems to say a enjoys a 50% membership grade in the union of S and S's complement—thinking along classical lines, $S \cup \overline{S}$ would encompass everything, including a, which may indicate to some that a's membership grade in $S \cup \overline{S}$ should certainly be 1, irrespective of what S actually might be.

Points such as these have led to various acrimonious debates between the proponents and the opponents of fuzzy systems. Fixes to the above problem, based on the notion of a triangular norm, shall be reviewed in detail later on in this section.

Fuzzy Logic

In classical logic, there is a close correspondence between *sets* and logic. Part III introduced the notion of an *interpretation* of a classical logic language. If F is a formula in such a logical language, then F denotes the set of all interpretations that satisfy it, where satisfaction is as defined in Part III. Formulas in fuzzy logic have exactly the same syntax as those of classical logic. However, they differ from classical logic in the following ways:

- An interpretation of a fuzzy language is a function, I, that maps ground atoms in the language to real numbers in the unit interval $[0, 1]$.

- The notion of satisfaction is fuzzy—if $Sat(F)$ denotes the set of interpretations that satisfy F, then each interpretation I of the language has a degree of membership in $Sat(F)$.

Therefore, strictly speaking, given any formula F, and an interpretation I, we should use the notation $\chi_{Sat(F)}(I)$ to denote the degree of membership of I in $Sat(F)$. However, in order to simplify notation, we will merely write $I(F)$ for this quantity.

Suppose I is an interpretation. If X is any set of real numbers between 0 and 1 inclusive, we will use the notation $\inf(X)$ (pronounced *infimum* of X) to denote the largest real number that is smaller than all elements of X. The notation $\sup(X)$ (pronounced *supremum* of X) denotes the smallest real number that is greater than or equal to all elements of X. Then $I(F)$ may be defined inductively as follows:

$$I(\neg A) = 1 - I(A)$$
$$I(A \wedge B) = \min(I(A), I(B))$$
$$I(A \vee B) = \max(I(A), I(B))$$
$$I(\forall x.F) = \inf\{I(F[x/a]) \mid a \text{ is a ground term}\}$$
$$I(\exists x.F) = \sup\{I(F[x/a]) \mid a \text{ is a ground term}\}$$

In view of the informal correspondence between fuzzy sets and fuzzy logic, you will not be surprised to learn that fuzzy logic exhibits some of the same anomalies as fuzzy sets. For example, consider the interpretation I that assigns 0.5 to A; then,

1. $I(\neg A) = 0.5$

2. $I(A \wedge \neg A) = 0.5$

   3. $I(A \vee \neg A) = 0.5$

   The results above may appear contradictory to some. However, fuzzy
sets and fuzzy logic do have the advantage that computing the fuzzy truth
value assigned to a complex formula by an interpretation I is a very simple
process that is linear in the size of the formula. In contrast, as we shall see
later on in Section 13.2.4, the situation with probabilities is substantially
more complicated.

Triangular Norms and Conorms

In the preceding section, we have already presented some apparent drawbacks of fuzzy logic. These drawbacks are based on the belief among logi-
cians and computer scientists that formulas such as $(A \wedge \neg A)$ and $(A \vee \neg A)$
must be assigned the truth values 0 and 1, respectively, in all interpretations.
In order to alleviate these problems, the concept of a *triangular norm (and
conorm)* was introduced.

   Basically, a triangular norm T is a function that intuitively captures the
notion of conjunction. T-norms take as input two real numbers in the $[0, 1]$
interval, and return another number in the same interval. For example, the
function min is a T-norm. A triangular conorm S is, likewise, a function
that intuitively captures the notion of disjunction. T-conorms also take as
input two real numbers in the $[0, 1]$ interval, and return another number in
the same interval. For example, the function max is a T-conorm. In this
book, we will assume that given any T-norm T, this uniquely determines a
T-conorm S. [1]

   A function T from $[0, 1] \times [0, 1]$ is said to be a *triangular norm* iff it
satisfies the following axioms:

   1. $T(x, y) = T(y, x)$, for all x, y

   2. $T(T(x, y), z) = T(x, T(y, z))$, for all x, y, z

   3. If $x_1 \leq x_2$, then $T(x_1, y) \leq T(x_2, y)$

   The intuition behind the above axioms is simple. The first axiom merely
states that conjunction is commutative, that is, the truth value of $(A \& B)$
is the same as the truth value of $(B \& A)$. The second axiom is also simple
and states that conjunction should be associative. The last axiom says that

---

[1] We note that in the literature, T-norms and T-conorms have often been independently
defined and later "connected up" to satisfy some conditions.

the function T should be monotonic in both arguments; if the truth value of one conjunct is increased, then the truth value of the entire conjunct should increase.

Suppose T is a triangular norm. Then the *triangular conorm S* given by T is defined by

$$S(x, y) = 1 - T(1 - x, 1 - y)$$

The intuition behind the above axiom defining S in terms of T is the following:

1. Recall that in classical logic, $A \vee B$ is equivalent to $\neg(\neg A \wedge \neg B)$. Suppose now that the truth value assigned to A is x and that assigned to B is y.

2. Then the truth values assigned to $\neg A$ and $\neg B$ are $(1 - x)$ and $(1 - y)$, respectively.

3. Thus, if we want the formulas $A \vee B$ and $\neg(\neg A \wedge \neg B)$ to be equivalent (i.e., always assigned identical truth values), we should have $S(x, y) = 1 - T(1 - x, 1 - y)$.

At this stage, the basic idea is the following: as in the case of fuzzy logic, an interpretation I assigns values in the $[0, 1]$ interval to all ground atoms. Let us now suppose that the person building a system has decided that they want to interpret conjunction in terms of some selected triangular norm T and disjunction in terms of the corresponding triangular conorm S. Then $I(F)$ is defined as

$$I(\neg A) = 1 - I(a) \qquad \text{A, B are ground atoms}$$
$$I(A \wedge B) = T(I(A), I(B))$$
$$I(A \vee B) = S(I(A), I(B))$$
$$I(\forall x.F) = \inf\{I(F[x/a]) \mid a \text{ is a ground term}\}$$
$$I(\exists x.F) = \sup\{I(F[x/a]) \mid a \text{ is a ground term}\}$$

$F[x/a]$ denotes the replacement of all free occurrences of x in F by the ground term a (chosen from the Herbrand universe of our underlying logical language).

It is easy to verify that fuzzy logic may be captured as a special case of triangular norms, by setting $T = \min$ and $S = \max$.

13.2.2 Lattice-Based Approaches

Another approach that generalizes the fuzzy set approach is based on lattices (described briefly below). In this approach, the designer of a system that reasons with uncertainty picks some complete lattice, $(L, \sqsubseteq)$, and designates this to be the set of truth values of interest. This allows the user a great deal of flexibility in choosing the granularity of the uncertainty lattice. Once a complete lattice $(L, \sqsubseteq)$ has been selected, we may define an interpretation I to be a map from ground atoms to L; that is, $I(A)$ is a member of L for ground atoms A. A logic similar to fuzzy logic may then be induced, using the members of the lattice as truth values. Before going into further details of lattice-based logics, we provide a quick introduction to lattices.

Lattices

Suppose L is a set that is partially ordered under an ordering $\sqsubseteq$. We say that $(L, \sqsubseteq)$ is a lattice if it satisfies certain conditions. Figure 13.1 shows a variety of different lattices that we will use to illustrate the basic definitions provided in this section.

Suppose X is any subset of L, and u is some element of L. u is said to be an *upper bound* for X iff for each element $x \in X$ it is the case that $x \sqsubseteq u$. An upper bound u_{min} is said to be a least upper bound of X iff there is no other upper bound u' of X such that $u' \sqsubseteq u_{min}$.

Similarly, an element $\ell \in X$ is said to be a *lower bound* for X iff for each element $x \in X$ it is the case that $\ell \sqsubseteq x$. A lower bound ℓ_{max} is said to be a greatest lower bound of X iff there is no other lower bound ℓ' of X such that $\ell_{max} \sqsubseteq \ell'$.

For instance, if we consider the lattice in Figure 13.1(b), and take $X = \{LLt, Lt\}$, then this set has three upper bounds, Lt, t, and $\top$. Of these, Lt is the only least upper bound. On the other hand, it has two lower bounds, LLt and $\bot$, and of these, LLt is the greatest lower bound.

If we consider the lattice in Figure 13.1(c), and take Y_i to be the set $\{L^j t \mid j \geq i\}$, then the set $Y_0 = \{t, Lt, LLt, \ldots\}$ has two upper bounds, t and $\top$. Of these, t is the least upper bound. On the other hand, Y_0 has only one lower bound, $\bot$, which therefore is also the greatest lower bound.

It is obvious that if X is a subset of $(L, \sqsubseteq)$, then X may have at most one least upper bound, and at most one greatest lower bound. To see why X may not have two or more least upper bounds, let us assume that u_1 and u_2 are both least upper bounds of X. By the definition of least upper bounds, we know that $u_1 \sqsubseteq u_2$ and $u_2 \sqsubseteq u_1$. As $\sqsubseteq$ is a partial ordering, it follows that $u_1 = u_2$. The same reasoning applies to greatest lower bounds.

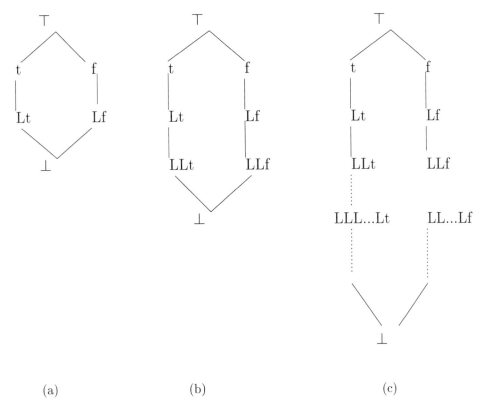

Figure 13.1: Some example lattices

$(L, \sqsubseteq)$ is said to be a *lattice* iff for every finite subset $X \subseteq L$, it is the case that X has a unique least upper bound, denoted $\sqcup(X)$, and a unique greatest lower bound, denoted $\sqcap(X)$. $(L, \sqsubseteq)$ is said to be a *complete lattice* iff for every subset (finite and infinite), it is the case that X has a unique least upper bound and a unique greatest lower bound.

Some examples of such (complete) lattices are shown below:

- SIX: This lattice is shown diagrammatically in Figure 13.1(a). As usual, the values t and f stand for true and false, respectively. The value $\bot$ means undetermined (or unknown). Similarly, the value $\top$ means overdetermined (or inconsistent). Lt and Lf stand, respectively, for likely to be true and likely to be false. The fact that Lt is below t in the ordering may be thought of as follows: if an interpretation I assigns Lt to some atom A, then I is "less informative" about A

than if it were to assign t to A. Of course, the $\top$ truth value is overly informative!

- FOUR: This lattice is obtained by eliminating the values Lt and Lf from the lattice SIX. This lattice was used extensively by Vassiliou [447] to characterize the semantics of null values.

- EIGHT: This lattice is identical to the lattice of SIX, except that it has two new truth values, LLt and LLf, standing for "likely to be likely to be true" and "likely to be likely to be false," respectively. This lattice may be viewed as a more fine-grained refinement of SIX.

- L^{∞}: This lattice is shown diagrammatically in Figure 13.1(c) and was introduced by Halpern and Rabin. Intuitively, the truth value $L^{i+1}t$ says "it is likely that $L^{i}t$ is true." This lattice may be viewed as a more fine-grained refinement of both SIX and EIGHT.

- $[0, 1]$: This lattice, with the usual less than or equals ordering on it, corresponds to the assignment of truth in fuzzy logic.

- $[0, 1] \times [0, 1]$: Consider this set with the ordering $(x_1, y_1) \sqsubseteq (x_2, y_2)$ iff $x_1 \leq x_2$ and $y_1 \leq y_2$. When interpretation I assigns (x, y) to an atom A, this means that I's degree of belief that A is true is x, and its degree of belief that A is false is y. Notice that no restrictions are placed on whether $x + y = 1$, $x + y \leq 1$, and so on.

Of course, the above is only a small list of examples of lattice-based strategies. Kifer and Subrahmanian have shown how these strategies may be used to capture reasoning with multiple agents and multiple modules, as well as reasoning with multiple representations of time. The definition of how interpretations assign truth values to complex formulas is as follows:

$$I(\neg A) = \sqcup\{x \mid x \sqcup I(A) = \top\}$$
$$I(A \wedge B) = \sqcap(I(A), I(B))$$
$$I(A \vee B) = \sqcup(I(A), I(B))$$
$$I(\forall x.F) = \sqcap\{I(F[x/a]) \mid a \text{ is a ground term}\}$$
$$I(\exists x.F) = \sqcup\{I(F[x/a]) \mid a \text{ is a ground term}\}$$

Here, we use the notation $\sqcap$ and $\sqcup$ to denote the greatest lower bound (glb) and least upper bound (lub) operators on the lattice $(L, \sqsubseteq)$. We may often use the notation $\mu_1 \sqcup \cdots \sqcup \mu_n$ to denote $\sqcup\{\mu_1, \ldots, \mu_n\}$, and $\mu_1 \sqcap \cdots \sqcap \mu_n$ to denote $\sqcap\{\mu_1, \ldots, \mu_n\}$.

13.2.3 Relationship to Fuzzy Logic

To see why the lattice-based approach generalizes fuzzy logic, we need to show that fuzzy logic can be expressed in terms of the lattice-based approach. To see this, we observe the following:

- First and foremost, the unit interval $[0, 1]$ of reals forms a complete lattice under the usual "less than or equals" ordering $\leq$. The least upper bound operator is the sup (supremum) operator on the reals, while the greatest lower bound operator is the inf (infimum) operator.

- If we fix our lattice to be the unit interval of reals under the $\leq$ ordering, then an interpretation (with respect to the lattice) is a mapping from ground atoms of our language to the unit interval $[0, 1]$. This coincides with the definition of a fuzzy interpretation. That is, if I_r is any lattice-based interpretation over $[0, 1]$, then it is a fuzzy interpretation as well.

- The only thing that we still need to show is that the lattice-based definition of satisfaction of formulas by I_r coincides with the definition of satisfaction by a fuzzy interpretation. However, this is easily verified to be true if we choose our complementation operator $\mathsf{com}(x) = 1 - x$. The truth values assigned by I_r are as follows:

  1. $I_r(A) = \mathsf{com}(I_r(A)) = 1 - I_r(A)$, which coincides with the fuzzy definition.
  2. $I_r(A \wedge B) = \sqcap\{I_r(A), I_r(B)\}$, which coincides with $\min(I_r(A), I_r(B))$ because greatest lower bound under the $\leq$-ordering on reals is min when applied to finite sets.
  3. $I_r(A \vee B) = \sqcup\{I_r(A), I_r(B)\}$, which coincides with $\max(I_r(A), I_r(B))$ because least upper bound under the $\leq$-ordering on reals is max when applied to finite sets.
  4. $I_r(\forall x.F) = \sqcap\{I(F[x/a])|a \text{ is a ground term}\}$. This coincides with $\inf(\{I(F[x/a]) \mid a \text{ is a ground term}\}$, which is what is assigned to this formula by a fuzzy interpretation.
  5. $I_r(\exists x.F) = \sqcup\{I(F[x/a])|a \text{ is a ground term}\}$. This coincides with $\sup(\{I(F[x/a]) \mid a \text{ is a ground term}\}$, which is what is assigned to this formula by a fuzzy interpretation.

Thus, we see that fuzzy logic is obtained as a special case of the lattice-based class of logics by picking as our lattice the unit interval $[0, 1]$ of reals under the ordering $\leq$, and picking as our definition of negation the operator $\mathsf{com}(x) = 1 - x$.

13.2.4   Probability Theory

Of all existing paradigms for reasoning about uncertainty and chance, probability theory is undoubtedly the best known and most studied. Researchers from the time of Aristotle and Euclid have delved into one or more aspects of probability theory. In probability theory, we have a space of possible events, $\mathcal{E}$, and a probability function, $\mathbf{P}$, that ascribes, to each event e in this space, a real number called the *probability* of event e. Compound events are *combinations* of events in e. For instance, $(e_1 \wedge e_2)$ refers to the event composed of e_1 and e_2 both occurring. Similarly, $(e_1 \vee e_2)$ refers to the compound event in which at least one of e_1, e_2 occur. Though probability theory deals extensively with various aspects of sampling, estimation, and statistical distributions, we will not go into those issues here—you are encouraged to refer to one of the numerous excellent texts on probability for this purpose.

The basic issue that we will consider in this section is the following: Suppose $\mathbf{P}$ is the probability associated with the event space $\mathcal{E}$. How should $\mathbf{P}$ be extended so as to assign probabilities to complex events?

There is no unique answer to the above question. Rather, an appropriate answer to this question depends upon our knowledge of the relationship between the events whose probability is being combined. In the rest of this section, we will present some elementary ways of computing the probabilities of compound events under different assumptions.

Independence

The most common assumption made in probability theory is the assumption that two events, e_1 and e_2, are independent (i.e., there is no connection between e_1 and e_2). In our example describing the faces of different individuals, the events

$$e_1 = \text{``John Smith occurs in the rectangle with lower-left}$$
$$\text{corner (10,10) and upper-right corner (20,20) of im1.gif''}$$
$$e_2 = \text{``Lynn Bloom occurs in the rectangle with lower-left}$$
$$\text{corner (10,10) and upper-right corner (20,20) of im3.gif''}$$

may well be considered independent if no additional information is available.

However, suppose e_3 is the event

$e_3 = $ "Mark Bloom occurs in the rectangle with lower-left
corner (10,10) and upper-right corner (20,20) of im1.gif"

In this case, e_1 and e_3 are not independent as only one person's face is allowed to appear in a rectangle.

Under the assumption of independence, probabilities of complex events are computed as follows:

$$\mathbf{P}(e_1 \wedge e_2) = \mathbf{P}(e_1) \times \mathbf{P}(e_2)$$
$$\mathbf{P}(e_1 \vee e_2) = \mathbf{P}(e_1) + \mathbf{P}(e_2) - \mathbf{P}(e_1) \times \mathbf{P}(e_2)$$
$$\mathbf{P}(\neg e_1) = 1 - \mathbf{P}(e_1)$$

Another well-known concept is *conditional probability*, which asks, "What is the probability that e_2 occurs given that e_1 has occurred?" Note that the probability of e_1 may not be 1—rather, conditional probabilities ask what the probability of e_2's occurrence is, if we know that e_1 has in fact occurred. The event "e_2 occurs, given that e_1 has occurred" is usually denoted $(e_2|e_1)$, and its probability, under the independence assumption, is defined as

$$\mathbf{P}(e_2|e_1) = \frac{\mathbf{P}(e_1 \wedge e_2)}{\mathbf{P}(e_1)}$$

The above formula assumes that $\mathbf{P}(e_1) \neq 0$; this assumption is reasonable as we are assuming that e_1 has occurred, and it is absurd to make such an assumption if we know that e_1's probability is 0, indicating that it is an impossible event.

Ignorance

Though the assumption that two events are independent is often appealing, it can only be used under rather limited circumstances. After all, in many cases, we may not even know what the relationship between two events is, if any. In the face example, it may very well be the case that the photographs were collected in some specific, ordering manner, and this may very well affect the computed probabilities. Alternatively, consider the events e_1 and e_2 given below:

$$e_1 = \text{Radar } r \text{ is a 200 KHz radar.}$$

$$e_2 = \text{Radar } r \text{ is detectable by sensor } s.$$

Here r may be an enemy radar, whose precise emitting frequency is not known to us. Each of the above events has a probability, but what is the probability that event $e_1 \wedge e_2$ occurs if we are ignorant about the relationship between events e_1 and e_2 ? We may compute this analytically as follows:

1. There are four possible worlds associated with this example. In the first world (w_1), neither e_1 nor e_2 is true; in the second world (w_2), e_1 is true, but e_2 is not; in the third (w_3), e_1 is not true, but e_2 is; in the last world (w_4), both e_1 and e_2 are true. By "event e is true," we mean that this event occurs in the world in question.

2. Suppose p_i denotes the probability that the "real" world is world w_i. Then we may create a linear program, LP, containing four constraints:

$$p_2 + p_4 = \mathbf{P}(e_1) \tag{13.1}$$

$$p_3 + p_4 = \mathbf{P}(e_2) \tag{13.2}$$

$$p_1 + p_2 + p_3 + p_4 = 1 \tag{13.3}$$

$$p_i \geq 0 \text{ for } i = 1, \ldots, 4 \tag{13.4}$$

Let us see why these constraints can be derived. Event e_1 occurs in two mutually exclusive worlds, w_2 and w_4, and as these two worlds are mutually incompatible, the probability of event e_1 is the sum of the probabilities of these two worlds being the "real" world. Notice, here, that $\mathbf{P}(e_1)$ and $\mathbf{P}(e_2)$ are constants, whose values are known to us, and p_1, p_2, p_3, and p_4 are unknown variables.

In light of the above discussion, what is $\mathbf{P}(e_1 \wedge e_2)$? $e_1 \wedge e_2$ is true in only one world, w_4. Hence, the probability $\mathbf{P}(e_1 \wedge e_2)$ is given by solving for the value of p_4 subject to the constraints $LP = \{$ 13.1, 13.2, 13.3, 13.4$\}$, given above. However, different solutions of LP may yield different values of p_4. For example, suppose $\mathbf{P}(e_1) = 0.3$ and $\mathbf{P}(e_2) = 0.6$. Then each of σ_1, σ_2, and σ_3, given below, is a solution of LP:

$$\sigma_1 = \{p_1 = 0.1; p_2 = 0.3; p_3 = 0.6; p_4 = 0\}$$
$$\sigma_2 = \{p_1 = 0; p_2 = 0.4; p_3 = 0.6; p_4 = 0\}$$
$$\sigma_3 = \{p_1 = 0.4; p_2 = 0; p_3 = 0.3; p_4 = 0.3\}$$

In addition to the above three solutions, LP has many other solutions. However, there is no solution in which p_4 has a value less than 0, and no solution in which p_4's value is over 0.3. Thus, the constraints listed above, and the information we have about e_1 and e_2's probabilities, only allow us to determine a precise range (rather than a point) for the probability of $e_1 \wedge e_2$. This range may be computed in the above case by solving two linear programming problems. These are

- **minimize p_4 subject to LP**
- **maximize p_4 subject to LP**

Generally speaking, we may determine the probability ranges of complex formulas from those of other known formulas by using the following method:

1. Suppose $\mathcal{E} = \{e_1, \ldots, e_k\}$ is the set of all elementary (i.e., noncomplex) events. Let $W = \{w_1, \ldots, w_n\}$ be the power set of $\mathcal{E}$, where $n = 2^k$.

2. Let **Known** be some set of events (simple and complex) such that, for each event $ev \in$ **Known**, we know a lower bound **lower**(ev) and an upper bound **upper**(ev) on ev's probability.

3. Notice that a world is just an Herbrand interpretation, and an event (simple or complex) is just a propositional formula constructed from the set of symbols in $\mathcal{E}$. Hence, we may use the same definition of satisfaction of a formula by an interpretation as presented in Part III to determine which events occur in which worlds.

4. Recall that we use the variable p_i to denote the probability of world w_i. With this in mind, we may now construct a set $LP(\textbf{Known})$ as follows:

   a. For each $ev \in$ **Known**, $LP(\textbf{Known})$ contains the constraint

   $$\textbf{lower}(ev) \leq \sum_{w_i \models ev} p_i \leq \textbf{upper}(ev)$$

b. $LP(\mathbf{Known})$ contains the constraint

$$\sum_{i=1}^{n} p_i = 1$$

c. For each $i = 1, \ldots, n$, $LP(\mathbf{Known})$ contains the constraint

$$0 \le p_i \le 1$$

5. To determine the probability of an arbitrary event $ev^\star$, solve the following two linear programming problems:

   a. **Lower Bound: Minimize $\sum_{w_i \models ev^\star} p_i$ subject to $LP(\mathbf{Known})$**

   b. **Upper Bound: maximize $\sum_{w_i \models ev^\star} p_i$ subject to $LP(\mathbf{Known})$**

Before giving an example, we provide some quick intuitions about the above approach. Let $\mathsf{lb}(ev^\star)$ and $\mathsf{ub}(ev^\star)$ denote the lower and upper bounds obtained above. $LP(\mathbf{Known})$ is a set of constraints that describes all the probabilities that we know apply to different events. Each solution of the constraint set $LP(\mathbf{Known})$ makes some probability assignment to the event $ev^\star$. However, different solutions may assign different values; the fact that $LP(\mathbf{Known})$ has multiple solutions reflects our uncertainty about the world. The lower bound above gives us the minimal possible probability of $ev^\star$, while the upper bound yields the maximal possible probability of $ev^\star$. Interestingly enough, for every probability $\mathsf{lb}(ev^\star) \le p \le \mathsf{ub}(ev^\star)$ that lies between the lower bound and upper bound of $ev^\star$'s probability, there exists a solution σ of $LP(\mathbf{Known})$ such that $p = \sum_{w_i \models ev^\star} v_i$, where v_i is the value assigned to the variable p_i by the solution σ. Thus, the interval $[\mathsf{lb}(ev^\star), \mathsf{ub}(ev^\star)]$ precisely captures the range of possible probability values that $ev^\star$ could even have.

To see how the above definitions may be used, consider the following three events:

$$e_1 = \text{Radar } r \text{ is a 200 KHz radar.}$$
$$e_2 = \text{Radar } r \text{ was built in South Africa.}$$
$$e_3 = \text{Radar } r \text{ was bought before 1989.}$$

There are eight worlds, $w_1, \ldots, w_8$, associated with these three events. They are

$$w_1 = \emptyset \qquad w_2 = \{e_1\}$$
$$w_3 = \{e_2\} \qquad w_4 = \{e_3\}$$
$$w_5 = \{e_1, e_2\} \qquad w_6 = \{e_1, e_3\}$$
$$w_7 = \{e_2, e_3\} \qquad w_8 = \{e_1, e_2, e_3\}$$

Suppose we know the following two facts: e_1's probability lies between 0.3 and 0.5, and $(e_2 \wedge e_3)$'s joint probability lies between 0.35 and 0.45. Then $LP(\mathbf{Known})$ is given by the following constraints:

$$0.3 \leq p_2 + p_5 + p_6 + p_8 \leq 0.5$$
$$0.35 \leq p_7 + p_8 \leq 0.45$$
$$p_1 + \cdots + p_8 = 1$$
$$0 \leq p_1, \ldots, p_8 \leq 1$$

If we wish to compute the probability that $(e_1 \wedge e_2)$ occur together, then we must attempt to

- **minimize** $(p_5 + p_8)$ **subject to** $LP(\mathbf{Known})$ to find the lower bound and

- **maximize** $(p_5 + p_8)$ **subject to** $LP(\mathbf{Known})$ to find the upper bound.

13.3 Bibliographic Notes

The study of multivalued logic stretches back hundreds of years. Rescher's excellent book [356] provides an excellent introduction to the formal theory of multivalued logic, with emphasis on the philosophical foundations. In particular, Rescher introduces several different types of multiple-valued logics and suggests applications to real-world reasoning situations.

In contrast to Rescher's philosophically motivated study are the excellent mathematical treatments of multivalued logic, based on Boolean algebras. In these works, best described by the Polish school of logic, the authors assume that classical two-valued logic may be extended to logic based on arbitrary Boolean algebras. Boolean algebras basically consist of a set, together with certain operations on the set that satisfy certain axioms. Sikorski's classic work [402], as well as Rasiowa's excellent mathematical treatment of logic based on Boolean algebras, are well summarized in [352].

Fuzzy logic may be viewed as a special case of a Boolean algebra. It was introduced by Zadeh in two pioneering papers [462, 463], both of which are eminently readable. The key difference between fuzzy logic and the above work on Boolean-valued logics is that Zadeh's paper makes several linguistic claims regarding fuzzy logic. For example, there are claims that statements such as "John is tall" may be captured through fuzzy logic—a claim that has generated some controversy. Kosko [254] provides an easy nontechnical introduction to fuzzy logic for the layperson. Other interesting aspects of fuzzy logic may be found in [26].

References [70, 334, 85, 191, 259] are all elegant introductions to probability theory. Schrijver [391] is a good text for learning more about linear programming (which we have used in this chapter). The relationship between logic and probability was pioneered by Boole as long back as 1854 [70, 204], and Carnap further developed the foundations of probability in a classic series of papers [85]. Later, Dempster [128] and Shafer [397] presented a comprehensive theory of how probabilities obtained as evidence from different sources may be combined, leading to what is today known as Dempster-Shafer theory. Nilsson [311] was one of the first to use probabilistic logics in artificial intelligence—an approach that has subsequently been developed extensively by Fagin, Halpern, and their coworkers [144].

The use of uncertainty in databases was motivated in large part through the desire to treat null values. In the relational model of data, we may not always know precisely the value of an attribute field A of a tuple t. However, we may know that $t.A$ is one of some set of values $v_1, \ldots, v_n$, and furthermore, there may exist a "confidence" or probability associated with each of these values. Lipski [267] and Vassiliou [447] both addressed this problem. More recently, Dyreson and Snodgrass [138] studied the issue of uncertainty in databases arising from temporal indeterminacy (see the example at the beginning of this chapter). The temporal database query language TSQL2 [409] provides syntactic constructs for reasoning with such types of uncertainty.

Lakshmanan, Leone, Ross, and Subrahmanian [260] have developed a system called ProbView [260], where users may request that relational algebraic operations be performed with respect to one or more user-specified probability assumptions.

13.4   Exercises

13.1. Suppose I is a fuzzy logic interpretation that assigns 0.3 to A and 0.4 to B. What does I assign to

    a. $A \wedge B$

    b. $A \wedge \neg B$

 c. $((A \wedge \neg B) \vee (\neg A \wedge B))$

13.2. Suppose I is a fuzzy interpretation and all you know is that $I((A \wedge B) \vee C) = 0.6$. Using this information, find

 a. Lower bounds on the truth value that I must assign A, B, C

 b. Upper bounds on the truth value that I must assign A, B, C

13.3. Suppose $(L, \sqsubseteq)$ is a complete (nonempty) lattice of truth values. A function $f : L \rightarrow L$ is said to be *monotonic* iff for all $x, y \in L$, $x \sqsubseteq y$ implies that $f(x) \sqsubseteq f(y)$. Show that if f is monotonic, then there exists an element $e \in X$ such that $f(e) = e$.

13.4. Consider the lattice L^{∞} presented in this chapter. Suppose we consider a logical language containing atoms $p(0), p(1), p(2), \ldots$ and $q(0), q(1), \ldots$. Suppose I is a lattice-valued interpretation that makes the following assignments: $I(p(j)) = L^j\text{t}$; $I(q(j)) = L^j\text{f}$. What is the truth value assigned by I to

 a. $(\exists x)p(x)$
 b. $(\forall x)q(x)$
 c. $(p(0) \vee p(2) \vee p(4))$
 d. $(p(0) \vee p(2) \vee p(4)) \vee (q(0) \vee q(2) \vee q(4))$

13.5. Consider the case of probabilistic reasoning, where we have three events ev_1, ev_2, ev_3. Suppose we know that $\mathbf{P}(e_1)$ lies between 0.2 and 0.4 (inclusive), $\mathbf{P}(e_2)$ lies between 0.1 and 0.5 (inclusive), and $\mathbf{P}(e_3)$ lies between 0.3 and 0.4 (inclusive).

 a. Enumerate the set of all possible worlds associated with these three events.

 b. Construct the linear program $LP(\mathbf{Known})$ defined in terms of the known information stated in this problem.

 c. Construct an objective function that captures the minimal possible probability of the complex event $\mathbf{P}(ev_1 \wedge \neg ev_2)$.

 d. Solve the above linear program.

Chapter 14

Uncertainty in Relational Databases

The relational model of data may be extended to incorporate uncertainty either at the tuple level or at the attribute level.

In the tuple-level approach, we extend each tuple to have one or more uncertainty attributes. Typically, the uncertainty attribute would either be a single real number $r \in [0,1]$ or an interval $[r_1, r_2]$ of real numbers, or a lattice element τ drawn from the complete lattice of truth values being considered. For example, the first approach would perhaps be preferred when fuzzy logic is the selected mode of uncertainty. On the other hand, as we have already seen, knowing the probabilities of events only allows us, in general, to infer a probability range for conjunctions; hence, you would expect that operations such as join and Cartesian product (both akin to conjunction), and union (similar to disjunction), would only allow us to infer the existence of probability ranges, rather than point probabilities, unless there is reason to believe that something like the independence assumption may be made.

In the attribute-level approach, however, we associate probabilities with individual items occurring in attribute slots. For example, we may wish (in the fuzzy case) to represent the table describing the `face` relation of Chapter 13 as shown in the following table:

File	Person	LLx	LLy	URx	URy
im1.gif	John Smith (0.3), Mark Bloom (0.6)	10	10	20	20
im1.gif	Mark Bloom (0.2), Ted Lewis (0.8)	30	10	40	20
im2.gif	Mark Bloom	50	10	50	20
im2.gif	Ted Lewis	10	10	20	20
im3.gif	Lynn Bloom (0.4), Elsa Bloom (0.5)	10	10	20	20

Suppose t_1 represents the first tuple listed above. This tuple may be interpreted as saying that

- t_1.File= $im1.gif$ with certainty 1

- t_1.Person= John Smith with certainty 0.3, and t_1.Person= Mark Bloom with certainty 0.6

- t_1.LLx= 10, t_1.LLy= 10, t_1.URx= 20, t_1.URy= 20, all with certainty 1

In the rest of this chapter, we will discuss extensions of the relational model of data to handle different types of uncertainty. Because the fuzzy set approach is nothing but a special case of the lattice-based approach, we will deal with lattice-based relational and deductive databases. However, in order to clearly illustrate the intuitions underlying the lattice-based approach, we will provide a fuzzy version of the `face` example above. Chapter 15 will later show how similar extensions to handle uncertainty may be made to the deductive database paradigm.

14.1   Lattice-Based Relational Databases

Suppose $(L, \sqsubseteq)$ is a complete lattice of truth values. Suppose R is a relation over schema $(A_1, \ldots, A_n)$. The *tuple-based lattice extension*, R^ℓ, of relation R is a relation over schema $(A_1, \ldots, A_n, Unc)$ where $dom(Unc) = L$. $A_1, \ldots, A_n$ are called the *data attributes* of R. Notice that R^ℓ handles uncertainty at the tuple level, not the attribute level. If, for example, $L = [0, 1]$, then the following table shows a tuple-level table that extends the `face` table described earlier in this chapter.

File	Person	LLx	LLy	URx	URy	Unc
im1.gif	John Smith	10	10	20	20	0.3
im1.gif	Mark Bloom	10	10	20	20	0.6
im1.gif	Mark Bloom	30	10	40	20	0.2
im1.gif	Ted Lewis	30	10	40	20	0.8
im2.gif	Mark Bloom	50	10	60	20	1
im2.gif	Ted Lewis	10	10	20	20	1
im3.gif	Lynn Bloom	10	10	20	20	0.4
im3.gif	Elsa Bloom	10	10	20	20	0.5

Two tuples t_1 and t_2 in relation R^ℓ are said to be *data identical* iff they are identical on all data attributes. We use the notation $\mathsf{DI}(t, R^\ell)$ to denote the set of all tuples in R^ℓ that are data identical to tuple t. In addition, the notation $\mu(t, R^\ell)$ denotes the truth value given by

$$\mu(t, R^\ell) = \sqcup\{t_i.Unc \mid t_i \in \mathsf{DI}(t, R^\ell)\}$$

Furthermore, if R^ℓ is a lattice-based relation, then we use the notation **Data_R^ℓ** to denote the (classical) projection of R^ℓ on its data attributes; that is, **Data_R^ℓ** is obtained from R^ℓ by merely dropping the Unc column. We may now define the standard relational operators as follows.

Selection

Suppose C is any selection condition (defined in the standard way) on relation R^ℓ. Then the selection operator $\sigma^\ell_C(R^\ell)$ is defined as

$$\sigma^\ell_C(R^\ell) = \{(a_1, \ldots, a_n, \mu(t, R^\ell)) \mid t = (a_1, \ldots, a_n) \in \mathbf{Data\_}{R^\ell}_1$$
$$\text{where } {R^\ell}_1 = \sigma_C(R^\ell)\}$$

In other words, whenever a selection operation is performed, it is implemented as follows:

1. *Naive select:* First perform a standard select (σ) by treating the relation R^ℓ as a standard relation, and identify all tuples that satisfy the selection condition.

2. *Grouping:* Group together all data-identical tuples.

3. *LUBing:* Examine each group of data-identical tuples. Suppose that $\{t_1, \ldots, t_r\}$ are data identical. Thus, each t_i is of the form $(a_1, \ldots, a_n, \mu_i)$. Return the tuple $t = (a_1, \ldots, a_n, \mu)$, where $\mu = \mu_1 \sqcup \cdots \sqcup \mu_r$. Do this for each group.

Projection

Let π denote the standard projection operation on relational databases. Then projection in our lattice-based setting may be defined as

$$\pi^{\ell}_{B_1,\ldots,B_r}(R^{\ell}) = \{(a_1,\ldots,a_r,\mu(t,R^{\ell}_1)) \mid t = (a_1,\ldots,a_n) \in \mathbf{Data\_}R^{\ell}_1$$
$$\text{where } R^{\ell}_1 = \pi_{B_1,\ldots,B_r}(R^{\ell})\}$$

The projection operator may also be expressed in the equivalent form:

$$\pi^{\ell}_{B_1,\ldots,B_r}(R^{\ell}) = \sigma^{\ell}_{\text{true}}\left(\pi_{B_1,\ldots,B_r,Unc}(R^{\ell})\right)$$

Thus, projection in our setting, denoted by the symbol π^{ℓ}, contains two steps:

1. *Project with uncertainty:* The first step performs a standard project on all the specified data attributes, $B_1,\ldots,B_r$, together with the additional attribute Unc.

2. *LUBing:* Subsequently, we merge all data-identical tuples in the result of the preceding step by replacing data-identical tuples by a single tuple whose uncertainty value is the lub of the uncertainty values of the tuples that are in a given group. (Note that the operation $\sigma^{\ell}_{\text{true}}$ automatically forces data-identical tuples to be grouped together and LUBed.)

Union

The union operation, $\cup^{\ell}$, is defined on lattice-based relations in terms of the standard union operator, $\cup$, as follows:

$$R^{\ell}_1 \cup^{\ell} R^{\ell}_2 = \{(a_1,\ldots,a_n,\mu(t,R^{\ell})) \mid t = (a_1,\ldots,a_n) \in \mathbf{Data\_}R^{\ell}\}$$
$$\text{where } R^{\ell} = R^{\ell}_1 \cup R^{\ell}_2$$

This definition may be alternatively expressed in the equivalent form:

$$R^{\ell}_1 \cup^{\ell} R^{\ell}_2 = \sigma^{\ell}_{\text{true}}(R^{\ell}_1 \cup R^{\ell}_2)$$

where R^{ℓ}_1, R^{ℓ}_2 are relations that are union-compatible in the classical sense (i.e., they share the same schema). The implementation of the union operator involves three steps—first, taking the standard union of the two relations, then grouping together all data-identical tuples, and finally taking the least upper bound of all these data-identical tuples.

Intersection

The intersection operation, $\cap^\ell$, is defined on lattice-based relations as follows:

$$R^\ell_1 \cap^\ell R^\ell_2 = \{(a_1, \ldots, a_n, \mu) \mid t_1 = (a_1, \ldots, a_n, \mu_1) \in \sigma^\ell_{\text{true}}(R^\ell_1) \text{ and}$$
$$t_2 = (a_1, \ldots, a_n, \mu_2) \in \sigma^\ell_{\text{true}}(R^\ell_2) \text{ and}$$
$$\mu = \mu_1 \sqcap \mu_2\}$$

In other words, the intersection of two relations R^ℓ_1 and R^ℓ_2 is created in the following way:

- *Grouping:* First group together all data-identical tuples in R^ℓ_1, R^ℓ_2.

- If there exists a tuple t_1 in $\sigma^\ell_{\text{true}}(R^\ell_1)$ and a tuple t_2 in $\sigma^\ell_{\text{true}}(R^\ell_2)$ that are data identical, then the intersection contains a tuple whose data fields are identical to those in t_1, t_2 and whose Unc field is the greatest lower bound of μ_1, μ_2.

Cartesian Product

The Cartesian product of two lattice-based relations R^ℓ_1, R^ℓ_2 is defined as follows:

$$R^\ell_1 \times^\ell R^\ell_2 = \{(a_1, \ldots, a_n, b_1, \ldots, b_m, \mu \mid (a_1, \ldots, a_n, \mu_1) \in R^\ell_1 \text{ and}$$
$$(b_1, \ldots, b_m, \mu_2) \in R^\ell_2 \text{ and}$$
$$\mu = \mu_1 \sqcap \mu_2\}$$

Difference

Difference is a somewhat more complicated operation than most because we must assume the existence of a complementation operator, com, on the lattice $(L, \sqsubseteq)$. The following table shows some possible complementation functions for some of the lattices described earlier:

Lattice	Definition of complement
SIX	$\text{com}(t) = f;\ \text{com}(f) = t;\ \text{com}(Lf) = Lt;\ \text{com}(Lt) = Lf;$ $\text{com}(\bot) = \top;\ \text{com}(\top) = \bot$
EIGHT	same as above, plus $\text{com}(LLf) = LLt;\ \text{com}(LLt) = LLf$
L^∞	$\text{com}(L^i f) = L^i t;\ \text{com}(L^i t) = L^i f;\ \text{com}(\bot) = \top;\ \text{com}(\top) = \bot$
$[0, 1]$	$\text{com}(e) = 1 - e$
$[0, 1] \times [0, 1]$	$\text{com}(e_1, e_2) = (e_2, e_1)$

We may now define the difference operator as follows:

$$R^\ell{}_1 -^\ell R^\ell{}_2 = R^\ell{}_1 \cap^\ell \{(a_1, \ldots, a_n, \text{com}(\mu)) \mid (a_1, \ldots, a_n, \mu) \in R^\ell{}_2\}$$

In other words, the difference of two relations $R^\ell{}_1, R^\ell{}_2$ (that have the same schema) may be captured by performing two steps:

- *Complement* $R^\ell{}_2$: Replacing the Unc field of each tuple by $\text{com}(Unc)$.

- *Intersection:* Taking the intersection of $R^\ell{}_1$ and the result of the preceding step.

14.1.1   An Example

Let us consider the above algebraic operations applied to the following simple example involving two relations, $R^\ell{}_1, R^\ell{}_2$.

$R^\ell{}_1$

A_1	A_2	A_3	Unc
r1	1989	200	0.3.
r1	1989	220	0.2.
r1	1989	230	0.5.
r1	1991	200	0.3.
r2	1989	220	0.4.
r2	1989	230	0.2.
r2	1989	200	0.3.

$R^\ell{}_2$

A_1	A_2	A_3	Unc
r1	1989	200	0.1.
r1	1989	210	0.3.
r1	1989	230	0.1.
r1	1991	200	0.4.
r2	1989	220	0.2.
r2	1989	230	0.2.
r2	1989	200	0.3.

The table on the left below shows the result of evaluating the algebraic expression $\pi^\ell_{A_1, A_2}(R^\ell{}_1)$, while the table on the right shows the result of evaluating the query $\pi^\ell_{A_1, A_2}(R^\ell{}_1 \cup^\ell R^\ell{}_2)$.

A_1	A_2	Unc	A_1	A_2	Unc
r1	1989	0.5	r1	1989	0.5.
r1	1991	0.3	r1	1991	0.4.
r2	1989	0.4	r2	1989	0.4.

Consider now, the problem of computing the difference of the previous two queries, that is, computing the query

$$\pi^\ell_{A_1,A_2}(R^\ell_1) - \pi^\ell_{A_1,A_2}(R^\ell_1 \cup^\ell R^\ell_2)$$

The table below shows the result:

A_1	A_2	Unc	$Comments$
r1	1989	0.5	$0.5 = \min(0.5, 1 - 0.5)$
r1	1991	0.3	$0.3 = \min(0.3, 1 - 0.4)$
r2	1989	0.4	$0.4 = \min(0.4, 1 - 0.4)$

14.1.2 Querying Lattice-Based Databases

As databases that contain lattice-based uncertainty look very much like ordinary relations and have no new operators in them, standard SQL may be used directly to express queries. However, there is one difference. Consider the following example.

Example 14.1   Find people who appear in the face database with certainty over 50%

> **SELECT** Person
> **FROM** face
> **WHERE** Unc $\geq$ 0.50

A query of the form shown above must be interpreted in terms of the lattice-based selection condition, rather than in terms of the standard select operator. Thus, in this case, the selection will involve finding all triples (File, Person, Unc) from the face relation (of Section 14.1), identifying and grouping together all tuples that are identical as far as the File and Person attributes are concerned, and then taking the lub of the uncertainty values of each such group. If we use the face relation given at the beginning of Section 14.1, then the computed answer to this query is shown in (a) below:

Mark Bloom	1
Ted Lewis	1

Mark Bloom	0.6
Ted Lewis	0.8
Mark Bloom	1
Ted Lewis	1

(a)   (b)

Had we treated `face` as an ordinary relation (i.e., not as a lattice-based relation) and interpreted the above query as a straight selection on the `face` relation without taking into account the theory developed in this section, we would instead have obtained the result shown in table (b) above. Note, in particular, that the correct result, table (a), is obtained by grouping the data-identical tuples in table (b) together, and then taking the least upper bound of the Unc field of each such group. For instance, one such group involves the first and third tuples of table (b)—they are grouped together as their data fields are identical (and equal "Mark Bloom"). The resulting lub is 1, which is exactly the uncertainty value associated with Mark Bloom in table (a).

In general, we may use standard SQL to query lattice-based relational databases as long as we are aware that the lattice-based analogs of the relational operators will be used to execute the query. Thus, even though the queries look as if they are expressed in standard SQL, they are implemented using the operations, described in this chapter, that differ from standard SQL implementations.

14.2   Probabilistic Relational Databases

In the preceding sections, we have studied how the relational model of data may be extended to handle lattice-based notions of uncertainty, including fuzzy notions of uncertainty. However, as we have already observed earlier in this chapter, probability theory is very different from fuzzy set theory. In particular, we have shown that given two events A and B, knowledge of the probabilities $\mathbf{Prob}(A)$ and $\mathbf{Prob}(B)$ alone is not adequate to accurately pinpoint the probability of $(A \wedge B)$, $(A \vee B)$, and so on. However, in some cases (e.g., knowledge that events A and B are independent), it is indeed possible to accurately specify these probabilities as single points. Thus, in general, the formula used to express the probability of a compound event depends upon our knowledge of the interrelationship or semantic dependency between the events in question. Because such formulas will need to be used when extending the relational model of data to handle probabilistic information, it is critically necessary that we allow users to specify such parameters in their queries. In other words, users should be able to express their queries in the form

equi join (handwritten note)

1. Compute the join of relations $R1$ and $R2$ when $R1.A1 = R2.A2$ under the assumption that all tuples in $R1$ and $R2$ are independent.

2. Compute the union of relations $R1$ and $R2$ under the assumption of ignorance.

If we examine these two examples, we observe that there is no hope of developing a probabilistic database system that captures both the above requests in a probabilistically valid way unless that model deals with interval probabilities rather than point probabilities. The reason for this is that the second query above cannot be computed without the use of interval probabilities. Though point probabilities are adequate for the first, they can just as easily be expressed with intervals—after all, the probability value p is equivalent to the probability interval $[p, p]$. Thus, in the following, we will describe a probabilistic model of uncertainty in relational databases that uses intervals rather than points. This model, called ProbView, is the work of Lakshmanan, Leone, Ross, and Subrahmanian [260].

Read their new papers! (handwritten note)

14.2.1 Probabilistic Relations

Read [331] (handwritten note)

Definition 14.1 *A data tuple* over the relation scheme $R = \{A_1, \ldots, A_n\}$ *is any n-tuple* $t = (a_1, \ldots, a_n)$*, where each* $a_i \in dom(A_i)$*. A data relation over* R *is a finite set of data tuples over* R*.*

Basically, a data relation is just a classical relation. On the other hand, a probabilistic tuple is defined somewhat more generally, as shown below. Before we introduce this definition, we introduce a piece of notation: $\mathcal{C}[0, 1]$ denotes the set of all closed subintervals of the unit interval $[0, 1]$.

Definition 14.2 *A probabilistic tuple over relation scheme* $R = \{A_1, \ldots, A_n\}$ *is an n-tuple* $(\mathbf{v_1}, \ldots, \mathbf{v_n})$*, where each* $\mathbf{v_i}$ *is a pair of the form* (V_i, h_i)*, with* $V_i \subseteq dom(A_i)$ *a finite set of values from* A_i*'s domain, and* $h_i : V_i \rightarrow \mathcal{C}[0, 1]$ *a function that maps each value in* V_i *to a probability range. A probabilistic relation over the scheme* R *is a finite set of probabilistic tuples over* R*. A probabilistic database is a finite set of probabilistic relations with associated schemes.*

Consider a probabilistic tuple $t_p = ((V_1, h_1), \ldots, (V_n, h_n))$. The events associated with this tuple are equalities of the form $t_p.A_i = c$, where A_i is one of the attributes and $c \in V_i$. Such an event says that the value of the tuple corresponding to attribute A_i is c. The probabilistic tuple t_p above says that

$$\mathbf{Prob}(t_p.A_i = c) = \begin{cases} h_i(c) & \text{if } c \in V_i \\ [0,0] & \text{otherwise, i.e., if } c \in dom(A_i) - V_i \end{cases}$$

For example, suppose we return to the image database example described earlier. In the preceding treatments of this example, no probabilities were present, though fuzzy notions of uncertainty were present. Below, we show how the previously introduced image database may be represented as a set of four probabilistic tuples:[1]

Tid	File	Person	LLx	LLy	URx	URy
t_1	im1.gif	John Smith, [0.3,0.4]	10	10	20	20
		Mark Bloom, [0.5,0.65]				
t_2	im1.gif	Mark Bloom, [0.3.0.35]	30	10	40	20
		Ted Lewis, [0.6.0.8]				
t_3	im2.gif	Mark Bloom, [1,1]	50	10	60	20
t_4	im2.gif	Ted Lewis, [0.1,0.2]	10	10	20	20
t_5	im3.gif	Lynn Bloom, [0.6,0.7]	10	10	20	20
		Elsa Bloom, [0.2,0.25]				

The first tuple, t_1, in the above table may be (informally) read as follows:

1. The probability of the event t_1.Person= John Smith lies in the interval $[0.3, 0.4]$, and

2. the probability of the event t_1.Person= Mark Bloom lies in the interval $[0.5, 0, 65]$, and

3. the probability of each of the events t_1.File= im1.gif and t_1.LLx= 10 and t_1.LLy= 10 and t_1.URx= 20 and t_1.URy= 20 are all equal to 1, and

4. all other events relating to tuple t_1 have probability 0.

It is now easy to see that a conventional (classical) tuple is a probabilistic tuple where V_i is always required to be a singleton, say $\{d_i\}$, and $h_i(d_i) = [1, 1]$, $i = 1, \ldots, n$.

---

[1]Obviously, the probabilities associated with these four probabilistic tuples are not related to the previous uncertainty values.

14.2.2 Annotated Relations

Though probabilistic relations are easy to understand from an intuitive point of view, they are not "flat" and hence are often difficult to manipulate. Rather than manipulate probabilistic tuples and relations directly, we will instead flatten them by an appropriate conversion procedure. The result of such a conversion will be what is called an *annotated relation*. In order to construct annotated relations from probabilistic ones, we need to introduce some definitions.

The first definition we introduce is that of a *world*. Let us consider any probabilistic tuple t_p, such as the tuple t_1 shown above. This tuple defines two possible worlds. In the first world (which we denote w_1), t_1.Person = John Smith, while in the second world (which we denote w_2), t_1.Person = Mark Bloom. Clearly these two worlds are incompatible, since only one face is contained in the rectangle specified in tuple t_1. Furthermore, these two worlds are mutually exclusive. Hence, by examining the probabilities attached to the components of the t_1.Person field, we may write the following constraints:

$$0.3 \leq p_1 \leq 0.4$$

$$0.5 \leq p_2 \leq 0.65$$

$$p_1 + p_2 = 1$$

$$p_1, p_2 \geq 0$$

When we minimize and maximize the values of the variables p_1, p_2 with respect to the above constraints, we notice that p_1 must lie between 0.35 and 0.4, while p_2 must lie between 0.6 and 0.65. Thus, the probability that world w_1 is the "right" world lies between 35% and 40%, while that of w_2 lies between 60% and 65%. Thus, instead of associating probabilities with the attribute slots of tuples, we may instead want to associate probabilities with the whole tuple itself, reducing tuple t_1 above to the following two tuples:

Tid	File	Person	LLx	LLy	URx	URy	LB	UB	Path
t_1'	im1.gif	John Smith	10	10	20	20	0.35	0.4	w_1
t_1''	im1.gif	Mark Bloom	10	10	20	20	0.6	0.65	w_2

The above informal intuition may now be realized formally as follows:

Definition 14.3 *Suppose $R = \{A_1, \ldots, A_n\}$ is a relation scheme and r is a probabilistic relation over scheme R. Suppose $t_p = ((V_1, h_1), \ldots, (V_n, h_n))$*

is a probabilistic tuple in r. Any member w of $V_1 \times V_2 \times \cdots \times V_n$ is called a tuple world. *Associated with each tuple world is a symbol called the* world-id *(wid) of that world.*

We will often abuse notation and use the same symbol to denote both a world and its wid.

Definition 14.4 *A* path *is a Boolean expression over wids. For a given database D, we use $\mathcal{P}_D$ to denote the set of all distinct paths over D. When the database is clear from the context, we drop the subscript D. A* path annotated tuple *(or just* annotated tuple, *for short) over $\{A_1, \ldots, A_n\}$ is an element of $dom(A_1) \times \cdots \times dom(A_n) \times \mathcal{U} \times \mathcal{U} \times \mathcal{P}$. The definition of annotated relations and databases is an obvious extension of the above notion. The relation scheme associated with an annotated relation contains all the attributes $A_1, \ldots, A_n$ and three special attributes* LB, UB, *and* path, *corresponding to the domains $\mathcal{U}$, $\mathcal{U}$, and $\mathcal{P}$.*

A path annotated tuple $(a_1, \ldots, \ell, u, p)$ is *consistent* provided $\ell \leq u$ and p is a consistent Boolean expression over world-ids.

Generally speaking, when a base probabilistic relation is converted to an annotated relation (using the procedure described in the next subsection), the resulting annotated relation will have only world-ids in its path column; that is, all paths will be world-ids, rather than Boolean formulas constructed from world-ids. However, when we pose queries over the annotated relations, the annotated relations resulting from materializing (i.e., computing) such queries may end up having complex Boolean formulas in their path attributes.

14.2.3   Converting Probabilistic Tuples to Annotated Tuples

We now address the important issue of converting probabilistic tuples to annotated tuples. This is done as follows:

1. *Linear program construction:* Suppose $t_p = ((V_1, h_1), \ldots, (V_n, h_n))$ is a probabilistic tuple in r. Associate with each t_p-world $w \in \mathbf{W}(t_p)$, a linear programming variable z_w (which ranges over the real numbers). Associate with tuple t_p a linear program $\mathsf{LP}(t_p)$ as follows:

   (a) For all $1 \leq i \leq n$ and for all $v \in V_i$, $\mathsf{LP}(t_p)$ contains the constraint

   $$\mathsf{lb}(h_i(v)) \leq \left(\sum_{w \in \mathbf{W}(t_p) \ \& \ w.A_i = v} z_w \right) \leq \mathsf{ub}(h_i(v))$$

where $h_i(v) = [\text{lb}(h_i(v)), \text{ub}(h_i(v))]$. This constraint is said to be *induced by* v and V_i.

(b) For each $w \in \mathbf{W}(t_p)$, the constraint

$$0 \leq z_w \leq 1$$

is present in $\text{LP}(t_p)$.

(c) Finally, add the constraint $\left(\sum_{w \in \mathbf{W}(t_p)} z_w \right) \leq 1$. You may have noticed that this constraint is a $\leq$-constraint rather than an equality constraint—as was the case previously. The reason for this is that when we consider the probabilistic tuple $t_p = ((V_1, h_1), \ldots, (V_n, h_n))$, there is no reason to believe that the V_i's represent all possible values of the ith attribute; rather, they represent values whose probabilities are known. Thus, the $\leq$-constraint leaves the door open for unknown possibilities.

2. *Finding lower and upper bounds for each tuple world:* For each t_p-world $w \in \mathbf{W}(t_p)$, set

$$\ell_w = \mathbf{minimize}\ z_w\ \mathbf{subject\ to}\ \text{LP}(t_p)$$
$$u_w = \mathbf{maximize}\ z_w\ \mathbf{subject\ to}\ \text{LP}(t_p)$$

3. *Annotated tuples:* The annotated representation of t_p contains, for each world $w = (v_1, \ldots, v_n) \in \mathbf{W}(t_p)$, the annotated tuple

$(v_1, \ldots, v_n)$	ℓ_w	u_w	w

Let us now return to the probabilistic relation described in Section 14.2.1. This probabilistic relation contains four tuples, $t_1, \ldots, t_4$. We have informally explained above how we might convert the probabilistic tuple t_1 into a set of annotated tuples. The table below shows the full annotated relation corresponding to the probabilistic relation of Section 14.2.1.

File	Person	LLx	LLy	URx	URy	LB	UB	Path
im1.gif	John Smith	10	10	20	20	0.35	0.4	w_1
im1.gif	Mark Bloom	10	10	20	20	0.6	0.7	w_2
im1.gif	Mark Bloom	30	10	40	20	0.3	0.35	w_3
im1.gif	Ted Lewis	30	10	40	20	0.65	0.7	w_4
im2.gif	Mark Bloom	50	10	60	20	1	1	w_5
im2.gif	Ted Lewis	10	10	20	20	0.1	0.2	w_6
im3.gif	Lynn Bloom	10	10	20	20	0.6	0.7	w_7
im3.gif	Elsa Bloom	10	10	20	20	0.2	0.25	w_8

14.2.4   Manipulating Annotated Relations

Now that we know how to convert probabilistic relations into annotated relations, we are in a position to define operations that can algebraically manipulate such annotated relations. As in the case of the lattice-based approach to uncertainty in databases, we will describe how each of the standard relational operators may be extended to the probabilistic case.

Selection

We use the expression *data selection condition* to refer to any traditional selection condition on the "data" component of an annotated relation (i.e., one that does not refer to either the LB, UB, or Path attributes). A selection condition may now be defined in terms of data selection conditions as follows:

- Every (data) selection condition $\mathcal{F}$ as defined above is a (probabilistic) selection condition.

- For a real number $n \in [0, 1]$, and $\theta \in \{=, >, <, \geq, \leq, \neq\}$, $LB \; \theta \; n$ and $UB \; \theta \; n$ are both conditions.

- Whenever $\mathcal{C}_1, \mathcal{C}_2$ are conditions, so are $(C_1 \wedge C_2), (C_1 \vee C_2)$, and $\neg C_1$.

Definition 14.5 *Let r be an annotated relation and $\mathcal{F}$ be any legal selection condition. Then $\sigma_{\mathcal{F}}(r) = \{t_a \in r \mid t_a \text{ satisfies } \mathcal{F}\}$.*

Note that the definition of selection on annotated relations is identical to classical selection.

Example 14.2   Selection on annotated relations

Let us now return to the annotated version R_a of the probabilistic relation described in Section 14.2.1. Let C be the selection condition

$$LB > 0.4 \wedge \texttt{Person} = \texttt{Mark Bloom}.$$

Then the result of applying the operation $\sigma_C(R_a)$ is

File	Person	LLx	LLy	URx	URy	LB	UB	Path
im1.gif	Mark Bloom	10	10	20	20	0.6	0.7	w_2
im2.gif	Mark Bloom	50	10	60	20	1	1	w_5

Projection

Projection too is similar to projection in standard relational algebra. However, there is one significant difference. We would like the result of any algebraic operation to be an annotated relation. In particular, this means that the result of a projection must contain the attributes LB, UB, and Path even if the user does not explicitly specify that these fields be projected out as well. Formally, suppose t_a is an annotated tuple over R, and $X \subseteq R$. Then the *restriction* of t_a to X, denoted $t_a[X]$, is obtained by deleting all components of t_a not corresponding to one of the attributes in X or to one of LB, UB, or Path.

Definition 14.6 *Let r be an annotated relation over the scheme R and let $X \subseteq R$. Then $\pi_X(r) = \{t_a[X] \mid t_a \in r\}$.*

Let us return to the annotated relation given in Section 14.2.1 and suppose we wish to compute $\pi_{Person}(r)$. The result of this projection is the annotated relation given below:

Person	LB	UB	Path
John Smith	0.35	0.4	w_1
Mark Bloom	0.6	.7	w_2
Mark Bloom	0.3	0.35	w_3
Ted Lewis	0.65	0.7	w_4
Mark Bloom	1	1	w_5
Ted Lewis	0.1	0.2	w_6
Lynn Bloom	0.6	0.7	w_7
Elsa Bloom	0.2	0.25	w_8

Cartesian Product

One of the most complicated operations within our probabilistic setting is the Cartesian product operation. The reason for this is the following. Suppose we consider two annotated relations R_1 and R_2, and suppose $(a_1, \ldots, a_n)$ and $(b_1, \ldots, b_m)$ are tuples that correspond to the data parts of the schemas of R_1 and R_2, respectively (i.e., these tuples do not contain the LB, UB, or Path attributes). If $(a_1, \ldots, a_n, \ell_1, u_1, p_1)$ is in R_1 and $(b_1, \ldots, b_m, \ell_2, u_2, p_2)$ is in R_2, then these tuples intuitively say that "the probability that $(a_1, \ldots, a_n)$ is in R_1 lies between ℓ_1 and u_1 if path p_1 is valid" and "the probability that $(b_1, \ldots, b_m)$ is in R_2 lies between ℓ_2 and u_2 if path p_2 is valid," respectively. When computing the Cartesian product of these two relations, we need to be able to define the probability that the data tuple

$$(a_1, \ldots, a_n, b_1, \ldots, b_m)$$

is in $R_1 \times R_2$. This Cartesian product reflects the conjunction of two events: the event that $(a_1, \ldots, a_n)$ is in R_1 and the event that $(b_1, \ldots, b_m)$ is in R_2.

In order to accurately compute the probability of the conjunction, we need to proceed under some assumptions on the relationship between these two events. The nature of this relationship is what will determine the probability associated with the tuple

$$(a_1, \ldots, a_n, b_1, \ldots, b_m)$$

being in the Cartesian product. A flexible probabilistic database system will allow the user to pick an appropriate strategy and allow the concept of Cartesian product to follow from the choice he has made. Thus, rather than pick one of the strategies, Lakshmanan, Leone, Ross, and Subrahmanian (LLRS) have developed a system called ProbView [260], where users may make the conjunction generic, with the motivation that, depending on the situation, the appropriate strategies can be applied.

Basically, these authors first define a conjunction strategy to be a function $\otimes$ that satisfies certain axioms. They then say the following:

1. Let the user pick any function $\otimes$ that satisfies these axioms.

2. This choice automatically induces a notion of Cartesian product. Different choices of a conjunction strategy $\otimes$ lead to different notions of Cartesian product.

Based on the work in [260], we are now ready to introduce the concept of a *generic probabilistic conjunction* as a function $\otimes : \mathcal{P} \times \mathcal{C}[0,1] \times \mathcal{P} \times \mathcal{C}[0,1] \rightarrow \mathcal{C}[0,1]$. Any such generic conjunction function must satisfy the *LLRS Postulates for Probabilistic Conjunction* listed below. In the following, $[\alpha_i, \beta_i]$ are arbitrary elements of $\mathcal{C}[0,1]$ and p, q, r are arbitrary elements of $\mathcal{P}$. Recall that $\mathcal{P}$ is the set of all paths (i.e., Boolean expressions over world-ids) over a probabilistic database D.

C1. *Bottomline*: It is always the case that $(p, [\alpha_1, \beta_1]) \otimes (q, [\alpha_2, \beta_2]) \le [min(\alpha_1, \alpha_2), min(\beta_1, \beta_2)]$. Here, $[a, b] \le [a', b']$ iff $a \le a'$ and $b \le b'$.

Intuitively, this axiom says that the probability of a conjunct cannot exceed the probabilities of the components of the conjunct.

C2. *Ignorance*: When nothing is known about the dependency between the events,

$$(p, [\alpha_1, \beta_1]) \otimes (q, [\alpha_2, \beta_2]) = (p, [\alpha_1, \beta_1]) \otimes_{ig} (q, [\alpha_2, \beta_2])$$

$$= [\max(0, \alpha_1 + \alpha_2 - 1), \min(\beta_1, \beta_2)]$$

which is the formula for conjunction under total ignorance and under no independence assumptions whatsoever. Here, $\otimes_{ig}$ refers to this specific combination strategy.

Intuitively, this axiom says that when no information is available about the relationship (or lack thereof) between two events, the standard formula for combining probabilities in a state of ignorance must be used.

C3. *Identity:* $(p, [\alpha, \beta]) \otimes (q, [1, 1]) = [\alpha, \beta]$, as long as $p \wedge q$ is consistent.

Intuitively, this axiom says that if one of the two conjuncts is certainly true, then the probability of the conjunction equals the probability of the other conjunct.

C4. *Annihilator:* $(p, [\alpha, \beta]) \otimes (q, [0, 0]) = [0, 0]$.

Intuitively, this axiom says that if one of the two conjuncts is certainly false, then the probability of the conjunction equals 0.

C5. *Commutativity:* $(p, [\alpha_1, \beta_1]) \otimes (q, [\alpha_2, \beta_2]) = (q, [\alpha_2, \beta_2]) \otimes (p, [\alpha_1, \beta_1])$.

This axiom makes the commonsense assertion that the probability of $(A \wedge B)$ must equal the probability of $(B \wedge A)$.

C6. *Associativity:* $((p, [\alpha_1, \beta_1]) \otimes (q, [\alpha_2, \beta_2])) \otimes (r, [\alpha_3, \beta_3]) = (p, [\alpha_1, \beta_1]) \otimes ((q, [\alpha_2, \beta_2]) \otimes (r, [\alpha_3, \beta_3]))$.

This axiom asserts that the order in which expressions are evaluated (left to right vs. right to left) should not affect the probabilities obtained.

C7. *Monotonicity:* $(p, [\alpha_1, \beta_1]) \otimes (q, [\alpha, \beta]) \leq (p, [\alpha_2, \beta_2]) \otimes (q, [\alpha, \beta])$ if $[\alpha_1, \beta_1] \leq [\alpha_2, \beta_2]$.

Intuitively, this axiom says the following: Suppose the probability of one event in a conjunction is increased while holding the other constant. Then the probability of the conjunction as a whole should also increase.

Any function $\otimes$ that satisfies the above axioms is said to be a *conjunction strategy*. Some example conjunction strategies are the following:

1. *Ignorance:* The conjunction can be performed by ignoring the path information and computing under total ignorance. This gives rise to

$$[\alpha, \beta] = (p_1, [\alpha_1, \beta_1]) \otimes_{ig} (p_2, [\alpha_2, \beta_2])$$

where $\otimes_{ig}$ is defined in postulate C2 for probabilistic conjunction.

2. *Positive correlation:* The strategy of positive correlation says that one event implies the other. Suppose the probability of the first event is in the interval $[\alpha_1, \beta_1]$ while the second is in the interval $[\alpha_2, \beta_2]$. If the first implies the second, then the probability of the second event must exceed that of the first, and the probability of the two occurring simultaneously will coincide with the lower probability value. This leads us to define the conjunction strategy based on positive correlation as

$$[\alpha, \beta] = (p_1, [\alpha_1, \beta_1]) \otimes_{pc} (p_2, [\alpha_2, \beta_2]) =_{def} [min(\alpha_1, \alpha_2), min(\beta_1, \beta_2)]$$

Here $\otimes_{pc}$ stands for probabilistic conjunction under the assumption of positive correlation, explained above.

This conjunction is performed by ignoring path information, but computing under the conservative assumption that the overlap between the two events is maximal, to the point where one of them implies the other.

3. *Path-based:* We can take the path information into account while computing probabilistic conjunction. Here, we may compute the probability of the conjunction in the following manner. If the paths are inconsistent, then the two events cannot possibly occur simultaneously (i.e., they are mutually exclusive and have probability 0). If one path is implied by the other, then this means that the strategy of positive correlation can be used. Finally, if path p_1 is consistent with path p_2 as well as with path $\neg p_2$, then we do not know the precise relationship between the paths, and hence we may assume that we are ignorant of the relationship between these two events, and apply the strategy of ignorance.

$$[\alpha, \beta] = \begin{cases} [0,0], & \text{if } p_1 \wedge p_2 \text{ is inconsistent} \\ (p_1, [\alpha_1, \beta_1]) \otimes_{ig} (p_2, [\alpha_2, \beta_2]), & \text{if } p_1 \wedge p_2 \text{ and } p_1 \wedge \neg p_2 \\ & \text{are both consistent} \\ (p_1, [\alpha_1, \beta_1]) \otimes_{pc} (p_2, [\alpha_2, \beta_2]), & \text{otherwise} \end{cases}$$

In all cases, the path attribute of the result is $(p_1 \wedge p_2)$.

Formally, suppose $\otimes$ is any conjunction strategy that satisfies the above axioms C1–C7. Let r and s be two annotated relations. Then the Cartesian product of r and s induced by $\otimes$ is defined as

$$r \times s = \{(d_r, d_s, \ell, u, p) \mid t_r = (d_r, \ell_1, u_1, p_1) \in r, t_s = (d_s, \ell_2, u_2, p_2) \in s \text{ and}$$
$$(p_1, [\ell_1, u_1]) \otimes (p_2, [\ell_2, u_2]) = (p, [\ell, u])\}$$

Note that the above definition of Cartesian product leads to different solutions, depending on which conjunction strategy $\otimes$ is chosen.

Here is a simple example of the Cartesian product of two single-tuple relations R_1 and R_2:

R_1:	a	b	0.4	0.7	w_1
R_2:	c	b	0.3	0.6	w_2

Suppose we wish to compute the Cartesian product of these two relations under the conjunction strategy $\otimes_{ig}$. The result is

a	b	c	b	0	0.6	$(w_1 \wedge w_2)$

However, had we performed this join under the conjunction strategy $\otimes_{pc}$, the result would have been

a	b	c	b	0.3	0.6	$(w_1 \wedge w_2)$

Under the assumption of independence, we would have obtained the following result:

a	b	c	b	0.12	0.42	$(w_1 \wedge w_2)$

Union

The operation of union is analogous to classical union. As usual, we say that two annotated relations r, s are union-compatible iff the classical relations underlying them (obtained by dropping the LB, UB, and Path attributes of r, s) are union-compatible. In this case, we define $r \cup s = \{t \mid t \in r \text{ or } t \in s\}$.

Note that unlike the classical case, where duplicates are eliminated, it is entirely possible that $r \cup s$ contains two tuples that are identical in their data components.

Compaction

This is a brand-new operator, denoted κ, that closely corresponds to the notion of duplicate elimination in classical relational databases. The aim of the compaction operator is to ensure that duplicate tuples are merged together in some reasonable way. For instance, duplicate tuples may arise when two different paths allow us to conclude two data-identical tuples. To see this, we present below the table described earlier when defining projection on annotated relations:

Person	*LB*	*UB*	*Path*
John Smith	0.35	0.4	w_1
Mark Bloom	0.6	0.7	w_2
Mark Bloom	0.3	0.35	w_3
Ted Lewis	0.65	0.7	w_4
Mark Bloom	1	1	w_5
Ted Lewis	0.1	0.2	w_6
Lynn Bloom	0.6	0.7	w_7
Elsa Bloom	0.2	0.25	w_8

Clearly, this table has only one data attribute (the field **Person**), and there are several distinct tuples that have the same data attribute but contain different probability/path attributes. In many applications, we may wish to merge these data-identical tuples into one. In the above example, this means that we may wish to have only one tuple with the **Person** field = "Mark Bloom" (instead of the three shown above) and only one tuple with the **Person** field = "Ted Lewis" (instead of the two shown above). Let us examine the two tuples about Ted Lewis. These tuples may be read as the following:

1. If path w_4 is valid, then Ted Lewis is in this relation with probability between 0.65 and 0.7.

2. If path w_6 is valid, then Ted Lewis is in this relation with probability between 0.1 and 0.2.

We are thus confronted with the question "What is the probability that Ted Lewis is in the relation if either path w_4 is valid or path w_6 is valid?" In order to answer this question, we must be able to describe the probabilities of disjunctions. However, as described earlier in the case of conjunctions, the probability of a disjunctive event depends very much on what is known about the interrelationship and/or dependencies between the primitive events in the disjunction. Therefore, we now propose a generic disjunction operator, called $\oplus$, that is similar to the generic conjunction operator defined earlier, except that it applies to disjunction, rather than to conjunction. Following are the *LLRS Postulates for Generic Disjunction*, where $[\alpha_i, \beta_i]$ are arbitrary elements of $\mathcal{C}[0,1]$ and p, q, r are arbitrary elements of $\mathcal{P}$.

D1. *Bottomline*: It is always the case that $(p, [\alpha_1, \beta_1]) \oplus (q, [\alpha_2, \beta_2]) \geq [max(\alpha_1, \alpha_2), max(\beta_1, \beta_2)]$. Here, $[a, b] \leq [a', b']$ iff $a \leq a'$ and $b \leq b'$.

D2. *Ignorance*: When nothing is known about the interdependence between the events,

$$(p, [\alpha_1, \beta_1]) \oplus (q, [\alpha_2, \beta_2]) = (p, [\alpha_1, \beta_1]) \oplus_{ig} (q, [\alpha_2, \beta_2])$$

$$= max(\alpha_1, \alpha_2), min(1, \beta_1 + \beta_2)]$$

which is the formula for disjunction under total ignorance and under no independence assumptions whatsoever. Here, $\oplus_{ig}$ refers to this specific disjunction strategy.

D3. *Identity*: $(p, [\alpha, \beta]) \oplus (q, [0, 0]) = [\alpha, \beta]$.

D4. *Annihilator*: $(p, [\alpha, \beta]) \oplus (q, [1, 1]) = [1, 1]$.

D5. *Commutativity*: $(p, [\alpha_1, \beta_1]) \oplus (q, [\alpha_2, \beta_2]) = (q, [\alpha_2, \beta_2]) \oplus (p, [\alpha_1, \beta_1])$.

D6. *Associativity*: $((p, [\alpha_1, \beta_1]) \oplus (q, [\alpha_2, \beta_2])) \oplus (r, [\alpha_3, \beta_3]) = (p, [\alpha_1, \beta_1]) \oplus ((q, [\alpha_2, \beta_2]) \oplus (r, [\alpha_3, \beta_3]))$.

D7. *Monotonicity*: $(p, [\alpha_1, \beta_1]) \oplus (q, [\alpha, \beta]) \leq (p, [\alpha_2, \beta_2]) \oplus (q, [\alpha, \beta])$ if $[\alpha_1, \beta_1] \leq [\alpha_2, \beta_2]$.

The intuition behind the above postulates are identical to that for the conjunction strategies. We may extend the operator $\oplus$ to annotated tuples that are data identical as follows. Let $(\vec{a}, \alpha_1, \beta_1, p_1)$ and $(\vec{a}, \alpha_2, \beta_2, p_2)$ be annotated tuples. Then $(\vec{a}, \alpha_1, \beta_1, p_1) \oplus (\vec{a}, \alpha_2, \beta_2, p_2) = (\vec{a}, \alpha, \beta, p)$, where $[\alpha, \beta] = (p_1, [\alpha_1, \beta_1]) \oplus (p_2, [\alpha_2, \beta_2])$, and $p = p_1 \vee p_2$.

As in the case of generic conjunction, here are some generic disjunction strategies. In the following, suppose $t_r = (\vec{a}, \alpha_1, \beta_1, p_1), t_s = (\vec{b}, \alpha_2, \beta_2, p_2)$. Let $t_{ann} = t_r \oplus t_s$, and let $[\alpha, \beta]$ be the probability interval associated with t_{ann}.

1. *Ignorance*: The disjunction can be performed by ignoring the path information and computing under total ignorance. This gives rise to

$$[\alpha, \beta] = (p_1, [\alpha_1, \beta_1]) \oplus_{ig} (p_2, [\alpha_2, \beta_2])$$

where $\oplus_{ig}$ is defined in postulate D2 for probabilistic disjunction.

2. *Positive correlation:* As in the case of conjunction earlier, consider the case when we are computing the probability of $(e_1 \wedge e_2)$ and where we know that e_1 implies e_2. In this case, if e_1 is true, then $\mathbf{P}(e_2) \geq \mathbf{P}(e_1)$, and hence $\mathbf{P}(e_1 \wedge e_2)$ equals $\mathbf{P}(e_2) = max(\mathbf{P}(e_1), \mathbf{P}(e_2))$. Otherwise, if e_1 is false (i.e., has probability 0), then the probability of $(e_1 \wedge e_2)$ equals the probability of e_2. This leads to

$$[\alpha, \beta] = (p_1, [\alpha_1, \beta_1]) \oplus_{pc} (p_2, [\alpha_2, \beta_2]) =_{def} [max(\alpha_1, \alpha_2), max(\beta_1, \beta_2)]$$

where $\oplus_{pc}$ stands for probabilistic disjunction under the assumption of positive correlation, explained above.

3. *Path-based:* Using the same intuitions as in the case of conjunction, we can take the path information into account while computing probabilistic disjunction. This leads to

$$[\alpha, \beta] = \begin{cases} (p_1, [\alpha_1, \beta_1]) \oplus_{nc} (p_2, [\alpha_2, \beta_2]), & \text{if } p_1 \wedge p_2 \text{ is inconsistent} \\ (p_1, [\alpha_1, \beta_1]) \oplus_{ig} (p_2, [\alpha_2, \beta_2]), & \text{if } p_1 \wedge p_2 \text{ and} \\ & \qquad p_1 \wedge \neg p_2 \text{ are consistent} \\ (p_1, [\alpha_1, \beta_1]) \oplus_{pc} (p_2, [\alpha_2, \beta_2]), & \text{otherwise} \end{cases}$$

where $(p_1, [\alpha_1, \beta_1]) \oplus_{nc} (p_2, [\alpha_2, \beta_2]) =_{def} [min(1, \alpha_1 + \alpha_2), min(1, \beta_1 + \beta_2)]$.

Let us now see how we combine the two tuples involving Ted Lewis into a single tuple. Using the strategy of ignorance, we get

Ted Lewis	0.65	0.7	$(w_4 \vee w_6)$

Surprisingly, under the strategy of positive correlation, we obtain the same result. However, under the strategy of independence, we obtain the result

Ted Lewis	0.685	0.76	$(w_4 \vee w_6)$

Formally, the compaction, $\kappa(r)$, of relation r may be computed as follows:

1. First, group together all tuples in r that are data identical.

2. For each such data-identical group, merge the tuples into one tuple by computing their disjunction.

Difference

Our final operator is difference. What should the difference of two relations be? To examine this question, let us first consider a simpler question. Suppose we have two tuples t_1 and t_2 that are data identical, as shown below:

$$t_1 = (\vec{a}, \ell_1, u_1, p_1); \quad t_2 = (\vec{a}, \ell_2, u_2, p_2)$$

What should the difference of these two tuples be? Clearly, for a tuple with data component $\vec{a}$ to be in $(t_1 - t_2)$, it must be the case that $p_1 \wedge \neg p_2$ is true. As soon as we realize this, we may immediately conclude that the probability range $[\ell, u]$ of this new tuple should be given by

$$(p_1 \wedge \neg p_2, [\ell, u]) = (p_1, [\ell_1, u_1]) \otimes (\neg p_2, [1 - u_2, 1 - \ell_2])$$

Here, $\otimes$ is any conjunction strategy.

In general, the difference between two relations r and s may be computed as follows:

1. Select any conjunction strategy $\otimes$ and any disjunction strategy $\oplus$.

2. For each tuple $t = (\vec{a}, \ell_1, u_1, p_1)$ in r, do the following:

    (a) Let $X[t]$ be the set of all tuples in s that are data identical to t.

    (b) Let $t' = (\vec{a}, \ell_2, u_2, p_2)$ be the single tuple obtained as a result of compacting $X[t]$ with respect to the disjunction strategy $\oplus$, i.e., $\kappa(X[t]) = \{t'\}$.

    (c) Let $t'' = (\vec{a}, \ell, u, p_1 \wedge \neg p_2)$, where $(p_1 \wedge \neg p_2, [\ell, u]) = (p_1, [\ell_1, u_1]) \otimes (\neg p_2, [1 - \ell_2, 1 - u_2])$ for the selected conjunction strategy $\otimes$.

    (d) If the path field of t'' is consistent, then insert t'' into $r - s$.

3. Return $(r - s)$.

14.2.5 Querying Probabilistic Databases

In the case of lattice-based relational databases, we were able to use SQL more or less directly to express queries, as shown in Section 14.1.2. There, the syntax of queries remained the same as in SQL, but the queries were executed somewhat differently from standard SQL.

In contrast, in the probabilistic case, we need to extend SQL if we wish to successfully execute queries. The reason for this is that the definition of operations like Cartesian product (and hence join) as well as union and difference depend upon the probabilistic assumptions (e.g., independence, ignorance, etc.) being made. An SQL query should indicate these assumptions explicitly. One possibility is to extend SQL through the addition of a special construct called **UNDER**. Thus, for instance, suppose the user wishes to perform a join of the following form:

Example 14.3   **Find all pictures of people making over $100,000 per year where the pictures correctly identify the person in question with over 70% probability**

    SELECT File,Salary
    FROM face F, emp E
    WHERE F.Person = E.Name **AND** F.LB > 0.7
        AND E.Salary > 100,000

This standard SQL query applies to two relations: the `face` relation as defined in Section 14.2, and a relation called `emp`, which is a standard relation whose LB and UB fields are all 1. The query basically asks for all pictures of people making over $100,000 per year where the pictures correctly identify the person in question with over 70% probability. Thus, this query is a join query. When we execute this query over probabilistic relations, the answer to the query will be a table consisting of three parts:

1. `File`: derived from the `face` relation

2. `Salary`: derived from the `emp` relation

3. `LB,UB,Path`: attributes derived from both the `face` relation and the `emp` relation

   In order to determine the LB, UB, and Path attributes of the resulting relation, we need to know the assumptions under which the join is to be computed. This may be done by extending SQL to include a special operator, called the **UNDER** operator.

Example 14.4   **Using the ignorance strategy for conjunction, find all pictures of people making over $100,000 per year where the pictures correctly identify the person in question with over 70% probability**

    UNDER conj=ignorance
    SELECT File,Salary
    FROM face F, emp E

> **WHERE** F.Person = E.Name **AND** F.LB > 0.7
>   **AND** E.Salary > 100,000

This says that conjunctions (and hence joins) should be computed under the policy of ignorance. In general, suppose our probabilistic relational system supports conjunction strategies $c_1, \ldots, c_n$ and disjunction strategies $d_1, \ldots, d_m$.

A conj-expression (or disj-expression) is a statement of the form `conj` $=$ `c`$_i$ (or `disj` $=$ `d`$_j$, respectively) for some $1 \leq i \leq n$ (or $1 \leq j \leq m$, respectively).

If C is a conj-expression and D is a disj-expression, then:

1. C is a prob-expression

2. D is a prob-expression

3. $(C$ **AND** $D)$ is a prob-expression.

Thus, a prob-expression is a conjunction of at most two atoms. At most one of these is a conj-expression and at most one of them is a disj-expression. We may now define a *probabilistic SQL* (ProbSQL) query inductively as follows:

1. If Q is any (ordinary) SQL query, then

   > **UNDER** *prob-expression*
   > Q.

   is a ProbSQL query.

2. If Q is a ProbSQL query, then

   > **COMPACT** Q

   is a ProbSQL query.

For instance, the following are syntactically correct ProbSQL queries:

UNDER conj=ignorance **AND** disj=positive correlation
SELECT File,Salary
FROM face F, emp1 E1, emp2 E2
WHERE (F.Person = E1.Name **AND** F.LB > 0.7 **AND** E1.Salary > 100,000)
    OR (F.Person = E2.Name **AND** F.LB > 0.7 **AND** E2.Salary > 100,000)

COMPACT
UNDER conj=ignorance **AND** disj=positive correlation
SELECT File,Salary
FROM face F, emp1 E1, emp2 E2
WHERE (F.Person=E1.Name **AND** F.LB > 0.7 **AND** E1.Salary $> 100,000$)
    OR (F.Person=E2.Name **AND** F.LB > 0.7 **AND** E2.Salary $> 100,000$)

However,

UNDER conj=ignorance **AND** disj=pos correlation **AND** conj=independence
SELECT File,Salary
FROM face F, emp1 E1, emp2 E2
WHERE (F.Person=E1.Name **AND** F.LB > 0.7 **AND** E1.Salary $> 100,000$)
    OR (F.Person=E2.Name **AND** F.LB > 0.7 **AND** E2.Salary $> 100,000$)

is not a syntactically valid ProbSQL query.

Thus, probabilistic SQL queries seamlessly extend SQL using the simple, nonintrusive **UNDER** and **COMPACT** operators, together with appropriate advice on how conjunctions and disjunctions are to be evaluated.

14.3   Bibliographic Notes

There has been a spectacular amount of work on uncertainty in databases and knowledge bases. This work has been done in two separate communities: the database community and the artificial intelligence community. The former has focused primarily on extensions of the relational model of data to handle uncertain information, while the latter (discussed in the next chapter) has largely focused on extending knowledge representation paradigms such as first-order logic, nonmonotonic logics, and neural networks (to name a few) to handle uncertain information. We hope the information below will enable you to pursue your interests in further detail. A recent excellent survey of the state of the art is Parsons [331], who presents a bird's-eye view of the whole field, without getting into too much technical detail.

Fuzzy Extensions of the Relational Model

Fuzzy extensions to the relational model were studied by a number of authors, such as Raju and Majumdar [345] and Dubois and Prade [132]. In almost all these cases, they extended the standard relational operators to handle uncertainty under different models of uncertainty (e.g., fuzzy vs. possibilistic logic).

Probabilistic Extensions of the Relational Model

Cavallo and Pittarelli [89] were among the first to propose an elegant theoretical model for probabilistic relational databases. In their model, tuples in a probabilistic relation are interpreted using an exclusive Or connective, meaning at most one of the data tuples is assumed to be present in the underlying classical relation.

The next advance came from Barbará et al. [42], who developed a probabilistic data model and proposed probabilistic operators. Their work is based on the following assumptions:

1. A central premise in their model is that every probabilistic relation has a set of deterministic attributes forming the key of the relation.

2. They use only discrete probabilities, which in effect amounts to assuming that probabilities of compound events can always be precisely determined, an assumption valid for few combination strategies.

3. When performing joins, they assume that Bayes' rule applies (and hence, as they admit up front, they make the assumption that all events are independent). Also, as they point out, unfortunately their definition leads to a "lossy" join.

Another important approach was developed by Lee [264], who showed how to define a probabilistic relational algebra based on Dempster-Shafer theory [397]. A tuple in Lee's framework is syntactically similar to a probabilistic tuple presented here, but probabilistic tuples allow interval probabilities (and hence errors in probability estimates), while Lee's framework doesn't. Lee's framework, like all the preceding frameworks, assumes that different events are independent.

Fuhr has recently proposed a probabilistic data model [176] in which he too makes the assumption of independence. Like the presentation in this chapter, he too associates constraints with tuples. However, the major difference here is that his constraints are Boolean constraints not over paths, but over tuple-ids. In contrast, the notion of a world-id used in this chapter is explicitly induced on an annotated relation from a probabilistic relation.

Dey and Sarkar [129] have recently proposed a probabilistic relational data model that removes, from the model of Barbará et al. [42], the restrictive assumption that two records should not have the same key.

The presentation of probabilistic databases given in this chapter is based on recent work of Lakshmanan et al. [260], who eliminated all the assumptions of Barbará et al. [42] and provided a very flexible probabilistic database paradigm where different probabilistic strategies automatically induced different notions of select, project, difference, join, union, and intersection operations. This was backed up by a prototype implementation, details of which are available from the authors.

Query Optimization in Fuzzy Databases

Almost no work has been performed to date on the topic of query optimization in fuzzy and multivalued databases. The reason for this has been that the foundations of such extensions of the relational model have still been evolving. Now that they have reached a reasonably mature state, they can (and must) lead to a detailed study of query containments and query equivalences with respect to fuzzy/lattice-based relational databases. A start has been made for probabilistic databases in [260]. However, very few ways of automatically rewriting queries so as to optimize them have been developed, and few, if any, join optimization techniques exist.

Temporal Probabilities

Dyreson and Snodgrass [138] have pointed out that probabilities are required to handle valid-time indeterminacy in temporal databases. One of the important assumptions they make (like most research in probabilistic databases) is that of statistical independence of events. For probabilistic databases, it has been shown in [260] that this assumption may be completely eliminated. The question of whether the elimination of the independence assumption can be applied to the case of valid-time indeterminacy still exists and needs to be investigated. Unfortunately, although the approach in [260] is theoretically sound, and is feasible in most cases where the value of an attribute of a tuple is known to fall into a relatively small set (e.g., a few hundred values, which suffices for most nontemporal applications), temporal indeterminacy poses special problems. Temporal indeterminacy may cause several million annotated tuples to result from a single tuple containing temporal indeterminacy (as even a "small" time interval such as a month may have millions of chronons). Thus, the removal of the statistical independence assumption from the Dyreson-Snodgrass framework [138] in a practically realizable manner remains a formidable challenge.

14.4   A Final Note

In this chapter, we have shown how relational databases may be neatly extended to handle

- lattice-based models of uncertainty, which include, as a special case, fuzzy logic approaches

- probabilistic modes of uncertainty that are flexible enough to allow users to specify, in their queries, the probabilistic conditions (e.g., independence, ignorance, positive correlation, etc.) under which extended versions of the relational operators are computed.

14.5 Exercises

14.1. Consider the fuzzy `face` relation shown in Section 14.1.

    a. Express, in fuzzy SQL (using the lattice-based version of SQL), the query that selects all tuples associated with the file im1.gif, and then projects out the Person field.

    b. What is the result of this query when executed using the definition of the relational operators for lattice-based relational databases provided in this chapter?

    c. What would an ordinary SQL interpreter have returned when processing this query?

14.2. Suppose Q is a query of the form $\pi^\ell_{B_1,\ldots,B_r}(R^\ell)$, where R^ℓ is a lattice-based relation and $B_1,\ldots,B_r$ are attributes of R^ℓ. Describe a necessary and sufficient condition C such that the following property holds: The result returned by evaluation query Q under the lattice-based semantics is equivalent to the result returned by computing $\pi_{B_1,\ldots,B_r,Unc}(R')$, where R' is identical to R^ℓ except that it has an extra data attribute (Unc).

14.3. What is the result of the query $\pi^\ell_{A_3}(R^\ell_1)$ of Section 14.1.1?

14.4. Compute the Cartesian product of the relations R^ℓ_1 and R^ℓ_2 of Section 14.1.1.

14.5. Consider the simple probabilistic relation R given below:

A_1	A_2	A_3
p1	q1, $[0.5, 0.7]$ q2, $[0.2, 0.4]$	r1, $[0.2, 0.4]$. r2, $[0.3, 0.5]$. r3, $[0.1, 0.25]$
p2	q1, $[0.1, 0.7]$ q2, $[0.4, 0.5]$	r1, $[0.3, 0.5]$. r2, $[0.3, 0.8]$.

Find the annotated representation (call it R_a) of the above probabilistic relation.

14.6. Continuing with the previous problem, express, using probabilistic SQL, the query that computes the compaction of the result of projecting out attribute A_2 under the assumption of ignorance. What is the result of executing this query under the assumption of ignorance?

14.7. Suppose S_a is the annotated relation shown below.

A_4	A_5	LB	UB	Path
q1	r1	0.2	0.4	$v_1 \wedge \neg v_6$
q1	r2	0.3	0.6	v_1

What is the join of R_a and S_a (with respect to the join condition $A_2 = A_4$) when we use

a. the assumption of ignorance?

b. the assumption of independence?

Chapter 15

Including Uncertainty in Deductive Databases

In the preceding chapter, we studied methods and techniques to extend the relational model of data to handle lattice-based (including fuzzy) uncertainty measures, as well as to handle probabilistic modes of uncertainty. In this chapter, we will show how the same techniques may be extended to the case of knowledge bases (KBs).

15.1 Generalized Annotated Programs (GAPs)

Let us suppose that $(L, \sqsubseteq)$ is a complete lattice (of truth values). In this section, we will define something called a generalized annotated program (GAP) that will allow us to reason about data when truth values are drawn from any such complete lattice. GAPs are defined using a two-sorted language.

First, there is a logical language, defined in the usual way, from a finite set of constant symbols and predicate symbols, and an infinite set of variable symbols. This language is used to define terms—a term is either a constant or a variable—and atoms. If p is an n-ary predicate symbol, and $t_1, \ldots, t_n$ are terms, then $p(t_1, \ldots, t_n)$ is an atom.

In addition to the above language, we allow the lattice $(L, \sqsubseteq)$ to generate another lattice language as follows:

1. *Lattice constants:* Every member of L is a lattice constant.

2. *Lattice variables:* We assume the existence of a set (infinite) of lattice variables.

3. *Lattice functions:* We assume the existence of some set of predefined, implemented functions $f_1, \ldots, f_k$ on the lattice L.

4. *Lattice terms:* These are defined inductively as follows:

   (a) Every lattice variable is a lattice term.

   (b) Every lattice constant is a lattice term.

   (c) If $t_1, \ldots, t_n$ are lattice terms, and f_i is an n-ary lattice term, then $f_i(t_1, \ldots, t_n)$ is a lattice term.

Thus, for example, if our lattice is the the set of real numbers, and if $\times, +, -, \mathrm{div}$ denote the operations of multiplication, addition, subtraction, and division, respectively, then the expression $((V + 5) * (V' + 2)) \,\mathrm{div}\, 4$ is a valid lattice term.

Definition 15.1 *Suppose A is an atom in the logical language, and $\mathcal{V}$ is a lattice term. Then $A : \mathcal{V}$ is an* annotated atom.

For example, if our lattice is the unit interval $[0, 1]$ with the usual $\leq$ ordering on it, then an annotated atom of the form $A : 0.3$ says, informally, that the truth value of A is at least 30%.

Definition 15.2 *If $A_0 : \mu_0, \ldots, A_n : \mu_n$ are annotated atoms, where $\mu_1, \ldots, \mu_n$ contain no lattice functions, then*

?why?

$$A_0 : \mu_0 \leftarrow A_1 : \mu_1 \wedge \cdots \wedge A_n : \mu_n$$

is called an annotated clause. *Each variable occurring in an annotated clause is assumed to be universally quantified at the front of the clause. A generalized annotated program (GAP) is a finite set of annotated clauses.*

For example, let us return to our face relation, and suppose that relation is named face. Suppose our lattice is the set of all closed intervals of $[0, 1]$. Then the following annotated clause finds all people with whom Person1 was seen.

$$\mathrm{seen}(\mathrm{Person1}, \mathrm{Person2}) : \frac{V_1 + V_2}{2} \leftarrow \mathrm{face}(\mathrm{File}, X1, Y1, X2, Y2, \mathrm{Person1}) : V_1 \wedge$$
$$\mathrm{face}(\mathrm{File}, X3, Y3, X4, Y4, \mathrm{Person2}) : V_2 \wedge$$
$$\mathrm{diff}(X1, Y1, X2, Y2, X3, Y3, X4, Y4)$$

Above, diff is a predicate that succeeds iff the rectangle with lower-left corner $(X1, Y1)$ and upper-right corner $(X2, Y2)$ is different from the rectangle with lower-left corner $(X3, Y3)$ and upper-right corner $(X4, Y4)$.[1] When the above rule is invoked with Person1 $=$ John Smith, then the set of people returned in the seen relation is

Person1	Person2	Unc
John Smith	Mark Bloom	$\frac{V_1+V_2}{2}$
John Smith	Ted Lewis	$\frac{V_1+V_3}{2}$

In the above example, V_1, V_2 and V_3 are the certainties associated with tuples 1, 3, and 4, respectively, of the relation face given at the beginning of this chapter.

In any complete lattice $(L, \sqsubseteq)$, we use the notation $\sqcup$ and $\sqcap$ to denote the least upper bound and greatest lower bound operators, respectively. We are now in a position to define the semantics of GAPs. We will define the semantics of GAPs using three paradigms: a declarative logical model theory, a declarative fixpoint theory, and finally, a query processing procedure.

15.1.1 Lattice-Based KBs: Model Theory

In this section, we will define a formal declarative semantics for GAPs using *logical model theory*. In the rest of this section, we assume that $(L, \sqsubseteq)$ is an arbitrary but fixed complete lattice of truth values. As usual, the Herbrand base of a GAP will denote the set of all ground atoms expressed using the constant and predicate symbols occurring in the GAP.

Definition 15.3 *An Herbrand interpretation is a map from the Herbrand base of a GAP to the set L.*

For example, consider the unit interval $[0, 1]$ of truth values under the usual ordering, and the GAP:

$$p(a) : 1 \leftarrow .$$
$$p(b) : 0.8 \leftarrow .$$
$$q(X) : \frac{V}{2} \leftarrow p(X) : V.$$

---

[1]We will not go into the definition of diff. The definition of this operator may be done on an application-by-application basis. For example, two rectangles that are almost identical (i.e., have a 90% or greater overlap) may be considered not different. We will assume therefore that diff is defined in some way based on the application developer's intuitions on when two rectangles should be considered to be different.

Here are two (of many) possible interpretations I_1 and I_2 associated with this GAP.

$$I_1(p(a)) = 1; I_1(p(b)) = 0.8; I_1(q(a)) = 0.7; I_1(q(b)) = 0.4$$

$$I_2(p(a)) = 1; I_2(p(b)) = 0.4; I_2(q(a)) = 0.2; I_2(q(b)) = 0.4$$

Definition 15.4 *Suppose I is an Herbrand interpretation.*

1. *I satisfies a ground atom $A : \mu$ iff $\mu \leq I(A)$.*

2. *I satisfies $(F \wedge G)$ iff I satisfies F and I satisfies G.*

3. *I satisfies $(F \vee G)$ iff I satisfies F or I satisfies G.*

4. *I satisfies $F \leftarrow G$ iff I satisfies F or I does not satisfy G.*

5. *I satisfies $(\forall x.)F[x]$ iff for all ground terms t from the domain over which x ranges, I satisfies $F[x/t]$. Here, $F[x/t]$ refers to the simultaneous replacement of all free occurrences of x in F by t.*

6. *I satisfies $(\exists x.)F[x]$ iff for some ground term t from the domain over which x ranges, I satisfies $F[x/t]$.*

It is important to recall that all annotated clauses occurring in a GAP contain an implicit universal quantifier in front. Thus, strictly speaking, the rule

$$q(X) : \frac{V}{2} \leftarrow p(X) : V.$$

in the GAP described earlier should be written

$$(\forall X)(\forall V)(q(X) : \frac{V + 1}{2} \leftarrow p(X) : V.)$$

Furthermore, note that here, X ranges over the set $\{a, b\}$, while V ranges over all real numbers in the unit interval $[0, 1]$. If we now return to the GAP given above, we observe that I_1 satisfies this GAP, but I_2 does not. To see why I_2 does not satisfy the GAP, consider the ground instance of the rule in the GAP:

$$q(a) : \frac{1}{2} \leftarrow p(a) : 1.$$

This ground instance is obtained by substituting a for X and 1 for V. I_2 satisfies the body because $1 \leq I_2(p(a)) = 1$. However, $I_2(q(a)) = 0.2 < 0.5$. Thus, neither of the two conditions defining satisfaction of an implication hold in this case, and hence, I_2 does not satisfy this rule.

An interpretation I is said to *satisfy* a GAP P iff I satisfies each and every annotated clause in P.

Given two interpretations I and I', we may extend the ordering $\sqsubseteq$ on the truth value lattice $(L, \sqsubseteq)$, so that it applies to interpretations, as follows:

$$I \sqsubseteq I' \text{ iff for all ground atoms } A, I(A) \sqsubseteq I'(A).$$

Thus, for example, suppose

$$I(p) = 0.3; I(q) = 0.4$$

$$I'(p) = 0.5; I'(q) = 0.45$$

$$I''(p) = 0.35; I''(q) = 0.3$$

Then,

- $I \sqsubseteq I'$

- $I'' \sqsubseteq I'$

- $I \not\sqsubseteq I''$

- $I'' \not\sqsubseteq I$.

Theorem 15.5 *Suppose P is a GAP and $\mathcal{I}$ is the set of all Herbrand interpretations associated with the language of P. Then $\mathcal{I}$ is a complete lattice under the ordering $\sqsubseteq$. In particular, if $X \subseteq \mathcal{I}$ is any set of interpretations, then the least upper bound and greatest lower bound of X are defined as*

$$\sqcup(\mathcal{I})(A) = \sqcup\{J(A) \mid J \in \mathcal{I}\}.$$
$$\sqcap(\mathcal{I})(A) = \sqcap\{J(A) \mid J \in \mathcal{I}\}.$$

In addition, suppose we consider a ground rule of the form

$$A : \mu \leftarrow B_1 : \mu_1 \wedge \cdots \wedge B_k : \mu_k.$$

Suppose I_1 and I_2 are two interpretations that satisfy the above rule. Then $I = I_1 \sqcap I_2$ must also satisfy this rule. To see why, suppose I satisfies the body of the above rule. Then $\mu_i \leq I(B_i)$ for all $1 \leq i \leq k$ by definition (of satisfaction), and as the above rule is ground. As $I = I_1 \sqcap I_2$, it follows that for all $1 \leq i \leq n$, $\mu_i \leq I_1(B_i)$ and $\mu_i \leq I_2(B_i)$; hence, both I_1 and I_2 satisfy the body of the above ground rule. As I_1, I_2 satisfy the above rule, it follows that they must satisfy the head of the above rule as well, that is, $\mu \leq I_1(A)$ and $\mu \leq I_2(A)$. Thus, μ is a lower bound of $\{I_1(A), I_2(A)\}$, and hence $\mu \leq \sqcap\{I_1(A), I_2(A)\} = I(A)$. Thus, I satisfies the head of the above rule, which means that I satisfies the above rule. This argument may be extended (with a small amount of work) to prove the following theorem.

Theorem 15.6 *Suppose I' is any interpretation. Then the set $\{I^\star \mid I^\star$ sat-isfies P and $I' \sqsubseteq I^\star\}$ has a unique $\sqsubseteq$-minimal element. As a consequence, P has a unique $\sqsubseteq$-minimal model.*

Intuitively, an interpretation specifies a possible meaning of a GAP. How-ever, as you may have already noticed, a GAP may have many possible interpretations that satisfy it. We say a GAP P has a formula F as a *logi-cal consequence* if every interpretation that satisfies P also satisfies formula F. Usually, we will be interested only in formulas that are conjunctions of atoms. If we return to our example GAP, we notice that the ground atoms that are logical consequences of it are

$$p(a) : 1; p(b) : 0.8; q(a) : 0.5; q(b) : 0.4$$

Intuitively, the logical consequences of a GAP are those formulas that are true in all interpretations that satisfy the GAP. You may, at this stage, feel that computing each and every interpretation that satisfies a GAP, and then checking to see which formulas are true in all of them, might be a rather cumbersome process. It is, but fortunately there is a way around this problem, using a technique called *fixpoint computation*.

15.1.2   Lattice-Based KBs: Fixpoint Theory

The semantics of programs have long been characterized by viewing the pro-gram as a function that maps states to states, and considering the meaning of the program to be a state that does not change when this function is ap-plied to that state. In the case of GAPs, interpretations capture the notion of a state. After all, we may view an interpretation as a "guess" about the meaning of the GAP, and the transformation as a map that determines what immediately "follows" from the guess. Fixpoints are those interpretations that intuitively remain unchanged by the state transformation.

The first step in rendering this informal intuition into a formal framework is to determine what operator should be associated with a GAP. Given a GAP P, we may associate with P a function, denoted T_P, that maps interpretations to interpretations. If I is an interpretation, then so is $T_P(I)$, and the formal definition of T_P is given by

$T_P(I)(A) = \sqcup\{\mu \mid A : \mu \leftarrow Body$ is a ground instance of an annotated clause in P such that I satisfies $Body\}$.

Informally, $T_P(I)(A)$ may be (inefficiently) computed by following the steps outlined below:

1. Let $S = \emptyset$.

2. First replace P by the (possibly infinite) GAP $grd(P)$ obtained by instantiating each annotated clause in P in as many ways as possible.

3. For each ground annotated clause in $grd(P)$ that has a head of the form $A : \mu$, do the following: if I satisfies the body of the clause, then put μ in S.

4. Compute the least upper bound of all elements of S and set $T_P(I)(A)$ to this value.

Example 15.1   Application of T_P

Suppose P is the GAP given by

$$p(a) : 1 \leftarrow .$$
$$p(b) : 0.8 \leftarrow .$$
$$q(X) : \frac{V}{2} \leftarrow p(X) : V.$$

Suppose I_1, I_2 are the interpretations given below:

$$I_1(p(a)) = 1; I_1(p(b)) = 0.8; I_1(q(a)) = 0.7; I_1(q(b)) = 0.4$$

$$I_2(p(a)) = 1; I_2(p(b)) = 0.4; I_2(q(a)) = 0.2; I_2(q(b)) = 0.4$$

Then $T_P(I_1)$ is given by

$$T_P(I_1)(p(a)) = 1$$
$$T_P(I_1)(p(b)) = 0.8$$
$$T_P(I_1)(q(a)) = 0.5$$
$$T_P(I_1)(q(b)) = 0.4$$

However, $T_P(I_2)$ is given by

$$T_P(I_2)(p(a)) = 1$$
$$T_P(I_2)(p(b)) = 0.8$$
$$T_P(I_2)(q(a)) = 0.5$$
$$T_P(I_2)(q(b)) = 0.2$$

Note that $T_P(I_2)(q(b)) = 0.2$ because $I_2(p(b)) = 0.4$, and hence $T_P(I_2)(q(b)) = \frac{0.4}{2} = 0.2$.

A slightly more complex example is given below:

Example 15.2   Infinite iterations of T_p

Suppose P is the very simple GAP given by

$$p(a) : 0 \leftarrow .$$
$$p(X) : \frac{V+1}{2} \leftarrow p(X) : V.$$
$$q(X) : 1 \leftarrow p(a) : 1.$$

Suppose I_0 is the interpretation such that $I_0(p(a)) = I_0(q(a)) = 0$. Let I_j denote the j-fold application of T_p to I_0, i.e., let us set

$$I_j = T_P^j(I_0)$$

Recall, from naive set theory, that ω is the smallest ordinal larger than all the natural numbers. We will use the notation I_ω to denote $\sqcup_{j<\omega}I_j$. Then, $I_{\omega+1}$ will denote $T_P(I_\omega)$, $I_{\omega+2}$ will denote $T_P(I_{\omega+1})$, and so forth.

For example, we can easily see that

$$I_1(p(a)) = 0.5; I_1(q(a)) = 0$$

$$I_2(p(a)) = 0.75; I_2(q(a)) = 0$$
$$I_3(p(a)) = 0.875; I_3(q(a)) = 0$$

$$\cdots$$

$$I_j(p(a)) = 1 - \left(\frac{1}{2}\right)^j ; I_j(q(a)) = 0$$

$$\cdots$$

$$I_\omega(p(a)) = 1; I_\omega(q(a)) = 0$$

$$I_{\omega+1}(p(a)) = 1; I_{\omega+1}(q(a)) = 1$$

$$I_{\omega+2} = I_{\omega+1}$$

Above, we use the notation I_ω to denote $\sqcup\{I_j \mid j < \omega\}$, i.e., ω is the smallest limit ordinal.

Proposition 15.7 *Suppose P is any GAP. Then,*

1. *T_P is monotonic, i.e., if $I_1 \sqsubseteq I_2$, then $T_P(I_1) \sqsubseteq T_P(I_2)$.*

2. *I satisfies P iff $T_P(I) \sqsubseteq I$.*

3. *$\{I \mid T_P(I) = I\}$ has a unique, $\sqsubseteq$-minimal element called the* least fix-point *of T_P, and denoted $\mathsf{lfp}(T_P)$.*

4. *For any ground atom A and any truth value μ, it is the case that $A : \mu$ is a logical consequence of the GAP P iff $\mu \sqsubseteq \mathsf{lfp}(T_P)(A)$.*

The first part of the above result says that as interpretations assign "higher" (in the lattice) truth values, $T_P(I)$ also likewise assigns higher truth values. The second part of the above result is more interesting. It says that the interpretations I satisfying P are exactly those having the property that $T_P(I) \sqsubseteq I$. This implies that to check for logical consequence, we merely need to examine whether $A : \mu$ is true in all interpretations I such that $T_P(I) \sqsubseteq I$. The third part of the above result is even more optimistic. It says that we do not, in fact, have to examine all interpretations I such that $T_P(I) \sqsubseteq I$—examining just one of them is enough, namely, $\mathsf{lfp}(T_P)$!

Example 15.3   Fixpoints of T_P revisited

Let us return to the GAP in Example 15.2. The T_P operator associated with this GAP has interpretation I_ω as its least fix-point.

As we have seen, the preceding proposition tells us that computing logical consequence of a GAP basically depends upon our ability to compute $\mathsf{lfp}(T_P)$. Fortunately, this is not very difficult. The procedure may be intuitively described by referring to what we did in Example 15.2. There, we first started out by assuming I_0, which in effect captures a state of complete ignorance.

15.1.3   Lattice-Based KBs: Query Processing

In this section, we will present a simple resolution-based query processing strategy that may be used to answer queries posed to GAPs.

Definition 15.8 *Suppose $(L, \sqsubseteq)$ is a lattice. An* atomic lattice constraint *is an expression of the form $t \sqsubseteq t'$ where t, t' are lattice terms. A* lattice constraint *is a Boolean combination of atomic lattice constraints.*

Definition 15.9 *If $A_1 : \mu_1, \ldots, A_n : \mu_n$ are annotated atoms, where each μ_i is a lattice element, and $X_1, \ldots, X_k$ are all the variables occurring in $A_1, \ldots, A_n$, and $\mathcal{C}$ is a lattice constraint (possibly empty), then*

$$(\exists X_1, \ldots, X_k)(A_1 : \mu_1 \wedge \ldots \wedge A_n : \mu_n) \wedge \mathcal{C}$$

is a query. *We will often write the above query as just $(A_1 : \mu_1 \wedge \ldots \wedge A_n : \mu_n) \wedge \mathcal{C}$, with the understanding that the variables in it are existentially quantified at the front of the conjunction.*

Notice that $\mu_1, \ldots, \mu_n$ are all lattice elements and do not include annotation variables. An example of a simple query is the conjunction

$$(\exists X, Y)p(X, Y) : 1 \wedge q(Y) : 0.8.$$

Informally, this query may be read as "Find X, Y such that $p(X, Y)$ is true with certainty 1 or more and $q(Y)$ is true with certainty 0.8 or more." Usually, we will assume that users' queries involve no lattice constraints. These will be introduced as the query gets processed.

More formally, if P is a GAP, then given the query $(\exists X_1, \ldots, X_k)(A_1 : \mu_1 \wedge \ldots \wedge A_n : \mu_n)$, we are looking for a ground substitution θ for the variables in the query such that

$$(\forall)(A_1\theta : \mu_1 \wedge \ldots \wedge A_n\theta : \mu_n)$$

is a logical consequence of the GAP P.

Example 15.4   Answers to GAP queries

Suppose we consider the GAP

$$p(X, Y) : V \leftarrow q(X, Z) : V \wedge r(Z) : V.$$
$$q(X, a) : 0.7 \leftarrow .$$
$$r(a) : 0.6 \leftarrow .$$

Suppose we consider the query $p(X, Y) : 0.6$. In this case, consider the substitution $\theta_1 = \{Y = a\}$. This is an answer to the query because $(\forall X)p(X, a) : 0.6$ is a logical consequence of P.

On the other hand, consider the query $p(X, Y) : 0.7$. In this case, θ_1 is not an answer to the query because $(\forall X)p(X, a) : 0.7$ is not a logical consequence of P and hence cannot be considered an answer to this query.

Definition 15.10 *Suppose Q denotes the query $(A_1 : \mu_1 \wedge \ldots \wedge A_n : \mu_n) \wedge \mathcal{C}$ and $\mathcal{C}$ is the annotated clause:*

$$A : \mu \leftarrow B_1 : \rho_1 \wedge \cdots \wedge B_m : \rho_m.$$

Further, suppose that $\mathcal{C}$ and Q share no variables (i.e., they are standardized apart) and that σ is an mgu of A_i and A for some $1 \leq i \leq n$. Then the query

$$(A_1 : \mu_1 \wedge \ldots \wedge A_{i-1} : \mu_{i-1} \wedge B_1 : \rho_1 \wedge \cdots \wedge B_m : \rho_m \wedge$$

$$A_{i+1} : \mu_{i+1} \wedge \ldots \wedge A_n : \mu_n)\sigma \wedge (\mathcal{C} \wedge \mu_i \sqsubseteq \mu)$$

is said to be an annotated resolvent *of Q and $\mathcal{C}$ via mgu σ.*

Example 15.5 Annotated resolvents of queries with GAPs

Let us return to the GAP of Example 15.4 and consider, once again, the query $p(X', Y') : 0.6$. The annotated resolvent of this query with the annotated clause

$$p(X, Y) : V \leftarrow q(X, Z) : V \wedge r(Z) : V.$$

is the query

$$q(X', Z) : V \wedge r(Z) : V \wedge 0.6 \sqsubseteq V.$$

Definition 15.11 *Suppose Q denotes a query, and P is a GAP. An* annotated deduction *from P with respect to Q is a finite or infinite sequence*

$$(Q_0, C_0, \theta_0), \ldots, (Q_j, C_j, \theta_j), \ldots$$

where

1. $Q_0 = Q$ and

2. C_j *is a renaming of an annotated clause in* P *for all* $j \geq 0$ *and*

3. Q_{j+1} *is an annotated resolvent of* Q_j *and* C_j *via mgu* θ_j.

An annotated refutation *of* Q *from* P *is a finite annotated deduction*

$$(Q_0, C_0, \theta_0), \ldots, (Q_{r-1}, C_{r-1}, \theta_{r-1})$$

($r \geq 1$) from P *with respect to* Q *such that the annotated resolvent of* Q_{r-1} *and* C_{r-1} *via mgu* θ_{r-1} *is the empty query (i.e., a query containing no annotated atoms, and a solvable constraint part). Such a refutation is said to be of length* r.

Intuitively, an annotated refutation is just a sequence of annotated resolution steps, leading to the empty query. A simple example may help here.

Example 15.6   An example annotated refutation

Let us return to the very simple GAP P in Example 15.4 and the query $Q = p(X', Y') : 0.6$. Here is a very simple annotated refutation of this query. We use Cl_1, Cl_2, Cl_3 to denote the first, second, and third clauses of P, respectively. We will also abuse notation slightly by not standardizing apart the clauses in P.

1. $(Q_0, Cl_1, \{X' = X, Y' = Y\})$.
2. $(q(X, Z) : 0.6 \land r(Z) : V \land 0.6 \sqsubseteq V, Cl_2, \{Z = a\})$.
3. $(r(a) : V \land (0.6 \sqsubseteq V \land V \sqsubseteq 0.7), Cl_3, \{\})$.
4. $(0.6 \sqsubseteq V \land V \sqsubseteq 0.7 \land V \sqsubseteq 0.6, -, -)$.

The last query above has no atoms (only a lattice constraint) and this lattice constraint is solvable.

Though annotated resolution may appear to be sound and complete, it turns out that completeness does not hold. There are two reasons for this:

- The first reason is that the operator T_P may lead to fixpoints at ordinals greater than ω, leading some atoms to have infinite justifications. To see why this is true, let us return to the GAP in Example 15.2. Here, $q(a) : 1$ is a logical consequence of this GAP. However, the justification for this is based on an infinite argument, as detailed in Example 15.2, and the argument cannot be captured in a finite way.

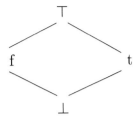

Figure 15.1: The lattice FOUR

- The second reason is that the notion of deduction does not allow us to "merge" multiple derivations. For example, consider a lattice such as the lattice FOUR shown in Figure 15.1, and consider the simple GAP P given by

$$p : t \leftarrow .$$
$$p : f \leftarrow .$$

It is easy to see that $p : \top$ is a logical consequence of this GAP. However, there is no annotated refutation of this query from P.

Given any function f on a complete lattice $(L, \sqsubseteq)$, we may define the *iterations* of f as follows:

$$f \uparrow 0 = \bot.$$
$$f \uparrow \alpha = f(f \uparrow (\alpha - 1)) \text{ for successor ordinals } \alpha.$$
$$f \uparrow \lambda = \sqcup_{\beta < \lambda} f \uparrow \beta \text{ for limit ordinals } \lambda.$$

Definition 15.12 *We say that a GAP P possesses the* fixpoint reachability *property if, whenever $\mu \sqsubseteq \mathsf{lfp}(T_P)(A)$, it is the case that $\mu \sqsubseteq T_P \uparrow k(A)$ for some integer k.*

Definition 15.13 *Suppose C_1, C_2 are two clauses in a GAP P having the respective forms:*

$$A_1 : \mu_1 \leftarrow Body1.$$
$$A_2 : \mu_2 \leftarrow Body2.$$

If A_1, A_2 are unifiable via mgu θ, then the clause

$$(A_1 : \mu_1 \sqcup \mu_2 \leftarrow Body1 \wedge Body2)\theta$$

is called a reductant *of C_1, C_2. The* closure *of P is defined to be $\Re^\omega(P)$ where*

1. *$\Re^0(P) = P$.*

2. *$\Re^{j+1}(P) = \Re^j(P) \cup \{C \mid$ there exist $C_1, C_2 \in \Re^j(P)$ such that C is the reductant of $C_1, C_2\}$.*

Thus, for example, with respect to the lattice FOUR described above, the clause

$$p : \top \leftarrow .$$

is a reductant of the clauses

$$p : t \leftarrow .$$
$$p : f \leftarrow .$$

We may now state the soundness and completeness of annotated resolution as follows:

Theorem 15.14 *Soundness and completeness of annotated resolution. Let P be any GAP and Q be a query.*

1. *Soundness: If there exists an annotated refutation of Q, then Q is a logical consequence of P.*

2. *Completeness: Suppose Q is a logical consequence of P and P satisfies the fixpoint reachability condition. Then there exists an annotated refutation of Q with respect to the closure of P.*

Note that in the statement of the completeness result above, resolutions are allowed with clauses in the closure of P, not just with clauses in P itself. In general, the closure of P may be somewhat larger than P. Fortunately, there are new advances, some by Adali and Subrahmanian, and also some by Lu, Murray, and Rosenthal, that allow us to avoid computing reductants and program closure. However, this topic is beyond the scope of this book. Section 15.3 will point to useful details.

Before concluding our section on lattice-based approaches to uncertainty in knowledge bases, we provide a quick example of annotated resolution with respect to the closure of GAPs rather than the GAPs themselves.

Example 15.7 **Annotated resolution with respect to closures**

Let us reconsider the GAP over the lattice FOUR defined by

$$p : t \leftarrow .$$
$$p : f \leftarrow .$$

Consider the query $p : \top$. First of all, observe that if we do not permit the use of reductants in constructing refutations, then there is no refutation of this query, even though it is a logical consequence of P. However, when we resolve with clauses in the closure of P instead of P itself, we may resolve this clause with the reductant,

$$p : \top \leftarrow .$$

which is in the closure of P, obtaining the empty query immediately.

15.2 Probabilistic Knowledge Bases

Though lattice-based approaches are very general and allow us to capture many different kinds of reasoning within a single theoretical framework, they do not allow us to capture probabilistic reasoning. The reason for this is that probabilities of compound events are not expressible in terms of least upper bounds and greatest lower bounds on a lattice. Rather, probabilities of complex events must be computed carefully, using somewhat more complex structures. In this section, we will introduce the concept of a probabilistic knowledge base and provide a formal syntax and a formal semantics for it. As in the case of GAPs, the formal semantics will consist of three parts: a formal logical model theory with an associated notion of logical consequence, a formal fixpoint theory, and a formal query processing procedure.

As in the case of GAPs, we will assume the existence of two languages, a logical language that is identical to that for GAPs, and an annotation language.

Annotated Language

This language has certain annotation variables that range over the reals in the unit interval $[0, 1]$ and annotation functions that are maps (of different arities) from $[0, 1]^n$ to $[0, 1]$. We assume that all annotation functions f

are computable in the sense that there is a fixed procedure P_f such that if f is n-ary, and if $\rho_1, \ldots, \rho_n$, all in $[0,1]$, are given as inputs to P_f, then $f(\rho_1, \ldots, \rho_n)$ is computed by P_f in a finite amount of time.

Definition 15.15 *ρ is called an* annotation item *if it is one of the following:*

1. *a constant in $[0,1]$, or*

2. *an annotation variable in the underlying language, or*

3. *of the form $f(\delta_1, \ldots, \delta_n)$, where f is an annotation function of arity n and $\delta_1, \ldots, \delta_n$ are annotation items.*

For c, d such that $0 \leq c, d \leq 1$, let the closed interval $[c, d]$ be the set $\{x \mid c \leq x \leq d\}$.

The closed interval $[\rho_1, \rho_2]$ is called an annotation (term) if $\rho_i (i = 1, 2)$ is an annotation item. If an annotation does not contain any annotation variables, the annotation is called a c-annotation. Otherwise, it is called a v-annotation.

For example, $[0.1, 0.2]$, $[0.7, \frac{V}{2}]$, and $[\frac{|V_1 - V_2|}{2}, \frac{|V_1 + V_2|}{2}]$ are all annotation terms as long as our vocabulary contains the variables V_1 and V_2 and the annotation functions of addition, subtraction, and division.

Logical Language

This language is generated by symbols in an underlying logical alphabet as described in the case of GAPs. We use the notation B_L to denote the set of all ground atoms in language L. We further use the notation $conj(B_L)$ and $disj(B_L)$ to denote the set of all conjunctions and disjunctions of atoms, respectively, that can be expressed in our language.

Definition 15.16 *We use the following notation:*

1. *$conj(B_L) = \{A_1 \wedge \ldots \wedge A_n \mid n \geq 1$ is an integer and $A_1, \ldots, A_n \in B_L$ and for all $1 \leq i, j \leq n, i \neq j \Rightarrow A_i \neq A_j\}$*

2. *$disj(B_L) = \{A_1 \vee \ldots \vee A_n \mid n \geq 1$ is an integer and $A_1, \ldots, A_n \in B_L$ and for all $1 \leq i, j \leq n, i \neq j \Rightarrow A_i \neq A_j\}$,*
   where all the A_i's are ground atoms.

Definition 15.17 *A* basic formula *of language L is any member of $conj(B_L) \cup disj(B_L)$.*

In other words, basic formulas are either conjunctions of atoms, or disjunctions of atoms, but not a mix of the two. We use the notation $bf(B_L)$ to denote the set $conj(B_L) \cup disj(B_L)$.

Definition 15.18 *If C is a conjunction of atoms, not necessarily ground, and μ is an annotation, then $C : \mu$ is called an* annotated conjunction. *Similarly, if D is a disjunction, not necessarily ground, then $D : \mu$ is called an* annotated disjunction.

We present a list of four different annotated basic formulas:

1. $at(25, 26, robot) : [0.3, 0.4]$: This annotated atom says that the probability that the robot is at location $(25, 26)$ lies in the range 30% to 40%.

2. $(at(25, 26, robot1) \wedge at(25, 36, robot2)) : [0.2, 0.25]$: This annotated conjunction says that the combined probability that robot1 is at location $(25, 26)$ and robot2 is at location $(25, 36)$ lies in the range 20% to 25%.

3. $(at(25, 26, robot1) \vee at(25, 36, robot2)) : [0.4, 0.45]$: This annotated conjunction says that the combined probability that either robot1 is at location $(25, 26)$ or robot2 is at location $(25, 36)$ lies in the range 40% to 45%.

4. $(at(25, 26, robot1) \vee at(25, 36, robot2)) : [\frac{|V_1 - V_2|}{2}, \frac{|V_1 + V_2|}{2}]$: This says that the combined probability that either robot1 is at location $(25, 26)$ or robot2 is at location $(25, 36)$ lies in the range $[\frac{|V_1 - V_2|}{2}, \frac{|V_1 + V_2|}{2}]$, where the values of V_1, V_2 are currently unknown.

There are some subtle differences between the new concept of an annotation and the old, as described in the section on lattice-based KBs. First and foremost, notice that annotations are pairs now. These pairs are composed of annotation terms of the old sort and denote an interval. Second, annotation variables range over the reals in the unit interval $[0, 1]$.

Definition 15.19 *pf-clauses and p-clauses.*

1. *If $F_0, \ldots, F_n$ are basic formulas, and $\mu_0, \ldots, \mu_n$ are annotations such that all the annotation variables that appear in μ_0 also appear in at least one of $\mu_1, \ldots, \mu_n$, then the clause $F_0 : \mu_0 \leftarrow F_1 : \mu_1 \wedge \ldots \wedge F_n : \mu_n$ is called a* pf-clause. *$F_0 : \mu_0$ is called the* head *of the clause, and $(F_1 : \mu_1 \wedge \ldots \wedge F_n : \mu_n)$ is called the* body.

2. *If F_0 is an atom, then the clause is called a* p-clause.

Intuitively, the prefix "p-" stands for "probabilistic," while the prefix "pf-" stands for probabilistic formula. The distinction lies in the fact that heads of p-clauses are annotated atoms, while in the case of pf-clauses, they may be annotated basic formulas.

Definition 15.20 *pKBs and pf-KBs.*

1. *A probabilistic knowledge base (pKB) is a finite set of p-clauses.*

2. *A pf knowledge base (pf-KB) is a finite set of pf-clauses.*

It is important to note that pf-KBs are more expressive than pKBs because a rule can directly make statements about the probability of a complex event without making any explicit statement about the probabilities of the primitive events that constitute the complex event. We have already shown in this chapter that computing probability ranges for complex events like $(A \land B)$ and $(A \lor B)$ from the probability ranges known for A and B is relatively straightforward. However, going the other way is not always obvious; computing probability ranges for A and B from known probability ranges for complex events like $(A \land B)$ and/or $(A \lor B)$ requires reasoning with linear programming. The fact that treating pf-KBs is significantly more complex than treating pKBs will become clear as we proceed through this section. *Throughout the rest of this section, we will assume that we are manipulating probabilities under conditions of ignorance.*

Here are some examples of p-clauses and pf-clauses that may help you to gain a better understanding of the intuition underlying probabilistic KBs:

- Consider the p-clause

$$object(a) : [\max(0, \frac{V_1 - 0.1}{2}), \frac{V_2 + 0.1}{2}] \leftarrow sensor1(a) : [V_1, V_1] \land$$
$$sensor2(a) : [V_2, V_2].$$

  This rule says if sensor1 reports that object a is present with probability V_1 and sensor2 reports that object a is present with probability V_2, then we may conclude that object a is present with a probability in the range : $[\max(0, \frac{V_1 - 0.1}{2}), \frac{V_2 + 0.1}{2}]$.

- Consider the rule

$$object(a) : [\max(0, \frac{V_1 - 0.1}{2}), \frac{V_2 + 0.1}{2}] \leftarrow (sensor1(a) \land$$
$$sensor2(a)) : [V_1, V_2].$$

This p-clause is slightly different from the previous one because it says that we may conclude that object a is present with a probability in the range : $[\max(0, \frac{V_1 - 0.1}{2}), \frac{V_2 + 0.1}{2}]$ if the *joint* probability that sensor1 and sensor2 detect object a is in the interval $[V_1, V_2]$.

- The statement

$$(object(a) \wedge object(b)) : [0.9, 1] \leftarrow .$$

  is a simple pf-clause that says that the probability that objects a and b will occur is over 90%.

15.2.1 Probabilistic KBs: Fixpoint Theory

Having informally explained the meaning of p-clauses and pf-clauses, we are now in a position to develop a formal semantics for pKBs and pf-KBs. We will first develop a fixpoint theory for pKBs and pf-KBs, and subsequently develop model-theoretic and proof-theoretic semantics.

Definition 15.21 *A* world *is any Herbrand interpretation of our underlying logical language. We assume that the set $\mathcal{W}$ of all worlds is enumerated in some arbitrary but fixed order, $W_1, \ldots, W_k$.*

Definition 15.22 *A world probability density function $WP : \{W_1, \ldots, W_k\} \longrightarrow [0, 1]$ assigns to each world W_j a probability $WP(W_j)$ such that for all $j = 1, \ldots, k$, $WP(W_j) \geq 0$ and $\sum_{j=1}^{k} WP(W_j) = 1$.*

To simplify our notation, we will henceforth use p_j to denote $WP(W_j)$ for W_j. (Recall that this is consistent with the notation used in Section 13.2.4.)

Intuitively, one may think of world probability density functions as follows. Everything in the real world is either true or false (i.e., there are no probabilities), but our knowledge of what is true and what is false is incomplete and/or uncertain. Thus, we may assign a probability to each possible world, denoting the probability that that world does in fact capture the "real" world. This is exactly what a world probability density function does: it assigns probabilities to different possible worlds, specifying the probability of these worlds being the right one.

A formula function, on the other hand, instead makes a direct guess about the probabilities of basic formulas (as opposed to worlds).

Definition 15.23 *A formula function is a mapping $h : bf(B_L) \longrightarrow C[0,1]$, where $C[0,1]$ denotes the set of all closed subintervals of the unit interval $[0,1]$.*

Formula functions may be "ordered" with respect to each other as follows:

Definition 15.24 *Given two formula functions h_1 and h_2, $h_1 \leq h_2$ iff $\forall F \in bf(B_L), h_1(F) \supseteq h_2(F)$.*

Intuitively, the relation $h_1 \leq h_2$ between family functions may be read as h_2 is sharper than h_1. This reading is consistent with the fact that for each basic formula, h_2 assigns a smaller range than h_1, and hence there is less uncertainty in the probability assignment made by h_1.

Fixpoint Operator for pKBs

Definition 15.25 *Suppose P is any pKB (not pf-KB!). We may associate with P an operator T_P that maps formula functions to formula functions, defined as follows:*

1. *For ground atoms A: $T_P(h)(A) = \cap\{[\ell,u]|A : [\ell,u] \leftarrow B_1 : \mu_1 \wedge \ldots B_k : \mu_k$ is a ground instance of some clause in P such that for all $1 \leq i \leq k$, $h(B_i) \subseteq \mu_i\}$.*

2. *For conjunctions $A \wedge B$: $T_P(h)(A \wedge B) = T_P(h)(A) \otimes_{ig} T_P(h)(B)$, where $\otimes_{ig}$ is the policy described earlier in Section 14.2.4 for computing conjunctions under the policy of ignorance.*

3. *For disjunctions $A \vee B$: $T_P(h)(A \vee B) = T_P(h)(A) \oplus_{ig} T_P(h)(B)$, where $\oplus_{ig}$ is the policy described earlier in Section 14.2.4 for computing disjunctions under the policy of ignorance.*

Informally speaking, the T_P operator works as follows when attempting to compute $T_P(h)(A)$ for a ground atom A:

1. First, find all ground instances of rules in P having a head of the form $A : [\ell,u]$ and whose bodies are satisfied by h, i.e., if $B_i : \mu_i$ occurs in the body of the ground rule, then $h(B_i)$ must be a subset of μ_i.

2. Collect the intervals $[\ell,u]$ for all rules satisfying the above condition.

3. $T_P(h)(A)$ is the intersection of all the intervals collected above.

Once $T_P(h)$ has been computed for ground atoms, we can assign probability ranges to complex formulas using the $\oplus_{ig}$ operation for basic formulas in $disj(B_L)$ and using the $\otimes_{ig}$ operation for basic formulas in $conj(B_L)$. (Note: In the rest of this chapter, we will use the notation $\otimes$ and $\oplus$ to denote probabilistic conjunction and disjunction, respectively, under the strategy of ignorance.)

Example 15.8   Application of the T_P operator for pKBs

Consider, for example, the simple pKB consisting of the following p-clauses:

$$object(a) : [\max(0, \frac{V_1 - 0.1}{2}), \frac{V_2 + 0.1}{2}] \leftarrow sensor1(a) : [V_1, V_1] \wedge$$
$$sensor2(a) : [V_2, V_2].$$
$$sensor1(a) : [0.6, 0.6] \leftarrow .$$
$$sensor2(a) : [0.4, 0.5] \leftarrow .$$

Suppose h is the formula function given by

$$h(object(a)) = [0, 0]$$
$$h(sensor1(a)) = [0.9, 0.9]$$
$$h(sensor2(a)) = [0.8, 0.8]$$

Then $T_P(h)$ is given by

$$T_P(h)((object(a)) = [0, 0]$$
$$T_P(h)(sensor1(a)) = [0.6, 0.6]$$
$$T_P(h)(sensor2(a)) = [0.4, 0.5]$$

We will use the notation $T_P \uparrow \alpha$ to describe iterations of the T_P operator. These iterations are formally described as

$$T_P \uparrow 0(A) = [0, 1]$$
$$T_P \uparrow \alpha(A) = T_P(T_P \uparrow \beta) \text{ if } \alpha \text{ is a successor ordinal with } \beta$$
$$\text{as its predecessor}$$
$$T_P \uparrow \alpha(A) = \sqcup\{T_P \uparrow \beta \mid \beta < \alpha\} \text{ if } \alpha \text{ is a limit ordinal}$$

The operator T_P may be extended to basic formulas in the obvious way that we have described earlier. The following result is easy to establish.

It says that as we make h "sharper," T_P returns sharper formula functions. Furthermore, the iterative application of T_P starting from the most uncertain interpretation (that assigns the entire $[0, 1]$ interval to all atoms), leads to successively sharper interpretations, until a fixpoint is reached.

Theorem 15.26 *Suppose P is a pKB.*

1. *If h_1, h_2 are formula functions such that $h_1 \leq h_2$, then $T_P(h_1) \leq T_P(h_2)$.*

2. *T_P has a least fixpoint, $\mathsf{lfp}(T_P)$, and furthermore, there exists an ordinal α such that $\mathsf{lfp}(T_P) = T_P \uparrow \alpha$.*

Fixpoint Operator for pf-KBs

The definition of a fixpoint operator for pKBs is relatively easy because every p-clause has an annotated atom in the head. In contrast, pf-clauses have annotated basic formulas in the head. As we have stated earlier, annotated basic formulas may impose constraints on the probability ranges of the atoms constituting that basic formula. We now show how the above fixpoint operator, T_P, may be extended to the case of pf-KBs. The extended operator will be denoted by V_P. This new operator V_P will be defined in three stages:

- *Stage 1:* In the first stage, we will define an operator, called S_P, that will merely behave like T_P, except that it will apply to basic formulas in the heads of pf-clauses as well. However, it will not attempt to derive probabilities associated with the atomic parts of such basic formulas.

- *Stage 2:* Once $S_P(h)$ is computed, the next step is to treat $S_P(h)$ as a set of events whose probabilities are known in the sense described in Section 13.2.4.

- *Stage 3:* We may then set up a linear program, denoted $LP(S_P(h))$ as described in Section 13.2.4, and for each basic formula, $F \in bf(B_L)$, in our language, we can compute a lower bound c_F and an upper bound d_F on the probability of F. $V_P(h)(F)$ is then set to $[c_F, d_F]$ and we are done.

When describing stage 1, where we define the intermediate operator S_P, we use the notation $\mathbf{min_Q}(Exp)$ and $\mathbf{max_Q}(Exp)$ to denote the minimization and maximization of the expression Exp subject to the set of linear constraints $\mathbf{Q}$.

Definition 15.27 *Suppose P is a pf-KB and h is a formula function.*

- *Stage 1: Definition of S_P. We define an intermediate operator S_P from formula functions to formula functions as follows:*
  For all $F \in bf(B_L)$, $S_P(h)(F) = \bigcap M_F$, where $M_F = \{\mu\sigma \mid F : \mu \leftarrow F_1 : \mu_1 \wedge \ldots \wedge F_n : \mu_n$ is in $grd(P)$, σ is a ground substitution to the set of annotation variables that occur in the body of the above clause such that $\mu\sigma \neq \emptyset$, and $\forall i, 1 \leq i \leq n, h(F_i) \subseteq \mu_i\sigma\}$. Note that if M_F is empty, then we set $S_P(h)(F) = [0, 1]$.

- *Stage 2: Linear program associated with S_P. Let $LP(S_P(h))$ be the linear program obtained, as described in Section 13.2.4, by assuming that for each formula F, $S_P(h)(F) = [\ell_F, u_F]$.*

- *Stage 3: Definition of V_P. We now define an operator V_P from formula functions to formula functions as follows:*

  a. *If $LP(S_P(h))$ has solutions, then for all $F \in bf(B_L)$, $V_P(h)(F) = [c_F, d_F]$, where*

  $$c_F = \mathbf{min}_{\mathbf{LP(S_P(h))}} \left(\sum_{W_j \models F \text{ and } W_j \in 2^{B_L}} p_j \right) \text{ and}$$

  $$d_F = \mathbf{max}_{\mathbf{LP(S_P(h))}} \left(\sum_{W_j \models F \text{ and } W_j \in 2^{B_L}} p_j \right).$$

  Note that this step involves the straightforward use of any linear programming package/algorithm, numerous implementations of which are available in the commercial marketplace.

  b. *Otherwise, if $LP(S_P(h))$ is empty, then for all $F \in bf(B_L)$, $T_P(h)(F) = \emptyset$.*

Once again, the intuition behind the use of the S_P operator above is to ensure that "global" consistency is checked. For instance, consider the very simple pf-KB

$$(a \wedge b) : [1, 1] \leftarrow .$$
$$a : [0, 0] \leftarrow .$$
$$b : [1, 1] \leftarrow .$$

Suppose $h(F) = [0, 1]$ for all basic formulas F. The behavior of the three steps in the computation of $V_P(h)$ may now be described as follows:

1. First, we compute $S_P(h)$ and notice that

$$S_P(h)((a \wedge b)) = [1,1]$$
$$S_P(h)(a) = [0,0]$$
$$S_P(h)(b) = [1,1]$$

It is immediately apparent that there is an inconsistency here. After all, the probability of the event $(a \wedge b)$ cannot be 1 if the probability of a is 0, as the second equality above seems to indicate.

2. The second and third steps in the definition of V_P are intended to correct such problems. In this case, **Known** (as defined in Section 13.2.4) consists of the three assignments shown above, and we set up the linear program $LP(S_P(h))$ as follows. Suppose w_1 is the world in which both a and b are false, w_2 is the world in which a is true, but b is false, w_3 is the world in which b is true, but not a, and w_4 is the world in which both a and b are true. Then the constraints generated are

$$p_4 = 1$$
$$p_2 + p_4 = 0$$
$$p_3 = 1$$
$$p_1 + p_2 + p_3 + p_4 = 1$$
$$p_i \leq 1 \text{ for } i = 1, \ldots, 4$$
$$p_i \geq 0 \text{ for } i = 1, \ldots, 4$$

3. As the set of constraints described above is unsolvable, $V_P(h)(F) = \emptyset$ for all basic formulas F. In general, if $V_P(h)(F) = [c_F, d_F]$, then this means that the probability of F lies in the interval $[c_F, d_F]$. However, when the interval is the empty interval, this reading leads to the statement: "The probability of F lies in the empty interval," which basically is impossible, thus indicating that an inconsistency has occurred.

On the other hand, suppose our pf-KB had been the program

$$(a \vee b) : [1,1] \leftarrow .$$
$$a : [0.2, 0.5] \leftarrow .$$
$$b : [0.4, 0.6] \leftarrow .$$

Suppose $h(F) = [0, 1]$ for all basic formulas F. The behavior of the three steps in the computation of $V_P(h)$ may now be described as follows:

1. First, we compute $S_P(h)$ and notice that

$$S_P(h)((a \lor b)) = [1, 1]$$
$$S_P(h)(a) = [0.2, 0.5]$$
$$S_P(h)(b) = [0.4, 0.6]$$

2. In this case, we may set up $LP(S_P(h))$ as follows, using the same notation as we used above.

$$p_2 + p_3 + p_4 = 1 \qquad 0.2 \leq p_2 + p_4 \leq 0.5$$
$$0.4 \leq p_3 + p_4 \leq 0.6 \qquad p_1 + p_2 + p_3 + p_4 = 1$$
$$0 \leq p_i \leq 1 \text{ for } i = 1, \ldots, 4$$

3. For each formula F, we may compute $V_P(h)(F)$ by finding c_F and d_F, where c_F is the minimal (d_F, the maximal) value of the expression

$$\sum_{w_j \models F} p_j$$

subject to the above constraints. The values of $V_P(h)(F)$ for some different F's are given below:

F	$V_P(h)(F)$
$(a \lor b)$	$[1, 1]$
a	$[0.4, 0.5]$
b	$[0.5, 0.6]$
$(a \land b)$	$[1,1]$

As in the case of the T_P operator, the V_P operator is monotonic.

Theorem 15.28 *Suppose P is any pf-KB. Then,*

1. *For all basic formulas F, and all formula functions h, $V_P(h)(F) \subseteq S_P(h)(F)$.*

2. *If h_1, h_2 are formula functions such that $h_1 \leq h_2$, then $V_P(h_1) \leq V_P(h_2)$.*

Earlier, we had defined the concept of upward iteration of arbitrary functions on complete lattices. In the case of the operator V_P, this means that

1. $V_P \uparrow 0 = \bot$, i.e., for all $F \in bf(B_L)$, $V_P \uparrow 0(F) = [0, 1]$

2. $V_P \uparrow \alpha = V_P(V_P \uparrow (\alpha - 1))$, where α is a successor ordinal whose immediate predecessor is denoted by $(\alpha - 1)$

3. $V_P \uparrow \lambda = \sqcup\{V_P \uparrow \alpha | \alpha < \lambda\}$, where λ is a limit ordinal

As in the case of the operator T_P that applies to pKBs, the operator V_P also is guaranteed to possess a least fixpoint.

Theorem 15.29 *Suppose P is any pf-KB. Then V_P has a least fixpoint, denoted* $\mathsf{lfp}(V_P)$. *Furthermore, there exists an ordinal α such that $V_P \uparrow \alpha = \mathsf{lfp}(V_P)$.*

Pf-KBs generalize pKBs by allowing p-clauses to have annotated basic formulas in their head, instead of annotated atoms. This comes at a huge price when fixpoints need to be computed:

1. First, every iteration of the application of the V_P operator requires writing down a linear program that is exponential in size (with respect to the number of ground atoms in the language). This exacts a huge price. In contrast, no linear programs at all need to be constructed when dealing with pKBs.

2. Second, for each basic formula F, when computing V_P, we need to solve two linear programming problems: one to obtain a lower bound on F's probability, and another to obtain an upper bound. This needs to be done in every iteration toward the fixpoint. It is well known that linear programming packages start falling apart when the number of variables (i.e., number of worlds) and/or the number of constraints in the linear program run into the tens of thousands. In our case, the number of Herbrand interpretations could well be very large.

Thus, the expressive power inherent in pf-KBs comes at a huge potential price—something that needs to be considered when applications are being built and we need to decide whether to use pKBs or pf-KBs.

15.2.2 Probabilistic KBs: Model Theory

Having provided a detailed description of the fixpoint theory associated with pKBs and pf-KBs, we are now ready to provide a formal model theory for them.

Let us now consider a world probability density function WP defined as in Definition 15.22. If our underlying logical language generates worlds $w_1, \ldots w_k$, then $WP(w_i)$ denotes the probability that world w_i is the "real" world according to WP.

Definition 15.30 *Let WP be a world probability density function. Extend WP to a probabilistic interpretation $I_{WP} : bf(B_L) \longrightarrow [0,1]$ (i.e., a mapping from all basic formulas to $[0,1]$) in the following way: for all basic formulas $F \in bf(B_L)$,*

$$I_{WP}(F) = \left(\sum_{W_j \models F \text{ and } W_j \in 2^{B_L}} p_j \right).$$

The intuition behind this definition is that each world probability density function WP in effect makes an assignment of a probability value to each basic formula. This is done by examining all worlds in which that formula is true, and summing up the probabilities of those worlds. Thus, for example, suppose we consider WP to be the function

$$WP(w_1) = 0.4$$
$$WP(w_2) = 0.1$$
$$WP(w_3) = 0.2$$
$$WP(w_4) = 0.3$$

Suppose that w_1 makes a, b false, w_2 makes a true but b false, w_3 makes b true but a false, and w_4 makes both a, b true. Then the interpretation I_{WP} associated with WP makes the following assignments:

$$I_{WP}(a) = 0.4$$
$$I_{WP}(b) = 0.5$$
$$I_{WP}(a \vee b) = 0.6$$
$$I_{WP}(a \vee \neg b) = 0.8$$

We are now ready to define what it means for a probabilistic interpretation I_{WP} to satisfy a formula.

Definition 15.31 *Suppose WP is a world probability density function and I is the probabilistic interpretation associated with WP. Further assume that $F_0, F_1, \ldots, F_n$ are in $bf(B_L)$, and $[c_0, d_0], [c_1, d_1], \ldots, [c_n, d_n]$ are closed subintervals of [0,1]. Finally, let C be a pf-clause as defined in Definition 15.19.*

1. $I \models_p F_1 : [c_1, d_1]$ iff $I(F_1) \in [c_1, d_1]$

2. $I \models_p (F_1 : [c_1, d_1] \wedge \ldots \wedge F_n : [c_n, d_n])$ iff for all $1 \leq j \leq n$, $I \models_p F_j : [c_j, d_j]$

3. $I \models_p F_0 : [c_0, d_0] \leftarrow F_1 : [c_1, d_1] \wedge \ldots \wedge F_n : [c_n, d_n]$ iff $I \models_p F_0 : [c_0, d_0]$ or $I \not\models_p (F_1 : [c_1, d_1] \wedge \ldots \wedge F_n : [c_n, d_n])$

4. $I \models_p (\exists x)(C)$ iff $I \models_p (C(x/t))$ for some ground term t, where x represents an object variable, and $C(x/t)$ denotes the replacement of all free occurrences of x in C by t

5. $I \models_p (\forall x)(C)$ iff $I \models_p (C(x/t))$ for all ground terms t, where x represents an object variable

6. $I \models_p (\exists V)(C)$ iff $I \models_p (C(V/c))$ for some $c \in [0, 1]$, where V represents an annotation variable

7. $I \models_p (\forall V)(C)$ iff $I \models_p (C(V/c))$ for all $c \in [0, 1]$ such that $\mu(V/c) \neq \emptyset$, where V represents an annotation variable occurring in annotation term μ. Here, if μ is an annotation term, then the notation $\mu(V/c)$ is the annotation term that is obtained by replacing all occurrences of V in μ by c and evaluating the resulting term (if it is ground).

In the case of probabilistic satisfaction of universally closed formulas, we point out one salient feature. Notice that a probabilistic interpretation I always assigns point probabilities to basic formulas. Thus, if we consider an annotated basic formula of the form $F : [V_1, V_2]$ where F is ground, but V_1, V_2 are annotation variables, then we observe that there is at most one time point, namely, $I(F)$, at which F is satisfied by I. Thus, in case 7 above, whether universal quantification over annotation variables is considered, or existential quantification is considered, makes little difference.

We have now introduced three types of semantic objects within our framework: formula functions, world probability density functions, and probabilistic interpretations. A natural question to ask is how these different concepts are related to one another.

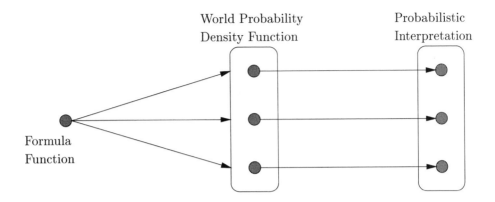

Figure 15.2: Relationship between semantic structures

As Figure 15.2 shows, it will turn out, that given any formula function h, there exists a set of world probability density functions that are determined by h; these world probability density functions are the solutions of a linear program associated with h. Subsequently, each world probability density function uniquely determines a probabilistic interpretation as we have described above. We now describe how this procedure occurs.

Definition 15.32 *A formula function h is* fully defined *iff for all basic formulas $F \in bf(B_L), \emptyset \subset h(F) \subseteq [0,1]$.*

Intuitively, a formula function h specifies, for each formula F, an interval $[c_F, d_F]$, and the informal reading of the assignment is that "according to h, F's probability lies in the interval $[c_F, d_F]$." However, if this interval $[c_F, d_F]$ is empty, then F's probability cannot possibly lie in the empty interval, and hence h's assignment does not make sense. Fully defined formula functions avoid this situation.

Generating World Probability Density Functions from Formula Functions

Every formula function determines a set of world probability density functions that are consistent with the assignments made by the formula function. The following definition shows how this is done:

Definition 15.33 *Suppose h is a formula function. Then the* set of world probability density functions determined by h, *denoted* WPD(h), *is given by*

WPD(h) = {WP | σ *is a solution of $LP(h)$ and $WP_\sigma(w_i) =$* p_i *for all w_i*}.

In other words, given a formula function h, we may compute the set, WPD(h), of world probability density functions associated with h using the following steps:

1. Construct $LP(h)$.

2. Find every solution of $LP(h)$.

3. For each solution σ of $LP(h)$, the function WP_σ defined by $WP_\sigma(w_i) = p_i$ is in WPD(h).

Generating Probabilistic Interpretations from Formula Functions

Just as a formula function determined a set of world probability density functions, it also determines a set of probabilistic interpretations. The contents of this set are specified by the definition below:

Definition 15.34 *Suppose h is a formula function. Then the* set of probabilistic interpretations, *denoted* PRI(h), *is given by* {I_{WP} | $WP \in$ WPD(h)}.

The following observation allows us to conclude that for pf-KBs, when we construct the fixpoint operator V_P, the set of constraints generated by the intermediate operator and the final operator V_P have the same set of solutions.

Proposition 15.35 *Suppose P is a pf-KB and h is a formula function. Then $LP(S_P(h))$ and $LP(V_P(h))$ have the same set of solutions.*

The following result tells us that $V_P(h)$ is fully defined iff the set of linear constraints generated by h has at least one solution.

Proposition 15.36 *Let h be a formula function. Then $V_P(h)$ is fully defined iff* WPD(h) $\neq \emptyset$.

The following result tells us that the intervals assigned by $V_P(h)$ to basic formulas F are the tightest possible intervals.

Proposition 15.37 *Suppose $V_P(h)$ is fully defined. Then for all basic formulas F, $V_P(h)(F)$ is the smallest interval that contains* {$I(F)$|$I \in$ PRI(h)}.

Relating Model Theory and Fixpoint Theory of pf-KBs

We are now in a position to start tying together the model theory of pf-KBs and the fixpoint theory of pf-KBs.

Theorem 15.38 *Suppose P is a pf-KB, and h is a fully defined formula function. Then each member of $\mathsf{PRI}(h)$ satisfies P iff $V_P(h) \le h$.*

This result tells us that a formula function h generates a set, $\mathsf{PRI}(h)$, of satisfying interpretations (i.e., models) of P iff $V_P(h) \le h$. As a consequence, from the monotonicity of V_P, we may easily state the following:

Theorem 15.39 *Suppose P is a pf-KB. Then*

1. *V_P has a unique least fixpoint denoted by $\mathsf{lfp}(V_P)$.*

2. *For any annotated basic formula $F : [c_F, d_F]$: $F : [c_F, d_F]$ is a logical consequence of P iff $\mathsf{lfp}(V_P)(F) \subseteq [c_F, d_F]$.*

The above theorem specifically tells us that in order to determine what the logical consequences of a pf-KB are, we need to merely examine the least fixpoint of V_P. However, recall that it is easy to write pf-KBs that are inconsistent. The following result tells us that a pf-KB is inconsistent iff $\mathsf{lfp}(V_P)$ is not fully defined.

Theorem 15.40 *Suppose P is a pf-KB. P is consistent (i.e., there exists a probabilistic interpretation that satisfies P) iff $\mathsf{lfp}(V_P)$ is fully defined.*

At this stage, we have presented a close relationship between the fixpoint characterization of pf-KBs, and the model-theoretic basis for pf-KBs. In particular, it is clear that logical consequence in pf-KBs is equivalent to checking for truth in the least fixpoint of the V_P operator. We are therefore ready to show how we may compute queries to pf-KBs.

15.2.3 Probabilistic KBs: Query Processing

In this section, we will first present techniques for query processing in pf-KBs. As we have already seen in the case of GAPs, the query processing procedure will be based on a resolution-style approach.

Unification in pf-KBs

One of the key components of resolution is the operation of unification. However, in the case of GAPs, only annotated atoms were unified against other annotated atoms. In contrast, in the case of pKBs as well as pf-KBs, we may wish to unify annotated basic formulas with annotated basic formulas. This causes complications because the order in which atoms occur in the basic formulas should not affect the outcome of the unification operator. After all, the basic formulas $(p(X) \wedge q(Y))$ and $(q(U) \wedge p(V))$ should certainly be considered unifiable, even though there is no substitution θ such that $(p(X) \wedge q(Y))\theta$ is syntactically identical to $(q(U) \wedge p(V))\theta$.

Thus, to avoid problems like this, we will first introduce a notion of unification for basic formulas. Subsequently, we will define a suitable resolution-based query processing procedure.

Definition 15.41 θ *is a* unifier *of annotated conjunctions* $C_1 \equiv (A_1 \wedge \ldots \wedge A_n) : \mu_1$ *and* $C_2 \equiv (B_1 \wedge \ldots \wedge B_m) : \mu_2$ *iff* $\{A_i\theta | 1 \leq i \leq n\} = \{B_i\theta | 1 \leq i \leq m\}$. *Similarly,* θ *is a* unifier *of annotated disjunctions* $D_1 \equiv (A_1 \vee \ldots \vee A_n) : \mu_1$ *and* $D_2 \equiv (B_1 \vee \ldots \vee B_m) : \mu_2$ *iff* $\{A_i\theta | 1 \leq i \leq n\} = \{B_i\theta | 1 \leq i \leq m\}$.

Thus, for example, suppose we consider the annotated conjunctions:

$$Exp1 = (p(X, a) \vee p(Y, b)).$$
$$Exp2 = (p(Z, Z) \vee p(c, W)).$$

Note that there are many ways in which these two basic formulas can be unified. For example, one unifier would "match up" $p(X, a)$ with $p(Z, Z)$, and $p(Y, b)$ with $p(c, W)$, leading to an mgu θ_1 given by

$$\theta_1 = \{X = a, Z = a, Y = c, W = b\}$$

On the other hand, had we chosen instead to match up $p(X, a)$ with $p(c, W)$, and $p(Y, b)$ with $p(Z, Z)$, we'd have obtained the equally legitimate but different mgu:

$$\theta_2 = \{X = c, Z = b, Y = b, W = a\}$$

As the following example shows, it is not necessary that the number of literals occurring in the expressions being unified be the same. For instance, the expressions

$$Exp1 = p(X, a)$$
$$Exp2 = p(b, V) \vee p(W, a)$$

are unifiable with unifier

$$\sigma = \{X = b, V = a, W = b\}$$

A consequence of the above discussion is that the notion of an "mgu" is not unique when we consider annotated basic formulas. Therefore, we define a notion of a maximally general unifier:

Definition 15.42 *Suppose F_1, F_2 are two basic formulas and $Uni(F_1, F_2)$ denotes the set of all unifiers of F_1, F_2. Suppose $\theta_1, \theta_2 \in Uni(F_1, F_2)$. We say the following:*

1. *$\theta_1 \leq \theta_2$ iff there exists a substitution γ such that $\theta_1 = \theta_2\gamma$.*

2. *$\theta_1 \equiv \theta_2$ iff $\theta_1 \leq \theta_2$ and $\theta_2 \leq \theta_1$. We use the notation $[\theta]$ to denote the equivalence class of θ, i.e., $[\theta] = \{\theta' \mid \theta \equiv \theta', \text{ where } \theta' \in Uni(F_1, F_2)\}$.*

3. *$[\theta] \leq [\theta']$ iff $\theta \leq \theta'$.*

4. *θ is a maximally general unifier (max-gu) of F_1, F_2 iff there does not exist $\theta_1 \in Uni(F_1, F_2)$ such that $[\theta] < [\theta_1]$.*

The following result guarantees us that if two basic formulas F_1 and F_2 are unifiable according to our definition above, then they are guaranteed to possess a max-gu, though the max-gu may not be unique.

Theorem 15.43 *If F_1, F_2 are basic formulas that are unifiable, then they have at least one max-gu.*

Resolution in pf-KBs

We are now ready to define the query processing procedure for pf-KBs. As in the case of GAPs where closures of GAPs needed to be computed, we first need to compile a pf-KB into a larger pf-KB. This is done by creating certain clauses called *constrained pf-clauses*.

Definition 15.44 *A* p-constraint *is a conjunction of constraints having the form: $\rho_1 \leq \rho_2$ or $\rho_1 = \rho_2$, where $\rho_i (i = 1, 2)$ is an annotation item.*

Definition 15.45 *A constrained pf-clause is an expression of the form*

$$F_0 : \mu_0 \leftarrow F_1 : \mu_1 \bigwedge \cdots \bigwedge F_n : \mu_n \bigwedge Con_C.$$

where

$$F_0 : \mu_0 \leftarrow F_1 : \mu_1 \bigwedge \ldots \bigwedge F_n : \mu_n$$

is a pf-clause and Con_C is a p-constraint.

We had previously defined what it means for a probabilistic interpretation to satisfy a pf-clause. The extension to constrained pf-clauses is natural: probabilistic interpretation I_{WP} satisfies the constrained pf-clause shown above if and only if for all ground substitutions σ (with respect to the annotation variables) such that $Con_C\sigma$ is true, I satisfies $(F_0 : \mu_0 \leftarrow F_1 : \mu_1 \bigwedge \ldots \bigwedge F_n : \mu_n)\sigma$.

Compiled Version of a pf-KB

In pf-KBs, two or more (ground instances of) rules might have an atom A in the head, and may have bodies that are logical consequences of the pf-KB P. The value of atom A in the least fixpoint of T_P may be obtained by taking the intersection of the annotations in the heads of such rules. The same situation may arise in the case of nonatomic basic formulas. In order to ensure that one rule in our pf-KB is responsible for the value assigned to an atom in the least fixpoint of T_P, we augment P by adding certain derived rules. The augmentation of P is called the *compiled version* of P and is denoted by $com(P)$. The definition of $com(P)$ requires some intermediate definitions, the first of which is given below.

Definition 15.46 *Let P be a finite but nonempty pf-KB, i.e., $P = \{ C_1, \ldots, C_k \}$, where for all $1 \leq i \leq k$, $C_i \equiv F_i : [\delta_i, \rho_i] \leftarrow Body_i$ and $[\delta_i, \rho_i]$ is an annotation term.*

1. *We may associate a set, $LP(P)$, of linear constraints with P as follows: for all $1 \leq i \leq k$, the inequality*

$$\delta_i \leq \left(\sum_{W_j \models F_i \text{ and } W_j \in 2^{B_L}} p_j \right) \leq \rho_i$$

is in $LP(P)$. In addition, $LP(P)$ contains the following constraints:

$$\sum_{W_j \in 2^{B_L}} p_j = 1, \text{ and}$$

$$(\forall W_j \in 2^{B_L}), p_j \geq 0.$$

2. The closure of P, denoted $cl(P)$, is now defined as follows. Let
$cl(P) = P \cup$
$\{ F : [\delta_F, \rho_F] \leftarrow Body_1 \wedge \ldots \wedge Body_k \wedge Con_{sol} \mid F \in bf(B_L),$

$$\delta_F = min_{LP(P)} \left(\sum_{W_j \models F \text{ and } W_j \in 2^{B_L}} p_j \right),$$

$$\rho_F = max_{LP(P)} \left(\sum_{W_j \models F \text{ and } W_j \in 2^{B_L}} p_j \right),$$

and Con_{sol} denotes the conjunction of constraints on the annotation terms for $LP(P)$ to have solutions. $\}$

It is easy to see that, in general, the closure of P is very large and is usually exponential with respect to the size of P. For example, consider the very simple pKB given by

$$a : [0.3, 0.6] \leftarrow c : [0.3, 0.4].$$
$$b : [0.4, 0.8] \leftarrow c : [0.1, 0.4].$$

The closure, $cl(P)$, contains one pf-clause, having each of the basic formulas $(a \vee b)$, $(a \wedge b)$, $(a \vee c)$, $(a \wedge c)$, $(b \vee c)$, $(b \wedge c)$, $(a \vee b \vee c)$, and $(a \wedge b \wedge c)$ in the head; all these pf-clauses have, in the body, the conjunction

$$c : [0.3, 0.4] \wedge c : [0.1, 0.4].$$

Furthermore, for each such pf-clause, we need to compute the annotation in the head by applying the $\otimes$ operator (for conjunctive basic formulas) and the $\oplus$ operator (for disjunctive ones). The closure of P, $cl(P)$, is listed below:

$$(a \vee b) : [0.4, 1] \leftarrow c : [0.3, 0.4] \wedge c : [0.1, 0.4].$$
$$(a \wedge b) : [0, 0.6] \leftarrow c : [0.3, 0.4] \wedge c : [0.1, 0.4].$$
$$(a \vee c) : [0.3, 1] \leftarrow c : [0.3, 0.4] \wedge c : [0.1, 0.4].$$
$$(a \wedge c) : [0, 0.6] \leftarrow c : [0.3, 0.4] \wedge c : [0.1, 0.4].$$
$$(b \vee c) : [0.4, 1] \leftarrow c : [0.3, 0.4] \wedge c : [0.1, 0.4].$$
$$(b \wedge c) : [0, 0.8] \leftarrow c : [0.3, 0.4] \wedge c : [0.1, 0.4].$$
$$(a \vee b \vee c) : [0.4, 1] \leftarrow c : [0.3, 0.4] \wedge c : [0.1, 0.4].$$
$$(a \wedge b \wedge c) : [0, 0.6] \leftarrow c : [0.3, 0.4] \wedge c : [0.1, 0.4].$$

Notice that as P contains no rules with c in the head, we assume that c's probability lies between 0 and 1 in the above computation, in keeping with Definition 15.46.

Definition 15.47 *Let P be a pf-KB.*

1. *Define $redun(P) = \{F : [0,1] \leftarrow \; | \; F \in bf(B_L)\}$.*

2. *Define the* compiled *version of P, denoted by $com(P)$, as follows: $com(P) = \bigcup cl(Q)$ for each subset Q of $redun(P) \bigcup grd(P)$.*

Intuitively, $com(P)$ is nothing more than an expanded version of P having the following property: for each basic formula F, if $F : \mu$ is a logical consequence of P, then there exists a single clause C in $com(P)$ having a ground instance, $C\sigma$, such that the head of $C\sigma$ is of the form $F : \mu'$ and $\mu \subseteq \mu'$. This makes it much easier to define a linear resolution-style query processing procedure, similar to GAPs, that is sound and complete.

Definition 15.48 *If $F_1 : \mu_1, \ldots, F_n : \mu_n$ are annotated basic formulas, and Con_Q is a conjunction of constraints on the annotation terms, then $\exists (F_1 : \mu_1 \wedge \ldots \wedge F_n : \mu_n \wedge Con_Q)$ is a constrained p-query.*

Definition 15.49 *Suppose*

$$C \equiv G_0 : \lambda_0 \leftarrow G_1 : \lambda_1 \wedge \ldots \wedge G_m : \lambda_m \wedge Con_C$$

is a constrained p-clause in $com(P)$, and

$$Q \equiv \exists (F_1 : \mu_1 \wedge \ldots \wedge F_n : \mu_n \wedge Con_Q)$$

is a constrained p-query such that C and Q are standardized apart. If G_0 and F_i are unifiable with max-gu θ, an SLDp-resolvent of C and Q on $F_i : \mu_i$ is the following constrained query:

$$\exists ((F_1 : \mu_1 \wedge \ldots \wedge F_{i-1} : \mu_{i-1} \wedge G_1 : \lambda_1 \wedge \ldots \wedge G_m : \lambda_m \wedge F_{i+1} :$$
$$\mu_{i+1} \wedge \ldots \wedge F_n : \mu_n)\theta$$
$$\wedge Con_C \wedge Con_Q \wedge \lambda_0 \subseteq \mu_i \;)$$

Definition 15.50 *An SLDp-deduction of a constrained query Q_1 from a pf-KB P is a sequence $\langle Q_1, C_1, \theta_1 \rangle, \ldots, \langle Q_r, C_r, \theta_r \rangle, \ldots$, where for all $i \geq 1$, C_i is a renamed version of a clause in $com(P)$, and Q_{i+1} is an SLDp-resolvent of Q_i and C_i through max-gu θ_i.*

Definition 15.51 *An* SLDp-refutation *of a constrained p-query Q_1 from a pf-KB P is a finite SLDp-deduction $\langle Q_1, C_1, \theta_1 \rangle, \ldots, \langle Q_n, C_n, \theta_n \rangle$, where the SLDp-resolvent of Q_n and C_n via max-gu θ_n, denoted by Q_{n+1}, satisfies the following two conditions:*

1. *The query part of Q_{n+1} is empty.*

2. *The constraint part of Q_{n+1} is satisfiable. $\theta_1 \ldots \theta_n$ is called the computed answer substitution.*

Theorem 15.52 *Let P be a pf-KB and Q_1 be a constrained query of the form $\exists (F_1 : \mu_1 \wedge \ldots \wedge F_m : \mu_m \wedge Con_Q)$, where the constraint part Con_Q may be null. Suppose there exists an SLDp-refutation*

$$\langle Q_1, C_1, \theta_1 \rangle, \ldots, \langle Q_n, C_n, \theta_n \rangle$$

of Q_1 from P. Let σ be any solution to the constraint part of Q_{n+1}, the SLDp-resolvent of Q_n and C_n via max-gu θ_n. Then it must be the case that $P \models_p \forall (Q_1 \sigma) \theta$, where θ is the computed answer substitution.

SLDp-refutations are complete only under certain conditions. The first condition, called compactness, is similar to the fixpoint reachability condition for GAPs. The second is the condition of fully definedness (i.e., consistency).

Definition 15.53 *A pf-KB P is* compact *if for all $F \in bf(B_L)$, there exists an integer $\alpha_F < \omega$ such that $lfp(T_P)(F) = T_P \uparrow \alpha_F(F)$.*

Theorem 15.54 *Let Q be a query and P be a consistent and compact pf-KB. Then if $P \models_p \exists Q$, there exists an SLDp-refutation of Q from P.*

15.3 Bibliographic Notes

As mentioned in the preceding chapter, there has been a spectacular amount of work on uncertainty in databases and knowledge bases. This work has been done in two separate communities: the database community and the artificial intelligence community. The former focuses on extensions of the relational model of data and has been discussed in the preceding chapter. The latter, which we focus on here, deals with extending knowledge representation paradigms such as first-order logic, nonmonotonic logics, and neural networks (to name a few) to handle uncertain information. We hope the information below will enable you to pursue your interests in further detail.

General Surveys

A recent excellent survey of the state of the art is Parsons [331], who presents a bird's-eye view of the whole field, without getting into too much technical detail. Pearl [334] provides an excellent overview of the Bayesian approach to uncertainty in AI (databases were not addressed in any detail by him), while the book of Dubois and Prade [134] presents a possibilistic (similar to fuzzy sets) approach.

Fuzzy Knowledge Bases

Logic knowledge bases have been extended to handle fuzzy modes of uncertainty since the early 1970s with the advent of the MYCIN and Prospector systems [136]. Shapiro was one of the first to develop results in fuzzy logic programming [400]. Baldwin [25] was one of the first to introduce evidential logic programming and a language called FRIL. Van Emden [440] was the first to provide formal semantical foundations for logic programs that were later extended by Subrahmanian [422] and then completely generalized in a succession of papers by Blair and Subrahmanian [63, 62], Fitting [169], and Ginsberg [190], and applied to databases by Kifer and Li [244] and Kifer and Subrahmanian [245].

Probabilistic Knowledge Bases

Probabilistic knowledge bases were studied extensively by the AI community, with elegant results on Bayesian nets reported widely in the Uncertainty in AI (UAI) conferences, and neatly summarized in [334, 331]. Fagin, Halpern, and others [146, 144] developed fundamental results on probabilistic logics and their complexity.

Kiessling and his group [242, 429, 388] have developed a framework called DUCK for reasoning with uncertainty. They provide an elegant logical axiomatic theory for uncertain reasoning in the presence of rules. They largely assume the Bayesian model. Ng and Subrahmanian, in a series of papers [305, 306], were the first to develop techniques for probabilistic databases under the assumption of ignorance between probabilistic relations.

Finally, we note that this part of the book is intended as a classroom introduction to the topic of probabilistic and uncertain reasoning in databases and knowledge bases, rather than an exhaustive survey. Thus, we have not mentioned several worthwhile efforts above. See Parsons' excellent bibliography [331] for a comprehensive description of different research efforts.

15.4 Research Directions

Though there has been extensive research on uncertainty in knowledge bases, the field of uncertainty in databases is relatively young. We present a few research topics below.

Hybrid Probabilistic Databases

Current work has shown how Datalog rules may be extended to include probabilities under a fixed assumption (e.g., independence, in the case of approaches described by Pearl [334], or ignorance, in the case of the Ng-Subrahmanian [305] approach). However, just as in the case of relational databases in the previous chapter, applications may require a mix of probabilistic strategies to be used. For example, a user may wish to specify a rule that says that the probability of event A lies between values $[\ell, r]$, where ℓ is the lower bound of events B and C occurring together (under ignorance) and r is the probability of events B and D occurring together (under independence). Existing frameworks cannot and do not allow a single rule or even different rules to evaluate probabilities of events under varying probabilistic assumptions.

Query Processing Techniques

The resolution-based technique for evaluating probabilistic rules as well as for GAPs presented in this chapter is inefficient. Tabling techniques for improving the performance of GAP query evaluation have been developed. Sophisticated query optimization techniques, such as magic sets and counting methods, have existed in the deductive database literature for many years, but have yet to be studied in any detail for probabilistic deductive databases, as well as GAPs. The development of such techniques will be critical to the successful implementation of probabilistic deductive databases and GAPs. Furthermore, these techniques will need to be extended to the case of hybrid probabilistic databases, such as those alluded to above.

Complexity and Expressiveness

Though GAPs, as well as probabilistic databases, have now been studied for several years, there is almost no existing work on the expressive power of such query languages. What classes of query languages can be expressed in these languages, and how complex is it to compute the answers to queries expressed in these languages? Are there tractable subsets of such deductive databases? These questions need to be addressed in coming years.

15.5 Summary

One of the best-known models of data is the deductive database model. In this chapter, we have described the extension of deductive databases in two ways: by the incorporation of lattice-based (and hence fuzzy) uncertainty and by the extension of probabilistic modes of uncertainty. In particular, we have shown how deductive databases may be extended in two ways:

- First, we have shown how given any complete lattice $(L, \sqsubseteq)$ of truth values, deductive databases may be extended to reason with uncertainty over this domain of truth values. As the unit interval of real numbers is a complete lattice, it follows immediately that fuzzy logic extensions of deductive databases are captured within the very general and powerful GAP paradigm described in this chapter.

- Second, we have described how we may incorporate probabilistic reasoning (assuming ignorance about the interdependency between events) into deductive databases. We have developed a formal theory for probabilistic knowledge bases, and described the semantics of such knowledge bases, as well as query processing procedures for them.

15.6 Exercises

15.1. Consider the complete lattice $[0, 1]$, under the usual $\leq$ ordering on the reals, and suppose P is the GAP shown below:

$$q(a) : 0.1 \leftarrow$$
$$q(b) : 0.6 \leftarrow$$
$$r(a) : 0.4 \leftarrow$$
$$r(b) : 0.4 \leftarrow$$
$$p(X) : min(V_1, \frac{V_1 + V_2}{2}) \leftarrow q(X) : V_1 \wedge r(X) : V_2.$$

Suppose I is the interpretation that assigns 0.1 to $q(a)$, 0.2 to $q(b)$, 0.3 to $r(a)$, 0.5 to $r(b)$, and 0 to both $p(a)$ and $p(b)$. Compute $T_P(I)$, $T_P(T_P(I))$, and $T_P(T_P(T_P(I)))$.

15.2. Find a maximal value v such that the GAP P (of Exercise 15.1) above has $p(a)$ as a logical consequence. Do the same for $p(b)$.

15.3. Compute the annotated resolvent of the query $p(b) : 0.4$ with the last clause of the GAP P of Exercise 15.1. Then find a full annotated refutation of this query with respect to P.

15.4. Suppose P is the pf-KB consisting of the rules:

$$(a \lor b) : [0.6, 0.7] \leftarrow (b \land c) : [0.1, 0.9].$$
$$b : [0.3, 0.6] \leftarrow$$
$$c : [0.2, 0.5] \leftarrow$$

Suppose h is the formula function that assigns $[0, 1]$ to all of a, b, c. Let $h_1 = T_P(h)$. What is h_1? If $h_2 = T_P(h_1)$, what is $T_p(h_2)$?

15.5. What is the closure, $cl(P)$, of the pf-KB P given in Exercise 15.4?

15.6. Is $(a \lor c) : [0.2, 0.7]$ a logical consequence of the pf-KB of Example 15.4? If so, give an SLDp-refutation of this p-annotated basic formula. Otherwise, construct a model of P in which this annotated basic formula is false.

Part VI

Schema and Database Evolution in Object Database Systems

Part VI has been written together with Fabrizio Ferrandina.[1]

There would be no life without evolution. Evolution means changes. Changes are part of our nature and occur at any time in life.

When we want to record a portion of the real world using a computer, we must take changes into account. If we store data in a database that is representing a real-life situation, we must be ready, and more importantly able, to change it to reflect the evolving nature of the real-life situation. We must be able to change both the structure and the value of the data stored in the database.

This part of the book is entirely dedicated to the problem of supporting changes when using a database. In particular, we will concentrate our attention on the class of databases called object-oriented, and study the problem of how to change the schema and consequently the database itself.

The interest in schema and database evolution for object database systems is rooted back when Roberto Zicari was visiting GIP Altair (now O_2 Technology) in 1989–1990. At that time, the initial motivation was to understand how to provide powerful schema update primitives for modifying the schema in an object database system while preserving the schema

---

[1]Computer Science Department, Johann Wolfgang Goethe University, Frankfurt am Main, Germany.

consistency. From 1991 to 1995, Roberto Zicari, together with Fabrizio Ferrandina, worked with the technical team of O_2 Technology in the design and implementation of the schema and database evolution mechanisms now part of the commercial O_2 object database release 4.6.

The following chapters aim at presenting both the problem of schema and database evolution for object databases in general, and the specific solution implemented in the O_2 database system.

Part VI is structured as follows: Chapter 16 gives an informal and brief introduction to the basic concepts of object databases, with which you are already probably quite familiar. It further introduces the problem of change management in general and explains the relationships with schema evolution. Chapter 17 discusses how a database schema can be modified by using schema modification primitives and what the invariants are that keep the schema consistent. Chapter 18 describes the problem of database inconsistency after a schema modification has been performed and presents the algorithms for enforcing database consistency. In Chapter 19, we present a detailed description of how to benchmark the performance of an object database with respect to database updates.

Chapter 16

Object Databases and Change Management

16.1 Why Changes Are Needed

Databases are normally used to store a variety of different information depending on the application domain chosen. Data often needs to be periodically changed—both in its structure and value—to accommodate changes in the application domain.

In using a database, the idea is to store information in a way that is as close as possible to the real-world data representation.

Relational database systems have proven to be very effective any time the information is naturally modeled as flat tables and does not change very often, which is typical in business applications.

However, if the information is complex and, moreover, needs to be changed frequently and in a involved way, which is typical in the design phase, pure relational database systems run into problems of two kinds: a lack of adequate support for changes and a decrease in performance.

In the past few years, with the advent of a new programming paradigm, object-oriented programming, a new class of database systems has been defined and implemented, *object database management systems* (ODBMSs), often referred to as *object databases*. Object database systems have been successfully used to support complex applications—engineering applications such as computer-aided design (CAD) and computer-aided software engineering (CASE), and multimedia systems such as geographical information systems (GIS) and document/image management systems, where one of the key requirements is the capability to make the system evolve.

The costs associated with maintaining applications and adapting them to changing requirements keeps increasing. Developing applications is expensive, and maintaining them and making them evolve is even more expensive.

Evolutionary changes to a database system can occur at various stages in the life cycle of the system for many reasons. First, experience shows how the system can be improved. Modeling reality is complex, and the ability of humans to cope with this complexity is limited. In particular, for object databases, an optimal schema is not always readily apparent for complex real-world situations, and its design is further complicated by the wealth of mechanisms provided by object-oriented data definition languages (DDLs). Second, user requirements can change, and additional functionalities have to be integrated. Finally, the application domain modeled by the system can change, and the system has to be adapted accordingly.

Any change to a software system is a source of new software faults and therefore must be followed by extensive regression testing as part of a revalidation and reverification process. As Ivar Jacobson observes, "a seemingly small change often results in a disproportionated expensive alteration." The big costs of these activities are a major reason why usually either the changes are not done, or the subsequent testing is reduced—both of which are unsatisfactory. The research into evolution, restructuring, and reorganization of object database systems addresses, therefore, an issue with important theoretical and practical implications.

Some of the results presented in this part of the book are derived from the work done in the multiyear project GOODSTEP (General Object-Oriented Database for Software Engineering Processes), whose primary goal was to enhance and improve the functionality of the O_2 object database to yield a platform suited for applications such as software development environments (SDEs).

The algorithms presented in this part of the book were first prototyped in 1994–1995. They were then reengineered in 1995 at O_2 Technology, Versailles, and included in the O_2 product release 4.6.

16.2   The Essence of Object Databases

If you already have a good grasp of the basics of object databases, you will probably want to skip Section 16.2.1. In case you are new to the subject, however, we wanted to provide a brief informal guide to the essential elements of object databases.

16.2.1 Basics of Object Databases

Since our main objective is to study the problem of changing the schema and the database, we will introduce in this section the basic concepts of an object database system that will be used in later chapters.

Our goal in this section is to guide you in defining a simple database schema, creating a simple base, and writing a simple application—all without considering changes either to the schema or to the database. Changes will be considered in later chapters.

Let's start by defining what an object database is. An *object database* is a database management system that is consistent with the object-oriented language paradigm.

In the rest of Part VI we always refer to the O_2 object database for a better understanding of the concepts and for the presentation of specific examples. It is relatively straightforward to apply the concepts presented in this part to other object database systems.

Objects

An object database system is made up of objects, as opposed to the records (tuples) in traditional relational database systems. An object encapsulates data and its behavior; a relational tuple simply contains data.

Some object databases, such as GemStone, provide a data model where data is defined in terms of objects only. Other systems, such as O_2 , distinguish between values and objects. We will consider this latter class of systems.

An object in the application domain corresponds to a real-life element. For example, the worker John Smith in a company can be represented by an object. And so can his car. If the company has more than one employee, they will be represented by separate objects. The same applies for cars.

Let's be more precise and give the definition of what an object is. An *object* is composed of an identity, a value, and a set of methods (see Figure 16.1). The *identity* of an object is simply an internal identifier that is transparent to the programmer. It is independent from the data contained in the object, enabling data to be modified without modifying the identifier. What is important is that each object has a unique identifier in the system. Objects refer to each other by their identifiers, and this allows object sharing.

Data contained in the object is the *value* of the object, and the definition of the structure of this value is called the *type*. The behavior of the data or

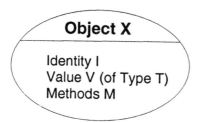

Figure 16.1: An object in the O_2 database

value is described by a set of *methods*. Methods are program modules. Any interaction with the data occurs through methods.

As you can see, this organization greatly differs from relational database systems, which manage information in data tuples.

Types

Object database systems provide a set of predefined types and allow for extensible types defined by the user.

Types are either basic (boolean, char, integer, real, string) or constructed (also called complex). Constructed types are defined applying *constructors*, such as tuple, list, bag, and set (a bag without replicates).

The following is a tuple built up from atomic types:

```
tuple (name: string,
       salary: integer)
```

This could be a type associated with an employee object, if we forget for the moment that an employee can have a car.

Tuples can be built up using other tuples, as shown in the next example, where the field `address` is made up of an inner tuple.

```
tuple (name: string,
       salary: integer,
       address: tuple (city: string,
                       street: string,
                       number: integer))
```

In the same way, the other constructors can be used to build up complex types.

Methods

Methods are just modular pieces of code. All data contained in an object can be accessed and manipulated through methods. This simple principle is called *object encapsulation.*

Encapsulation is the principle that data and operations (methods) should be modeled at the same time. Typically, an object has an interface part and an implementation part. The interface part provides the visibility of the objects from the outside world, while the implementation part specifies the internal part of the object, that is, the attributes and the implementation of the methods.

A method is composed of two parts: a method signature and a method body. The method signature is the specification of the method; the implementation is in the method body.

Normally, the method body is defined separately from the method signature, and within a class description only the signature of the methods are given. The signature of a method basically defines the name of the method and the type of the parameters. This is an example of a simple method signature:

```
method public set_name (name: string);
```

The key word `public` indicates that the method is part of the visible interface of the class. This definition assumes that the method has been defined inside a class. This method could, for example, be used to extract the name of an employee object.

While the signature of a method simply defines the visible interface, the actual code of the method is defined in the method body. Typically, method bodies are defined using an object-oriented language, such as C++, properly extended to include special database operations.

Classes

Since several objects may have similar structure, it is convenient to assemble objects with the same value and with the same set of methods together into a *class* (see Figure 16.2).

Therefore, an object is always associated with a class. The definition of a class includes its type definition, methods definition, and different relationships with other classes. We have already seen the definition of a type and of methods. A class specification can be divided up as follows:

- a class name

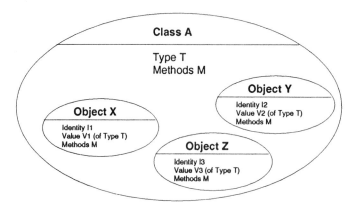

Figure 16.2: A class in the O_2 database

- a class type

- public and private attributes and methods

Let's now define a class modeling "worker" objects. In our example, each worker object has a name and a monthly salary. Such a class can be defined as follows:

```
class Worker
    type tuple (name:  string,
                read salary: integer)
    method public set_name(name: string),
                get_name: string,
                set_salary(salary: integer),
                compute_annual_salary: integer
end;
```

If we would like to model the fact that a worker object may be driving a car, a possible design is to introduce a new class, named `Car`, to represent car objects, and link the `Worker` class to the `Car` class to represent that each worker object drives a car object. We assume that a car is represented by a name, a price, and its horsepower. This can be done as follows:

```
class Car
    type tuple (public name:  string,
                public price: real,
                public hpw: integer) \nopagebreak
```

```
end;

class Worker
   type tuple (name:   string,
               read salary: integer,
               public car: Car)
   method public set_name(name: string),
               get_name: string,
               set_salary(salary: integer),
               compute_annual_salary: integer
end;
```

The class `Worker` is associated with a tuple type that defines the structure of the class itself. When embedded in a class, the tuple fields `name`, `salary`, and `car` are usually referred to as the class attributes. Both attributes `name` and `salary` are defined using the built-in types string and integer. Attribute `car`, instead, is declared to be of type `Car`, where `Car` is the other class in the database schema. In this case, we say that objects of class `Worker` refer to objects of class `Car` by means of attribute `car`.

By default all attributes of a class are private. Attributes' visibility can be modified by adding the keyword `read` or `public` before the attribute definition.

To access `Worker`'s attributes and/or to associate behavior to the class, the designer associates methods to the class `Worker` after the keywords `method public`.

The implementation of the class's methods is generally defined outside the definition of the class itself. In O_2, the implementation of the method `compute_annual_salary` can be defined, for example, as follows:

```
method body compute_annual_salary: integer in class Worker {
    return (self->salary*12);
}
```

The method simply computes and returns the yearly salary. The class definitions, including specifications of class types and methods (with method code), as well as the different relationships between these classes, is called the *database schema*.

After the definition of a database class in the schema, no instances of that class are present yet in the database. To populate the database with objects, an application must be defined to perform the task.

We have defined our first two classes. Let's now create objects corresponding to class `Worker` and class `Car`.

Say we want to model two workers. The first one is John Smith, with a monthly salary of $6,000 and driving a Mercedes S 280. The second one is Paul Willis, with a monthly salary of $5,600 and driving a BMW 328i Cabriolet. The database can be populated, as follows, using an O_2 script:

```
run body {
    /* code creating two objects of class
       Worker and two objects of class Car */

    o2 Worker worker1 = new Worker;
    o2 Worker worker2 = new Worker;
    o2 Car car1 = new Car ("Mercedes S 280");
    o2 Car car2 = new Car ("BMW 328i Cabriolet");

    /* code to initialize the state of the two objects of
       class Worker */

    worker1->set_name("John Smith");
    worker1->set_salary(6,000);
    worker1->car = car1;

    worker2->set_name("Paul Willis");
    worker2->set_salary(5,600);
    worker2->car = car2;

    /* code to initialize the state of the two objects of
       class Car */

    car1->price = 100,000;
    car2->price = 55,000;

    /* code that uses the created objects */
    ...
}
```

By running the script above, we created and initialized two objects of class `Worker` and two objects of class `Car`. An object is created by applying a `new` operator specifying the appropriate class. The object identifier is given by the system and is not visible to the user. The initial database values of an object are either passed as a parameter to the new operator, or a specific method needs to be used. Note that in the example, worker1 refers to car1 and worker2 refers to car2, which corresponds exactly to our requirements: John Smith drives a Mercedes, and Paul Willis drives a BMW.

If we want to know the yearly salary of John Smith modeled by worker1, we invoke the appropriate method on the desired object:

```
...
worker1->compute_annual_salary();
...
```

The result is (assuming a 12-month salary per year) $72,000.

We will see later in this chapter how to handle the situation when the object for whom we want to execute a method is not known a priori. A typical example would be the following query: "Find the yearly salary of employees who are driving cars with horsepower greater than 120."

So far, we have seen an example of how to create simple objects. However, objects can represent more complex structures.

Complex objects are instances of classes whose attributes are defined by applying constructors to simple types or to other classes. Supporting complex objects also requires that appropriate operators must be provided for dealing with such objects. Operators on a complex object must also transitively be applicable to all of its components.

Let's define another class Worker_with_address that represents complex objects:

```
class Worker_with_address
    type tuple (name: string,
                read salary: integer,
                public car: Car,
                public address: tuple (city: string,
                                       street: string,
                                       number: integer)
    method public set_name (name: string),
                get_name: string,
                set_salary (salary: integer),
                compute_annual_salary: integer
end
```

The first three attributes of the class have been defined using the simple types string and integer and the Car class definition. The fourth attribute, namely `address`, makes the class represent complex objects because it is defined using the tuple constructor.

Object Identity

As already described before, the origin of object identity is based on the distinction between the identity of an object and its value. The identity remains the same throughout the life of an object, while the value can be modified. In the example of the `Worker` objects, the object identity never changes, but the value of the object (say, the `salary` attribute) can.

Let's modify the script below to reflect a price rise of the BMW 328i Cabriolet. This can be accomplished by adding the following lines of code to the previous example:

```
run body {
    ...

    /* code that increases the price of car2 */

    car2->price = 61,000;
}
```

The value but not the object identifier of `car2` has been modified. Therefore, the object `worker2` representing Paul Willis continues referring to the same object `car2` as before.

Inheritance and Class or Type Hierarchies

All object databases support inheritance. Inheritance is the key for code reusability. Most of the current object database systems support multiple inheritance, that is, the ability to have multiple superclasses for the same subclass. When this is provided, care must be taken to avoid name collisions, that is, to avoid having attributes or methods defined with the same name in the superclasses all being inherited in the subclass.

Assume the designer wants to add employees and consultants in the schema. These entities are, by definition, a specialization of the workers concept previously described. The two new entities can be modeled by defining two classes, `Employee` and `Consultant`, that both inherit from class `Worker`.

```
class Employee inherit Worker
    type tuple (work_addr: string,
```

```
                    emp_no: integer)
    method public ...
end;

class Consultant inherit Worker
    type tuple (work_addr: string,
                specialization: integer)
    method public ...
end;
```

In the definition of both `Employee` and `Consultant`, there is no need to include attributes such as `name`, `salary`, and so on. These attributes are automatically inherited from class `Worker`.

Concepts such as manager and manager/consultant can be defined in the database schema by further specializing classes `Employee` and `Consultant`:

```
class Manager inherit Employee
    type tuple (car: Exp_car,
                bonus: integer)
    method public ...
end;

class ConsulManag inherit Consultant, Manager
    type tuple (car: Exp_car)
    method public ...
end;
```

Class `Manager` is derived from class `Employee`; class `ConsulManag` is derived from both `Consultant` and `Manager`. Note that in class `Manager` the inherited attribute `car` has been redefined to refer to expensive cars only. We assume here that class `Exp_car` is a subclass of class `Car`. The definition of class `ConsulManag` is a typical example of multiple inheritance. The explicit definition of attribute `car` solves the ambiguity of having the attribute `car` inherited from two different class paths, namely the one involving classes `Worker` and `Consultant` and the one with classes `Worker`, `Employee`, and `Manager`.

Overriding, Overloading, Late Binding

Object databases support overriding, overloading, and late binding. Simply stated, *overloading* is the ability to use the same name for different method implementations, *overriding* is the ability to redefine the implementation of a method without changing its name, and *late binding* is the ability of the database system, given a method name, to select at run-time the appropriate implementation. The three features combined together ensure database extensibility, that is, adding new types and methods, without changing the applications.

Let's reconsider the two classes `Manager` and `Employee`. We assume the computation of the annual salary for managers to be different from the one for regular employees because managers obtain a performance bonus at the end of the year. In our running example, this is modeled by overriding the method `compute_annual_salary` in class `Manager`:

```
class Manager inherit Employee
    type tuple (car: Exp_car,
                bonus: integer)
    method public compute_annual_salary: integer
end;

method body compute_annual_salary: integer in class Manager {
    return (self->salary*12 + self->bonus);
}
```

Persistence

The obvious difference between an object-oriented programming language and an object database system is that objects in an object database system have to be made persistent.

There are various ways in which an object database system defines an object (or a set of objects) to be persistent. We will look at *persistency by reachability*—that is, to become persistent, an object must be attached directly or transitively to a persistent *root*. These roots are declared in a schema by giving an explicit name to them. In this way, persistence becomes transparent.

In the following example, we create an `Employee` and a `Consultant` persistent object as well as two persistent sets for employees and consultants. In O_2, objects are made persistent by using the **name** command:

```
name employee1: Employee;      /* root named object */
name consultant1: Consultant;  /* root named object */

name Employees: set(Employee);     /* root set */
name Consultants: set(Consultant); /* root set */
```

Objects `employee1` and `consultant1` can now be used and initialized with the **new** instruction. The name gives persistence to the object as well as quick access to it. This can be implemented as follows:

```
run body {
    /* Declaration and instantiation of three transient Car
        objects and one transient Worker object*/

    o2 Car car1 = new Car("VW Passat");
    o2 Car car2 = new Car("Opel Corsa");
    o2 Car car3 = new Car("Fiat Bravo");
    o2 Worker worker3 = new Worker;

    /* Instantiation of the two persistent objects employee1 and
        consultant1 */

    employee1 = new Employee;
    consultant1 = new Consultant;

    /* Assignment of car1 to employee1, car2 to
        consultant1, and car3 to worker3. Both car1 and
        car2 become persistent by reachability. Objects car3
        and worker3 are transient */

    employee1->car = car1;
    consultant->car = car2;
    worker3->car = car3;

    /* employee1 and consultant1 are now inserted in the
        corresponding name sets */

    Employees += set(employee1);
    Consultants += set(consultant1);
}
```

Ad Hoc Query Facility

We now show you how to query the database to get the information stored.

There are basically two ways to query the database, either by calling appropriate methods or by using a declarative query language. In the first case, we can use a navigational approach using C++ as DML language; in the second case, we can use an SQL-like query language. Let's see how it can be done.

Assume we collected all the employees and the consultants in the two named (i.e., persistent) sets called `Employees` and `Consultants`. Here is an example of a declarative query, expressed in the O_2 query language (OQL), which asks for employees named "Steven Arm" who earn more than \$7,000 a month.

```
select e
from e in Employees
where e.name = "Steven Arm" and
      e.salary > 7,000
```

Now let's look at an example of an object-oriented join query returning the set of employees who have the same name as a consultant:

```
select e
from e in Employees,
     c in Consultants
where e.name = c.name
```

Creating a Schema

We are now ready to create our first simple schema. We want to pull together all the classes defined before into one single schema. First of all, a schema normally has a single root class, called `Object`. All other classes are connected directly or indirectly to the root class `Object`.

We want to define a schema called `Workers` representing the class `Worker` with subclasses `Consultant`, `Employee`, and class `Car` with subclass `Exp_car`. Moreover, we want class `Employee` to have a subclass `Manager`, and `Consultant` and `Manager` to both have a common subclass `ConsulManag`. The complete schema is defined as follows:

```
schema Workers;
class Worker
   type tuple (name:  string,
               read salary: integer,
               public car: Car)
   method public set_name(name: string),
               get_name: string,
               set_salary(salary: integer),
```

```
                    compute_annual_salary: integer
end;

class Employee inherit Worker
   type tuple (public work_address: string,
               public emp_no: integer)
end;

class Consultant inherit Worker
   type tuple (public work_address: string,
               public specialization: string)
end;

class Manager inherit Employee
   type tuple (public car: Exp_car,
               bonus: integer)
   method public set_bonus(bonus: integer),
               get_bonus: integer,
end;

class ConsulManag inherit Consultant, Employee
   type tuple (public car: Exp_car)
end;

class Car
   type tuple (public name: string,
               public price: real,
               public hpw: integer)
end;

class Exp_car
   type tuple (public optionals: Options)
end;
```

Creating a Base

Now that we have created the schema, we need to start populating the base. Objects are created in accordance to the definition of the classes defined in the schema. Let's start creating two objects for class Worker and two objects for class Car, where worker "Steve Millis" drives a "Fiat 500" and worker "Paul John" drives a "Ford Fiesta." Further, we create an object "Jim Steven" of class Manager who drives a "Ferrari F40," which, as one probably can guess, is an instance of class Exp_car.

```
base DB_workers;
name workJohn: Worker;
name workMillis: Worker;
name mngSteven: Manager;

name carFerrari: Exp_car;

run body {
    /* Instantiation of transient car objects */

    o2 car1 = new Car("Fiat 500");
    o2 car2 = new Car("Ford Fiesta");

    /* Instantiation of persistent car objects */

    carFerrari = new Car("Ferrari F40");

    /* Instantiation of two persistent Worker and one
       persistent Manager objects */

    workJohn = new Worker;
    workMillis = new Worker;
    workSteven = new Manager;

    /* Code to initialize the state of the two worker and
       one manager objects */

    workJohn->set_name("Paul John");
    workJohn->car = car1;        /* car1 becomes persistent */

    workMillis->set_name("Steve Millis");
    workMillis->car = car2;      /* car2 becomes persistent */

    workSteven->set_name("Jim Steven");
    workSteven->car = carFerrari;
}
```

We now add a fourth object, "Paul Whilm" of class `ConsulManag`. "Paul Whilm" drives an expensive car, exactly the same as "John Smith."

```
name cnsmngWhilm: ConsulManag;

run body {
    /* Instantiation of persistent consulmanag objects */

    cnsmngWhilm = new ConsulManag;

    /* Code to initialize the state of consulmanag objects */

    cnsmngWhilm->set_name("Paul Whilm");
    cnsmngWhilm->car = carFerrari;
}
```

Creating a Simple Application: Increase Salary of Employees

Now that we have written our first schema, created our first base, and know how to query the database, it is time to test what we have done with a simple application. It is important to remember that a schema and related base are meaningful if there is at least one application using them. This is how, in practice, we check if the defined schema is what it was intended to be—by testing it with a simple application.

In our simple application, we want to find all the employees who drive a car worth more than $50,000 and who have a yearly salary less than $100,000 and increase their salary by 10%. A simple way to write such an application is first to run a query to extract the employees satisfying the requirements and subsequently to increase their salary.

This can be done as follows:

```
application incr_salary_emps
{
  o2 set(Employee) res_employees;  /* set containing
                                      the query result */
  o2 Employee it_emp;              /* set iterator */
  o2 integer new_salary;           /* support variable */

  /* run the embedded query using the O2query command */
```

```
o2query (res_employees,
        "select e
         from e in $1
         where e->car->price > 50,000 and
               e->salary < 100,000", Employees);

for (it_emp in res_employees)
{
   new_salary = it_emp->salary + it_emp->salary/10;
   it_emp->set_salary(new_salary);
}
}
```

To conclude this chapter, let's review a few remaining concepts.

Computational Completeness

Object database systems implement computational completeness by having a connection (language binding) to one or more (usually) object-oriented languages, such as C++ or Smalltalk.

Secondary Storage Management, Concurrency, and Recovery

Of course, we have not described in this chapter other important aspects of an object database system: all object database systems must handle the storage of objects on disk and provide concurrent access to objects and a recovery mechanism.

However, since the focus of this part of the book is on schema and database evolution, we will not cover these aspects here. The details of the internal implementation of an object database system will be considered in Chapter 18.

Advanced Database Features

What we have seen until now are the essential features that every object database system must have.

Commercial database systems, however, do support a richer set of more advanced features, most of them not available (or only partially available) in conventional relational database systems:

- Versioning

- Integrity constraints and triggers

- Advanced transaction management

- Schema and database updates

- Views and authorization mechanisms

- Advanced graphical facilities

- Metadata handling

In Chapters 17 and 18 we will focus our attention on the problem of how to support schema and database updates in an object database system. Schema and database updates are a part of a broader topic known as *change management*. Change management encompasses several of the advanced topics listed previously and some of the topics covered in other chapters of this book, such as views, versioning, triggers, and, to some extent, deductive capabilities.

16.2.2   Standards

One of the problems with objects is the lack of a unique, accepted definition. In fact, object orientation is a set of paradigms.

Since object database systems depend heavily on the object model chosen (for example, C++ or Smalltalk), they all differ from one another.

This is in contrast with the relational database systems, which, broadly speaking, are all based on a single accepted definition of the relational data model.

Object database vendors have recognized the importance of supporting a standard object model, as opposed to each vendor supporting a slightly different object model. In 1994, the majority of the object database vendors agreed on an object database standard, called ODMG-93, revised in 1996, which addresses five issues:

1. a common object model

2. an object definition language

3. an object query language

4. a C++ language binding

5. a Smalltalk language binding

At this time, the ODMG standard is only partially supported by the object database vendors.

Another standard that needs to be taken into consideration is SQL3. The new definition of SQL contains several new object features. Although SQL3 is not yet implemented in any commercial database system, it may, if integrated with the ODMG standard, be a way to bridge relational and object database systems together.

16.2.3   Change Management in Object Database Systems

Change management in object database systems encompasses all those functionalities that allow the system to evolve. Two criteria are discussed in the literature that differentiate system evolution into a vertical and a horizontal evolution. The former basically copes with evolution within a single system; the latter concentrates on evolution issues derived from the integration of cooperative systems. Horizontal evolution is out of the scope of this chapter.

Vertical evolution can be considered at three different levels: application evolution, schema evolution, and database evolution (see Figure 16.3).

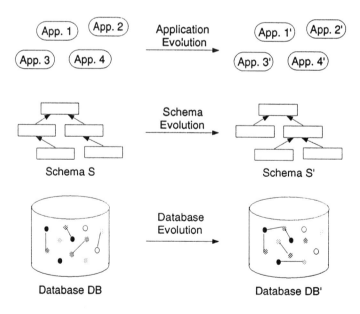

Figure 16.3: Vertical evolution in object databases

Schema Evolution

The schema of a software system focuses upon the essential characteristics of the system itself, relative to the perspective of the designer. The schema represents an abstraction of the system that helps the designer cope with its complexity. Its focus on the essential characteristics makes the system ideal for reasoning about evolution. In order to factor out the different processes occurring during evolution, we will use the term "schema evolution" strictly for the modifications of the database schema: *schema evolution* is the process of changing the schema of an object database while maintaining its consistency. The goal of schema evolution is thus to evolve a schema from one consistent state to the next. We call this *conceptual consistency*. Examples of systems providing rules for schema consistency are Gemstone, ORION, and O_2 . Schema evolution can be accomplished by making use of the following approaches:

1. *Schema evolution primitives* allow the schema to be modified incrementally and locally, by allowing, for instance, a single property to be added to a class. Schema evolution primitives are normally interpreted by the system and allow the schema to be modified on-line. This is a very important issue for those application domains where an application shutdown is considered critical. Systems providing schema evolution primitives are, among others, Versant' and O_2.

2. *Schema restructuring*, where the schema is changed globally, requires a complete recompilation of the schema itself. During recompilation, applications need to be suspended. The ObjectStore object database is the most representative example of a schema restructuring supporting system.

3. In *schema* and/or *class versioning*, a history tree of schemas and/or classes is kept by the system, and modifications to schemas and/or classes always imply the creation of a new schema/class. This schema evolution technique allows applications not to be suspended, since the information of the schema/class to be modified is only copied into the new version. One example of a commercially available system supporting schema versioning is the Objectivity database. To our best knowledge, there are no commercial systems available supporting class versioning because of the high overhead required for managing such complexity.

4. *Schema views* allow a database designer to virtually restructure the

schema and the database by using a special view definition language or by making use of queries as in the relational approach. So far, no commercially available object database supports view mechanisms for schema evolution.[1] We are aware that O_2 Technology is considering integrating views in a future release of the O_2 database.

Database Evolution

After a schema change, database objects have to be adapted to be consistent with the modified schema. We call this *structural consistency*. If schema evolution primitives or schema restructuring are used, then objects in the database have to be physically transformed to conform to the modified schema. In the case of schema versioning, objects generally do not have to be physically transformed, but some emulation is required if objects conforming to one schema version have to be seen as objects of a different schema version. Schema views do not generally require the underlying database to be transformed, but only when a schema view has to be materialized.

Application Evolution

Another type of consistency, known as *behavioral consistency*, concerns the dynamic aspect of objects. For instance, if an attribute is deleted or modified, a method referring to that attribute in its implementation would no longer be consistent in terms of the current schema. Commercially available object databases where methods are compiled face this problem by making the designer recompile the entire schema along with its methods. In particular, O_2 provides compiler options that determine the behavior of the compiler in the situation where a schema change affects the validity of a method. The system administrator can opt for an automatic recompilation of those methods that have been affected by the schema change, or for a warning notification mechanism where only messages are issued but no recompilation is performed. Other, more advanced program restructuring techniques that analyze the behavioral aspects of methods and their interactions have been proposed in the literature. Another technique proposed in the literature is known as *change avoidance*. As opposed to program restructuring, change avoidance tries to "fix" inconsistencies before they occur. Thus, change avoidance can be characterized as an active, as opposed to reactive, update mechanism. In the database area, some of the work on views

---

[1]As in relational databases, schema views are a useful means not only for schema evolution, but also for (1) managing authorization to critical or private data, and (2) for allowing schema integration in a heterogeneous environment.

has been extended so that the views support a limited independence between manipulation programs and schema. In the programming language area, the adaptive software solution supports change avoidance by providing a kind of metaprogramming, minimizing dependencies between the program text and the class structure. Adaptive software is generally written at a higher, schematic level that abstracts the details of object traversal and navigation.

The following chapters concentrate exclusively on the first two kinds of evolution, namely, schema and database evolution. References to relevant related work on application evolution will be given throughout the book.

16.3 Bibliographic Notes

Change management in object databases is described in [127, 209, 224, 219, 431].

As regards horizontal evolution, which is out of the scope of this chapter, the reader is referred to [10, 19, 45, 211, 261, 268, 287, 298, 344, 386, 387, 390, 401, 458].

For vertical evolution, references [3, 32, 127, 161, 209, 403, 451, 472, 473] exhaustively cover the topic of schema evolution. Schema views are treated in [54, 370, 389, 413, 412]. Database evolution is well described in [166, 163, 162, 165, 209, 417, 403]. Application evolution has been extensively studied in [17, 219, 216, 266, 343, 403, 424, 432, 451, 461].

References to the O_2 object database are [312, 313, 193]. Other systems such as Gemstone, Versant, ObjectStore, Objectivity, ORION, and Itasca are covered in [77, 448, 314, 315, 31, 223].

An initial reading for the GOODSTEP project is [193, 312].

16.4 Exercises

16.1. Define a schema that models the structure of a small company. Use the following classes: `Building`, `Room`, `Person`, `Employee`, `Manager`. Represent the following relationships: an employee is a person, and a manager is an employee. Each employee works in a room. The office building has several rooms.

16.2. Define for each class in the schema of Exercise 16.1 an appropriate set of methods. Write the signature and the body of each method separately.

16.3. Populate the database, creating objects for each class defined in the schema of Exercise 16.1. Give to each object an initial value.

16.4. Write a simple application that uses the schema of Exercise 16.1 and the database created.

Chapter 17

How to Change the Schema

The definition of a database schema is an evolutionary design activity. More than one design increment and iteration is needed to properly capture the relevant properties of complex real-world situations. Once defined, modifications to the database schema have to be taken into account in the project life cycle to adapt the schema to changes coming from the user requirements and from the application domain. This chapter covers the topic of schema evolution, with particular emphasis on the schema evolution primitives supported by object databases. Section 17.1 presents the taxonomy of schema evolution primitives supported by the majority of object databases. Section 17.2 describes the concept of schema invariants and rules for preserving them in case schema evolution primitives are applied. Finally, Section 17.3 summarizes the semantics associated with each schema evolution primitive.

17.1   Changing the Schema Using Primitives

In a relational database, the primitives offered for manipulating the schema are used primarily for the creation and deletion of relations and for adding or deleting attributes to relations. It is normally fairly simple to manage this limited type of changes, since modifications to a relation have no effect on other relations. The SQL-2 standard, for instance, provides the primitives `create table` and `drop table` for inserting and deleting tables in the schema. Attributes in the tables can be added or deleted with the primitives `alter table ... add column` and `alter table ... drop column`. The modification of a column with the primitives `alter table ... alter column` gives the possibility of overriding the default column initialization only. Commercially available relational databases already support the operation to modify a column domain.

The situation is more complex in an object database, since the repertory of possible schema modifications is significantly larger because of the increased complexity of the object data model and because modifications to a class may involve changes in other classes in the schema. If, for instance, an attribute is modified/deleted in one class, the same attribute must be modified/deleted in all its subclasses. Concepts such as inheritance and composition links in the object model require new schema modification primitives to be defined other than the ones used for relational databases. Another important issue concerns those mechanisms for on-line execution of schema modifications where no shutdown of running applications is possible. This is a mandatory requirement for critical applications such as medical or process-controlling applications.

17.1.1   Taxonomy of Schema Modifications

The definition of a set of classes, attribute and method declarations, and method implementations is a highly complex design task prone to errors. A structuring mechanism is therefore needed to allow breaking down this task into subtasks and to support its successive development over time.

However, a schema is not fixed once defined, but evolves over time in order to capture the changing user requirements or the changing model of the application domain. New classes and/or attributes are introduced, old classes and/or attributes deleted, methods modified, errors eliminated, and so forth.

In the literature, taxonomies of schema changes have been exhaustively discussed. The taxonomy we use in this chapter has been partly integrated in the O_2 object database. With some simplifications, the taxonomy is defined as follows:

1 Modifications to attributes of a class

    1.1 Creation of an attribute

    1.2 Deletion of an attribute

    1.3 Renaming of an attribute

    1.4 Modification of the domain of an attribute

2 Modifications to methods of a class

    2.1 Creation of a method

2.2 Deletion of a method

2.3 Renaming of a method

2.4 Modification of the signature of a method

3 Modifications to the class inheritance graph

3.1 Creation of a new superclass/subclass relationship between classes

3.2 Deletion of a superclass/subclass relationship between classes

4 Modifications to classes

4.1 Creation of a class

4.2 Deletion of a class

4.3 Renaming of a class

Attributes and methods are treated almost in the same way in O_2. Therefore, in what follows, we have deliberately omitted the treatment of modifications of methods mainly because they do not affect the structural consistency of the underlying database.

When executing modifications to a schema, the proposed changes must maintain the schema in a consistent state. In ORION, GemStone, and O_2, rules have been defined for schema consistency. Consistency rules are referred to as *schema invariants*.

17.1.2 Schema Evolution Primitives in O_2

As an example, in this section we briefly present the schema update commands supported by O_2. Both the syntax used and the list of commands are not complete.

Creating a Class

To create a class in O_2, the developer can use the command:

create class *Class_name*
[Class_inheritance]
[Class_renaming]
end

where *Class_inheritance* is defined as

inherit *Class_name [, Class_name ...]*

The developer uses this *Class_inheritance* clause to position the new class in the class hierarchy by specifying its immediate superclass(es).

The *Class_renaming* clause to rename any inherited attributes is defined as follows:

rename *attribute_renaming [, attribute_renaming ...]*

where *attribute_renaming* is defined as

attribute *attribute_name* as *new_attribute_name*

Deleting a Class

To delete the definition of a class, the developer can use the following command:

delete class *Class_name*

To delete the definition of a class along with all its subclasses, the following command can be used:

delete classes from *Class_name*

Inheritance of Class

The inheritance graph of a schema can be changed by modifying the direct superclass of a class as follows:

create inherit *Class_name Superclass_name*

A link between a superclass and a class can be deleted with the following command:

delete inherit *Class_name Superclass_name*

Modifying Class Definitions

To modify a class, the developer can use the modify class command:

modify class *Class_name [Class_inheritance] [Class_renaming]* end

This redefines the specified class *Class_name*. It works in exactly the same way as the create class command, whose grammar is given above.

Attribute Primitives

Attributes of a class may be added, deleted, renamed, or modified. For creating one or more attributes in a class, the following command can be used:

create attribute *attribute_name* : *type_spec* in class *Class_name*

To remove an attribute from a class, O_2 provides the command

delete attribute *attribute_name* in class *Class_name*

To rename or modify an attribute, the developer uses the commands

rename attribute *attribute_name* as *new_attribute_name*
in class *Class_name*

modify attribute *attribute_name* : *type_spec* in class *Class_name*

17.2 Schema Invariants

In this section, schema invariants and rules for preserving them are presented for the O_2 database. However, concepts presented here are general and applicable to a broader class of object databases. For a better presentation of the concepts, we make use of Figure 17.1, which illustrates part of a schema called Workers. We will use the graphical notation of Figure 17.1 throughout the rest of this book. Classes are denoted by boxes. Class names are defined in bold. Inherited attributes can be distinguished from local ones because they are embedded in gray boxes. Arrows in the graph model inheritance links. The schema in Figure 17.1 presents all the classes already used in Chapter 16. To keep the exposition simpler, all the methods have been omitted.

In O_2 the following invariants have been defined:

- *I1—Class hierarchy invariant:* The class hierarchy in the schema is a *rooted* and *connected directed acyclic graph* with classes that are named. The inheritance hierarchy has only one root, a system-defined class called Object. The class hierarchy is connected (i.e., there are no isolated classes). Classes are named, and each class in the class graph has a unique name.

- *I2—Distinct name invariant:* All attributes of a class, whether defined or inherited, have distinct names.

- *I3—Single origin invariant:* All attributes of a class have a single distinct origin. Consider, for instance, the schema Workers in Figure 17.1. Class ConsulManag can inherit attribute name from either class Consultant or from class Manager. However, in both these superclasses, name has the same origin, namely, attribute name of

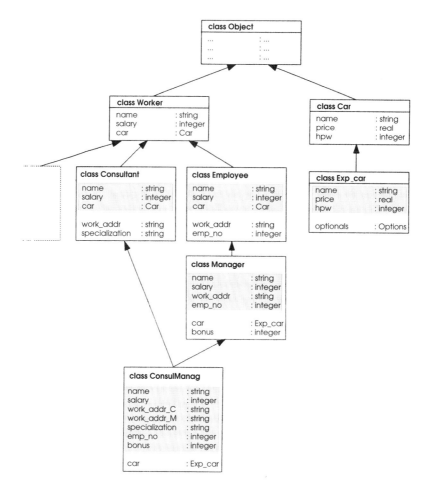

Figure 17.1: Inheritance hierarchy in the `Workers` schema

class `Worker`, where `name` was originally defined. Therefore, class `ConsulManag` must have only one occurrence of attribute `name`.

- *I4—Complete inheritance invariant:* A class X inherits all attributes from each of its superclasses, except when complete inheritance violates the distinct name and single origin invariant. Two different cases can occur:

  1. Two attributes have a different origin but the same name in two different superclasses. Both of them are inherited. In this case, one of the two attributes, or both of them, must be renamed

because of the distinct name invariant (see attribute `work_addr` in classes `Consultant` and `Manager`).

2. Two attributes have the same origin in two different superclasses. Only one of them is inherited (see attribute `name` in class `Consultant` and `Manager`). If one of them has been locally redefined, then there must be a local definition of the attribute in class `X`. Consider, in fact, attribute `car` in class `Consultant` and `Manager`. The origin of attribute `car` is class `Worker`, but the attribute has been redefined in class `Manager`. Therefore, attribute `car` must be redefined in class `ConsulManag` as well.

- *I5—Domain compatibility invariant:* If an attribute `att_i` appears both in class `X` and `Y`, with `X` subclass of `Y`, then the domain of `att_i` in `X` must be either the same as the one in `Y` or a subtype of it (see attribute `car` in classes `Employee` and `Manager`).[1]

When defining a mechanism for schema evolution, rules must be specified in such a way that, when schema modification primitives are applied, schema invariants are preserved. In what follows, we present the rules defined for the O_2 object database. Rules have been divided into three groups as outlined below.

Multiple Inheritance Rules

The first group of rules concerns the resolution of conflicts caused by multiple inheritance and the redefinition of attributes in a subclass:

- *Rule R1:* If an attribute is locally defined in a class `X` and its names corresponds to the name of an inherited attribute of one of its superclasses, the locally defined attribute overrides the inherited one.

- *Rule R2:* If two or more superclasses of a class `X` have attributes with the same name but distinct origin, both attributes are inherited and renamed. The system assigns new default names to the inherited attributes by postponing system default information to the name themselves. Alternatively, the designer can also assign new names to inherited attributes.[2]

---

[1]In O_2, both classes and types can be defined in the schema. Types do not belong to the class hierarchy.

[2]A similar rule has been presented in the literature, where only one attribute is inherited, namely, the one belonging to the first superclass among conflicting superclasses. In this case, an order among superclasses must be implicitly kept by the system.

- *Rule R3:* If two or more superclasses of a class X has attributes with the same name, but with the same origin, the attribute is inherited only once. If one of these attributes has been locally redefined in these classes, then the attribute must be redefined in class X.

Attribute Propagations Rules

This second group of rules concerns the propagation of modifications to subclasses:

- *Rule R4:* A modification to an attribute of a class X is always propagated to all its subclasses, except to those in which the attribute has been locally redefined.

- *Rule R5:* A creation of an attribute att_i in a class X requires that no locally defined attribute with the same name is present in class X. Further, it requires the presence of no more than one subclass of X containing an attribute with the same name.

- *Rule R6:* Only locally defined attributes can be deleted from a class.

- *Rule R7:* A modification of the name of an attribute att_i in a class X is not propagated to its subclasses.

Class Hierarchy Manipulation Rules

The third group of rules concerns the aggregation and deletion of inheritance relationships between classes and the creation and removal of classes:

- *Rule R8:* If a class Y is added to the list of superclasses of a class X, any conflict of inheritance is resolved by Rules R1, R2, and R3.

- *Rule R9:* The deletion of a class Y from the list of superclasses of a class X removes the inherited attributes in X and its subclasses. If Y is the last superclass in the list, the removal of class Y makes X a direct subclass of the root class Object. The root class Object cannot be removed from the list of superclasses of any class.

- *Rule R10:* New classes can be created only as leaf classes in the class graph. If a new class X is created without any indication of which class(es) it should inherit from, X becomes a subclass of the root class *Object.*

- *Rule R11:* Only leaf classes can be removed from the schema. The root class `Object` cannot be removed.

17.3 Semantics of Schema Modifications

In this section, the schema modification primitives presented above in Section 17.1.1 are discussed in more detail. Primitives, when applied locally to a class, may imply a complex modification to the whole schema. For example, the simple deletion of an attribute in a class implies that this attribute is deleted from all its subclasses as well.

We provide below an analysis of schema modification primitives and discuss the consequences of their execution on the schema.

Modifications to Attributes of a Class

1.1 – Creation of an attribute: A new attribute `att_i` can be created in a class X only if class X does not contain a locally defined attribute with the same name (Rule R5). If class X contains an inherited attribute with the same name, then the new created attribute overrides the inherited one (Rule R1). The class modification propagates to all subclasses of X, except to those where `att_i` is already locally defined (Rule R4). If the attribute can be inherited from X through more than one inheritance path, then the attribute is inherited only once according to Rule R3. Finally, if the attribute causes a name conflict as specified in Invariant I4 (case 1), then the attribute is automatically renamed (Rule R2).

1.2 – Deletion of an attribute: An attribute `att_i` that has to be deleted from a class X must have been defined locally in class X (Rule R6). Deleting an attribute from a class results in the attribute being deleted from all its subclasses, except from those where the attribute has been locally redefined (Rule R4). If class X has only one superclass with an attribute with the same name, then this attribute is inherited according to Rule R4. If more than one superclass contains attributes with the same name, then these attributes are inherited according to Rules R2 and R3. The same holds for any subclass of X where attribute `att_i` is not locally defined.

1.3 – Renaming of an attribute: Renaming of an attribute `att_i` in class X can only take place if no name conflicts are created; that is, if there is no attribute with the same name in class X that is locally defined or inherited. The modification of the name of an attribute is not propagated to subclasses (Rule R7).

1.4 – Modification of the domain of an attribute: The modification of the domain of an attribute can be done only if the domain compatibility invariant (Invariant I5) is preserved. The modification of the domain is propagated to those subclasses in accordance with Rule R4.

Modifications to the Class Inheritance Graph

3.1 – Creation of a new superclass/subclass relationship between classes: The creation of a superclass/subclass relationship between class Y and X can only be carried out if they do not cause cycles in the inheritance hierarchy; that is, class Y must not be a subclass, whether direct or indirect, of class X. All attributes of Y are inherited in X and its subclasses on the basis of Rule R8.

3.2 – Deletion of a superclass/subclass relationship between classes: The deletion of a superclass/subclass relationship between class Y and class X makes class X and its subclasses lose the attributes inherited from Y (Rule R9). The deletion of an inherited attribute does not take place if the attribute can be inherited through a different inheritance path (Rule R3). If class Y is the last class in the list of X's superclasses, then Y becomes a direct subclass of the root class `Object` (Rule R9).

Modifications to Classes

4.1 – Creation of a class: If no superclass is specified for the creation of a class X, then X becomes a direct subclass of `Object` (Rule R10). If, however, one or more superclasses have been specified, then X becomes a direct subclass of these classes and inherits their attributes. Inheritance conflicts are resolved in accordance with Rules R1, R2, and R3.

4.2 – Deletion of a class: Only leaf classes can be deleted from the class graph (Rule R11). Alternatively, the designer can delete in one step a class along with all its subclasses. This does not contradict Rule R11 since the deletion of a class subgraph (which has to be a leaf subgraph) is only a shortcut for deleting more than one class by starting always from leaf classes.

4.3 – Renaming of a class: This operation can be carried out if other classes do not have the same name according to Invariant I2.

17.4 Bibliographic Notes

Primitives on how to change the schema have been studied in [1, 32, 55, 77, 161, 290, 335, 471, 472, 473]. In [127] an approach is discussed on how to make schema modification primitives parametrized. In [73, 74, 75, 76] other primitives are presented that are suitable for change management in software development environments and ought to support more declarative and advanced operations used in analysis and design processes. Examples of such primitives are the generalization, specialization, and merge of two or more classes, the deletion of a class in the middle of the class hierarchy, and so on. The rationale behind these high-level primitives comes from similar operations used in object-oriented methods such as OMT [369], Booch [69], and Jacobson [224], and from operations adopted in conceptual database design [44].

17.5 Exercises

17.1. Given the schema defined in Figure 17.1, apply the following primitives:

  a. Create a new class `Student` as a subclass of `Object`, with attributes `name`, `address`, and `university`

  b. Create a new class `Person` as a subclass of `Object` with attributes `name`, `address`, and `birthday`

  c. Make classes `Student` and `Worker` subclasses of class `Person`

  d. Create an attribute `car` in class `Student` referring to class `Car`

17.2. Given the schema defined in Figure 17.1, identify for each of the following primitives (1) which rules are applied that preserve the schema invariants and (2) the state of the schema after applying the primitives:

  a. Create attribute `salary` in class `Worker`

  b. Create attribute `specialization` in class `Employee`

  c. Delete attribute `car` in class `ConsulManag`

17.3. Consider the complete inheritance invariant (Invariant I4). Modify the invariant so that only one attribute is inherited when the two attributes have a different origin but the same name in two different superclasses.

17.4. Redefine the rules affected by the modification of the complete inheritance invariant (Invariant I4) in Exercise 17.3.

Chapter 18

How to Change the Database

Now that we know how to change a schema, we need to turn our attention and analyze what happens to the database after the schema is changed. While the activity of verifying the consistency of the schema is similar to that of a traditional compiler's semantic analysis, the enforcement of the consistency between the schema and the underlying database(s) is a typical database problem because objects are persistent. Consider the example of an attribute being added to a class. A drastic method to obtain consistency is to delete all objects of the modified class. Since the information contained in the persistent objects may represent an enormous value for a company, this clearly is an inappropriate measure. This chapter covers in detail the issue of database evolution and describes the basic mechanisms for the implementation of a database transformation. The rest of the chapter is structured as follows: Section 18.1 illustrates the relevant aspects related to two techniques for changing the database: immediate and deferred database transformations. Section 18.2 categorizes the schema evolution primitives into those that preserve the structural consistency and those that do not. Section 18.3 describes how the database is transformed either with default rules or with the input of the user. Section 18.4 illustrates the design and implementation issues used in the O_2 object database. Finally, Section 18.5 presents relevant related work.

18.1 Immediate vs. Deferred Transformations

When the schema of an object database system is modified, the database needs to be changed in such a way that the schema and the database remain consistent with each other. There are mainly two approaches for implementing a database transformation: immediate and deferred.

18.1.1   Immediate Database Transformation

The whole database, or the part of it that is affected by the schema change, must be transformed immediately after the schema modification. The database remains locked until the database transformation is finished. All running programs have to be suspended until the application that updates the database terminates. The time when the database is locked can be very long depending on specific parameters (e.g., size of the database, type of update performed, object retrieving strategy, etc.). Since all objects of the modified classes have to be updated at once, this could be expensive, especially if the system does not manage class extensions.[1]

Consider, for example, the case where an attribute of a class has changed its type. If no class extensions are maintained by the system, in the worst case the whole database has to be locked and all the objects of the database have to be accessed to find those that underwent a class modification. For small databases that fit into the client cache, the immediate transformation is always slower than the deferred one.

A clear advantage of the immediate database transformation is that after the transformation of all the objects, the entire database is in a state consistent with the new schema.

18.1.2   Deferred Database Transformation

With this approach, objects are expected to logically conform to the new modified schema, but they are physically transformed only when they are effectively used. If and only if an object is accessed and it is in an old format, then it is transformed to conform to its current definition in the schema. Note that the schema may undergo in the meanwhile several changes before an object is used. The advantage of this solution is that the entire database does not have to be locked during the transformation.

However, there is the need to store and remember the history of all schema updates that have been performed in the system. Every time an object is accessed by an application, a test has to be done in order to check

---

[1]A *class extension* is the set of objects that belong to a particular class. Some of the object-oriented database programming languages have taken the approach of not maintaining class extensions automatically on the grounds that this is conceptually cleaner and that it is easy for the programmer to maintain the extension when needed.

whether the object is already in the new format/value or not (i.e., if the object has to be updated or not).

If the deferred database transformation is used, then the cost for the transformation itself strongly depends on the object access rate performed by application programs.

We will return to this in detail in Chapter 19, where we will present a performance evaluation study of immediate and deferred database transformations.

18.2 Preserving Structural Consistency

When a schema is modified through the schema modification primitives presented in Section 17.1.1, structural consistency might be affected by the schema change. We deliberately say "might" since primitives such as the creation of a class in the schema do not imply any modification in the underlying database(s). Let's now reconsider the schema modification primitives presented in Section 17.1.1. We classify them into primitives that, when applied, never require the database to be transformed and primitives that, when applied, might require the system to transform the database in such a way that the schema and the database remain consistent with each other. We call the former *structural consistency preserving primitives* and the latter *structural consistency modifying primitives*.

18.2.1 Structural Consistency Preserving Primitives

Structural consistency preserving primitives (SCPPs) never require the underlying database to be transformed as a consequence of the schema change. For example, the creation of a new class in a schema preserves the structural consistency because the class can be created only as a leaf class (because of Rule R10, as defined in Section 17.2) and because its extension is empty by definition. All the renaming primitives (i.e., the renaming of a class and the renaming of an attribute) are structural consistency preserving. Attributes and classes will be accessed by applications by making use of the new name, but the structure of objects in the database remains unaltered since both the number of attributes in the class itself and the domain of its attributes have not been changed after the schema modification.

18.2.2   Structural Consistency Modifying Primitives

Structural consistency modifying primitives (SCMPs) might require the restructuring of the database to make it consistent with the modified schema. As an example, consider the class Worker already introduced in Section 16.2.1 and an instance worker (see Figure 18.1).

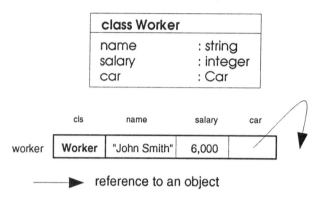

Figure 18.1: Definition of class Worker and object worker

Assume now a new attribute address of type string is added to the class Worker. To keep the database and the schema containing class Worker consistent with each other, objects belonging to class Worker must be restructured to contain the new attribute address. By default, this attribute is initialized with the system default value, for example, with an empty string (see Figure 18.2).

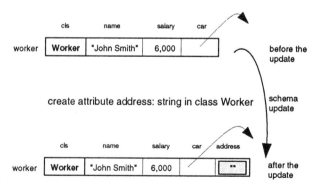

Figure 18.2: Transformation of object worker after the creation of attribute address in class Worker

As another example, objects must be restructured also when an attribute is deleted from a class. In Figure 18.3, the attribute salary is deleted from class `Worker`. In some systems such as ORION, objects are not restructured after the deletion of an attribute, but deleted attributes are filtered out from being used by applications. This technique is known as *screening*.

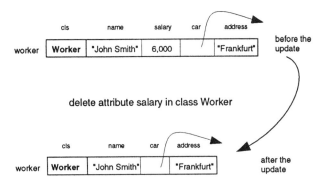

Figure 18.3: Transformation of object `worker` after the deletion of attribute `salary` in class `Worker`

We said that structural consistency modifying primitives might require the restructuring of the database because there are cases where the execution of such primitives does not affect the underlying base at all. Consider, for example, the simple case where the deletion of an attribute from a class causes an attribute with the same name and type to be inherited from a superclass. In this case, the structure of the class does not change since the deleted attribute is replaced by the inherited one. No database modification is therefore required.

Table 18.1 shows the impact on the database when applying the schema modification primitives presented in Section 17.1.1.

The schema modification primitives 1.3 (renaming of an attribute), 4.1 (creation of a class), and 4.3 (renaming of a class) do not affect the underlying database. The primitive 1.4 (modification of the domain of an attribute) requires in general that objects are modified.[2]

The schema modification primitives 1.1 (creation of an attribute) and 1.2 (deletion of an attribute) imply a corresponding database modification only if the attribute in question is not present in the class's superclass(es). The same holds for the primitives 3.1 (creation of a new superclass/subclass relationship between classes) and 3.2 (deletion of a superclass/subclass relationship between classes). In fact, a database modification is required only if the subclass does not locally provide all the attributes of the superclass.

---

[2]In some systems, the generalization of an attribute's domain does not imply a corresponding database modification.

Schema Modification	Objects Modified ?
(1.1)	in general yes (a)
(1.2)	in general yes (a)
(1.3)	no
(1.4)	yes
(3.1)	in general yes (b)
(3.2)	in general yes (b)
(4.1)	no
(4.2)	(c)
(4.3)	no

(a) Objects are not modified if attributes with the same name and type are present in a superclass.

(b) Objects are not modified if the subclass locally provides all the attributes of the superclass.

(c) Objects must be deleted from the database.

Table 18.1: Schema modification primitives and their impact on the database

Finally, the schema modification primitive 4.2 (deletion of a class) requires objects either to be deleted or to be filtered out from the database.

18.3   User-Defined and Default Transformations

The semantics of updating the database after a schema change depends on the application(s) that use(s) the schema. In most object databases, the basic mechanism to update the database is very simple: the designer may program *conversion functions* that are associated with modified classes in the schema and define how objects have to be restructured. If no conversion functions are provided by the designer, the system provides *default conversion functions*, where no user programming is required. Instead, default transformation rules are applied to objects of modified classes.

User-defined database conversion functions can be found in O_2, GemStone, ObjectStore, and OTGen; Versant and Itasca offer features that are similar to default conversion functions only. Sections 18.3.1, 18.3.2, and 18.3.3 will focus on the transformation mechanisms implemented in the O_2 object database.

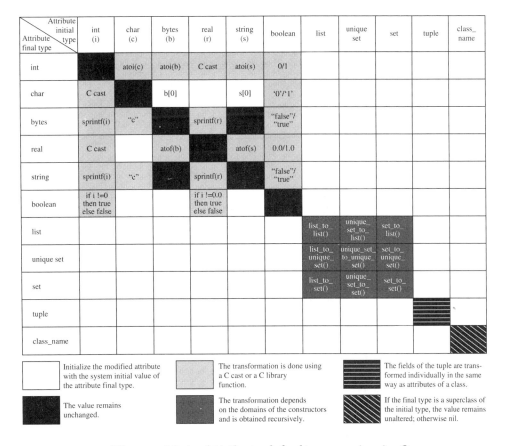

Attribute final type \ Attribute initial type	int (i)	char (c)	bytes (b)	real (r)	string (s)	boolean	list	unique set	set	tuple	class_name
int		atoi(c)	atoi(b)	C cast	atoi(s)	0/1					
char	C cast		b[0]		s[0]	'0'/'1'					
bytes	sprintf(i)	"c"		sprintf(r)		"false"/"true"					
real	C cast		atof(b)		atof(s)	0.0/1.0					
string	sprintf(i)	"c"		sprintf(r)		"false"/"true"					
boolean	if i !=0 then true else false			if i !=0.0 then true else false							
list							list_to_list()	unique_set_to_list()	set_to_list()		
unique set							list_to_unique_set()	unique_set_to_unique_set()	set_to_unique_set()		
set							list_to_set()	unique_set_to_set()	set_to_set()		
tuple											
class_name											

▢	Initialize the modified attribute with the system initial value of the attribute final type.
◼	The value remains unchanged.
▨	The transformation is done using a C cast or a C library function.
▨	The transformation depends on the domains of the constructors and is obtained recursively.
▤	The fields of the tuple are transformed individually in the same way as attributes of a class.
▨	If the final type is a superclass of the initial type, the value remains unaltered; otherwise nil.

Figure 18.4: Attribute default conversion in O_2

18.3.1 Default Database Transformations

In this section we describe what we call *default database conversion functions*. If no user-defined conversion functions are specified, the system transforms the objects in the database using default transformation rules. When a class in the schema is modified, the system compares each attribute of the class before and after the modification of the class and transforms the values of the object attributes according to the following default rules:[3]

- An attribute defined in a class before its modification and not present in the class after the modification (i.e., a deleted attribute) is ignored.
- An attribute that is not present in a class before its modification and present after its modification (i.e., a new attribute) is initialized with

---

[3]Note that, in O_2, after a class modification has been performed, two attributes are considered the same attribute if they have the same name.

default initial values (i.e., 0 for an integer attribute, nil for an attribute referring to a class, etc.).

- An attribute present in the class both before the change and after the change is transformed according to the rules in Figure 18.4.

In Figure 18.4, *attribute initial type* refers to the type of an attribute before the class modification; *attribute final type* refers to the type of the same attribute after the modification of the class. If, for instance, an attribute of a class is declared of type real (the attribute initial type), and after a schema modification its type is transformed to integer (the attribute final type), a C cast function is applied, which truncates the real value. For those attributes where an empty entry appears in Figure 18.4, the system initial value for the final type is used.

Let's redefine the schema Workers already presented in Chapter 16. We assume that two classes Vendor and Car have been defined at time t_0:

schema creation at time t_0:

```
create schema Workers;

class Vendor type tuple (name: string,
                         address: tuple(city: string,
                                        street: string,
                                        number: real),
                         sold_cars: list(Car))
end;

class Car type tuple(name: string,
                     price: real,
                     hpw: integer)
end;
```

Assume we only have one object in the database for class Vendor, with the following values: name = "Volkswagen";   address = tuple(city: "Frankfurt", street: "Goethe", number: 5.0); sold_cars = list([1]: Golf_id, [2]: Passat_id, [3]: Corrado_id); where Golf_id, Passat_id, Corrado_id are references to Car objects.

Suppose at time t_1 the class `Vendor` in the schema is modified as follows:

schema modification at time t_1:

```
modify class Vendor type tuple(name: string,
                               address: tuple(street: string,
                                              number: integer),
                               sold_cars: set(Car))
end;
```

After the change of class `Vendor`, the type of the attribute `address` is now a tuple where the tuple field `city` has been deleted, and the tuple field `number` has become an integer instead of a real. Moreover, the attribute `sold_cars` is now a `set` instead of a `list`.

Since no user-defined conversion functions have been associated with the modified class `Vendor`, a default conversion function is applied. The object of class `Vendor` in the database is then automatically converted as follows: the attribute `name` keeps the value `"Volkswagen"`, the tuple field `number` of attribute `address` is transformed from 5.0 to 5, and the attribute value of `sold_cars` becomes the `set(Golf_id, Passat_id, Corrado_id)`, that is, without order among values.

18.3.2 User-Defined Database Transformations

At any time, the schema designer can override the default database transformations by explicitly associating user-defined conversion functions with the class just after its change in the schema.

In this case, the update to a class in the schema is performed in two phases. The first phase is the update to the class (i.e., using schema update primitives). This phase is called the *class modification phase*. The second phase is when user-defined conversion function(s) are associated (i.e., defined and compiled) with the modified class(es). This second phase is called the *conversion functions definition phase*.

We show the definition of user-defined conversion functions by further modifying the schema `Workers`. Assume at time t_2 the schema designer decides to delete the attribute `hpw` in class `Car`, but to retain the information by adding the attribute `kW` in class `Car` instead. This can be done as follows:

schema modification at time t_2:

```
begin modification in class Car;
delete attribute hpw;
```

```
create attribute kW: integer;
conversion functions;
conversion function mod_kW (old: tuple(name: string,
                                       price: real,
                                       hpw: real)) in class Car
{
   self->kW = round( old.hpw / 1.36);
};
end modification;
```

Two schema update primitives for class `Car` are used after the command `begin modification in class Car`. The command `conversion function` associates the user defined conversion function mod_kW with class `Car` after the change. In the body of the conversion function, "`->`" returns the attribute value of an object. The input parameter `old` of the conversion function refers to a tuple value conforming to the type of class `Car` before the modification has been performed. The variable `self` refers to an object of class `Car` after its modification. In the conversion function, the transformation is not defined for all the attributes of class `Car` but only for the attribute kW because a default transformation is executed in any case on objects before a user-defined conversion function is executed. This simplifies the writing of use-defined conversion functions. In the example, there is no need to write trivial transformations such as

```
        self->name = old.name,
        self->price = old.price.
```

These transformations are performed by the default conversions.

The command `conversion functions` is optional. If not present, the system transforms the database using default transformations instead. The command `end modification` specifies the end of the class transformation(s). Conversion functions are logically executed at the end of a modification block. The real execution time of the conversion functions depends on the implementation strategy chosen, as described in Section 18.4.

Suppose now the attribute `sales` is added to the class `Vendor` at time t_3:

schema modification at time t_3:

```
begin modification in class Vendor;
modify class Vendor type tuple(name: string,
                               address: tuple(street: string,
```

```
                                           number: integer),
                    sold_cars: set(Car),
                    sales: real)
end;

conversion functions;
conversion function compute_sales (old: tuple (
                    name: string,
                    address: tuple (street: string,
                                    number: integer),
                    sold_cars: set(Car))) in class Vendor
{
    o2 Car c;
    for (c in old.sold_cars) {
        self->sales += c->price; }
};

end modification;
```

At time t_3 class Vendor has been modified as a whole with the primitive modify class instead of using the primitive create attribute sales in class Vendor. The user-defined conversion function associated with class Vendor stores in sales the sales turnover for the vendor.

Note the difference between the conversion function mod_kW associated with Car at time t_2 and the conversion function compute_sales associated with Vendor at time t_3. For the first one, the value of the "updated" object is computed using only values locally defined to the object. The second conversion function instead uses the value of objects belonging to another class in the schema.

Two types of user-defined conversion functions can therefore be identified:

- *Simple conversion functions*, where the object transformation is performed using only the local information of the object being accessed (the conversion function mod_kW, defined at time t_2).

- *Complex conversion functions*, where the object transformation is performed using objects of the database other than the current object being accessed (the conversion function compute_sales, defined at time t_3).

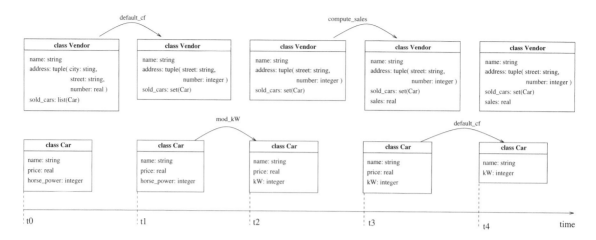

Figure 18.5: Schema evolution until time t_4

The above is an important distinction when implementing conversion functions, as we will see in Section 18.4.

Suppose now we make a final schema modification at time t_4 by deleting the attribute `price` in class `Car`:

schema modification at time t_4:

```
delete attribute price in class Car;
```

At time t_4 we did not associate any user-defined conversion function with class `Car`. The default conversion is then used for the transformation of the objects.

Figure 18.5 is a graphical representation of the schema modifications performed on the two classes. Classes connected by a solid arrow mean a modification has been performed on them; the label on the arrow indicates the presence of default or user-defined conversion functions.

The designer in O_2 has the ability to specify the execution time for conversion functions. In particular, O_2 offers a command to execute conversion functions immediately:

```
transform database;
```

After the database transformation is completed, all objects in the database conform to the last schema definition. The default implementation modality for the execution of conversion functions is the deferred approach, as described in Section 18.4.3.

18.3.3 User-Defined Object Migration Functions

So far, we have seen how objects of a class are updated as a consequence of a class modification using conversion functions. It is also possible in O_2 to update objects by migrating them to other classes in the schema. This is addressed in this section. *Object migration* refers to the possibility for an individual object to change its class during its lifetime. O_2 offers two ways to migrate objects:

- a single object can change its class

- an entire class extension (or a part of it) can be migrated to another class

We start by looking at the first possibility, and then we consider class extensions.

We can define a system method `migrate()` associated with the root class `Object` that, when invoked for a particular object, allows the object to migrate from its class to any of its subclasses (if any). In the method `migrate()`, the name of the target subclass must be given as an input parameter. Migrations of objects are allowed to subclasses only, to avoid the possibility of run-time type errors if objects were allowed to migrate freely to any class in the schema.

Notwithstanding this limitation, this feature is particularly useful when (1) a new class is added to the schema and the existing objects of the class's superclasses need to be moved down to the new class, and (2) a class is deleted and objects of that class must be retained by migrating them to subclasses.

The other possibility is to migrate an entire class extension (or a part of it) to other subclasses with a *migration function*. The use of migration functions can be explained using our example. Suppose at time t_5 the designer creates a new class `Sports_car` in the `Car_showroom` schema. After the creation of the class, he wants to migrate powerful cars (i.e., those cars with `kW` $\geq$ `100`) from class `Car` to class `Sports_car`. This can be achieved as follows:

schema modification at time t_5:

```
class Sports_car inherit Car
                type tuple(speed: integer)
end;
```

```
migration function migrate_cars in class Car
{
   if (self->kW >= 100)
      self->migrate("Sports_car");
};
```

The migration function `migrate_cars` is associated with class `Car`. In the body of the migration function, the system method `migrate` is called to migrate each object satisfying the selection condition to the subclass `Sports_car`.

The example shows the importance of having object migration when new classes are added to the schema. Let's consider the case of the deletion of a class. Suppose the designer wants to delete class `Car`, but retain some of the objects in the database by moving them to another class. By creating class `Sports_car` and migrating `Car` objects to it, if the designer deleted class `Car` from the schema, he would lose only part of the objects, namely, the ones whose attribute `kW` is lower than 100. Without migration, there would be no chance to retain any object of class `Car`.

As in the case of conversion functions, migration functions can be executed either with an immediate or a deferred modality. By default, O_2 uses a deferred approach for the migration of objects. It is, however, possible to migrate objects immediately by explicitly calling the `transform database schema` command.

18.4   Implementing Database Updates in O_2

In this section we look in detail at how we can implement database updates as a consequence of schema changes. We will describe the implementation done for the O_2 object database. O_2 supports both the immediate and the deferred database transformation previously defined. However, the basic principle followed in the implementation of database updates in O_2 is the following: whatever transformation strategy is chosen for implementing a database transformation, there should be no difference for the schema designer as far as the result of the execution of the conversion functions is concerned. From this principle the notion of the *correctness* of a deferred database transformation can be derived. A correct implementation of a deferred database transformation satisfies the following criteria: The result of a database transformation implemented with a deferred modality is the same as if the transformation were implemented with an immediate modality.

18.4.1 Problems with Deferred Database Transformations

In Section 18.3.2 we made the distinction between simple and complex conversion functions because implementing complex conversion functions for a deferred database transformation requires special care.

To explain the problems that can arise with the deferred database transformation, consider in our usual example two objects, v of class Vendor and c of class Car, conforming to the respective class definitions at time t_2. Object v refers to c through the attribute sold_cars. If object c were accessed by an application at time t_a, with $t_4 < t_a$, the system would transform the object to conform to its last class definition, deleting the attribute price from it. If, at time t_b, with $t_a < t_b$, object v is accessed, v will be restructured as well, and its new value will be computed by applying the conversion function compute_sales.

The problem is that compute_sales accesses object c through the attribute price. But c now no longer has all the information required for the transformation of v because it has lost the attribute price when it was transformed at time t_a. In this special case, the execution of compute_sales would result in a run-time type error. In general, using default values, as described in Section 18.3.1, for the restructured object v does not solve the problem, as it could result in an incorrect database transformation.

Let's consider again the database at time t_2, and assume the immediate database transformation had been used to transform objects v and c. If at time t_3 the system had transformed the object v immediately by executing the conversion function compute_sales, no run-time type error would have occurred because at time t_3 the object c accessed by the conversion function would have had the attribute price. The deletion of price at time t_4 would therefore not affect the execution of previously defined conversion functions. This is the correct transformation of the database.

In Section 18.4.2 we will present in detail the data structures and in Section 18.4.3 the algorithm used in O_2 for implementing simple and complex conversion functions using deferred database updates, which guarantees a correct database transformation. The basic idea is to physically retain the deleted or the modified information in the object in a *screened part*. This implementation strategy is commonly known as *screening*. Applications running against the database do not have access to the screened information, but conversion functions do have access to the screened information in order to perform a correct database transformation.

When some information is deleted and/or modified in the schema, it is only screened out, but not physically deleted in the database. When, for instance, a deletion of an attribute (or a change in the type, which would correspond to a deletion and an addition of the same attribute) is performed, the update is not physically executed on the object structure, but simply a different representation of the object is presented to applications. Using screening, O_2 manages the different representations of an object, one representation visible to applications and one representation visible to conversion functions only.

18.4.2 Data Structures

The physical format of an object (i.e., as it is internally stored in the database) contains two parts: the *object header* and the *object value*, the value itself being composed of an *existing value* and a *screened value* (see Figure 18.6).

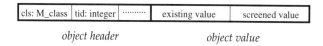

object header   *object value*

Figure 18.6: Structure of an O_2 object

The object value part is used for storing values that reside within the object, such as attribute values. The object header contains, among other information, the identifier of the object's class descriptor (`cls`) and the type entry identifier (`tid`), according to which format the object itself is stored. Both of these two can be viewed as somewhat special fields in the physical format of the object.

The main principle in the implementation of deferred updates is to keep track of the evolution of the schema. The O_2 schema manager manages a persistent symbol table containing schema components, such as class definitions, type definitions, and so on.

A simple integer variable, called the *schema state*, is associated with each schema. The schema state is incremented every time a class in the schema undergoes a change.

All components of a schema are internally maintained as metaobjects. Each class in the schema is internally represented by a class descriptor, which can be considered as an instance of the O_2 class `Meta_class`:

```
class Meta_class type tuple (
   :
   :
   sch      : integer,            /* schema-id */
   name     : string,             /* name of the class */
```

```
  visib      : char,                 /* access mode */
  type       : Meta_type,            /* type of the class */
  properties: list(Meta_property), /* attributes and methods */
  parents    : list(Meta_class),     /* direct superclasses */
  children   : list(Meta_class),     /* all subclasses */
  ancestors : list(Meta_class),      /* all superclasses */
  ispartof   : list(Meta_class),     /* classes with a component
                                          of this class */

  :          :
  cur_tid    : integer,                    /* current tid */
  history    : list(Meta_history_entry), /* type history */
  :
  : )
end;
```

The class `Meta_class` contains all the information related to a class (i.e., its name, its type, its visibility (private vs. public), the list of its parent classes, etc.). In particular, to implement a deferred database transformation, each class descriptor contains a field `cur_tid`, which is used for testing whether an object in the database conforms to the last class definition in the schema or not. Other important information in the class descriptor is stored in the field `history`, the list of history entry descriptors containing the information of the class as it was defined in the past.

A history entry descriptor can be considered as an instance of the class `Meta_history_entry`:

```
class Meta_history_entry type tuple (
  tid   : integer,
  type  : Meta_type,
  ex_type: Meta_type,
  struct : list(Meta_property_entry),
  cf    : Meta_conversion,
  mf    : Meta_migration )
end;

class Meta_property_entry type tuple (
  pid       : integer,
  sch_state: integer,
  offset    : integer,
  type      : Meta_type,
  status    : {existing, screened} )
end;

class Meta_conversion type tuple (
```

```
  next_state: integer,
  function   : Meta_binary )
end;

class Meta_migration type tuple (
  sch_state: integer,
  function : Meta_binary )
end;
```

A history entry descriptor contains the following fields:

- The type entry identifier `tid`, a simple integer number, which helps in identifying to which entry an object of the class belongs to. When a class undergoes a change, the schema state is assigned to the `tid`.

- The type `type`, which corresponds to the type of the class visible by applications.

- The type `ex_type`, which corresponds to the extended type of the class including the screened information.

- The entry `struct`, which contains a list of property entry descriptors.

- A field `cf`, which contains a reference to a conversion function descriptor that is used to convert objects to conform to a subsequent entry in the history.

- A field `mf`, which contains a reference to a migration function descriptor that is used to migrate objects to conform to the appropriate entry in the history of a subclass.[4]

A property entry descriptor belonging to the `struct` list of a history entry descriptor can be considered as an instance of the class `Meta_property_entry`. It contains the following information:

- The `pid` of the attribute, which is used so that the external name of a property can be changed without affecting the identity of a property.

- The `sch_state`, that is, the state of the schema when the attribute has been created. The information (`pid`, `sch_state`) identifies an attribute in a nonambiguous way.

- The `offset` of the attribute, that is, the physical position of the attribute in the object itself.

---

[4]In Section 18.4.3 we describe how O_2 infers the history entry in the target class when executing a migration function.

- The `type` of the attribute.

- The `status` of an attribute, indicating whether the given attribute can be accessed by both application and conversion functions (in this case the value is set to `existing`), or by conversion functions only (in this case the value is set to `screened`).

The last two components of a history entry descriptor, `cf` and `mf`, are the descriptors of a conversion and a migration function, which can be considered as instances of the classes `Meta_conversion` and `Meta_migration`. In a conversion function descriptor, the field `next_state` indicates to which entry in the class history the conversion function, stored as a binary file in the field `function`, is supposed to transform objects. The same applies for a migration function descriptor. The `sch_state` field indicates the state of the schema when the migration function has been associated with the class. The `sch_state` information is used by the system to determine to which history entry of a subclass an object has to be migrated.

Recall the example taken from the `Car_showroom` schema. Figure 18.7 illustrates the class descriptor of `Car` after the migration function `migrate_cars` has been defined at time t_5.

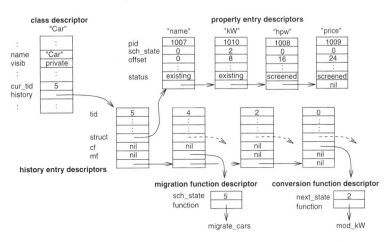

Figure 18.7: Descriptor of class `Car` along with its history

The field `cur_tid` of the class is equal to 5 and corresponds to the schema state just after the migration function `migrate_cars` has been associated with the class. The field `history` points to a list of four history entry descriptors; the one with `tid = 0` identifies the original class information when it has been created at time t_0. The following history entry descriptors identify the information of the class after each class modification or after the association of a migration function with the class. For reasons of readability, we show only the `struct` information related to the first history entry descriptor, whose `tid` = 5. The field `struct` points to the list of property entry descriptors belonging to the class. The first two property entry descriptors refer to attributes in the class that are visible by applications. This can be recognized by the value `existing` in the `status` field. The last two property entry descriptors refer to screened attributes visible by conversion functions only. It is important to note that screened attributes are always physically stored after visible attributes; that is, their offset in the chunk of memory representing an object is always greater than the one of a visible attribute.

The conversion function descriptor for `mod_kW` and the migration function descriptor for `migrate_cars` are associated with the appropriate history entry descriptors.

18.4.3   The Deferred Database Update Algorithm

Before we present the algorithm implemented in O_2 for deferred database updates, we need to introduce some definitions.

The most recent entry in a class history is called the *current history entry*. An entry in a class history is called *input relevant* if this entry holds a conversion or a migration function. The current history entry is defined as input relevant as well. From now on, the class descriptor of a class X is referred to as X_desc.

When a new class X is created, the schema manager of O_2 instantiates a class descriptor with the appropriate information (i.e., the name of the class, the list of parent and ancestor classes in the hierarchy, etc.). In particular, the field `cur_tid` is initialized with the schema state associated with the schema, and a first entry is created in the history of the class.

After a modification is performed on a class X, the schema state is incremented, and a new entry in the class history is created for the modified class X and for all of its subclasses that have effectively undergone a modification. The newly created entry becomes the current history entry, and its `tid` is initialized with the schema state. For those subclasses where no modification has taken place (e.g., because an attribute has been added to X that is already present in its subclasses), no new entry in the class history is created. If a conversion function is associated with the class modification, the schema manager instantiates and initializes a conversion function descriptor and assigns it to the `cf` field of the history entry descriptor that chronologically precedes the current history entry. The `function` field of the conversion function descriptor contains a pointer to the binary code of the conversion function. The field `next_state` contains the `tid` of the current history entry.

The same happens for a migration function. When a migration function is associated with a class X, the schema state is incremented, and a new entry in the history of X is created. The newly created entry becomes the current history entry, and its `tid` is initialized with the schema state. The schema manager instantiates and initializes a migration function descriptor that is then assigned to the `mf` field of the history entry descriptor that chronologically precedes the current history entry. The `function` field of the migration function descriptor contains a pointer to the binary code of the migration function. The field `sch_state` contains the `tid` of the current history entry.

Basic Deferred Update Algorithm

The algorithm used by O_2 when an object o of class X is accessed by an application is the deferred update algorithm:

```
while (o->tid <> o->cls->tid) do    /* o is not in current format */
  for (X_his_desc in o->cls->history where X_his_desc->tid == o->tid)
    {
      break;    /* find the history entry descriptor to which o
                   conforms */
    }
  if (X_his_desc->mf <> nil) then
    /* a migration function has to be applied */

    apply the migration function X_his_desc->mf->function;
    if (object o has not been migrated) then
      modify the tid of the object to correspond to the tid
      belonging to the chronologically following entry;
    endif;
  else
    /* a default or user-defined conversion function
       has to be applied */

    copy the value of o in a variable old; /* old is used by the cf's */
    if (X_his_desc->cf <> nil) then
      /* a user-defined cf has to be applied */
```

```
            restructure o to conform to the entry in the history whose tid
            corresponds to X_his_desc->cf.next_state;
            apply the default conversion function;
            apply the conversion function X_his_desc->cf->function;
            o->tid = X_his_desc->cf.next_state;
        else
            /* a default conversion function has to be applied */
            restructure o to conform to the next input relevant entry in
            the class history;
            /* entry with a migration or user-defined conversion function */

            apply the default conversion function;
            update the tid to correspond to the one found in the
            next input relevant entry;
        endif;
    endif;
endwhile;
```

The algorithm first checks whether an object conforms to its last class definition in the schema. If yes, the object can be used by the application that accessed it without being first transformed. If not, O_2 identifies the appropriate history entry descriptor in the history of class X to which object o conforms. Three alternatives are then possible:

1. The history entry descriptor contains a migration function that implies a possible migration of o to a subclass of X.

2. The history entry descriptor contains a conversion function that implies that o must be restructured to conform to a more recent entry in the history of class X.

3. The history entry contains neither a conversion nor a migration function; object o must be restructured and reinitialized using a default conversion function to conform to the next input relevant entry in the history.

Note that, because of how class descriptors are maintained by O_2, no entry will ever contain both a conversion and a migration function.

Implementing Complex Conversion Functions

The deferred update algorithm presented before works fine if only simple conversion functions have been defined when evolving the schema. In the case of complex conversion functions, instead, the transformation of objects accessed by complex conversion functions must be stopped before reaching the state corresponding to the current history entry to avoid database inconsistencies or run-time type errors.

Suppose that a complex conversion function `cf` associated with a history entry with `tid` $= i$ of a class X transforms objects of that class to conform to a history entry with `tid` $= j$, where $j > i$. If other objects are accessed by `cf`, their transformation should not be propagated up to the current history entry, but it must be stopped at a history entry that is the one visible by the conversion function `cf` at the time it was defined. The concept of visibility is modeled by the `tid` attached to each entry in the history of a class.

The nth history entry of a class Y in the schema is visible by `cf` if

$$\texttt{Y\_desc->history[n]->tid} \leq j$$

and the chronologically subsequent entry (if any)

$$\texttt{Y\_desc->history[n-1]->tid} > j$$

where `history[n]` indicates the nth history entry descriptor in the history list of a class and `history[n-1]` indicates the entry that chronologically follows `history[n]`.[5]

In order to stop the transformation of objects to the visible history entry, O_2 maintains a stack associated with each application. Before the execution of an application or of a conversion function, the system pushes in the stack the appropriate entry number signaling up to which entry in the history an object has to be transformed (the actual schema state for the application, or a smaller number for a conversion function). This number is removed from the stack after the execution of a conversion function or the execution of an application.

Reconsider the example in Section 18.3.2 where the complex conversion function `compute_sales` accesses objects of class Car to perform the computation of the vendor's turnover. Since the conversion function `compute_sales` is supposed to transform objects of class Vendor to conform to the history entry with `tid` $= 3$,[6] the schema manager of O_2 pushes the value 3 on the

---

[5]It might happen that objects accessed by a `cf` have a `tid` $\geq j$. In this case no transformation is triggered on them because they are already containing the information needed by `cf`.

[6]After the modification of class Vendor at time t_3, the schema state is equal to 3.

stack. When an object c of class Car is accessed by the conversion function, c is transformed to conform to the history entry visible by compute_sales (i.e., the one with tid $= 2$).

Implementing Object Migration

We now look at how to implement object migration. If an object o conforming to the history entry descriptor of class X with tid $= i$ has to migrate to a target class Y because of the presence of a migration function descriptor, the deferred update algorithm executes the migration function stored in the mf field of the history entry descriptor. When migrating an object, the schema manager of O_2 must decide to which history entry of the target class Y a migrated object has to conform. This is not necessarily the current history entry of Y because between the definition of the migration function and its execution, class Y might have been changed. The schema manager of O_2 identifies the history entry of the target class Y as the one whose tid j is the greatest satisfying the condition $j \leq s$, where s is the value stored in the field sch_state of the migration function descriptor (i.e., the state of the schema at the time the migration function has been defined).

As shown in Section 18.3.3, the real migration of an object is performed by the execution of the system's method migrate, which is called within a migration function.

The method migrate, when executed on an object o that has to migrate from class X to class Y, is responsible for the following:

- Copy the value of o in a variable old.

- Find the appropriate target history entry where o has to be migrated.

- Restructure o to conform to the target history entry of class Y.

- Perform the default transformation on o using the information present in old.

- Update the class identifier cls in the header of o to be the one of the target class.

- Update the type identifier tid in the header of o to be the one of the target history entry of class Y.

Implementing Class Deletions

So far, we have discussed how to transform objects in the database when a class in the schema has been modified. Another important issue is how O_2 implements a class deletion.

Basically, when using the deferred database transformation, there is no way to control when objects are accessed by applications, that is, when conversion functions are effectively executed. In particular, the execution of a complex conversion function might require the information of objects whose class has been deleted in the schema. Further, since migration of objects is implemented using a deferred modality as well, objects of a deleted class can be migrated to subclasses of the deleted class.

To accomplish a deferred database transformation when classes are deleted in the schema, the deletion of a class is not physically performed, but classes are only screened out from being used by applications. Only conversion and migration functions are allowed to access the information of screened classes. If class `Car` were deleted from the schema `Car_showroom`,[7] the schema manager of O_2 would only set the field `visib` of the class descriptor to `deleted`. This would imply that conversion functions accessing objects of class `Car` can still read the information needed for the transformation.

Optimization Issues

There is no need to screen all deleted classes but only those ones whose objects might be accessed by complex conversion functions or by migration functions. Therefore, O_2 internally maintains a *dependency graph* associated with each schema, which allows the schema manager to understand when deleted classes have to be screened. The dependency graph is defined as follows:

Definition 18.1: *The dependency graph G is a tuple (V, E), extended by a labeling function $l : (V \times V) \to A$. V is a set of class vertices, one for each class in the schema. E is a set of directed edges (v, w) $v, w \in V$. A is a set of attribute names and the special value "mf", which identifies a migration function. An edge (v, w) indicates that there exists at least one complex conversion function associated with class w that uses the value of objects of class v or that a migration function is associated with class v that migrates objects to class w. The function $l(v,w)$ returns the names of the attributes of class v used by conversion functions associated with class w and/or "mf" if objects have to be migrated to class w.*

Evolution of the schema implies changing the dependency graph associated with the schema. By looking at the dependency graph, it is possible to

---

[7]Note that in the current version of O_2 only leaf classes can be deleted. To delete class `Car` would therefore imply first removing the link with its subclass `Sports_car`.

identify when classes have to be screened because of a definition of a complex conversion function or a migration function.

The use of the graph is shown with our usual example, the `Car_showroom` schema. In Figure 18.8 the evolution of the dependency graph for the schema `Car_showroom` from time t_0 till time t_5 is illustrated. The conversion function defined at time t_1 uses only local defined attributes; therefore, no edge appears in the graph. At time t_3, the edge is added to the graph because of the definition of the complex conversion function `compute_sales`. At time t_5, a new edge is added to the dependency graph because of the definition of the migration function `migrate_cars`.

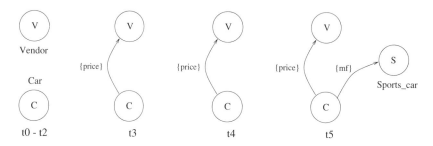

Figure 18.8: Evolution of the dependency graph of schema `Car_showroom`

The dependency graph has to be checked by the system in the following cases: (1) a class is modified along with a complex conversion function, (2) a class is deleted from the schema, (3) a migration function is associated with a class. If, for instance, class `Vendor` is deleted from the schema, the schema manager of O_2 recognizes that there is no outgoing arrow for class `Vendor` in the dependency graph and therefore the class can be really removed along with its extension.

If no space optimization is taken into account when using screening (i.e., if the information is never deleted in the objects), the size of the database risks growing continuously.

The schema manager of O_2 optimizes space by physically deleting the information in those objects that will never be accessed by any complex conversion function. This can be easily obtained by checking the dependency graph. Objects of classes that do not have any outgoing arrow in the dependency graph should not contain screened attributes because no conversion function will ever use them. Objects of classes that have an outgoing arrow in the dependency graph contain only screened attributes whose name appears to be returned by the labeling function associated with the arrow. Moreover, every time the immediate database transformation is launched,

O_2 transforms all the objects to conform to the last schema definition. After the transformation, the system deletes the edges in the dependency graph, and therefore the screened part can be dropped from all the objects in the database. As a consequence of the immediate database transformation, all histories of the class descriptors are updated to contain only one history entry, namely, the current history entry with the information of the class as visible by applications.

Implementing Immediate Database Updates

In O_2, the immediate database transformation is implemented using the algorithm defined for the deferred database transformation. When the designer specifies the schema command `transform database`, the schema manager of O_2 launches an internal tool that is responsible for accessing all objects in the database that are not up-to-date. When accessed, objects are transformed according to the algorithm defined for the deferred database transformation.

The tool follows basically two strategies for accessing objects that are not up-to-date. If class extensions are maintained by the system,[8] extensions of updated classes have to be iterated to access all objects of that class. If extensions are not maintained by the system, the tool accesses objects in the database starting from appropriate roots of persistence and following the composition links between objects.

As already mentioned, after an immediate database transformation, the dependency graph is updated. Further, the history of all classes is deleted, and the deleted part of screened objects is dropped.

18.5   Related Work

Not all available object database systems provide the feature of adapting the database after a schema modification has been performed. For those that do it, they differ from each other in the approach followed for updating objects. Some commercial systems support the possibility of defining object versions to evolve the database from one version to another; examples are Objectivity and GemStone. Objectivity does not provide any tool to automatically update the database, besides providing object versions. The designer has to write a program that reads the value `old_val` of objects of the old version, computes the new value `new_val`, and assigns it to the corresponding ob-

---

[8]Note that O_2 does not automatically maintain extensions associated with classes. It is the responsibility of the designer to inform the system if extensions are to be kept or not.

jects of the new version. The program can be written in order to transform the database both immediately and lazily. GemStone, on the other hand, provides a flexible way for updating object instances. It provides default transformation of objects and the possibility of adding conversion methods to a class. Conversion methods can update objects either in groups (for instance, the whole extension of a class) or individually. The transformation of the database is performed in a deferred mode but manually; that is, objects are transformed on demand only when applications call the transformation methods. The problems pointed out in this chapter do not occur when versioning is used because objects are never transformed, but a new version is created instead. Therefore the information for the transformation of an object can always be found in its corresponding old version.

The majority of the existing commercially available systems, however, do not use versioning for updating the database. Applications can run on top of the schema as defined after the last modification. Instances are converted either immediately or lazily. ObjectStore makes use of the immediate database transformation. Transformation functions, which override the default transformation, can be associated with each modified class. Objects are not physically restructured, but a new object (conforming to the definition of the modified class) is created instead. The transformation function reads the value in the old object and assigns it (after having made some modification on it) to the new object. All references to the object have to be updated in order to point to the newly created object. This technique resembles the one used by those systems providing versions; the only difference is that, after the transformation, the old objects are discarded. Deferred transformation of objects is provided in systems like Itasca and Versant. They both do not provide the user with flexible conversion functions like the one presented in this chapter. Instead, they have the possibility of overriding a default transformation assigning new constant values to modified or added attributes of a class.

Among research prototype systems, Avance, CLOSQL, and Encore all use object versioning. ORION uses a deferred approach where deletion of attributes is filtered. Information is not physically deleted, but it is no longer usable by applications. No conversion functions are provided to the schema designer.

18.6 Bibliographic Notes

Problems arising with the deferred database transformation have been discussed in [32, 166, 163, 417]. A formal approach covering database updates is illustrated in [162]. Three algorithms for performing deferred database transformations have been presented in [163], whereby the screening approach has also been treated in [32]. The concrete implementation in the O_2 object database is presented in [165].

18.7 Exercises

18.1. Given the schema defined in Figure 17.1, create a small base conforming to the schema. Apply some structural consistency preserving primitives to the schema Workers.

18.2. Given the schema defined in Figure 17.1, identify which of the following structural consistency modifying primitives do actually imply a database transformation:

    a. Create attribute pr_addr in class Worker.

    b. Create attribute optionals in class Car.

    c. Delete attribute car in class Manager.

18.3. Given the schema defined in Figure 17.1 and an associated base, consider the following schema modifications:

    a. Modify attribute price: integer in class Car.

    b. Modify attribute salary: string in class Worker.

    c. Delete attribute car in class Manager.

Transform the database according to the default transformation rules.

18.4. Given the schema defined in Figure 17.1 and an associated base:

    a. Create a class Address with attributes city, street, and number in a modification block.

    b. In the same modification block, modify the attribute address of class Vendor to refer to the new created Address.

    c. Write a conversion function that transforms the data of the modified class Vendor.

Chapter 19

How to Change the Database Fast: A Performance Evaluation

In this chapter, we present a performance evaluation study for the two techniques to change the database shown in Chapter 18: immediate and deferred database transformations. The study attempts to identify those parameters that most influence the performance of the system when the database needs to be changed as a consequence of a set of schema modifications. This chapter is structured as follows: Section 19.1 describes the relevant factors that influence a database transformation. Section 19.2 illustrates how to benchmark database updates. Sections 19.3 and 19.4 report the results of the benchmark and conclude with some final considerations.

19.1   Factors Influencing the Performance of a Database Transformation

Before going into details on the benchmark organization, let's understand from a qualitative point of view what the main factors are that affect a database reorganization as a consequence of a schema modification.

Consider, for instance, the simple database in Figure 19.1, consisting of 12 objects stored in four pages. Let's assume, for the moment, that the client cache is not big enough to contain all four database pages.

At time t_1 we assume a schema modification occurred that implies that some objects in the database do no longer conform to the new modified

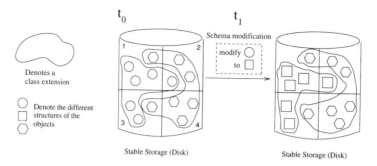

Figure 19.1: Immediate transformation of 12 objects in four pages: with class extensions, only the three pages containing objects that are outdated (i.e., pages 1, 2, and 3) have to be fetched from the disk

schema. In general, the time cost for performing a database transformation is mainly determined by the page fetch/flush operations from/into the disk.

19.1.1   Immediate Database Transformation

Suppose we use an immediate database transformation. If class extensions are maintained by the schema manager, only those pages containing class extensions affected by the schema change need to be fetched/flushed. In the worst case, when class extensions are not supported by the database,[1] all pages of the database need to be fetched from the disk, but only those containing objects that have been modified need to be flushed back into the disk.

19.1.2   Deferred Transformation

Alternatively, if the deferred database transformation is used, then the cost for the transformation itself strongly depends on the object access rate performed by the application programs.

Figure 19.2 illustrates the same database where the client cache holds one slot only. We assume the slot contains exactly one page of the disk.

Suppose, as in the previous example, that at time t_1 the same schema modification occurred that makes part of the database objects no longer conform to the new schema. Since we use a deferred strategy, the system does not need to change the database at this time. If, at a later time t_2, an object

---

[1]In the O_2 object database, extensions are not automatically maintained by the system, but the schema designer has the possibility of maintaining explicit class extensions as collections.

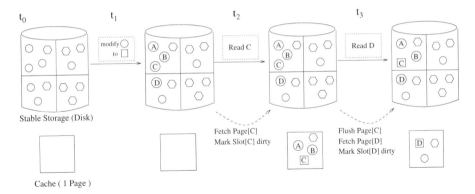

Figure 19.2: Deferred transformation of 12 objects in four pages

in the database, say C, is read by an application, then the page containing C needs to be fetched from the disk into the cache. After the transformation of object C, one possible strategy followed by the cache manager is to mark the slot containing the page as "dirty."[2] The page in the slot is flushed back to the disk only if a dirty slot in the cache is needed for a new page. In the worst case, the number of page I/O operations may equal the number of object accesses.

19.1.3 Hybrid

Another third possible implementation strategy for transforming the database is the hybrid approach, which behaves exactly as the deferred approach except that it transforms all the objects on a page when any of them are accessed. This would avoid the I/O overhead of possibly writing out a page more than once. Figure 19.3 shows the results of the database transformation if the hybrid approach is used.

The difference between the database transformations illustrated in Figures 19.2 and 19.3 can be seen after time t_2, when the page containing C is fetched from the disk. With the hybrid approach, all objects in the page are updated when object C is accessed.

Systems like ObjectStore use exclusively the immediate database transformation; other systems like Itasca, Versant, and OTGen make use of the deferred transformation. In the new release of the O_2 object database, both transformation possibilities are provided.

---

[2]Other strategies are possible, depending on the recovery policy supported by the system.

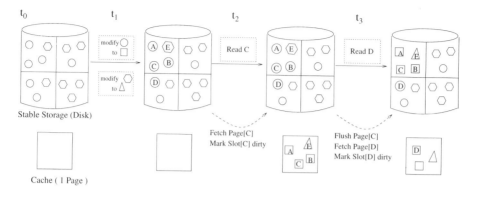

Figure 19.3: Hybrid transformation of 12 objects in four pages

19.2   How to Benchmark Database Updates

In this section, we describe the rationale used for measuring the performance of the system when database updates are executed as a consequence of changes to the schema.

In general, to measure the performance of a system, we need to identify the key parameters to be measured and how to organize the benchmark on these parameters. Then, we have to run experiments on a sample database and look at the experimental results. We need finally to interpret the results so that we can give some heuristics or guideline that should help the database designer to choose a database update strategy.

To benchmark database updates, we have adapted a general benchmark for object databases known as OO1. OO1 is a general benchmark used for measuring the performance of engineering applications. Since it is difficult or even impossible to design an application whose performance would be representative of many different applications, OO1 measures the operations that are expected to be frequent in engineering applications, such as inserting objects, looking up objects, and traversing connections between objects.

More complete and complex benchmarks for object databases have been defined, such as OO7 or the HyperModel. For our purposes, the OO1 has proved a good basis for defining our specific benchmark. The findings of the study are summarized in Section 19.3.

19.2.1   Basic Benchmark Organization

For our benchmark we used an ad hoc schema object storage system developed at the University of Frankfurt called OSLOT (Object Storage with

Lazy Object Transformations). OSLOT is developed on top of EOS using Tcl/Tk and [incr Tcl].[3] The schema modification primitives supported by OSLOT resemble the one provided by O_2. After a schema modification, OSLOT can perform both the immediate and the deferred database transformations. The schema manager of OSLOT supports the definition of user-defined database conversion functions that override automatically generated default conversion functions.

We have run experiments with both small and large databases using an adapted version of the OO1 benchmark. We used the OO1 lookup query to randomly access objects in the database. In addition, we slightly modified the OO1 lookup query to make sure to access more than one object in a page. We call this a cluster query. We run the cluster query for the specific case where half of the objects in a page are transformed, as opposed to only one. The cluster query is therefore useful to infer the results of the hybrid database transformation approach, that is, when all (and not only half) of the objects affected by a schema change in a page are transformed. We did not use the traversal query of the OO1 benchmark mainly because we wanted to keep control of the number objects accessed on a page and, as a consequence, of the number of pages fetched from the disk.

We instantiated the OO1 benchmark for a small and a large database. The small database holds 20,000 objects of class `Part` in approximately 4 MB. This a good representative of an engineering database working set that fits entirely in main memory. The large database holds 200,000 objects of the same class `Part` in approximately 40 MB.

The class `Part` is defined as follows:[4]

```
class Part type tuple( id    : integer;
                       type  : string;
                       x,y   : integer;
                       build : date;
                       to    : list(tuple(p      : Part;
                                          type   : string;
                                          length : integer));
                       from  : list(Part))
   end;
```

As defined in the OO1 benchmark, an object of class `Part` contains a unique `id` and exactly three connections to other randomly selected parts.

---

[3]EOS has been currently replaced by BeSS (Bell Labs Storage System).
[4]The syntax used for the definition of class `Part` is O_2C.

These connections are stored by the two lists `to` and `from`; the `from` list allows a reverse traversal. The other field values are selected randomly from a given range (e.g., `x`, `y`, `length`: [0..99999], `build`: 10-year range).

In Figure 19.4, five objects of class `Part` are presented with their connections. One of the objects is illustrated in detail.

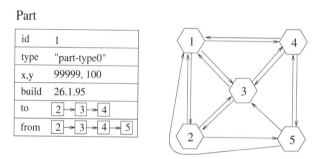

Figure 19.4: Objects in the OO1 benchmark

The following operations characterize the lookup query, which resembles the one defined in the OO1 benchmark:

Lookup: Read 1,000 randomly selected objects.

- Generate 1,000 random part object identifiers (ids).
- For each of these ids,
  - read the corresponding part object from the database
  - call a null procedure passing `x`, `y` positions and the type of the part

The following operations characterize the cluster query, which implements a special lookup where it is guaranteed to access at least half of the objects in the page itself:

Cluster: Read 1,000 "clustered" objects.

- Generate 100 random page ids.
- For each of these page ids,
  - fetch the corresponding page from the disk
  - read the first or last 10 part objects on this page (one page containing 19 objects)
  - call a null procedure passing `x`, `y` positions and the type of the part

To give a rough idea of the difference between the two kind of queries, note that when running the lookup query against a large database, almost every object access caused a page fault (about 880 for each lookup query). With the cluster query, it is guaranteed to have at most 100 page faults (about 90 pages for each cluster query).

For the benchmark, we used the following configuration: a Sun Sparc 10 (86 Mips) with 32 MB of main memory; a Seagate ST11200N disk, 1 GB, 10.5 ms avg. seek time; running SunOS 4.1.3. In contrast to what was specified in the OO1 benchmark, the server and the client run on the same machine. During the tests, the machine has been exclusively reserved for benchmarking. The caches of the server and the client have been set to 5 MB (1,250 pages, 4 KB each).

19.2.2   How to Run the Benchmark

To consider the effects of schema modifications, we first run the queries without any schema modification. The same queries have been started after 1, 2, and 5 modifications on the schema. The benchmarking steps were always executed in the following order:

1. Clear the operating system cache (e.g., read a large file).

2. Open the database (includes reading of schema and system information).

3. Execute 10 queries (to avoid cold-start effects).

4. Perform 0, 1, 2, or 5 schema modifications to the class **Part**. Objects are transformed after each schema modification in the immediate transformation only. In the deferred transformation, objects are accessed after the last schema modification (see next step).

5. Execute 60 more queries. This is relevant for the deferred transformation only to access objects in the database.

For the immediate database transformation, only the first four steps are relevant, since all objects affected by a single schema modification are transformed immediately after the schema modification itself in step 4. Since in the deferred database transformation objects need to be accessed after the schema modification(s), this is obtained in step 5 by means of 60 queries.

Performance has been measured with respect to the following parameters: response time,[5] number of objects transformed, number of pages fetched from the server, and number of pages flushed to the server.

19.3 Performance Evaluation

In this section, we report and interpret the results of the benchmark for small and large databases. General considerations and guidelines for the database designer are presented in Section 19.4.

19.3.1 Small Databases

In our experiments, the immediate database transformation locks the database for the time needed to perform the transformation itself. After each schema modification, the database is brought to a state consistent with the modified schema. In the deferred transformation, the database is not locked, and objects are accessed by lookup and cluster queries after the last schema modification. To better understand the results presented later in this section in Table 19.1, consider Figure 19.5, showing both the response time associated with each lookup query in the presence of 0, 1, 2, and 5 schema modifications and the number of object transformations per query.

In Figure 19.5(a), the curve describing the lookup response time without schema modifications, the cold and warm effects are clearly illustrated. After 10 lookup queries the response time keeps constant. We omitted the cold-start effect for the curves describing the response time with one or more schema modifications. The downward trend of these curves stems from the fact that at the beginning almost all accessed objects do not conform to the new schema definition and must therefore undergo a transformation. In subsequent queries, part of the objects accessed have already been transformed with preceding queries (see Figure 19.5(b)).

Table 19.1 illustrates the results for a small database while running the lookup query. N denotes the number of schema modifications performed by the designer. Time T indicates the time needed to transform all the objects with an immediate database transformation; ΔT indicates the time needed by the 60 queries for performing a deferred database transformation. ΔT is

---

[5]The response time is the real time elapsed from the point where a program calls the database system with a particular query, until the results of the query, if any, have been placed into the program's variables.

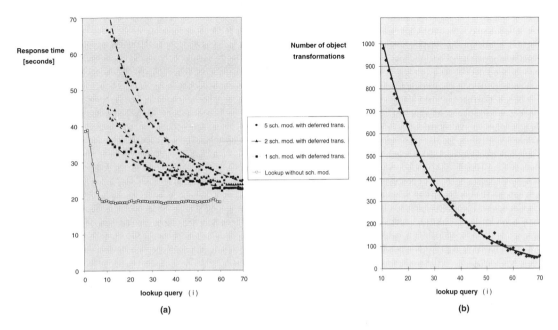

Figure 19.5: Response time and number of objects transformed for the lookup query in small databases

computed as follows:

$$\Delta T = \sum_{i=11}^{70} \Delta t_i \qquad (19.1)$$

where Δt_i is obtained by subtracting the average response time $\bar{t}_{Lookup}$ of one lookup query without any schema modification (in this case, objects do not have to be transformed) from the real response time t_i of the same query obtained after one or more schema modifications (in this case, objects have to be transformed):

$$\Delta t_i = t_i - \bar{t}_{Lookup} \qquad (19.2)$$

The summation in Equation 19.1 goes from 11 to 70 to avoid cold-start effects from being considered. Let $\#Obj$ denote the total number of objects transformed after the lookup queries; then the average cost for the transformation of one object $\bar{t}\ (\overline{\Delta t})$ is computed by dividing $T\ (\Delta T)$ by $\#Obj$.

We do not report the results obtained for a cluster query in a small database since the results do not largely differ from the ones obtained with the lookup query.

N	Immediate Transformation		Deferred Transformation		
	T (min)	$\bar{t}$ (ms)	ΔT (min)	$\overline{\Delta t}$ (ms)	ΔT^* (min)
1	7.5	22.6	8.0	25.2	8.4
2	14.8	44.5	11.1	34.9	11.6
5	36.7	110.7	19.4	61.0	20.3
Time/N	≈ 7.4	≈ 22.2	$\Delta T/N \to 3$	$\overline{\Delta t}/N \to 9.1$	$\Delta T^*/N \to 3$

Table 19.1: Time needed for transforming objects in a small database (in the immediate transformation, all the 20,000 objects have been accessed; in the deferred transformation, the number of accessed objects is only 19,048)

For small databases, results presented in Table 19.1 can be interpreted as follows:

- The cost for the immediate database transformation grows linearly with the number of schema modifications. Except for one schema modification, the deferred database transformation always performs better than the immediate database transformation (see values for ΔT and T).

- For each schema modification, the immediate transformation takes about 7.4 minutes for the database. The deferred database transformation takes about 8 minutes if only one schema modification is considered. For more than one schema modification, the average cost for each schema modification $\Delta T/N$ decreases with N and asymptotically approaches the value of 3 minutes.

- On the average, each object transformation for each schema modification takes about 22 ms in the case of the immediate transformation, and $\overline{\Delta t}/N$ in the case of the deferred transformation. For only one schema modification, it takes 25.2 ms for an object to be transformed; this time decreases with N and asymptotically approaches the value of 9.1 ms.

- With the immediate transformation, all 20,000 objects are transformed in one go just after the schema modification, while with the deferred transformation only a portion of the objects, namely 19,048, are accessed by the lookup query. The total cost for the deferred database transformation must therefore include the cost for transforming the remaining 952 objects, as denoted in Table 19.1 by the parameter ΔT^*. It is not worthwhile to consider ΔT^* here for small databases since its value does not considerably differ from ΔT. For large databases, ΔT^* will be much more significant.

For small databases, the immediate database transformation is significantly slower than the deferred database transformation. This is mainly because the deferred database transformation in one step can restructure an object whose class might have undergone several modifications. In the immediate database transformation, single objects have to be brought up to conform to the schema soon after the schema has been modified. Further, in the deferred database transformation, the operation to read an object from the local cache to main memory is considered not part of the database transformation itself but rather of the application that caused the object to be read. A graphical representation of the results given in Table 19.1 is shown in Figure 19.6.

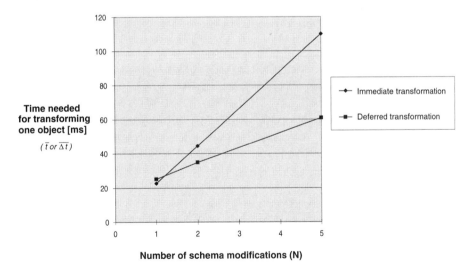

Figure 19.6: Time needed for transforming an object in small databases

19.3.2   Large Databases

As opposed to small databases that fit in the client cache, performance in large databases is mainly affected by the number of page I/O operations carried out for the transformation itself. Figure 19.7 illustrates the response time and number of objects transformed using the lookup query when running the deferred database transformation.

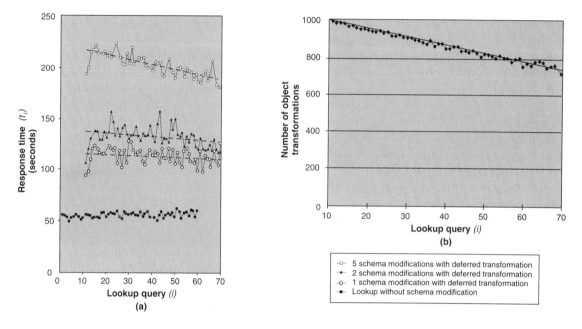

Figure 19.7: Response time and number of objects transformed for the lookup query in large databases

In Figure 19.7(b), the curve describing the number of objects transformed shows a moderate linear downward trend since the probability of finding objects that have already been updated is pretty low. The number of page I/O operations reflects the same trend (see Figure 19.8(a)). The decreasing number of I/O operations justifies the downward trend of the response time curve in Figure 19.7(a).

Table 19.2 summarizes the results obtained with a lookup query in a large database. For large databases, the results presented in Table 19.2 can be interpreted as follows:

- The immediate database transformation might block the database for a considerable amount of time (for one schema modification for about 2 hours). This is not acceptable for most of the applications.

- As opposed to what was presented for small databases, the deferred transformation performs better ($\Delta T^* = 564$ minutes) than the immediate one ($T = 575$ minutes) only if more than five schema modifications are considered.

N	Immediate Transformation		Deferred Transformation		
	T (min)	$\bar{t}$ (ms)	ΔT (min)	$\overline{\Delta t}$ (ms)	ΔT^* (min)
1	115	34.5	57.4	66.3	221
2	230	69.0	76.6	88.4	295
5	575	172.5	146.6	169.3	564
Time/N	≈ 115	≈ 34.5	$\Delta T/N \to 21.7$	$\overline{\Delta t}/N \to 25$	$\Delta T^*/N \to 83$

Table 19.2: Time needed for transforming objects in a large database: In the immediate transformation, all 200,000 objects have been accessed; in the deferred transformation, the number of accessed objects is only 51,955

- For each schema modification, the immediate transformation takes about 115 minutes for the database to be transformed. The estimated time ΔT^* for transforming all the objects with the deferred transformation after one schema modification is 221 minutes. The average cost for the deferred transformation for each schema modification $\Delta T^*/N$ asymptotically approaches the value of 83 minutes.

- On the average, each object transformation for each schema modification takes about 34.5 ms in the case of the immediate transformation. For one schema modification, the deferred transformation takes 66.3 ms; this time decreases with N and asymptotically approaches the value of 25 ms.

The results of our experiments can be explained by considering the number of page I/O operations. When the immediate transformation is used, all objects of a page are transformed together, and therefore a page is fetched and flushed only once. In the deferred transformation, a page can be fetched and flushed several times—in the worst case, as many times as objects stored on the page itself. Each lookup query, for instance, was required to fetch 880 pages on average from the server because almost every object access caused a page fault. When more schema modifications are performed, the deferred transformation takes advantage of the fact that in one step it can restructure an object whose class might have undergone several modifications (i.e., the number of page faults for the complete object transformation is at most one). Further, the time ΔT considers the time for flushing a page only. The time to fetch a page is considered as part of the time needed by the query to be processed.

If a query reads more objects in one page, as in the cluster query, then the deferred transformation performs better because the number of page I/O operations decreases. In Figure 19.8, page faults are shown for both lookup and cluster queries.

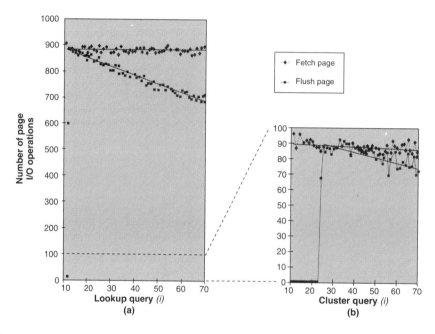

Figure 19.8: Page faults for each lookup and cluster query in the large database

In the lookup query, 880 pages on the average are fetched. The cache of 5 MB contains 1,250 pages, and the size of the entire database corresponds to 10,527 pages. With these values, the probability that a page of an accessed object is not in the cache can be computed as follows: $p = 1 - 1,250/10,527 = 0.88$. The downward trend of the flush curve reflects the decreasing number of objects to be transformed after each query. In the cluster query, Figure 19.8 clearly shows that the number of fetch/flush operations improves by an order of magnitude. In the case of the cluster query, each page will be flushed at most two times. Although the cost for the immediate transformation is still smaller for one schema modification, already after two schema modifications the deferred transformation shows better results.

Results for the cluster query are presented in Table 19.3.

The main results of this chapter shown in Tables 19.2 and 19.3 are graphically summarized in Figure 19.9. Figure 19.9 illustrates the average time

N	Deferred Transformation			
	ΔT (min)	$\#Obj$	$\overline{\Delta t}$ (ms)	ΔT^* (min)
1	34.7	51,636	40.3	134
2	38.4	51,636	44.6	148
5	66.2	51,636	76.9	256
Time/N	$\Delta T/N \to 7$		$\overline{\Delta t}/N \to 8$	$\Delta T^*/N \to 27$

Table 19.3: Time needed for transforming clustered objects in large databases

for the transformation of a single object in a large database. The decision about which transformation approach is the most suitable depends, among other things, both on the number of schema modifications that have to be performed and on the kind of query used to access the database (random vs. clustered access to objects).

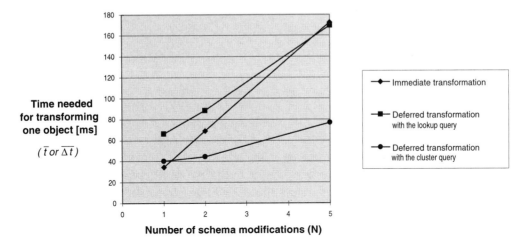

Figure 19.9: Time needed for transforming an object in a large database

19.4 Open Problems

This chapter presented a proposal for how to benchmark database updates and gave some results for the two most used approaches for transforming the database after a schema modification, the immediate and the deferred database transformation.

The main results of the study can be summarized as follows:

- The deferred database transformation always performs better for small databases. In a large database, the deferred database transformation works pretty well if several schema modifications are performed before objects are accessed (e.g., when developing an application).

- For the deferred database transformation, good response times are obtained also for cluster queries, that is, those queries accessing more than one object per page (e.g., in the hybrid transformation approach). The immediate database transformation, on the contrary, seems to provide better results in a large database when the number of schema modifications is limited (e.g., a database in a production mode when changes are usually rare).

- From a more qualitative point of view, it must be considered that the immediate database transformation might block the database for a considerable amount of time. This is not acceptable for most applications. The deferred database transformation, on the other hand, seems to be not suitable for some other applications (e.g., real-time applications) where the response time of a query plays an important role. For such applications, no additional unpredictable amount of time can be dedicated for the transformation of the objects.

Other experiments can be run by slightly modifying the benchmarking scenario. The experiments we presented in Section 19.3 using the deferred transformation strategy assumed that applications did not access objects between two schema modifications. An interesting scenario that could be considered is that part of the database is actually used between two schema modifications. In the development phase, where experiments and simulations are required, schema modifications are supposed to be more frequent. In this scenario, it is, for instance, assumed that only a small part of the database (30%) is accessed. In production mode, instead, it is assumed that almost all the objects in the database (80%) are used. An intermediate scenario, where only 50% of the database is accessed, can also be experimented with. A preliminary result we have obtained so far is that the total cost for the deferred database transformation increases with the percent of objects accessed between two schema modifications, since the number of page faults for the complete transformation of an object can be greater than one, as in the case where objects are not accessed between schema modifications.

Another interesting experiment is to consider update queries (i.e., queries where applications modify the value of objects). With these queries, the deferred database transformation performs better than the immediate one because costs with update queries do not depend on fetch/flush operations. In fact, when a page is fetched from the disk because of an object's access, the page is marked as dirty no matter whether the object has to be transformed because of a schema modification or not. Costs for the object transformation include, therefore, only the execution of conversion functions, which implies in memory operations only. To our best knowledge, the benchmark and results presented in this chapter are the first attempt to address the specific problem of measuring the performance of database updates because of schema modifications.

19.5 Bibliographic Notes

The OO1 benchmark has been discussed in [88]. More complete and complex benchmarks for object databases have been defined, such as OO7 [84] or the HyperModel [18].

Informations about EOS and BeSS can be found in [59] and [58]. Tcl/Tk and [incr Tcl] are treated, respectively, in [326] and [282].

Qualitative performance studies have been presented in [209] and [219].

Bibliography

[1] S. Abiteboul and R. Hull. Restructuring Hierarchical Database Objects. *Theoretical Computer Science* 62(1, 2), December 1988.

[2] S. Abiteboul, R. Hull, and V. Vianu. *Foundations of Databases.* Addison-Wesley, Reading, MA, 1995.

[3] S. Abiteboul, P. Kanellakis, and E. Waller. Method Schemas. In *Proceedings ACM SIGACT-SIGMOD-SIGART Symposium on Principles of Database Systems*, pp. 16–27, Atlantic City, NJ, 1990.

[4] S. Abiteboul and V. Vianu. Non-Determinism in Logic Based Languages. *Annals of Mathematics and Artificial Intelligence* 3:151–186, 1991.

[5] R. Agrawal, R. J. Cochrane, and B. G. Lindsay. On Maintaining Priorities in a Production Rule System. In G. M. Lohman, A. Sernadas, and R. Camps (eds.), *Proceedings International Conference on Very Large Data Bases*, pp. 479–487, Barcelona, Spain, September 1991.

[6] R. Agrawal, C. Faloutsos, and A. Swami. Efficient Similarity Search in Sequence Databases. In *Proceedings Foundations of Data Organization and Algorithms Conference*, pp. 69–84, Evanston, IL, October 1993.

[7] R. Agrawal, S. Ghosh, T. Imielinski, B. Iyer, and A. Swami. An Interval Classifier for Database Mining Applications. In *Proceedings International Conference on Very Large Data Bases*, pp. 560–573, August 1992.

[8] R. Agrawal, T. Imielinski, and A. Swami. Mining Association Rules Between Sets of Items in Large Databases. In *Proceedings ACM SIGMOD International Conference on Management of Data*, pp. 207–216, May 1993.

[9] R. Agrawal and R. Srikant. Fast Algorithms for Mining Association Rules in Large Databases. In *Proceedings International Conference on Very Large Data Bases*, pp. 487–499, September 1994.

[10] R. Ahmed, P. De Smedt, W. Du, W. Kent, M. A. Ketabchi, W. A. Litwin, A. Rafii, and M. C. Shan. The Pegasus Heterogeneous Multidatabase System. *IEEE Computer* 24(12), December 1991.

[11] I. Ahn and R. T. Snodgrass. Performance Evaluation of a Temporal Database Management System. In C. Zaniolo (ed.), *Proceedings ACM SIGMOD International Conference on Management of Data*, pp. 96–107, May 1986.

[12] A. V. Aho and M. J. Corasick. Fast Pattern Matching: An Aid to Bibliographic Search. *Communications of the ACM* 18(6):333–340, June 1975.

[13] A. Aho and J. D. Ullman. Universality of Data Retrieval Languages. In *Proceedings ACM SIGACT-SIGMOD-SIGART Symposium on Principles of Programming Languages*, 1979.

[14] A. Aiken, J. Widom, and J. M. Hellerstein. Behavior of Database Production Rules: Termination, Confluence, and Observable Determinism. In M. Stonebraker (ed.), *Proceedings ACM SIGMOD International Conference on Management of Data*, pp. 59–68, San Diego, May 1992.

[15] K. K. Al-Taha, R. T. Snodgrass, and M. D. Soo. Bibliography on Spatiotemporal Databases. *International Journal of Geographical Information Systems* 8:195–203, January–February 1994.

[16] H. Aly and Z. M. Özsoyoğlu. Synchronized Counting Method. In *Proceedings IEEE International Conference on Data Engineering*, pp. 366–373, 1989.

[17] J. Andany, M. Léonard, and C. Palisser. Management of Schema Evolution in Databases. In G. M. Lohman, A. Sernades, and R. Camps (eds.), *Proceedings International Conference on Very Large Data Bases*, pp. 161–170, Barcelona, Spain, September 1991.

[18] A. T. L. Anderson, et al. The HyperModel Benchmark. In *Proceedings International Conference on Extending Database Technology*, Venice, Italy, March 1990. Springer-Verlag, New York. LNCS.

[19] M. Andersson, Y. Dupont, S. Spaccapietra, K. Yètongnon, M. Tresch, and H. Ye. The FEMUS Experience in Building a Federated Multilingual Database. In *Proceedings IEEE Workshop on Research Issues on Data Engineering: Interoperability in Multidatabase Systems*, Vienna, Austria, April 1993.

[20] K. R. Apt, H. A. Blair, and A. Walker. Toward a Theory of Declarative Knowledge. In J. W. Minker (ed.), *Foundations of Deductive Databases and Logic Programming*, pp. 89–184, Morgan Kaufmann, San Francisco, 1988.

[21] M. Arya, W. Cody, C. Faloutsos, J. E. Richardson, and A. Toga. Qbism: A Prototype 3-D Medical Image Database System. *IEEE Data Engineering Bulletin* 16(1):38–42, March 1993.

[22] M. Arya, W. Cody, C. Faloutsos, J. E. Richardson, and A. Toga. Qbism: Extending a DBMS to Support 3-D Medical Images. In *Proceedings IEEE International Conference on Data Engineering*, pp. 314–325, February 1994.

[23] R. Baeza-Yates and G. H. Gonnet. A New Approach to Text Searching. *Communications of the ACM* 35(10):74–82, October 1992.

[24] I. Balbin and K. Ramamohanarao. A Generalization of the Differential Approach to Recursive Query Evaluation. *Journal of Logic Programming* 4(3):259–262, 1987.

[25] J. F. Baldwin. Evidential Support Logic Programming. *Journal of Fuzzy Sets and Systems* 24:1–26, 1987.

[26] J. F. Baldwin (ed.). *Fuzzy Logic*. John Wiley & Sons, New York, 1996.

[27] D. Ballard and C. Brown. *Computer Vision*. Prentice Hall, Englewood Cliffs, NJ, 1982.

[28] F. Bancilhon. Naive Evaluation of Recursively Defined Relations. In M. Brodie and J. Mylopoulos (eds.), *On Knowledge Base Management Systems*, pp. 165–178. Springer-Verlag, New York, 1986.

[29] F. Bancilhon, D. Maier, Y. Sagiv, and J. D. Ullman. Magic Sets and Other Strange Ways to Implement Logic Programs. In *Proceedings ACM SIGACT-SIGMOD-SIGART Symposium on Principles of Database Systems*, pp. 1–15, 1986.

[30] F. Bancilhon and R. Ramakrishnan. Performance Evaluation of Data Intensive Logic Programs. In J. W. Minker (ed.), *Foundations of Deductive Databases and Logic Programming*, pp. 439–518, Morgan Kaufmann, San Francisco, 1988.

[31] J. Banerjee, H.-T. Chou, J. F. Garza, W. Kim, D. Woelk, N. Ballou, and H.-J. Kim. Data Model Issues for Object-Oriented Applications. *ACM Transactions on Office Information Systems* 5(1):3–26, January 1987.

[32] J. Banerjee, W. Kim, H.-J. Kim, and H. F. Korth. Semantics and Implementation of Schema Evolution in Object-Oriented Databases. In U. Dayal and I. Traiger (eds.), *Proceedings of ACM SIGMOD International Conference on Management of Data*, pp. 311–322, San Francisco, May 1987.

[33] C. Baral and M. Gelfond. Representing Concurrent Actions in Extended Logic Programming. In R. Bajcsy (ed.), *Proceedings IJCAI'93*, pp. 866–871, Morgan Kaufmann, San Francisco, 1993.

[34] C. Baral and J. Lobo. Formal Characterization of Active Databases. In D. Pedreschi and C. Zaniolo (eds.), *Proceedings International Workshop on Logic in Databases (LID'96)*, pp. 195–216, Springer-Verlag, New York, 1996.

[35] E. Baralis, S. Ceri, P. Fraternali, and S. Paraboschi. Support Environment for Active Rule Design. *International Journal of Intelligent Systems*, Kluwer, to appear.

[36] E. Baralis, S. Ceri, G. Monteleone, and S. Paraboschi. An Intelligent Database System Application: The Design of EMS. In W. A. Litwin and T. Risch (eds.), *Proceedings International Conference on Applications of Databases*, pp. 172–189. LNCS 819, Springer-Verlag, New York.

[37] E. Baralis, S. Ceri, and S. Paraboschi. ARACHNE: A Tool for the Analysis of Active Rules. In *Proceedings International Conference on Applications of Databases*, Santa Clara, CA, December 1995.

[38] E. Baralis, S. Ceri, and S. Paraboschi. Improved Rule Analysis by Means of Triggering and Activation Graphs. In T. Sellis (ed.), *Proceedings Workshop on Rules in Database Systems*, LNCS 985, pp. 165–181, Athens, Greece, September 1995.

[39] E. Baralis, S. Ceri, and S. Paraboschi. Run-time Detection of Non-Terminating Active Rule Systems. In *Proceedings on Deductive and Object-Oriented Databases*, LNCS 1013, pp. 38–54, Singapore, December 1995.

[40] E. Baralis, S. Ceri, and S. Paraboschi. Modularization Techniques for Active Rules Design. *ACM Transactions on Database Systems* 21:1, March 1996.

[41] E. Baralis and J. Widom. An Algebraic Approach to Rule Analysis in Expert Database Systems. In *Proceedings International Conference on Very Large Data Bases*, pp. 475–486, Santiago, Chile, September 1994.

[42] D. Barbará, H. García-Molina, and D. Porter. The Management of Probabilistic Data. *IEEE Transactions on Knowledge and Data Engineering* 4:487–502, 1992.

[43] F. Barbic and B. Pernici. Time Modeling in Office Information Systems. In S. B. Navathe (ed.), *Proceedings ACM SIGMOD International Conference on Management of Data*, pp. 51–62, Austin, TX, May 1985.

[44] C. Batini, S. Ceri, and S. B. Navathe. *Conceptual Database Design.* Benjamin/Cummings, Redwood City, CA, 1992.

[45] C. Batini, M. Lenzerini, and S. B. Navathe. A Comparative Analysis of Methodologies for Database Schema Integration. *ACM Computing Surveys* 18(4), December 1986.

[46] M. Baudinet, J. Chomicki, and P. Wolper. Temporal Deductive Databases. In [427], Chapter 13, pp. 294–320.

[47] R. Bayer. Query Evaluation and Recursion in Deductive Database Systems. Technical report, Technical University of Munich, Germany, 1985.

[48] N. Beckmann, H.-P. Kriegel, R. Schneider, and B. Seeger. The R*-Tree: An Efficient and Robust Access Method for Points and Rectangles. In *Proceedings ACM SIGMOD International Conference on Management of Data*, pp. 322–331, May 1990.

[49] C. Beeri and R. Ramakrishnan. On the Power of Magic. In *Proceedings ACM SIGACT-SIGMOD Symposium on Principles of Database Systems*, pp. 269–283, 1987.

[50] A. Belussi and C. Faloutsos. Estimating the Selectivity of Spatial Queries Using the 'Correlation' Fractal Dimension. In *Proceedings International Conference on Very Large Data Bases*, pp. 299–310, September 1995.

[51] E. Benazet, H. Guehl, and M. Bouzeghoub. VITAL: A Visual Tool for Analysis of Rules Behavior in Active Databases. In T. Sellis (ed.), *Proceedings Workshop on Rules in Database Systems*, LNCS 985, pp. 182–196, Athens, Greece, September 1995.

[52] J. L. Bentley. Multidimensional Binary Search Trees Used for Associative Searching. *Communications of the ACM* 18(9):509–517, September 1975.

[53] J. L. Bentley. Multidimensional Binary Search Trees in Database Applications. *IEEE Transactions on Software Engineering* SE-5(4):333–340, July 1979.

[54] E. Bertino. A View Mechanism for Object-Oriented Databases. In A. Pirotte, C. Delobel, and G. Gottlob (eds.), *Proceedings International Conference on Extending Database Technology*, pp. 136–151, Vienna, Austria, March 1992. Springer-Verlag, New York. LNCS 580.

[55] E. Bertino and L. Martino. *Object-Oriented Database Systems: Concepts and Architectures.* International Computer Science Series. Addison-Wesley, Reading, MA, 1993.

[56] G. Bhargava and S. K. Gadia. Relational Database Systems with Zero Information Loss. *IEEE Transactions on Knowledge and Data Engineering* 5(7):76–87, February 1993.

[57] T. Bially. Space-Filling Curves: Their Generation and Their Application to Bandwidth Reduction. *IEEE Transactions on Information Theory* IT-15(6):658–664, November 1969.

[58] A. Biliris, W. O'Connell, and E. Panagos. *BeSS Reference Manual, Version 0.4.0 (Beta).* AT&T Bell Laboratories, Murray Hill, NJ, 1995.

[59] A. Biliris and E. Panagos. *EOS User's Guide, Release 2.1.* AT&T Bell Laboratories, Murray Hill, NJ, 1993.

[60] G. Birkoff. *Lattice Theory.* American Mathematical Society, Providence, RI, 1984.

[61] H. A. Blair and P. Cholak. The Complexity of the Class of Locally Stratified Prolog Programs. *Fundamenta Informaticae* 21(4):333–344, 1994.

[62] H. A. Blair and V. S. Subrahmanian. Paraconsistent Foundations for Logic Programming. *Journal of Non-Classical Logic* 5(2):45–73, 1988.

[63] H. A. Blair and V. S. Subrahmanian. Paraconsistent Logic Programming. *Theoretical Computer Science* 68:135–154, 1989.

[64] M. H. Böhlen. The Temporal Deductive Database System ChronoLog. Ph.D. dissertation, Departement Informatik, ETH Zurich, 1994.

[65] M. H. Böhlen. Temporal Database System Implementations. *SIGMOD Record* 24(4):53–60, December 1995.

[66] M. H. Böhlen, R. T. Snodgrass, and M. D. Soo. Coalescing in Temporal Databases. In *Proceedings International Conference on Very Large Data Bases*, pp. 180–191, Bombay, India, September 1996.

[67] A. Bolour, A. T. L. Anderson, L. J. Dekeyser, and H. K. T. Wong. The Role of Time in Information Processing: A Survey. *SigArt Newsletter* 80:28–48, April 1982.

[68] A. Bonner and M. Kifer. An Overview of Transaction Logic. *Theoretical Computer Science* 133, 1994.

[69] G. Booch. *Object Oriented Analysis and Design with Application, Second Edition*. Benjamin/Cummings, Redwood City, CA, 1994.

[70] G. Boole. *The Laws of Thought*. Macmillan, London, 1854.

[71] R. S. Boyer and J. S. Moore. A Fast String Searching Algorithm. *Communications of the ACM* 20(10):762–772, October 1977.

[72] H. Branding, A. P. Buchmann, A. Kudrass, and J. Zimmermann. Rules in an Open System: The Reach Rule System. In [333], pp. 111–126.

[73] P. Brèche. Schema Update Primitives for ODB Design. Technical Report 7, Fachbereich Informatik, University of Frankfurt, Frankfurt am Main, Germany, May 1995.

[74] P. Brèche. Advanced Primitives for Changing Schemas of Object Databases. In *Proceedings of the CAiSE'96 Conference*, Heraklion, Crete, May 1996. Springer-Verlag, New York.

[75] P. Brèche, F. Ferrandina, and M. Kuklok. Simulation of Schema Change Using Views. In N. Revell and A. M. Tjoa (eds.), *Proceedings International Conference on Database and Expert Systems Applications*, pp. 247–258, London, September 1995. Springer-Verlag, New York. LNCS 978.

[76] P. Brèche and M. Wörner. How to Remove a Class in an Object Database System. In *Proceedings International Conference on Application of Databases*, San Jose, CA, December 1995.

[77] R. Bretl, D. Maier, A. Otis, D. J. Penney, B. Schuchardt, J. Stein, E. H. Williams, and M. H. Williams. The GemStone Data Management System. In W. Kim and F. H. Lochovsky (eds.), *Object-Oriented Concepts, Databases, and Applications*, Chapter 12, pp. 283–308, ACM Press, New York, September 1989.

[78] T. Brinkhoff, H.-P. Kriegel, R. Schneider, and B. Seeger. Multi-Step Processing of Spatial Joins. In R. T. Snodgrass and M. Winslett (eds.), *Proceedings ACM SIGMOD International Conference on Management of Data*, pp. 197–208, May 1994.

[79] T. Brinkhoff, H.-P. Kriegel, and B. Seeger. Efficient Processing of Spatial Joins Using R-Trees. In *Proceedings ACM SIGMOD International Conference on Management Data*, pp. 237–246, May 1993.

[80] A. Brogi, V. S. Subrahmanian, and C. Zaniolo. Modeling Sequential and Parallel Plans. *Journal of Artificial Intelligence and Mathematics* 19(3/4), April 1997.

[81] E. W. Brown, J. P. Callan, and W. B. Croft. Fast Incremental Indexing for Full-Text Information Retrieval. In *Proceedings International Conference on Very Large Data Bases*, pp. 192–202, September 1994.

[82] L. Gottesfeld Brown. A Survey of Image Registration Techniques. *ACM Computing Surveys* 24(4):325–376, December 1992.

[83] A. R. Butz. Alternative Algorithm for Hilbert's Space-Filling Curve. *IEEE Transactions on Computers* C-20(4):424–426, April 1971.

[84] M. J. Carey, D. J. DeWitt, and J. F. Naughton. The OO7 Benchmark. In S. Nishio and A. Yonezawa (eds.), *Proceedings ACM SIGMOD International Conference on Management of Data*, pp. 12–21, Washington, DC, May 1993. ACM Press, New York.

[85] R. Carnap. *The Logical Foundations of Probability*. University of Chicago Press, Chicago, 1962. Second edition.

[86] F. Casati, S. Ceri, B. Pernici, and G. Pozzi. Workflow Enactment by Active Rules. In *Proceedings International Conference on Database Expert Systems and Applications*, September 1996.

[87] M. Castagli and S. Eubank. *Nonlinear Modeling and Forecasting.* Addison-Wesley, Reading, MA, 1992.

[88] R. G. G. Cattell and J. Skeen. Object Operations Benchmark. *ACM Transactions on Database Systems* 17(1):1–31, March 1992.

[89] R. Cavallo and M. Pittarelli. The Theory of Probabilistic Databases. In *Proceedings International Conference on Very Large Data Bases*, 1987.

[90] J. Celko. Regions, Runs, and Sequences. Chapter 22 of *SQL for Smarties: Advanced SQL Programming.* Morgan Kaufmann, San Francisco, 1995.

[91] S. Ceri, E. Baralis, P. Fraternali, and S. Paraboschi. Design of Active Rule Applications: Issues and Approaches. In *Proceedings International Conference on Deductive and Object-Oriented Databases*, pp. 1–18, Singapore, December 1995.

[92] S. Ceri and P. Fraternali. *Designing Database Applications with Objects and Rules: The IDEA Methodology.* Series on Database Systems and Applications. Addison-Wesley, Reading, MA, 1997.

[93] S. Ceri, P. Fraternali, S. Paraboschi, and L. Tanca. Automatic Generation of Production Rules for Integrity Maintenance. *ACM Transactions on Database Systems* 19(3):367–422, September 1994.

[94] S. Ceri and R. Manthey. Consolidated Specification of Chimera, the Conceptual Interface of Idea. Technical Report IDEA.DD.2P.004, ES-PRIT Project Number 6333 Idea, June 1993.

[95] S. Ceri and R. Manthey. Chimera: A Model and Language for Active DOOD Systems. In *Proceedings East/West Database Workshop*, pp. 3–16, 1994.

[96] S. Ceri and J. Widom. Deriving Production Rules for Constraint Maintenance. In D. McLeod, R. Sacks-Davis, and H. Schek (eds.), *Proceedings International Conference Very Large Data Bases*, pp. 566–577, Brisbane, Australia, August 1990.

[97] S. Ceri and J. Widom. Deriving Production Rules for Incremental View Maintenance. In G. M. Lohman, A. Sernadas, and R. Camps (eds.), *Proceedings International Conference on Very Large Data Bases*, pp. 577–589, Barcelona, Spain, September 1991.

[98] S. Ceri and J. Widom. Deriving Incremental Production Rules for Deductive Data. *Information Systems* 19(6):467–490, November 1994.

[99] S. Chakravarthy, Z. Tamizuddin, and J. Zhou. A Visualization and Explanation Tool for Debugging ECA Rules in Active Databases. In T. Sellis (ed.), *Proceedings Workshop on Rules in Database Systems*, LNCS 985, pp. 197–209, Athens, Greece, September 1995.

[100] A. Chandra and D. Harel. Computable Queries for Relational Data Bases. *Journal of Computer and System Sciences* 21(2), 1980.

[101] A. Chandra and D. Harel. Structure and Complexity of Relational Queries. *Journal of Computer and System Sciences* 25(1):99–128, 1982.

[102] C. Chatfield. *The Analysis of Time Series: An Introduction.* Chapman and Hall, London & New York, 1984. Third edition.

[103] W. Chen and D. S. Warren. Tabled Evaluation with Delaying for General Logic Programs. *Journal of the ACM* 43(1):20–74, January 1996.

[104] D. Chimenti, R. Gamboa, and R. Krishnamurthy. Towards an Open Architecture for LDL. In *Proceedings International Conference on Very Large Data Bases*, pp. 195–204, 1989.

[105] D. Chimenti, R. Gamboa, R. Krishnamurthy, S. Naqvi, S. Tsur, and C. Zaniolo. An Overview of the LDL System. *Data Engineering* 10(4):44–52, 1987.

[106] J. Chomicki. Polynomial-Time Computable Queries in Temporal Deductive Databases. In *Proceedings ACM SIGACT-SIGMOD-SIGART Symposium on Principles of Database Systems*, 1990.

[107] J. Chomicki. Temporal Query Languages: A Survey. In H. J. Ohlbach and D. M. Gabbay (eds.), *Proceedings International Conference on Temporal Logic*, pp. 506–534. Lecture Notes Artificial Intelligence 827, Springer-Verlag, New York, July 1994.

[108] S. Christodoulakis and C. Faloutsos. Design Considerations for a Message File Server. *IEEE Transactions on Software Engineering* SE-10(2):201–210, March 1984.

[109] K. Clark. Negation as Failure. In J. M. Nicolas, H. Gallaire, and J. W. Minker (eds.), *Logic and Databases*, pp. 293–332, Plenum Press, New York, 1978.

[110] J. Clifford and A. Croker. The Historical Relational Data Model (HRDM) and Algebra Based on Lifespans. In *Proceedings International Conference on Data Engineering*, pp. 528–537, Los Angeles, CA, February 1987.

[111] J. Clifford and T. Isakowitz. On the Semantics of (Bi)Temporal Variable Databases. In M. Jarke, J. Bubenko, and K. Jeffery (eds.), *Proceedings International Conference on Extending Database Technology*, Cambridge, U.K., pp. 215–230, March 1994. Springer-Verlag, New York. LNCS 779.

[112] W. Clocksin and C. Mellish. *Programming in Prolog*. Springer-Verlag, New York, 1981.

[113] R. J. Cochrane and N. Mattos. ISO-ANSI SQL3 Change Proposal, ISO/IEC ITC1/SC21/WG3 DBL KHR-89, X3H2-95-458, An Execution Model for After Triggers, December 1995.

[114] R. J. Cochrane, H. Pirahesh, and N. Mattos. Integrating Triggers and Declarative Constraints in SQL Database Systems. In *Proceedings International Conference Very Large Data Bases*, Bombay, September 1996.

[115] E. F. Codd. A Relational Model of Data for Large Shared Data Banks. *Communications of the Association of Computing Machinery* 13(6):377–387, 1970.

[116] E. F. Codd. Further Normalization of the Relational Data Model. In R. Rustin (ed.), *Data Base Systems*, Prentice Hall, Englewood Cliffs, NJ, 1972.

[117] E. F. Codd. Relational Completeness of Database Sublanguages. In R. Rustin (ed.), *Data Base Systems*. Prentice Hall, Englewood Cliffs, NJ, 1972.

[118] D. Coleman, P. Arnold, S. Bodoff, C. Dollin, H. Gilchrist, F. Hayes, and P. Jeremaes. *Object-Oriented Development: The Fusion Method*. Prentice Hall, Englewood Cliffs, NJ, 1994.

[119] C. Collet, T. Coupaye, and T. Svensen. NAOS: Efficient and Modular Reactive Capabilities in an Object-Oriented Database System. In

J. B. Bocca, M. Jarke, and C. Zaniolo (eds.), *Proceedings International Conference on Very Large Data Bases*, pp. 132–143, Santiago, Chile, 1994.

[120] D. Comer. The Ubiquitous B-Tree. *ACM Computing Surveys* 11(2):121–138, 1979.

[121] S. Cook and J. Daniels. *Designing Object Systems*. Prentice Hall, Englewood Cliffs, NJ, 1994.

[122] W. S. Cooper. On Deriving Design Equations for Information Retrieval Systems. *JASIS*, pp. 385–395, November 1970.

[123] L. Corciulo, F. Giannotti, and D. Pedreschi. Datalog with Non-Deterministic Choice Compute NDB-PTime. In S. Ceri, K. Tanaka, and S. Tsur (eds.), *Proceedings International Conference on Deductive and Object-Oriented Databases* pp. 49–66, Springer-Verlag, New York, 1993.

[124] D. Cutting and J. Pedersen. Optimizations for Dynamic Inverted Index Maintenance. In *Proceedings SIGIR*, pp. 405–411, 1990.

[125] U. Dayal, M. Hsu, and R. Ladin. Organizing Long-Running Activities with Triggers and Transactions. In H. Garcia-Molina and H. V. Jagadish (eds.), *Proceedings ACM SIGMOD International Conference on Management of Data*, pp. 204–214, Atlantic City, NJ, May 1990.

[126] S. Deerwester, S. T. Dumais, G. W. Furnas, T. K. Landauer, and R. Harshman. Indexing by Latent Semantic Analysis. *Journal of the American Society for Information Science* 41(6):391–407, September 1990.

[127] C. Delcourt and R. Zicari. The Design of an Integrity Consistency Checker (ICC) for an Object Oriented Database System. In P. America (ed.), *Proceedings European Conference on Object-Oriented Programming*, pp. 97–117, Geneva, Switzerland, July 1991. Springer-Verlag, New York. LNCS 512.

[128] A. P. Dempster. A Generalization of Bayesian Inference. *Journal of the Royal Statistical Society* Series B(30):205–247, 1968.

[129] D. Dey and S. Sarkar. A Probabilistic Relational Model and Algebra. *ACM Transactions on Database Systems* 21(3):339–369, 1996.

[130] O. Diaz, A. Jaime, and N. W. Paton. DEAR: A DEbugger for Active Rules in an Object-Oriented Context. In [333], pp. 180–193.

[131] K. R. Dittrich, S. Gatziu, and A. Geppert. The Active Database Management System Manifesto. In [396], pp. 3–17.

[132] D. Dubois and H. Prade. Certainty and Uncertainty of Vague Knowledge and Generalized Dependencies in Fuzzy Databases. In *Proceedings International Fuzzy Engineering Symposium*, pp. 239–249, Yokohama, Japan, 1988.

[133] D. Dubois and H. Prade. Default Reasoning and Possibility Theory. *Artificial Intelligence* 35:243–257, 1988.

[134] D. Dubois and H. Prade. *Possibility Theory: An Approach to the Computerized Processing of Uncertainty*. Plenum Press, New York, 1988.

[135] R. O. Duda and P. E. Hart. *Pattern Classification and Scene Analysis*. John Wiley & Sons, New York, 1973.

[136] R. O. Duda, P. E. Hart, and N. J. Nilsson. Subjective Bayesian Methods for Rule-Based Inference Systems. In *Proceedings of National Computer Conference*, pp. 1075–1082, 1976.

[137] C. R. Dyer. The Space Efficiency of Quadtrees. *Computer Graphics and Image Processing* 19(4):335–348, August 1982.

[138] C. E. Dyreson and R. T. Snodgrass. Valid-time Indeterminacy. In *Proceedings of the International Conference on Data Engineering*, pp. 335–343, Vienna, April 1993.

[139] R. D. Edwards and J. Magee. *Technical Analysis of Stock Trends*. John Magee, Springfield, MA, 1966. Fifth edition, second printing.

[140] P. Elias. Universal Codeword Sets and Representations of Integers. *IEEE Transactions on Information Theory* IT-21:194–203, 1975.

[141] R. Elmasri and S. B. Navathe. *Fundamentals of Database Systems*. Benjamin/Cummings, Redwood City, CA, 1994. Second edition.

[142] E. Emerson. Temporal and Modal Logic. In J. van Leeuwen (ed.), *Handbook of Theoretical Computer Science*, Vol. B, Chapter 16, pp. 995–1072, Elsevier/MIT Press, Amsterdam/Cambridge, MA, 1990.

[143] J. Ewing, S. Mehrabanzad, S. Sheck, D. Ostroff, and B. Shneiderman. An Experimental Comparison of a Mouse and Arrow-Jump Keys for an Interactive Encyclopedia. *International Journal of Man-Machine Studies* 24(1):29–45, January 1986.

[144] R. Fagin, J. Y. Halpern, and N. Megiddo. A Logic for Reasoning about Probabilities. *Information and Computation* 87(1/2): 78–128, 1990.

[145] R. Fagin, J. Nievergelt, N. Pippenger, and H. R. Strong. Extendible Hashing—A Fast Access Method for Dynamic Files. *ACM Transactions on Database Systems* 4(3):315–344, September 1979.

[146] R. Fagin and J. Y. Halpern. Uncertainty, Belief and Probability. In *Proceedings International Joint Conference on Artificial Intelligence*, pp. 1161–1167, Morgan Kaufmann, San Francisco, 1989.

[147] C. Faloutsos. Access Methods for Text. *ACM Computing Surveys* 17(1):49–74, March 1985.

[148] C. Faloutsos. Gray Codes for Partial Match and Range Queries. *IEEE Transactions on Software Engineering* 14(10):1381–1393, October 1988.

[149] C. Faloutsos. Signature Files. In W. B. Frakes and R. Baeza-Yates (eds.), *Information Retrieval: Data Structures and Algorithms*, Prentice Hall, Englewood Cliffs, NJ, 1992.

[150] C. Faloutsos. Analytical Results on the Quadtree Decomposition of Arbitrary Rectangles. *Pattern Recognition Letters* 13(1):31–40, January 1992.

[151] C. Faloutsos. *Searching Multimedia Databases by Content.* Kluwer Academic, Norwell, MA, 1996.

[152] C. Faloutsos, R. Barber, M. Flickner, J. Hafner, W. Niblack, D. Petkovic, and W. Equitz. Efficient and Effective Querying by Image Content. *Journal of Intelligent Information Systems* 3(3/4):231–262, July 1994.

[153] C. Faloutsos and S. Christodoulakis. Optimal Signature Extraction and Information Loss. *ACM Transactions on Database Systems* 12(3):395–428, September 1987.

[154] C. Faloutsos and V. Gaede. Analysis of the Z-Ordering Method Using the Hausdorff Fractal Dimension. In *Proceedings International Conference on Very Large Data Bases*, September 1996.

[155] C. Faloutsos, H. V. Jagadish, and Y. Manolopoulos. Analysis of the N-Dimensional Quadtree Decomposition for Arbitrary Hyper-Rectangles. CS-TR-3381, UMIACS-TR-94-130, Department of Computer Science,

University of Maryland, College Park, MD, December 1994. To appear in *IEEE Transactions on Knowledge and Data Engineering*.

[156] C. Faloutsos and I. Kamel. Beyond Uniformity and Independence: Analysis of R-trees Using the Concept of Fractal Dimension. In *Proceedings ACM SIGACT-SIGMOD-SIGART Symposium on Principles of Database Systems*, pp. 4–13, May 1994.

[157] C. Faloutsos, M. Ranganathan, and Y. Manolopoulos. Fast Subsequence Matching in Time-Series Databases. In R. T. Snodgrass and M. Winslett (eds.), *Proceedings ACM SIGMOD International Conference on Management of Data*, pp. 419–429, May 1994.

[158] C. Faloutsos and Y. Rong. Dot: A Spatial Access Method Using Fractals. In *Proceedings IEEE International Conference on Data Engineering*, pp. 152–159, Kobe, Japan, April 1991.

[159] C. Faloutsos and S. Roseman. Fractals for Secondary Key Retrieval. In *Proceedings ACM SIGACT-SIGMOD-SIGART Symposium on Principles of Database Systems*, pp. 247–252, March 1989.

[160] C. Faloutsos, T. Sellis, and N. Roussopoulos. Analysis of Object Oriented Spatial Access Methods. In *Proceedings ACM SIGMOD International Conference on Management of Data*, pp. 426–439, May 1987.

[161] F. Ferrandina and S.-E. Lautemann. An Integrated Approach to Schema Evolution for Object Databases. In *Proceedings of the Third International Conference on Object Oriented Information Systems*, London, December 1996.

[162] F. Ferrandina, T. Meyer, and R. Zicari. Correctness of Lazy Database Updates for an Object Database System. In M. Atkinson, D. Maier, and V. Benzaken (eds.), *Persistent Object Systems*, pp. 284–301, Tarascon, France, September 1994. Springer-Verlag, New York.

[163] F. Ferrandina, T. Meyer, and R. Zicari. Implementing Lazy Database Updates for an Object Database System. In J. Bocca, M. Jarke, and C. Zaniolo (eds.), *Proceedings International Conference on Very Large Databases*, pp. 261–272, Santiago, Chile, September 1994. Morgan Kaufmann, San Francisco.

[164] F. Ferrandina, T. Meyer, and R. Zicari. Measuring the Performance of Immediate and Deferred Updates in Object Database Systems. In *Proceedings OOPSLA Workshop on Object Database Behavior, Benchmarks, and Performance*, Austin, TX, October 1995.

[165] F. Ferrandina, T. Meyer, R. Zicari, G. Ferran, and J. Madec. Schema and Database Evolution in the O_2 Object Database System. In U. Dayal, P. M. D. Gray, and S. Nishio (eds.), *Proceedings of the International Conference on Very Large Databases*, pp. 170–181, Zurich, Switzerland, September 1995.

[166] F. Ferrandina and R. Zicari. Object Database Schema Evolution: Are Lazy Updates Always Equivalent to Immediate Updates? In *Proceedings of the OOPSLA Workshop on Supporting the Evolution of Class Definitions*, Austin, TX, October 1995.

[167] J. R. Files and H. D. Huskey. An Information Retrieval System Based on Superimposed Coding. In *Proceedings AFIPS FJCC*, pp. 423–432, 1969.

[168] S. J. Finkelstein, N. Mattos, I. S. Mumick, and H. Pirahesh. Expressing Recursive Queries in SQL. ISO/IEC JTC1/SC21 WG3 DBL MCI Report X3H2-96-075r1, 1996.

[169] M. C. Fitting. Logic Programming on a Topological Bilattice. *Fundamenta Informatica* 11:209–218, 1988.

[170] M. Flickner, H. Sawhney, W. Niblack, J. Ashley, Q. Huang, B. Dom, M. Gorkani, J. Hafner, D. L. Lee, D. Petkovic, D. Steele, and P. Yanker. Query by Image and Video Content: The QBIC System. *IEEE Computer* 28(9):23–32, September 1995.

[171] P. W. Foltz and S. T. Dumais. Personalized Information Delivery: An Analysis of Information Filtering Methods. *Communications of the ACM* 35(12):51–60, December 1992.

[172] A. C. Fong and J. D. Ullman. Induction Variables in Very High-Level Languages. In *The ACM SIGACT-SIGMOD-SIGART Symposium on Principles of Database Systems*, pp. 104–112, 1976.

[173] W. Frakes and R. Baeza-Yates. *Information Retrieval: Data Structures and Algorithms*. Prentice Hall, Englewood Cliffs, NJ, 1992.

[174] P. Fraternali and L. Tanca. A Structured Approach for the Definition of the Semantics of Active Databases. *ACM Transactions on Database Systems* 20(4):414–471, December 1995.

[175] E. Fredkin. TRIE Memory. *Communications of the ACM* 3(9):490–500, September 1960.

[176] N. Fuhr. Models for Integrated Information Retrieval and Information Systems. *IEEE Data Engineering Bulletin*, pp. 3–13, 1996.

[177] K. Fukunaga. *Introduction to Statistical Pattern Recognition.* Academic Press, San Diego, CA, 1990. Second edition.

[178] K. Fukunaga and P. M. Narendra. A Branch and Bound Algorithm for Computing K-Nearest Neighbors. *IEEE Transactions on Computers* C-24(7):750–753, July 1975.

[179] V. Gaede. Optimal Redundancy in Spatial Database Systems. In *Proceedings International Symposium on Spatial Databases*, pp. 96–116, 1995.

[180] V. Gaede and O. Günther. Survey on Multidimensional Access Methods. Technical Report ISS-16, Institut fuer Wirtschaftsinformatik, Humboldt-Universitaet zu Berlin, August 1995.

[181] V. Gaede and W. F. Riekert. Spatial Access Methods and Query Processing in the Object-Oriented GIS GODOT. In *Proceedings of the AGDM Workshop*, pp. 40–52, Delft, The Netherlands, 1994. Netherlands Geodetic Commission.

[182] H. Gallaire, J. W. Minker, and J. M. Nicolas (eds.). *Logic and Databases.* Plenum Press, New York, 1978.

[183] H. Gallaire, J. W. Minker, and J. M. Nicolas (eds.). *Advances in Database Theory*, volume 1. Plenum Press, New York, 1981.

[184] I. Gargantini. An Effective Way to Represent Quadtrees. *Communications of the ACM* 25(12):905–910, December 1982.

[185] N. Gehani and H. V. Jagadish. ODE as an Active Database: Constraints and Triggers. In G. M. Lohman, A. Sernadas, and R. Camps (eds.), *Proceedings International Conference on Very Large Data Bases*, pp. 327–336, Barcelona, Spain, September 1991.

[186] M. Gelfond and V. Lifschitz. The Stable Model Semantics for Logic Programming. Joint International Conference and Symposium on Logic Programming, pp. 1070–1080, Seattle, WA, 1988.

[187] M. Gelfond and V. Lifschitz. Representing Action and Change by Logic Programs. *Journal of Logic Programming* 17:301–322, 1993.

[188] A. Geppert, M. Krasolfer, and D. Tombros. Realization of Cooperative Agents Using an Active Object-Oriented Database Management System. In [396], pp. 327–341.

[189] F. Giannotti, D. Pedreschi, D. Saccà, and C. Zaniolo. Non-Determinism in Deductive Databases. In C. Delobel, M. Kifer, and Y. Masunaga (eds.), *Proceedings Deductive and Object-Oriented Databases, Second International Conference, DOOD'91*, pp. 129–146, Springer-Verlag, New York, 1991.

[190] M. Ginsberg. Multivalued Logics: A Uniform Approach to Reasoning in Artificial Intelligence. *Computational Intelligence* 4:265–316, 1988.

[191] B. V. Gnedenko and A. Y. Khinchin. *An Elementary Introduction to the Theory of Probability*. Dover Publications, Mineola, NY, 1962.

[192] G. H. Gonnet and F. W. Tompa. Mind Your Grammar: A New Approach to Modelling Text. In *Proceedings International Conference on Very Large Data Bases*, pp. 339–346, September 1987.

[193] The GOODSTEP Team. The GOODSTEP Project: General Object-Oriented Database for Software Engineering Processes. In *Proceedings IEEE Asia-Pacific Software Engineering Conference*, pp. 410–420, Tokyo, Japan, 1994.

[194] S. Greco and C. Zaniolo. Optimization of Linear Logic Programs Using Counting Methods. In *Proceedings International Conference on Extending Database Technology*, 1992.

[195] T. Griffin and L. Libkin. Incremental Maintenance of Views with Duplicates. In M. Carey and D. Schneider (eds.), *Proceedings ACM SIGMOD International Conference on Management of Data*, pp. 328–339, San Jose, CA, May 1995.

[196] H. Gunadhi and A. Segev. A Framework for Query Optimization in Temporal Databases. In *Proceedings International Conference on Statistical and Scientific Database Management Systems*, pp. 131–147, Springer-Verlag, New York, April 1990. LNCS 420.

[197] H. Gunadhi and A. Segev. Query Processing Algorithms for Temporal Intersection Joins. In *Proceedings International Conference on Data Engineering*, Kobe, Japan, 1991.

[198] O. Günther. The Cell Tree: An Index for Geometric Data. Memorandum No. UCB/ERL M86/89, University of California, Berkeley, December 1986.

[199] U. Guntzer, W. Kiessling, and H. Thone. New Directions for Uncertainty Reasoning in Deductive Databases. In *Proceedings ACM SIGMOD International Conference on Management of Data*, pp. 178–187, 1991.

[200] A. Gupta, D. Katiyar, and I. S. Mumick. Counting Solutions to the View Maintenance Problem. In *Proceedings Workshop on Deductive Databases (in Conjunction with the Joint International Conference and Symposium on Logic Programming)*, Washington, DC, November 1992.

[201] A. Gupta, I. S. Mumick, and V. S. Subrahmanian. Maintaining Views Incrementally. In P. Buneman and S. Jajodia (eds.), *Proceedings ACM SIGMOD International Conference on Management of Data*, pp. 157–166, Washington, DC, May 1993.

[202] A. Guttman. R-trees: A Dynamic Index Structure for Spatial Searching. In B. Yormack (ed.), *Proceedings ACM SIGMOD International Conference on Management of Data*, pp. 47–57, Boston, MA, June 1984.

[203] R. Haddad and J. F. Naughton. Counting Methods for Cyclic Relations. In *Proceedings ACM SIGACT-SIGMOD-SIGART Principles of Database Systems*, pp. 333–340, 1988.

[204] T. Hailperin. Probability Logic. *Notre Dame Journal of Formal Logic* 25(3):198–212, 1984.

[205] P. A. V. Hall and G. R. Dowling. Approximate String Matching. *ACM Computing Surveys* 12(4):381–402, December 1980.

[206] R. W. Hamming. *Digital Filters*. Signal Processing Series, Prentice Hall, Englewood Cliffs, NJ, 1977.

[207] J. Han. Selection of Processing Strategies for Different Recursive Queries. In *Proceedings International Conference on Data and Knowledge Bases*, Jerusalem, Israel, 1988.

[208] M. C. Harrison. Implementation of the Substring Test by Hashing. *Communications of the ACM* 14(12):777–779, December 1971.

[209] G. Harrus, F. Vélez, and R. Zicari. Implementing Schema Updates in an Object-Oriented Database System: A Cost Analysis. Technical report, GIP Altair, Versailles, France, 1990.

[210] R. L. Haskin and L. A. Hollaar. Operational Characteristics of a Hardware-Based Pattern Matcher. *ACM Transactions on Database Systems* 8(1):15–40, March 1983.

[211] D. Heimberger and D. McLeod. A Federated Architecture for Information Management. *ACM Transactions on Information Systems* 3(3), 1985.

[212] L. Henschen and S. Naqvi. On Compiling Queries in Recursive First-Order Databases. *Journal of the ACM* 31(1):47–85, 1984.

[213] K. Hinrichs and J. Nievergelt. The Grid File: A Data Structure to Support Proximity Queries on Spatial Objects. In *Proceedings International Workshop on Graph Theoretic Concepts in Computer Science*, pp. 100–113, 1983.

[214] L. A. Hollaar. Text Retrieval Computers. *IEEE Computer Magazine* 12(3):40–50, March 1979.

[215] J. E. Hopcroft and J. D. Ullman. *Introduction to Automata Theory, Languages, and Computation.* Addison-Wesley, Reading, MA, 1979.

[216] R. Hull, K. Tanaka, and M. Yoshikawa. Behavior Analysis of Object-Oriented Databases: Method Structure, Execution Trees, and Reachability. In *Proceedings International Conference on Foundations of Data Organization and Algorithms*, pp. 39–46, Paris, France, June 1989. Springer-Verlag, New York. LNCS.

[217] A. Hume and D. M. Sunday. Fast String Searching. *Software—Practice and Experience* 21(11):1221–1248, November 1991.

[218] G. M. Hunter and K. Steiglitz. Operations on Images Using Quad Trees. *IEEE Transactions on PAMI* PAMI-1(2):145–153, April 1979.

[219] W. L. Hürsch. *Maintaining Behavior and Consistency of Object-Oriented Systems During Evolution.* Ph.D. thesis, College of Computer Science, Northeastern University, Boston, MA, 1995.

[220] IBM. *IBM DATABASE 2 SQL Guide for Common Servers, Version 2*, 1995.

[221] Illustra. *Illustra User's Guide, Server Release 2.1*, June 1994.

[222] Informix. *Informix Guide to SQL, Syntax, Version 6*, March 1994. Part No. 000-7597.

[223] Itasca Systems, Inc. OODBMS Feature Checklist, Itasca Systems Technical Report Number TM-92-001. Rev 1.1. December 1993.

[224] I. Jacobson, M. Christerson, P. Jonsson, and G. Övergaard. *Object-Oriented Software Engineering: A Use Case Driven Approach.* Addison-Wesley, Reading, MA, 1992.

[225] H. V. Jagadish. Spatial Search with Polyhedra. In *Proceedings IEEE International Conference on Data Engineering*, February 1990.

[226] H. V. Jagadish. Linear Clustering of Objects with Multiple Attributes. In *Proceedings ACM SIGMOD International Conference on Management of Data*, pp. 332–342, May 1990.

[227] H. V. Jagadish. A Retrieval Technique for Similar Shapes. In *Proceedings ACM SIGMOD International Conference on Management of Data*, pp. 208–217, May 1991.

[228] R. Jain and W. Niblack. NSF Workshop on Visual Information Management, February 1992.

[229] J. S. N. Jean. New Distance Measure for Binary Images. *International Conference on Acoustics, Speech and Signal Processing*, Volume 4, April 1990. Paper no. M5.19.

[230] C. S. Jensen, J. Clifford, R. Elmasri, S. K. Gadia, P. Hayes, and S. Jajodia (eds.). A Glossary of Temporal Database Concepts. *SIGMOD Record* 23(1):52–64, March 1994.

[231] C. S. Jensen and R. T. Snodgrass. Temporal Specialization and Generalization. *IEEE Transactions on Knowledge and Data Engineering* 6(6):954–974, December 1994.

[232] C. S. Jensen and R. T. Snodgrass. Semantics of Time-Varying Information. *Information Systems* 21(4):311–352, 1996.

[233] C. S. Jensen, R. T. Snodgrass, and M. D. Soo. The TSQL2 Data Model. In [409], pp. 157–240, Chapter 10.

[234] C. S. Jensen, M. D. Soo, and R. T. Snodgrass. Unifying Temporal Models via a Conceptual Model. *Information Systems* 19(7):513–547, December 1994.

[235] F. Kabanza, J.-M. Stévenne, and P. Wolper. Handling Infinite Temporal Data. *Journal of Computer and Systems Sciences* 51(1):3–17, 1995.

[236] K. Kahn and G. A. Gorry. Mechanizing Temporal Knowledge. *Artificial Intelligence*, pp. 87–108, 1977.

[237] I. Kamel and C. Faloutsos. On Packing R-Trees. In *Proceedings International Conference on Information and Knowledge Management*, November 1993.

[238] I. Kamel and C. Faloutsos. Hilbert R-tree: An Improved R-tree Using Fractals. In *Proceedings International Conference on Very Large Data Bases*, pp. 500–509, Santiago, Chile, September 1994.

[239] A. P. Karadimce and S. D. Urban. Conditional Term Rewriting as a Formal Basis for Analysis of Active Database Rules. In *Proceedings International Workshop on Research Issues in Data Engineering*, pp. 156–162, Houston, TX, February 1994.

[240] R. M. Karp and M. O. Rabin. Efficient Randomized Pattern-Matching Algorithms. *IBM Journal of Research and Development* 31(2):249–260, March 1987.

[241] D. Kemp, K. Ramamohanarao, and P. Stuckey. ELS Programs and the Efficient Evaluation of Non-Stratified Programs by Transformation to ELS. In *Proceedings on Deductive and Object-Oriented Databases: DOOD95*, pp. 91–108, Singapore, December 1995.

[242] W. Kiessling, H. Thone, and U. Guntzer. Database Support for Problematic Knowledge. In *Proceedings International Conference on Extending Database Technology*, pp. 421–436, LNCS 580, Springer-Verlag, New York, 1992.

[243] M. Kifer and G. Lausen. F-Logic: A Higher Order Language for Reasoning about Objects, Inheritance and Schema. In *Proceedings ACM SIGMOD International Conference on Management of Data*, pp. 134–146, 1989.

[244] M. Kifer and A. Li. On the Semantics of Rule-Based Expert Systems with Uncertainty. In M. Gyssens, J. Paredaens, and D. Van Gucht (eds.), *Proceedings International Conference on Database Theory*, pp. 102–117, Bruges, Belgium, 1988. Springer-Verlag, New York, LNCS 326.

[245] M. Kifer and V. S. Subrahmanian. Theory of Generalized Annotated Logic Programming and Its Applications. *Journal of Logic Programming* 12(4):335–368, 1992.

[246] W. Kim, N. Ballou, H.-T. Chou, J. F. Garza, and Darrell Woelk. Features of the ORION Object-Oriented Database System. In W. Kim and F. H. Lochovsky (eds.), *Object-Oriented Concepts, Databases, and Applications*, pp. 251–282. Chapter 3, Addison-Wesley, Reading, MA, 1989.

[247] R. E. Kimbrell. Searching for Text? Send an N-Gram! *Byte* 13(5):297–312, May 1988.

[248] N. Kline. An Update of the Temporal Database Bibliography. *ACM SIGMOD Record* 22(4):66–80, December 1993.

[249] N. Kline and R. T. Snodgrass. Computing Temporal Aggregates. In *Proceedings IEEE International Conference on Database Engineering*, Taipei, Taiwan, March 1995.

[250] D. E. Knuth. *The Art of Computer Programming, Volume 3: Sorting and Searching.* Addison-Wesley, Reading, MA, 1973.

[251] D. E. Knuth, J. H. Morris, and V. R. Pratt. Fast Pattern Matching in Strings. *SIAM Journal of Computing* 6(2):323–350, June 1977.

[252] C. P. Kolovson and M. Stonebraker. Segment Indexes: Dynamic Indexing Techniques for Multi-Dimensional Interval Data. In *Proceedings ACM SIGMOD International Conference on Management of Data*, pp. 138–147, May 1991.

[253] H. F. Korth and A. Silberschatz. *Database Systems Concepts.* Computer Science Series. McGraw-Hill, New York, 1991. Second edition.

[254] B. Kosko. *Fuzzy Thinking: The New Science of Fuzzy Logic.* Hyperion, New York, 1993.

[255] M. Koubarakis. Database Models for Infinite and Indefinite Temporal Information. *Information Systems* 19(2):141–173, 1994.

[256] M. Koubarakis. Complexity Results for First Order Theories of Temporal Constraints. In *Proceedings International Conference on Principles of Knowledge Representation and Reasoning (KR-94)*, Bonn, Germany, pp. 379–390, 1994.

[257] R. Krishnamurthy and S. Naqvi. Non-Deterministic Choice in Datalog. In *Proceedings International Conference on Data and Knowledge Bases*, 1988.

[258] A. Kumar, V. J. Tsotras, and C. Faloutsos. Access Methods for Bi-Temporal Databases. In *Proceedings International Workshop on Temporal Databases*, September 1995.

[259] H. Kyburg. *The Logical Foundations of Statistical Inference*. D. Reidel, Hingham, MAP 1974

[260] L. V. S. Lakshmanan, N. Leone, R. Ross, and V. S. Subrahmanian. ProbView: A Flexible Probabilistic Database System. To appear in *ACM Transactions on Database Systems*, 1997.

[261] T. Landers and R. L. Rosenberg. An Overview of Multibase. In *Proceedings International Symposium on Distributed Data Bases*, Berlin, Germany, September 1982.

[262] D.-L. Lee and C. W. Leng. Partitioned Signature File: Designs and Performance Evaluation. *ACM Transactions on Information Systems* 7(2):158–180, April 1989.

[263] R. M. Lee, H. Coelho, and J. C. Cotta. Temporal Inferencing on Administrative Databases. *Information Systems* 10(2):197–206, 1985.

[264] S. K. Lee. An Extended Relational Database Model for Uncertain and Imprecise Information. In *Proceedings International Conference on Very Large Databases*, pp. 211–220, Vancouver, Canada, 1992.

[265] C. Y. T. Leung and R. R. Muntz. Stream Processing: Temporal Query Processing and Optimization. In [427], pp. 329–355, Chapter 14.

[266] L. Ling, R. Zicari, W. L. Hürsch, and K. Lieberherr. The Role of Polymorphic Reuse Mechanisms in Schema Evolution in an Object-Oriented Database. To appear in *IEEE Transactions on Knowledge and Data Engineering*, 1997.

[267] W. Lipski. On Semantic Issues Concerned with Incomplete Information Databases. *ACM Transactions on Database Systems* 4(3):262–296, 1979.

[268] W. A. Litwin, L. Mark, and N. Roussopoulos. Interoperability of Multiple Autonomous Databases. *ACM Computing Surveys* 22(3), September 1990.

[269] J. W. Lloyd. *Foundations of Logic Programming*. Springer-Verlag, New York, 1987. Second edition.

[270] M. L. Lo and C. V. Ravishankar. Spatial Joins Using Seeded Trees. In R. T. Snodgrass and M. Winslett (eds.), *Proceedings ACM SIGMOD International Conference on Management of Data*, pp. 209–220, May 1994.

[271] D. B. Lomet and B. Salzberg. The hB-Tree: A Multiattribute Indexing Method with Good Guaranteed Performance. *ACM Transactions on Database Systems* 15(4):625–658, December 1990.

[272] R. Lowerance and R. A. Wagner. An Extension of the String-to-String Correction Problem. *Journal of the ACM* 22(2):3–14, April 1975.

[273] U. Manber and S. Wu. Glimpse: A Tool to Search through Entire File Systems. In *Proceedings USENIX Technology Conference*, 1994. `ftp://cs.arizona.edu/glimpse/glimpse.ps.Z`

[274] B. Mandelbrot. *Fractal Geometry of Nature*. W. H. Freeman, New York, 1977.

[275] A. Marchetti-Spaccamela, A. Pelaggi, and D. Saccà. Worst-Case Complexity Analysis of Methods for Logic Query Implementation. In *Proceedings ACM SIGACT-SIGMOD-SIGART Symposium on Principles of Database Systems*, pp. 294–301, 1987.

[276] V. W. Marek and M. Truszczynski. *Nonmonotonic Logic*. Springer-Verlag, New York, 1995.

[277] A. Martelli and U. Montanari. An Efficient Unification Algorithm. *ACM Transactions on Programming Languages and Systems* 4(2):258–282, 1982.

[278] Mathematical Committee on Physical and NSF Engineering Sciences. *Grand Challenges: High Performance Computing and Communications*. National Science Foundation, 1992. The FY 1992 U.S. Research and Development Program.

[279] J. McCarthy. Applications of Circumscription to Formalising Common Sense Reasoning. *Artificial Intelligence* 26:89–116, 1986.

[280] E. M. McKenzie. Bibliography: Temporal Databases. *ACM SIGMOD Record* 15(4):40–52, December 1986.

[281] E. M. McKenzie and R. T. Snodgrass. An Evaluation of Relational Algebras Incorporating the Time Dimension in Databases. *ACM Computing Surveys* 23(4):501–543, December 1991.

[282] M. J. McLennan. *[incr Tcl]—Object-Oriented Programming in Tcl.* AT&T Bell Laboratories, Murray Hill, NY, 1993.

[283] J. Melton (ed.). Working Draft: Database Language SQL (SQL3) ISO/IEC ITC1/SC21/WG3 DBL LHR-004, X3H2-95-368. October 1995.

[284] J. Melton (ed.). SQL/Temporal. ISO/IEC JTC 1/SC 21/WG 3 DBL-MCI-0012. July 1996.

[285] J. Melton and A. R. Simon. *Understanding the New SQL: A Complete Guide.* Morgan Kaufmann, San Francisco, CA, 1993.

[286] T. Meyer. Schema Updates in Object Database Systems—A Comparison Between Immediate and Deferred Object Transformations. Master's thesis, J. W. Goethe University of Frankfurt, Fachbereich Informatik, Robert-Mayer Str. 1995. In German.

[287] R. J. Miller, Y. E. Ioannidis, and R. Ramakrishnan. The Use of Information Capacity in Schema Integration and Translation. In R. Agrawal, S. Baker, and D. Bell (eds.), *Proceedings International Conference on Very Large Databases*, pp. 62–72, Dublin, Ireland, August 1993.

[288] J. W. Minker. On Indefinite Databases and the Closed-World Assumption. In D. Loveland (ed.), *Proceedings Conference on Automated Deduction*, 1982.

[289] J. W. Minker. Logic and Databases: A 20 Year Retrospective. In D. Pedreschi and C. Zaniolo (eds.), *Proceedings International Workshop on Logic in Databases (LID'96)*, Springer-Verlag, New York, pp. 5–52, 1996.

[290] G. Moerkotte and A. Zachmann. Towards More Flexible Schema Management in Object Bases. In *Proceedings IEEE International Conference on Data Engineering*, pp. 174–181, Vienna, Austria, April 1993.

[291] A. Montanari and B. Pernici. Temporal Reasoning. In [427], pp. 534–562, Chapter 21.

[292] G. Monteleone and E. Baralis. A Dynamic Electrical Network Description: Analysis and Design. Technical Report IDEA.DD.1T.005, TXT Ingegneria Informatica, Milano, Italy, August 1993.

[293] C. Mooers. Application of Random Codes to the Gathering of Statistical Information. Bulletin 31, Zator Co, Cambridge, MA, 1949. Based on M.S. thesis, MIT, January 1948.

[294] B. Moon, H. V. Jagadish, C. Faloutsos, and J. H. Saltz. Analysis of the Clustering Properties of Hilbert Space-Filling Curve. Technical Report CS-TR-3611, Department of Computer Science, University of Maryland, College Park, 1996.

[295] K. Morris. An Algorithm for Ordering Subgoals in NAIL! In *Proceedings ACM SIGACT-SIGMOD-SIGART Symposium on Principles of Database Systems*, pp. 82–88, 1988.

[296] K. Morris, J. D. Ullman, and A. Van Gelder. Design Overview of the NAIL! System. In *Proceedings International Conference on Logic Programming*, pp. 554–568, Springer-Verlag, LNCS 225, New York, 1986.

[297] I. Motakis and C. Zaniolo. Composite Temporal Events in Active Database Rules: A Logic-Oriented Approach. In *Proceedings of the Conference on Deductive and Object-Oriented Databases*, LNCS 1013, pp. 19–37, Singapore, December 1995.

[298] A. Motro. Superviews: Virtual Integration of Multiple Databases. *IEEE Transactions on Software Engineering* 13(7):785–798, July 1987.

[299] F. Murtagh. A Survey of Recent Advances in Hierarchical Clustering Algorithms. *The Computer Journal* 26(4):354–359, 1983.

[300] J. Mylopoulos, A. Borgida, M. Jarke, and M. Koubarakis. Telos: Representing Knowledge about Information Systems. *ACM Transactions on Office Information Systems* 8(4):325–362, October 1990.

[301] S. Naqvi. A Logic for Negation in Database Systems. In *Proceedings Workshop on the Foundations of Deductive Databases and Logic Programming*, 1986.

[302] S. Naqvi and S. Tsur. *A Logic Language for Data and Knowledge Bases*. Computer Science Press, New York, 1989.

[303] J. F. Naughton. Compiling Separable Recursions. In *Proceedings ACM International Conference on Management of Data*, pp. 312–319, 1988.

[304] S. B. Navathe and R. Ahmed. A Temporal Relational Model and a Query Language. *Information Sciences* 49:147–175, 1989.

[305] R. Ng and V. S. Subrahmanian. Probabilistic Logic Programming. *Information and Computation* 101(2):150–201, 1993.

[306] R. Ng and V. S. Subrahmanian. Stable Semantics for Probabilistic Deductive Databases. *Information and Computation* 110(1):42–83, 1995.

[307] W. Niblack, R. Barber, W. Equitz, M. Flickner, E. Glasman, D. Petkovic, P. Yanker, C. Faloutsos, and G. Taubin. The QBIC Project: Querying Images by Content Using Color, Texture and Shape. In *Proceedings International Symposium on Electronic Imaging: Science and Technology, Conference 1908, Storage and Retrieval for Image and Video Databases*, February 1993.

[308] J. M. Nicolas, H. Gallaire, and J. W. Minker (eds.). *Advances in Database Theory*, volume 2. Plenum Press, New York, 1983.

[309] J. M. Nicolas, H. Gallaire, and J. W. Minker. Logic and Databases: A Deductive Approach. *ACM Computing Surveys* 16(1):154–185, 1984.

[310] J. Nievergelt, H. Hinterberger, and K. C. Sevcik. The Grid File: An Adaptable, Symmetric Multikey File Structure. *ACM Transactions on Database Systems* 9(1):38–71, March 1984.

[311] N. J. Nilsson. Probabilistic Logic. *AI Journal* 28:71–87, 1986.

[312] O_2 Technology. *O_2 C Reference Manual, Version 4.6*, Versailles Cedex, France, October 1995.

[313] O_2 Technology. *System Administration Guide, Version 4.6*, Versailles Cedex, France, October 1995.

[314] Object Design, Inc. *ObjectStore User Guide, Release 3.0*, chapter 10, December 1993.

[315] Objectivity, Inc. *Objectivity, User Manual, Version 2.0*, March 1993.

[316] K. Obraczka, P. B. Danzig, and S.-H. Li. Internet Resource Discovery Services. *IEEE Computer*, September 1993.

[317] V. E. Ogle and M. Stonebraker. Chabot: Retrieval from a Relational Database of Images. *IEEE Computer* 28(9):40–48, September 1995.

[318] A. V. Oppenheim and R. W. Schafer. *Digital Signal Processing*. Prentice-Hall, Englewood Cliffs, NJ, 1975.

[319] Oracle Corporation. *Oracle 7 Server SQL Language Reference Manual*, December 1992. Part Number 778-70, Redwood City, CA.

[320] Oracle Corporation. *Oracle 7 Server Concepts Manual*, December 1992. Number 6693-70.

[321] J. A. Orenstein. Spatial Query Processing in an Object-Oriented Database System. In *Proceedings ACM SIGMOD International Conference on Management of Data*, pp. 326–336, May 1986.

[322] J. A. Orenstein. Redundancy in Spatial Databases. In *Proceedings ACM SIGMOD International Conference on Management of Data*, May 1989.

[323] J. A. Orenstein. A Comparison of Spatial Query Processing Techniques for Native and Parameter Spaces. In *Proceedings ACM SIGMOD International Conference on Management of Data*, pp. 343–352, 1990.

[324] J. A. Orenstein and F. A. Manola. Probe Spatial Data Modeling and Query Processing in an Image Database Application. *IEEE Transactions on Software Engineering* 14(5):611–629, May 1988.

[325] J. A. Orenstein and T. H. Merrett. A Class of Data Structures for Associative Searching. In *Proceedings ACM SIGACT-SIGMOD-SIGART Symposium on Principles of Database Systems*, pp. 181–190, April 1984.

[326] J. K. Ousterhout. *Tcl and the Tk Toolkit*. Addison-Wesley, Reading, MA, 1994.

[327] K. Owens and S. Adams. Oracle 7 Triggers: Mutating Tables? *Database Programming and Design* 7(10), 1994.

[328] G. Özsoyoğlu and R. T. Snodgrass. Temporal and Real-Time Databases: A Survey. *IEEE Transactions for Knowledge and Data Engineering* 7(4):513–532, August 1995.

[329] B. Pagel, H. Six, H. Toben, and P. Widmayer. Towards an Analysis of Range Query Performance. In *Proceedings of ACM SIGACT-SIGMOD-SIGART Symposium on Principles of Database Systems*, pp. 214–221, May 1993.

[330] R. Paige and J. T. Shwartz. Reduction in Strength of High-Level Operations. In *Proceedings of ACM SIGACT-SIGMOD-SIGART Symposium on Principles of Programming Languages*, pp. 58–71, 1977.

[331] S. Parsons. Current Approaches to Handling Imperfect Information in Data and Knowledge Bases. *IEEE Transactions on Knowledge and Databases* 8(3):353–372, 1996.

[332] N. W. Paton, O. Diaz, M. H. Williams, J. Campin, A. Dinn, and A. Jaime. Dimensions of Active Behaviour. In [333], pp. 40–57.

[333] N. W. Paton and M. H. Williams (eds.). *Proceedings of Workshop on Rules in Database Systems*, WICS, Edinburgh, Scotland, August 1993. Springer-Verlag, Berlin.

[334] J. Pearl. *Probabilistic Reasoning in Intelligent Systems: Networks of Plausible Inference*. Morgan Kaufmann, San Francisco, 1988.

[335] D. J. Penney and J. Stein. Class Modification in the GemStone Object-Oriented DBMS. In N. Meyrowitz (ed.), *Proceedings ACM International Conference on Object-Oriented Programming Systems, Languages, and Applications*, pp. 111–117, Orlando, FL, October 1987. Special Issue of *SIGPLAN Notices* 22(12), December, 1987.

[336] F. C. N. Pereira and D. H. D. Warren. Parsing as Deduction. In *Proceedings Annual Meeting Association for Computational Linguistics*, pp. 137–144, 1983.

[337] E. G. M. Petrakis and C. Faloutsos. Similarity Searching in Large Image Databases. To appear in *IEEE Transactions on Data and Knowledge Engineering*. Also available as technical report at MUSIC with # TR-01-94, 1994, and at Univ. of Maryland with # UMIACS-TR-94-134, CS-TR-3388, 1994.

[338] G. Phipps, M. A. Derr, and K. A. Ross. Glue-Nail!: A Deductive Database System. In *Proceedings International ACM SIGMOD Conference on Management of Data*, pp. 308–317, 1991.

[339] J. Pinto and R. Reiter. Temporal Reasoning in Logic Programming: A Case for the Situation Calculus. In *Proceedings International Conference on Logic Programming*, pp. 203–221. MIT Press, Cambridge, MA, 1993.

[340] W. H. Press, B. P. Flannery, S. A. Teukolsky, and W. T. Vetterling. *Numerical Recipes in C*. Cambridge University Press, Cambridge, England, 1988.

[341] T. C. Przymusinski. On the Declarative and Procedural Semantics of Stratified Deductive Databases. In J. W. Minker (ed.), *Foundations of Deductive Databases and Logic Programming*, pp. 193–216, Morgan Kaufman, San Francisco, CA, 1988.

[342] T. C. Przymusinski. Extended Stable Semantics for Normal and Disjunctive Programs. In *Proceedings of the International Conference on Logic Programming*, pp. 459–477, 1990.

[343] Y.-G. Ra and E. A. Rundensteiner. A Transparent Object-Oriented Schema Change Approach Using View Evolution. Technical Report R-94-4, Department of Electrical Engineering and Computer Science, The University of Michigan, Ann Arbor, MI, April 1994.

[344] E. Radeke and M. H. Scholl. Federation and Stepwise Reduction of Database Systems. In *Proceedings International Conference on Parallel and Distributed Information Systems*, Austin, TX, September 1994.

[345] K. V. S. V. N. Raju and A. Majumdar. Fuzzy Functional Dependencies and Lossless Join Decomposition of Fuzzy Relational Database Systems. *ACM Transactions Database Systems* 13(2), June 1988.

[346] R. Ramakrishnan. *Applications of Logic Databases*. Kluwer Academic, Norwell, MA, 1995.

[347] R. Ramakrishnan, F. Bancilhon, and A. Silberschatz. Safety of Recursive Horn Clauses with Infinite Relations. In *Proceedings ACM SIGACT-SIGMOD-SIGART Symposium on Principles of Database Systems*, pp. 328–339, 1987.

[348] R. Ramakrishnan, C. Beeri, and R. Krishnamurthy. Optimizing Existential Datalog Queries. In *Proceedings ACM SIGACT-SIGMOD-SIGART Symposium on Principles of Database Systems*, pp. 89–102, 1988.

[349] R. Ramakrishnan, D. Srivastava, and S. Sudanshan. CORAL—Control, Relations and Logic. In *Proceedings of International Conference on Very Large Databases*, pp. 238–250, 1992.

[350] R. Ramakrishnan, D. Srivastava, S. Sudanshan, and P. Seshadri. Implementation of the CORAL Deductive Database System. In *Proceedings of the International ACM SIGMOD Conference on Management of Data*, pp. 167–176, 1993.

[351] R. Ramakrishnan and J. D. Ullman. A Survey of Research in Deductive Database Systems. *Journal of Logic Programming* 23(2):125–149, 1995.

[352] H. Rasiowa. *An Algebraic Approach to Non-Classical Logics*. Polish Scientific Publishers, Warsaw, Poland, 1974.

[353] E. Rasmussen. Clustering Algorithms. In W. B. Frakes and R. Baeza-Yates (eds.), *Information Retrieval: Data Structures and Algorithms*, pp. 419–442, Prentice Hall, Englewood Cliffs, NJ, 1992.

[354] R. Reiter. On Closed World Data Bases. In J. W. Minker and H. Gallaire (eds.), *Logic and Databases*, pp. 55–76, Plenum Press, New York, 1978.

[355] R. Reiter. Towards a Logical Reconstruction of Relational Database Theory. In J. W. Schmidt, M. L. Brodie, and J. L. Mylopoulos (eds.), *On Conceptual Modeling*, pp. 163–189, Springer-Verlag, New York, 1984.

[356] N. C. Rescher. *Many-Valued Logic*. McGraw-Hill, New York, 1969.

[357] N. C. Rescher and A. Urquhart. *Temporal Logic*. Springer-Verlag, New York, 1971.

[358] J. E. Richardson and M. J. Carey. Persistence in the E Language: Issues and Implementation. *Software—Practice and Experience* 19(12):1115–1150, December 1989.

[359] R. L. Rivest. Partial Match Retrieval Algorithms. *SIAM Journal of Computing* 5(1):19–50, March 1976.

[360] J. T. Robinson. The k-D-B-Tree: A Search Structure for Large Multidimensional Dynamic Indexes. In *Proceedings ACM SIGMOD International Conference on Management of Data*, pp. 10–18, 1981.

[361] J. J. Rocchio. Performance Indices for Document Retrieval. In G. Salton (ed.), *The SMART Retrieval System—Experiments in Automatic Document Processing*, Chapter 3, Prentice Hall, Englewood Cliffs, NJ, 1971.

[362] J. F. Roddick. Schema Evolution in Database Systems—an Annotated Bibliography. *ACM SIGMOD Record* 21(4):35–40, December 1992.

[363] Y. Rong and C. Faloutsos. Analysis of the Clustering Property of Peano Curves. Technical Report CS-TR-2792, UMIACS-TR-91-151, University of Maryland, December 1991.

[364] K. A. Ross. Modular Stratification and Magic Sets for Datalog Programs with Negation. *Journal of ACM* 41(6):1216–1266, 1994.

[365] K. A. Ross and Y. Sagiv. Monotonic Aggregation in Deductive Databases. In *Proceedings ACM SIGACT-SIGMOD-SIGART Symposium on Principles of Database Systems*, pp. 114–126, June 1992.

[366] N. Roussopoulos, S. Kelley, and F. Vincent. Nearest Neighbor Queries. In *Proceedings ACM-SIGMOD International Conference on the Management of Data*, pp. 71–79, May 1995.

[367] N. Roussopoulos and D. Leifker. Direct Spatial Search on Pictorial Databases Using Packed R-Trees. In *Proceedings ACM SIGMOD International Conference on Management of Data*, May 1985.

[368] D. Rozenshtein, A. Abramovich, and E. Birger. Loop-Free SQL Solutions for Finding Continuous Regions. *SQL Forum* 2(6), November–December 1993.

[369] J. Rumbaugh, M. Blaha, W. Premerlani, F. Eddy, and W. Lorensen. *Object-Oriented Modeling and Design.* Prentice Hall, Englewood Cliffs, NJ, 1991.

[370] E. A. Rundensteiner. Multiview: A Methodology for Supporting Multiple Views in Object-Oriented Databases. In L.-Y. Yuan (ed.), *Proceedings International Conference on Very Large Databases*, pp. 187–198, Vancouver, Canada, August 1992. Morgan Kaufmann, San Francisco.

[371] M. B. Ruskai, G. Beylkin, R. Coifman, I. Daubechies, S. Mallat, Y. Meyer, and L. Raphael. *Wavelets and Their Applications.* Jones and Bartlett Publishers, Boston, MA, 1992.

[372] D. Saccà and C. Zaniolo. Magic Counting Methods. In *Proceedings ACM SIGMOD International Conference on Management of Data*, pp. 49–59, 1987.

[373] D. Saccà and C. Zaniolo. Differential Fixpoint Methods and Stratification of Logic Programs. In *Proceedings International Conference on Data and Knowledge Bases*, 1988.

[374] D. Saccà and C. Zaniolo. The Generalized Counting Method of Recursive Logic Queries for Databases. *Theoretical Computer Science*, pp. 187–220, 1988. Preliminary version appeared in ICDT86.

[375] D. Saccà and C. Zaniolo. Stable Models and Non-Determinism in Logic Programs with Negation. In *Proceedings ACM SIGACT-SIGMOD-SIGART Symposium on Principles of Database Systems*, 1990.

[376] D. Saccà and C. Zaniolo. Deterministic and Non-Deterministic Stable Models. *Journal of Logic and Computation*, 1997.

[377] R. Sacks-Davis, A. Kent, and K. Ramamohanarao. Multikey Access Methods Based on Superimposed Coding Techniques. *ACM Transactions on Database Systems* 12(4):655–696, December 1987.

[378] R. Sacks-Davis and K. Ramamohanarao. A Two Level Superimposed Coding Scheme for Partial Match Retrieval. *Information Systems* 8(4):273–280, 1983.

[379] G. Salton. Relevance Feedback and the Optimization of Retrieval Effectiveness. In [380], Chapter 15.

[380] G. Salton. *The SMART Retrieval System—Experiments in Automatic Document Processing.* Prentice Hall, Englewood Cliffs, NJ, 1971.

[381] G. Salton and M. J. McGill. *Introduction to Modern Information Retrieval.* McGraw-Hill, New York, 1983.

[382] G. Salton and A. Wong. Generation and Search of Clustered Files. *ACM Transactions on Database Systems* 3(4):321–346, December 1978.

[383] B. Salzberg and V. J. Tsotras. A Comparison of Access Methods for Time Evolving Data. *ACM Computing Surveys*, to appear, 1997.

[384] D. Sankoff and J. B. Kruskal. *Time Warps, String Edits and Macromolecules: The Theory and Practice of Sequence Comparisons.* Addison-Wesley, Reading, MA, 1983.

[385] N. Sarda. Extensions to SQL for Historical Databases. *IEEE Transactions on Knowledge and Data Engineering* 2(2):220–230, June 1990.

[386] H.-J. Schek and M. H. Scholl. Evolution of Data Models. In *Proceedings International Symposium on Database Systems for the 90's*, Berlin, Germany, November 1990. Springer-Verlag, New York. LNCS 466.

[387] H.-J. Schek and M. H. Scholl. From Relations and Nested Relations to Object Models. In H. J. Butterworth-Heinemann (ed.), *Proceedings British National Conference on Databases*, Wolverhampton, UK, July 1991. Springer-Verlag, New York.

[388] H. Schmidt, W. Kiessling, U. Guntzer, and R. Bayer. Combining Deduction by Uncertainty with the Power of Magic. In *Proceedings International Conference on Deductive and Object-Oriented Databases*, pp. 205–224, Kyoto, Japan, 1987.

[389] M. H. Scholl, C. Laasch, and M. Tresch. Updatable Views in Object-Oriented Databases. In C. Delobel, M. Kifer, and Y. Masunaga (eds.), *Proceedings International Conference on Deductive and Object-Oriented Databases*, pp. 189–207, Munich, Germany, December 1991. Springer-Verlag, New York. LNCS 566.

[390] M. Schrefl. *Object-Oriented Database Integration*. Ph.D. thesis, Technische Universitat Wien, Vienna, Austria, June 1988.

[391] A. Schrijver. *Theory of Linear and Integer Programming*. John Wiley and Sons, New York, 1986.

[392] M. Schroeder. *Fractals, Chaos, Power Laws: Minutes from an Infinite Paradise*. W. H. Freeman and Company, New York, 1991.

[393] B. Seeger and H.-P. Kriegel. The Buddy-Tree: An Efficient and Robust Access Method for Spatial Database Systems. In *Proceedings International Conference on Very Large Data Bases*, pp. 590–601, August 1990.

[394] A. Segev, G. Himawan, R. Chandra, and J. Shanthikumar. Selectivity Estimation of Temporal Data Manipulations. *Information Sciences* 74,(1–2), October 1993.

[395] A. Segev and A. Shoshani. Logical Modeling of Temporal Data. In U. Dayal and I. Traiger (eds.), *Proceedings ACM SIGMOD International Conference on Management of Data*, pp. 454–466, San Francisco, CA, May 1987.

[396] T. Sellis (ed.). *Proceedings of Second Workshop on Rules in Database Systems*, Athens, Greece, September 1995. LNCS, Springer-Verlag, Berlin.

[397] G. Shafer. *A Mathematical Theory of Evidence*. Princeton University Press, Princeton, NJ, 1976.

[398] C. A. Shaffer. A Formula for Computing the Number of Quadtree Node Fragments Created by a Shift. *Pattern Recognition Letters* 7(1):45–49, January 1988.

[399] C. A. Shaffer, H. Samet, and R. C. Nelson. Quilt: A Geographic Information System Based on Quadtrees. Technical Report CS-TR-1885.1, Department of Computer Science, University of Maryland, July 1987.

[400] E. Shapiro. Logic Programs with Uncertainties: A Tool for Implementing Expert Systems. In *Proceedings International Journal Computational Artificial Intelligence*, pp. 529–532, Morgan Kaufmann, San Francisco, 1983.

[401] A. P. Sheth and J. A. Larson. Federated Database Systems for Managing Distributed, Heterogeneous, and Autonomous Databases. *ACM Computing Surveys* 22(3), September 1990.

[402] R. Sikorski. *Boolean Algebras*. Academic Press, San Diego, CA, 1964.

[403] A. H. Skarra and S. B. Zdonik. The Management of Changing Types in an Object-Oriented Database. In N. Meyrowitz (ed.), *Proceedings International Conference on Object-Oriented Programming Systems, Languages, and Applications*, pp. 483–495, Portland, OR, September 1986. ACM, New York. Special Issue of *SIGPLAN Notices* 21(11), November 1986.

[404] A. H. Skarra and S. B. Zdonik. Type Evolution in an Object-Oriented Database. In B. Shriver and P. Wegner (eds.), *Research Directions in Object-Oriented Programming*, pp. 393–415, MIT Press, Cambridge, MA, 1987.

[405] R. T. Snodgrass. The Temporal Query Language TQuel. *ACM Transactions on Database Systems* 12(2):247–298, June 1987.

[406] R. T. Snodgrass. Temporal Databases. In A. U. Frank, I. Campari, and U. Formentini (eds.), *Theories and Methods of Spatio-Temporal Reasoning in Geographic Space*, pp. 22–64, LNCS 639, Springer-Verlag, New York, September 1992.

[407] R. T. Snodgrass. Temporal Object-Oriented Databases: A Critical Comparison. In W. Kim (ed.), *Modern Database Systems: The Object Model, Interoperability and Beyond*, pp. 386–408, Chapter 19, Addison-Wesley/ACM Press, Reading, MA/New York, 1995.

[408] R. T. Snodgrass and I. Ahn. Temporal Databases. *IEEE Computer* 19(9):35–42, September 1986.

[409] R. T. Snodgrass (ed.), I. Ahn, G. Ariav, D. S. Batory, J. Clifford, C. E. Dyreson, R. Elmasri, F. Grandi, C. S. Jensen, W. Käfer, N. Kline, K. Kulkanri, C. Y. T. Leung, N. Lorentzos, J. F. Roddick, A. Segev, M. D. Soo, and S. M. Sripada. *The TSQL2 Temporal Query Language*, Kluwer Academic, Norwell, MA, 1995.

[410] M. D. Soo. Bibliography on Temporal Databases. *ACM SIGMOD Record* 20(1):14–23, March 1991.

[411] M. D. Soo, R. T. Snodgrass, and C. S. Jensen. Efficient Evaluation of the Valid-Time Natural Join. In *Proceedings International Conference on Data Engineering*, pp. 282–292, February 1994.

[412] C. Souza dos Santos. Design and Implementation of Object-Oriented Views. In N. Revell and A. M. Tjoa (eds.), *Proceedings International Conference on Database and Expert Systems Applications*, pp. 91–102, London, September 1995. Springer-Verlag, New York. LNCS 978.

[413] C. Souza dos Santos, S. Abiteboul, and C. Delobel. Virtual Schemas and Bases. In M. Jarke, J. Bubenko, and K. Jeffery (eds.), *Proceedings International Conference on Extending Database Technology*, pp. 81–94, Cambridge, United Kingdom, March 1994. Springer-Verlag, New York. LNCS 779.

[414] S. M. Sripada. A Logical Framework for Temporal Deductive Databases. In *Proceedings International Conference on Very Large Data Bases*, pp. 171–182, Los Angeles, 1988.

[415] R. Stam and R. T. Snodgrass. A Bibliography on Temporal Databases. *IEEE Database Engineering* 7(4):231–239, December 1988.

[416] C. Stanfill and B. Kahle. Parallel Free-Text Search on the Connection Machine System. *Communications of the ACM* 29(12):1229–1239, December 1986.

[417] B. Staudt Lerner and A. N. Habermann. Beyond Schema Evolution to Database Reorganization. In N. Meyrowitz (ed.), *Proceedings ACM International Conference on Object-Oriented Programming Systems, Languages, and Applications* and Proceedings European Conference on Object Oriented Programming, pp. 67–76, Ottawa, Canada, October 1990. Special Issue of *SIGPLAN Notices* 25(10).

[418] L. Sterling and E. Shapiro. *The Art of Prolog*. MIT Press, Cambridge, MA, 1986.

[419] S. Stiassny. Mathematical Analysis of Various Superimposed Coding Methods. *American Documentation* 11(2):155–169, February 1960.

[420] M. Stonebraker, T. Sellis, and E. N. Hanson. Rule Indexing Implementations in Database Systems. In *Proceedings International Conference on Expert Database Systems*, Charleston, SC, April 1986.

[421] R. Sturm, J. A. Mulle, and P. C. Lockemann. Temporized and Localized Rule Sets. In [396], pp. 131–146.

[422] V. S. Subrahmanian. On the Semantics of Quantitative Logic Programs. In *Proceedings IEEE Symposium on Logic Programming*, pp. 173–182, Computer Society Press, Washington, DC, 1987.

[423] V. S. Subrahmanian. Paraconsistent Disjunctive Deductive Databases. *Theoretical Computer Science* 93:115–141. February 1992.

[424] K. J. Sullivan and D. Notkin. Reconciling Environment Integration and Software Evolution. *ACM Transactions on Software Engineering and Methodology* 1(3):229–268, July 1992.

[425] D. M. Sunday. A Very Fast Substring Search Algorithm. *Communications of the ACM* 33(8):132–142, August 1990.

[426] Sybase. *Sybase SQL Server: Transact-SQL User's Guide, Release 10.0*, February 1994.

[427] A. Tansel, J. Clifford, S. K. Gadia, S. Jajodia, A. Segev, and R. T. Snodgrass (eds.). *Temporal Databases: Theory, Design, and Implementation.* Database Systems and Applications Series. Benjamin/Cummings, Redwood City, CA, 1994.

[428] A. Tarski. A Lattice-Theoretical Fixpoint Theorem and Its Applications. *Pacific Journal of Mathematics* 5:285–309, 1955.

[429] H. Thone, W. Kiessling, and U. Guntzer. On Cautious Probabilistic Inference and Default Detachment. *Annals of Operations Research* 55:195–224, 1955.

[430] A. Tomasic, H. García-Molina, and K. Shoens. Incremental Updates of Inverted Lists for Text Document Retrieval. In R. T. Snodgrass and M. Winslett (eds.), *Proceedings ACM SIGMOD International Conference on Management of Data*, pp. 289–300, May 1994.

[431] M. Tresch. *Evolution in Objekt-Datenbanken: Anpassung und Integration bestehender Informationssysteme*, volume 10 of *Teubner-Texte zur Informatik*. Teubner, 1995.

[432] M. Tresch and M. H. Scholl. Schema Transformation without Database Reorganization. *SIGMOD Record* 22(1):21–27, March 1993.

[433] H. Tsai and A. M. K. Cheng. Termination Analysis of OPS5 Expert Systems. In *Proceedings AAAI National Conference on Artificial Intelligence*, Seattle, WA, 1994.

[434] D. Tsichritzis and S. Christodoulakis. Message Files. *ACM Transactions on Office Information Systems* 1(1):88–98, January 1983.

[435] V. J. Tsotras and A. Kumar. Temporal Database Bibliography Update. *ACM SIGMOD Record* 25(1), March 1996.

[436] S. Tsur. Deductive Databases in Action. In *Proceedings ACM SIGACT-SIGMOD-SIGART Symposium on Principles of Programming Languages*, pp. 142–154, 1991.

[437] J. D. Ullman. *Principles of Data and Knowledge-Base Systems*, volume 1. Computer Science Press, New York, 1988.

[438] J. F. K. A. Van Benthem. *The Logic of Time: A Model-Theoretic Investigation into the Varieties of Temporal Ontology and Temporal Discourse*. Reidel, Hingham, MA, 1982.

[439] L. van der Voort and A. Siebes. Termination and Confluence of Rule Execution. In *Proceedings International Conference on Information and Knowledge Management*, Washington, DC, November 1993.

[440] M. H. Van Emden. Quantitative Deduction and Its Fixpoint Theory. *Journal of Logic Programming* 4(1):37–53, 1986.

[441] M. H. Van Emden and R. Kowalski. The Semantics of Predicate Logic as a Programming Language. *Journal of the ACM* 23(4):733–742, 1976.

[442] A. Van Gelder. Negation as Failure Using Tight Derivations for General Logic Programs. In *Proceedings IEEE Symposium on Logic Programming*, pp. 127–139, 1986.

[443] A. Van Gelder. The Alternating Fixpoint of Logic Programming with Negation. In *Proceedings ACM SIGACT-SIGMOD-SIGART Symposium on Principles of Database Systems*, pp. 1–10, 1989.

[444] A. Van Gelder, K. A. Ross, and J. S. Schlipf. The Well-Founded Semantics for General Logic Programs. *Journal of ACM* 38:620–650, 1991.

[445] A. Van Gelder and R. Topor. Safety and Correct Translation of Relational Calculus Formulas. In *Proceedings ACM SIGACT-SIGMOD-SIGART Principles of Database Systems*, pp. 313–328, 1987.

[446] C. J. Van Rijsbergen. *Information Retrieval*. Butterworths, London, England, 1979. Second edition.

[447] Y. Vassiliou. Null Values in Database Management, A Denotational Semantics Approach. In *Proceedings of ACM-SIGMOD International Conference on Management of Data*, pp. 162–169, 1979.

[448] Versant Object Technology. *Versant User Manual*, Menlo Park, CA, 1992.

[449] L. Vielle. Recursive Axioms in Deductive Databases: The Query-Subquery Approach. In *Proceedings International Conference on Expert Database Systems*, pp. 253–268, 1986.

[450] G. K. Wallace. The JPEG Still Picture Compression Standard. *Communications of the ACM* 34(4):31–44, April 1991.

[451] E. Waller. Schema Updates and Consistency. In C. Delobel, M. Kifer, and Y. Masunaga (eds.), *Proceedings International Conference on Deductive and Object-Oriented Databases*, pp. 167–188, Munich, Germany, December 1991. Springer-Verlag, New York. LNCS 566.

[452] A. S. Weigend and N. A. Gerschenfeld. *Time Series Prediction: Forecasting the Future and Understanding the Past*. Addison-Wesley, Reading, MA, 1994.

[453] Y.-W. Whang and E. N. Hanson. A Performance Analysis of the Rete and TREAT Algorithms for Testing Database Rule Conditions. In *Proceedings of the IEEE International Conference on Data Engineering*, pp. 88–97, Tempe, AZ, February 1992.

[454] M. White. *N-Trees: Large Ordered Indexes for Multi-Dimensional Space*. Application Mathematics Research Staff, Statistical Research Division, U.S. Bureau of the Census, December 1981.

[455] J. Widom and S. Ceri. *Active Database Systems*. Morgan Kaufmann, San Francisco, August 1996.

[456] J. Widom, R. J. Cochrane, and B. G. Lindsay. Implementing Set-Oriented Production Rules as an Extension to Starburst. In G. M. Lohman, A. Sernadas, and R. Camps (eds.), *Proceedings International Conference on Very Large Data Bases*, pp. 275–285, Barcelona, Spain, September 1991.

[457] J. Widom and S. J. Finkelstein. Set-Oriented Production Rule in Relational Database Systems. In H. García-Molina and H. V. Jagadish (eds.), *Proceedings ACM SIGMOD International Conference on Management of Data*, pp. 259–270, Atlantic City, NJ, May 1990.

[458] K. Wilkinson, P. Lyngbaek, and W. Hasan. The IRIS Architecture and Implementation. *IEEE Transactions on Knowledge and Data Engineering*, 2(1), March 1990.

[459] S. Wolfram. *Mathematica.* Addison-Wesley, Reading, MA, 1991. Second edition.

[460] S. Wu and U. Manber. Text Searching Allowing Errors. *Communications of the ACM* 35(10):83–91, October 1992.

[461] C. Xiao. *Foundations for Adaptative Object-Oriented Software.* Ph.D. thesis, College of Computer Science, Northeastern University, Boston, MA, September 1995.

[462] L. A. Zadeh. Fuzzy Sets. *Information and Control* 8:338–353, 1965.

[463] L. A. Zadeh. Fuzzy Algorithms. *Information and Control* 12:94–102, 1968.

[464] C. Zaniolo. Safety and Compilation of Non-Recursive Horn Clauses. In *Proceedings International Conference on Expert Database Systems*, pp. 167–178, 1986.

[465] C. Zaniolo. Design and Implementation of a Logic Based Language for Data Intensive Applications. In *Proceedings International Conference on Logic Programming*, 1988.

[466] C. Zaniolo. A Unified Semantics for Active and Deductive Databases. In *Proceedings International Workshop on Rules in Database Systems*, pp. 271–287, 1993.

[467] C. Zaniolo. Transaction-Conscious Stable Model Semantics for Active Database Rules. In *Proceedings International Conference on Deductive Object-Oriented Databases*, 1995.

[468] C. Zaniolo. Active Database Rules with Transaction-Conscious Stable-Model Semantics. In *Proceedings of the Conference on Deductive and Object-Oriented Databases*, pp. 55–72, LNCS 1013, Singapore, December 1995.

[469] C. Zaniolo, N. Arni, and K. Ong. Negation and Aggregates in Recursive Rules: the LDL++ Approach. In *Proceedings International Conference on Deductive and Object-Oriented Databases, DOOD'93*, 1993.

[470] P. Zezula, F. Rabitti, and P. Tiberio. Dynamic Partitioning of Signature Files. *ACM Transactions on Office Information Systems* 9(4):336–369, October 1991.

[471] R. Zicari. Schema Updates in the O_2 Object Oriented Database System. Technical Report 89-057, Politecnico di Milano, Milano, Italy, October 1989.

[472] R. Zicari. A Framework for Schema Updates in an Object Oriented Database System. In *Proceedings International Conference on Data Engineering*, pp. 2–13, April 1991.

[473] R. Zicari. A Framework for Schema Updates in an Object-Oriented Database System. In F. Bancilhon, C. Delobel, and P. Kanellakis (eds.), *Building an Object-Oriented Database System—The Story of O_2*, pp. 146–182, Morgan Kaufmann, San Francisco, 1992.

[474] J. Zobel, A. Moffat, and R. Sacks-Davis. An Efficient Indexing Technique for Full-Text Database Systems. In *Proceedings International Conference on Very Large Data Bases*, pp. 352–362, August 1992.

Author Index

Subject Index

About the Authors

After two decades of industrial experience, **Carlo Zaniolo** joined the UCLA Computer Science Department in 1991 and was appointed to the Friedmann Chair in Knowledge Sciences. Before joining UCLA, he was associate director in the Advanced Computer Architecture Program of the Microelectronics and Computer Technology Corporation (MCC) in Austin, Texas, where he was responsible for the Logical Data Language (LDL) project. Before MCC, he was with AT&T Bell Laboratories in Murray Hill, New Jersey, where he designed the system GEM, featuring one of the earliest object-oriented data definition and manipulation languages for databases. Carlo Zaniolo has been active in the areas of databases, knowledge bases, and intelligent databases from the time he completed his Ph.D. at UCLA in 1976. He served as the program chairman for the 1986 ACM SIGMOD conference and as the American program chair for the VLDB 1981 and 1994 conferences.

Stefano Ceri is full professor of database systems at the Dipartimento di Elettronica e Informazione, Politecnico di Milano; he was visiting professor at the Computer Science Department of Stanford University between 1983 and 1990. His research interests are focused on extending database technology to incorporate data distribution, deductive and active rules, and object orientation. He is author of several articles in international journals and conference proceedings, and he is co-author of the books *Distributed Databases: Principles and Systems* (McGraw-Hill), *Logic Programming and Databases* (Springer-Verlag), *Conceptual Database Design: An Entity-Relationship Approach* (Benjamin/Cummings), *Active Database Systems* (Morgan Kaufmann), *The Art and Science of Computing* (Addison-Wesley, in preparation), and *Designing Database Applications with Objects and Rules: The IDEA Methodology* (Addison-Wesley, in preparation). He is a member of the VLDB Endowment, EDBT Foundation, and DOOD Steering Committee; he was an associate editor of *ACM Transactions on Database Systems* (1989-92) and is currently an associate editor of several international journals. He is project manager at the Politecnico of the Esprit project P6333, IDEA: Intelligent Database Environments for Advanced Applications.

Christos Faloutsos received the B.Sc. degree in electrical engineering from the National Technical University of Athens, Greece, and the M.Sc. and Ph.D. degrees in computer science from the University of Toronto, Canada. Since 1985 he has been with the Department of Computer Science at the University of Maryland, College Park, where he is currently an associate professor. In 1989 he received the Presidential Young Investigator Award from the National Science Foundation. His research interests include physical database design, searching methods for text, geographic information systems, and indexing methods for medical and multimedia databases.

Richard T. Snodgrass received his Ph.D. from Carnegie Mellon University in 1982 and joined the University of Arizona in 1989, where he is a professor of computer science. He chaired the TSQL2 Language Design Committee, edited the book *The TSQL2 Temporal Query Language* (Kluwer Academic Press), and is now working closely with the ISO SQL3 committee to add temporal support to that language. He initiated the SQL/temporal part of the SQL3 draft standard. He is co-editor of *Temporal Databases: Theory, Design, and Implementation* (Benjamin/Cummings). Richard Snodgrass is an associate editor of the *ACM Transactions on Database Systems* and is on the editorial boards of the *IEEE Transactions on Knowledge and Data Engineering* and the *International Journal on Very Large Databases*. He chaired the program committees for the 1994 ACM SIGMOD conference and the 1993 International Workshop on an Infrastructure for Temporal Databases. He co-directs TIMECENTER, an international center for the support of temporal database applications on traditional and emerging DBMS technologies. His research interests include temporal databases, query language design, query optimization and evaluation, storage structures, database design, and software development databases.

V. S. Subrahmanian received his Ph.D. in computer science from Syracuse University in 1989. Since then, he has been a member of the faculty of the Computer Science Department at the University of Maryland, College Park, where he currently holds the rank of associate professor. He received the prestigious NSF Young Investigator Award in 1993. He has worked extensively in knowledge bases, bringing together techniques in artificial intelligence and databases, and in dealing with incomplete and uncertain information in databases and knowledge bases. More recently, he has been working on the problem of integrated heterogeneous data and software located across the Internet. He has proposed formal theoretical models for such integrations, as well as led the HERMES project for heterogeneous reasoning and mediator systems. Finally, he has worked extensively on multimedia systems and made fundamental contributions to scalable implementation of such systems. Professor Subrahmanian has over 80 published/accepted papers in leading journals and conferences. He has edited two books, one on non-monotonic reasoning (MIT Press) and a recent one on multimedia databases (Springer-Verlag). He has given invited talks and served on invited panels at various conferences. In addition, he has served on the program committees of various conferences. He is on the editorial board of *IEEE Transactions on Knowledge and Data Engineering*.

Roberto Zicari is full professor of computer science at the Johann Wolfgang Goethe University in Frankfurt, Germany. Previously he was an associate professor at Politecnico di Milano, Italy; visiting scientist at IBM Almaden Research Center and UC Berkeley; visiting professor at EPFL (Lausanne, Switzerland) and National University of Mexico City. Professor Zicari is the editor-in-chief of *Theory and Practice of Object Systems* (John Wiley) and the technical director of the Esprit project Goodstep. He is an internationally recognized expert in the field of object database systems. He has consulted and lectured in Europe, North America, and Japan. Roberto Zicari holds a doctor of engineering degree from Politecnico di Milano.